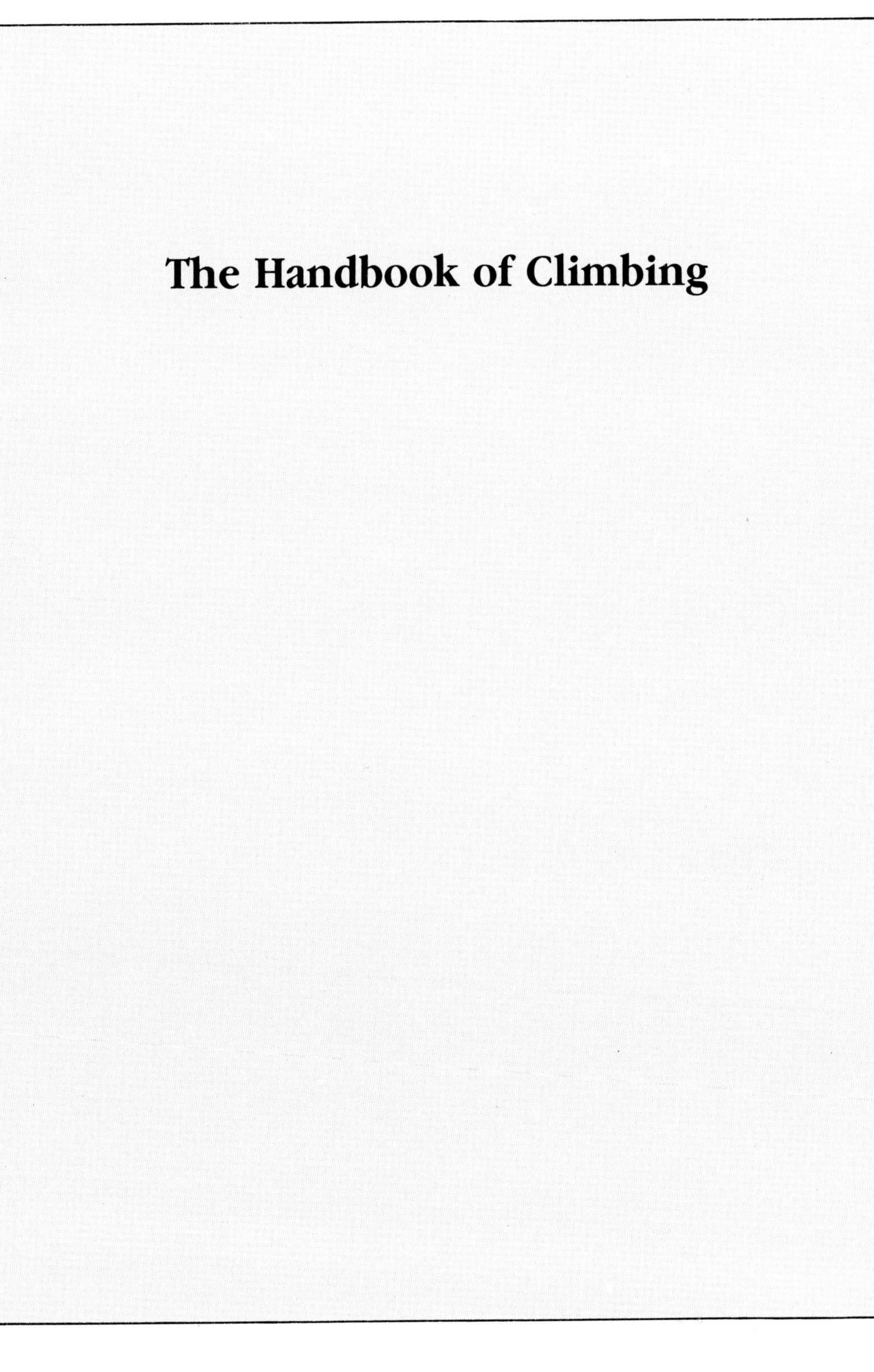

The Handbook of Climbing

The Handbook of Climbing

ALLEN FYFFE
and
IAIN PETER

Fully endorsed by the British Mountaineering Council

PELHAM BOOKS
Stephen Greene Press

PELHAM BOOKS/Stephen Greene Press
Published by the Penguin Group
27 Wrights Lane, London W8 5TZ, England
Viking Penguin Inc., 40 West 23rd Street, New York, New York 10010, USA
The Stephen Greene Press Inc., 15 Muzzey Street, Lexington, Massachusetts 02173, USA
Penguin Books Australia Ltd, Ringwood, Victoria, Australia
Penguin Books Canada Ltd, 2801 John Street, Markham, Ontario, Canada L3R 1B4
Penguin Books (NZ) Ltd, 182–190 Wairau Road, Auckland 10, New Zealand

Penguin Books Ltd, Registered Offices: Harmondsworth, Middlesex, England

First published 1990

Made and printed in Singapore by
Kyodo-Shing Loong Printing Industries Pte Ltd

Typeset by KeyStar, St Ives, Cambridge

A CIP catalogue record for this book is available from the British Library.

ISBN 0 7207 1805 8

Library of Congress Catalog Card Number: 89-64184

Contents

ACKNOWLEDGEMENTS

The authors would like to thank the following for their assistance with the black and white photography: Alex Gillespie, James Hepburn, Adrian Liddell, Andrew Cunningham, Giles Green, Willy Todd, Mark Diggins, Martin Doyle, Donald Stewart and Libby Healey. The colour photographs are individually credited with the captions. All line drawings and two-colour illustrations are by Douglas Godlington.

Note on the use of colour in the illustrations:
Orange is used for Rock Climbing, blue for Snow, Ice and Winter Climbing, and green for Alpine Climbing. Grey tints are used in the Appendices and for some of the more technical diagrams in Sections I, II and III.

Foreword

by Hamish MacInnes

It is good to find a manual on mountaineering which is both up to date and very comprehensive. *The Handbook of Climbing* is, in my opinion, one of the best to be produced in the English language. Its scope is wide, the text lucid and the mass of information is the culmination of years of experience by experts used to instructing mountaineering.

You certainly cannot learn to climb safely by reading a text book on the subject, but you can absorb a tremendous amount of information which can be used to advantage on mountains and crags. The sections on Training and Psychological Skills are of particular interest in these days of specialised climbing and have in the past been neglected subjects. But it is not just a book for the beginner, even the experienced mountaineer will find gems of information and the excellent Glossary and Index make it also a comprehensive reference work.

GLENCOE, ARGYLL
SCOTLAND

Introduction

This book has been written as a technical handbook of climbing skills. Climbing is taken to mean the ascent of rock, snow or ice which generally requires the use of the hands for progress or for safety. Skill, as defined in the dictionary, is the knowledge of any art or science and dexterity in the practice of it. Climbing is neither an art nor a science but an activity which is a combination of both, and climbing skills are a reflection of this. There are few hard and fast rules; there are general principles which are usually followed, but sometimes even these may have to be abandoned. In many climbing situations the unusual or unexpected may arise, though it can often be anticipated. Experience allows you to foresee or deal successfully with these situations; a technical repertoire should enable you to solve individual problems in a safe, quick and efficient manner. This is true throughout climbing from the unusual move to the most complex of rope manoeuvres.

Safety, too, is related to experience and an easy answer to many questions about climbing is that experience will tell you the best thing to do. Yet gaining the relevant experience presents the greatest risk, particularly when starting climbing or when moving on to a different aspect of the sport. Experience, however, is best gained by participation. Reading about techniques can, of course, help speed up the learning process, but practice, controlled progress and an inquiring and questioning attitude are the best ways to learn. The most effective aid to learning to climb safely is the ability to look at a situation, ask the question, 'What would happen if ...?', and work out a solution based on the knowledge and skills at your disposal. If you increase the techniques at your disposal, so you increase your problem solving ability.

Climbing is unlike most other sporting activities in that it takes place in an inherently dangerous environment, be it on a rock face or a high mountain. The risks generally lessen as experience is gained, but climbing can never be totally safe. Part of the attraction of climbing can be the sense of danger; to remove this risk would alter the activity itself.

In the course of a climb, whether it is on rock, snow or ice, there are a number of parts which are linked together to provide a safe system. This interlocking is often referred to as the safety chain and, like any chain, is only as strong as its weakest link. Because of the interconnected nature of the parts, however, it is difficult to explain one section in isolation, and to describe the complete system with all its variations is too complex and confusing. Each chapter of this book mainly concerns itself with its subject matter in relative isolation but in a way which should allow a total picture of the sport to be built up.

Climbing and mountaineering have a long and fascinating history which is well documented in books, journals and magazines. For anyone interested in climbing, this literature can provide an insight into it; and an understanding of the history and background is one of the safeguards of the sport as it can act as a reminder to us all of the risks and rewards involved. Climbing literature also serves as the second-best source of the joys, rewards, sorrows and set-backs of the sport. The best aspects of climbing are your personal experiences. No attempt has been made in this book to describe what climbing can give to its participants: that is for you to discover, and it has been very well described by others. What we have tried to do is to detail the techniques by which these personal experiences may be safely gained.

We have written this book for anyone who wishes to improve their climbing from the point of view not only of personal performance but also of gaining knowledge of the sport's technical aspects, such as the intricacies of rope management and the use of equipment, the facets of climbing which are 'unnatural' and need to be learned. Often there is no single correct way to do something in climbing but rather several acceptable ways, one of which will be better than the others in a particular situation. Because of this, and to allow for personal preference, we have tried to describe the most useful techniques and methods so that the reader will be in a position to weigh up the pros and cons, try them out in the appropriate places and come to his own conclusions. Uniqueness is a feature of climbing and it is part of its appeal: every move, every climb, every situation encountered is likely to be different from any other and for this reason having a range of techniques under your belt is important.

Our aim in this book has been to facilitate an understanding of the general principles of climbing. This approach has also been extended to include our treatment of equipment. Modern climbing is a fast-developing activity with regard to the range of equipment now available. Some of this gear is here to stay, other items may fall by the wayside and advances in materials and design will continue. Because of this changing scene we have tried to avoid trade names where possible and refer to general rather than specific types of equipment except where the name is so well established that it has come to mean all gear of that type. How a piece of equipment works and how it is used are more important than its name or the latest variation which will probably be superseded in the near future. The wide range of climbing magazines are in a better position than a book to provide up-to-date information on the latter. Those with an interest in the latest developments and fashions may also consult equipment reviews and surveys, and many manufacturers provide technical information with their products.

There are four sections to this book: 'Rock Climbing'; 'Snow, Ice and Winter Climbing'; 'Alpine Climbing' and 'Appendices'. Their order is not meant to imply any development in difficulty or worth of the branches of climbing but rather that it is easier and simpler to learn and develop the basic skills on warm rock rather than in winter or in high mountains. The basic techniques are the same throughout: it is the environment in which they are applied that becomes increasingly hostile.

Section IV contains information which is peripheral to actual climbing skills and techniques and is not applicable to all aspects of the sport. Some of it, however, is essential for anyone moving from climbing into mountaineering with its greater arenas and increased dangers and demands.

Finally, we must apologise for referring to the climber throughout the book as 'he'. Although climbing is still a male-dominated activity, there are more and more women taking to the rocks and the mountains and it is not our intention to cause offence to female readers but simply to keep the text as uncluttered and easy-to-understand as possible.

SECTION ONE

Rock Climbing

1 Personal Equipment

The amount of personal equipment required for rock climbing is fairly limited, and at a basic level virtually any sensible clothing and footwear can be used. However, for anything more than the briefest of introductions to climbing some pieces of special equipment are required, the most important of which is a pair of rock boots. For those who wish to make rock climbing part of their wider mountaineering activities, the footwear and clothing is basically the same as that required for snow and ice or winter climbing (see Chapter 11). The only real difference is that less insulating clothing is required. Those who move on to rock climbing from hill walking are likely already to possess the necessary attire whereas others may have to make a few purchases or adaptations.

APPROACH FOOTWEAR

Since rock boots are notoriously uncomfortable to walk in and also too important and expensive to use for this job, a pair of training shoes or light walking boots is needed to walk to most low level cliffs. For mountain crags the same footwear may suffice but slightly better or more specialised boots may be worthwhile or even necessary for some cliffs.

CLOTHING

Within certain limits, clothing for rock climbing is chosen primarily as protection from the weather rather than anything else. As long as it gives sufficient insulation, protection from the sun and wind and does not restrict movement, any practical clothing will do. Preferably it should be of a closely woven material which is smooth enough not to snag easily on the rock, yet not so slippery that it provides little friction when this is required. It should be close-fitting or cut in such a way that it does not obscure your feet. After these criteria have been met, it is the weather you climb in which decides what you wear and what you take with you.

For warm rock, shorts and shirt are all that is needed and are ideal as they allow complete freedom of movement. However, some harnesses are uncomfortable when worn against the skin, as are some ways of carrying equipment when wearing a shirt with no collar. If a good deal of rock/body contact is expected then more clothing or padding may be required. Knee pads are invaluable in some areas and for some types of climbing. Track suit trousers are extremely popular and practical for climbing in, particularly those which are tight-fitting and stretchy. Loose, baggy bottoms are less suitable as they snag more readily and can obscure your feet. Purpose-made climbing trousers or tights are also available for those with more flamboyant tastes.

Various types of fibre-pile tops and trousers are also suitable for use in slightly colder conditions but some, although light and warm, are not very windproof. The top in particular can be augmented with a light, windproof smock to give a good combination. Thermal underwear is warm and comfortable when worn beneath a more windproof layer such as track suit trousers. Having several layers is always the best combination because of the flexibility this gives. When climbing you can become very hot yet cool rapidly when not actually moving. Hat and gloves can be useful when stationary, particularly if in the wind or the shade.

If climbing in colder or wetter conditions, full mountain gear with a waterproof outer shell and layers of insulation underneath will be required. Again, freedom of movement is of prime importance. In very hot conditions loose-fitting, non-restrictive clothing as protection from the sun is best, but it should be cut to allow you to move freely and see your feet.

Before starting a climb it is best to remove any watches or rings you may be wearing. Watches get broken, scratched or pulled off on rock climbs, while rings can also be damaged and cause nasty accidents in slips or falls when they catch on the rock. Rings have even been known to get stuck in cracks and trap their owners on the route.

RUCKSACKS

A rucksack to carry the climbing gear and spare equipment to and perhaps up the route is not essential but certainly useful. One with clean, uncluttered lines which will not snag is best, although most people do not climb with a rucksack except on longer mountain routes. The rucksack should be large enough to carry your share of the gear, spare clothing and food and drink. About 25 litres capacity should be enough, but a larger sack of about 40 litres gives greater versatility. Compression straps on the side which can be used to alter the volume are useful, as is a waist belt which can make the load more stable. However, the extra belt round your waist may be restrictive and uncomfortable, especially when you are wearing a harness. It can always be fastened round the sack rather than round you to keep it out of the way when it is not needed.

ROCK BOOTS

Of all a climber's personal equipment, boots are the most important as footwork is fundamental in every aspect of the sport. At one time, when rock climbing was part of the greater game of mountaineering, routes were usually climbed in heavy mountain boots. In the early days these had nailed soles but after the Second World War the more adaptable Vibram soles gained popularity. Big boots were fairly cumbersome to climb in but performed better on positive edges where their stiffness was an advantage. Friction climbing in stiff boots was much more difficult and many of the harder routes of this period were done wearing plimsolls or even with the feet bare. More specialised lightweight rock boots with rope or felt soles were favoured in some Continental climbing areas such as the Dolomites. Another boot which bridged the gap between mountaineering and pure rock was the *Kletterschuh*, a light leather or suede boot with a thin Vibram sole.

The forerunner of the modern rock boot, designed by Pierre Allain and Emil Bordenau, made its first appearance in the 1930s in the bouldering arena of Fontainebleau near Paris. The PA and later the EB was a tight-fitting boot of canvas and leather with a thin, smooth, rubber sole which could be flexed for maximum rock/rubber contact. The EB was the most popular boot for hard rock climbing all over the world until the 70s when other boots began to challenge its supremacy. The great change came at the start of the 80s when the Firé rock boot from Spain hit the scene. Instead of a fairly hard, carbon rubber sole, the new type of sole was made of butyl rubber which has superior frictional properties, and 'sticky rubber' is now standard on most rock boots. At present there is a wide range of footwear to choose from, often in radical designs and colours which are changed and updated with increasing regularity. This has resulted in an unprecedented degree of specialisation. To climb the hardest routes now it is almost necessary to use different boots for every rock type. The ideal boot for a friction slab is not the same as the one for an overhanging, pocketed limestone wall.

This element of choice, however, has led to complications for the rock climber who just wants to buy one good pair of boots. The ideal rock boot would be comfortable, retain its size and shape, be flexible for friction work but almost rigid both laterally and longitudinally for use on edges. It would have pointed toes for pockets, sticky but long-lasting soles which retained a good edge, and would allow maximum ankle flex yet protect the ankle and be light and robust. This perfect boot would also have a good rand for friction at the sides which would not interfere with the capacity of the boot to twist when required. One boot cannot have all these features and so the choice must be a compromise. The user has to select the footwear which is most appropriate for his style and type of climbing [*fig. 1.1*].

When starting climbing, or if you climb on a wide variety of rock types, a good general-purpose boot is the obvious choice, one which will perform reasonably well both on positive edges and on friction holds. Some boots have a removable stiffener which allows a greater versatility in use. Today's range of boots, catering for every foot shape, should enable you to select a

pair which suits your feet. They should fit snugly, with no empty spaces which will affect performance. A lined boot can be worn comfortably either over very thin socks or bare feet. Beware of choosing too narrow a boot which may bulge at the sides and inhibit the use of the edge on small holds, or too wide a boot where the sides of the closure touch and prevent the laces from being pulled tight enough.

The uppers are usually made of leather, suede, nylon, canvas or a mixture of these materials and they can be lined or unlined. Most boots stretch with use, particularly those of unlined suede, but these can be shrunk, at least temporarily, by soaking in water for a few hours. Lacing boots up too tightly will tend to speed up this stretching. Comfort is a personal matter when it comes to rock boots and depends on the type of routes for which they are to be used. On long, multi-pitch climbs it is important that the boots are comfortable; on short, technical routes it may be worth enduring some pain for the improved performance a tight boot can give. However, wearing boots that are too tight for too long can lead to foot problems. The strength of your feet and ankles will also influence your choice of boot: those who have strong feet can use a boot which has a less stiff sole and a more flexible upper – qualities often possessed by a friction boot. With any boot larger sizes tend to bend more than the same boot in a small size. In any case a close, firm fitting means that the foot itself stiffens the boot.

Fig 1.1 ABOVE: *A small selection of rock climbing footwear, showing (clockwise from top left) a lightweight, elasticated rock slipper, a rock shoe, a flexible friction boot and an edging boot with a low-cut ankle and a removable stiffener.*

The lacing system should allow the boot to be pulled firm all round the foot. If the eyelets are not reinforced with metal, broad, flat laces will prevent the material from tearing when you tighten the boot and also reduce pressure points.

Boots which are primarily for use on small, positive holds, edging boots, are fairly stiff both laterally (across the width of the sole) and longitudinally (along the length of sole) so that small ledges can be stood on with security and comfort. Smearing boots are softer and more flexible to allow maximum sole-to-rock contact. More flex is also achieved by a soft upper or one which is low cut. With an edging boot the rubber may be harder to preserve the edge for longer. The rand is also important, particularly in cracks where it provides friction and protection. Having the rand cut away at the instep allows easier twisting when using the toes in thin cracks. A shaped cup to hold the heel firmly in place and facilitate heel hooking is a feature common to many boots.

With increased specialisation at the highest grades of rock climbing and the resultant desire to reduce weight, climbing footwear of a different sort has appeared: the shoe and the slipper. The shoe is similar to the boot in most respects except that it gives maximum ankle flex but less ankle protection and may be lighter in weight. It may have a rand only at the front and have a thinner sole than a boot. The slipper is more extreme, being something like a ballet shoe; very light and close-fitting, it is a second skin of high-friction rubber, particularly good when sensitivity is required.

Care of Boots

Rock boots are a vital and expensive piece of equipment, so it makes sense to look after them to obtain the best performance and prolong their life. Many boots have well-made uppers which can be re-soled and re-randed but, although this may be expertly done, the repaired boot is unlikely to be as good as it once was. The rand in particular is unlikely to be of the same quality as the original, so a re-sole before the rand needs repair is a good idea. Re-soled boots can always be used for training.

To get the best performance from the boot, particularly on friction moves, the sole should be clean and the pores in the rubber free from dirt. The sole and rand should be washed and scrubbed regularly after use. Just before a climb, clean any dirt or grit from the sole: these act like ball-bearings and readily attach themselves to the sticky sole. The same applies when leaving any dirty ledge: hands, clothes or a cloth, carried for this purpose, can be used. Water, a brush and a cloth with which to clean the sole may be worth taking to some areas where the foot of the cliffs could be muddy, and having something to stand on while cleaning the boots prior to stepping on to the rock allows a clean start. If your boots get wet with sea water, they should be washed thoroughly with fresh water to remove any salt which can corrode eyelets and stitching.

HELMETS

Whether or not to wear a climbing helmet is, in some situations, a matter of choice but one which should be based on an appreciation of the facts rather than fashion or prejudice. In other situations, however, helmets can be considered essential equipment. Head injuries are unfortunately common in climbing accidents and a large proportion of these are fatal. A helmet will protect the head from some of the effects of falling stones and lessen the chance of severe injury if the head hits the rock in a fall. It will not, however, save the wearer from large falling rocks or long falls. Wearing a helmet should not make you feel immune to these hazards and so venture into places where you would not normally go. Helmets unfortunately can be heavy, hot and uncomfortable, and they can also limit vision and feel obstructive, although these drawbacks usually lessen with familiarity.

The decision whether to wear a helmet or not should be based on the type of climbing to be done. On many cliffs there is little danger of stone fall and on many of the harder climbs the rock is so steep that there is little likelihood of being hit by anything from above or from striking the rock in a fall. On less difficult climbs, however, head injuries from a fall are more likely as the rock tends to be easier-angled and have more ledges and projections. In some places, such as mountain cliffs and on Alpine routes where stone fall is common, helmets are essential, as they are on winter and snow and ice routes where falling material is to be expected. Climbing behind others is another situation in which falling objects are not uncommon.

Helmets are of two main types: those made of GRP (fibreglass) and those which have some type of plastic shell. Fibreglass helmets absorb the energy of a falling object by the breaking of the shell, while plastic helmets absorb less energy themselves but transfer this energy to the cradle which stretches. This means that fibreglass helmets can be made more compactly than plastic ones which must allow for this stretch and the deformation of the shell and so sit higher on the head. In both cases the protection provided by the helmet is lost after one severe impact and both types are subject to deterioration with age.

Climbing helmets are a compromise between their ability to absorb energy and the limits of acceptable size and weight. There is no point in having an ultra-strong helmet if it is too heavy and uncomfortable to wear. The ideal helmet is light, strong, has a comfortable cradle and a chin strap which prevents the helmet from being pushed back off the forehead in a fall. Those which cover the vulnerable temples are safer but feel more restrictive to some wearers. If the helmet is to be worn in a variety of conditions, such as in summer and winter, an adjustable cradle to allow for additional hats and Balaclavas is necessary to ensure a good fit at all times. For Alpine and winter climbing some form of attachment for a head torch is needed and ventilation holes are an advantage in hot weather [*fig. 1.2*].

CHALK

Chalk (light magnesium carbonate) came to climbing from gymnastics where it is used to give a better grip on the apparatus. On rock it is used for the same purpose: that is, to improve the grip on hand holds, especially when it is hot or the climber's hands are sweating. Its use gradually spread through the climbing world from the USA, where it was initially adopted, and it is now common in most climbing areas. At first it tended to be used by climbers at the top of the sport and its use gradually filtered down through the grades. It is of most benefit where the holds are small, slippery or sloping, but usually unnecessary on large holds. Chalk is not normally used on easier climbs, where it is not needed.

Unfortunately, the continual use of chalk on holds, especially those in a sheltered position which are seldom rain-washed, builds up a slippery deposit which itself encourages the further use of chalk. Also, on many climbs, a line of chalked-up holds can form a visual scar besides making the way more obvious and route-finding ability less important. This can either be a good or a bad thing, depending on your point of view. Although it is now in common use, chalk is still frowned on in some places and local ethics should be respected by visiting climbers.

Chalk comes in powder or block form and is usually white, but rock-coloured chalk is available and may well become more popular on aesthetic grounds. It is carried in a chalk bag at the waist where it is accessible to both hands [*fig. 1.3*]. The bag should be wide and deep enough for the whole hand, have a stiffened rim so that it stays open when necessary and a secure closure to prevent spillage when not in use, particularly when the climber is sitting down on a stance or on a descent path. A fibre-pile lining helps when chalking up.

Although chalk is useful on hand holds, this is not the case when the holds are subsequently stood on. Holds used for both the hands and the feet should be chalked as lightly as possible. If a foot hold is to be marked for ease of finding when moving on to it, the rock above the hold rather than the hold itself should be chalked. Devotees of bare-footed climbing can chalk their feet in the usual way!

Besides its physical use on holds, many climbers finding chalking-up a mental help as well: something to do while working out moves, getting their minds under control, making decisions or simply putting off what is to come. Chalk and chalking-up may not ruin your health but it can be addictive.

Fig 1.2 OPPOSITE PAGE ABOVE: *The two main types and shapes of climbing helmet: a fibreglass helmet with an adjustable cradle (left) and a plastic helmet.*

Fig 1.3 OPPOSITE PAGE BELOW: *Chalk bags and chalk in block form. Both have fibre-pile lining and secure closures to prevent spillage.*

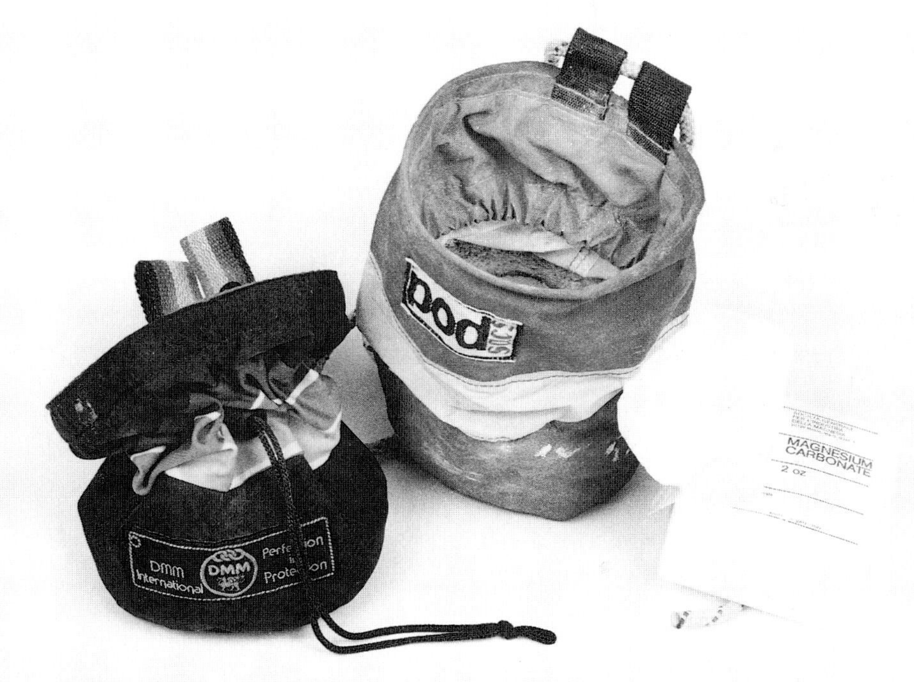

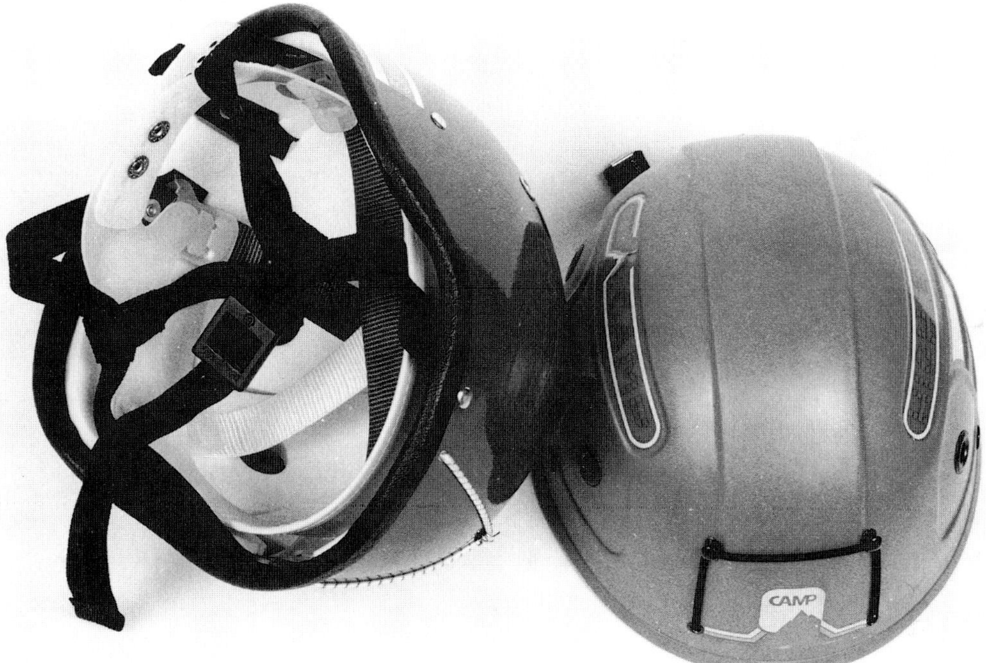
CAMP

pod
DMM
International
DMM
MAGNESIUM
CARBONATE
2 oz

2 Rock Climbing Technique

Rock climbing is a very natural activity and, to begin with, few specialised techniques are required. Using the hands for balance while stepping up using the legs is the basis of much rock climbing. For more difficult climbs less natural techniques have to be learned. Whether this is by trial and error, watching others, reading instructional books or by receiving tuition does not really matter. Some people pick up these methods of movement very quickly, almost instinctively, as in the case of 'natural' climbers; others have to work hard to perfect their technique; but the end result may well be climbers of equal ability. It is the experience of actually climbing that is most important in the acquisition of climbing techniques: every rock climb, virtually every move on rock is unique, so the more you do, the more you learn. It is practice that allows you to improve and progress, to harder climbs and bigger routes perhaps, or simply to climbing with more grace, control and skill. Climbing is for enjoyment and it is up to each individual to follow the line that they wish. 'Harder is better' is not the only philosophy available: people climb for the thrill of being close to nature, battling against the elements, for the pleasure of physical movement, for companionship or for a host of other equally valid reasons, but good and varied technique will enhance everyone's enjoyment.

ATTITUDE

Rock climbing is not simply about physical ability. To climb well you must want to do it and have the mental control to complement the desire. It is this blend of the physical and the mental challenges that gives climbing much of its appeal. With determination, hard work, training and, most importantly, time on the rock, your standard and ability will improve. If you do not really enjoy tackling the problems presented by climbs, strength will only take you so far. Confidence born of experience and knowledge of your ability is as great an asset on many routes as actual physical capability.

USING THE EYES

It has been said, with a great deal of truth, that you climb first with your eyes. Seeing and recognising is essential to all climbing at all different levels. You must first look to see where the climb goes and pick out from the cliff the different rock features that make up the route. This is best done at a distance, for once below the cliff foreshortening can make the climb harder to distinguish. The higher the cliff, the further away you will need to be. Even if you are using a good guide-book, this initial viewing is still invaluable.

When you are actually on the rock (or snow and ice), the eyes lead the way. Holds must be seen – and recognised before they can be used. Although blind moves are by no means uncommon, they are not the norm. The hold, once discovered, must then be used correctly for the situation. With experience the ways in which holds can be utilised will increase and the range of features that can be used as holds will likewise multiply. It is practice that teaches you how small a hold you can pull on or stand on in a given situation, but these holds must first be found.

Many people discover when they begin to climb, or when on a route which they find very difficult, that it is the process of looking, selecting and using the holds properly that lets them down. Their attention focuses on too small an area of rock, usually just in front of their eyes, and they fail to see or recognise holds which are further away. Holds need not be directly in front of the body to be usable and often the solution to a particular problem may lie not straight above but to the side. The area of rock containing viable holds is often much larger than is at first thought.

BODY POSITION

Correct body position is essential for efficient climbing. Basic rock climbing can be compared to climbing a ladder. The body is held vertically with the weight above the feet. This upright posture

Fig 2.1 A good, relaxed position on a slab. The centre of gravity is over the feet pushing them on to the rock; the arms are low to help maintain this position and the eyes are looking down for foot holds, the main means of progress on rock of this nature.

Fig 2.2 By turning the hips at right angles to the rock it is easier to use the sides of the feet and take a higher step without putting so much outwards pressure on the hand holds. This way of climbing suits some individuals, particularly those who are less flexible.

accomplishes two important things: the centre of gravity is kept above the feet so that they are pressed firmly on to the foot holds; and there is space between the body and the rock so that holds can be seen and there is room to lift the feet up on to them. Ideally the hands and arms are kept at about shoulder level and used for balance rather than pulling [*fig. 2.1*]; this is also less strenuous than holding them above head height. If the arms are stretched up too much, the body is pulled towards the rock: this obscures the holds and tends to push the feet outwards and even off the hold. However, on vertical or overhanging rock the upright body position cannot be maintained. At these angles the arms must work harder to stop you from falling backwards but the legs and the feet are still the main means of progress.

Climbing is a dynamic activity and any body position adopted must be easily adaptable so that you can progress easily, using the holds available. A fully extended position is usually one which inhibits fluent movement by obscuring the rock and stopping the legs from pushing effectively. However, there is no fixed, 'correct' posture. When climbing you change body position continually to find the best way to use the holds. Although much climbing is done face-on to the rock, turning sideways-on in some situations can be beneficial, particularly when the holds are also positioned to the side [*fig. 2.2*]. Size, strength, flexibility and personal preference all influence how you climb and the position you adopt.

BALANCE

Much of climbing is about balance and this primarily means standing so that the body is evenly placed over one or both feet and the arms are doing the minimum amount of work maintaining this position. Body position and footwork are the two main ingredients in this. Climbers often talk of 'balance climbing' or 'balance moves', and this generally means climbing on slabby rock where good hand holds are few and the feet do most of the work.

If the body's centre of gravity runs through your base, you will be in balance; if this base is small, such as one foot, you must act to put the centre of gravity over that foot, either to move or stay still unless the hands are also used. This can be done in a variety of ways, depending on the rock, but in a pure balance position over one foot the body is leant to one side while the free leg counter-balances to the other side.

The only way to step up with no hand holds is to have the centre of gravity over the base foot. When holds are available they make the body position less critical but put strain on the arms. Balance in climbing is a continual shifting of body position to allow progress to be made in the most efficient manner.

HOLDS

Progress up rock is made by means of holds for the hands and the feet. Sometimes one hold can be used by the hands followed by the feet. Other holds may be perfect for the hands yet unsuitable as foot holds and vice versa. A crack under a roof may be pulled on but not stood on; a sloping friction hold may give a good foot placement but be useless as a hand hold.

Holds can be used in a variety of ways besides pulling down on and standing up on them, particularly when they become smaller, further apart, less obvious or sloping. With experience and practice you will develop the skill to distinguish which holds to use, how and in what order. The ways in which holds are used depends to some degree on your physique, strength and reach. Climbers of different builds can use the same set of holds in different ways to suit their body and style of climbing. Provided that holds are used in a way which minimises the output of energy and allows progress on to the next holds, there is no right or wrong method. However, it is often the case on harder climbs that the holds can be used only in a particular sequence, in which case the right way is the only way.

Holds need not be a succession of horizontal edges that the hands can curl round and the feet stand on, but can be a whole range of sizes, shapes, angles and configurations. They are, however, most useful when pulled or pushed on in the direction opposite to the one which they face: in other words, a horizontal hold is best pulled down on, a vertical edge or side pull best used for leaning sideways. The climber must approach the rock in an imaginative way in order to make the best use of what is available. This means continual movement of the body and limbs as the holds are used, balance is established and the next holds are seen, recognised and reached in an appropriate manner. Climbing has been called a vertical dance and it is the rock and the holds that choreograph the dance.

Foot Holds

Precise, accurate foot work is essential for good climbing style. The foot should be placed accurately on the hold to make the best use of it and this is best done while actually looking at the hold. Decide on the best way to use the hold before stepping on to it. The smaller the hold, the more accurate the foot placement should be, and when on it the foot should be kept still. On marginal holds a small shift may be enough to cause a slip. Where hand holds allow it, leaning out slightly puts some inward pressure on the hold and increases the security of the foot.

Foot holds are used in two basic ways: edging and smearing. Edging is primarily used on positive holds which are relatively sharp-edged or when wearing stiff footwear. It is usually the inside edge of the boot under the big toe and the ball of the foot that make contact, although it can be any part of the sole. Using the inside edge gives good support yet does not strain the legs, particularly the calves, too much. If the toe is used, such as in small pockets or on tiny incut holds, it can become tiring and painful because of the increased leverage on the feet and legs. It does, however, put the body slightly further out from the rock which can be advantageous in some situations. When edging, the ankle is normally kept above the level of the hold to maintain pressure down on to it [*fig. 2.3*].

Smearing is the technique employed on sloping or rounded holds, although it can be used on some edges as well. As much of the sole as possible is placed over the hold [*fig. 2.4*]. The

Fig 2.3 Edging on a small hold, using the side of the boot under the ball of the foot so as to keep leverage at a minimum. Some inwards pressure helps to keep the foot on the hold.

friction between the rock and the rubber and the sole moulding itself round tiny rugosities provide the grip. When smearing, the toe is generally placed uppermost with ankle flexed to give maximum rock/rubber contact. On marginal smearing holds the foot may well feel as if it is about to slip off and it is only when fully weighted that its true potential is realised. The boot may even begin to slip as the weight is being transferred on to or off it, making this type of climbing feel very precarious and committing. Smearing takes place not only on sloping holds but also in a wide variety of situations which involve 'pressure' climbing.

Many holds can be either edged or smeared and the actual way of using the foot depends on your own preference, how strong your feet are, the type of footwear worn and how good the edges are. Generally, however, the stiffer the boot, the easier it is to edge; the more flexible it is, the better it is for smearing.

Hand Holds

Hand holds come in many different forms but the easiest to use are those that are basically horizontal and incut. The more they slope outwards, the less reassuring they feel. If the hold is big enough

Fig 2.4 Smearing on a sloping slab. The ankle is flexed so that as much sole as possible is put on to the rock.

to accept the whole hand, that is what is used; if smaller, try to get as many fingers on as possible [*fig. 2.5*]. Putting some fingers on top of one another will strengthen the grip and even the little finger can help to make the hand more stable on the hold. On these small holds, flexing the top knuckle inwards is more secure and using the thumb, the strongest finger, will help even more: it can be pressed hard into the index finger on small holds or spread out on to another part of the rock to utilise any other possibilities [*fig. 2.6*]. On the tiniest holds, such as those found on difficult slabs, the thumb itself may be placed on the hold and the other fingers stacked on top of it to bring more of the muscles of the forearm into play. The wrist and arm should be arranged so that the pull comes downwards on the hold and minimises the outward force which would make it less secure. On larger but sloping holds, friction plays an important role, so as much of the fingers and hand as possible is placed on the rock [*fig. 2.7*]. This is known as palming. Even with finger holds, valuable support can be gained from pressing the heel of the hand on to the rock below the hold itself.

The amount of use that can be made of a hold depends not only on the hold itself but also on the

Fig 2.5 ABOVE: *Pulling hard on a vertical edge. The top finger joints are flexed inwards and the thumb is pressed into the index finger for added strength.*

Fig 2.6 BELOW: *Pulling on the same edge as in fig. 2.5, but this time the fingers and thumb are spread to get a better grip. The way a hold is used can vary according to the position of the body in relation to the hold.*

angle of the rock and your body position. On slabs, tiny holds can be used to gain a lot of height; on steep rock the distance for which they can be used is less as they are best while the pull is downwards unless they have an edge to pull out on. Small, flat holds generally become less helpful when moving up past them because of the increased outwards force when the body reaches a certain level. Other holds however, become more useful as height is gained.

Vertical or diagonal holds give side pulls. These can be formed by the edges of cracks, flakes, ribs or other rock features and can range from holds good enough to curl the hand round to poor friction or palming holds. Although these are gripped in the same way as a horizontal hold, the

Fig 2.7 LEFT: *Palming a large, sloping hold to get as much friction as possible from the hands.*

Fig 2.8 BELOW: *Using a vertical edge to lean off to one side. Hanging off this side pull with a straight arm means less muscle strain. The feet are positioned to take as much weight as possible and maintain balance.*

body position is more likely to be leaning off to one side [*fig. 2.8*]. The holds may be difficult to pull directly up on but, if combined with careful footwork and balance, can often be used from above the head to below waist level even on overhanging rock. Sometimes side pulls can be improved by placing the thumb on a feature at one side of the edge: this is the start of a pinch grip where a flange or a rib of rock is gripped between the fingers and the thumb. The more defined the flange, the better the hold, but it is strenuous as the hand must grip tightly. Horizontal holds can be improved if they can be pinched [*fig. 2.9*], and pinching a hold also increases its range of use. Side pulls and pinch grips merge into each other and which is used depends on where the body is in relation to the hold: if the hold is in front of the body, more of a pinch-type of grip must be used. As rock shows an infinite variety of forms, so holds and the ways in which they can be used vary from one technique to another. Some holds offer a range of uses: pockets, for example, can be pulled up on, used as side pulls and finally used as undercuts.

Fig 2.9 Pinching a horizontal flange with the left hand to improve the grip on a poor, sloping hold. The other hand is crossed over to reach a hold further up and to the side as this is easier than trying to change hands on the pinch.

Not all holds are for pulling on. Many can be used for downwards pressure and some can only be used in this fashion. When applying pressure, the hand can be placed on the hold in several ways, depending on the rock's configuration. On pure pressure holds where friction is important, using the palm and heel of the hand with the fingers pointing downwards is most effective. On small pressure holds it may be the fingertips which are the points of contact with the rock.

A hold may start off being pulled down on, then the pull changed to a push when the hold is about shoulder level. The epitome of this is a pure mantelshelf where a hold above the head is eventually stood on without the use of any other holds. To mantelshelf on to a ledge on a smooth wall, pull up on the hold while running your feet up the rock. Once the hands are below the shoulders, push up on to straight arms. When on an extended arm above the hold, the locked bones take the load rather than the muscles. Then get a foot on the ledge, rock the body over the top of it and stand up. If there are other holds available, they will make every part of this easier, otherwise a mantelshelf is strenuous and dynamic to start and requires delicate balance to finish [*figs. 2.10 and 2.11*].

CRACKS

Cracks can be used as holds in a variety of ways, some of which are obvious and natural, others of which are not. A horizontal crack can be used as a normal hold and a vertical crack can give a side pull. However, these use only one side of the crack; if the whole crack is used, a wide range of different holds become possible.

Jamming, in its simplest form, is putting part of the body such as a hand or foot in a crack and manipulating it so that it sticks or jams. If the crack narrows, insert at the wide point and pull or push until a jam is formed. Not all cracks, however, are so accommodating, and more complex techniques must therefore be learned for those which are parallel-sided or flared.

Cracks are basically of two types: the straight-in or face crack as found in walls; and the crack situated in a corner or groove. Although the actual jam may be the same in both cases, the way

Fig 2.10 ABOVE LEFT: *A dynamic pull/push action to get up on straight arms and draw one foot on to the ledge is the start of this mantelshelf.*

Fig 2.11 ABOVE RIGHT: *The mantelshelf is finished by turning the base hand to palm down with fingers out and the arm locked on the bones. In this stable position balance can be established over the foot on the ledge; in this case it is made much easier by the use of the diagonal edge for the other hand.*

Fig 2.12 LEFT: *Jamming in a straight-in crack. The top hand is jammed with the thumb down and the lower hand with the thumb up. The hands can be crossed over or moved up the crack in that order. The lower foot is smearing into a corner to get as much contact between the rock and the sole and rand of the boot as possible.*

in which the arms are used may be different. In a straight-in crack the hands can be crossed over alternately, as though climbing a rope [*fig. 2.12*]; in a corner crack the hands may be kept in the same order and moved up the crack one at a time. Which hand is on top will depend on which way the crack goes; when facing the crack, the outer hand is on the top. That is, if the right shoulder is against the rock the left hand will be on top.

However, these are only general pointers and the shape of the crack and the actual manoeuvre dictate how the arms are placed.

Cracks come in various widths, defined by climbers according to what part of the body can be jammed in them. On many rock types, however, cracks vary in size and depth over a short distance: they may lean one way or the other, zig-zag, fade out, flare or merge into other features. The actual technique used to climb a crack will depend on several factors, including the rock architecture. Ample face holds may make jamming unnecessary and more conventional climbing methods viable. The size of your hands also affects the type of jam used – one person's hand jam may be another's fist size and so on. Jams can be used in vertical, diagonal or horizontal cracks but they do demand a fair amount of practice.

Finger Cracks

The narrowest usable cracks are those which accept the tips of the fingers. If there is a constriction, pull the fingers down so that the knuckles wedge above it; if not, twist the fingers to lock them in place. This is usually done with the thumb down and the wrist kept close to the rock so that by twisting the wrist and keeping the elbow down the fingers are torqued more securely. With the thumbs-up position, however, it is possible to reach slightly further [*fig. 2.13*] and, although the jam initially feels less secure, it can improve as you move up on it. But often the size, shape and location of the crack dictates which way the fingers must go. Any irregularities in the crack or places where the edge is more pronounced can be used to improve the jam.

Fig 2.13 Finger-tip jam in a very narrow crack. This jam is placed thumb up so that the little finger can be inserted into the crack.

Fig 2.14 Finger jam in which three fingers are stacked on top of each other to improve the grip. As the forearm pulls down, the fingers are twisted more securely across the crack.

The next size up in cracks is that where it is possible to insert the fingers up to the first knuckle and use them to jam. Stacking fingers on top of each other helps make the jam more secure by bringing more of the forearm muscles into play [*fig. 2.14*].

Off-Hand Cracks

These are cracks which are too big to finger jam but too small to get the whole hand into and so are a difficult size to use comfortably. Any method of off-hand jamming is liable to be strenuous and feel insecure, especially if there are no constrictions against which some part of the hand can be locked.

Finger torquing is done by placing the fingers in the crack as far as possible. The arm then levers down and twists the fingers across the crack giving a very strenuous jam. An alternative is the seemingly absurd thumb lock where the thumb is inserted vertically in the crack, bent across it and the index and middle fingers placed on top of the thumb knuckle. Pulling down with the fingers and twisting with the forearm makes this lock. The third form of off-hand jam is the knuckle jam where two or three fingers are put in the crack, preferably above a constriction. The fingers are horizontal with the palm facing the rock and they are then curled into a small fist to expand the knuckles and jam them. This will probably be painful as so little of the hand is in contact with the rock and taking the strain.

Hand Cracks

The classic, most versatile and least precarious type of jam is where the whole hand is put in the crack. Any constriction against which it can be pulled will improve holding power, and placing the thumb down will twist the hand more firmly against the sides of the crack. Irregularities inside the crack can also give added security.

Hand jams come in various sizes. In the narrowest cases the hand is pushed into the crack with the fingers flat, pointing upwards, and then pulled down to wedge it in place. In wider cracks the hand size is increased by folding the thumb into the palm [*fig. 2.15*]. In cracks that are wider still the hand is cupped so that the jam is maintained by powerful pressure on the back of the knuckles on one side and the heel of the hand and the fingertips on the other. To make this bridge more secure the thumb can be pressed on the lower end of the index finger.

Fist Cracks

For the smallest fist cracks the hand is made into a fist with the thumb tucked across the palm. This is placed in the crack and turned so that the sides of the hand lock against the sides of the crack. For the basic fist jam, the hand is put in the crack, palm up or down, and a fist formed so that the sides of the hand wedge in the crack. Pushing the little finger into the palm helps to push out the fleshy part of the hand and make a fatter fist [*fig. 2.16*]. Further increase in size can be obtained by moving the thumb out and pressing it against the side of the index finger. Changing the actual position of the fingers within the fist will also vary the size.

Fig 2.15 Classic hand jam with the thumb tucked into the palm of the hand.

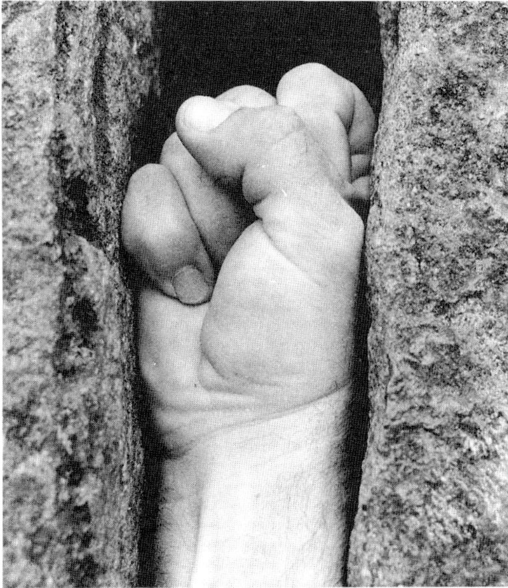

Fig 2.16 Fist jam in a wide crack. The little finger is pushed into the palm to expand that side of the hand.

Foot Jams

The feet can also be jammed in cracks when other holds are absent. If the crack is too thin to admit any part of the boot, the edges of the crack must be used. In the case of a straight-in crack that is not too steep, the inside edge of the boot, toe down, is smeared. If the crack is steep, the boot edge, toe up, is used for friction. In the case of a crack in a corner or groove the toe is wedged in, heel down, and the sole and rand of the boot smeared on to the rock [*fig. 2.12,* page 15]. In all these cases, changes of angle or indentations can be used to improve the hold.

Thin cracks can be jammed by putting the toe in the crack with the outside of the ankle down. By standing up and keeping the heel low the toe is twisted more securely into the crack. In wider cracks the foot is turned, so that the front of the boot can be placed in the crack and twisted to secure it. These jams can make the feet and ankles sore. In even broader cracks the boot can be placed horizontally and the friction between the rand and the side walls used. If the opening is wider than the foot, the jam must be kept in place by twisting the leg, so that the foot is diagonal and the inside and outside of the boot are putting pressure on the sides of the crack. Alternatively, a jam can be formed between the inside edge of the sole and the outside of the ankle. It is worth noting that foot jams can be very secure and sometimes difficult to remove. This can be dangerous in the event of a fall.

Off-Width Cracks

Off-width cracks are greater than fist-width but too narrow to admit the whole body. In general they are strenuous, feel insecure and require the whole body to be used correctly for efficient progress. The hands, arms, feet and legs must all work together in a controlled and organised manner.

In an off-width crack you face sideways, this direction being determined by the crack itself. If one edge protrudes, keep your back to it; if it leans, face downwards but also investigate the interior for alternative holds. Any helpful irregularities in this size of crack should be used gratefully.

There are several ways to use the hands and arms in an off-width. Normally the inside arm jams and the outer hand is held about shoulder level and pulls on the outside edge of the crack. In the narrowest off-widths an arm bar can be used. The inside arm is put in the crack as far as the shoulder: the palm of the hand presses on one side while the elbow, back of the upper arm and shoulder press on the opposite wall [*fig. 2.17*]. The forearm lock is made by putting the arm in the crack, palm up and horizontal, then bending it back towards the shoulder to expand the muscle and produce the jam. In wider cracks the arm lock can be used. Here the elbow is bent and, with the palm facing away from the body, put in the crack. By pulling the arm out slightly the angle at the elbow is opened and the jam created [*fig. 2.18*]. In the shoulder lock, which is a variation of this, the arm is placed vertically, elbow up, palm down, and wedged by pulling down on it [*fig. 2.19*]. This is the least strenuous of these off-width techniques and useful for resting. In off-width cracks, combinations of jams using both hands can be employed, such as placing one hand against one side and putting a fist or hand jam between it and the rock [*fig. 2.20*], or even putting two fist jams side by side to fill up the crack.

As these jams can only be made by the arms in the crack, the feet and legs must not just move you up the crack, but must also hold you in place while the next jam is formed. The inside leg is kept in the crack with the knee bent and jammed by twisting the foot diagonally across the crack. Or a knee can be jammed by bending the leg then bringing the foot up towards the body, expanding the muscles at the side of the knee. Alternatively, the lower leg can be jammed by placing it in the crack and expanding the calf muscle.

The outside leg is used to heel and toe jam. The foot is put across the crack with the toe lower than the heel and jammed by pressing down and twisting [*fig. 2.21*]. If there are holds on the edge or the outside, it is usually better to use these. If the crack is too wide to heel and toe jam, the feet can be T-stacked: one foot is placed horizontally in the crack and the other foot wedged between it and the opposite wall.

To progress using off-width techniques, rhythm is important. The feet are brought up in a knees-bent position below the body and jammed. The arm is loosened slightly, the legs straightened, the body pushed upwards. The arm jam is then re-secured for the feet to be brought up and the cycle repeated to pump you up the crack.

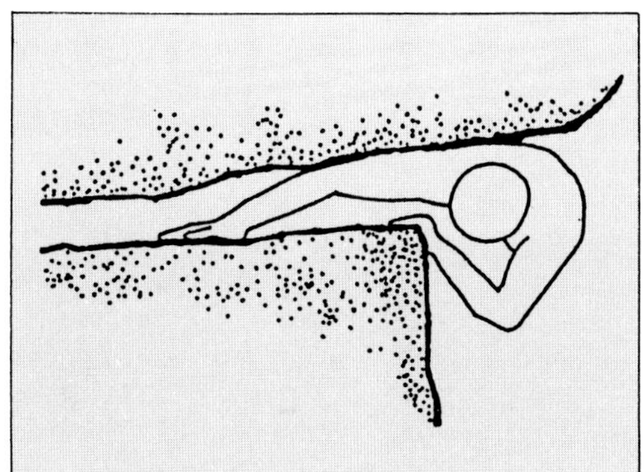

Fig 2.17 Using an arm bar with the inside arm in an off-width crack while the outer arm pulls on the edge of the crack.

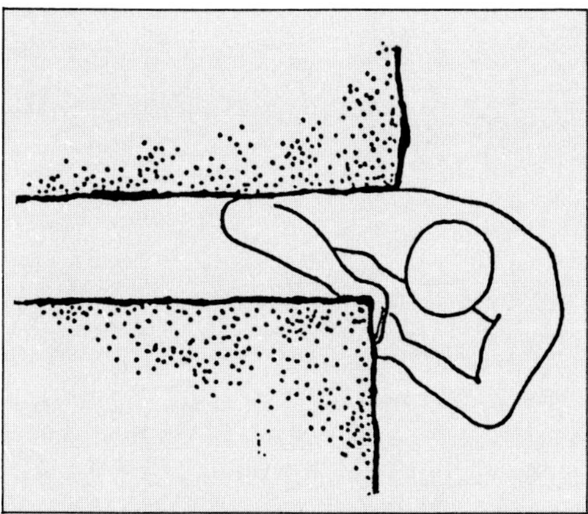

Fig 2.18 An arm lock in an off-width crack.

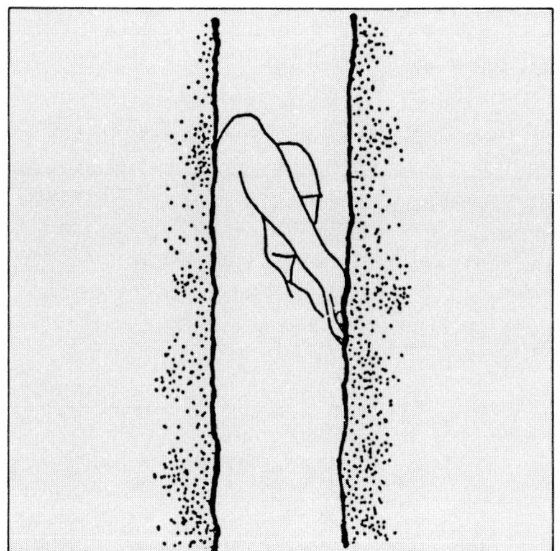

Fig 2.19 A shoulder lock in an off-width crack.

CHIMNEYS

When a fissure is wide enough to permit the entry of a body, it is known as a chimney. Chimneys can vary from the tight squeeze type, almost claustrophobic in their embrace, to openings as wide as you can span. By virtue of the fact that there is a lot of rock within reach there may also be more holds, which means that chimneys may form fairly amiable means of progress. However, like cracks, chimneys present the opportunity to use more specialised techniques which, once mastered, have a wide range of applications elsewhere.

Chimneys can be climbed by the conventional use of holds or by opposed pressure by pushing outwards against both walls. Movement is by releasing pressure at one place to progress part of the body, then re-applying pressure and relaxing another part in order to move it up. The actual combination used depends on the width of the chimney.

In a squeeze chimney it is difficult to move any part of the body; often it is as difficult to fall out as it is to move up. Even chest expansion can wedge you securely, so progress is by a shuffling, squirming action. The feet can heel and toe or T-stack, the hands are kept low and palmed on the rock or used for arm bars. Sometimes, if the fault is deep enough, a diagonal movement can be used. The lower body is brought up to one side, the upper body moved to the vertical above it and the process repeated. Staying on the outside,

Fig 2.20 A fist and hand jammed side by side to fill up a wide crack.

Fig 2.21 In a squeeze chimney the hands are used to push the body up and the feet heel and toe jam.

Fig 2.22 Back and knee position in a chimney. A safe position but painful on unprotected knees.

Fig 2.23 Back and foot in a wider chimney which flares outwards and so calls for more careful use of the feet.

however, normally offers more opportunities to use holds on the edges [*fig. 2.21*].

In wider chimneys, back and knee technique is employed. With the back and the boot soles on one wall and the knees and hands on the other, pressure can be exerted [*fig. 2.22*]. To ascend, either squirm or alternately lock and raise the top and the bottom parts of the body. The next width up can be climbed using back and foot. With the back on one wall, feet on the opposite and the hands on holds or pressing on the wall at the climber's back [*figs 2.23 and 2.24*], progress is made by pushing forward to move up the back, then walking the feet up to start a new cycle. Again the principle of maintaining pressure with one part of the body while raising another part applies. It is also possible to put one foot on the wall behind and one on the wall in front. Other variations can be discovered fairly easily and normally feel quite safe and secure.

In a chimney that is too wide to back and foot, bridging (stemming) can be used. Instead of facing across the chimney, face either in or out depending on where most holds are liable to be found, with a foot and a hand on each wall. The feet are kept as flat as possible for maximum friction and the hands are palmed on the walls or used on any holds. Progress is by moving the arms and legs alternately, or both legs then both arms.

If a fault is too wide to bridge, it may be

climbed by spanning the gap in a horizontal position, feet on one wall, hands on the opposite. Progress is made by walking these points of contact up the rock. This is strenuous, scary and fortunately does not often have to be resorted to, although on occasion it may be used in deep grooves.

OPPOSED PRESSURE

There are several climbing techniques which use opposed pressure. The majority of these involve vertical features such as cracks, corners, flakes or arétes. Opposed pressure means pulling or pushing with one part of the body while countering this with a pull or a push from another part. Chimney techniques such as back and foot or bridging are opposed pressure techniques, as are various types of holds and jams. A pinch grip, for instance, where the fingers are on one side of a projection and the thumb on the other, requires pressure. In a crack a sprag can be used: the fingers grip one edge while the thumb presses against the other side to form a hold [*fig. 2.25*]. Closely spaced cracks can be used by pulling outwards on each edge; fins of rock can be used by pushing inwards on each side. On a narrow ridge 'à cheval' uses opposed pressure by pushing inwards with the legs while sitting astride the ridge.

Fig 2.24 Back and foot in a chimney.

Bridging

Although bridging is a fairly obvious technique when there are two walls facing each other, as in a chimney, it can be used in many other situations. In the bridging position the legs and feet are straddled out to each side and the weight of the body pushing downwards presses them against the rock. Even the hands and arms, if placed in this position, can bridge. Most features which are deep enough and have two walls, such as grooves and corners, can be bridged. And more subtle bridges are possible: two parallel cracks, ribs and vertical or diagonal edges offer bridging potential. Although positive holds are an advantage, much bridging, especially in corners, is done by smearing on either wall [*fig. 2.26*]. Even in overhanging corners it is possible to maintain a vertical body position if the feet are kept towards the outside edge, and surprisingly steep rock can be climbed in a balanced fashion.

Bridging can be hard on the legs which are usually kept fairly straight, but resting a knee on the rock helps relieve the strain. On the plus side, even on steep rock adopting a bridging position helps to take some of the strain off the arms.

Fig 2.25 A sprag: the thumb presses on one side of the crack while the fingers pull against the opposite edge.

Fig 2.26 Bridging on smearing holds in an open groove.

Fig 2.28 A layaway on the edge to allow a higher bridging position to be achieved. This requires careful foot work to prevent swinging out and off.

Laybacking

Laybacking, perhaps the purest form of opposed pressure technique, is where the arms pull against an edge while the feet press against the rock. It is strenuous and should be done forcefully and quickly or failure can result, either through strength running out or by compromising technique in trying to save strength. The most obvious type of layback feature is a corner with a crack at its back. With the hands in the crack and the feet pushing against the wall, the feet are walked up the rock and the hands shuffled up the crack. The pull with the arms is countered by the press of the legs. The higher the feet, the more securely they are pressed against the rock but the more strength is used; if the feet are kept low, less effort is required but there is a greater chance of them slipping off. Any positive holds should be used for the feet so that a more upright and less strenuous position can at times be adopted [*fig. 2.27*].

Fig 2.27 A simple layback in a slabby corner where a fairly upright body position can be adopted.

Laybacks can also be used on more open features such as flakes. A problem here is that the body can swing round out of balance as there is no side wall to maintain stability. To counteract this tendency to swing, or 'barn-door', the foot further away from the edge is placed out to the side.

Even arêtes and edges can be laybacked: the hands pull across and down while the feet smear or use any available holds. Here the question of balance is even more critical and the feet must be

Fig 2.29 An undercling can be used to gain a good deal of height, particularly if the feet can be worked high up to beneath the hands.

placed carefully to resist the tendency to swing out and off.

Layaways

The layaway is the layback's little brother; here the layback type of position is adopted for a single move. Using an edge, the body is leant away from it so that a foot can be brought up to a hold and the body pulled up and across into a higher position. While moving up, the side pull can be used for quite a long time if you continue to lean away from it until balance is regained or new holds reached [*fig. 2.28*].

Underclings or undercuts

These are basically holds which are upside-down and, like other holds, the best are incut and the worst rounded or sloping. By leaning out on an undercut, the feet are walked up the rock to close below the hands and the legs then push and straighten, with the arm still pulling, so that progress is made. When held above the head with an extended arm, undercuts are both strenuous and insecure, but, as height is gained, they improve and become more useful when below waist level. The climber can then lean out from the rock to reach holds above. Like any hold, the more it is incut the better it is to use, but even sloping undercuts can be palmed in some situations [*fig. 2.29*].

OVERHANGS

Climbers describe overhangs in several ways depending on their actual shape and the rock on which they lie. They can be bulges, overlaps, overhangs, roofs or ceilings, and each description implies a slightly different form. For example, an overlap is most usually associated with slabby rock, while a roof is a near-horizontal feature but may vary considerably in size. The way in which overhangs are climbed depends on several factors such as the rock itself, the features they contain and their position as regards other features. The climb may be made using holds, or by bridging, jamming, chimneying or laybacking; in fact any technique may need to be employed, but some points are applicable to overhangs in general

That overhangs are strenuous is obvious, so decide what to do before launching out: get the feet as high as possible under the overhang for maximum reach and keep them on the rock. Any weight taken on the feet is a saving on the arms. If the feet do slip off, the resultant swing may cause the hands to be pulled off as well. No matter how radical the rock, foot-work is still vital.

One manoeuvre that overhangs encourage is the heel-hook. The boot heel is placed on a high hold, even above head level, and used to take some of the weight off the arms [*fig. 2.30*]. Heel-hooking underneath a roof or over the lip of an overhang can make reaching out, or pulling round from the horizontal to the vertical, less tiring. In fact, heel- or toe-hooking have a number of applications where balance is difficult to maintain, as when laybacking an edge or leaning a long way to one side to reach other holds. The more imaginative you are, the greater the opportunities for their use.

OTHER MOVES

Several other types of move exist which are more specialised than those already described and tend to be confined to harder routes and boulder problems.

Fig 2.30 A heel hook on an overhanging wall is used to take some of the weight off the hands and arms.

Dynos

Occasionally a climber meets a situation where the next hold is completely out of reach with no way of getting to it. The choice is then to retreat or make a dynamic move or a dyno. These used to be referred to as jumps or lunges, but in recent years have gained respectability and are now recognised moves. To dyno you should first be sure that what you are going for is a hold and that, if you fail to reach it or hold on to it, the consequences will not be too dire. Sink down slightly and, with the legs pushing and the arms pulling, extend towards the hold. Bouncing up and down a few times can help to prepare you for this sudden upward motion. This type of move is used more often on the harder routes, but your size is obviously a factor: shorter climbers tend to do more dynos. Dynos also require some practice to establish just how far you can extend and how effectively you can maintain a grip when you get to the hold. Timing is critical in these dynamic movements and they can vary from being an extension upwards with nothing for the hands to a no-points-of-contact leap. This type of manoeuvre is likely to be used when bouldering and on climbing walls, but as climbs continue to increase in difficulty, dynos seem destined to become more usual and more sophisticated.

Rock-over

A rock-over is basically an extremely high step up on to a hold with little or nothing in the way of holds above. The foot is placed on the hold, even being helped up with the use of the hand if it is really high, and the body moved sideways and up until it is over the foot and the hold. Once in balance over this foot you can stand up. This move often has to be done in a dynamic manner to get established over the hold and, as with any high step, 'toe jabs' with the lower foot can help to maintain balance and momentum. The extreme flexion involved can be damaging to the knee.

Locking Off

Locking off is not so much a move as a static position between moves which is held so that one hand can be freed to reach as high as possible. Locking off can be very tiring as the position must be held with the arm bent, and the poorer the foot holds and the steeper the rock, the greater the strain on these arm muscles. When in this position, using the outside edge of the boot can enable you to get your body closer into the rock and so reach a little further.

TRAVERSING

Traversing basically means going across the rock and most techniques can be used to achieve it. However, the holds are used only for support, not to gain height, so it may be possible to use smaller holds. The usual body position is adopted but, on a traverse, one side of the body leads while the other follows.

If there is a continuous hold or line of holds for the hands, a hand traverse may be called for. The hands pull on the holds while the feet are kept high and push against the rock for friction. Hand traverses can be very tiring if there are no foot holds [*fig. 2.31*] and they should be done powerfully and swiftly. If there are enough holds, each hand can have its own but if not they will have to change over. Swapping hands can be done by progressively removing the lead hand while replacing it with the following one. (This sharing of holds can be done on ascent as well.) Alternatively, it may be possible to cross arms in front of the body to reach the next hold [*fig. 2.9,* page 13]. To reach a little further the following arm can be

Fig 2.31 ABOVE: *On a hand traverse where there is an excellent continuous crack for the hands the feet must be pushed as flat as possible against the rock to use what friction they can.*

Fig 2.32 BELOW: *Traversing on a steep wall. The top climber is in a good balanced bridging position; the lower climber is using more strength in a somewhat constricted body position.*

crossed in front of the body but under the leading arm. The body has to turn sideways-on to the rock for this and so there is more outwards force on the gripping hand, making this a more strenuous position to adopt.

On continuous foot ledges it may be possible to shuffle along, one foot at a time. With the feet on small holds, a little hop can be made to replace the leading foot with the following one. Another way is to step the following foot past the leading one on to the next hold. Whether the foot goes between the body and the rock or behind the body depends on the configuration of the rock and the quality of the hand holds. Because of the nature of traversing, the bridging position is one that tends to be used quite a lot, particularly when regaining a balanced position [*fig. 2.32*].

DOWN CLIMBING

The techniques of down climbing are little different from those of ascent, although the holds may be more difficult to see from above. Climbing down rock already ascended is made easier by knowledge of the holds, but some types of move, such as the mantelshelf, can be more difficult to reverse. It is generally easier to lower yourself on small holds than pull up on them, as gravity helps rather than hinders, and this is true for several strenuous manoeuvres. Balance moves, on the other hand, may be harder to reverse.

When descending, you can face different ways, depending on the angle of the rock. On easy terrain it is best to face out so that the holds are more easily seen. The hands are kept low and used for pressure. On steeper ground facing sideways still permits good visibility but allows holds to be used in a satisfactory manner. If this feels too precarious, it is best to face in; this may, however, mean leaning out further than usual to see holds. If the rock is too difficult to down climb safely, an abseil is probably necessary.

RESTING

Climbing can be tiring, not just physically but mentally as well. Being able to rest allows you to regain strength and drive for the next section, and resting places permit the rock to be broken down into more manageable portions. Many modern routes do not have any resting places, whereas easy climbs may have resting possibilities after almost every move, but the majority of climbs lie somewhere between these two extremes.

If a resting place is obvious, such as a large ledge, there is no problem once this is reached; stand or sit on it until you have recovered, then carry on. Many resting places, however, require more thought and imagination. Any of the chimneying techniques allow the arms to be rested, perhaps even the legs as well, and it is often possible to use these in much more open situations than the confines of a chimney – corners and grooves being two of the more frequently occurring examples. Bridging is also an extremely useful resting position as it offers the chance to get the body weight balanced over the feet [*fig. 2.33*]. Simply altering the method of climbing, to use another set of muscles, also helps: changing from laybacking to bridging or jamming is one way to rest at least some of the upper body muscles. A change may not be as good as a rest but it does help.

It is the arms which are most likely to tire, and if a hands-off rest is not possible, the arms can be

Fig 2.33 Using a bridging position to rest by employing holds out from the corner to get into a position where the hands are not needed.

rested alternately. Hang on with one and let the other recover; the resting arm should be hung low, the hand shaken and the fingers flexed to encourage the blood circulation back into the overworked muscles. The working arm should be kept straight so that most of the weight is taken on the skeleton (hanging on a bent arm means that the arm muscles are still working). Alternate the arms until ready to continue, but remember that energy is still being used while hanging there, so that it may become a case of diminishing returns after a time. This straight arm position is also adopted on steep rock when good holds are kept at arm's length while the feet are sorted out.

The feet and legs can become tired if using small holds for a long time. If a hold large enough to rest on cannot be found, the feet are rested alternately or a different part of the foot used to take the strain. If the heel can be used, this is good for resting the calf muscle. Changing from edging to smearing also spreads the strain.

Many resting positions are not obvious and ingenuity can pay dividends. A change of angle, a different width of crack, a corner, even an overhang can provide a much needed resting place if approached with an open, inventive mind and a good repertoire of climbing techniques. Knee locks in cracks, jamming and wedging your head under an overhang, lying along narrow slots and ledges or even hanging from your feet can be a form of rest but mental relaxation and breathing control are vital for effective recuperation.

PROBLEM ROCK

Loose, brittle or unsound rock is a problem which every active climber will encounter sooner or later: even the best cliffs will probably have dubious holds somewhere. Some loose rock can be climbed safely if the holds are used correctly and this usually means pulling or pushing them in the correct direction. If a loose hold must be used, determine the direction in which it is strongest and use it that way – often an outward pull is unsafe when a downward pull may be relatively secure. If a hold is suspect, hit it firmly with the heel of the hand to see if it moves or vibrates; if it does, treat it with care.

Brittle rock, in many ways, is more difficult to deal with as the holds may fail suddenly and this is hard to anticipate. On such rock look carefully at the holds and work out how, and why, they might fail, and treat all holds with respect. Jamming in a crack rather than climbing on face holds is often the better alternative; avoid powerful moves if possible. Distribute your weight as evenly as you can and do not rely too much on one hold. Climb gently, avoid any sudden, violent moves and try to maintain three points of contact with the rock.

Vegetation can also be a problem, particularly when it is wet. Large trees and bushes can be a positive help on some routes, but smaller shrubs and grasses can be dangerous as they are unreliable hand holds and slippery under foot. If they must be used, grip as much of the vegetation as near to the earth as possible to reduce leverage and spread the load. If the soil is soft enough, dig the fingers down into the ground among the roots for extra security. Before pulling on any vegetation determine whether it is sitting firmly on a ledge or lying on sloping rock: in the latter case you may have to clear it off to see if it is obscuring holds. When leaving vegetated ledges, clean and dry your boots as you did when starting off from the ground. Even standing on a few blades of grass can have a serious effect on sole friction.

ROCK TYPES

Climbing and holds cannot be divorced from the rock on which they lie and an understanding of basic geology will help you to get more out of routes. Different rocks run to different types of holds and have different frictional properties. Sedimentary rocks such as gritstone, limestone and sandstone often exhibit their original bedding in one way or another; granite shows distinctive cracks, flakes and featureless slabs; volcanic rocks such as rhyolite give varied and interesting climbing often on good rough rock; soluble rocks like limestone frequently show the results of water action, while metamorphic rocks such as schists and slates may split easily along certain lines. When starting to climb on an unfamiliar type of rock, it is often worth lowering your standard for a few routes until you are familiar with the types of hold, moves and friction that the rock provides. Friction climbing up a bald granite slab can feel very different from muscling up some overhanging limestone wall, even though both routes may be of the same degree of difficulty.

3 Climbing Equipment

THE ROPE

The rope, more than anything else, is the piece of equipment most closely associated with climbing. The first ropes used for climbing were of natural fibres such as manila and hemp but their low energy-absorbing characteristics ensured that the security they provided was more psychological than real – for the leader at least. Because of this and because of the lack of worthwhile protection there arose the maxim that the leader must not fall. This state of affairs continued until after the Second World War when nylon ropes became generally available. These ropes, like the earlier ones, were of hawser-laid construction in which three bundles of fibres were twisted or laid together [*fig. 3.1*]. The new ropes were a vast improvement as they could be relied upon to stop a fall without breaking but they tended to kink badly, stretch excessively and, because of their laid construction, spin when hung on. In the 1950s the first of the modern type of climbing ropes were made. These are of a kernmantel construction in which a braided sheath, the mantel, surrounds more loosely laid bundles of fibres, the kern or the core. For modern climbing, kernmantel ropes are used almost exclusively and are the type referred to throughout this book.

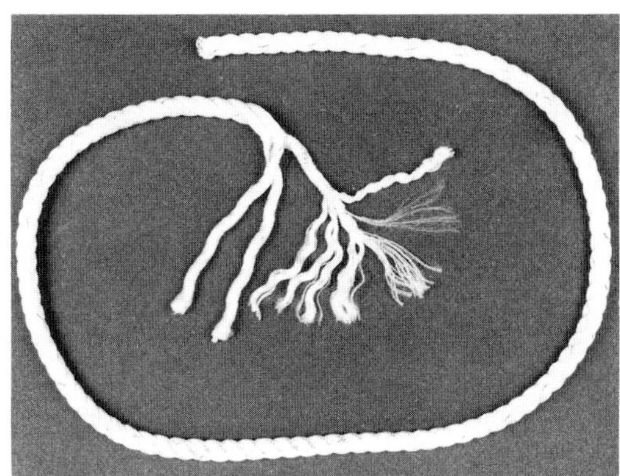

Fig 3.1 Hawser-laid rope constructed of three bundles of twisted nylon fibres.

Rope Sizes and Lengths

The ropes used in climbing are either single or half-ropes. A single rope, which can be used on its own for climbing, has an approximate diameter of 11mm. Half-ropes are about 9mm in diameter and these must be used double to give a safe system. (These diameters may in fact vary from about 11.5mm down to 8.5mm.) The ends of a climbing rope should be marked with '1' or '½' to indicate whether it is a single or a half-rope.

Ropes come in a variety of lengths, usually 40m, 45m and 50m. The first is suitable for outcrop climbing, but for longer routes 45m is commonly used. Ropes of 50m, however, are becoming more usual and have several advantages, particularly in the Alps and other areas where long pitches are to

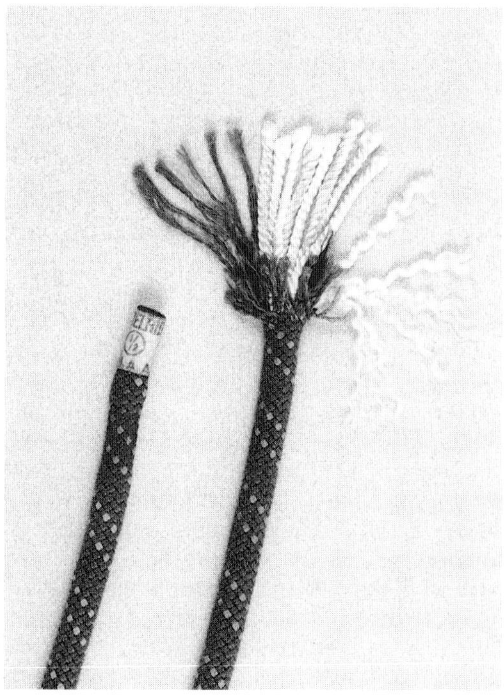

Fig 3.2 Kernmantel rope. Note the bundles of loosely laid continuous fibres which make up the core surrounded by the woven sheath. The other end of this 9mm rope is marked with '½', showing that it is a half-rope.

be expected and on snow and ice climbs when belays may be difficult to arrange. Ropes of 55m are also becoming more popular where belays are far apart or on climbs which have fixed anchor points 50m apart.

Rope Construction

A kernmantel rope is made up of bundles of loosely laid continuous nylon fibres which form its core and this is surrounded by a braided sheath [*fig. 3.2*]. The core provides most of the strength and weight of the rope – about 70–75 per cent – and is responsible for most of its dynamic properties: that is, its ability to stretch under load. The sheath which surrounds the core protects it and gives the rope its handling characteristics and colour; it must be constructed so that it will not readily slip over the core. A tightly woven sheath makes a rope stiff and resistant to abrasion; a sheath of a looser and more open weave makes a rope more supple and more easily managed which will knot well but be more liable to snag on the rock. It may also allow grit to work its way into the rope and so damage it. A softer sheath is also more liable to slip over the core and this can result in bulges in the rope which will wear more readily.

The core of the rope is usually white as the dyeing of the fibres produces some strength loss. The sheath, however, is coloured; this makes the rope easier to see and any cuts in the sheath more obvious as the white core shows through. Ropes may also be made waterproof to cut down water absorption and the associated increase in weight. The fibres in these treated ropes are impregnated with silicone, paraffin or Teflon either before or after construction.

Rope Strength

The breaking strength of a modern rope is well above any force which should be created in a fall. A single rope has a breaking strength of about 2300kg and a half-rope about 1500kg. Knots in the rope, however, cause a decrease in strength of between 25 and 45 per cent, depending on the knot used. Running the rope over an edge also causes a loss of strength – about 30 per cent when over a 5mm radius edge such as a karabiner. The sharper the edge, the greater the strength loss. This is because the rope is not stressed evenly, the fibres on the outer part of the curve being stretched more than those on the inside, so only part of the rope's cross-section absorbs energy. However, in the extremely unlikely event of a well-cared-for modern rope breaking, it would almost certainly occur over an edge rather than at a knot. Ropes which are saturated with water or frozen also show a significant loss of strength.

Energy Absorption

The rope's ability to absorb the energy created in a fall depends on how much it stretches. This stretch occurs as the fibres themselves lengthen and because of the way in which the rope is constructed. A rope which stretches a lot will arrest a fall relatively gently, while a rope which stretches only a little will cause an abrupt stop. The maximum force exerted on a rope when arresting a fall is known as the impact force and the resultant stretch is the impact force elongation. Low impact force means large impact force elongation: that is, the more a rope stretches, the less the force will be taken by the falling climber and all parts of the belay system to which the rope is attached. Unfortunately, the more the rope stretches, the further the climber will fall, so increasing his chance of hitting the ground or a rock projection. In a fall of medium severity the rope elongation is between 10 and 15 per cent.

The actual breaking strength of a rope is of less importance to the climber than the impact force. A rope could be made incredibly strong, but if it stopped a falling body too quickly it would impart unacceptably high forces to that body. Forces higher than 8G (8 times body weight) will inflict serious injury and the maximum impact force that a climbing rope should have is 1200kg.

Fall Factors

Fall factors are a useful concept in understanding the forces involved in a fall. While the energy developed in a fall is proportional to the distance fallen, the rope's ability to absorb that energy is proportional to the length of rope involved. The fall factor is the length of the fall divided by the length of rope available and this can vary between 0 and 2 under normal conditions [*fig. 3.3*]. For example, a leader 5m above a belay with no intermediate protection would fall 10m should he slip: this gives a fall factor of 2. Likewise a fall of 30m from 15m above a belay would also give a fall factor of 2. However, if the leader in the latter situation had intermediate protection 5m below him, the fall would be 10m with 15m of rope out to give a fall factor of 0.6. Fall factors can be increased even above 2 if any rope is taken in while a fall is actually occurring as this decreases the amount of rope available to absorb the energy created by the fall. The fall factor gives an indication of the severity of the load on the climber, the rope and the belay system. The smaller the fall factor, the smaller the force; fall factors of 1 and above are serious.

Fig 3.3 Fall factors:
(a) A fall factor of 2: the length of the fall, 8m, divided by the length of rope available.
(b) A factor 1 fall: a fall of 4m with 4m of rope involved.
(c) A fall factor of 0.5, where the fall is 2m.

While the concept of fall factors is a useful tool in understanding what happens in a fall, it does not give the complete picture. A longer fall, for example, will increase the time during which the force is high , the time during which the rope and

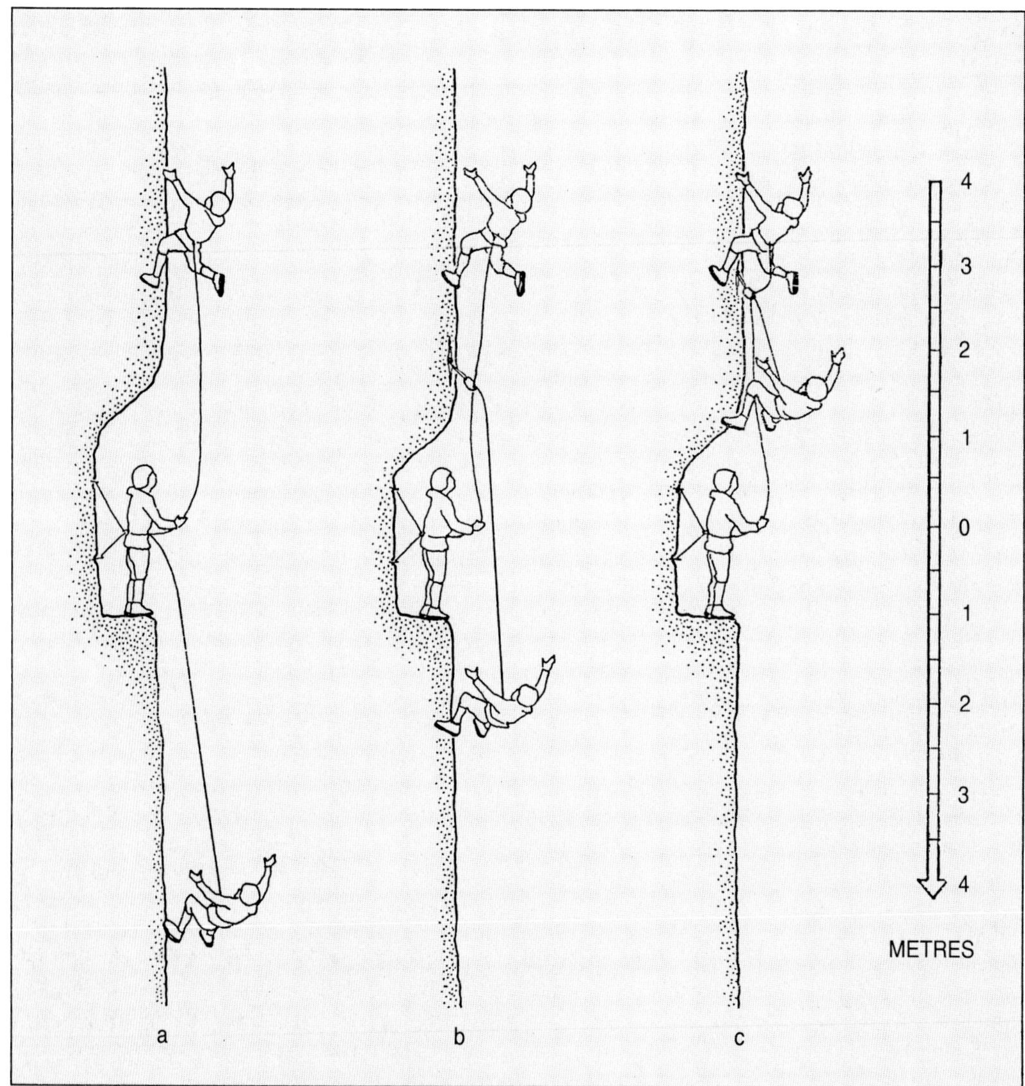

belay system are loaded when holding a fall. This can make the fall more difficult to arrest. Also, the longer the fall, the faster the climber will be travelling and therefore the harder he will impact with any projections or ledges.

Rope Tests

Standards for rope performance are laid down by the Union Internationale des Associations d'Alpinisme (UIAA). The main test to which a rope is subjected is the drop test which simulates a leader fall. In this a weight is dropped free for 5m with 2.8m of rope in use. The rope is attached to a fixed point and passed through an orifice plate with a smooth-finished 5mm radius rubbing edge 0.3m above it. This gives a fall factor of 1.78. A rope must withstand five falls like this without breaking. The number of falls held gives an indication of the rope's safety reserves. The weight used is 80kg for a single rope and 55kg for a half-rope. During the first test fall the impact force must not exceed 12 kilo Newtons.

The ropes are also tested for their static elongation, again using a 80kg weight: this should not exceed 8 per cent for a single and 10 per cent for a half-rope. However, this test shows only how much a rope will stretch when it is hung on, not when it is fallen on. The impact force elongation is more important to climbers. Some rope manufacturers quote the impact force elongation of their products, which is normally in the region of 20 per cent. Elongation at breaking point is about 40–50 per cent. Ropes are also tested for knotability, which gives an indication of the rope's flexibility. An overhand knot is tied in the rope and weighted with 10kg for one minute. Then the load is decreased to 1kg and the inside diameter of the knot is measured. The clear space in the knot must be less than the rope's diameter and the smaller this area, the more flexible the rope is. Sheath slippage, which is also tested, should be less than 40mm in 2.2m of rope.

Rope Wear and Care

The rope is such a vital piece of equipment that its care is of prime importance. For a start, only ropes which meet UIAA specifications should be used for climbing and the history of the rope should be known to the user. Several factors affect the life-span of a rope and, although it will not rot, a nylon rope deteriorates with time no matter how it is treated. Other types of mechanical damage during use are inevitable.

Nylon has a low melting point – about 250°C – and so can easily be melted by flames, hot metal and friction. Sufficient heat to melt a rope can be created by friction, as when one rope is pulled rapidly across another. Holding a fall can damage a rope, particularly the sheath, which can fuse to give hard, shiny patches which make it less pleasant to handle. Chemicals also cause damage, so keep nylon equipment away from acids, alkalis, bleach, oils and the like. Battery acid from cars is known to have been the cause of rope failure, so take care when carrying ropes in motor vehicles.

Sunlight and especially the ultra-violet component of sunlight damages ropes. This is one reason why rope and other nylon equipment found on a cliff can never be trusted: it may have been seriously weakened by ultra-violet although it can appear to be unaffected. This deterioration becomes greater as altitude is gained and less ultra-violet is blocked by the earth's atmosphere. Ropes should be stored in cool, dry, dark, well ventilated places, remembering that glass does not cut out the damaging effects of sunlight.

Ropes become worn and abraded with normal use. This shows primarily as 'furring' – that is, fine fibres in the sheath wear through and their ends stick up. This will eventually cause some loss in strength but may improve the rope's handling and gripping qualities. Some ropes are treated chemically to make them more slippery and supple to slow down the furring process. The amount of furring can give an indication of the amount of use a rope has had [*fig. 3.4*]. Ropes are quickly abraded or cut by running over sharp edges, so route them away from such features. Grit and rock particles can work their way into the rope and damage it from the inside, particularly when it is compressed or stretched. Never stand on a rope, and be extremely careful when wearing crampons. Ropes which are dirty are more prone to kinking, stiffening and are more difficult to handle. Superficial dirt can be removed by rinsing the rope in clean water; engrained dirt can be removed by washing in warm water (30–40°C) with mild soap. This can be done by hand or in a washing machine at a delicate setting. The rope should then be rinsed well and hung up to dry

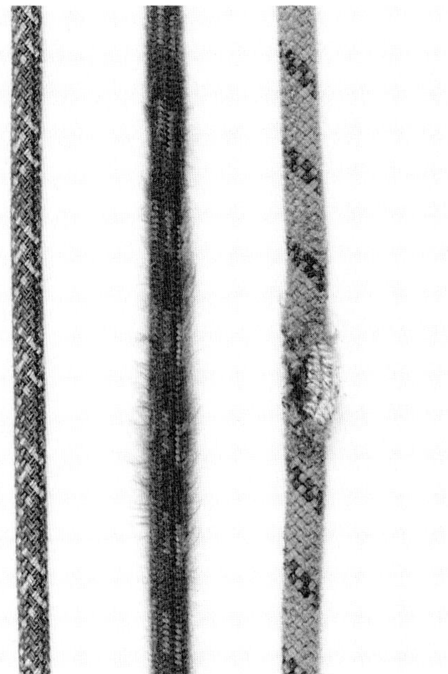

Fig 3.4 Three half-ropes: a new 9mm rope, a furred rope of the same diameter at the end of its useful life and a rope damaged by a fall over a sharp edge.

away from direct heat and sunlight.

Ropes suffer damage when they hold a fall, during which some of the nylon fibres are irreversibly stretched. This is seen in drop tests when progressively higher impact forces are recorded and the rope loses its ability to absorb energy. Eventually it will break. If fallen on, a rope should be given time to recover – at least ten minutes; if possible, untie and re-tie any knots in the rope which have tightened up and so lost their ability to absorb energy. It may even be better to change ends of the rope if the fall was fairly high (above fall factor 0.5).

Ropes handle best when free from kinks, spiral twists which are created when the rope is twisted round its longitudinal axis. This can happen through bad rope management or when it is pulled over an edge at an angle to its long axis. The screw-like action across an edge, such as a karabiner, puts opposite twists before and after the edge and these build up in the rope. If a rope gathers kinks, they can be removed by hanging it down a vertical drop or pulling it over suitable ground such as a grass field to let the kinks work their way along the rope to the end where they can untwist and come out.

The rate at which a rope wears out will depend on the type of use it has had, the kind of rock it was used on, its construction, its care and the climate in which it was most used. If a rope is cut, it should be retired from use or shortened to the cut. The ends may be sealed during this process by the use of a hot knife. A rope should be discarded if it has been in contact with chemicals. Parts of a rope which feel much softer than the rest are also a cause for concern. If it has held a fall of fall factor 1 or greater, it should no longer be used for climbing. As a rough guide, no rope over five years old should be considered safe; with occasional careful use a rope will last about two to four years, about two years with normal weekend use and with heavy use it may last from as little as three months to one year. Ropes may be retired from leading on to other uses such as abseiling or top roping, but should be marked so that they cannot get back into use as lead ropes.

Static Ropes

The ropes used for climbing are dynamic; however, for some non-climbing situations, static ropes are preferable. These have minimal stretch when loaded, although they are of similar strength and construction to climbing ropes. They are useful when a great deal of ascending or descending of the rope must be done and are also used in mountain rescue when very long ropes may be required. Static ropes are widely used in caving but are totally unsuitable for climbing as they transmit an unacceptably high impact force if fallen on.

Accessory Cord and Tape

Accessory cord is usually static rope of kernmantel construction which has various uses with protection equipment. While climbing ropes are made from continuous filament yarn, accessory cord may have joins in one or more of its yarns. It is generally available in sizes from 9mm down to 3mm in diameter. Because of its minimal elongation when loaded, it has poor energy-absorbing qualities but is very strong, flexible and easy to knot. Other materials such as Kevlar and Spectra are extremely strong and, because of their lightness and lack of bulk, are well suited to use with some types of protection. Like accessory cord these are not suitable for use in long lengths where they could be shock-loaded.

Nylon accessory tape or webbing, which is also used for protection, is of flat construction and woven from flat or round yarn. Its strength comes from the fibres which run the length of the tape, the crossways fibres giving the tape its shape and stability. It is available in widths of 10–50mm, in standard or super thickness and of flat or tubular construction [*fig. 3.5*]. These various factors determine its strength, handling characteristics and resistance to abrasion. Other types of even stronger tape are becoming available but they need to be sewn as they knot very poorly. Some tapes are now coded to show their minimum breaking strength, each line of marking thread denoting 500kg strength.

Accessory cord and tape are subject to the same deterioration as rope and should be cared for similarly. However, because of its large surface area, tape is particularly liable to abrasion and damage by ultra-violet radiation.

A selection of rope and tape sizes with approximate breaking strengths:

Rope type	*Breaking strength* (kg)
11mm dynamic	2000–2250
9mm dynamic	1450–1750
11mm static	3000–3100
9mm static	1950–2250
7mm static	900–1200
5.5mm static	650
5.5mm Kevlar	2045
25mm tape (solid)	1500–2400
25mm tape (tubular)	1800–2250

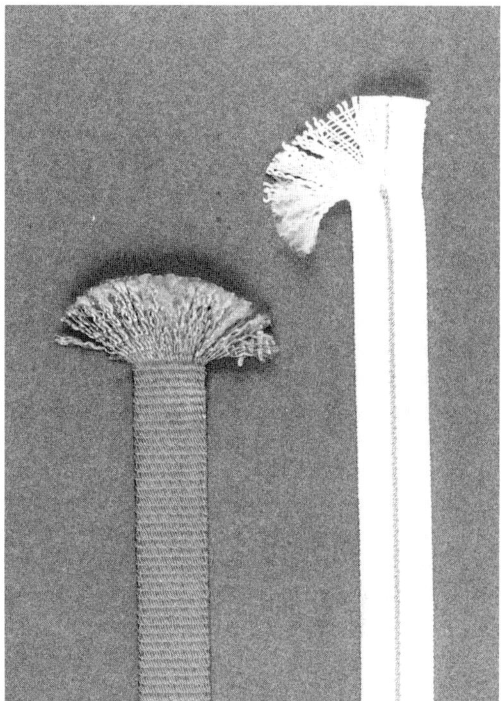

Fig 3.5 Construction of the two main types of nylon tape: the white tape is tubular and the coloured tape is solid (flat).

Coiling a Rope

A rope is usually coiled in some manner for ease of carrying and storing. A variety of ways are possible but the best method of storing a rope is to feed it directly into a bag or rucksack. This makes the rope very readily accessible and does not put kinks into it; however, it is not a practical way to carry a rope in many situations and there are several possible methods of coiling a rope.

Mountaineer's Coil

The traditional mountaineer's coil is made by laying a double arm's length of rope, a span, into one hand in the form of a loop and continuing this until all but 2m are coiled. Double about 0.5m of the first end back on itself and whip the remaining rope round all the loops. Work back towards the doubled end loop, pulling tight each time, and eventually feed the end through the doubled end loop. Pull one side of this to secure the whipping, which should be six to eight turns to keep the coils together [*fig. 3.6*]. If neat coils are desired, the rope is rolled between thumb and forefinger when the loop is being placed in the holding hand but, to reduce subsequent kinking, it may be better to let the rope lie naturally in figure-of-eight loops. A quick but less neat method to coil a rope in this fashion is to sit with the knees well apart and coil the rope round them. Alternatively, stand and use the back of the neck and one hand, palm down at waist level, around which to form the coils. Neat coils are useful when carrying the rope over the shoulder.

Rucksack Coil

A rucksack coil is made by first finding the middle of the rope and coiling it as if making a mountaineer's coil but with double rope. When about

4m of rope are left, whip the whole coil together near the top, push a bight through the coils and pull the ends through that. Alternatively take a bight (an open-ended loop of rope) through the coils at the top, loop it over them and pull tight. The ends can be tied round the shoulders and waist like a rucksack. This is a useful method of carrying a rope when climbing or scrambling, but the rope must be pulled through from one end before it can be used without the risk of tangling.

Double Hank

A double hank, butterfly or lap coil is formed by starting with the middle of the rope, or about 4m from the two single ends, and draping it back and forth across the hand until it can be finished as for a rucksack coil [*fig. 3.7*]. It is usually possible to use the rope once the whipping has been undone without the need to pull the rope through. Because this method of coiling is fast and does not kink the rope, it has much to recommend it. To make a rope easier to carry it can be coiled in two halves, leaving about 0.5m between the coils which can be hung over the top of the rucksack.

Chain Coil

A chain coil can be made with the rope single or doubled. Tie an overhand slip knot in one end, then put a bight of rope through the loop so formed. Continue like this to the end, then secure [*fig. 3.8*]. By pulling the final end when the securing knot is released, the whole chain will unravel. This is a useful method of coiling very long ropes.

Uncoiling a Rope

Coiling and uncoiling a rope provides a good opportunity to examine it for damage as the whole rope can be both looked at and felt as the loops pass through the hands. When uncoiling a rope prior to use, it is best first to undo the whipping and put this end well to one side where it can be found easily. Uncoil one loop at a time, flaking the rope on to a pile. The leader then takes the top end which will run freely from the pile. As the second's end is out to one side, this prevents knots being inadvertently formed by pulling the end up through the pile. If the whipping is undone and the coils simply laid on the ground, they can easily become knotted and tangled.

Fig 3.6 ABOVE: *Coiling a rope in mountaineer's coils: (a) Loops of rope about a span in length are laid into one hand, the neat loop being formed by twisting the rope between the thumb and forefinger.*
(b) OPPOSITE PAGE ABOVE: *To finish off, one end of the rope is doubled back on itself.*
(c) OPPOSITE PAGE BELOW: *The other end is whipped tightly round the bundle and put through the loop that is left. One end of the loop is pulled to trap this end and the coils are secured.*

KNOTS

Knots form the link which connects the climber to the rope and ultimately to the rock. The ability to tie and recognise a variety of knots is fundamental to safe climbing. Any knot used should have several important properties: it should be as strong as possible yet still be small and neat; it

should not come undone during normal use yet still untie easily after its job is finished; and it should be appropriate to the situation. Knots are only temporary connections and most have the disconcerting ability to work loose on their own so they must be checked regularly. The stiffer the rope or tape in which they are tied, the more likely this is to happen. All knots weaken the rope by between 25 and 45 per cent, depending on the knot itself and the size of the rope in which it is tied. This weakening is due to the bends put into the rope by a knot: the tighter the turn, the weaker the knot.

Knots which are used to form a permanent join, such as when tying rope or tape to form a sling, should be tied as tightly as possible. Knots used in other situations are worked tight by pulling the individual strands forming them. These knots should be firm but not overtight, so that if they

Fig 3.7 LEFT: *Using double hanks to coil a rope:*
(a) Hanks of the doubled rope about a span in length are laid back and forth across the hand.
(b) BELOW LEFT: *When about 4m of rope are left, they are whipped round the top of the hanks, a bight pushed through the hole and the ends pulled through to secure.*

Fig 3.8 BELOW: *Chain coils formed by putting a bight through the loop.*

3.9

are loaded they can tighten up further and thus absorb some of the energy of a fall.

The following knots are the main ones used in climbing.

Overhand Knot

The simplest of all knots, the overhand can be used as a stopper knot to secure a rope end after another knot has been tied. It is also known as a thumb knot [*fig. 3.9*].

Overhand Loop

The overhand loop is the simplest way to form a safe closed loop in a rope. Of medium strength, it is difficult to undo after it has been loaded [*fig. 3.10*].

Double Overhand Knot

Tie as for the overhand knot, but take the end twice round the ropes before feeding it through. This is a better stopper knot than the overhand as it is less likely to work loose [*figs. 3.11a, 3.11b*].

Stopper Knot

This is either an overhand or a double overhand knot tied in the tail end of another knot such as a bowline. It is tied round the rope to which the tail

3.10

3.11a

3.11b

3.12a

3.12b

lies parallel and its main function is to increase the security of the main knot [*figs. 3.13c, 3.15d*].

Figure-of-Eight

The figure-of-eight is the basic yet the most versatile climbing knot. It has a distinctive shape, is easy to tie, strong and fairly easy to untie after it has been loaded. Also, if tied wrongly with either one turn too few or too many, it will still produce a usable knot, an overhand loop or a figure of nine. It is better if the main rope lies on the outside of the first bend in the knot.

A figure-of-eight can be tied anywhere in the rope, but if tied in the rope end the tail should be secured with a stopper knot which is then worked up close to the main knot. Although this stopper knot does not make the main knot any stronger, it does ensure that a sufficiently long tail has been left. Too short a tail could work itself loose. This should more correctly be known as a figure-of-eight loop but is almost universally called a figure-of-eight by climbers [*figs. 3.12a, 3.12b*].

Figure-of-Eight Re-threaded

Also known as a re-woven figure-of-eight, this is another way to tie the same knot. A figure-of-eight is tied in a single rope and the end follows the knot back through itself. It is used when the figure-of-eight must be tied round something, such as when tying into a climbing harness. As with any figure-of-eight, it is awkward to adjust for tightness and should be finished with a stopper knot [*figs. 3.13a, 3.13b, 3.13c*]. A variation of this can be used to join two rope ends. In this case the single figure-of-eight is followed through by the end of the second rope.

Figure-of-Nine

A figure-of-nine knot is a figure-of-eight tied with an extra turn in it. It is stronger than the figure-of-eight knot but little used because of its greater bulk [*fig. 3.14*].

Bowline

The bowline is a strong knot which is easy to adjust and easy to untie after it has been loaded. It is a popular means of tying on to the rope. However, if tied wrongly it can be unsafe, it can work loose fairly easily and it does not function well if subject to a three-way loading, when it can

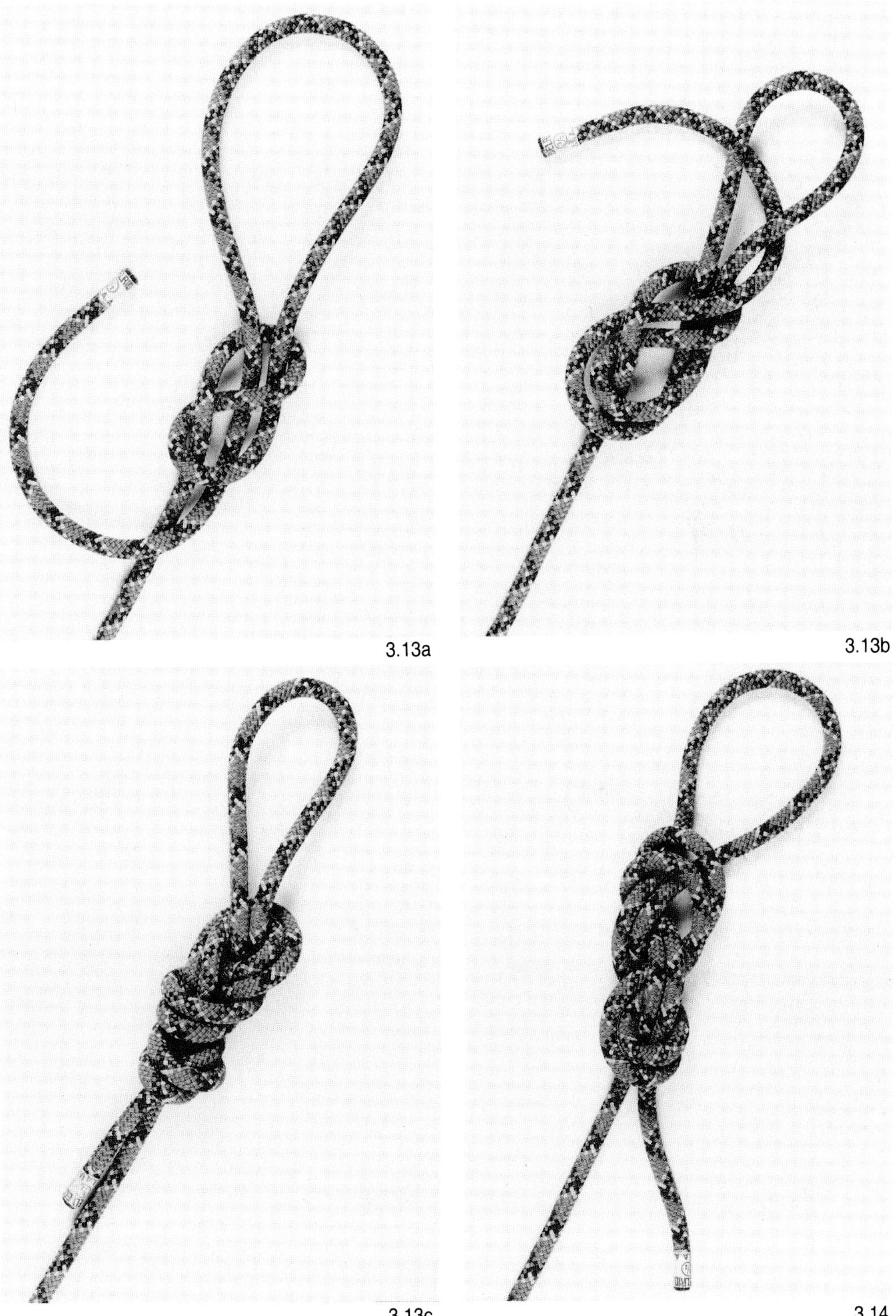

3.13a

3.13b

3.13c

3.14

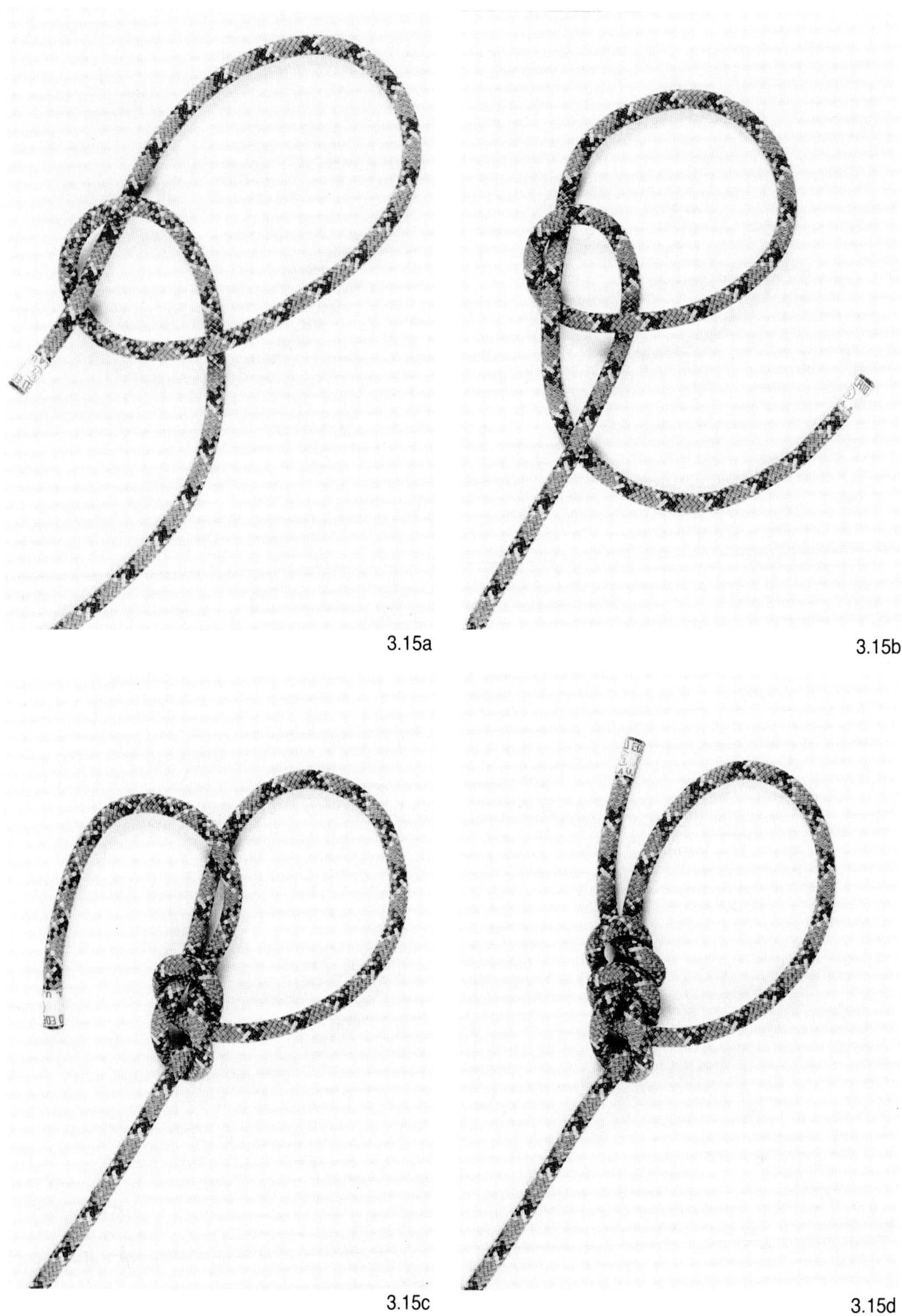

3.15a

3.15b

3.15c

3.15d

3.16a

3.16b

3.17

slip or even invert. It should be secured with a stopper knot tied round the rope in the loop [*figs. 3.15a, 3.15b, 3.15c, 3.15d*].

A bowline can be tied anywhere in the rope by doubling it and tying a bowline in this bight of rope. A variation used for tying on is the double-knotted bowline in which a second loop is laid on top of the initial turn and completed as for the standard bowline. This is stronger than the basic knot and less prone to inverting [*figs. 3.16a, 3.16b*].

Fisherman's Knot

The simplest knot for joining two rope ends is the fisherman's. It is two overhand knots, each tied round the other rope and pulled tight [*fig. 3.17*].

Double Fisherman's Knot

A double fisherman's knot is good for joining two ropes. Two double overhand knots, each round the other rope, are tied and pulled tight. This does not work loose easily but sufficiently long tails (approximately eight times the rope's diameter) should be left. The knot can be tightened by

3.18a

3.18b

3.18c

applying body weight, after which it can be extremely difficult to untie. It is also known as a grapevine knot [*figs. 3.18a, 3.18b, 3.18c*].

Tape Knot

The tape knot is the most suitable for joining tapes. An overhand knot is tied in one end and the other end then follows it through. This knot can work loose very easily and long tail ends must be left (approximately five times the tape's width). Load with at least body weight to tighten, check regularly and re-tie if the ends become too short. It is also known as a ring bend or water knot and can be used for joining rope as well as tape [*figs. 3.19a, 3.19b, 3.19c*].

Sheet Bend

The sheet bend is used occasionally to join rope or tape. The double version is more secure but both can work loose easily. It is an easy knot to adjust [*figs. 3.20a, 3.20b*].

Clove Hitch

Although not a particularly strong knot, the clove hitch is very useful as it is easily adjusted when in

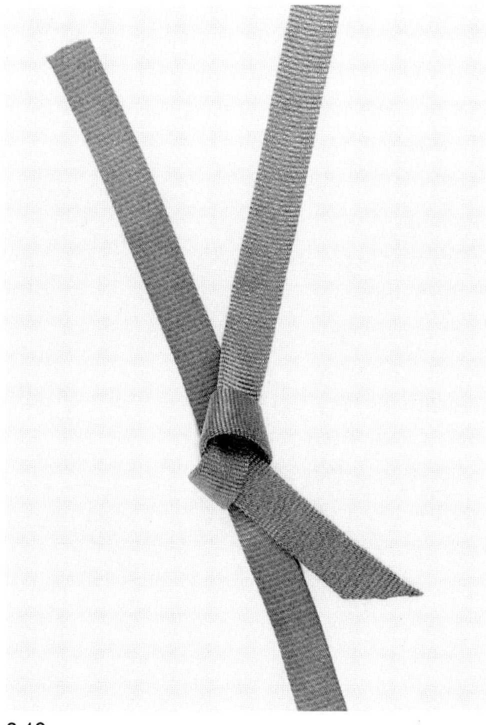

3.19a

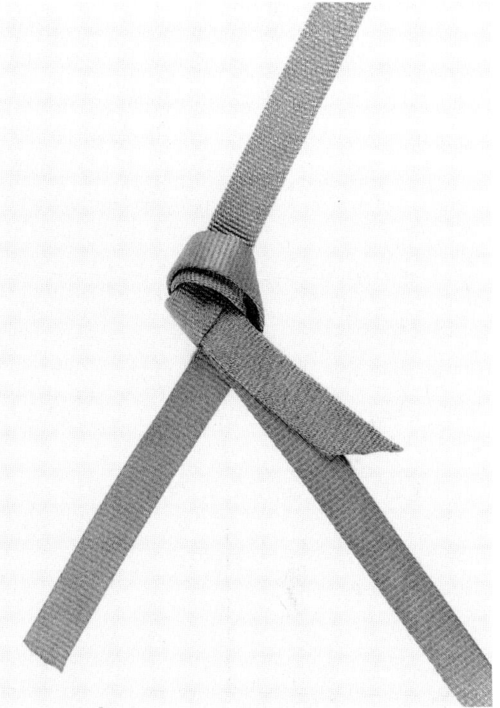

3.19b

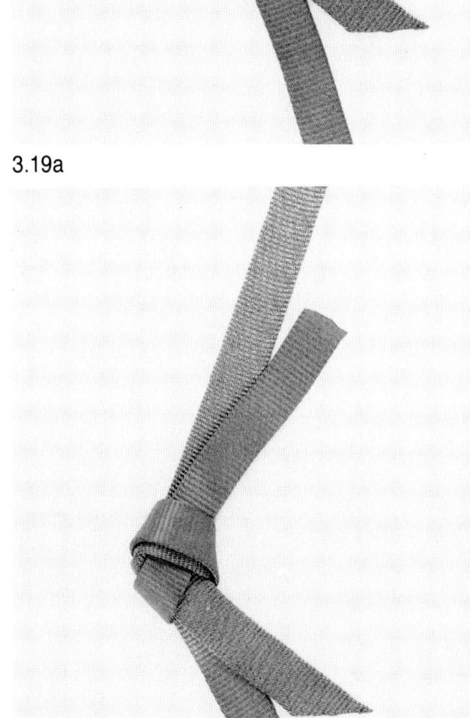

3.19c

place. It ties best in soft, flexible ropes. If only one side of the knot is to be loaded, it is best put on with the diagonal part of the knot at the bottom. If both sides are to be loaded, the diagonal is best at the top as it will then tighten rather than open up. Always ensure that it is tightened before use because it can run if loaded when loose [*figs. 3.21a, 3.21b, 3.21c*].

Lark's Foot

The lark's foot is a very simple but weak knot which is generally best avoided, although it can be tied quickly and so has some uses [*fig. 3.22*].

Alpine Butterfly

A useful mid-rope knot, the Alpine butterfly's main advantage is the ease with which it can be untied after it has been loaded. It can be loaded along either of the main strands of the rope or by the loop. It has several variations which all look similar and depend on exactly which method is used to tie it. In the method shown strand A is taken up through the hole X formed by the two overlapping loops [*figs. 3.23a, 3.23b, 3.23c, 3.23d*].

3.20a

3.20b

Knot Strengths

Although all knots weaken a rope, the actual strength of the knot is not the sole consideration when deciding which one to use. Factors such as reliability, speed, convenience, ease of untying and the amount of rope available all affect the choice. Generally the strength of the knot is not a serious consideration as there are weaker elements in the climbing system. However, for single kernmantle rope, the approximate breaking strengths of the main knots are given in the table below. These strengths vary according to the diameter of the rope in which they are tied, but knots in small-diameter rope can slip before breaking.

Knot strengths (percentages)

Knot	Strength
Unknotted rope	100
Figure-of-eight	75–80
Bowline	70–75
Double fisherman's knot	65–70
Fisherman's knot	60–65
Clove hitch	60–65
Overhand	60–65

TYING ON

When using a rope, you must attach yourself to it in a way which is safe, secure, convenient and appropriate to the situation, which still allows the freedom of movement necessary to climb efficiently. For example, the type of tie-on suitable for a one-pitch slab climb will probably be unsuitable for a big Alpine route.

Waist Tie-on

Most of the methods of tying on round the waist are quick, convenient, inexpensive and permit complete freedom of movement. However, they can be very dangerous in a long fall or if hanging free. In the first case the force of the fall is concentrated round the waist, and the soft internal organs and even the ribs and spine can be damaged. In the second instance the attachment will ride up over the rib cage and constrict breathing. After a period of some ten minutes or so, consciousness is lost and suffocation will follow.

The simplest waist tie-on is to use the rope itself tied round the narrowest part of the waist

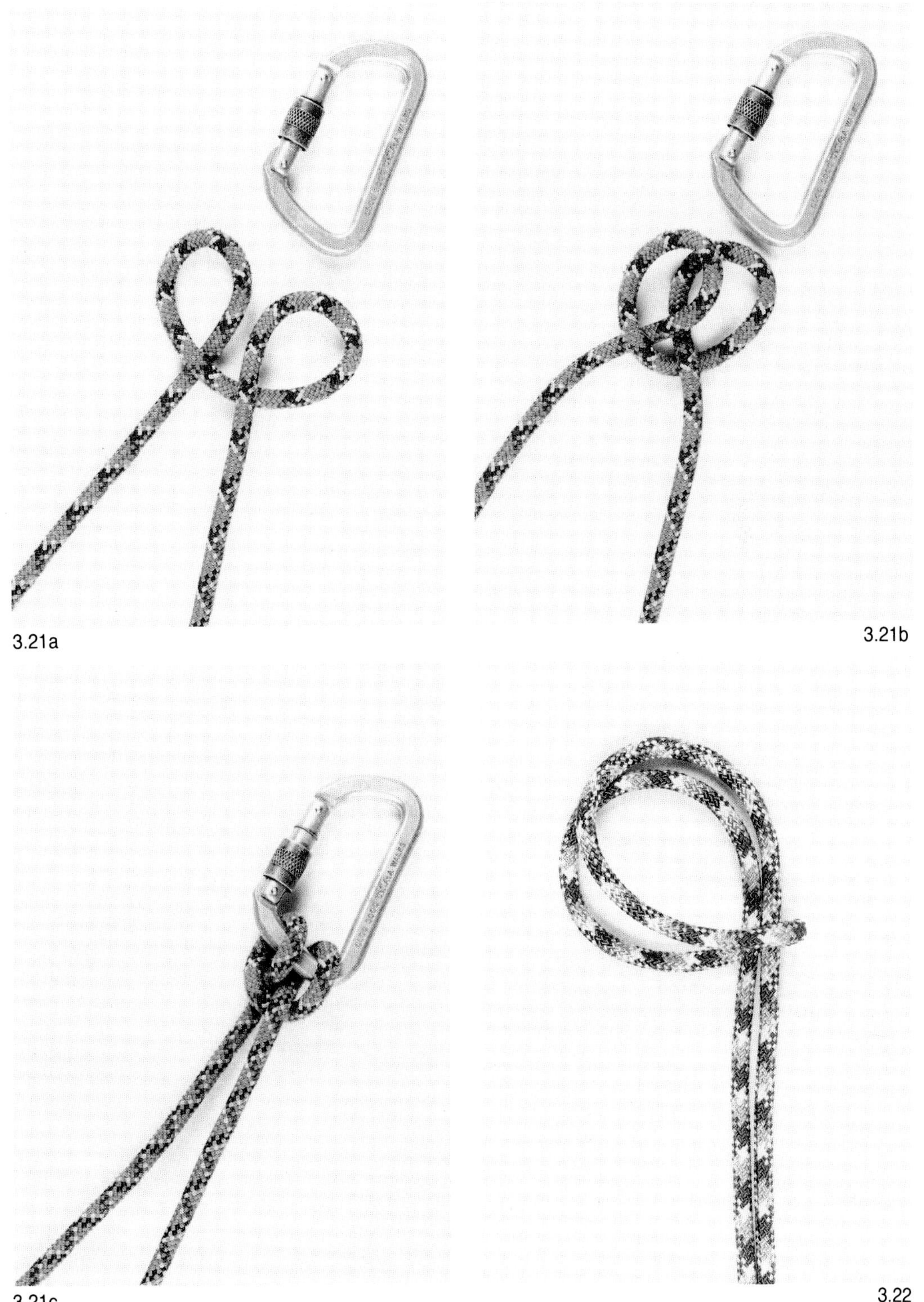

3.21a

3.21b

3.21c

3.22

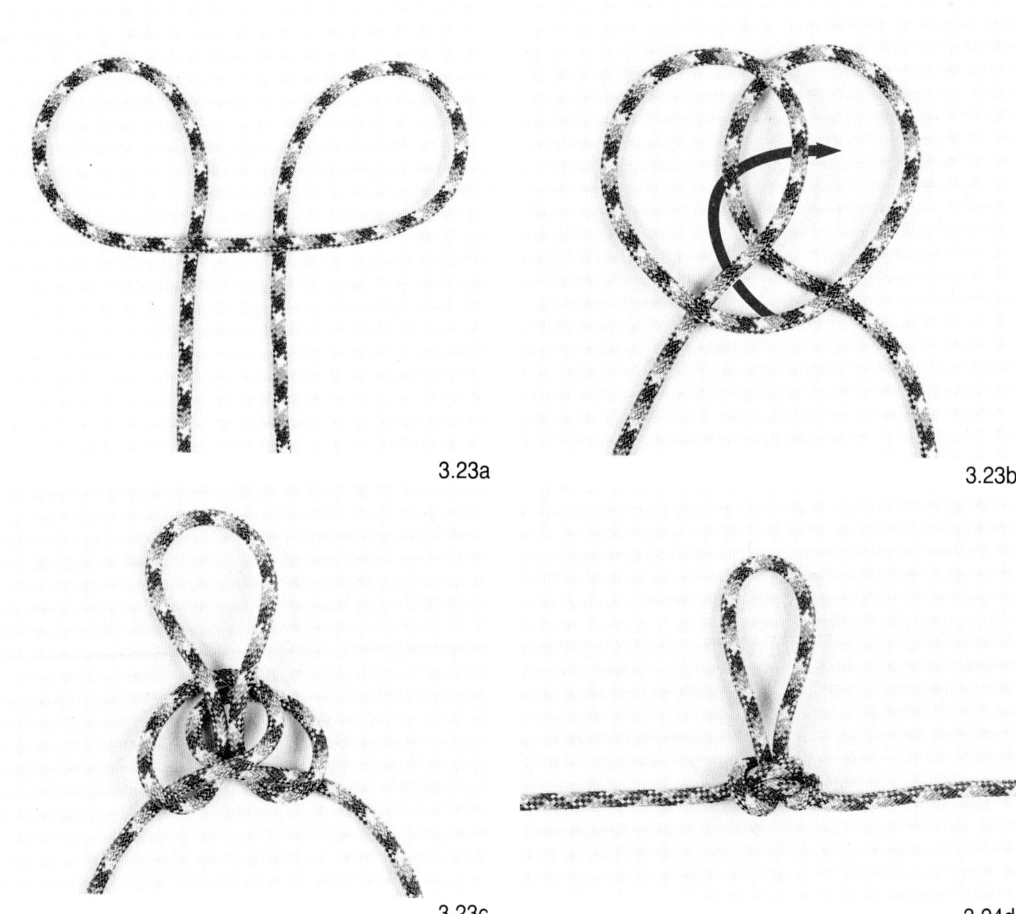

3.23a

3.23b

3.23c

3.24d

and secured with a stoppered figure-of-eight or bowline. This should be made as tight as possible without causing discomfort. A better method is to use a swami belt. This is a number of turns of tape wound round the waist, tied with a tape knot. About 6m of 25cm-wide tape or 5m of 50cm-wide tape is used for this [*fig. 3.24*]. The swami has the advantage of being wider, so spreading the load more. It also means that if you untie from the rope, you still have the means to secure yourself.

Simple waist belts are available and these are usually of wide tape which may be padded or protected by some form of covering and secured by a buckle. Always ensure that the buckle is closed according to the manufacturer's instructions. The rope is attached to the belt or swami by a bowline or a figure-of-eight finished with a stopper knot. A screw-gate karabiner can be used for convenience to link the rope to the belt as when top-roping a number of short climbs. However, it introduces an unnecessary link into the system, is less comfortable, especially if fallen on, and can be less safe.

Harnesses

Sit Harnesses

Sit, seat or thigh-loop harnesses are preferred for most rock climbing and harder winter or snow and ice routes. A harness generally consists of a wide waist belt, which may be padded for comfort, and two leg loops. The majority of waist belts are adjustable for size, though not all leg loops are. The loops can be connected, or separate so that the belt can be used on its own. Some can be put on and fastened in place, others have to be stepped into; some use the rope for closure, others have a buckle or tape system to fasten the harness. For any harness, however, the same criteria should apply: it must be safe, strong, well-fitting, comfortable, convenient and not too complex. One harness may not meet all your requirements. A good harness for rock may not be suitable for winter use when more clothing is worn and the harness needs to be put on when wearing crampons or even skis. It is vital to wear a harness when crossing glacial terrain.

Harnesses are normally made of several sections of securely sewn broad tape which may have some method of size adjustment such as buckles. A good harness is comfortable, non-restrictive and safe to fall on as it distributes the force of a fall round the thighs and buttocks, the part of the body best able to cope with it. However, in some falls you could be whipped upside-down or sideways with an increased chance of spinal whiplash or head injuries. This inversion is generally caused by a low point of attachment and is more likely to happen when you are wearing a rucksack or are unconscious. In a normal fall tensing yourself or holding the rope should prevent this from happening. Harnesses can also be less convenient in some belay situations.

The tie-on arrangement will depend on the exact type of harness, but always follow the manufacturer's instructions. The stoppered bowline or figure-of-eight is the usual tie-on knot, the latter being safer but less easily adjusted [*figs. 3.25, 3.26*].

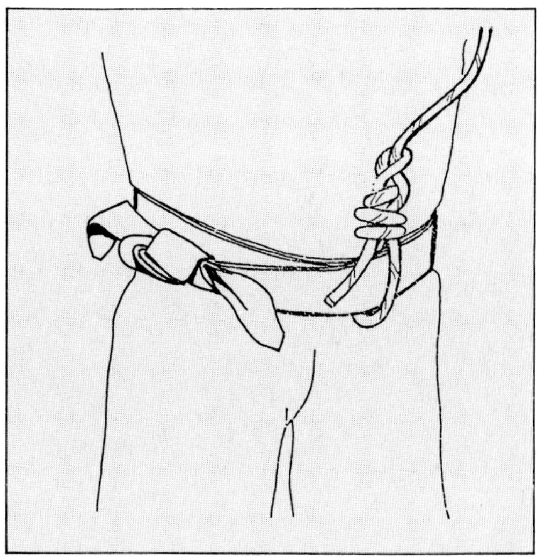

Fig 3.24 Swami belt of wide tape wrapped three times round the waist and tied with a tape knot. The ends of the knot must be sufficiently long to eliminate any chance of them pulling through. The rope is tied on with a stoppered bowline.

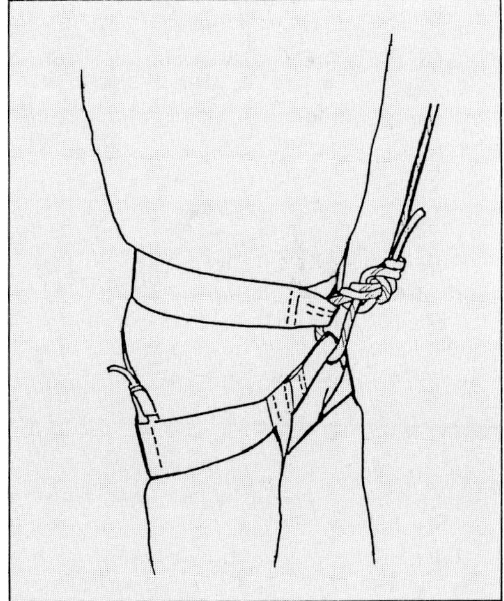

Fig 3.25 A two-piece non-adjustable harness consisting of a waist belt and leg loops. The rope is attached with a stoppered figure-of-eight. If the rope is not attached to a harness like this, a karabiner or sling is needed to stop the leg loops falling down. The knot loop formed by the rope connects the waist and the leg loops.

Full Body Harnesses

A full harness undoubtedly gives the best free-hanging position (at about 20° to the vertical) for an unconscious person, prevents inversion (particularly if the climber is wearing a rucksack) and distributes the force of a fall over a wide area, especially the buttocks and thighs. Unfortunately, it tends to be more cumbersome, heavier and more restrictive than a sit harness. It may be more complex to put on and adjust and can be awkward if you have to relieve yourself on a route and in some belay situations. It also makes it harder to hold a fall when moving together as it tends to pull you to the ground head first. Also, the pull down on the shoulders if there is a lot of rope drag can make climbing more difficult.

Full body harnesses can be either one-piece or a combination of a sit and a chest harness [*fig. 3.27*]. The latter system gives the greatest flexibil-

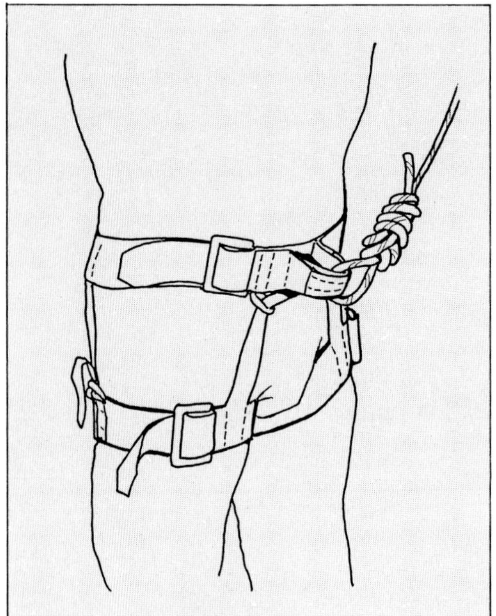

Fig 3.26 A fully adjustable harness. You can put this on without having to step into it.

ity as the sit harness can be used on its own if required. Chest harnesses must not be used on their own.

To tie on the harness, follow the maker's instructions. There are different methods, depending on whether the harness has a one- or two-point attachment system. In spite of its drawbacks, the safety aspects of the full harness cannot be overlooked, especially when climbing with a heavy rucksack or where a long fall is a possibility – especially if the ground is broken or not very steep.

Equipment Loops

Harnesses and belts are usually fitted with gear-carrying loops. These should be handy, easy to use and of wide enough diameter to avoid snagging the gates of karabiners. Those of a stiffened construction are the most convenient to use as long as they do not catch the rock in constricted situations.

The Knot Loop

When tying the end of a rope into a harness, a loop is formed by the knot. This is known as the central loop or the knot loop, the latter term being the one used in this book. This is an important attachment point for several procedures [*see figs. 3.24, 3.25, 3.26, 3.27*].

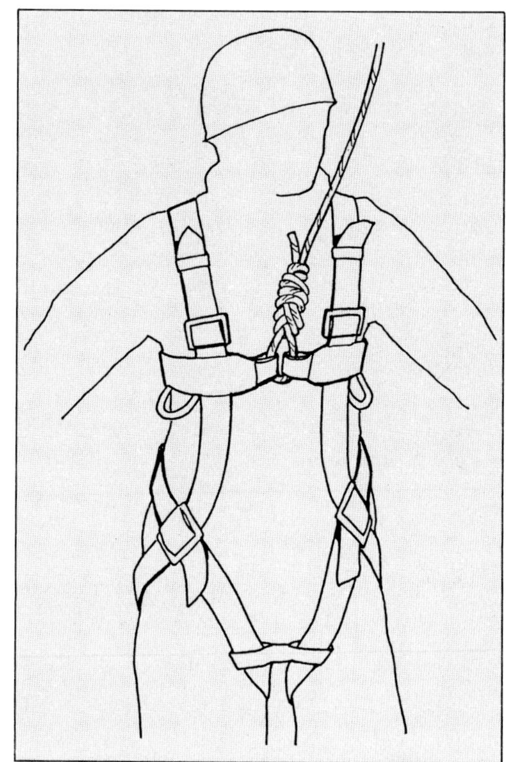

Fig 3.27 A one-piece full body harness with the rope attached using a stoppered figure-of-eight knot.

Hanging Free

An important consideration when choosing a method with which to tie on is the possibility of ending up hanging free in space, unable to get lowered to safety. If this is a possibility, a harness should be worn in preference to a waist tie-on [*fig. 3.28*].

KARABINERS

In modern roped climbing the karabiner is the universal means of attachment. Every piece of equipment used on a route will have a karabiner linking it to the rope and so the climber to the rock [*fig. 3.29*]. Karabiners (or krabs, biners or snap links) are made of steel or aluminium alloy.

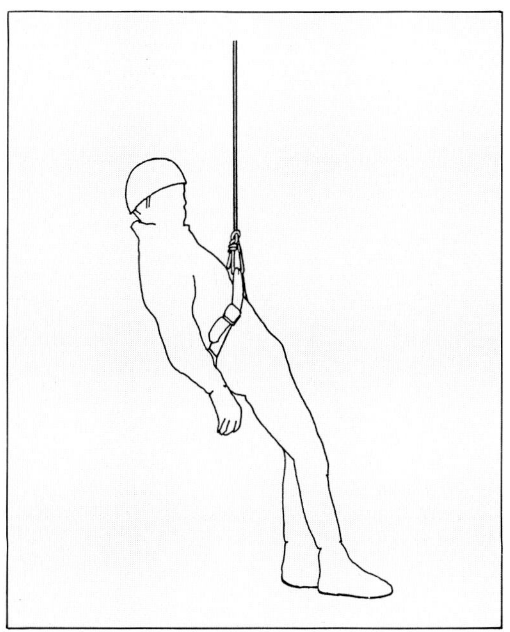

Fig 3.28 Hanging free in various types of tie-on methods:
(a) With a simple buckled belt round the waist. The belt pulls up under the chest and will quickly lead to suffocation.

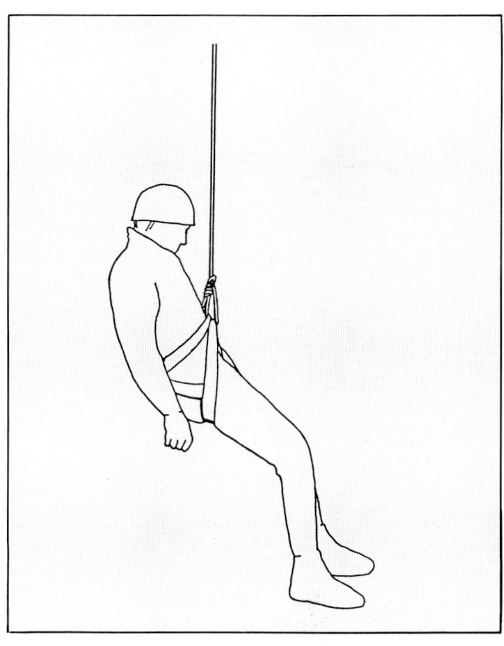

(b) With a sit harness the climber is supported with most of his weight on the thighs but will only maintain this position if he tenses his muscles.

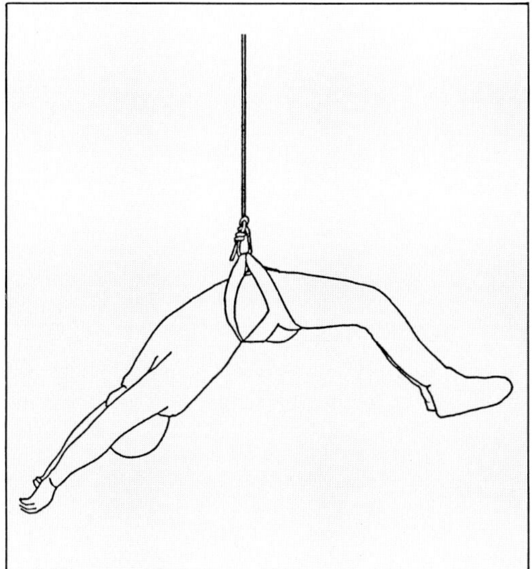

(c) If the climber is unconscious and wearing a sit harness, he will tip back in this manner unless the attachment point is above his centre of gravity. A fall in this manner can be extremely dangerous and result in spinal injuries.

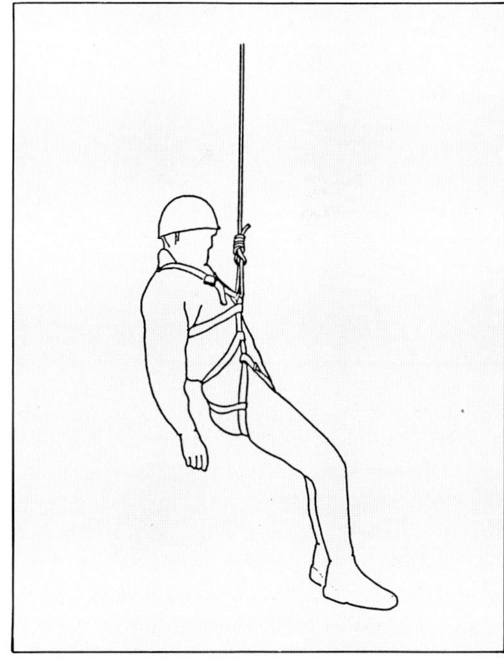

(d) With a full body harness the high attachment point gives a good free-hanging position whether the climber is conscious or unconscious.

Steel karabiners, although hard-wearing, are now little used because of their weight; alloy karabiners are as strong but much lighter. However, being softer, the latter can be damaged by some activities, particularly heavy use with wet, muddy ropes which can abrade them, and salt water can corrode them.

There are basically three types of karabiner: normal, lightweight and locking, all of which have the same basic form. Although the three types are basically interchangeable, some karabiners are better in certain situations than others and their suitability is usually determined by their size and shape. The size is generally given as the diameter of the material from which the karabiner is made – for example, 9mm, 10mm, 11mm or 12mm. All karabiners should be free from burrs or sharp edges which could cut the rope. The gate should have a smooth action with no sticking or jamming and have an efficient securing system such as a latch and pin. It is an advantage if the correct end of the keeper can be located by feel alone provided that this does not interfere with its use. Some karabiners are anodised or have coloured gates to make gate identification easier. The gate opening should be large enough to make the insertion of the rope easy.

Karabiner Shapes

Although the strength of a karabiner is related to the strength of the material from which it is made, its shape is also important. There are four main karabiner shapes. Of these shapes, the D and off-set D are by far the most popular for normal and lightweight karabiners.

Fig 3.29 A karabiner.

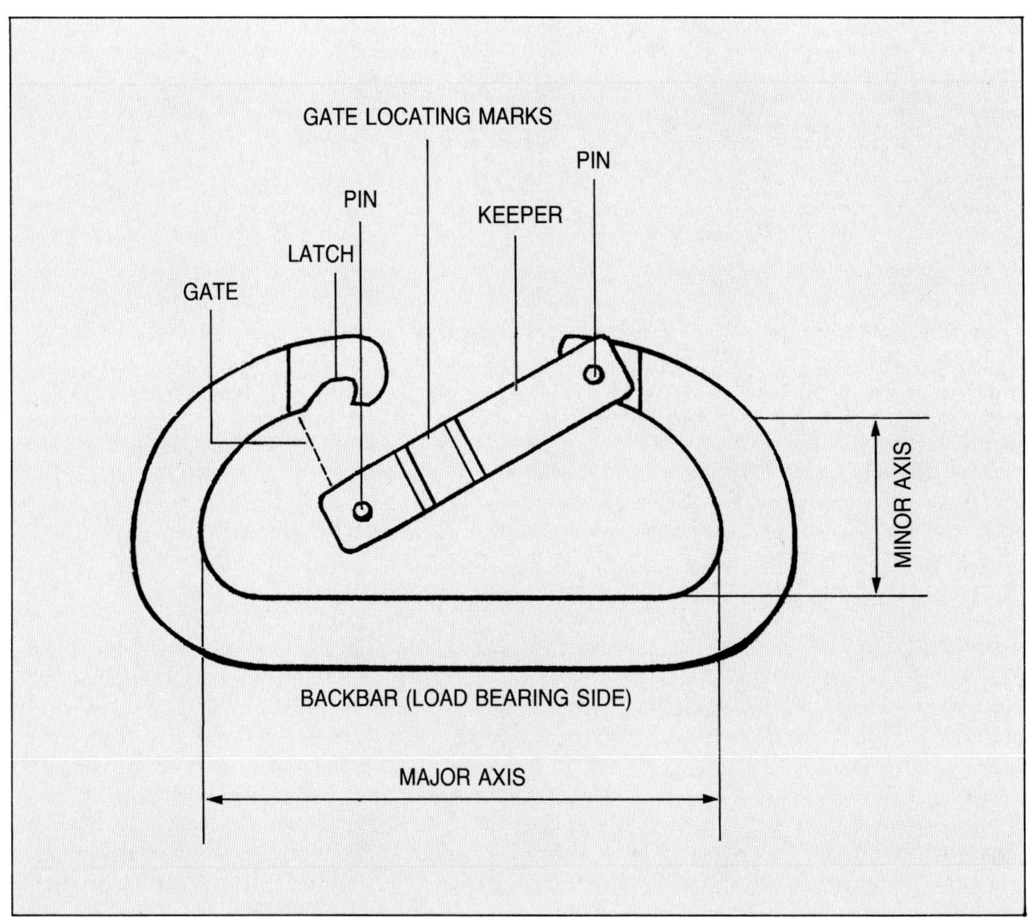

Oval Karabiners

Oval is the original classic shape which is nice to handle with no sharp angles. Unfortunately it is a weak shape as the load is shared between the back bar and the gate side which is less strong. It is good for artificial climbing [*fig. 3.30a*].

D-shaped Karabiners

The D is a strong shape as most of the load is taken on the solid back bar rather than on the gate. Its main disadvantage is that a sharp angle in the D can make it difficult to manoeuvre in some places [*fig. 3.30b*].

Off-set D

The off-set D is very similar to the D-shaped karabiner except that there is more room at one end [*fig. 3.30c*].

Pear-shaped

The pear is a weaker shape now found only in some locking karabiners of a particular type.

Bent Gate Karabiners

In these karabiners the keepers are curved, angled, bent or off-set to make the gate opening larger so that insertion of the rope is easier [*fig. 3.30d*].

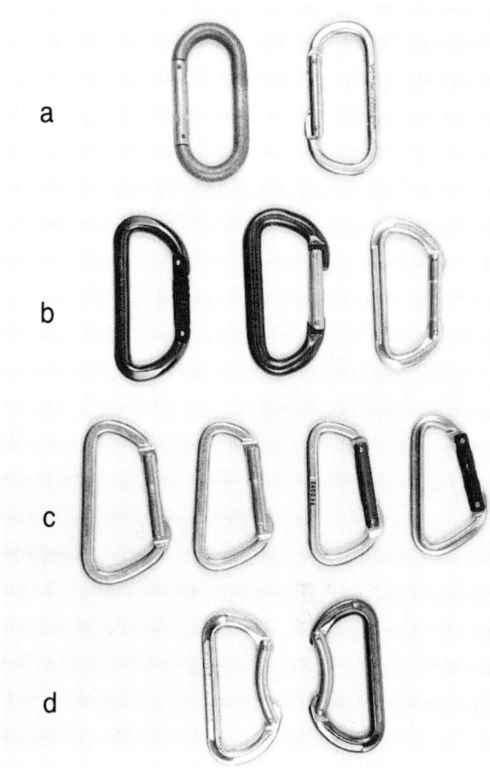

Fig 3.30 A selection of karabiners showing the main shapes:
(a) Oval.
(b) D-shaped.
(c) Off-set D-shaped.
(d) Bent-gate.

Locking Karabiners

Locking karabiners can be of any shape, but D and off-set D are the most usual because of the strength of this design. They are used in situations such as belaying and abseiling to eliminate the chance of the rope coming out when subjected to a force or twisting action and to prevent the karabiner being loaded when the gate is open. Any karabiner will be much weaker if loaded in this manner. The locking device may be a threaded sleeve which can screw up over the free end of the gate or down over the hinge; in this case the karabiner is commonly referred to as a screw-gate karabiner. Other types are fitted with a sprung sleeve which automatically keeps the gate closed unless twisted or pulled open.

Screw-gate karabiners are normally done up till the sleeve is just finger-tight. However, when loaded, the sleeve tends to slacken as the karabiner deforms slightly. If the sleeve is fully tightened and then the load removed, it will be difficult to release unless the karabiner is again loaded. This is less likely to happen if the sleeve locks over the hinge. Pear-shaped or HMS locking karabiners are designed specifically for use with the friction hitch when belaying [*fig. 3.31*].

Opposed-gate Karabiners

If a locking karabiner is needed but not available, two normal karabiners can be arranged so that they perform the same function. The karabiners are placed with the gates opening in opposite directions so that no force or twist can displace the rope; these are known as opposed-gate or 'back to back' karabiners [*fig. 3.32*]. When using D-shaped or off-set D-shaped karabiners, it may be better to put them together so that the back bars are on the same side but the gates open in

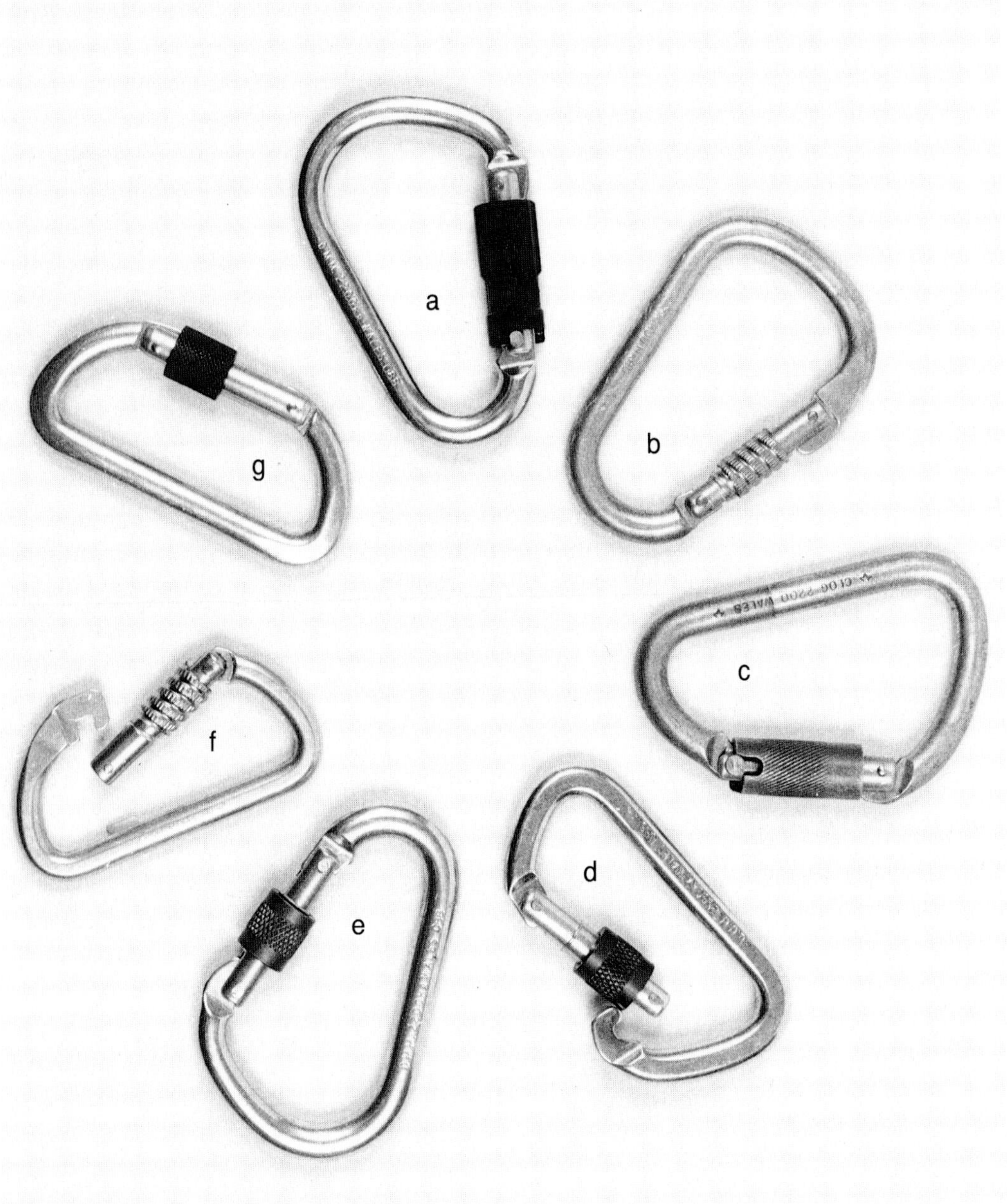

Fig 3.31 A selection of locking karabiners showing different locking methods, shapes and cross-sections:
(a) Pear-shaped HMS type with plastic twist lock closure.
(b) Pear-shaped karabiner with screw closure which locks over the hinge.
(c) Off-set D-shaped metal sleeve twist lock.
(d) D-shaped screw-gate.
(e) HMS with screw sleeve.
(f) D-shaped screw-gate held open by sleeve over hinge.
(g) D-shaped screw-gate closed by the sleeve.

Fig 3.32 Opposed-gate karabiners. In the case of symmetrical karabiners the gates are put on opposite sides and open in different directions. With asymmetric karabiners the gates are on the same side but open in different directions.

Fig 3.33 A karabiner which is three-way loaded and so weakened. The likelihood of failure would be even greater if the wide tape were at the gate end of the karabiner.

opposite directions. This keeps the pull along the back of the karabiner and also means that they sit together better.

Karabiner Strengths

Karabiners are strongest along their major axis – that is, along their length – and only work properly with the gate closed. Their strength across the minor axis is considerably lower and, with the gate open, a karabiner will have a breaking strength of only 600–700kg. The load-bearing side of the karabiner may be thicker than the gate side to increase its strength and the cross-sectional shape may be round, oval, T-shaped or roughly triangular or rectangular. The ends of the karabiner where the rope touches it should be rounded and have a radius of at least 4.5mm.

The gate is important as, by its very nature, it is the weakest part of the karabiner and should have a well-designed closure which is unlikely to snag and which will lock securely when loaded. This secure fit is important for, in a fall, if the gate is opened – even for an instant – it will be held open. This gate open strength is important, particularly with lightweight karabiners which, although strong enough with the gate closed, can be dangerously weak (600–650kg for a 9mm diameter karabiner) if the gate is held open when loaded. This gate opening can occur accidentally for a variety of reasons, especially in a fall situation; the gate can be pushed open by contact with the rock, the whiplash effect as the karabiner is moved violently in a fall or by vibration caused by jerks such as other gear failing or pulling out. A latch and pin is the most usual type of closure, although the pin can be on either the keeper or the body. The spring in the keeper should not be too strong as this can be more tiring to use, but it should be firm enough to prevent accidental opening in the event of a whipping or twisting force when shock-loaded. Tests have shown that a gate can open because of vibrations set up by a rope running through a karabiner during a fall.

Karabiners, particularly D-shaped ones, are strongest if the load is applied as near as possible to the back bar or spine, but all karabiners are weakened considerably if subjected to a three-way loading. In this situation the gate side is liable to fail [*fig. 3.33*]. Karabiners, especially off-set D-shaped ones, are weakened if the load is applied through a broad band such as wide tape or twin ropes when some of the load acts outwards, particularly on the weaker gate side. This is particularly the case with lightweight karabiners.

The UIAA sets standards for karabiners. To gain the UIAA stamp a karabiner should have a minimum gate opening of 15mm and accommodate two 12mm ropes without their interfering with the gate mechanism. It must survive loads of 22 kilo Newtons and show no deformation at 14kN. Karabiners must also pass tests concerning their deformation after loading and their strength across the minor axis when they must take a load of 6kN without the keeper opening or breaking. Most karabiners have their strength along the major axis stamped on the back bar and many also display the strength across the minor axis as well. Gate-open strength will also be shown in future.

Care of Karabiners

Karabiners should be checked every so often to ensure that they are free from burrs and sharp edges which could damage the rope. Keep them clean and free from grit by washing in warm water. An occasional spray of silicon lubricant helps keep the gate operating smoothly, but always wipe off the excess. Any karabiner which is suspect should be discarded or relegated to a non-load-bearing job. However, unless very well marked, they can, if not discarded, work their way back into regular use where they could be a danger. Alloy karabiners are particularly vulnerable to damage from salt water so should be washed thoroughly after use on sea cliffs where even spray in the air can affect them. Keep them well clear of corrosive substances such as acids.

4 Protection Equipment

THE CLIMBING SYSTEM

The usual system of roped climbing is based on the principle that only one person at a time is climbing and while doing so is protected by the rope. The rope is attached to both climbers, and while one person climbs, the other, who is securely tied to the cliff, manages the rope in such a way that, should a fall occur, it can be arrested. The method of doing this is basically the same whether on a 1000m cliff or a 10m outcrop.

In this system there are some specialised terms which unfortunately tend to be rather imprecise and some of the words have different shades of meaning depending on the context in which they are used. To avoid confusion the following terms are used in this book:

Anchor

A naturally occurring or specially constructed attachment point by which the climber can secure himself to the cliff.

To Be Anchored

To be tied on to one or more anchor points and secured to the cliff.

To Belay

To manage the rope in such a way that, should the person on the other end fall off, he can be stopped by the rope.

The Belayer

The climber who belays the rope.

The Belay

The complete system consisting of anchors, belayer and the method of rope management which allows the rope to be used to hold a fall.

Stance

A ledge where there are anchors and where a belay can be arranged.

Pitch

The distance between stances.

Running Belay

Points of intermediate protection through which the climbing rope is run to limit any falls. They are usually called runners.

In normal roped climbing belaying, rope management and protection in the form of running belays all form an integrated system in which these components are mutually dependent. One part of the system cannot be removed without making the other part ineffective. Climbing is unlike many other activities in that the system is basically the same at all standards. When you start climbing, the belaying, rope management and protection may well be straightforward but it is basically the same system as used on the hardest of climbs. Its purpose is always the same – to reduce the risk to life and limb – and as such there is no real progression from beginner to expert. The system must work at all levels or it is not worth using.

Unfortunately, to describe any part of the system means referring to the other parts as well and any divisions must, to some extent, be arbitrary. There is no real beginning or end as the parts are interlinked. For the convenience of description, however, the climbing system has been divided up into anchors, belaying and rope management, and protection.

Routes also can be categorised in terms of size into single- and multi-pitch climbs.

Single-Pitch Climb

On a single-pitch climb – that is, a route short enough to be done in one rope length – climbers A and B tie on to opposite ends of the rope. Climber B anchors himself at the foot of the climb and belays A who then climbs. If A fell at this point, he would hit the ground [*fig. 4.1a*]. As A continues, he places a running belay and clips his rope through it. A slip now would mean that A would fall at least twice the distance he is above the runner, but he would be stopped by B, still anchored at the foot of the climb [*fig. 4.1b*]. At the top of the climb A anchors himself and belays B while he climbs up after removing his anchors

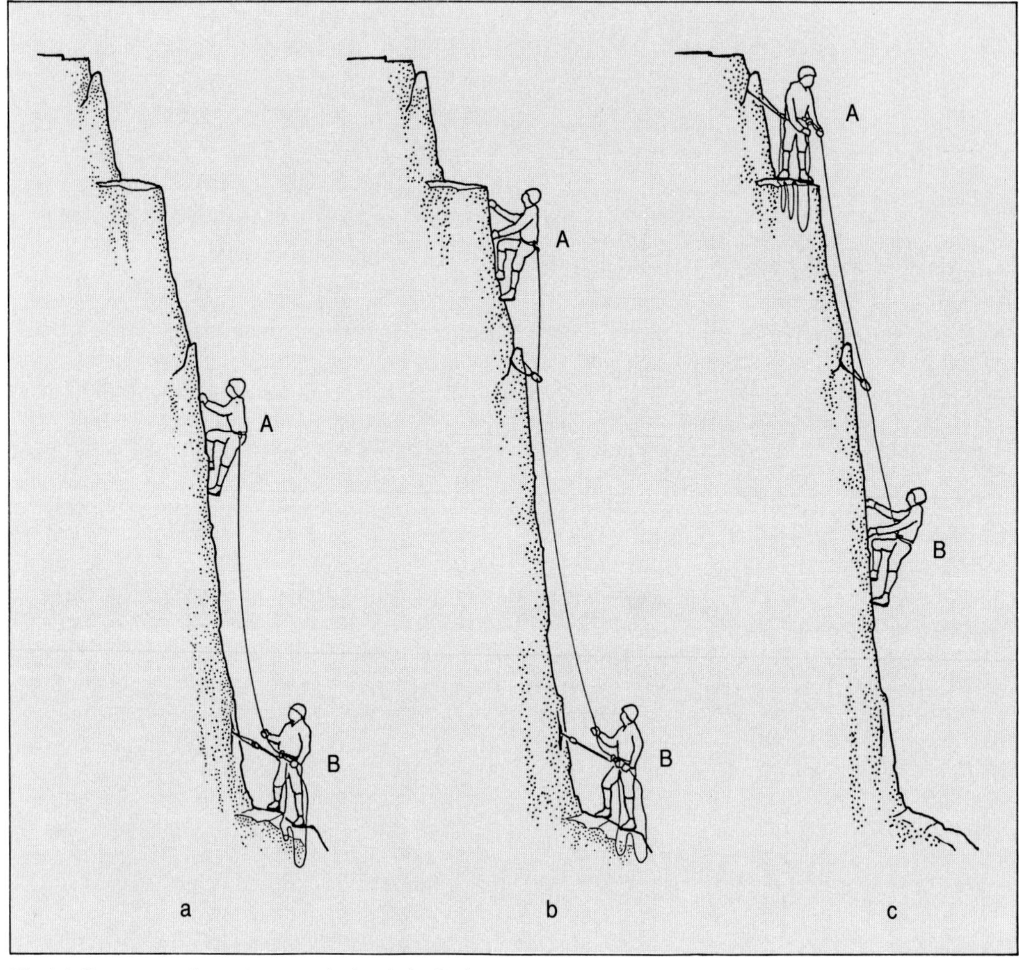

Fig 4.1 Sequence of events on a single-pitch climb.

and, when he reaches them, the running belays. If B were to fall, he would be held by A [*fig. 4.1c*].

Multi-Pitch Climb

On a cliff too high to be climbed in a single rope length, the route is broken into pitches. At the end of each pitch is a ledge or stance where anchors can be found and belays organised. As on a single-pitch climb, the second climber, B, is anchored and belays A while he leads the pitch [*fig. 4.2a*]. At the stance A places anchors, ties himself to them and belays B while he seconds the pitch [*fig. 4.2b*]. As they are sharing the role of leader, leading through, B continues up the next pitch, placing runners where possible [*fig. 4.2c*]. When B reaches the next stance, he secures himself as before and belays A as he climbs the pitch [*fig. 4.2d*]. They then carry on in this fashion until the climb is completed. If A were leading the whole route, A and B would change places at each stance and B would always climb protected by a rope from above.

USES OF PROTECTION EQUIPMENT

The use of protection equipment is fundamental to all aspects of climbing (apart from soloing). This gear has two main uses: it allows belays to be arranged by providing the means of anchoring

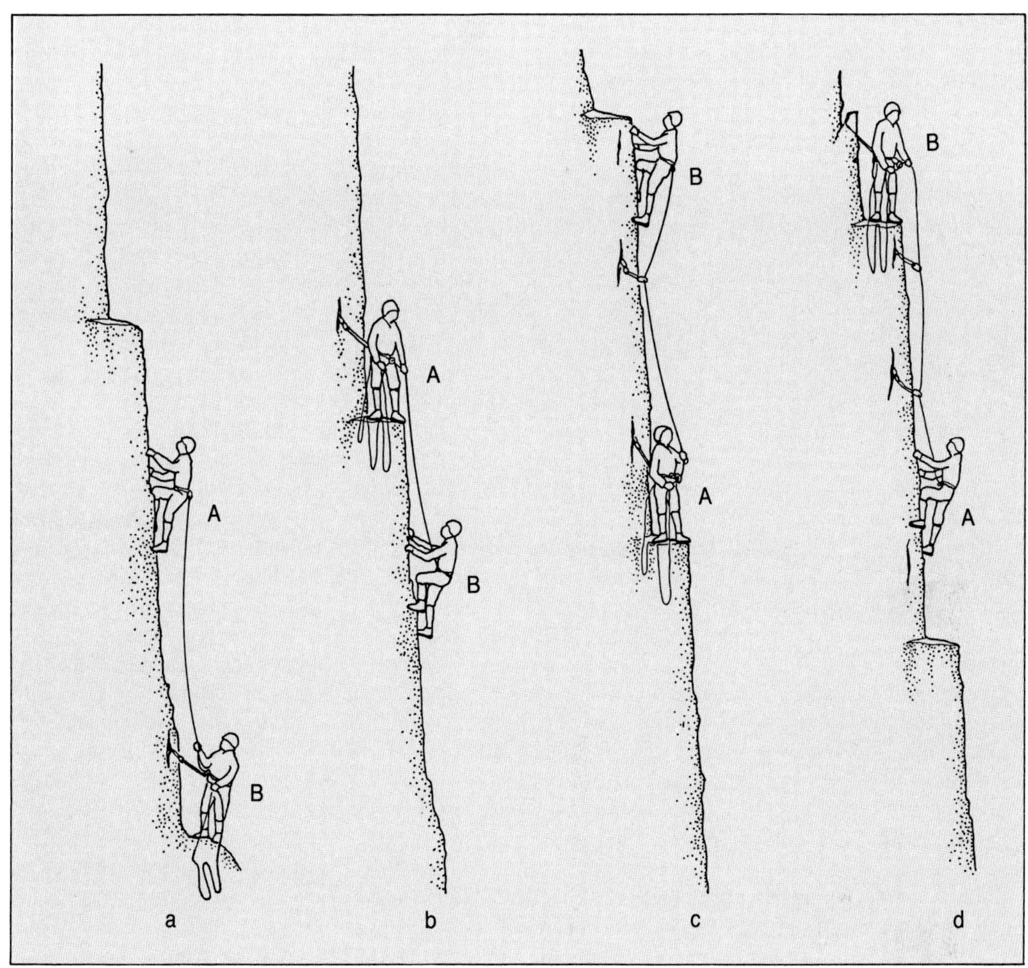

Fig 4.2 Sequence of events on a multi-pitch climb.

yourself to the rock and it protects the leader as he progresses up a pitch. These anchors and runners are placed in the same way: a belay anchor is usually placed from a position of relative comfort and security on a stance but a runner may be placed while hanging on with one hand with dwindling strength in a potentially serious situation.

Another difference is that in a belay situation, failure of the anchors will normally be extremely serious and for this reason it is normal to use several anchors to share the load and get a totally secure and trustworthy anchor for the belay. The failure of a runner may not be too serious, depending on the situation, but this is dependent on a host of other factors, the main ones being the frequency and quality of the other runners. However, runners are usually loaded individually, while in a belay situation load sharing is common.

The vast majority of protection equipment does both jobs but some gear (notably micro nuts) is normally used only for runners because of their lower strength. Short slings or extensions are used almost exclusively with runners because there is no real point in using them on belay anchors where all they do is introduce another link into the system.

In some ways the use of this gear is one of the more difficult things to learn when starting to climb. Although it is basically simple, there are many factors which affect how a piece of gear is used to gain the maximum benefit from it.

Experience is the key to runner placement and the arrangement of belay anchors. Judging size, selecting the correct piece of gear quickly, placing it correctly first time and using it to maximum advantage all take time and practice. The more you use gear, the better you will become at using it, but on some climbs the finding, placing and using of gear may occupy more time than the actual climbing.

PROTECTION DEVELOPMENT

The history of climbing and its advances in standards is closely linked with advances in equipment and protection techniques. The means to limit falls and make climbing safer has gone hand in hand with increased difficulty, and even climbs which are essentially unprotected have increased in standard as a result of the confidence and self-awareness that climbers have gained on better-protected routes.

In the earliest days, climbing protection was virtually non-existent and the rope the only equipment used. Routes tended to follow faults and lines of weakness where this lack of protection was less apparent: typically gullies and chimneys with their enclosing walls and short pitches often separated by easier terrain. As standards increased and climbers moved out on to steeper and more open faces, the practice of using rock anchors became more accepted and the shoulder belay became the norm. However, for the leader there were still few options for intermediate protection. The rope could be directed behind spikes, flakes or trees, or it could be untied, threaded behind a chockstone in a crack and then re-tied round the leader's waist. Karabiners and pre-tied slings made this much easier, but the number of features that could be used in this way were limited and, on some rock types, almost non-existent.

Pegs made an early appearance, particularly in the limestone of the Eastern Alps. In areas such as the Dolomites they were used to make some very impressive ascents, being employed both for protection and for direct aid to overcome sections of rock which were unclimbable at the standards of the day. While pegs were embraced enthusiastically in some areas, other places resisted or limited their use. This resistance was usually strongest in areas where the climbs tended to be on crags rather than on the bigger faces where a more liberal attitude prevailed. However, until the mid-1960s pegs were an important means of protection and their use was almost – though not quite – universal.

After the Second World War, when nylon ropes and cords became more generally available, protection improved. Thin yet strong nylon slings could be fitted behind smaller flakes and chockstones. This idea of threading chockstones was taken a stage further by wedging pebbles in cracks and then threading slings behind them. The next step was to have ready-threaded chockstones which could be placed, used and removed by the climbing party, and so the first nuts, or chocks, appeared. These were machine nuts with the internal thread removed and put on to a sling. From this basic yet brilliant idea came, in the mid-1960s, the first nuts specifically produced for climbing. Initially of fairly simple design, hexagonal, rounded or wedge-shaped, these changed into today's more sophisticated and versatile forms and have ousted most other means of protection. The concept of 'clean climbing', where the rock was left unaltered by the passage of climbers, was now a reality and swept the rock climbing world.

Although by the mid-1970s cracks from about 3mm to 10cm wide could be protected, the crack had to have a constriction to allow the nut to jam in place. Some nuts could be placed in parallel or even flared cracks, but the size tended to be critical and they could be difficult to place, especially if using one hand. This gap in the protection armoury was filled in the late 1970s with the appearance of Friends. These spring-loaded active camming devices could be placed in cracks which did not constrict and so provided protection where previously none was available. While they were not the first nuts to utilise the idea of camming to direct the force of a fall outwards on to the sides of the crack, Friends, in spite of their strange appearance and expense, soon became extremely popular.

Since then, equipment has continued to develop. Other camming devices have appeared: some involve similar ideas, others different ones, as the search for protection to use in thin cracks continues. Now a wide range of active camming units (ACUs) are available which give fast-to-place and safe-to-fall-on protection. Today's climber has a vast array of protection available to him, from the simple sling to items designed by computer and constructed with space-age materials. But it is still the person with the gear who must place and use it as and when he sees fit and as his ability and experience permit. Placing and using protection is an integral part of the climbing experience in most parts of the world.

Although nut protection is feasible where there are suitable cracks, where there are not, as is sometimes the case, pegs occasionally have to be used. Many protection pegs are relics of the pre-nut era and have gained a kind of historical legitimacy; others are genuinely needed. Today pegs are much less used than previously on rock climbs, although in some facets of the sport, such as big-wall climbing, winter climbing and Alpinism, they are still found.

The remaining means of protection, however, is one of the most contentious issues in climbing today. Bolts and how and where they are placed are subjects of much debate and controversy. The argument for their use is that they provide secure protection on routes which would otherwise be unprotected and so make this rock usable: the climber on a bolted route can concentrate on the moves and so increase his standard. Against this, bolts can change climbs to risk-free rock gymnastics and remove the element of boldness from the sport: anything is possible if enough time and bolts are used. These points are but a fraction of the debate about bolts which will no doubt continue for a long time. In some places their use is widespread, in others it is totally opposed. Bolts should never be placed on existing climbs and their use on new routes is a decision that first ascentionists should think long and hard about in the light of local opinion on the matter. To some the basic fabric of rock climbing is being destroyed by the use of bolts; to others, their use is the way forward. However, how and where bolts are used today will certainly have a bearing on the nature of the sport in years to come.

SLINGS

Although the sling was the first piece of protection equipment, even today slings are widely used and are invaluable in some situations. They can be draped over spikes and flakes, threaded through holes and round chockstones, attached to trees and bushes or used to extend other types of protection. They are light, cheap, convenient and extremely useful.

Most slings are now made of tape from about 15mm to 25mm wide and of either flat or tubular construction. They can be bought as sewn loops, which are stronger, lighter and less bulky than knotted slings. They can also be tied using a tape knot and personalised for length. This type can always be untied to give a single piece of tape, useful for tight threads and in some abseil situations. The tape knot, however, is prone to working loose and should be tightened with body weight when first tied and checked regularly. The ends of the knot can be taped or lightly stitched down for security. The breaking strength of a knotted sling is twice the strength of the rope or tape multiplied by the relative strength of the knot. This can be between 50 and 75 per cent and, for safety, is assumed to be the smaller value. This makes the strength of the sling about the same as that of the material from which it is made. Sewn slings are stronger, with strengths ranging from 1800kg for 14mm tape to 2500kg for 26mm tape slings. Spectra tape slings, which are even stronger, are available only as sewn loops.

Slings are usually of two basic loop sizes, though they can be of any length you care to make them. A standard or single sling is 120cm in length and a double sling 240cm. (These are often referred to as 4-foot and 8-foot slings.) It is worth having a few different lengths and thicknesses of sling to cope with tiny flakes and huge spikes. Tapes which have a small sewn loop at each end (snake slings) are slightly more versatile in the lengths in which they can be used.

All tape gear is vulnerable to abrasion and cutting on sharp edges so these should be padded if possible: the sewn join or the ends of the knot can be placed over any sharp edge to act as padding. Rope slings are less liable to damage in this way but they fit in fewer places because of their thickness, are bulkier and the double fisherman's knot used to tie them is inconveniently large in 9mm or 11mm rope. Any sling which shows signs of wear should be replaced.

When used on spikes, flakes or pinnacles, the sling is draped over the top and a karabiner used to attach the rope to it. The narrower the angle formed at the bottom of the sling, the better – ideally it should be less than 60° [*fig. 4.3*]. The wider the angle, the greater the load on each side of the sling. If the angle is too great, use a longer sling. The longer the sling used and the more the force is directed downwards rather than outwards, the better. Chockstones should be treated in a similar manner, at least for a downwards pull.

Check the placement carefully for cracks, particularly round its base, thump it with the heel of your hand to see if it moves and if it is loose reject it.

If a sling is used through any type of thread, it is better if the two ends of the loop are clipped together [*fig. 4.4*]. If one end is taken through the other, a lark's foot (a weaker way to use a sling) is formed. A small wired nut can often be used to help push a sling through narrow or awkward threads.

When using a sling round a tree or bush, put it on as close to the bottom of the trunk as possible to reduce leverage. If there is a problem with it riding up the trunk, an extra turn will hold it in place. It is better to tie it round the trunk rather than a branch as even quite large branches can be ripped off with a downwards force. Although trees can form very solid protection, it is as well to realise that even large trees have pulled out when loaded, especially in unusual conditions such as very wet or very dry soil.

A lark's foot may, however, be useful to keep the sling in place when you are using rounded knobs of rock such as chicken heads, although a clove hitch can also be used.

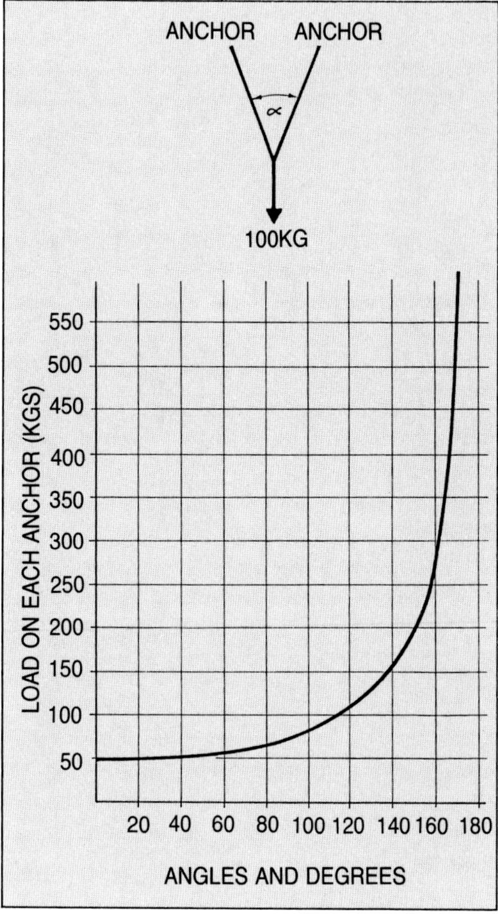

Fig 4.3 Graph showing the changing load on two anchors as the angle between them changes.

Short Slings

Short slings, variously known as extensions, extenders, quick-draws, express slings or tie-offs, are used in conjunction with other protection to increase the distance between the runner and the rope. This can be to reduce rope drag or to prevent the gear from being lifted out or unseated by the action of the rope. They can be tied in tape or cord, but are usually sewn tape loops between 10 and 30cm long and from about 15 to 25mm wide. Although they are basically simple loops, there are variations which offer some advantages. They can be sewn through both parts of the loop to give closed-end loops and a stiffer middle which stops the attached karabiners moving about; others have a 90° twist in one end so that one karabiner lies at right angles to the rock for ease of clipping. Some are thinner at the ends than in the centre so that any loading is along the back of the karabiner and does not increase the leverage which weakens the karabiner, particularly if the gate is open when a load is applied [*fig. 4.5*].

Shock slings are short slings whose central section is sewn in a concertina fashion with weaker stitching which is designed to rip in a fall and so absorb some of the force. They are of most use on marginal or poor yet important runners. They will act as shock slings for only one fall but may be suitable as normal extensions afterwards [*fig. 4.6*].

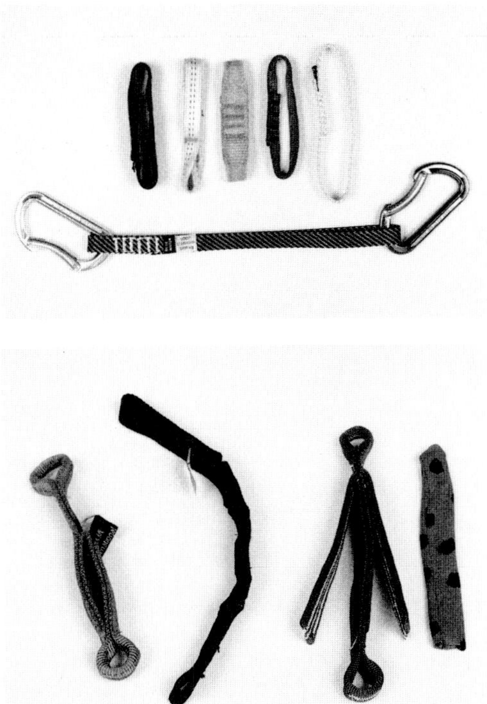

Fig 4.4 ABOVE: *Sewn tape sling round a thread.*

Fig 4.5 ABOVE RIGHT: *Selection of short slings.*

Fig 4.6 RIGHT: *Selection of shock slings showing various types of concertina-like stitching designed to tear when shock-loaded.*

NUTS (CHOCKS)

Nuts (or chocks) work by wedging or jamming in a crack, usually above a constriction, but there are more subtle ways of placing them. Modern nuts come in two main forms, basically wedge-shaped or roughly hexagonal. In both cases the original symmetrical forms have been superseded by more versatile, asymmetric shapes. Although there is an overlap in size in the middle of the range (15–25mm), smaller nuts tend to be wedges and larger ones polycentric. Nuts may be on wire or rope loops, but the smallest are wired and the largest on rope.

Roped Nuts

If a nut is sold loose, it has to be put on a sling which will generally be 6–9mm cord or 15–25mm tape unless the thinner but very strong Kevlar or Spectra cord is used. Some manufacturers recommend the diameter of cord to use to give optimum strength. Normally the thickest cord which can be threaded neatly should be used: overthick cord crammed through may actually be weaker. When using Kevlar or Spectra, the cord can be put through a vinyl insert to give a better fit in the holes. About 1–1.25m of rope are needed for the loop and the double fisherman's knot used to tie it. The exact length will vary with the diameter of the rope used and personal preference. Tape can also be used to sling nuts but it is more susceptible to abrasion and the tape knot liable to slippage, and so requires frequent inspection. It is useful on rock where the cracks tend to constrict sharply and cord is too thick for the placements. If slinging your own nuts, it is best to have each size on different-coloured slings for easy, quick identification. The slings on roped or taped nuts should be checked and renewed regularly as they are subject to more wear than climbing rope. Roped nuts can be wrapped in adhesive tape or slipped into a tube of nylon tape to protect them from abrasion – this is neat but heavier [*fig. 4.7*].

Wired Nuts

Most medium to small nuts are on wire cable which has the advantage of being far stronger than

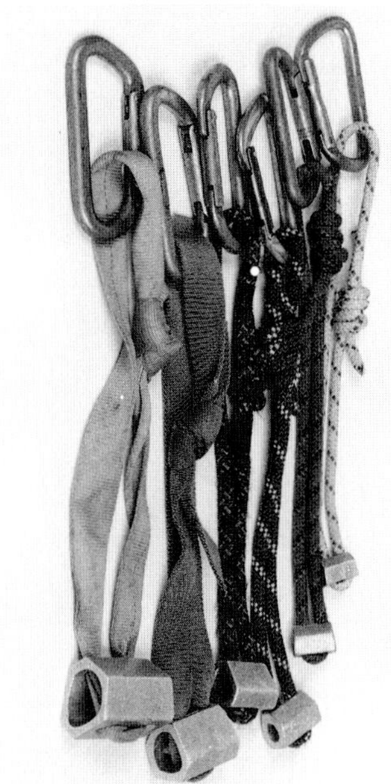

Fig 4.7 Selection of nuts on rope and tape. These nuts are the middle-sized range of Hexcentrics.

Fig 4.9 A Hexcentric in a parallel-sided crack. When loaded, the nut will be twisted more securely across the crack.

rope of equivalent size. Nuts on 2.5mm cable have a breaking strength of about 700kg; and on 3.2mm wire, the more usual thickness, a breaking strength of around 1200kg [*fig. 4.8*]. As the wire is fairly stiff, these nuts can be placed deep in the back of cracks or above full stretch where roped nuts could not be put.

Many wired nuts have a colour-coded plastic sleeve to indicate their size, but if not it is worth marking them for easy recognition, especially when sorting them out at stances or before starting a route.

Wedge-Shaped Nuts

Wedge-shaped nuts are extremely popular and versatile. Modern wedges have changed their original straight-sided shape and now have a convex and a concave face [*fig. 4.8*]. This permits a wider range of placements, particularly if there are irregularities in the crack. Edges are rounded to catch less when being placed and removed, and are more likely to seat better rather than get hung up on the actual edge. Although usually used to wedge above a narrowing, their shape means that they will often fit better one way round than the other. Getting as much of the nut in contact with the rock as possible, so that the load is shared over a greater surface area, is a good start to safe nut placing.

Another advantage of this shape is that when loaded the nut can rock or cam on the convex face and jam more securely. This means that wedge-shaped nuts can be used in near-parallel-sided cracks. To use this camming action they are positioned with the convex face down in horizontal and diagonal cracks.

Wedges are also tapered along the side faces, so can be used this way round in shallow cracks. However, the smaller sizes of nut can be deformed and the holes pushed closer together when loaded. This can lead to the nut pulling out or to the failure of the wire, which is forced into a tighter curve. In pockets wedge-shaped nuts can often be keyed in place if they are inserted and then turned on to their wider face so that they are locked in place.

Polycentric Nuts

The first commercially produced nuts took their shape from machine nuts and were hexagonal, but while these worked well in cracks which tapered, they had no real advantage over wedges. This

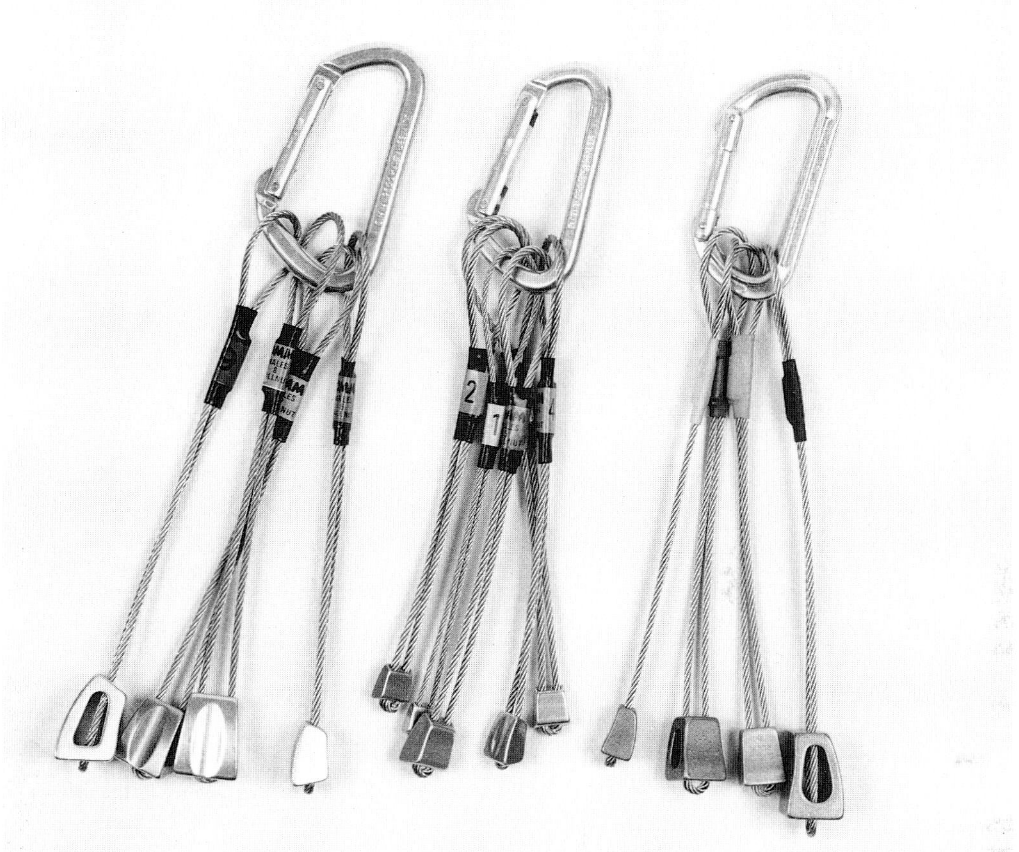

Fig 4.8 A selection of wired, wedge-shaped nuts.

state of affairs changed when the hexagonal shape was modified to produce Hexcentrics – asymmetric nuts whose side faces are of different sizes. Because they had slightly different sizes across the diagonals, their possibilities were increased and, more importantly, they could cam when loaded so that they could be used in parallel-sided cracks [*fig. 4.9*]. This only works well in vertical cracks if the fit is good enough to hold the nut in place until loaded, but in horizontal placements this camming is extremely useful. In a horizontal crack the rope should come out of the nut at the side nearer the top. Because Hexcentric nuts have a taper on the end face, they can also be used sideways in shallow cracks or when keyed in pockets, so in fact they will fit in three different-sized cracks. It is important that Hexs are placed with the faces and not the edges in contact with the rock.

Micro Nuts

Micro nuts are also wedge-shaped but generally have straight faces and work by pure wedging. Most are made of brass but they may also be of alloy or steel. There are some variations in design and they may have flattened, nearly square, asymmetric or scooped faces, each generally with some advantages [*fig. 4.10*]. A problem can be that the faces have so little surface (the smallest are only 3mm in size) that they may be resting on small irregularities in the crack which could fail or pull through when loaded.

All micro nuts are on wire; some are on wire of looped construction and others on trapped wire where the ends are silver-soldered or pressed into the head. The smallest of these nuts, on 1.3mm wire, have a breaking strain of about 250kg, rising to about 1000kg for nuts on 3mm cable [*fig. 4.11*].

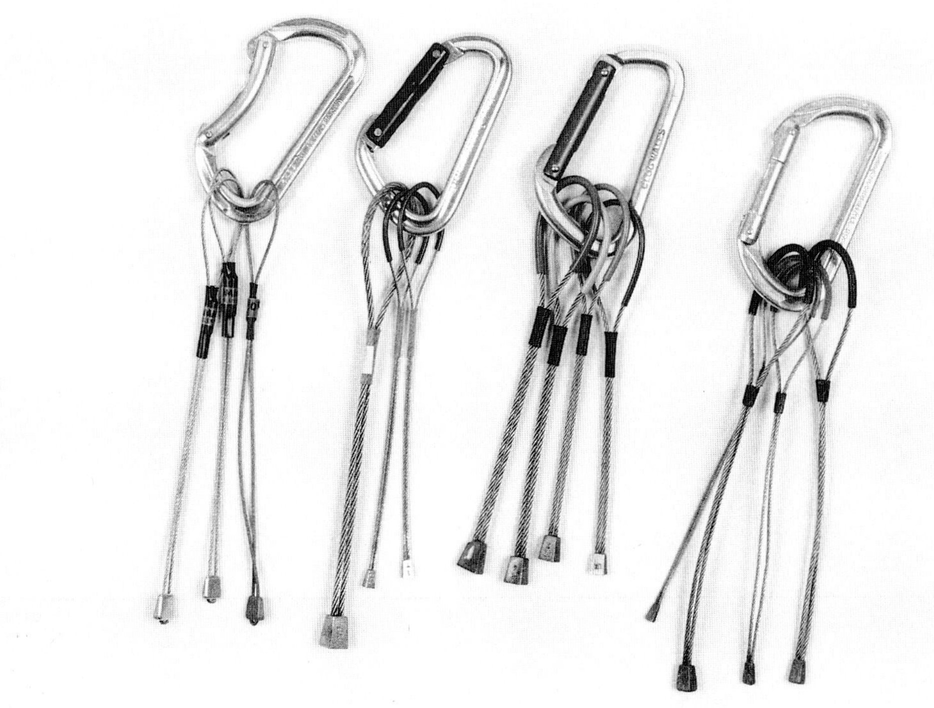

Fig 4.10 Selection of micro nuts showing some different nut shapes and the two main methods of wire attachment, swaged loops and trapped wire. Some of the micro nuts have a coloured plastic sleeve for easy identification.

Fig 4.11 A well placed micro nut, in this case an RP.

CAMMING DEVICES

Although Hexs and some wedge-shaped nuts have a camming action, this is not usually their prime function. Active camming devices, however, work only by this action directing any pull on the device outwards against the sides of the crack. If spring-loaded so that they are held in position before a load is applied, they have the potential for rapid placement and will work in cracks which do not constrict. They will hold in parallel-sided cracks and even in cracks which flare. Since friction plays a part in their action, the degree to which they can cope with a flare will also depend on the roughness of the rock [*fig. 4.12*].

Fig 4.12 RIGHT: *A selection of camming devices (from right to left): a Rock 'n' Roller, two TCUs with one- and two-finger trigger retraction, a Camalot, a flexible Friend and a rigid Friend.*

Tri-Cams

Tri-cams are remarkably simple yet effective. The nut has a curved face from the top of which runs a tape and, when loaded, this pulls the nut into a cammed position. Although slightly awkward for the unpractised to place, they can be used in shallow cracks, pockets and slots where nothing else will fit. They may need a hard jerk to seat them at first [*fig. 4.13*].

Fig 4.13 ABOVE: *A Tri-cam in a horizontal break. When the tape is loaded, the nut will be cammed to create a size increase which will hold it in place.*

Friends

The best-known and most popular camming devices are Friends, which cover a range from 13 to 100mm with nine sizes. They consist of four independently sprung cams on an axle attached to a stem. Each cam has a constant angle curve which means that it is in contact with the rock at the same angle wherever it touches it and, having two cams on either side of the shaft, gives the device a degree of stability. As each cam operates independently, a Friend can accommodate irregularities in a crack [*fig. 4.14*]. These cams are operated by a trigger by which they can be pulled smaller. To place a Friend, use the thumb and two fingers to pull back the trigger bar and close the

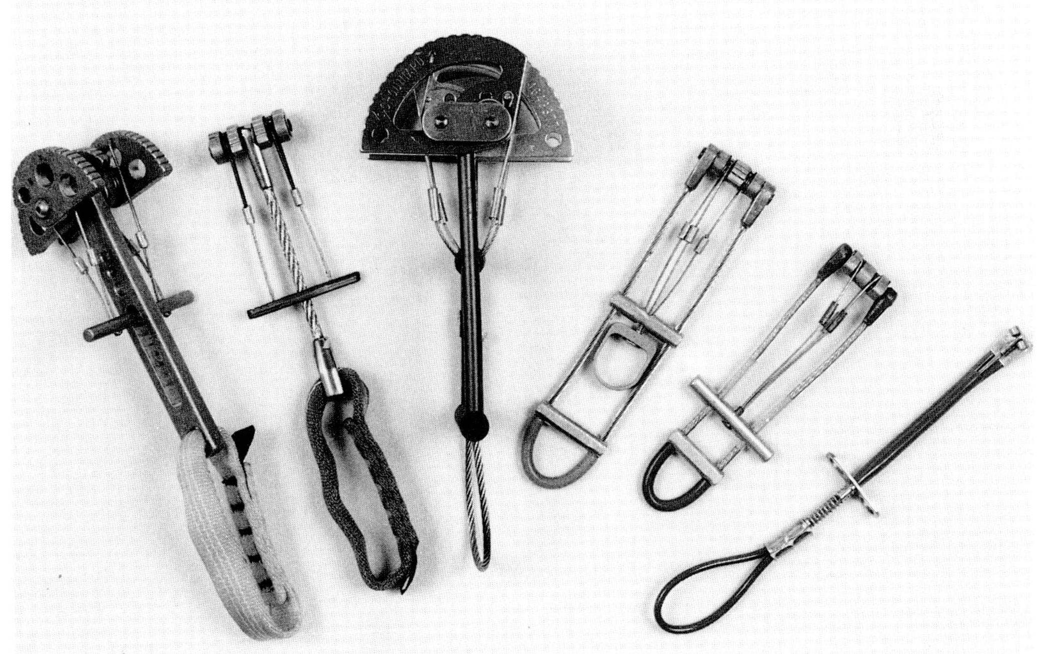

Fig 4.14 A large Friend in a crack which flares both downwards and outwards and so would be useless for a nut which works by pure wedging.

Fig 4.15 Placing a Friend.

cams, put it in the crack and let the cams expand and grip [*fig. 4.15*]. To remove, use the same actions to pull the trigger, contract the cams and then lift it out. Sometimes a small inward push while retracting the cams will assist removal.

Although Friends are simple and fast to place, the best performance is obtained if certain points are noted. They should be positioned so that the stem is aligned in the direction of loading, that will normally be almost straight down in a vertical crack. The cams should be as symmetrical as possible on either side of the stem and it is best if the trigger lies in the middle third of its slot. If only the tips of the cams are in contact with the rock, the device cannot expand further and grip properly; if the Friend is placed with the cams fully depressed, it may be impossible to remove as it cannot be reduced in size [*fig. 4.16*]. If a cam inverts, it will not work properly and should be removed and replaced.

One problem with Friends is that they can 'walk' into cracks if subject to any rocking action – from the rope, for example. If the crack expands inside, they can drop out, but more common is the trigger moving out of reach: this is particularly awkward with the smaller sizes of Friend. A small loop of cord attached to either side of the trigger can ease the removal of the device from a tight spot. If deep in a crack with the trigger out of reach, it can be pulled back by looping a wire nut over each side of the bar and pulling on those; alternatively, some nut keys have a double hook specifically for this job. The very careless could invest in one of the tools designed for Friend removal.

Care must also be taken when using Friends in horizontal cracks. If the stem protrudes too far, it could fail because of the leverage over the edge. It can be tied off using a sling but this tends to damage the trigger wires and is awkward to put on. An alternative is to put a short 4mm cord loop through the first hole above the trigger slot and use this: it can be taped out of the way for normal use.

This problem has been overcome by the Flexible Friend which has a stainless-steel cable instead of a rigid stem. As this will bend over an edge, the leverage problem is solved, but in vertical cracks it is not quite so predictable in the way that the load will be applied to the cams in a fall. The Flexible Friend can, however, be used in shallower pockets where the rigid stem cannot be aligned properly.

Friends can be repaired if damaged, the trigger wires being particularly vulnerable. If they become stiff and awkward to operate, they can be sprayed with a silicon-based lubricant.

Camalots

Camalots all have flexible wire frames, a double axle so the cams cannot invert and a trigger system that permits one-finger retraction. They are used in the same way as Friends but the double axle permits a greater range of size movement and they can be used as passive nuts with the cams fully open. They cover from about 25–125mm in four sizes.

Other Camming Devices

Although Friends work well in deep cracks, there are difficulties in using them in cracks too short to accept all four cams, and this gap in the protection armoury has given rise to smaller and narrower devices usable in these situations. There are two main types of device for thin and shallow cracks: they either work on the same camming principle as Friends or use opposed wedges.

Three- or technical cam units (TCUs) work in a similar way to Friends in directing the force of a fall outwards against the rock [*fig. 4.17*]. Having only three cams, they are narrower so can be used in shallower placements. Most have a cable loop attached to the axle and may have a one- or two-finger trigger action. However, they do seem less stable than four cams and they can rotate and so come out of placements which are near the top end of their range as the two cam side grips better than the single one. This is less likely to happen in tight placements.

Spring-loaded opposed wedges work on the principle of two wedges which, when pulled away from each other, will expand and jam. With passive wedges it is possible to get a placement in near-parallel-sided cracks: two nuts are placed side by side, the larger positioned normally but the smaller is placed upside-down. They are then jammed in place by pulling them away from each other [*fig. 4.18*]. The problem is to get them to stay in place and this is solved by using a spring to provide the initial pressure. Devices which use

Fig 4.16 A Friend in an overtight placement. The next size down would be a better fit and easier to remove.

Fig 4.17 TCU in a horizontal crack. The flexible stem removes the problem of leverage over the edge of the crack.

Fig 4.18 Two wedge-shaped nuts in a parallel-sided crack. The larger nut, when loaded, will pull against the smaller one and the sides of the crack and jam in place.

Fig 4.19 Rock 'n' Roller in a near-vertical parallel-sided placement. The spring holds it in place until loaded, when it works on the opposed-wedge principle.

this idea in some form may employ wedges, wedges and rollers or various combinations of curved shapes, but they have only one moving part which is spring-loaded. Their main advantage is that they can be used in thin, shallow, parallel-sided cracks. These devices have different strengths and weaknesses, but all require a bit of practice in their use to get the best out of them [*fig. 4.19*].

Various four cam devices similar to Friends are now becoming available. Most of these have flexible wire frames rather than rigid stems but function in much the same way as Friends.

Some camming devices have a sewn tape loop attached to the frame or stem. If a device does not have a tape loop it will normally have to be lengthened with karabiners and an extension to cut down on rope drag and stop the device 'walking' into the crack.

Emergency Nuts

If you run out of nuts, anything which can be jammed in a crack can be used. The most useful is probably jammed knots made by tying a suitable knot in a sling and wedging it in a crack. These are fairly versatile, can be tied to the desired size and hold remarkably well. In some areas such as Czechoslovakia, where metal nuts would destroy the soft sandstone, they are the main type of running belay [*fig. 4.20*].

Nuts in Opposition

Sometimes it may be necessary to use two nuts facing in opposite directions and connected so that they hold each other in place – perhaps in a vertical crack where a nut needs to be prevented from lifting out. This is done by tensioning the main or upper nut against a lower one placed to resist a pull in an upwards direction. The two nuts can be connected by a sling which is clove hitched tightly to each one or by a sling made to the correct length with an overhand knot [*fig. 4.21*]. Slings can also be tied down in this way.

In horizontal cracks placements can be found which will take a pull to the side. Two nuts, each of which can take a pull towards the other, can be linked so that the result is an anchor which will resist an outwards and downwards force. With roped nuts the sling of one can be put through the karabiner on the second one and the rope clipped through the other karabiner [*fig. 4.22*]. This is simple but does increase the load by acting as a pulley. Wired nuts or those further apart can be linked using a sling and clove hitches or an overhand knot.

Slings can also be used in this manner on horizontally facing spikes and flakes which would not take a downwards force. They can be linked as previously described.

Fig 4.20 RIGHT: *A jammed knot in a crack. In this case an overhand knot has been used, but any knot will do, its size being the important consideration.*

Fig 4.21 BELOW: *Two opposed nuts in a horizontal crack. The sling connecting them is tied with an overhand knot to maintain tension on them and keep them in place.*

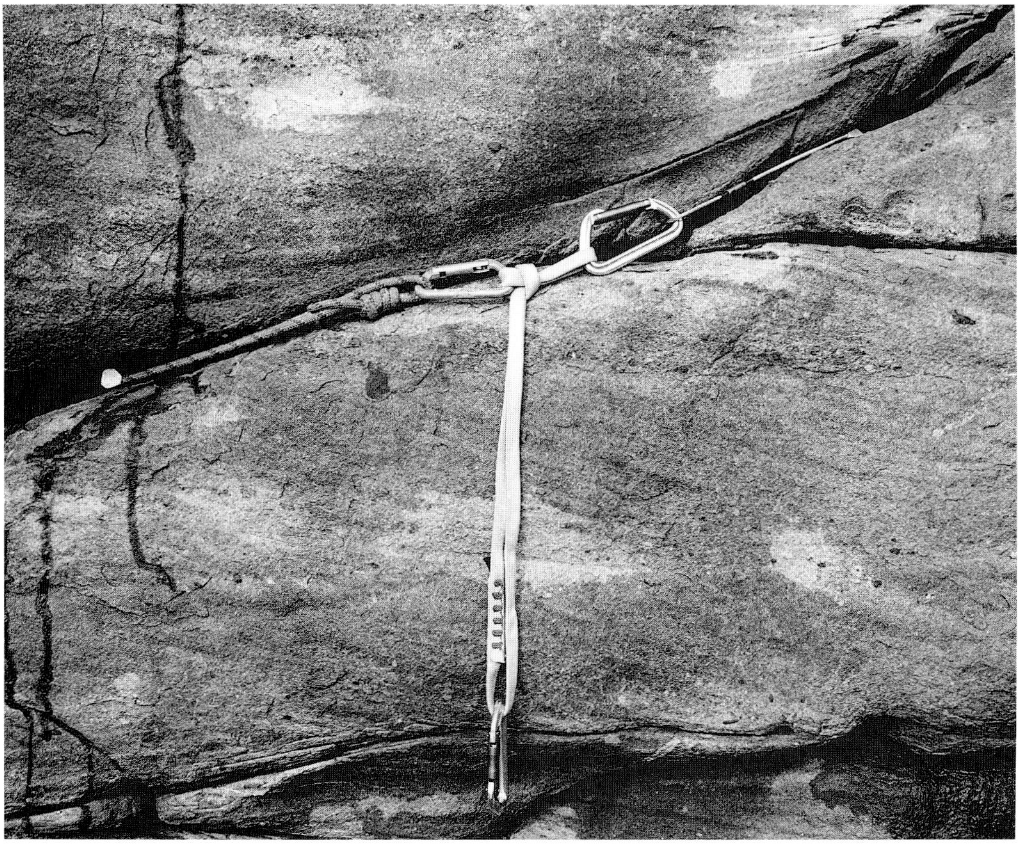

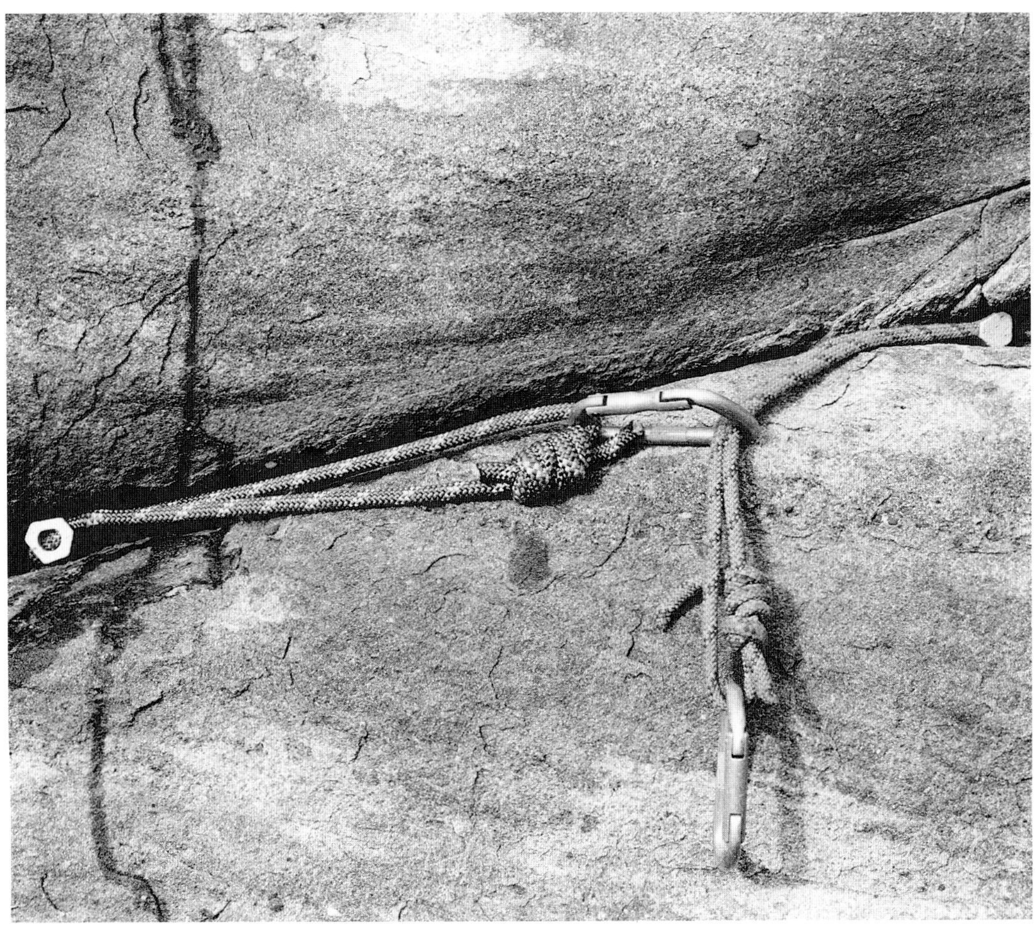

Fig 4.22 Two opposed nuts: the force is directed by threading one sling through the other. This works only if they will stay securely in place without tension. The left hand nut, the Hexcentric, is placed so that, when loaded, the sling will cam the nut more securely into the crack.

With camming devices which work well in horizontal cracks and are much less liable to work loose, nuts in opposition are less usual now but can still be useful in thin cracks or for vital but poorly seated placements.

PREVIOUS PAGE: *Chalking up on a strenuous boulder problem. Considerable strength is required in this type of dynamic climbing.* (Niall Ritchie)

ABOVE: *Bouldering is available in many places. Here in a disused quarry.* (Rab Anderson)

ABOVE RIGHT: *Much good bouldering is available on quarried rock, in this case limestone. The climber is pinch-gripping and toe-jamming in the cracks left by the saw used to cut the blocks of this soft rock.* (Chris Forrest)

BELOW: *Some rock types, such as gritstone, lend themselves to an athletic style of climbing. Here the leader is using a heel hook to take the weight off his arms.* (Allen Fyffe)

INSET RIGHT: *Although good footwork can reduce the strain on the arms, some types of climbing will always be strenuous. Here the climber uses a pinch grip and a side pull in conjunction with sloping footholds.* (Niall Ritchie)

RIGHT: *On the crux of a climb it is sometimes useful to have the protection selected and readily available. Here the necessary gear, complete with extension, is clipped to the shirt so that it is instantly accessible and can be quickly placed.* (Keith Geddes)

ABOVE LEFT: *In some parts of the world, where climbs are very direct, it is normal to climb on a single rope. When this is the case, extensions should be used, in this case in conjunction with bolts, to minimize rope drag.* (Stuart Wagstaff)

LEFT: *Steep strenuous wall climbing on small holds. The leader is arranging protection on both ropes, in the same horizontal breach. This is especially important when, as in this case, the gear is not ideal: the stem of the Friend protrudes too far from the crack.* (Richard Mansfield)

ABOVE: *Rock climbing on an easy ridge. Climbing of this nature is accessible to everyone and offers a progression from hill-walking to technical rock climbing.* (George Reid)

RIGHT: *The leader should always try to belay so that the second is in sight, thus making communication and rope management much easier. Full use has been made of the double-ropes to maximize the available protection and minimize rope drag.* (Martin Doyle)

ABOVE: *On many rock types the protection may be dubious because of the quality of the rock itself. This photo of steep wall climbing shows a climber on slate, a very friable rock which can fail unexpectedly.* (Martin Burrows-Smith Collection)

ABOVE LEFT: *Good rope management is important when climbing. Here the belayer is well positioned and anchored for a pull in any direction. The leader has made a sensible choice of protection and the appropriate rope has been used. In common with many sea cliff climbs this route has been approached by abseil on a separate rope.* (Adrian Liddell)

LEFT: *Climbing at a very high standard on bolt-protected rock. Weight is kept to a minimum with a single rope and a few extensions and karabiners.* (Rab Anderson)

RIGHT: *When climbing on rough rock, the wear and tear on the hands may make it necessary to tape them up to prevent damage. Here the climber is lay-backing a flake crack, protected by a Friend.* (Alastair Cain)

OVERLEAF: *On bulging rock it is often difficult for the belayer to get positioned so as to see the second. In this case a virtual hanging stance is necessary.* (Adrian Liddell)

5 Belaying and Rope Management

Belaying is fundamental to roped climbing and is one of the more complex parts of a safe climbing system. At any point on a climb any person tied on to the rope is either anchored or belayed. Setting up a belay consists of several parts: finding and placing anchors, tying on to them, belaying the rope and adopting the correct position.

The first belaying systems were primitive affairs – the ropes were weak, of little good to the leader and often created a dangerous bond rather than a safe connection. The earliest belays were simple, the rope being run behind a spike or flake of rock, or the belayer taking up as secure a position as possible. In the first case the rope was liable to break over the edge; in the second the belayer was likely to be pulled off. Then came the development of the shoulder belay, which was an improvement on holding the rope in the hands, and after this the body belay where the friction and braking force of the rope running round the body allowed longer falls to be held. This was a dynamic belay since, once a certain force had been reached, the rope would run, creating friction, and so use up some of the fall energy. This type of belay and the introduction of the better nylon ropes made climbing a safer activity, but the correct use of the body belay was a skilled process which required some strength and intelligent application as well as practice.

Towards the end of the 1960s the first belay plate, the Sticht, made its appearance. This mechanical belay device was a great step forward in terms of safety: it is strong, simple and does not rely on the belayer's strength or weight to function effectively. About this time, as well, the friction hitch made its appearance and provided another safe, simple and convenient way to belay. Although the friction hitch and the belay plate are the most popular and safest type of belay system, the body belay still has some uses.

BELAY MECHANICS

If a fall is stopped statically – that is, with no movement of the rope – all the energy has to be taken up by the rope system and its attachments. This puts great stress on everything connected to the rope, including the person who has fallen off. It is far better to arrest a fall dynamically and transform some of the fall energy into friction by rope movement. There are several ways of belaying which provide this dynamic element, but in all cases the more rope that runs through or round any belay system, the slower the fall is stopped and the lower the forces will be. Unfortunately, the longer the fall and the greater the speed reached, the greater the chance of injury from hitting something.

When climbing, the rope running to the climber, whether a leader or a second, is known as the live or active rope. After the rope has passed round or through the belay system, it is known as the dead or inactive rope. The hands holding these ropes are known as the live (or feeling) and dead (or braking) hands. Right and left are irrelevant as it is the part of the rope held that is important. The terms live and dead are used in this book.

TYPES OF BELAY

There are three main types of belay which differ in how much of the energy created by a fall is transmitted to the belay anchors. Although these methods are interchangeable in many cases, they are not always so. Each method has different advantages and disadvantages and it is important to know when each can be used safely.

Direct Belays

With a direct belay, the force of a fall is taken directly on the anchor. In its simplest form it can be the rope run behind a spike, flake, pinnacle or tree and the fall held by the friction between the rope and the rock [*fig. 5.1*]. Alternatively, a sling is put on an anchor and the rope arranged in the karabiner in a way which will provide friction. There are several different ways in which this can be done using combinations of twists or turns in the rope, but the friction hitch (see 'Belay

Methods', page 74) is probably the best method [*fig. 5.2*]. The advantage of this method is the speed with which it can be set up, though it relies on having an absolutely solid, single-point anchor. It is often used in Alpine climbing where speed is important.

Semi-Direct Belay

A semi-direct belay is commonly used when wearing a harness and using a mechanical belay device. The ropes from the anchors are tied into the harness or the loop formed by the knot used to tie in with, referred to as the knot loop. The

Fig 5.1 LEFT: *A direct belay used to protect a short, steep section. In this case the belayer is using a body belay but relying mainly on the friction of the rope on the rock.*

Fig 5.2 BELOW: *A direct belay with a sling on a spike. A friction hitch is the actual belay method used here.*

Fig 5.3 ABOVE: *Semi-direct belay to a second where the force of a fall would be straight on to the anchors. The tie-on is with two figure-of-eight knots tied into the knot loop. The dead hand controlling the rope through the belay plate is the uphill hand.*

Fig 5.4 ABOVE RIGHT: *Semi-direct belay to a leader. In this case the belayer would be lifted up if the leader fell off on to runners. The tie-on to the first anchor is a figure-of-eight and the second anchor is tied in with a clove hitch. A friction hitch is being used to belay the leader.*

belay device is attached to this knot loop and, with the belayer standing to the side, any force downwards goes straight on to the anchor [*fig. 5.3*]. A force in an upwards direction, however, will involve the belayer by lifting, or attempting to lift him, into the air [*fig. 5.4*].

Indirect Belay

In an indirect belay the belayer's body is positioned between the anchors and the force and so will absorb some of the fall energy and cushion the anchors. This is an advantage when the anchor is not totally reliable or cannot be inspected or tested adequately. An indirect belay is usually used with a snow anchor, for example. With any anchors, however, if a body belay is used, the belay must be indirect as the force of a fall always

Fig 5.5 An indirect belay in which the belayer is attached to the rope by a waist belt, and after tying on to the anchors the knot loop and attached knots have been pushed round to the centre of the back. A body belay is being used; to prevent the rope being whipped upwards in a fall a karabiner could be clipped into the belt behind the live hand and the live rope clipped into this.

comes on to the belayer's body before the anchor points [*fig.* 5.5, page 73].

To give an indirect belay it is better if the belayer's attachment to the anchors comes from the centre of his back so that any force on the belayer does not subject him to a twisting action.

BELAY METHODS

There are several methods of belaying but not all of them are of practical use. However, it is worth being familiar with more than one way of belaying because of the greater flexibility this gives. The following methods have shown themselves to be versatile and popular and do not rely too heavily on specialised pieces of equipment.

The Body Belay

In the body belay, also known as the waist or hip belay, the rope is taken round the belayer's back at the top of the hips but below the softer, more vulnerable parts of the waist. It is essential that the rope is put round the back above the ropes to the anchors and thus is prevented from being pulled down underneath the belayer and so dropped. A twist of rope can be taken round the dead arm to increase friction. In even a small fall, friction burns are a very real danger, so the arms should be covered and gloves worn [*fig.* 5.5].

To hold a fall using a body belay, the dead hand is brought across the front of the body [*fig.* 5.6]. This increases rope/body contact and consequently the braking friction. This is normally a fast action but it can be slowed down to increase the amount of rope let out and so decrease the force of a fall, though it does increase the length. Even when this braking action is done as quickly as possible, at a certain force the belay is dynamic as rope is pulled round the belayer's body.

In a leader fall, the belay rope can be whipped upwards across the back and under the arm on the live side. To prevent this, a karabiner can be clipped to the front of the tie-on arrangement and the live rope clipped in to it. This will redirect the rope and also increase rope/body contact. Holding falls with a body belay is not only painful but is also a technique which needs to be practised in a safe, controlled situation before it can be relied upon. This is particularly the case if one climber is heavier than his partner as strength and weight are factors in its effectiveness.

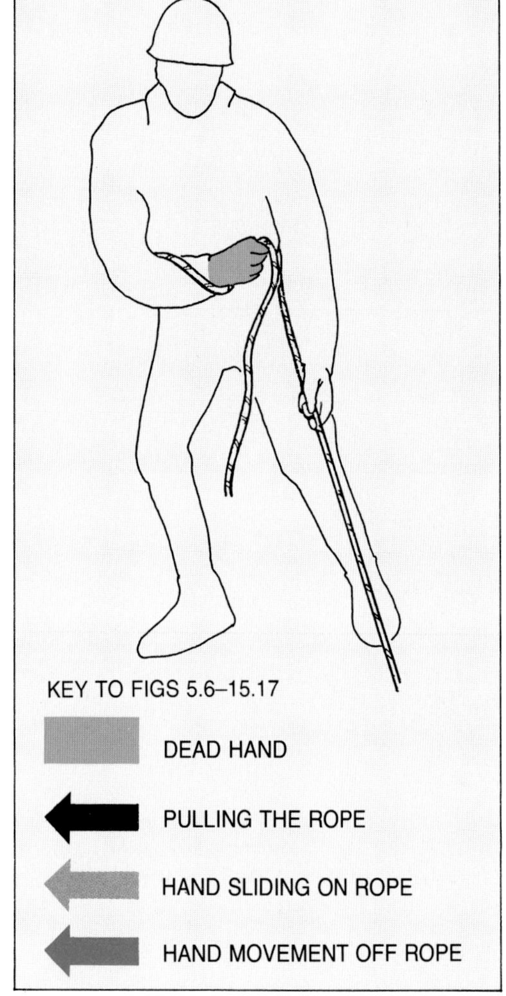

Fig 5.6 The body belay with the dead hand brought across the front of the body in the braking position. Standing with the live leg forward and the other at 45° gives a stable position.

When using the body belay, the dead hand, which does the braking, must never be taken off the rope. Paying out the rope is done by the live hand which slides back up the rope towards the body, grasps the rope and pulls out the required amount. To make this easier, the live hand can pull out to the side before moving in an arc to the front. This reduces friction between the rope and the body.

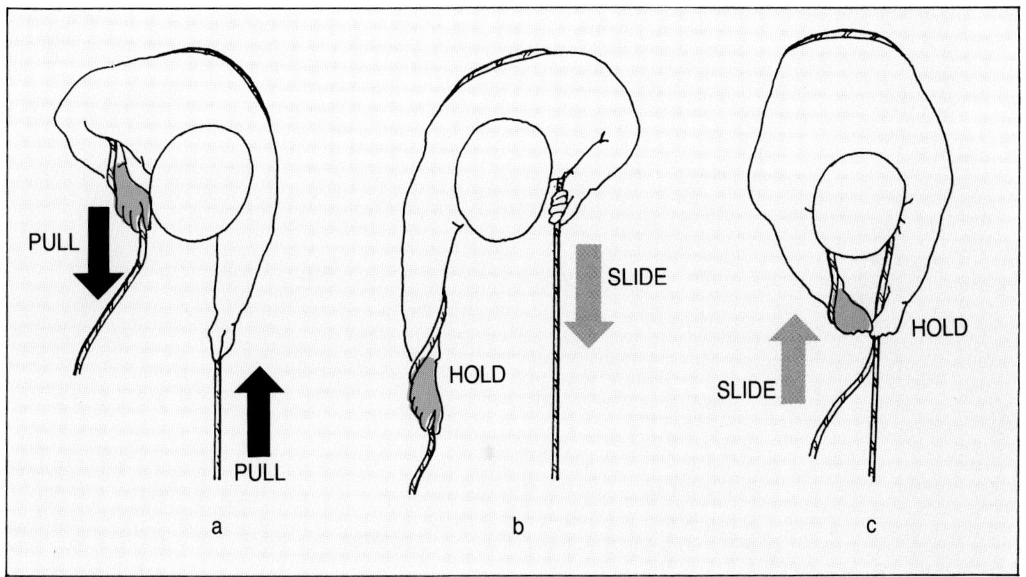

Fig 5.7 The sequence of actions for taking in using a body belay:
(a) The live hand pulls the rope up and the dead hand pulls forward.
(b) The dead hand stays forward and the live hand slides down the rope until it is further from the body.
(c) The live hand grips the dead rope lightly under the thumb so that the dead hand can be slid back to begin the next cycle.

Fig 5.8 RIGHT: *Front to rear conversion of a harness tied on to an anchor with a clove hitch.*

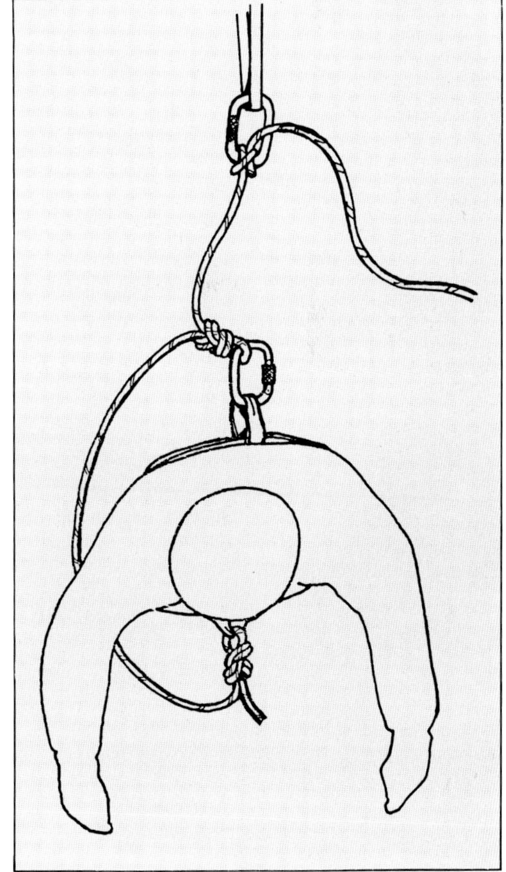

When taking in, the live hand pulls the rope in while the dead hand moves away from the body. The live hand is then slid back down the rope and grasps the dead rope lightly. This allows the dead hand to be slid back up towards the body while keeping close contact with the rope. The dead rope is then released from the live hand and the cycle begins again [*figs. 5.7a, 5.7b, 5.7c*]. The live hand, which holds both ropes, traps the dead rope under the thumb and does not hold it in the palm. This ensures that the dead hand can take the rope across the body at any time. A turning motion of the wrist makes holding the rope under the thumb an easy and natural action as the dead rope is at an angle to the live rope, not parallel to it.

If a harness is worn, it must be adapted so that the front-point attachment is changed to a rear-point attachment. This is done by attaching a short sling and a locking karabiner to the main

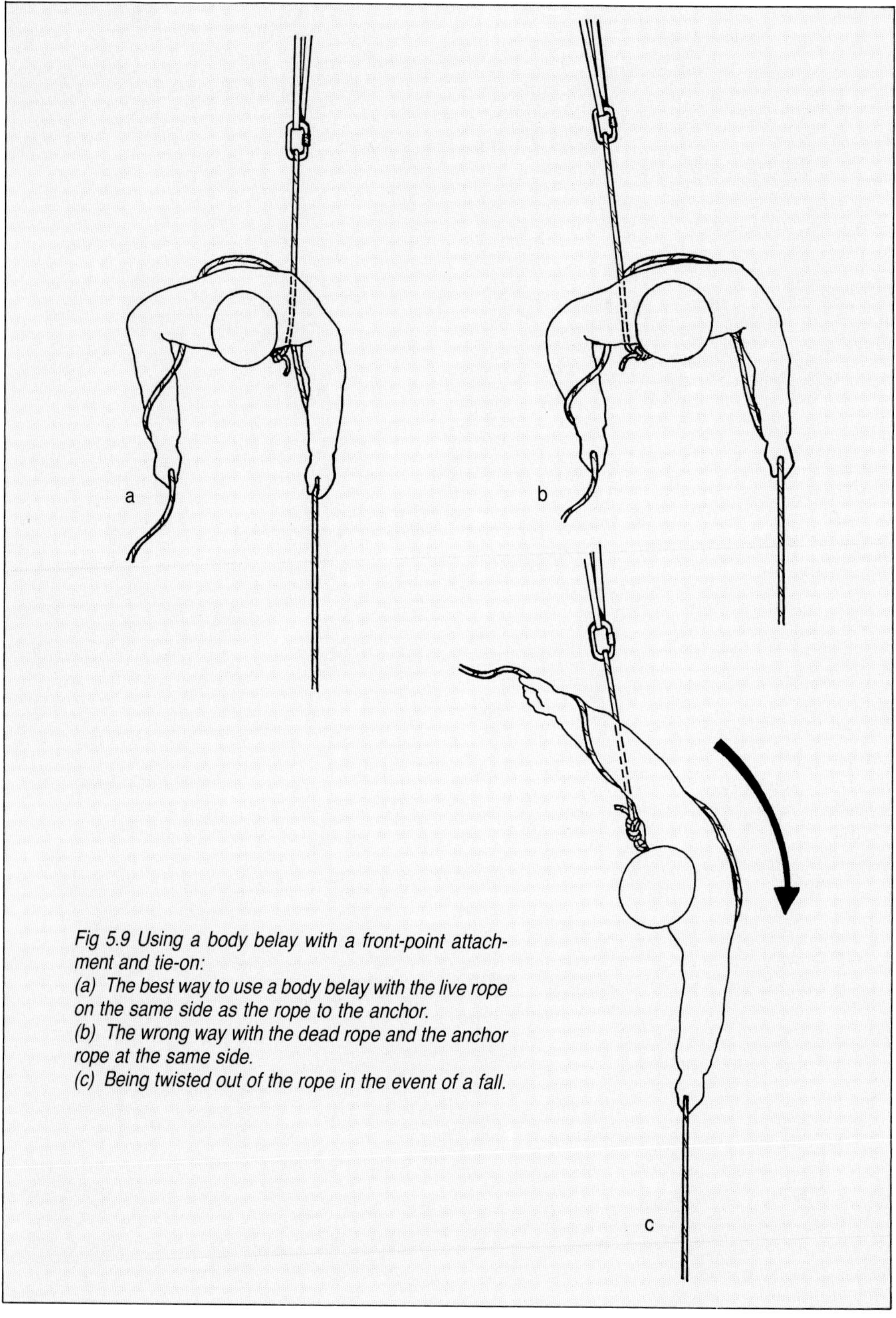

Fig 5.9 Using a body belay with a front-point attachment and tie-on:
(a) The best way to use a body belay with the live rope on the same side as the rope to the anchor.
(b) The wrong way with the dead rope and the anchor rope at the same side.
(c) Being twisted out of the rope in the event of a fall.

Fig 5.10 A selection of belay plates.

body of the harness at the back. A figure-of-eight knot tied in the rope about 2m from the front is then clipped into the karabiner at the back. This karabiner now becomes the attachment point of the rope to the harness and is used as the tie-in point to the anchors [*fig. 5.8*]. If a harness is worn and this is not done, great care must be taken when giving a body belay. The rope must run round the body so that the ropes going to the anchors are on the same side as the live rope. In this case, in a downwards fall, the belayer will be twisted into the rope [*fig. 5.9a*]; if the live rope is held on the opposite side from the anchor ropes, the belayer will be spun round in the event of a fall into a position in which it is impossible to hold the rope and control the fall [*fig. 5.9b, 5.9c*]. However, even if the live rope is arranged correctly for a downwards fall, it is still not safe for a big upwards pull unless it is clipped through a karabiner at the front to redirect it. It is seldom a good idea to use a body belay while wearing a harness which has not been adapted.

The main application of the body belay is any situation when the impact forces must be kept low. This can be on snow and ice climbs or at any time when the anchors are suspect. It is also useful when frozen ropes make other methods unusable, but letting the rope run deliberately is a skilled process and will always result in longer falls.

Belay Plates

Belay plates are an excellent means of belaying: they are light, simple, multi-purpose and the belayer's strength plays little part in their effectiveness. Using a belay plate is probably now the standard way of belaying on rock climbs, especially if a harness is worn. All belay plates work in basically the same way and are available in a variety of forms [*fig. 5.10*]. A bight of rope is pushed through the plate or tube and clipped into a locking karabiner. The best type of karabiner to use is one with a smooth, rounded shape such as

Fig 5.11 A belay plate attached to the knot loop and the rope held in the braking position for a downwards force.

the HMS type. This is attached to a suitable load-bearing part of the harness or the loop of rope (the knot loop) formed when tying on [*fig. 5.3*, page 73]. The plate should also have a short length of cord or wire attached for carrying and to prevent it from sliding down the rope out of reach. To hold a fall, the dead hand is pulled back; this forms an S shape in the rope and provides the required friction [*fig. 5.11*]. The braking force provided by the plate is usually between 200 and 400kg but can be lower, especially with plates which are old and worn. It is important that there is always space for the dead hand to move in order to brake. Belaying in constricted stances, such as tight chimneys or hard against the rock, require more organisation to ensure that this can happen.

To pay out, the live hand pulls through the necessary rope while the dead hand holds the dead rope parallel to it for easy running. The dead hand must never leave the dead rope and must always be in a position to brake.

To take in, several methods are possible, but in all cases the dead hand must not lose contact with its rope. The same system as for the body belay can be used: the live hand pulls in as the dead hand pulls out from the body. The live hand is then slid forward to hold the dead rope under the thumb while the dead hand is moved back towards the plate to begin the next cycle. A turn of the wrist aids this action and the thumb traps the rope firmly enough to permit this but not limit the braking action [*fig. 5.12*].

An alternative is to cross the live hand over to hold the dead rope while the dead hand is slid down to just above the plate to pull more rope through for the next cycle [*fig. 5.13*].

A variation of this is to cross the live hand over the front of the body to hold the dead rope while the dead hand is taken off the rope and then replaced just above the plate ready to start again. In this case the live hand can take the rope back into the braking position so the rope can always be locked effectively [*fig. 5.14*].

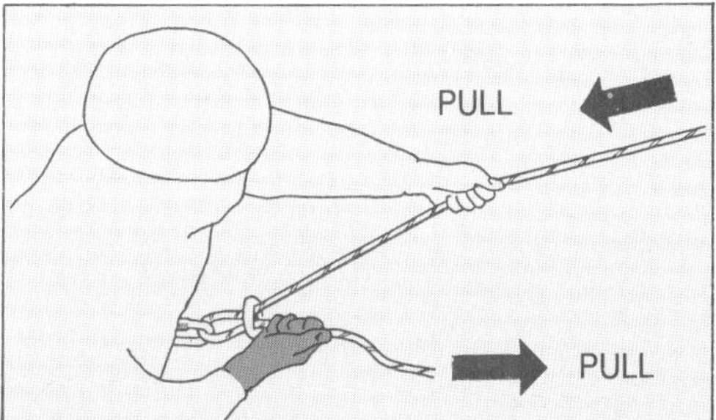

Fig 5.12 Taking the rope in using a belay plate:
(a) The live hand pulls back and the dead hand pulls forward.

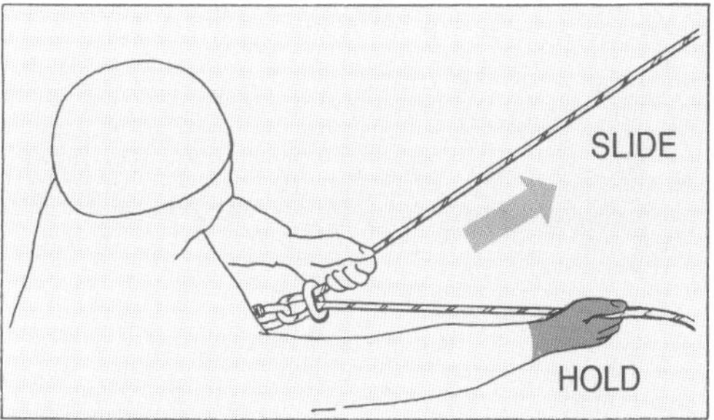

(b) The dead hand holds the rope and the live hand is slid away from the body.

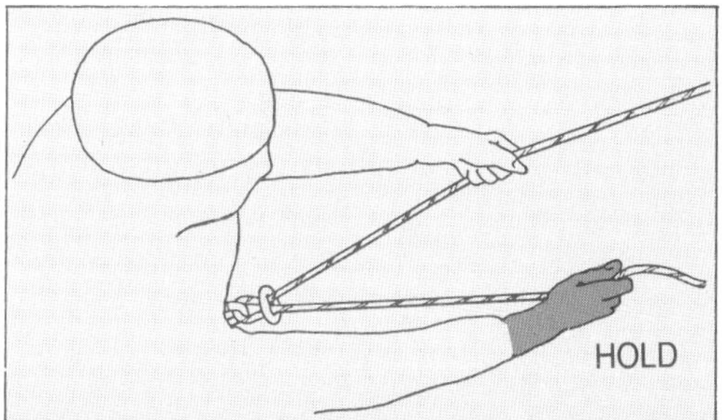

(c) The live hand is slid down the rope until it is slightly further forward of the dead hand.

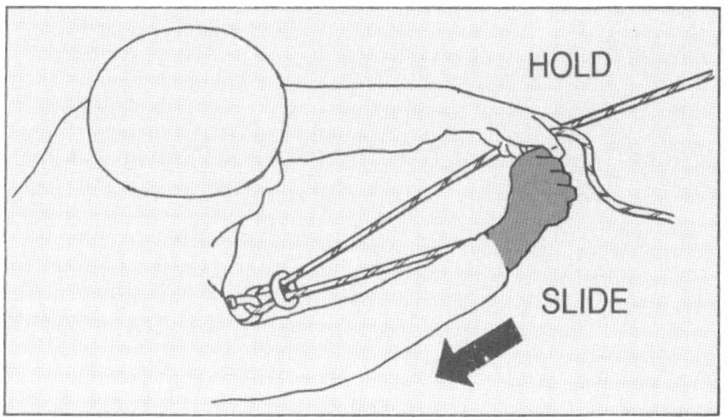

(d) The live hand grips the dead rope lightly under the thumb to provide enough tension to allow the dead hand to be slid back to the plate to begin the next cycle.

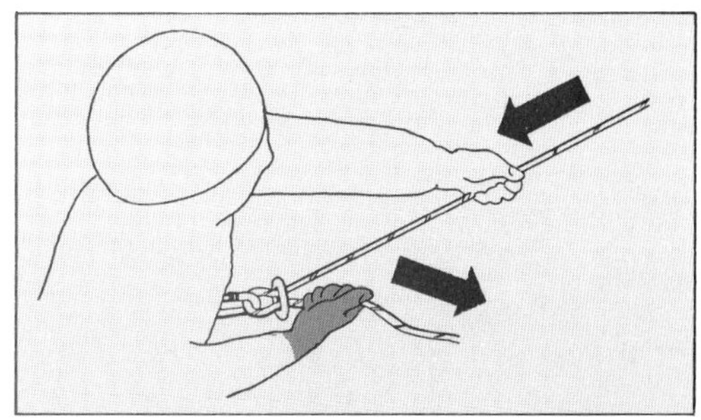

Fig 5.13 Taking the rope in using a belay plate:
(a) The live hand pulls back and the dead hand pulls forward.

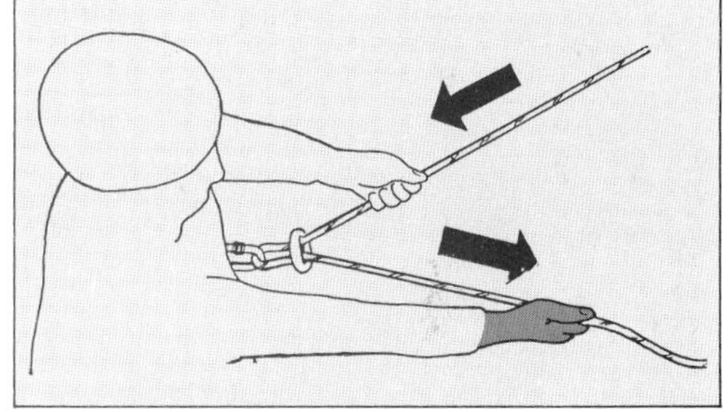

(b) The dead hand holds the rope and the live hand is slid away from the body.

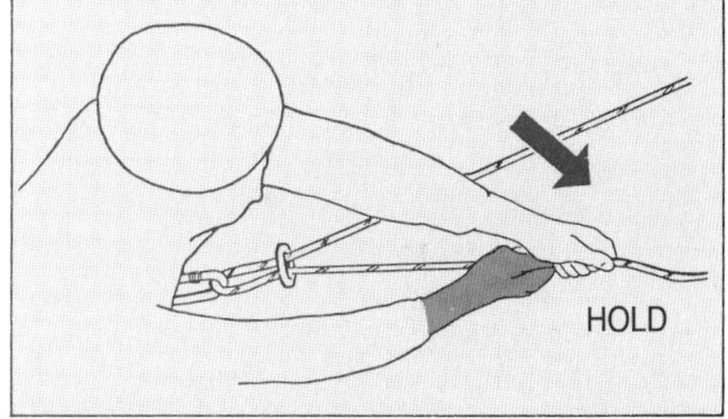

(c) The live hand is crossed over and holds the dead rope above the dead hand.

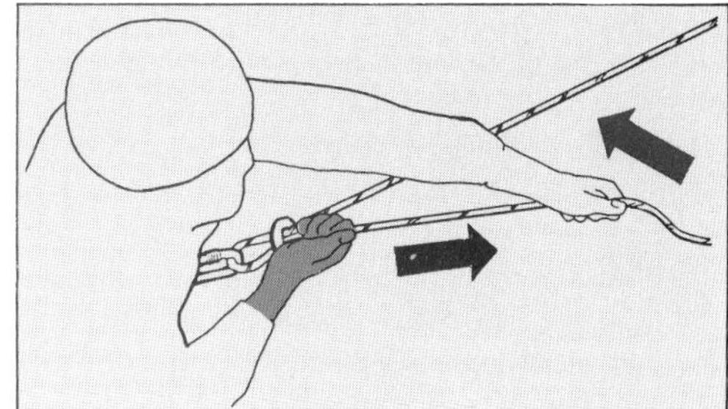

(d) The dead hand is slid back down to the plate while the live hand keeps the rope tight enough for this to be done easily.

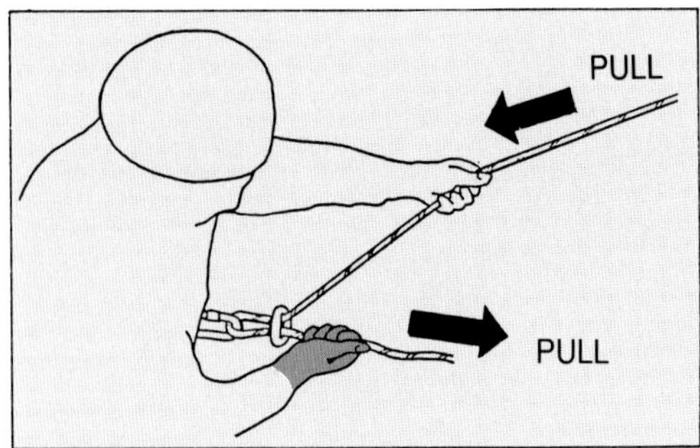

Fig 5.14 Taking the rope in using a belay plate:
(a) The live hand pulls back and the dead hand pulls forward.

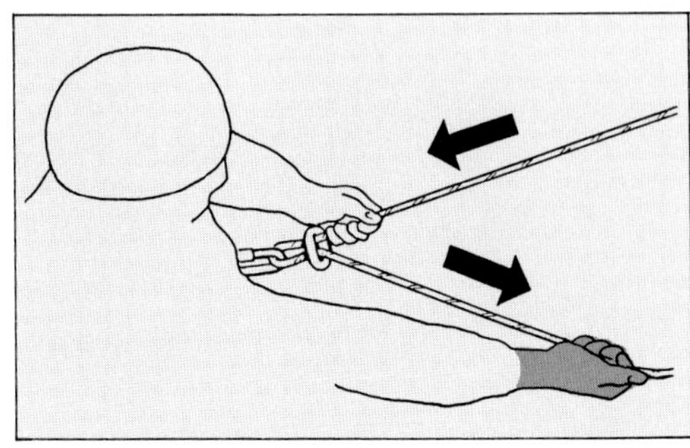

(b) The dead hand holds the rope and the live hand is slid away from the body.

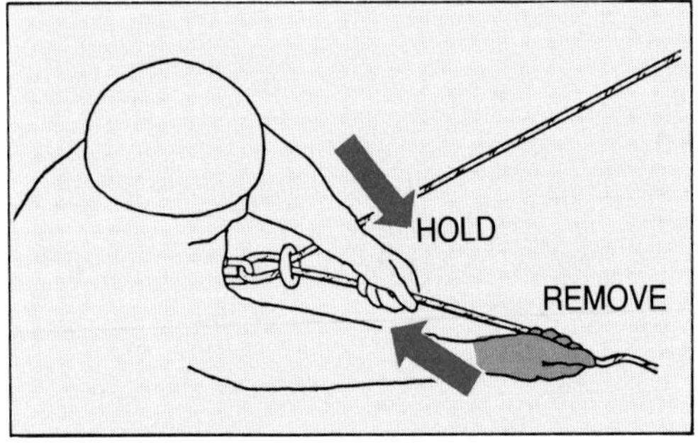

(c) The live hand is crossed over and holds the dead rope below the dead hand.

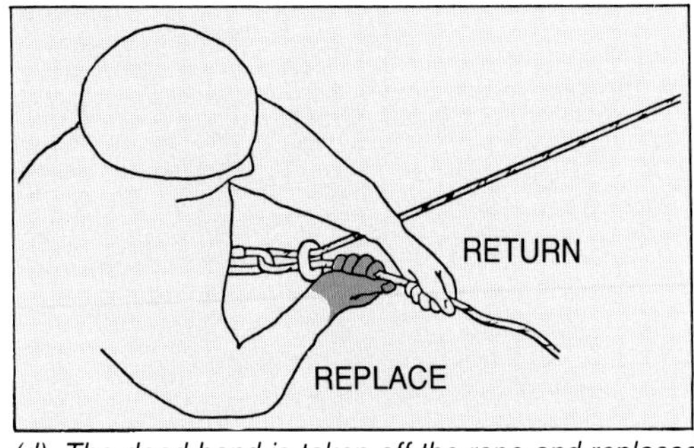

(d) The dead hand is taken off the rope and replaced nearer the plate to begin the next cycle.

The last method is to slide the dead hand back up to the plate after the arm has been extended. The disadvantage of this method is that it is easy to open the hand too much and lose control of the rope in a fall. If there is enough tension in the rope – if it is hanging down a cliff, for example – it is fairly safe to use this method. In other situations, such as sitting on a stance with the rope lying on it, it is not advisable as the dead rope is so slack it is difficult to move the dead hand without loosening it too much. Practice may well make this the preferred method but it must always be done with care and attention. If the dead rope is released in a fall, it is extremely difficult to regain control of it, and in any case the fall will be further than necessary. When starting to use a belay plate, it is strongly advised that one of the positive methods of rope handling is used and this more convenient system only adopted when sufficient experience and expertise in rope management has been gained.

Belay plates are probably the easiest and safest system to use with double-rope technique as they enable the ropes to be manipulated independently. (See 'Rope Systems', page 110.) However, it is still possible to make dangerous mistakes with belay plates. There should be no twists or crosses in the rope which could cause a plate to fail to operate properly; a locking karabiner must be used, preferably a screw-gate which is done up, and it must be attached to a part of the harness or belay that is capable of bearing the full force of a fall.

The Friction Hitch

The friction hitch, also known as the Italian or Munter hitch, is a safe and simple belay method which needs only a locking karabiner. This preferably should be of the pear-shaped HMS type designed for this task. The knot is tied [*fig. 5.15*] and put into the karabiner attached to the harness or the knot loop and the gate secured [*fig. 5.4*, page 73]. Once on the karabiner, the knot can be used to take in or pay out as it will 'capsize' to align itself correctly. To arrest a fall, the dead rope is held firmly. If taken away from the body to lie

a

b

c

Fig 5.15 Tying a friction hitch:
(a) A loop is formed in the rope.
(b) A strand is taken across the main rope and follows the loop.
(c) The friction hitch is put on a suitable locking karabiner.

parallel with the live rope, maximum braking is obtained [*fig. 5.16*]. The braking force needed to make the knot run is 300–400kg but there is some danger of friction melting and damaging the sheath in a big fall as there is with a belay plate. To pay out, the rope is pulled through with the live hand; to take in, any of the methods used with the belay plate can be adopted [*fig. 5.17*].

This system works best with a single rope or with twin ropes where a single knot is tied using both ropes. (See 'Rope Systems', page 110.) If used with double ropes, each must have a separate knot to allow them to work independently in a taking-in/paying-out situation. This should be on a large HMS karabiner which has enough room for both ropes. Another method is to use one karabiner for each knot and keep them separate by putting a third karabiner between them to act as a spacer. However, neither method is particularly convenient.

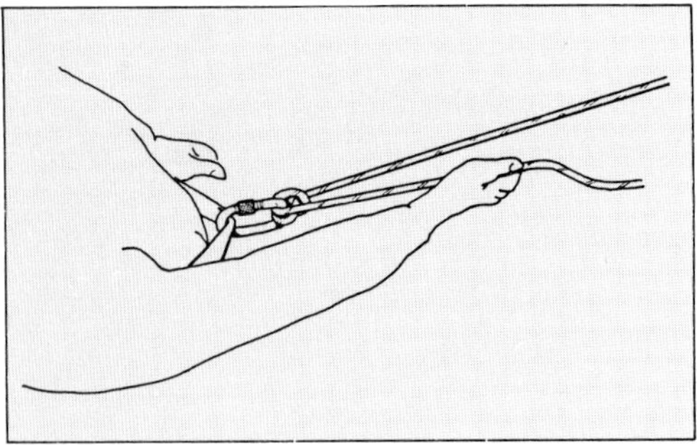

Fig 5.16 A fully braked friction hitch clipped on to a waist belt as would be the case when using one to give an indirect belay.

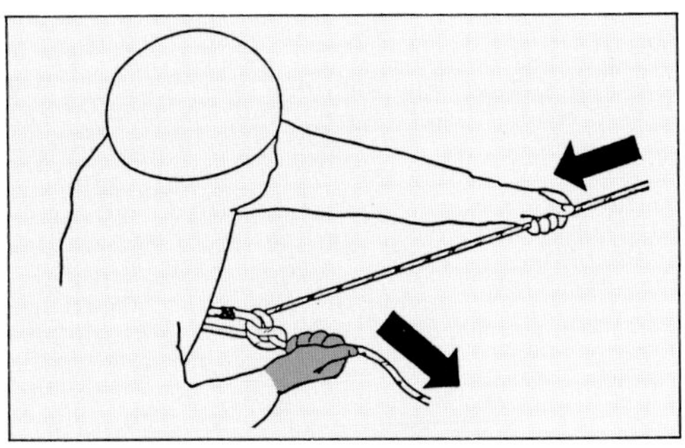

Fig 5.17 Taking in using a friction hitch:
(a) The live hand pulls towards the body while the dead hand pulls away.

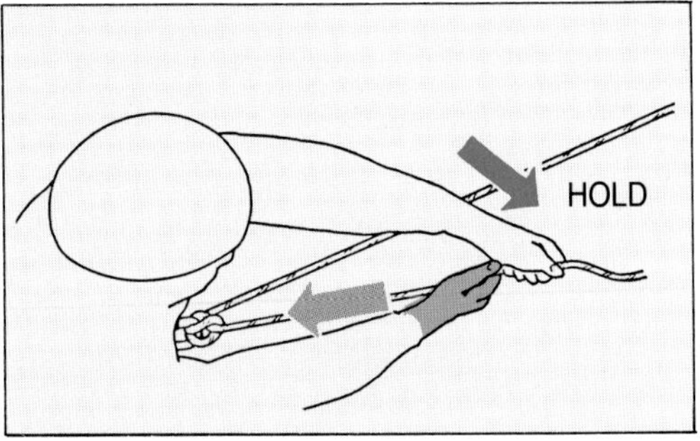

(b) The live hand is crossed over to hold the dead rope above the dead hand.

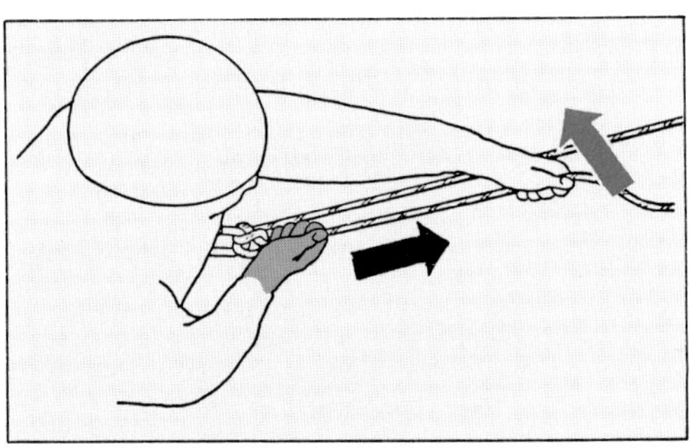

(c) The live hand holds the rope while the dead hand is slid down to begin a new cycle.

Figure-of-Eight Descender

Although primarily an abseil device, the figure-of-eight descender can also be used in belaying. The rope is put through the descender as normal and a fall held by pulling the dead hand back into the braking position. The rope is taken in or paid out with the same actions as are used with a belay plate. However, the descender is heavy, kinks the ropes, is awkward when using double ropes and may not provide the correct amount of friction and stopping power in some situations. The braking force can vary between 80 and 200kg. On some types of descender the small hole can be used as an improvised belay plate.

Other Devices

Other belay methods are possible and other belay devices are used in some areas, but the methods described above are the most popular ones in English-speaking countries. Any belay device should come with the maker's instructions which should be followed, but it is worth practising with any new device before committing yourself to it as they all have slightly different handling characteristics.

ATTACHMENT TO ANCHORS

When setting up a belay, several factors must be considered, one of which is the direction of pull in the event of a fall. The largest force created in a fall occurs when a leader falls with no runners, or with runners which fail. This force will be downwards and outwards. A fall on to runners will produce a lesser force acting in an upwards direction. It is better to belay with the first case – the worst possible situation – in mind and therefore with the main anchors placed to take a downwards and outwards pull.

The main anchor points should be above waist level so that they can resist this downward and outward force. If the anchors are below the waist, you could be inverted when holding a fall. In this case, a sitting position should be adopted. This is usually more comfortable and secure anyway. When standing, the best position is with the legs apart for stability and flexed at the knees. If giving a body belay, stand with the appropriate leg forward along the line of the live rope and the other leg angled out at about 45° to the side [*fig. 5.6*, page 74].

You must be tied on to the anchor points as tightly as possible so that you cannot be moved. (See 'Tying On', page 84.) If the rope from you to the anchor is slack, you could be jerked forward violently in the event of a fall. In certain situations the belayer being pulled can absorb some energy, particularly if in a good, braced position. In other cases this forward movement of the belayer can increase the load on the anchors, particularly if he is caught unawares. However, it is always best to be tied tightly to the anchors because there is an increased chance of injury if you are pulled violently in the event of a fall, which can also increase the possibility of a rope handling mistake. If pulled off a ledge, you are more likely to be concerned with your own safety than with the rope management.

The belay and the anchor points must be in line with the direction of any force. If they are not, the only non-fixed part of the system – you – will be moved so that the line is straight [*fig. 5.18*]. This could cause problems if you were pulled off the stance or into some obstruction such as a corner. When setting up a belay, note how the rope runs up to the stance or up the pitch above, and position yourself accordingly.

Fig 5.18 If the anchor and the belayer are not in the same line as a force on the rope, it will be the belayer that will be moved in the event of a fall.

Ideally, from a stance, you should be able to watch your partner climbing: this is not always possible, or even necessary, but it does make rope management easier. If you can get in a position to see clearly, then do so, but only if the other more important safety considerations are not compromised.

When using a friction hitch or a body belay, the braking action is to take the hand forward or across the front of the body and this should always be possible. With a belay plate, however, the braking hand has to be moved back and this means that there must be space on one side to do so. Belaying in a corner, for example, may mean that the rope cannot be braked effectively on one side. The other problem is that the belayer's own body can restrict the movement of the braking hand in a semi-direct belay when the body is to one side of the rope. When bringing up a second, the uphill hand should be the braking hand [*figs. 5.3*, page 73; *5.22*, page 86]; when belaying a leader, the downhill hand has the greater freedom of movement and so should be the braking hand controlling the dead rope [*fig. 5.4*, page 73]. The hand nearest the climber should be the live hand when facing to the side and using a semi-direct belay.

TYING ON

There are several methods of tying on to belay anchors which allow the belayer to keep the rope tight between himself and the anchors. Some are more appropriate in certain situations than others and the exact method used will vary from stance to stance and will depend on factors such as the nature of the anchors, the amount of rope available, the size of the stance or even the number of slings carried. The number of climbers in the party and whether the route is being led by one person or the leads are being shared can also influence the method of tying on.

Single Anchor

The following methods can be used when one anchor point is sufficiently secure. Sometimes a sling and locking karabiner can link the anchor and the belayer, the karabiner being attached to the knot loop. A figure-of-eight on a bight tied in the rope and clipped into the anchor point can also be used. These methods are satisfactory if the sling or the knotted rope is the correct length or if you can move forward to take up any slack. This is not always possible unless on a large stance and when the position of the belayer does not matter. A better method is to use a clove hitch which can be adjusted without taking it off the karabiner, but this is convenient only if the anchor is fairly near so that the hitch can be adjusted easily. The clove hitch should be tied so that the loaded part of the hitch is nearest the back bar of the karabiner as this is stronger.

However, it is often the case that the anchor is not within easy reach, so it is better to tie the adjusting knot at the belayer rather than at the anchor. The rope can be tied tightly into the anchor from anywhere on the stance, making this a versatile system.

One method of tying the adjustment knot at the waist uses a figure-of-eight knot tied in a bight of

Fig 5.19 Tying on using a figure-of-eight on a bight which is tied round one strand of the rope which forms the knot loop.

Fig 5.20 Tying on using a clove hitch tied round a locking karabiner clipped into the knot loop. The load rope is positioned nearer the back bar of the karabiner.

rope. Clip the rope into a karabiner on the anchor and move to where you want to be. A bight of rope about 1m long is then taken through the knot loop and a figure-of-eight tied round this and adjusted to keep you tight on to the anchor [*fig. 5.19*]. When tying this knot, there are certain points to watch. Tie the figure-of-eight round both the ropes: that is, the two ropes taken through to form the bight are tied round their continuation on the other side of the knot loop. When forming the knot initially, work as close as possible to the rope that it is being tied round as this helps to keep the whole system tight. The tail end of the figure-of-eight should be at least 25cm long so that there is no danger of it working loose: it should be worked firm by first pulling each side of the tail end, then the main part of the rope, then the rope which goes to the anchor.

The advantage of this method is that it is totally adjustable, requires no extra gear and can be used in any situation. The figure-of-eight in the bight can be tied round other places such as a waist belt or the front loop found on many harnesses, but the narrower the band it is tied round, the better, for it can then be more easily firmed up. The knot, if only firmed rather than overtightened, can absorb some energy in a fall if it can tighten up further.

A clove hitch can also be used as the adjustment knot at the waist. A large, strong, locking karabiner is clipped into the knot loop and the clove hitch tied into this. Ideally, the loaded part of the hitch should be nearest to the back bar of the karabiner [*fig. 5.20*].

If a large feature such as a flake or a block too big to take a sling is to be used as an anchor, the rope can be taken round it and tied back into the knot loop with either a figure-of-eight on a bight or a clove hitch and a locking karabiner.

Multiple Anchors

In many situations two anchors are needed and it is necessary to tie in to each point so that the rope is tight to both and any load is shared between them. If only tight to one, then it will take all the force in a fall and should it fail the second anchor will then be shock-loaded. This could create a

Fig 5.21 Tied on to take a downwards or an upwards pull. In this case the belayer is tied tightly to both anchors using figure-of-eight knots tied into the knot loop.

Fig 5.22 A hanging stance: tied on using two clove hitches and belaying the rope with a belay plate to bring up a second. The uphill hand, the one which can most easily be taken into the braking position, is the dead hand and the spare rope is hung in double hanks round one foot to keep it out of the way.

domino effect in which a series of anchors fail.

When using multiple anchors, the figure-of-eight on a bight or the clove hitch method can be used. Each anchor is tied back to the belayer in exactly the same way as a single anchor but ensuring that the tension in all the ropes is the same. It is important not to change position after tying in as this will alter the tension in the ropes to the anchors [*figs.* *5.3*, page 73; *5.21*].

There are other methods which save either time or rope. When using a figure-of-eight, the tail end can be made the appropriate length and clipped into the second, and nearer, anchor. Alternatively, you can tie in to the second anchor using a clove hitch provided that it is near enough to adjust without too much difficulty [*fig.* *5.4*, page 73].

The rope can be clove hitched on to the first anchor point and then clove hitched into the second point. The rope then goes from the second point to the belayer where it is tied with either a figure-of-eight on a bight or a clove hitch on to a locking karabiner. The rope between the two anchors should be slack so that it does not alter the way in which the anchors are pulled. This uses slightly less rope than the previous method [*fig.* *5.22*].

Other Considerations

When using a double rope, these systems are used in exactly the same way but with one rope to each anchor and tied back with a figure-of-eight or a clove hitch [*fig.* *5.23*]. If using two ropes to one anchor point, greater versatility can be achieved if the ropes are tied off separately rather than in one big knot. It is then possible to stay belayed, but remove one rope from the system.

If short of rope, slings can be used to lengthen any or all of the anchor points and can also be used to equalise the load on double anchors if they are not placed too far apart. A sling is clipped into both points, the tension equalised and an overhand or figure-of-eight tied in the bottom of the sling and used as the attachment point [*fig.* *5.24*]. This works only if the anchors are close

Fig 5.23 A semi-hanging stance facing uphill while belaying a leader – using double ropes where each rope is clove hitched on to an anchor. The danger here is that the belayer could be pulled up and into the rock in the event of a leader fall and hit his face on the overhang at head level.

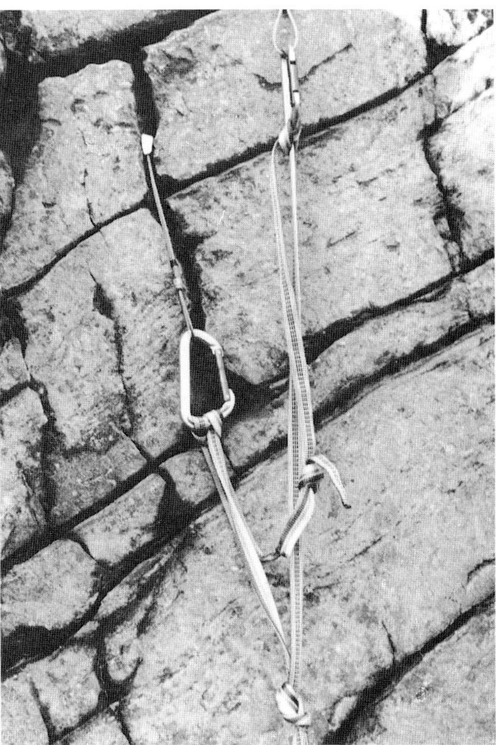

Fig 5.24 Two anchors connected to form a single point. The slings are equalised and an overhand knot used to form the single point. The clove hitch used on each of the anchor points is superfluous in this situation.

together or the sling is long. Another way is to clove hitch the single sling on to both points and put an overhand, figure-of-eight or clove hitch at the appropriate point [*fig.* 5.25]. Care must be taken when using a sling in these ways to ensure that the angle created between the anchor points is not too great – preferably less than 60°. Too wide an angle will increase the load on the anchors and could load them in an inappropriate direction.

A third method is to form the sling into an 'eight' shape and clip one loop to each point and put a karabiner through both loops so formed [*fig.* 5.26]. This then gives a self-equalising belay as the karabiner can move and keep the tension on both

Fig 5.25 RIGHT: *Two anchors taken to a single point using a clove hitch on each karabiner and a figure-of-eight used to form the loop at the bottom.*

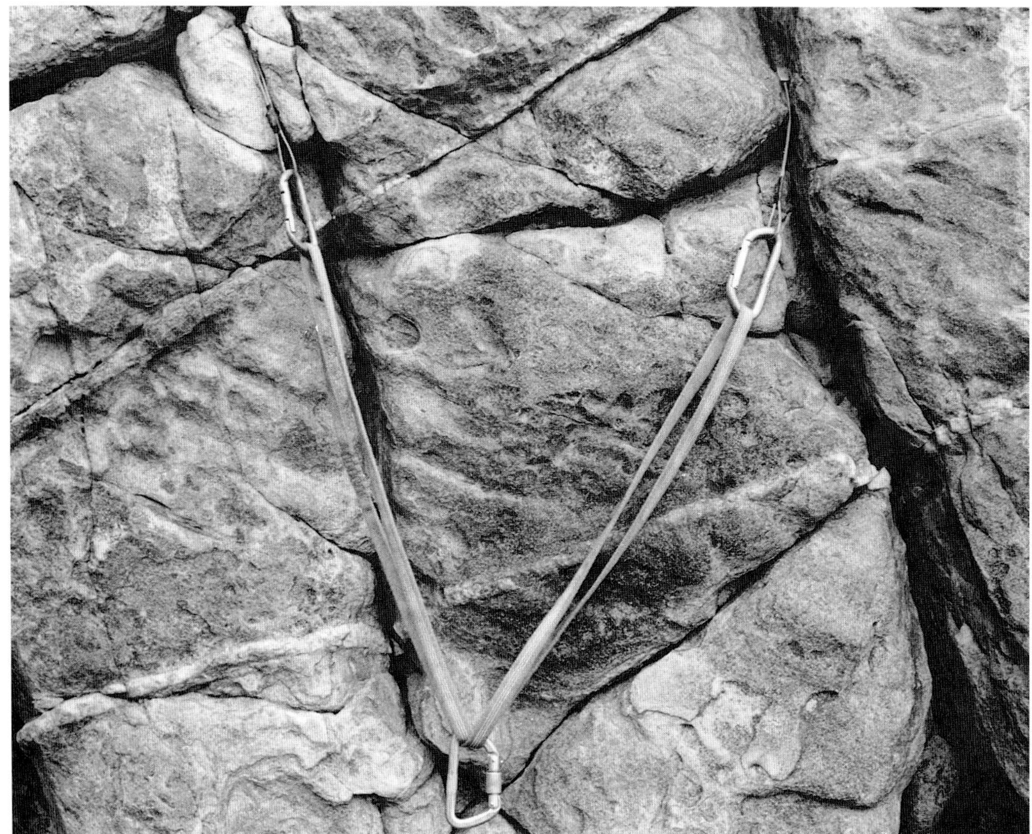

Fig 5.26 A self-equalising anchor point. The two anchors are connected by a sling which is formed into a figure-of-eight shape and the locking karabiner which is the attachment point clipped through both loops of the eight.

sides the same. It must be stressed that this should be done only with two equally secure anchors. If one anchor failed when loaded, the second would be shock-loaded as the belayer was pulled forward.

If more than two anchors have to be used to produce a secure belay, they are tied into using any of the previous methods which ensure that the load is shared among them and the tension in all the ropes to anchors is the same.

In an ideal situation, locking karabiners would be used on every anchor point, but this is not usual. They are safer as the gate cannot open and so there is no chance of a drastic reduction in strength should the karabiner be loaded in a gate-open position. If using a single-point belay, a locking karabiner or back-to-back karabiners should be used. If there is one locking karabiner but several anchor points, it should be used on the anchor point which cannot absorb any twisting action – a peg, for example – rather than on a tape which can turn. Otherwise the locking karabiner is used on the strongest of the anchor points. It is vital in any belay not to link two karabiners together: these can very easily unclip themselves with a twisting action. The only possible combination of karabiners that could be clipped together in a belay situation is two screwgate karabiners, and this can usually be avoided by other and better ways of tying in.

BELAY ORGANISATION

Belay anchors are placed in the same way as running belays, but while a runner is normally placed on its own to take a downwards force, belays need to be arranged so that they can resist a force from more than one direction. A belay anchor must also be totally secure so one piece of equipment will seldom be sufficient. There is little point in using a rope system which will take over 2000kg yet trusting yourself to an anchor which does not match this strength. Besides, there is always the strength of the equipment itself to consider: nuts and karabiners may be weakened by hidden corrosion, slings may be cut and abraded and even ropes have been known to detach themselves from anchors. The principle of backing up vital links is only common sense.

Ideally a belay anchor is constructed so that it can take a force from any direction, or at least from the main direction in which a pull could come. This will normally be up and down but can be diagonally or horizontally, as in the case of a belay at the end of a traverse. Anchors should be placed with these directions of pull in mind, not only for the pitch just completed, but also for the direction of the pitch to come. It is sometimes necessary to re-organise the belay before leading the next pitch.

Multi-directional anchors include items like threads, pegs, chockstones, trees, bolts and sometimes camming devices. Nuts in vertical cracks are usually good only for a pull in a downwards direction; so, if the belay has to resist an upwards pull, a nut will have to be placed specifically for this. A nut placed to take an upwards pull must be tied into tightly to stop it from dropping out [*fig. 5.21*, page 86]. Nuts in horizontal cracks are usually good for an up and a down pull, but not for a pull from the side.

Another consideration when using nuts (or pegs) is that, as far as possible, each placement should be in a separate crack. This depends a great deal on rock type, but on rocks of a blocky nature it can be important. If there are nuts in cracks on either side of a block, failure of the block could result in total belay failure. Look carefully at the rock and try to get independent anchors which are in no way connected. In some situations this is not possible or even necessary, as with a single crack splitting a huge sheet of granite. In other places, such as on some limestone and dolerite cliffs, it is sensible not to have all your eggs in one basket. Often it is only a matter of looking a little more carefully or going slightly further to get a really sound anchor.

When you reach a stance or decide that a belay is necessary, anchors must be found and placed. As soon as one anchor is in place, clip the rope in to act as a runner while you look for more or organise yourself. It is still possible to fall off a stance, especially as you tend to relax your concentration once the pitch is over. Once a suitable anchor has been arranged, decide where you are going to stand or sit. Sometimes the stance will dictate your position and what you can do, but there are three basic requirements which must be met: the anchors must be solid, you must not be pulled so that you could be injured and you must always be able to operate the belay system. It must always be possible to brake when the pull comes downwards, as with a second fall or a leader with no runners, and also when the pull is upwards, as with a fall on to runners. Other considerations are the need to see the climber; shelter from debris from above; ease of swopping over the lead or the belay; direction of the next pitch; communications or even shelter from the sun or the wind.

To some extent the position adopted on the stance depends on the type of belay used. In the usual rock climbing situation when wearing a harness and using a belay plate or friction hitch – that is, a semi-direct belay – the belayer normally faces to the side. When bringing up a second or belaying a leader who has no runners and would create a downwards pull in a fall, the plate is arranged so that the uphill hand, the one nearest the rock and the anchors, is the braking hand. This hand can move back to brake, whereas on the downhill side the braking action is blocked by the belayer's own body [*figs. 5.3,* page 73; *5.22,* page 86].

When belaying a leader who is protected by runners, the downhill hand now holds the dead rope as this hand can now move freely back and down to operate the brake. This means that if the second is leading through, the rope has to be taken out of the plate and replaced the correct way round. While this is being done the climber should be anchored, and it is often worth having a spare attachment point organised before the second starts up the pitch. Doing this, however, puts the hands in the wrong position to hold a factor 2 fall. If a runner cannot be placed soon after leaving the stance, the rope can be clipped into a belay anchor so that the pull will always be upwards.

If using a friction hitch as the belay method, face to one side; again it is better if the downhill or outside hand holds the dead rope [*fig. 5.4*, page 73].

On a small or hanging stance it is still possible and comfortable to adopt this sideways-facing position [*fig. 5.22*, page 86]. However, many climbers prefer to face directly uphill. In this case it is important that the leader places a runner immediately, as a factor 2 fall in such a situation can be dangerous – the belayer could be subjected to large twisting forces or rope burns. When bringing up a second, the rope will run over the side of the belayer's body unless redirected through a runner or kept between the legs.

There are, however, some very real dangers in facing the cliff when belaying, especially in the event of a large fall. You are more vulnerable to anything dropped from above; in a fall you can be pulled up and into the rock which could cause injury, and the more the pull is towards the rock, the more dangerous it is likely to be; being pulled against the rock can hamper rope management or even prevent the fall from being arrested properly. If you are pulled violently towards the rock, it is a natural reaction to try to protect yourself by putting out your hands to shield your vulnerable face and head, thus dropping the rope. In the worst case, a factor 2 fall on to a belayer facing uphill, you could be subject to very powerful twisting forces and the subsequent risk of injury [*fig. 5.23*, page 87].

If using an indirect belay, whether it is a body belay, friction hitch or belay plate, face down and out from the cliff on all occasions, whether you are a second or a leader. The live hand should be at the same side as the climber so that in a fall factor 2 situation the rope is round the correct side of the body and not stripped off. This is more likely to be used on a snow and ice or winter route, and facing downhill presents the back to falling ice liable to be encountered in these situations [*fig. 5.5*, page 73].

With a direct belay, the belayer can face whichever way he wants provided that he can operate the belay effectively. It is preferable even in this situation for the belayer to be anchored, but this tends to negate the direct belay's advantage which is the speed with which it can be set up.

If the second is not going to lead through, the belay has to be changed over. This is a simple operation but one that can be potentially dangerous as a mistake can result in both climbers becoming detached from the rope. The stages in a belay change-over are:

1 The leader anchored and belaying the second.

2 Both anchored and the second off the belay.

3 The leader belayed by the second but still tied on to the anchors.

4 The leader belayed and about to climb.

The bigger the stance, the easier this is to carry out safely. If the leader prepares the anchors before bringing up the second, it is again easier as he has more space to work in at this stage. Putting extra karabiners on each anchor point is handy when changing over and it decreases the chance of the wrong rope being inadvertently unclipped. Once the change-over is completed, spare karabiners are removed for use later on.

All the points made in this section, however, are only guidelines as every set of belays, anchors, stances and pitches is unique and what may be ideal in one situation may not be so in another. Each situation has to be considered on its own merits, what the rock gives you to work with and what your requirements are. When setting up a belay, you must consider the direction of any forces that could be created by a fall, remembering that the direction can change as the pitch progresses. Placing the first runner on the lead changes the pull from down to up; removing the last runner from a traverse to a stance changes the pull from horizontal to, eventually, downwards. The belayer should try to anticipate what will happen should a fall occur and the direction of the resultant forces, and arrange things accordingly. Continually looking at the climber, the rope and the protection in relation to the stance and the anchors helps to develop an awareness of what could occur. Asking yourself the question, 'What would happen if ...?' will help alert you to problems that can arise.

CLIMBING CALLS

Clear, concise communication between climbers is important both for safety and to save time. This can sometimes be difficult on long pitches, where the climbers are out of sight of each other or where there is noise from the wind, the sea or even traffic. On short climbs with good visibility the calls can be shortened or abandoned, and climbers who are used to each other's ways can get by with the minimum of calls. However, a simple, standardised system is helpful when you are a beginner to climbing or when you have a new partner. Calls should be short, simple and distinctive with no chance of misunderstandings. All calls are a form of code and actually mean more than the words themselves.

'Taking In'

The call by the leader to indicate that he has reached the belay, is secured and no longer needs to be belayed. It also means he is about to take in the unused rope between himself and his second. At this call the second can stop belaying and take the rope from his belay system. The leader will take the rope in hand-over-hand, the quickest and easiest way.

'That's Me'

The second's reply when the rope comes tight on him. It lets the leader know that the rope is not caught up anywhere.

'Climb When Ready'

The leader's call when he is actually belaying the rope. The second then begins to take off his belay, untying the knots and removing the anchors in the reverse order to which they went on. As this is happening the leader takes in the rope so that the spare is lifted clear and slack is not allowed to develop between them. As the leader will have passed this belay, he should have a good idea how much rope needs taking in.

'Climbing'

The second's call when he actually starts climbing.

'OK'

The leader's confirmation of the fact that the second has started to climb.

The calls 'Safe' and 'On belay' can be used when the leader first secures himself. The second replies with 'Take in' when the rope is free from the belaying device. These add a little to the basic calls, especially if the leader, after 'Taking in', pauses long enough to let the second get the rope out of the belay device, or off his body belay, before pulling up the slack rope.

There are other calls commonly used:

'Slack'

Either the leader or the second requires more rope.

'Take In'

Usually used by the second to indicate that the rope is not tight enough, but may be used by a leader who is climbing down.

'Tight'

The same as 'Take in' but only a second's call.

'Runner On'

A leader's call when he places the first running belay on a pitch. It lets the second know that, in the event of a fall, the pull would be in an upwards direction.

'Below'

A loud cry to warn others that something is falling down the cliff.

Because these calls have different numbers of syllables, even if they are not heard distinctly it is often possible to work out what they are by their length, the order in which they come and what the rope does after each call. They can also be related to the length of rope run out and the guidebook description of the climb. When verbal communication does not work, a system of tugs can be used. An unmistakable number of strong pulls on the rope can be used for 'Climb when ready', the most important call, and the other calls dispensed with. Four or five tugs, which cannot be confused with normal rope movement, are satisfactory, but it is a system used by a leader to a second and not vice versa.

BELAYING AT THE START OF A ROUTE

If a climb starts from a steep slope, a common occurrence on many mountain crags, it is best to belay normally with the second tied on so that he

can take a pull in an upwards or downwards direction. If there is no chance of a downwards pull, an anchor for an upwards pull may be all that is needed. This is usual on climbs which start from flat ground. Even an anchor for an upwards force may not be necessary and it may be better for the second not to be tied down or to be tied down slackly to the anchor. In a fall, the second can be lifted into the air, thus making the belay more dynamic and so putting less strain on the system. There is, however, a danger to the belayer if he is lifted violently upwards into the rock, especially if it overhangs. There is also the danger to the leader who will fall further, particularly if he is heavy and the belayer light. In places where there are no suitable anchors at the foot of a route, light seconds have been tied to a pack full of rocks to provide the necessary ballast. If in any doubt, it is safer to belay. This at least will prevent inattentive seconds from moving about and inadvertently pulling their leader off.

Belayers have on occasion prevented injury or worse by running downhill and so shortening his fall distance when their leader fell off. This, however, increases the force on the runner and is really a last-ditch effort when disaster is on its way!

When belaying at the top of a climb, it is usually necessary to anchor only for a downwards pull if no leading is to be done above that point.

Whether or not the belayer is anchored at the start of a route, he must take care where he positions himself. It is better to be slightly to one side, out of line of anything falling from above and close in to the foot of the rock. Then, if there is a fall, the rope acts in the best way on the runners. If a belayer stands out from the foot of the climb, the rope will, in the event of a fall, attempt to make a straight line with the highest, loaded runner and so can lift the lower runners up and out [*fig. 5.27*]. This could leave the leader hanging on a single runner. A way round is to make a low runner, one which will take a pull in any direction – a thread or a Friend, for example – which will redirect the rope. This situation is only liable to occur at the start of a climb unless on a huge stance which allows the belayer to be further out from the face.

Fig 5.27 OPPOSITE PAGE: *Belayer too far out from the foot of the climb so that, in the event of a fall, the protection could be lifted up and out of its placement.*

TOP-ROPING

Using a top rope is a simple climbing system in which a route is not lead but safeguarded by a rope from above. This is a convenient way of giving beginners a taste of climbing or of attempting climbs that are too hard for you to lead; it is also useful in training. However, it can be an ethically dubious practice where a route is top-roped prior to leading to work out the moves and protection.

The rope can be set up by belaying at the top of the climb and dropping the rope down, in which case the person at the top is anchored and belaying the rope as normal. A direct belay may be used where good anchors are available. Alternatively, belaying can be done from the bottom of the climb. In this case the belayer at the foot of the cliff may not need to be anchored but this depends on the comparative weights of the climber and the belayer and the amount of friction on the ropes. When setting up in this manner, the anchor point at the top must be carefully arranged. It must be secure with either locking or back-to-back karabiners and it should be located so that it lies below the top edge of the cliff to reduce rope wear and the chance of it knocking down rocks. This suspension point should be above the top of the climb and not off to one side as a fall on to it could cause a swing to the side which could knock down debris and also damage the rope. All the usual advice about setting up and equalising anchors applies to this top point. Remember that this point will have to take up to twice the weight of the climber because it acts like a pulley [*fig. 5.29*].

When belaying from below, it is often easier to lower the climber off when he has finished the route, but if using a tree as the top anchor always put a sling round it as lowering straight from it can ring the bark and so kill the tree.

Although top-roping has a place in climbing, it is not the same as leading which is what climbing is really all about. When top-roping, avoid monopolising a route for long periods, especially if there are others there who wish to climb it properly. Leading should have priority over top-roping. Using a top rope as training on classic or popular routes is also to be avoided as it adds to the polishing of the holds. Using less frequented

Fig 5.28 Degrees of safety in climbing. Soloing, leading and a second top-roping a climb while belayed from the ground.

routes may in fact clean them up a bit and will cause less damage and, perhaps, ill feeling.

On short routes even if the climb has been led, the leader may lower off and belay the second from the ground where he may be more comfortable and can see the second climbing. By taking the runners out on his way down he can often make the climbing more enjoyable for the second [*fig. 5.28*].

Fig 5.29 Top-roping.

6 Protecting the Climb

When leading a route, a great deal of time and energy, both physical and mental, is taken up with finding, placing and using running belays. As much time can be spent on these as actually climbing and for some this is a barrier between themselves and the rock, an interruption in the flow of the climbing. For others, however, there is a certain satisfaction in protecting a climb efficiently and effectively. While rock climbs in some areas, particularly certain parts of Europe, are often equipped with *in situ* protection, mostly bolts, this is not the case in most other countries. Protection placed on the lead is the norm in rock climbing as it is in all mountaineering. Protecting climbs effectively is vital and has to be practised and thoroughly learned. In fact this aspect of climbing can stop some beginners from climbing at their full potential as their ability to protect a climb has not caught up with their ability to move on rock.

PLACING RUNNERS

Placing runners quickly and efficiently can be the deciding factor in the success or failure on a climb. The harder and more strenuous the route,

Fig 6.1 Placing runners can be strenuous, time-consuming and frustrating, especially on steep rock. In this instance the leader is trying to place a wire nut from the bunch he is holding in his teeth.

the more this will be true [*fig. 6.1*]. Although fairly simple in theory, placing runners may not always be so easy in practice. Find a crack, then look for a constriction or narrowing in it, select the nut which will fit best in the wide part of the crack and which most nearly corresponds to the crack's shape, put the nut in, work it into place, give it a sharp tug to seat it firmly, clip the rope to it, relax and carry on climbing. If the crack has no narrowing, use a camming device instead. Although it is usual to use the biggest nut which will fit the crack comfortably, this is not always the best solution. If the crack is thin and also has to be used as a hold, the smallest nut that gives a good fit should be used to leave enough space for the fingers. After placing a runner above head height or where it is out of sight, always check it when you can get in a position to see it. What can look good from below may turn out to be useless on closer inspection.

When using slings, make sure that the spike or flake is solid enough to use, that the runner is long enough to fit correctly and that it will not lift off as you move above it. If the feature is rounded or poorly shaped, the sling can be weighted down with heavy or excess gear to prevent it from being lifted off by the rope's movement [*fig. 6.2*].

Skill in arranging runners effectively comes with experience in judging the size of cracks, selecting the right piece of gear, placing it fast and clipping in quickly. All these are subject to mistakes, time wasting and the squandering of physical and mental energy, but there is no real short-cut to learning by practice. The more runners you place, the better you become at placing them; the more you actually load them, the better you become at judging their strength and reliability.

Although trial and error is the main teacher in placing runners, some aspects can be worked on. What to look for and where runners are liable to be found on different rock types will come with practice. Knowledge of what runners you have, what you have used lower down and where everything is on the rack can all help save time, but using your eyes is the greatest asset. Although on many popular routes the nut placements may be very obvious slots in the rock that are polished and worn from repeated use, on other climbs they may be much harder to locate. Any break, crack or pocket may be considered as a potential placement, but only experience will tell you when to persevere with a difficult runner and when to move on to more fruitful ground. As when looking for holds, consider the rock all around, not just the small area in front of your face or the first crack you come across.

Fig 6.2 OPPOSITE PAGE: *On a steep wall climb a long, weighted sling is used on a poor, rounded but important flake. This reduces the chance of rope drag lifting the sling off.*

EXTENDING RUNNERS

Sometimes it is necessary to lengthen or extend runners to reduce the friction between the connecting karabiner and the climbing rope. Ideally the rope should run from the climber to the belayer in as straight a line as possible. The sharper the angle that it goes through at a runner, the greater the resultant friction. This can have two unpleasant effects: the leader must expend extra energy dragging up the rope and there is an increased chance of runners being lifted out [*fig. 6.4*].

Wired nuts in particular are liable to be lifted out by rope drag because of the stiffness of the wire. Wired nuts should be attached to the rope in such a way that there is some sort of hinge to absorb this lifting action. The most common way of doing this is by using a tape extension with a karabiner in each end, which means that each wired nut needs two karabiners to link it to the rope [*fig. 6.3*]. Sometimes two karabiners can be used to provide the link and a hinge; very occasionally the rope can be clipped directly to the wire, but only on a very straight pitch when rope drag will not be a problem and the nut is so well keyed in that it could not be pulled out accidentally. Even in this situation there is the danger that the rope could fall across the gate of a single karabiner and unclip itself. This is less likely to happen when using extensions which are more flexible.

Friends too may need extending as the rocking action of the rope running through the karabiner can cause the Friend to 'walk'. To avoid this it should be extended enough to prevent the rope from moving it.

The usual way of lengthening runners is to carry a selection of extensions and slings and clip the appropriate one to any runner that is too short. Slings can always be doubled if too long, but they are never threaded through wires. However, they can be doubled through roped nuts without too great a loss in strength provided that the rope is thick enough. Roped nuts can be used as emergency extensions by pulling the nut down from the end to give a simple loop of rope

Fig 6.3 OPPOSITE PAGE: *Using extensions on wire nuts to reduce rope drag and prevent them from lifting. The nearer runner clearly shows the way in which the rope can lift runners upwards.*

Fig 6.4 RIGHT: *Too short an extension on the right-hand rope will lead to excessive rope drag and also kinking as the rope is pulled across the sharp edge of rock.*

Fig 6.5 BELOW: *Where the route is devious or bulges and overhangs need to be negotiated, long slings may be required for extensions to reduce rope drag.*

or tape. Never clip two karabiners straight into a nut sling to use as an extension, as the pull could then come across the sling rather than along its length and the sharp angles the rope, or tape, makes when going through the nut would reduce the strength of the sling.

The nature of the climbing is the main factor in deciding how much extension will be needed: the more direct the pitch, the less extending is required; the more the pitch weaves about, either from side to side or in and out, crossing ledges and overhangs, the more runners will have to be lengthened [*fig.* 6.5]. Runners placed deep in grooves or chimneys are liable to lifting if you are climbing up the outside of the feature when an upwards and outwards force is put on the protection. The equipment and the rope system used will also have an effect. Nuts on rope slings may not need much lengthening, whereas wired nuts almost certainly will.

The best way to avoid a problem of this nature is by planning ahead. Look to see where the pitch goes and where any sharp changes in direction occur. Start extending runners early on rather than just where the change is. Keep the rope running in curves that are as smooth as possible. Although extending a runner will cut down on friction, it also increases your potential fall distance. The idea is to minimise fall potential without increasing rope drag.

The problem of the rope lifting out nuts, particularly those that are loosely seated, is also lessened by using extensions. The rope or tape takes up most of the lift caused by friction, so the nut is affected less.

In the event of a fall, poorly extended runners can cause further problems. When the rope is tensioned through a runner, there will be a force on the runner which bisects the angle made by the rope at that runner [*fig.* 6.6]. This can even happen when moving up above a runner [*fig.* 6.7.]. If this is sharp enough and the force acts outwards, it can lift a nut out. Should this occur in a fall, the runners below the top one, which holds the fall, can be pulled out unless they can take an outwards force – for example, if they are camming devices. This can result in a longer fall as the rope takes a straighter line up the cliff and could even leave a fallen leader hanging from a single, top runner. This lifting is particularly likely with runners placed low at the back of ledges where

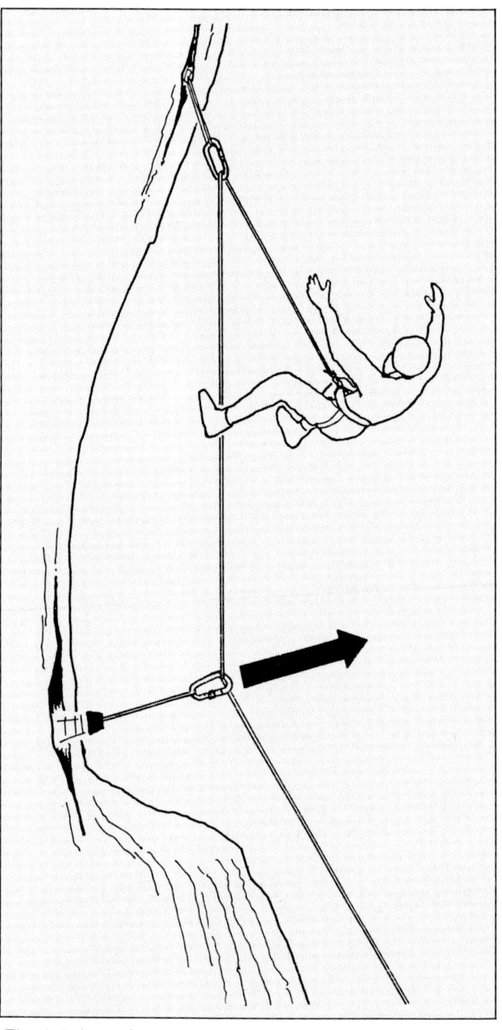

Fig 6.6 In a fall there is a force on a runner which bisects the angle made by the rope as it goes through the karabiner on the runner. This can easily lift the runner out.

the pull is directed upwards and outwards. Runners under roofs which are not extended enough for the rope to clear the edge can be pulled hard against the lip and the rope damaged if the edge is sharp enough.

Whenever a runner is used, ensure that the karabiners, particularly the one into which the rope is clipped, are positioned away from any projections that could open the gate in a fall. Always clip the karabiner so that its gate is away from the rock [*fig.* 6.8].

Fig 6.7 Even moving up can unseat runners, particularly when leaning out and making a high step up.

Fig 6.8 A projection or edge can easily open a karabiner gate when it is loaded.

CLIPPING IN

Once the runner has been placed and extended if necessary, the rope has to be clipped to it as quickly and efficiently as possible. This is made easier if the karabiner into which the rope goes has its gate facing away from the rock and the opening at the bottom. This is the easiest way to clip the rope and, as already explained, reduces the chance of accidental opening of the gate. The karabiner between an extension and the runner is also clipped with the back bar against the rock, but in this case the gate opening can be at the top, the easiest way to clip it to a runner. When you are using extensions, they can be racked for easy use with the karabiner clipped to the rack with its gate opening at the top ready to go on to the runner.

If both hands are free to clip the rope in, there is little difficulty in doing this. Pull up enough spare rope, steady the karabiner with one hand and clip the rope to it with the other. If only one hand can be freed, clipping in is more awkward. First, you must pull up enough spare rope using your free hand and your teeth. The call 'Rope!' to the second should alert him to your intentions; if double ropes are used, the rope's colour can be used as the call. Once enough rope is available, there are several ways to clip it to the runner, but usually the karabiner must be steadied in some manner. The rope can be draped across the back of the knuckles, the index finger steadies the karabiner and the thumb pushes the rope through the gate aided by gravity and a further lifting of the hand to roll the rope forward [*fig. 6.9*]. Another way is to steady the karabiner between the thumb and the middle finger and use the index finger to push the rope through the gate [*fig. 6.10*]. An alternative method is to clip the extension and karabiners on to the rope first, slide the hand up to the top karabiner, lift it up and clip it to the protection. With fixed protection the extension and karabiners can be clipped to the rope and a harness gear loop, so that when needed the rope can be clipped into the gear with one action. Care is needed when doing this to avoid inadvertently putting a twist into the rope and this system is not so good if there is a lot of rope drag or a heavy weight of rope to lift.

These are only some of the ways to clip a rope into gear and other variations are possible, the

Fig 6.9 Clipping a karabiner by steadying it with the index finger and pushing the rope in with the thumb.

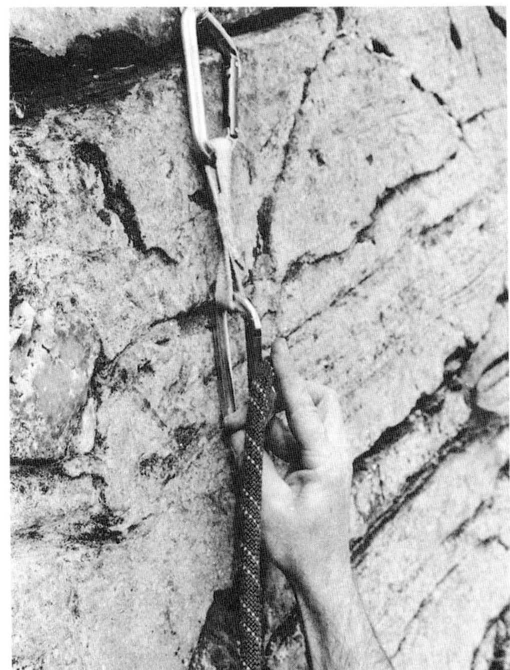

Fig 6.10 By steadying the karabiner with the middle finger you can push the rope into the karabiner with the index finger. This is made easier by pulling the karabiner upwards and sliding the rope down over the top of the knuckles.

actual method used often being dictated by the situation at the time but any technique will benefit from practice and having the karabiner facing the right way. It is in this situation that karabiners which have a wide opening, such as the bent-gate type, and a smooth action are an advantage.

FREQUENCY OF RUNNERS

The number of runners placed on a pitch depends on many factors: the opportunities offered by the rock, how difficult and sustained the climbing is, the climber's ability and boldness, the potential for injury, the likelihood of rope drag, the chance of a fall and so on. These and other considerations all interact to make any pitch a different experience for every climber. The optimum number of runners, however, will be that which will prevent an injury yet not detract from the climbing experience. It is possible to overprotect or underprotect many pitches. The skill is in ensuring that, should a fall occur, the consequences will not be too dire as a result of underprotection; and at the same time in not using up strength and time unnecessarily in overprotecting a pitch, so making a fall more likely.

The rock itself is the main factor in dictating the frequency of protection. If cracks or protrusions do not exist, protection is either absent or man-made; in the latter case, as with bolts, it can then effectively be anywhere. If, however, protection is abundant, as on a pitch following a good continuous crack, runners should not be spaced evenly throughout but placed to keep the fall factor relatively low. This means that they should be more frequent near the start of the pitch but could be further apart nearer the top when more rope is available to absorb the energy of a fall, as shown in the tables below.

The fall factor and the distance fallen are primarily of importance when there is no danger of hitting any projection as on overhanging rock or smooth walls. Runners should be placed to prevent a falling climber from hitting ledges or projections, but the greater the length of rope run out, the further he will go in a fall because of the stretch of the rope and the slack in the system. However, these are rather academic considerations for, when leading, the majority of climbers will put in more runners when sufficiently scared and fewer when the climbing is easy. Whatever the difficulty of the climb, there should always be sufficient runners to keep the potential fall factor below 1, which can be considered serious. It is seldom worth passing up an easily placed and obvious runner; unexpected falls caused by slips or holds breaking tend to be more serious than those resulting from the difficulty of the climbing.

FIXED PROTECTION

Fixed protection is of three main types: *in situ* threads, pegs and bolts. Nuts *in situ* are usually there because someone has been unable to remove them rather than as protection placed for the benefit of others. Threads are often found on limestone which tends to have more tunnels and holes than other rocks: often they are through small tunnels which could not easily be utilised when leading [*fig. 6.11*]. Threads may be of chain but are more usually of rope or tape, and must be taken on trust to some extent. Nylon deteriorates in time and any thread that looks very faded, frayed or otherwise affected should not be trusted. If you feel the need to replace an old thread, remove it completely rather than simply adding a new one and littering the cliff with bundles of decaying nylon.

Pegs must also be taken on trust and the only guide to their likely security is their appearance, lack of cracks and rusting. (See 'Pegs', page 155.) When you are using pegs for runners, they should always be extended [*fig. 6.12*].

The third type of fixed protection is bolts which are common on many cliffs in continental Europe, though much less so in most of Britain and the USA. A bolt consists of a metal sleeve which is placed in a drilled hole in the rock and expanded to grip the rock. Screwed into this is a threaded fixing bolt which attaches a hanger to it. The shape of the hanger will determine how the bolt is clipped. Those which have the eye at right angles to the rock are clipped from the side like pegs, while those which are angled may need to be clipped from above or below and the karabiner

Fig 6.11 Clipping an in situ *thread on a pocketed limestone wall.*

Fig 6.12 A route protected by in situ *pegs. By keeping his feet high and in contact with the rock, the climber is taking some of his weight off his arms.*

Fig 6.13 A bolt-protected climb, in this case an old aid route which has been climbed free. On steep rock like this a rest is something to enjoy!

then flipped over to face the right way. Some hangers, especially older ones, have a small eye and will take only narrow-nosed karabiners. If a hanger is missing, a small wired nut with the head pulled down can be slipped over the bolt stub and the head slid back up to hold it in place. Usually a karabiner/extension/karabiner is used on bolts, but in some situations a locking karabiner, which cannot accidentally release with the rope running over the gate, can be used. This system is most useful on straight routes where rope drag is not a problem [*fig. 6.13*].

Bolts should be completely safe if placed properly but this, unfortunately, is not always the case. They can deteriorate with corrosion and stress through overuse. Any bolt which protrudes from the rock will be weaker than it should be, and a bolt which is angled, rather than flush with the rock, will also be less secure. Small differences in placement can make significant differences to the strength of a bolt: overtightening, for example, can cause a loss of strength.

With fixed protection the natural desire is to clip it as soon as possible, but this is not always the easiest way. Sometimes it is placed so that it is clipped when the waist is level with the gear. This can reduce the effort required by the climber as less rope then has to be pulled through by hand. It can be useful to have a karabiner whose gate can be made to stay open for the really long reaches where a karabiner has to be held in the tips of the fingers.

Bolts and pegs should always be extended as there is a danger that the rope could run across the gate in a fall and so unclip itself, particularly in the case of bent-gate karabiners.

FALLS AND FORCES

In a fall on to a runner you will not simply drop twice the distance you are above that point. The fall can be significantly further because of rope

Relationship of rope available, length of fall and fall factor

Rope out (m)	Runner height (m)	Fall length (m)	Fall factor
4	3	2	0.5
6	5	2	0.33
12	10	4	0.33
18	15	6	0.33
24	20	8	0.33
35	30	10	0.29
45	40	10	0.22

While the actual length of fall increases, the fall factor decreases with height gained.

Relationship of rope available, fall factor and a constant distance fallen

Rope out (m)	Runner height (m)	Fall length (m)	Fall factor
4	3	2	0.5
6	5	2	0.33
11	10	2	0.2
16	15	2	0.13
21	20	2	0.1
31	30	2	0.06
41	40	2	0.05

The length of fall remains constant but the fall factor decreases as height is gained. In practice, however, the length of fall would increase because of rope stretch.

stretch, the rope straightening its line, the amount of rope which runs through the belay device, the tightening-up of harnesses and the belay system and perhaps the belayer being lifted up. Depending on the rope run out and the rope system used, in a short fall – that is, from a couple of metres or so above the runner – the distance fallen below it can be about twice the distance that you were above it. This stretch in the system can mean that the first runner which will stop a ground fall must be placed at about 3m above the ground but will be effective only for a short distance before another must be placed, the distance between runners gradually increasing as height is gained. The same applies to runners placed above easy angled rock. Runners placed lower than this 3m level, however, may still be useful as they can prevent a falling leader toppling over backwards, which can cause greater injury. When you leave any stance, you should place a runner as soon as possible as this will immediately reduce the fall factor and change the direction of pull on the belayer from downwards to upwards, which is easier to deal with.

Another point which arises from consideration of fall factors and runner placements is that it is better to do the harder climbing, where the chance of a fall is greater, nearer the top of a pitch than at the start. Given the choice, it is better to belay after a crux rather than before it. Although a fall may be longer due to increased rope stretch, the forces involved will be less.

However, fall factors are only a guide to the forces liable to be encountered in a fall. The actual distance fallen is usually of greater significance. The longer the fall, the more ground it will cover, so the chances of hitting an obstruction will be increased. You will, up to a point, be travelling faster the further you fall. The impact time is also greater and so all parts of the belay system are loaded for longer, which can in turn increase their chance of failing.

It is important to appreciate that runners should be capable of withstanding a load of about twice the impact force, the load on the runner being the sum of the force on the rope from the faller to the runner and the force from the belayer to runner. As this can be in the region of 1000kg in the worst case, the runner might have to withstand a force of 2000kg. The more dynamic parts there are in the system, the more this force will be reduced. If a belay were static for some reason, such as the rope catching in a crack, binding across a sharp edge due to poor runner placement, a knot jamming in the belay device or all the rope being run out, the load on a runner can easily cause it to fail.

In a fall to one side of a runner, as on a traverse, the climber will pendulum in an arc centred on the runner. In this case, with no actual vertical fall, the belay chain is loaded only with centrifugal force and this will not be greater than twice the penduluming weight. A poor runner which may hold a fall from a traverse may not stop a shorter fall from above it. Many falls are a combination of a vertical fall and a pendulum, but it is the former that is important for the forces involved. The pendulum, though, can be the dangerous part if the climber swings into the rock [*fig. 6.14*].

CARRYING EQUIPMENT

The way in which gear is carried can play an important part in the success or failure of a climb, particularly a strenuous one, when the time spent selecting and placing the right runner can be vital. It is worth spending time organising your gear and a logical method of carrying it. Methods of racking and carrying gear can be very individual but the main systems are: on a bandolier over the shoulder, on the gear loops supplied on most modern harnesses, or a combination of both. Each method has its pros and cons and the type of route to be tackled is often the deciding factor in the organisation of gear, which is fundamental to any system [*fig. 6.15*].

Bandoliers can be bought or made; they can be single, double, adjustable, padded, anatomically designed in shape or consist simply of a single sling. They should be long enough to allow the gear to hang comfortably under one arm, not restrict movement, yet be short enough so that the attached equipment cannot swing round in front of you and get in the way. The part on to which the karabiners clip should be round, smooth and thick enough to ensure that the gates do not snag on it. It is all the more convenient if it is strong enough to be used as a sling if necessary. The main advantages of the bandolier are that gear can be swapped over quickly when leading through on long routes and, by using a bandolier

Fig 6.14 ABOVE: *On a traverse a fall would not load the runners as much as a fall from above. The danger is in hitting something while swinging across the rock.*

Fig 6.15 LEFT: *A well-organised rack of gear with the larger pieces such as Friends on the bandolier, nuts racked in bunches at the front and extensions at the rear of the harness. As this climb follows a thin crack, the smaller nuts are the most ready to hand.*

over each shoulder, large amounts of equipment can be carried, as when on an aid pitch or a big wall. The disadvantage is that gear can swing round to the front and obscure your feet on a slab or disappear round your back on an overhang. A heavy bandolier on one side can make you feel lop-sided and can exert a greater load on your arms on overhanging rock.

Gear racks on harnesses are useful if smaller amounts are to be carried as they keep everything in place and so make speedy location easy. However, heavy gear will tend to drag the harness waist belt down, and nuts on longer slings can get in the way more. A combination of bandolier and harness loops is a good compromise, but it is worth experimenting to find the system that suits you and the type of routes you climb.

The way that gear is organised on the rack can also save you much time and effort. No matter what carrying system is used, it is best to rack the gear in the same way each time so that you know exactly where everything is. On a bandolier, rack roped nuts and Friends in order of size from back to front so that the bigger ones at the back get in the way less and do not obscure the smaller ones. It even helps if the length of nut slings graduate slightly from the smaller to the larger. Each nut is carried on a karabiner which goes on to the rack the same way each time. If the karabiner is clipped on so that the gate faces up and in, when you remove it the action takes it away from the body and so it is less liable to snag.

Wired nuts can be racked in several ways. If only a few are to be taken on a pitch, having each nut on a single karabiner is convenient and they can be carried with the extension already in place. Alternatively, the range of nuts can be carried two or three to each karabiner in descending order of size, or all the nuts of about the same size can be carried on one karabiner. The advantage of bunching wired nuts is that if you do not select the right one first time, there is still a good chance that the one that you do need is on the same karabiner. The disadvantage is that once the nut is placed, it must then be taken off the karabiner, the karabiner returned to its place on the rack, a karabiner, extension and karabiner clipped to the nut and then the rope clipped in. The advantage that roped nuts have over wired nuts is that they can be clipped almost immediately they are placed. With enough practice and experience the correct nut can be selected first time, but this does require a good eye for sizes, particularly with the smaller nuts. It is worth clearly colour coding wired nuts and trying a few different systems.

Extra karabiners can be carried in pairs at the front of the bandolier. Any gear that does not have to be looked at to be selected is best carried out of the way, so extensions with karabiners can be carried at the back although there can be an advantage in having one or two handy at the front for a quick clip.

When using harness loops, the same logic applies: the smallest should be at the front and the largest at the rear, some extensions and spare karabiners should be conveniently situated at the front and the rest out of the way at the back.

Slings are carried over the opposite shoulder from the bandolier, each with a karabiner on it and so ready to use. Double slings are draped over the shoulder and the ends clipped together so that they can be pulled out from under the single ones. The bandolier is put on first, then the double sling and then the single ones, so that all the gear is accessible. Personal gear not needed while climbing, such as belay plate and nut key, are carried at the back where they are out of the way.

MATCHING GEAR

When organising a rack of gear, it is worth considering the relative strength of the various pieces of equipment and putting nuts, slings and extensions on karabiners of similar strength to get the best possible performance out of them. This would not be done, however, when using wired micro nuts. With these large karabiners are used as smaller, lighter karabiners with their narrower diameter put the thin wire through a sharper angle which reduces its strength. A 5–10 per cent difference in breaking strength has been recorded in tests using a 12mm compared with a 10mm diameter karabiner.

AMOUNT OF GEAR

There is no one answer to the question of how much gear to take on a climb, but there are several points worth bearing in mind when trying to decide. First, there is little point in taking anything that you obviously will not need: forget the big Hexs and Friends on a finger crack for example. If spare or extra gear is to be taken, remember that slings are light and versatile and a bunch of small wired nuts does not weigh too much. If only a few medium-to-large nuts may be required, note that camming devices are more versatile and fit a wider range of crack sizes than passive nuts. These points are more applicable to one-pitch routes, especially if the whole pitch can be seen. A multi-pitch climb, however, will probably require you to carry more equipment.

As each belay may require two or more points of attachment, at times at least four items will be used on main anchors alone. Carrying a huge rack may get round the problem, but this extra weight is an obvious hindrance to enjoyable or hard climbing. The more you know about the route and the rock, the more you can plan ahead. Paradoxically, some well-protected climbs may require carrying less gear than a less well-protected one as the placements may happily accept a range of nut sizes. Other placements may only take one specific nut and if you do not have that nut then nothing else will fit.

As an extremely rough guide as to how much to carry, consistently using up three-quarters of your rack on a pitch indicates that you either have good judgement or are pushing your luck, whereas having three-quarters left at the end indicates overcaution or bad planning.

REMOVING GEAR

The greatest aid to removing gear is the ability to look at a placement and see how the nut went in. It can then usually be removed by reversing the insertion procedure. If this does not work, it may have to be tapped loose from its seating, especially if it has been loaded or fallen on. Larger nuts can be loosened by tapping with a karabiner, but smaller ones may need to be prised out using a nut key [*fig. 6.16*]. In fact, a nut key will make most extractions easier, particularly when the nut is deep in the crack and needs to be hooked or lifted to remove it. When removing wired nuts, avoid jerking them sharply upwards, which can cause permanent bending in the wire. This is especially true in the case of micro nuts as the wire below the nut can become bent, stressed and even begin to break up. Having said that, however, brute force can occasionally be the easiest way to remove stubborn nuts. Destroying the rock to remove a piece of gear is never acceptable, so if a nut will not come out without damaging the rock or the nut it is better to leave it in place. If a runner is to be left in, it is better that it is usable and safe rather than partially destroyed but blocking up a slot.

Fig 6.16 A selection of nut keys (right to left): a nut key with a double hook for removing Friends; a simple nut key; and a device for removing Friends which allows inaccessible triggers to be reached.

To make wired nuts easier to remove, the nut can be glued to the wire, so preventing the wire from sliding up through the nut, particularly in a tight placement. (This is more likely to happen with the larger-sized nuts.) There are occasions, though, when being able to slide the nut down the wire is an advantage, as when using the wire as a thread in small tunnels or even to thread the eye of a badly placed peg.

When removing nuts from a pitch, the second should try to get in a good position which allows one or both hands to be free. If this is not possible, he may have to take tension so that he is able to work efficiently. On one-pitch routes it may be easier if the gear is left in place and then removed by abseil or lowering down. This at least means that the second can enjoy the climbing and not be relegated to the role of gear-removing machine On strenuous pitches it can be worthwhile quickly taking the nuts out and leaving them hanging on the rope, then re-racking them when you are in a resting position. If the rope through the karabiner is tight and so putting pressure on the nut and holding it in place, it is best to unclip the rope before trying to remove it. Unfortunately this increases the chance of dropping it. Camming devices in particular are hard to remove if under any form of tension.

Besides being handy for a second, a nut key can be of benefit to a leader, especially when threading awkward small holes or when on mountain or less popular routes where grit, earth and vegetation need to be removed from the placement.

FALLING OFF

Falling off is something that happens to most climbers, especially those who are trying to push up their standard. To some, climbing at or near their limit with the ever-present risk of falling is one of the thrills of rock climbing. Others prefer a lower level of risk, but even they may reach their limit on occasions. This may be through choice or by accident: being off form, being on a badly graded climb, straying off route, losing concentration, attempting to use loose holds and simply being careless are some of the more common reasons. With modern protection falling off is much safer than it once was and many climbers happily fall from climbs repeatedly. However, there is still a degree of danger in any fall. This danger is more acute in the case of beginners and on easier climbs. Harder routes tend to be steeper, smoother and with fewer ledges. In a fall, the real danger is what you may hit and how fast you are travelling when you hit it [*fig. 6.17*].

Rope work and protection should limit the danger of a fall, but it is important to have a realistic appreciation of how good they are. This understanding will come with experience of using the gear but also, unfortunately, with having fallen on it. Blind faith in runners is not enough and should be guarded against, especially in the case of fixed gear which is often regarded as being totally secure when this may not be the case. However, overprotection can waste time and energy and so increase the chances of a fall because the climber is tired. The happier you are about your protection, the more relaxed your climbing will be. Worrying about a fall can make you stiff and tense and so increase the chance of the fall actually happening.

Fig 6.17 Falling off: the climber is just on the point of coming tight on to the right-hand rope. This runner pulled out and he was held on the runners on the left-hand rope.

Falls can be roughly divided into two types, predictable and unpredictable. In the former case you realise that you are about to fall and can in some way influence the outcome, if only by alerting your second. The latter type happens totally unexpectedly as when a hold breaks off. This can result in an uncontrolled fall in which you may come off in any manner – backwards, sideways or even upside-down. This is more dangerous as hitting the rock then can be more serious and you can be whipped round violently when the rope comes tight, further increasing the chance of injury. If you fall when wearing a rucksack and so have a higher centre of gravity, the risk of injury is a little greater.

In a predictable fall, in which you have an instant to do something, it is best if your feet leave the rock before, or at least at the same time as, your hands to ensure that you drop in an upright position. A push away from the rock may help maintain this position which should mean that the impact is taken on the buttocks and thighs when wearing a sit harness. The danger is still in hitting the rock, since it does not take much to break an ankle or wrist. There is also the danger of swinging under an overhang or into a corner. Try to cushion any such blow by using your legs rather than your arms. If you hold the rope lightly just above the knot in a fall, which seems a fairly natural thing to do, this helps keep you in an upright position. In fact, it may be that you hold the rope like this automatically without any conscious thought. However, do not try to grasp the 'up rope' which goes through the runners.

In a fall, the position of the rope is very important. Having the rope in front of you is best as you should face the rock as you fall, not turn round to face out as you would if jumping off a boulder when you would be looking for a landing spot. If a rope runs between your legs, not only will it flip you upside-down, but it can also cause rope burns. These can be very painful and even severe. You can easily get the rope in the wrong position when you are pulling it up to clip into a runner or in a traverse situation where the rope can easily loop itself on to the outside of your leg.

Often the hardest part of any fall is the psychological aspect. To be relaxed and comfortable about a fall not only requires an appreciation of what is about to happen and the equipment that will limit the fall, but also practice. This falling practice can be ignored – many climbers do not do it – or it can be gained on routes or in a controlled situation. In the latter case a solid runner is placed in a suitable situation: a smooth impending wall for example. You get up to a short way above the runner with your rope through it and then fall off, gradually increasing the fall length with subsequent drops. This, unfortunately, does take some of the life out of the rope, the runner and even the rock. It is wise to have the load-bearing runner backed up in case of failure and a separate rope can be used as a further safety precaution.

ROPE SYSTEMS

There are three rope management systems used in climbing and, although there are differences between them, they have overlapping applications. One of the main differences is how they are used in conjunction with protection.

Single Rope

Single-rope technique, which uses one rope of between 10 and 11mm diameter, is the basic rope management system. It is simple to use: only one rope has to be clipped into runners, and belaying is confined to either paying out or taking in. Its main application is on routes which follow fairly straight lines and these tend to be dependent on rock type [*fig. 6.18*]. At one time single ropes were the choice for easier routes but now they are also used on many of the hardest climbs which are very direct or have bolt protection. In this type of climb the light weight of a single rope is an advantage: 1m of 11mm rope weighs 75–80g and 1m of 10.5mm rope weighs about 70g. The diameter and weight of ropes strong enough to be designated as single ropes are decreasing all the time as rope construction methods improve.

The main drawback to the single-rope system is in dealing with more complex situations. If a route follows a devious line, friction through the runners can cause prohibitive rope drag and also put sideways pull on runners which may cause them to lift out [*fig. 6.19*]. To overcome this, large numbers of slings or extensions may need to be carried to extend each runner. This is as liable to

Fig. 6.18 A single rope used on a simple and straight-forward route.

occur on a moderately difficult or classic climb as on a hard one.

As there is only one rope available for protection for both the leader and second – for example, on a traverse – one or both may be put at greater risk. Some rope manoeuvres are more difficult to arrange as are most self-rescues. The maximum abseil possible is only half the length of the rope and it is more vulnerable to damage in stone fall or when the rope runs over an edge in a fall. All your eggs are in one basket with a single rope but there is a certain pleasing simplicity in working this way.

Double Rope

Double-rope technique normally employs two 9mm half-ropes, although different combinations such as one single and one half-rope can be used for increased security. This is the heaviest rope system, 1m of 9mm rope weighing about 50g. The advantages of double ropes are numerous; the main drawback is the weight and the increased complexity of the rope management. Two ropes obviously allow longer abseils and the extra rope can be put to good use in self-rescues, but it is in safety and protection that the real benefits are seen. With double ropes, runners can be clipped alternately, consecutively or in a varying pattern to eliminate rope drag [*fig. 6.20*].

This requires a degree of forward planning and consideration of what rope goes where, otherwise confusion and massive drag can result, especially if ropes are crossed. The actual rope clipped in any runner will depend on the exact situation, but the system is very flexible [*fig. 6.21*]. If both ropes, however, are to be clipped through the same runner, it is best to have each rope in a separate karabiner. This should reduce the risk of rope damage caused by the ropes running against each other at different rates as a result of differing lengths of rope being run out. It also prevents loading the karabiner away from its main axis in a fall.

Protection for the second is easier to arrange, particularly when a pitch has a traverse when one rope can be left basically free of runners to give protection from above. Double ropes also make clipping runners near the ground or a large ledge safer as the leader can be protected by one rope while pulling up the other to clip gear above his head. The same applies when using a dubious runner: in this case the leader is safeguarded by one rope while clipping the next runner up. If a fall should occur at this point, he will still be held on the second rope, whereas on a single rope the amount pulled up to clip will increase the potential fall length. Likewise, if a pitch cannot be completed because of weather deterioration, difficulty or lack of time, a leader can be lowered off a poor runner while still protected by the other rope through other, hopefully better, runners. There is, however, the danger of clipping one rope far more than the other and ending up effectively climbing on a half-rope with the increased chance of rope failure or a longer fall due to the increase in rope stretch. A fall approaching fall factor 1 can seriously damage a half-rope as these are meant to be used in pairs, not singly. Because different lengths of rope may be involved in a fall, the dynamics of the two ropes used will be different.

The second will have a more complex task to perform if the ropes are to be properly managed. When the leader is moving up below a clipped runner, for example, one rope will have to be taken in while the other is payed out until the

leader's waist is level with the runner when both ropes will be payed out. This is easier to do with a belay plate than by means of other belaying methods. In all cases the dead hand should remain in contact with the dead rope but the live hand can be crossed over to assist with the rope handling.

Double ropes are safer in the event of a fall as it is extremely unlikely that both would run over the same edge and be cut through. The same applies in stone-fall situations when it is less likely that both ropes would be cut by falling rocks.

Fig 6.19 OPPOSITE PAGE: *Using single rope on a route whose crux is a traverse. This creates rope drag, increases the chance of runners lifting out and means that the second is less well protected on this section of the climb.*

Fig 6.20 BELOW: *Wide bridging on friction holds in an open corner with a poor pinch grip for the left hand. The wired nut is lengthened with an extension to prevent it lifting out. This situation is ideal for using double ropes: the right-hand rope goes into runners in the right crack while the left-hand rope is used for the left-hand crack and runners.*

Fig 6.21 BELOW RIGHT: *The greater versatility of double ropes on a more complex pitch cuts down on rope drag. Even so long slings still have to be used to allow the ropes to run more freely. The climber is chalking up in a strenuous position but minimising the strain by hanging on a straight arm and using good footwork, edging with one foot and smearing with the other.*

Twin Ropes

The twin-rope system shares some of the features of both single and double ropes but uses two sub 9mm ropes as a single rope. In this case the weight falls somewhere between the other two systems at about 48g per metre. The twin ropes are used in exactly the same manner as a single rope, being belayed in the same way and clipped into runners as one rope. The main advantage is the increased safety. The two strands, having an increased surface area, are less likely to be damaged in a fall over an edge or in a stone fall and the figure-of-eight-shaped cross-section is easier to grip. There is also increased rope available in emergency situations and abseils. With runners, both ropes are normally clipped through a single karabiner and the two ropes treated as one. However, in the situation where the fall factor is sufficiently low, the ropes can be separated and used as a double rope to reduce rope drag. This is most likely to occur towards the top of a pitch when a fair amount of rope has been run out. However, to use the ropes in this fashion means that they have to be belayed separately from the start and both ropes must be running free and not twisted. The ability to use the ropes twisted is one of the advantages of this system as it speeds up organisation.

PROTECTING THE SECOND

Runners can be placed to safeguard the second, particularly on a traverse to prevent or limit a pendulum which can be dangerous if there is an obstruction in the path of the swing. The best situation for the second is to have a rope as directly above him as possible. The leader should, if there is no serious increase in danger to himself, avoid placing runners at the end of a traverse and for as far up the climb after that point as is possible. This will lessen the second's swing potential. Using a double rope makes this easier: one rope is used to protect the leader while the other is left free to protect the second [*figs. 6.22, 6.23*]. Another safeguard is for the second to tie on to a bight of spare rope dropped down from the stance.

If the leader needs runners for his own safety, the second has to arrange his own protection. With two ropes, one can sometimes be pulled through the runners and thrown back down to the second who ties on to it again [*fig. 6.24*]. That rope then runs more directly to the stance. This works only if the stance is above the traverse. If it is necessary to belay at the end of a hard traverse, the second may have to use a back rope. One rope is left through a runner at the start of the traverse and the leader takes in on one rope while paying out on the back rope as the second climbs. This back rope limits any pendulum and is recovered by untying and pulling the end through. For ease of running it is often necessary to leave a karabiner on the back rope anchor.

If using a single rope, the second ties on to the rope as far along it as possible, then unties from the end. This end is used as the back rope but the

Fig 6.22 BELOW: *Alternate clipping of each rope on a traverse.*

Fig 6.23 OPPOSITE PAGE: *By using two ropes the second is protected from above on the traverse as one rope has been left free.*

Fig 6.24 OPPOSITE PAGE: *Protecting a traverse by using two belayers. In this case one of a pair of ropes was pulled up then thrown down to the second who then had one rope above him at the start.*

second will have to manage it himself. This can be done using a friction hitch or belay plate through which the rope can be paid out as the traverse is crossed. A French prusik can also be used to control the back rope and is often the easiest method. If enough rope is available, a long bight can be used to provide the back rope. This allows everything to be done without untying from any rope. In all cases the back rope anchor has to be abandoned.

Runners can also be placed simply to show the second where the route goes, particularly if the leader has been out of sight. In this situation, runners placed off the route can be very misleading as can well-chalked-up holds on neighbouring climbs. Good communications are important when out of sight of your partner.

DOWN CLIMBING

Protection for down climbing is placed and arranged as on the ascent but the person to descend last is, in effect, the leader. Runners are placed to limit falls and more are placed about and below the difficult sections and towards the bottom of the pitch. When down climbing, it is possible to leave runners in place until below them before taking them out. Gear can also be used to lower off; if the runner is poor, it is better to lower yourself rather than have the belayer do it as this puts less load on the runner. This means abandoning gear, but the advantage over an abseil is that poorer gear can be used to assist descending, especially if lowering yourself on one rope while still protected by another. Sometimes it is possible to take tension from a sling round a spike, then flick it off when safely below it.

TENSION TRAVERSE

Sometimes the rope must be used not only for safety but also to give actual support. A tension traverse is an example of this. The leader takes tension from the rope through an anchor point somewhere above him. This support allows side-

Fig 6.25 A tension traverse. The climber is leaning away from the rope for support and using friction to try to reach holds on the left edge.

ways movement on rock which cannot be crossed by conventional means. The climbing is often effected by leaning sideways and using friction and any available holds. The higher the anchor is above the traverse, the more it supports the leader, but the longer the traverse, the harder it becomes. The second pays out the rope to the leader as it is required [*fig. 6.25*].

To follow a tension traverse, some form of back-roping is often needed. A friction device can be used by the second for tension or to lower himself from the anchor which is left in place, until he can climb or prusik up to the stance. The more directly the leader belays above the end of the traverse, the better. If the stance is at the same level as the tension traverse, the second may have to pull himself across using the ropes. Double ropes are an advantage in this manoeuvre.

The anchor from which the tension is taken must be secure and more than one point may be required – for the leader at least. On some tension traverses runners may be placed to limit any pendulum, should the leader fall off. The danger here is that the swing could take him back into an obstruction such as a corner. Another problem is that a tension traverse may be impossible to reverse. Doing one on a long or serious route is a way of ensuring commitment to the rest of the climb.

PENDULUMS

A pendulum is used to cross an area of rock too steep and holdless to allow the use of a tension traverse. First the leader is lowered the appropriate distance from a secure anchor. The pendulum is built up by running and swinging across the rock, using holds that are available to augment this action, particularly to begin with. Repeated swings may be needed to build up momentum on a long pendulum. When the leader reaches the objective, he reverts to normal climbing. If using a single rope, he should go to above the pendulum point before fixing any runners. This makes seconding easier and reduces rope drag. Using two ropes is preferable for this manoeuvre as the pendulum can be done on one rope while protected by the other. There is also a danger of rope damage if the pendulum rope runs against the rock. When the leader is being lowered, it is important that he does not go too low. It is easy for the second to lower him further if required, but more difficult to raise him to the correct level.

If the pendulum ends on a ledge below the pendulum point, the second can cross by penduluming in the same manner. If not, the anchor is used as a lowering point for the second to back-rope himself down to below the leader and then climb or prusik up the remainder of the pitch. This lowering can be done using a friction device. Simply penduluming across from the anchor is frightening, abrasive and dangerous.

Fig 6.26 On a Tyrolean traverse which has a steep finish the climber has to use prusik loops for progress, one to the harness and one to the foot. Using a chest sling would make this less strenuous.

TYROLEAN TRAVERSE

The Tyrolean traverse is used to cross gaps, such as between pinnacles and the mainland; it is also used for crossing gorges and even rivers. It is, however, often performed for its spectacular nature rather than through any real need. A rope is fixed and, hanging below it in a harness, you can cross the gap. A short sling between your harness and the tensioned rope can make progress easier – you pull yourself across hand over hand or by using prusik loops or clamps. (See Chapter 8, page 131.) On a long Tyrolean traverse a chest harness can give extra support [*fig. 6.26*].

Unless tensioned using some pulley system, the rope will stretch a good deal when you reach the mid-point. While it can be easy to slide down to the middle, the uphill section can be fairly strenuous. It is best to cross using a safety rope in case of rope or anchor failure or the need for assistance. This safety rope should be attached to both sides of the crossing to eliminate the risk of a dangerous swing into the side should the tensioned rope or an anchor fail. If the tension rope has to be retrieved afterwards, it will have to be used doubled.

Large forces can be created when a horizontal rope is tensioned, and the load on the rope and the anchors can be many times the climber's weight. The nearer the rope is to the horizontal, the greater this loading will be, so any rope should only be stretched as tight as is required and not over-tensioned. When any tensioned rope has to be secured at an anchor, it is best to attach it in such a way that it can be untied when still under tension in case something goes wrong. Using a locked-off friction hitch is a suitable way to do this.

7 Abseiling

Abseiling is the technique used to descend a rope, the speed of descent being controlled by friction between the rope and the climber's body or some form of abseil device. It is also known as rappelling or roping down. An abseil is usually done on a doubled rope so that the rope can be retrieved from below. It is an integral part of climbing and is used in a variety of situations when down climbing is not practicable or advisable. It can be used when a climb cannot be completed, to reach the foot of a sea cliff or gorge, to get down from a peak, pinnacle or sea stack, or even to return to the ground when the good climbing is over.

Unfortunately, abseiling can be dangerous, and may vary from being exhilarating to terrifying. A specifically set-up abseil with all safety precautions can be good fun; an abseil down a long unknown descent in worsening weather with limited equipment can mean hours of nerve-wracking uncertainty. In no other aspect of climbing are you so totally reliant on your gear for such a length of time. Once an abseil is started, you are dependent on your attachment to the rope down which you are moving and the rope's attachment to the cliff. Even in a fall on a climb, the rope is loaded only for a short time, and with reasonable runners and anchors a failure in one part of the system may not be catastrophic. A failure of any part of the abseil system usually is. If the anchor pulls, if the rope is cut, if you let go or fail to stop before the rope's end, disaster usually results. It has been said that more top climbers have been killed in abseil accidents than by any other cause. This is probably true. However, most of the dangers can be guarded against and good abseil practice can minimise the risks. Abseiling is something that most active climbers will be required to do at some stage, so it is as well to be familiar with the techniques involved and practise them in a controlled situation.

An abseil can be considered to consist of four parts: rigging the abseil, descending the rope, safeguarding the descent and retrieving the rope.

RIGGING AN ABSEIL

The first consideration is the line that the abseil should take. The ideal would be down steep, smooth, solid rock from good ledge to good ledge, each supplied with secure anchors. This is seldom found. If descending by the route of ascent, the location of the stances and anchors will be known, but on unknown ground they will have to be located on the way down. Good visibility and an uncomplicated rock structure will aid this. Loose and broken rock, trees and bushes, or anything that can snag the rope, will be a hazard. Abseiling above another climber is an anti-social and dangerous activity though unfortunately often necessary on popular routes in areas such as the Alps.

Once the line of descent has been selected, the next requirement is a solid anchor or anchors from which the rope can be suspended. As with belay anchors, features such as spikes, threads, chockstones or trees are the obvious choices. Because the rope has to be pulled down afterwards, these will almost certainly have to be equipped with a sling through which the rope can be doubled. If the rope is simply put round the rock, friction makes it difficult, if not impossible, to recover. Any natural spike or thread should be checked for sharp edges that could abrade or cut the sling and these should be padded or rounded off. With a thread, check that the sling cannot be pulled into a sharp constriction and cut. Old abseil slings should seldom be trusted as sunlight, chafing in the wind and friction burning from previous rope retrievals can seriously weaken them. Abseiling from loose blocks of any form is best avoided as even large boulders have been known to move if sufficient force is applied at the correct angle.

If no natural anchor is available, nuts or pegs have to be used. In this case it is best to have two (or even more) separate points linked so that they share the load. This should be done in such a way

Fig 7.1 Two wired nuts linked by a sling to form a safe abseil anchor. In this case the sling was untied, threaded through the nuts, re-tied, and the tension equalised and then maintained by tying an overhand knot in the bottom.

that the failure of one point would not shock-load the other. Any form of linking used in belaying can be employed [*fig. 7.1*]. A problem, however, does arise with the reluctance of climbers to leave expensive equipment behind; but gear can be replaced, lives cannot. In some climbing areas fixed bolts are used for abseil descents. Usually there are two bolts which should be linked in a load-sharing manner. If they are linked by a fixed chain, it is vital to put the rope through the chain and never run it over the top, for if one bolt pulls out, the rope will simply slide off the loose end.

Whatever type of anchor is used, ensure that the rope will run smoothly on retrieval. It will run more easily over wide tape or rope than thin slings, and if wired nuts are used a sling or karabiner will be needed. It is best that the point where the abseil ropes leave the anchor point is in space rather than held against the rock as this may cause excessive friction and make rope recovery difficult.

Make sure that the load on the rope is pulling the anchor in the direction in which it will best take the strain. This usually means as near straight down as possible. The anchor points should be fairly high above the ledge, and the bigger the ledge, the higher they should be. A sharp edge to the ledge should be padded as the sawing caused by the descent could badly abrade or even cut the ropes. In some situations it may even be necessary to round off the edge to prevent this, although the most serious abrasion tends to happen lower down where the sawing effect is greater.

Where abseils are to be expected, as in the Alps, it is normal to climb on, or at least have, two ropes because an abseil can only be half the total length of available rope if they are to be retrieved. These ropes must be joined together and the normal method is to use a double fisherman's knot [*fig. 7.2*]. This is a safe knot but it does become very tight after repeated use. An alternative is to tie the ropes together first with a reef knot and leave long tails which are then tied in a double fisherman's knot on either side of the reef knot. This is much easier to untie [*fig. 7.3*]. Another method is to use a figure-of-eight to join the ropes: a figure-of-eight in one end is followed through by the other end to produce a flat knot which does not snag so easily. Ensure that long tails are left if using this version of the figure-of-eight.

After joining the ropes through the abseil sling, they must then be put down the descent and there can be a danger of their tangling or becoming hung up on a projection or in a crack. There are several ways to get the ropes down but an organised method works best. If the ropes are flaked out first and then thrown in neat hanks or coils, there is less chance of their tangling. The ropes can be thrown separately or together but it is better to put the upper half down first and then throw down the bottom end. If the rope is thrown in an arc away from the cliff, it should fall clear of the rock. On steep rock a bight can be payed out from the anchor and only the bottom end then needs to be dropped down. When the ropes are down, check that they are hanging clear down the cliff. If not, it may be necessary to pull one or both up and try again.

If it is very windy, it may be necessary to weight the bottom end of the rope, though this increases the chance of its snagging on its way down. Another way of getting the rope down is to carry

Fig 7.2 TOP: *A double fisherman's knot used to join two ropes for an abseil.*

Fig 7.3 ABOVE: *A double fisherman's knot tied on either side of a reef knot. Although bulky, this is an easy knot to undo.*

it in hanks, paying it out as you descend. Always stand clear of ropes being thrown down and watch for them knocking down rocks. If other climbers are in the area, wait till they are clear or shout 'Rope below' to warn them of the possible danger of rocks being dislodged.

Once the rope is in place it can then be descended.

DESCENDING THE ROPE

There are many different methods of descending the rope, all of them using friction as a means of control. This can be between the rope and the body, some form of braking device or a combination of the two. Some methods require specialised pieces of equipment, but the best use equipment carried anyway. Unless you are performing a classic abseil, the first requirement is a seat to support your weight. Abseiling on a waist belt alone is dangerous as the belt will constrict breathing which can lead to unconsciousness and ultimately death. If you wear a harness, the normal attachment point for the rope is used for the brake, but ensure that it is safe and distributes the weight properly: most of the weight should be taken on the thighs, not the waist. Many harnesses have a sewn loop which connects the belt and leg loops and provides a good suspension point. If using only a waist belt, a sit sling must be constructed. This can then be clipped into the waist belt to improve the security and the position of the sit sling. (See Chapter 9, page 140.)

The means of descending the rope is basically the same in all cases. The climber controls the rate of descent with the hand held after the friction-producing system. This is known as the braking hand. The other hand (the balance hand) holds the tight rope from the anchor at about chest level. This hand does not grip tightly but merely steadies the descent. Keep the feet about twice hip width apart, again to aid stability, and gradually lean back so that your weight comes on to the brake and the rope. This leaning back is continued until the legs are at about 45° to the rock and the body is just back from the vertical. The knees are kept flexed and the descent is made by walking backwards and controlling the speed of the rope by movement of the braking hand. The feet are kept fairly flat against the rock and small backward steps are taken. If the body is too upright, the feet may slip downwards, causing a swing into the rock; too much backward lean, on the other hand, is strenuous and may even lead to your inverting with unpleasant consequences. Walk steadily and smoothly and avoid unnecessary jerks on the rope which put more load on the system, particularly the anchors. This is particularly important at the start where the system is

Fig 7.4 A free abseil.

less dynamic. Unnecessary leaps into space can load the anchor with as much as two and a half times the abseiler's weight, whereas the proper use of the feet can mean a load on the anchor of less than body weight. If the abseil goes down clear of the rock you will be in a sitting position suspended in the harness. In such a free abseil spinning on the rope is liable to occur but is usually of little consequence [*fig. 7.4*].

If an overhang is encountered, it may be necessary to push out with the legs and slide quickly to a position below it before proceeding normally. Failure to judge this correctly can be painful. It is better to let one leg fold right up while the other reaches under to make contact with the rock there. If the overhang is too big for this, turn side-on to the rock and descend carefully, using the side of your body to keep your face and the brake clear of the rock.

Often the most difficult part of an abseil is getting started. If the anchor points are high above the ledge or the angle rounds off gradually, it is easy to attain the correct position by leaning back against the rope. If the anchor points are low on the ledge, a different way of starting may be used. Sit on the ledge with your legs over the edge and the brake as high up the rope as possible. Then move on to the hip nearest the rope and gradually transfer your weight on to the rope, at the same time turning round to face the rock. It may help to descend a little at this point. Then, from a position below the edge, get your feet on the rock, push back into the correct position and descend normally. Care must be taken to avoid trapping the balance hand between the rope and the rock or snagging the abseil device on the edge.

Several factors affect the speed of descent: the angle of the rock, the braking system, the condition of the rope and the weight of rope below you being the main ones. Thicker ropes give more friction than thinner ones; ropes which are old and furred give a slower descent; gritty or muddy ropes do likewise and can even groove an abseil device. New, smooth ropes can give a faster-than-expected abseil; and icy or wet ropes can be either faster or slower, depending on the degree to which they are affected. One system of braking on double 11mm ropes may be immovable but on a single 9mm rope it could be dangerously fast. Experience and having a range of techniques at your disposal will allow you to deal with any situation.

Classic Abseil

The classic abseil is a basic method that needs no equipment other than the rope, but it can be dangerous and painful because of the friction and heat generated as the rope passes round the body, particularly the thigh and shoulder. It is, however, the only method that allows a knot in the rope to be passed with no extra manoeuvring. To get into the starting position, stand astride the ropes facing uphill and lift the ropes from behind up round one thigh. Then pass the ropes diagonally across the chest, over the opposite shoulder and down the back to the hand at the side which has the rope round the thigh. Extra friction can be created by taking a twist of rope round this arm. The thigh and shoulder should be padded, hair and beard tucked clear of the rope and the side of the neck well covered up. Wearing gloves is usually advisable. Once the rope is in place, lean back into the correct position and walk backwards down the rope. By turning the body out and towards the braking hand you can make the position more secure and also see the way down more clearly [*fig.* 7.5].

Figure-of-Eight Descender

The figure-of-eight descender is a simple, popular and easily controlled abseil device whose large size makes it efficient at dissipating the heat created by friction. It can be used on most combinations of rope sizes. If a very thin rope is to be used, the device can be inverted and the ropes put through the small eye. The disadvantage of the figure-of-eight, however, is its weight and lack of other real use. It also twists the ropes and these twists can create problems if allowed to build up. Another danger is that it can accidentally lock if the rope is forced up over the shoulder of the big eye where it forms a lark's foot; and it cannot be released until the weight is taken off the rope and the eight. This accidental locking can happen if the rope catches on an obstruction such as the lip of an overhang and is more likely to occur if the rope crosses the central bar on the side away from the body but nearer the rock. Some types of figure-of-eight are designed to prevent this happening and others to keep the two ropes separate [*fig.* 7.6].

To put on the device, stand parallel to the abseil ropes with the hand you want as the braking hand at the downhill side. Hold the figure-of-eight under the ropes, take a bight down through the big eye and up over the small one, then connect it to your harness with either a locking karabiner or two back-to-back karabiners. The braking hand, which is below the figure-of-eight, moves up to go faster and down towards the thigh to slow down. Pulling the ropes against the thigh further increases friction [*fig.* 7.7].

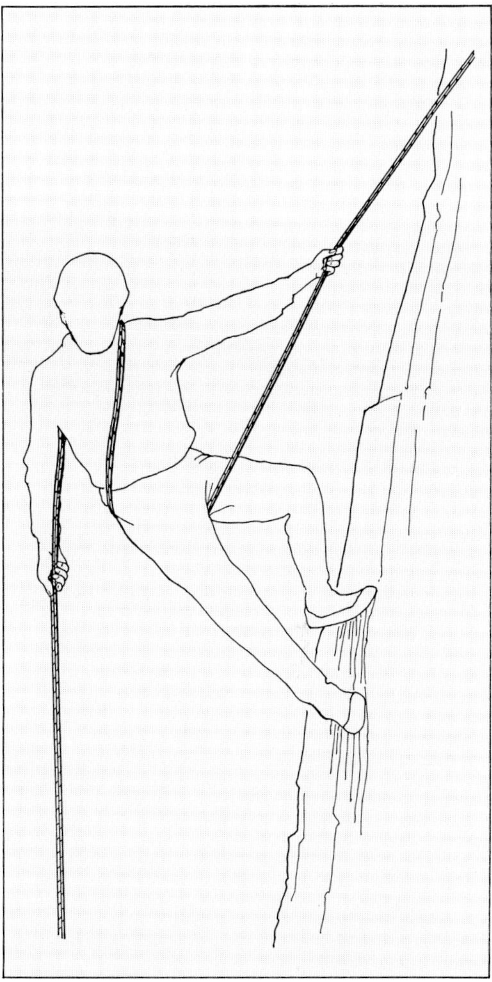

Fig 7.5 A classic abseil which is painful and not very secure but requires no equipment apart from the rope. By turning to face the side you can make it slightly easier and safer.

Belay Plate

The belay plate, a piece of equipment normally carried, provides a convenient way of abseiling. Bights of rope are pushed through the slots and connected to a locking karabiner on the harness. If this is done while the climber is standing parallel to the rope, the hand on the downhill side will be the braking hand. This holds the rope below the plate and moves down towards the thigh to brake and up to run more freely. It does, however, tend to give a jerky descent unless the ropes are held in just the correct position. This jerkiness is reduced slightly with a plate which has a spring attached. One way to make the ropes run more smoothly is to clip a karabiner in the bight of rope below the plate but above the locking karabiner [*fig.* 7.8]. This can be used to adjust the amount of braking but it is better to have too much rather than too little, for in the former case the rope can be fed into the plate and the descent continued. Also, the ropes always run

Fig 7.6 A selection of figure-of-eight descenders: a simple eight, a large eight with lugs to prevent the rope sliding up and so forming a lark's foot, and an eight with lugs and the two rings at right angles to each other.

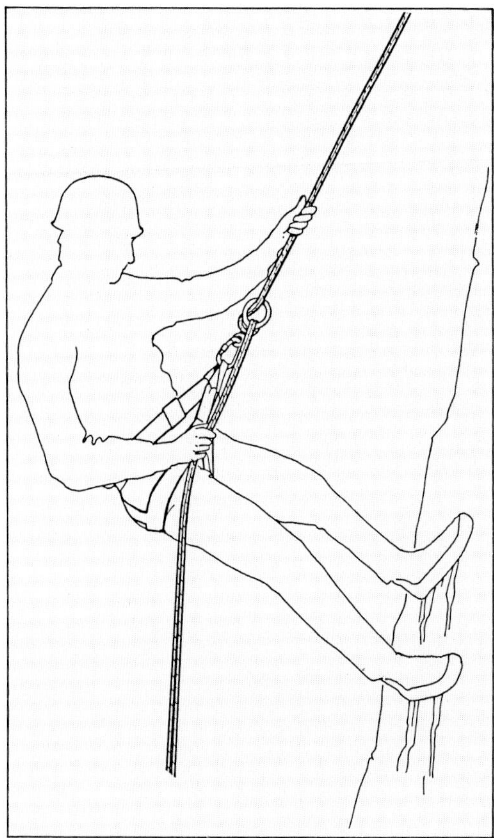

Fig 7.7 Using a figure-of-eight descender. The rope is put through the device so that it crosses the main bar on the side nearest the climber and thus cannot accidentally snag.

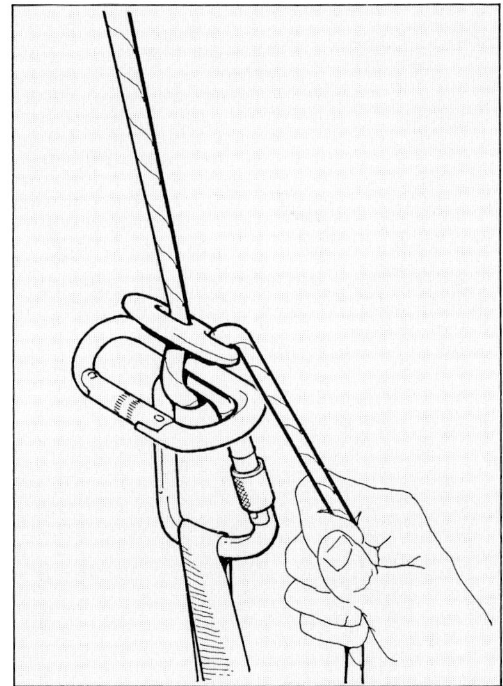

Fig 7.8 An extra karabiner put into the bight of rope through the belay plate to prevent it from jamming and so give a smoother descent.

more easily as you descend. This extra karabiner can even be placed during an abseil if you can stand on the rock and get your weight off the rope. The extra karabiner can then be clipped or unclipped if the angle of the abseil changes dramatically, such as from a free abseil on to a slab or vice versa.

The disadvantage of the plate is its small size and tendency to heat up. This could damage the rope, but it can be guarded against by carefully controlling your speed and letting the plate cool down between abseils. If abseiling on two ropes of different diameters, the thinner rope will tend to slide through more quickly unless watched carefully. This could be dangerous near the end of a descent if one rope becomes a lot shorter than the other and it could burn or melt the abseil sling if it ran rapidly across it.

Friction Hitch

The friction hitch is convenient for the occasional abseil but not for multi-pitch descents. It is tied as a single hitch in both ropes and attached to the harness with a locking karabiner, preferably one of the HMS type. The gate is positioned as far from the rope as possible. The braking hand holds the rope after the hitch and pulls back against the thigh to brake. Although holding the braking rope parallel to the load rope produces maximum braking, this is a difficult and tiring position to maintain. Gripping the rope more tightly or pulling it at an angle across the karabiner will also increase the braking effect. The friction hitch gives a smooth descent but too much speed can cause excessive heating of the karabiner; more importantly, however, it twists and kinks the rope quite badly [*fig. 7.9*].

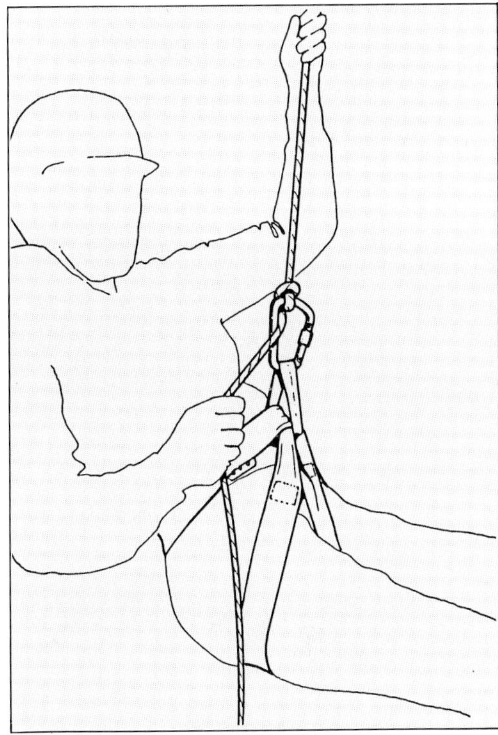

Fig 7.9 When abseiling with a friction hitch the rope is pulled against the back bar of the karabiner to give more friction. This also keeps it away from the gate. When abseiling on two ropes, a single hitch is tied in both ropes.

Karabiner Brakes

Karabiner brakes form a fairly simple system which uses normal climbing gear and can be built up to give varying degrees of braking power to suit the rope and the descent. The basic form uses two karabiners: first, lay one over the rope with the long axis parallel to it, take a loop of rope up through it and clip the second karabiner across the first so that its gate faces down and the rope runs over its back bar [*fig. 7.10*]. If locking karabiners are available, they should be used and placed so that the rope would tighten the screw sleeve if touched by the rope as it moves [*fig. 7.11*]. To make the basic form safer, double up on both karabiners. If oval karabiners are used, one gate can be at either side; if D-shaped karabiners are used, both gates are at the same side but open in opposite directions. The rope always runs over the back bar on the karabiners at right angles to the rope.

If one brake does not give enough friction, a second or third brake can be linked to it in series. If D-shaped karabiners are used, the rope should be on the gate side of the linking karabiners. If on the back bar side, the rope gets pinched in the corner and the brake locks [*fig. 7.12*]. The brake is attached to the harness by a locking karabiner or by two karabiners back to back.

Braking is carried out by pulling the ropes down towards and against the thigh. This method can also be used in conjunction with a belay plate

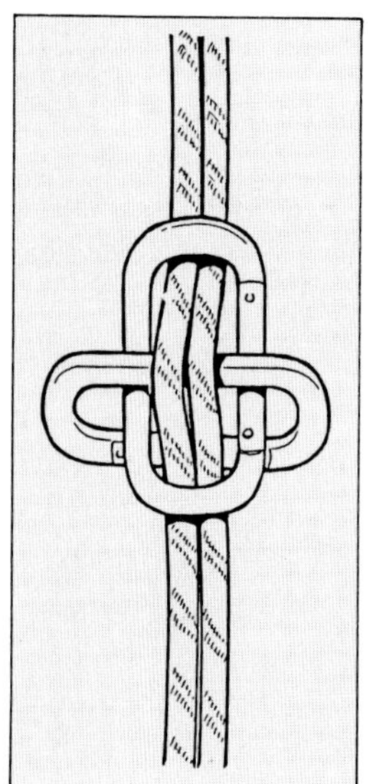

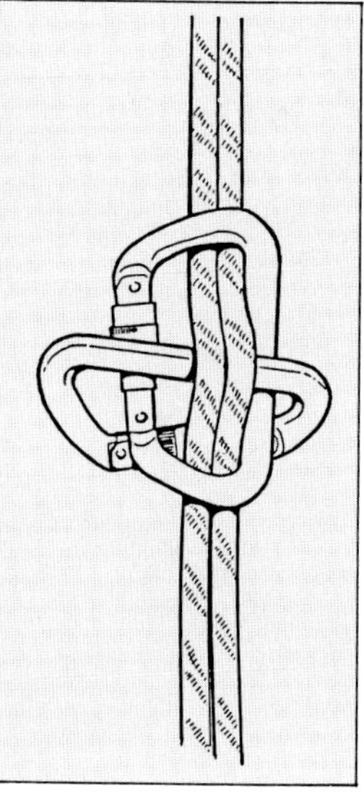

Fig 7.10 LEFT: *The basic karabiner brake.*

Fig 7.11 RIGHT: *A brake made with screw-gate karabiners which are arranged so that if the rope did touch them it would screw the sleeves tighter rather than loosen them.*

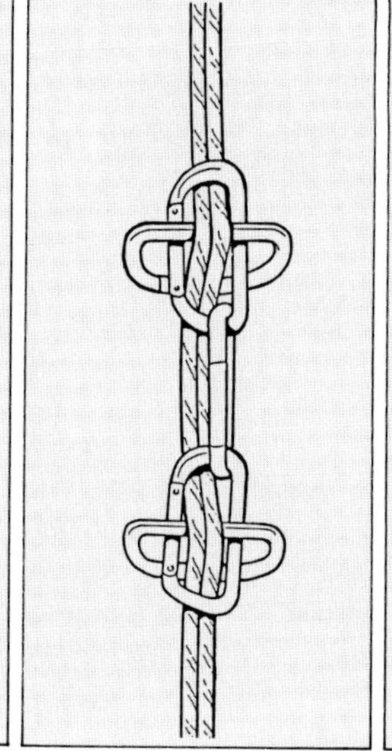

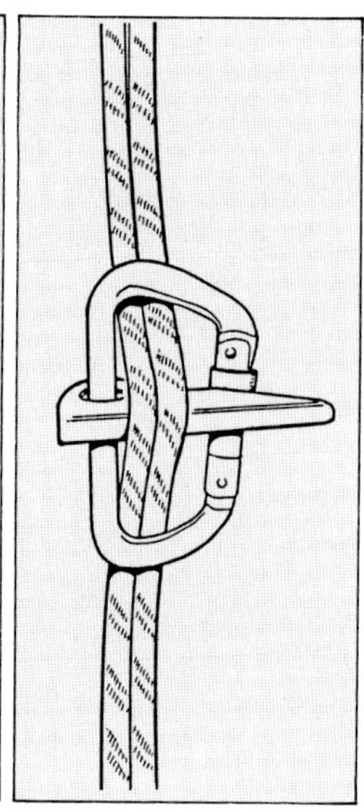

Fig 7.12 LEFT: *A larger brake built up from the basic form. The linking karabiner is put on the back bar side so that it does not pinch the rope.*

Fig 7.13 RIGHT: *A brake bar made with a baby angle peg.*

or figure-of-eight descender to provide extra friction. In this case it is placed above the abseil device and linked into it or the same harness attachment point as the other device.

The karabiner brake gives a very smooth descent but some experience is required to estimate how big to make it. It does not twist or kink the rope, but at the end of the abseil always dismantle the brake rather than pulling the ropes through as this can result in karabiners being dropped as the brake falls to pieces. However, it can also come to pieces if forced against the rock, so great care is necessary when starting off, particularly if the ropes run across any edges.

A variation of the karabiner brake is to use an angle peg as the braking bar by clipping the karabiner through the eye and laying the peg across the karabiner. Make sure that the peg is smooth and free from sharp edges and is large enough so that it cannot twist out of the karabiner. Standard and baby angles are suitable, depending on the karabiner size. It is worth remembering, however, that karabiners are not made to take heavy loads sideways across the gate, therefore using the locking type is always advisable [*fig. 7.13*].

Extra Friction

On some abseils the amount of friction supplied by the device may not be quite enough for a comfortable descent, especially near the foot of an abseil when the weight of rope hanging below the brake is less. Without setting up anything special you can hold the ropes in different ways which will give more control. Take both hands to one side to hold the rope below the brake or take the rope round the back and hold it at the opposite side of the body. In this case the free rope can hang between your legs and both hands can be used if required. None of these affects the way the rope is controlled but simply provide some more friction between the rope and the climber.

Extra friction can be gained by linking different types of brake: for example, a karabiner brake can be put above a belay plate as long as both are linked into the same suspension point. An alternative is to attach a friction hitch below a belay plate, descender or similar item to give greater control. It can be clipped into the side of the harness or a leg loop.

Several specialised abseil devices are available,

such as karabiner bars, rack descenders and autolock descenders, but these are advantageous only if very long descents are contemplated. Methods of safely descending extremely long pitches are well covered in caving literature.

SAFEGUARDING THE ABSEIL

There are some dangers in an abseil that it is not possible to guard against other than by using a safety rope from a separate anchor. This is not always practical and does not help the last man down. However, it is the only precaution that can be taken against anchor or rope failure. The latter can easily happen if a tensioned rope is hit by falling rock. Picking a good line out of stone-fall danger is important, as is the selection of good anchors. In some situations, such as a long unplanned abseil or retreat, it may not be practical to double up on each anchor because of lack of equipment. A partial solution here is to rig the abseil so that one anchor takes the load but is backed up by another. If the main anchor fails, the back-up should take the weight with a minimum of shock-loading. The heaviest person normally descends first and the last man down removes the back-up on the assumption that the main anchor will take his weight [*fig. 7.14*].

Fig 7.14 An abseil sling backed up with a Friend which would be removed before the last person descends. The back-up is not quite tight so that the sling takes the load but would not be shock-loaded if the first anchor failed.

If a brake is being used, the danger of sliding off the rope end can be avoided by tying a large knot such as a figure-of-eight about 2m from the rope ends. This will jam in the brake provided that it is large enough, the only problem being the increased chance of the rope snagging when thrown down. The ends below the knot can be useful in an emergency. The knot can be tied in both ropes or in each rope separately, in which case any kinks formed in the rope can spin out at the ends more easily. With any abseil method, if the rope ends are tied together the climber can clip a karabiner round one rope and so be attached to the huge loop. This also helps to keep the ropes separated to aid retrieval.

A method of self-protection is to use a prusik loop (see Chapter 8, page 131) from the climber to the ropes. The traditional way is to tie a prusik knot round both ropes above the brake and attach it to the harness. The knot is held open with the upper hand which moves it down the ropes. If it is released, the knot will lock and halt the descent. The prusik and attachment should not be longer than an arm's length, for if it accidentally locks up it may require the use of another prusik loop to release it and get the weight back on the rope to continue descending. The French prusik, which can be moved when loaded, is the best knot for this. A mechanical device called a shunt performs the same function [*fig. 7.15*].

A better alternative is to put the prusik on the ropes below the brake and keep it moving down with the braking hand. This works particularly well when using a belay plate or figure-of-eight descender for, when released, the prusik simply holds the rope in the locked-off position and your weight remains on the brake. As it takes little strain, it is easily slackened off and can never get out of reach. The loop can be attached to any strong point on the harness such as a leg loop, but ensure that it is not long enough to go into the brake and foul it up or fail to grip the rope properly [*fig. 7.16*]. An even simpler safeguard is

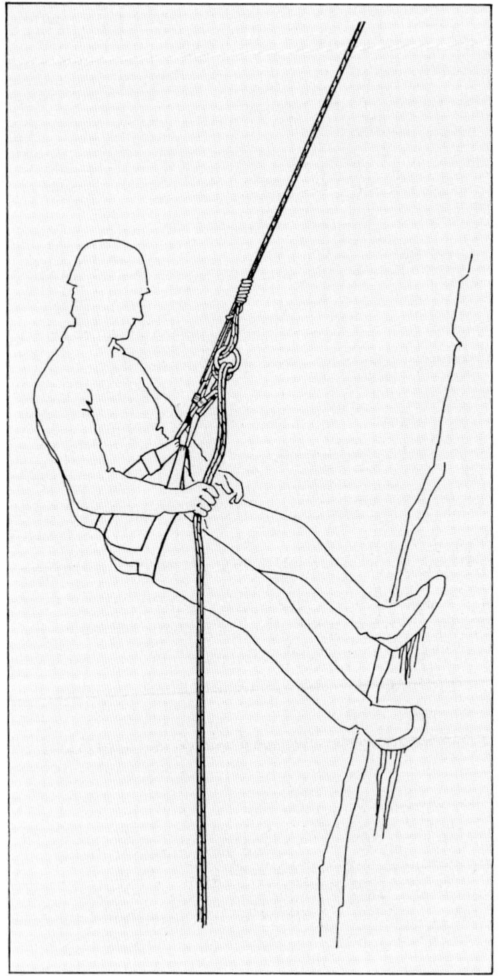

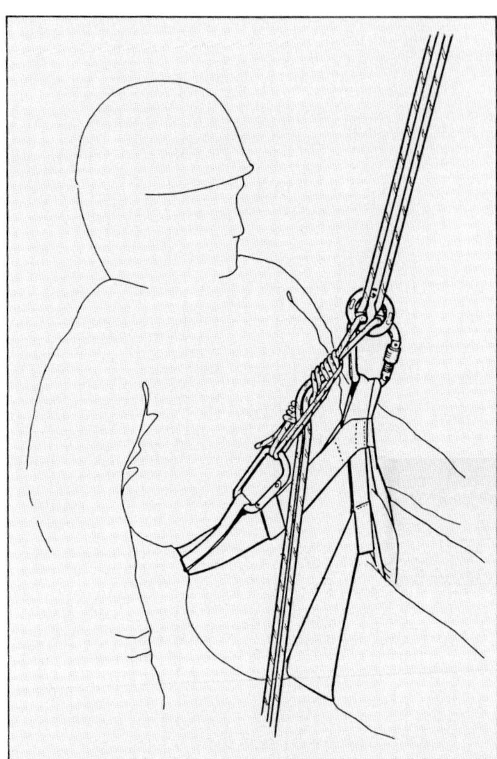

Fig 7.15 LEFT: *Protecting an abseil with a prusik loop attached to both ropes above the figure-of-eight descender.*

Fig 7.16 ABOVE: *Protecting an abseil with a French prusik tied round both ropes below the belay plate. In this case the prusik is attached to a sling which has been clipped into a suitably strong point at the back of the harness.*

to take a loop of rope right round the body at waist level just above the harness. The rope's weight will lock off the abseil device but conversely it will have to be fed round the body and into the brake to descend. This works less well near the bottom of the rope when there is insufficient weight to lock off effectively. This method is particularly handy if a lot of stops have to be made on the way down the abseil.

An abseil can also be safeguarded by a person at the bottom if he holds the rope and applies tension should anything go wrong. This tension can be used to lock off the brake or even control the rate of descent; the method does not work with the classic abseil, however. If you wish to stop for some time on the way down, your position can be maintained by wrapping the rope three or four times round the thigh (painful after a while) or locking off the brake as when belaying [*fig. 7.17*].

RETRIEVING THE ROPE

Retrieving the rope is probably the aspect of abseiling which can cause more problems than any other. The rope can refuse to move when pulled or, worse, move some distance and then jam. The best way to avoid this happening is careful preparation when setting up the abseil. Make sure that the rope is not binding against the rock near the anchor point and that the knot will clear the edge of any ledges. If an edge is sharp or cracked, it may be necessary to move the knot to below the possible obstruction and climb down to below it with the rope through the brake and locked off. Start the abseil proper when below the knot and the obstruction. Note carefully which rope to pull down and when abseiling keep the ropes separate. The first person down should test the ropes to ensure that they run before the last person starts his descent. If on the ground, move out as far as possible before pulling the rope and ensure that the rope going up is free from twists and kinks which can catch. Ropes which are twisted around each other can cause enough friction to make them immovable. As the rope comes free, watch out for the falling rope and any rocks that may be dislodged.

If the ropes jam and cannot be moved by normal methods, such as extra people pulling, a change of angle, or one person flicking the loose end while the other pulls, it may be necessary to go back up to sort them out. This can be done by ascending using prusiks tied round both ropes or climbing back up. Both ways can be safeguarded by tying into the ropes at regular intervals. Tie a figure-of-eight or a clove hitch in both ropes, clip it into your harness and climb to the first convenient stopping place. Tie another knot, clip into this, release the first knot and untie it and continue in this manner till the problem can be sorted out. If one end has pulled out of reach before jamming, climbing up protected by what rope is available is the only solution. Although the rope may not pull down, it could still come free if prusiked on.

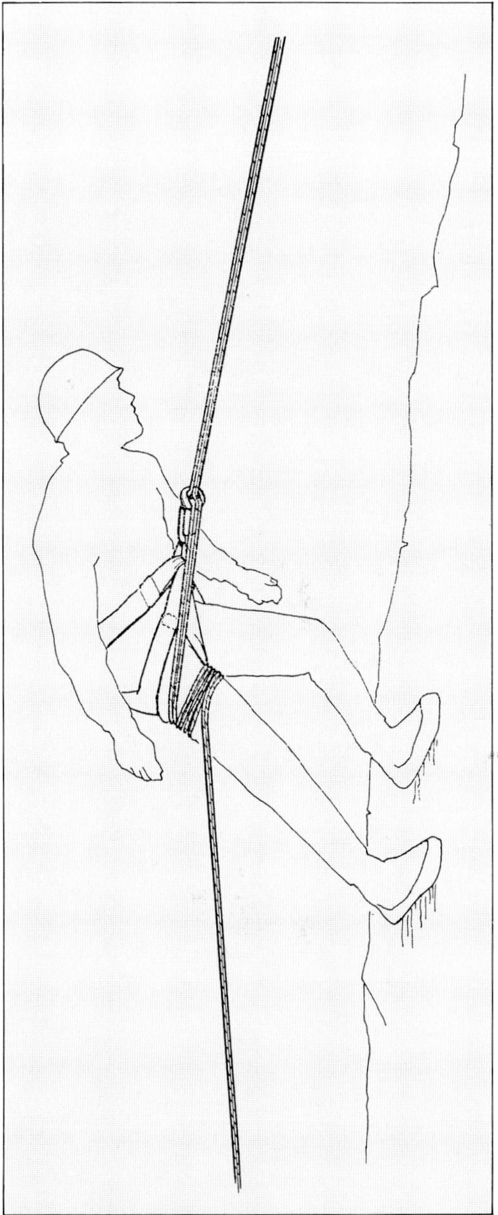

Fig 7.17 An abseil rope locked off by wrapping the rope round the thighs.

MULTI-PITCH ABSEILS

On long descents it is necessary to go from secure anchor to secure anchor and this is made easier by stances to work from. If the rock overhangs, the first person down, who will carry gear to set up the next abseil, can descend on a single rope and be protected with the other. As it can be difficult to start a swinging motion when hanging free, you may have to start this before you lose contact with the rock. Each time you touch the rock, push out and slide down so that the pendulum action eventually takes you in to the desired ledge. When the next person descends, he can be pulled in by the one already in place. If the rock overhangs considerably, placing runners to hold the rope in close to the cliff or down climbing may be necessary.

A diagonal movement may be needed on some descents to link up abseil points. This can be done by swinging back and forth or by locking off the brake and climbing sideways to reach the next point. All these actions put extra strain on the anchors and increase abrasion of the rope over edges and the chance of rocks being dislodged.

If a series of abseils is expected, it is worth carrying a length of tape and a knife to make slings rather than use up climbing gear. On multi-stage abseils the first person down takes the gear and sets up the next anchor, clipping into it before removing the locked-off brake from the abseil ropes. When the rope is pulled down, the lower end can be fed through the abseil sling so that the next abseil is partially set up when the ropes come free. This also decreases the chance of the ropes being accidentally dropped. If no ledges are available, hanging stances must be taken. This increases the fear factor but the system is the same. Each person at all times is either clipped into an anchor or a brake on the abseil rope.

When abseiling with a heavy pack, especially down steep rock, it is easy to become inverted because of the high centre of gravity. Using a chest harness clipped to the ropes prevents this.

Sometimes abseils must be done from anchors that are considered marginal at best and no amount of searching will produce anything better and safer. One slight help, if you are unlucky enough to find yourself in such a predicament, is to use friction from the rock to reduce the load on the anchor. Use as long a piece of sling or rope as you can spare and ensure that it runs over as much rock as possible. You may be able to do this with the rope rather than a separate sling but you might have difficulty in retrieving the rope after the abseil is over.

SIMULTANEOUS ABSEILS

Simultaneous or see-saw abseils may be used in certain places where there are no acceptable anchors. It can normally be used for only one pitch and must be down something which has a fairly flat top and two opposite sides such as a pinnacle, a sea stack or even some seracs. It can be done in two ways. Both climbers abseil carefully at the same speed down opposite sides of the feature using a rope draped across the top so that they can balance each other. Alternatively, one person abseils or is lowered while his partner uses his weight to augment a poor anchor. The first person down then anchors the end of the rope or uses his weight to allow his partner to abseil down the opposite side. Two sides are still needed with this second system but it allows the rope to be re-arranged once one person is down and it gets round the difficulties caused by two climbers of very different weights. Obviously a great deal of care has to be taken and it is used from necessity, not choice.

8 Ascending Techniques

A method of ascending a rope is something with which every climber should be familiar for a variety of reasons, particularly if attempting long and serious routes. It is even possible to fall off relatively easy climbs and end up hanging in space, and when crossing a glacier there is a chance of dangling on the end of the rope down a crevasse. These situations are not too difficult to deal with if a little time and effort has been spent practising the relevant techniques. The knots used are simple to tie and require little, if any, extra equipment. In fact, these sliding friction or prusik knots are also fundamental to all techniques of improvised and self-rescue.

However, rope ascending techniques are not limited to self-rescues but may be used as a matter of choice. Mechanical ascending devices are used to save time and energy when seconding a pitch on a long and technically demanding climb and on fixed ropes. The use of mechanical ascenders is also widespread in mountain-rescue. In all these cases the equipment required is carried specifically for the job and tailored to meet the needs of the user.

ASCENDING KNOTS

The original ascending knot, a sliding friction knot, was invented by the Austrian climber, Dr Karl Prusik, who gave it his name. But 'prusik knot' has come to be the generic name for all knots of this type and the ascending of ropes using them is often called 'prusiking'.

Prusik knots work on the principle of winding a thinner rope round a thicker one so that it will grip when loaded. They are usually tied in loops which are made from cord of a smaller diameter than the rope to be ascended. Prusik loops are generally of 5mm, 6mm or 7mm rope and from 0.5 to 1.5m in length. One factor which affects how well they grip the rope is their stiffness: loops of a soft construction generally grip best. If prusik loops are not available, slings, nuts on rope or tape, bootlaces or chalk-bag cord can be used instead. The condition of the main rope also affects how well prusiks work. On wet or muddy ropes the knots tend to tighten up and jam; on icy ropes they may slip. Most knots tighten up with use and it is necessary to slacken them off periodically to ensure that they slide easily.

As all these knots have slightly different properties, it is worth being familiar with a variety of them. When tying them, ensure that the knot used to form the loop is not included in the prusik knot. In most cases a karabiner can be incorporated in the knot to allow it to be slackened off more easily and provide a handle.

The Prusik Knot

In a prusik knot the loop is put behind the rope and then threaded through itself twice [*fig. 8.1*]. Ensure that the knot is kept symmetrical and that there is no overlapping of the turns, otherwise it will not grip properly. This knot is simple and effective and, with practice, can be tied with one hand. If the basic two-wrap prusik does not work well, an extra turn can be taken round the rope to form the slightly better three-wrap prusik knot [*fig. 8.2*]. However, both tend to jam easily, especially on wet or muddy ropes. A karabiner can be included in the knot by tying the loop round the rope and the back bar of the karabiner.

The Kleimheist

To tie a Kleimheist, wind the loop in a spiral down round the main rope, then pass the end back up through itself at the top [*fig. 8.3*]. The number of turns dictates the amount of friction and grip and three or more complete turns are usually required. The advantage of this knot is that it can be tied with any size of tape used for slings. A variation is the Zwangill knot, in which the ends are tied in a sheet bend. This is easier to loosen and less liable to jam.

The Kreuzklem

The Kreuzklem is the opposite of the Klemheist as the loop is wound up the rope and then threaded down through itself. Fewer turns are needed with this knot, so even the short slings on nuts can be used [*fig. 8.4*].

8.1a

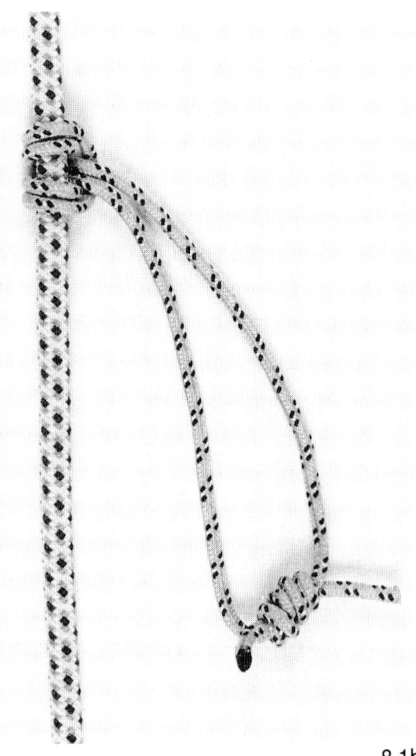

8.1b

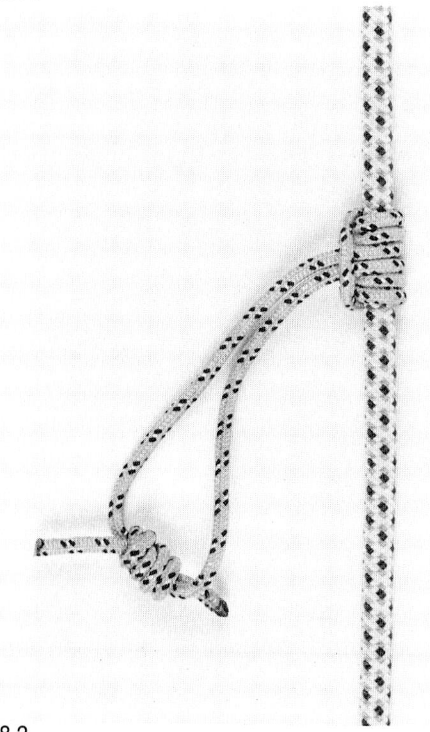

8.2

The French Prusik

An extremely useful knot, the French prusik is the only one which can usually be moved by hand when under tension. A short loop is wound in a spiral round the rope and the two end loops clipped into a karabiner [*fig. 8.5*]. Three turns or more are usually required but it is the length of unwrapped ends left before clipping together that affects how well this knot grips. The French prusik is best tied with a short loop, for if too long the knot opens out and stretches excessively when loaded. However, a long loop with a lot of turns releases more easily.

The Bachmann

In the Bachmann the loop is clipped to a karabiner and wound down in a neat spiral round the rope and the back bar. Three turns are usually sufficient, but more can be added. It is a good knot to use on wet and icy ropes and it slackens off quickly when unweighted [*fig. 8.6*].

The Alpine Clutch

Although not an ascending knot, the Alpine clutch is similar in some ways. Two karabiners, prefer-

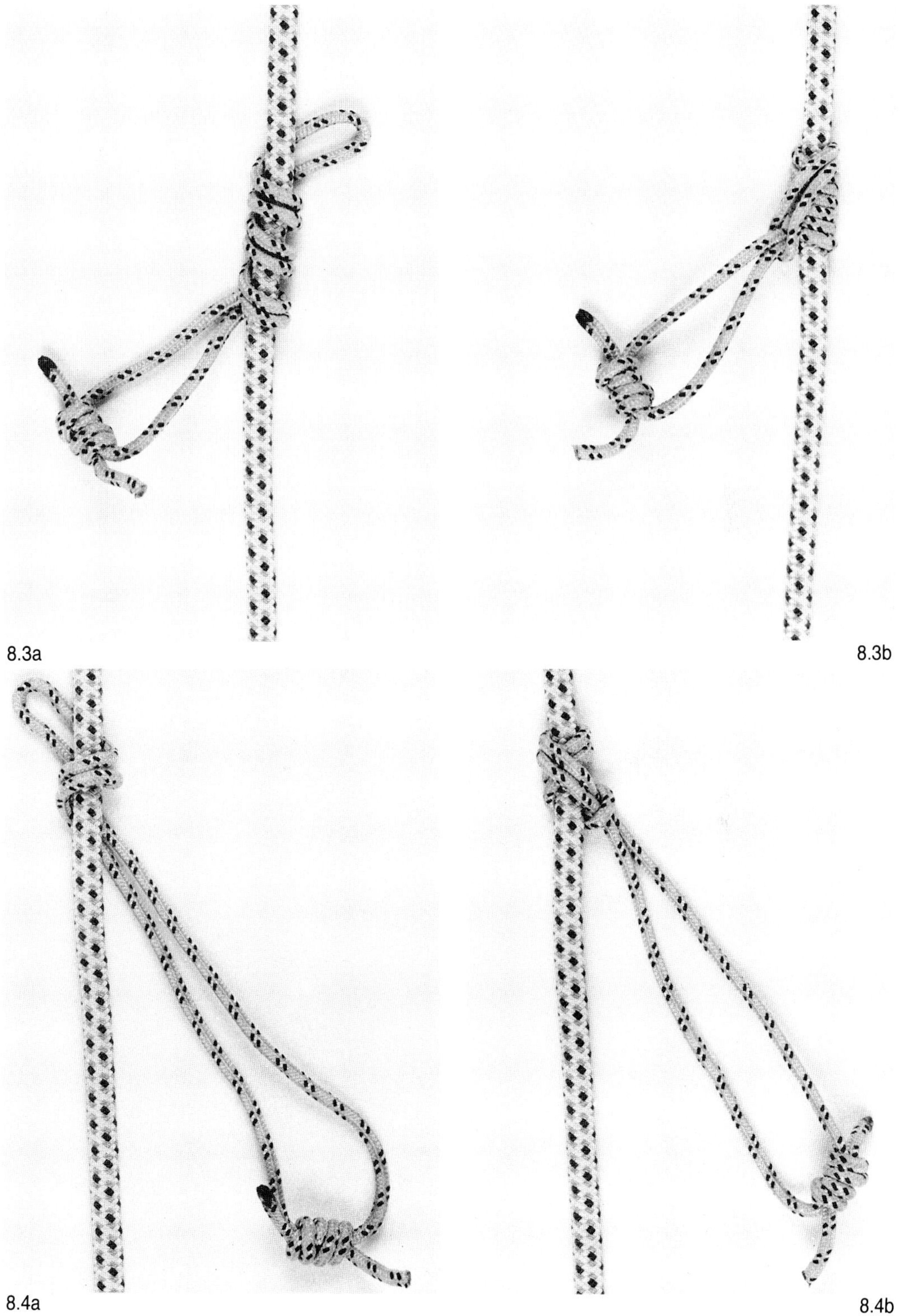

8.3a

8.3b

8.4a

8.4b

8.5a

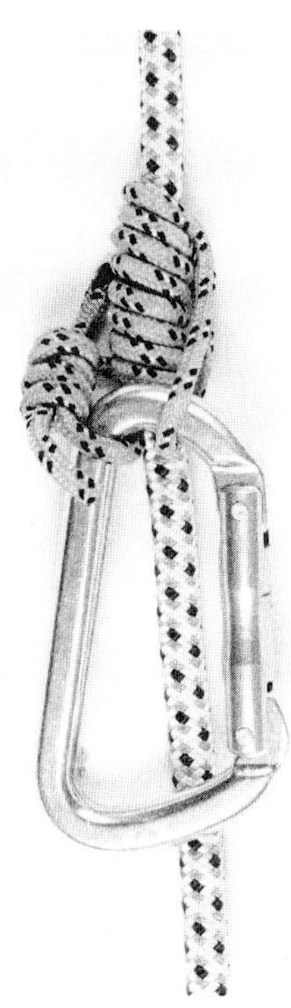

8.5b

ably identical, are used. The rope is clipped through both karabiners, under both and then clipped through the first again. When loaded, the rope is trapped between the karabiners [*fig. 8.7*]. This shape tends to change when the clutch is loaded and the ropes move up round the back bars of the karabiners. However, the rope can move through it in only one direction and it can be put only on to a slack rope. It can also invert and become useless unless the rope is kept under tension and bent through 180° at the clutch while it is moved.

ASCENDING THE ROPE

There are a number of possible situations in which the rope itself may have to be ascended. As a second you may not be able to climb a pitch because of injury, weather, darkness or difficulty. There are many instances in which a fall would, if long enough, leave you in space so that you would have to climb the rope to regain contact with the rock, and there is always the danger of falling into a crevasse when on glacial terrain.

There are several ways to ascend a rope but

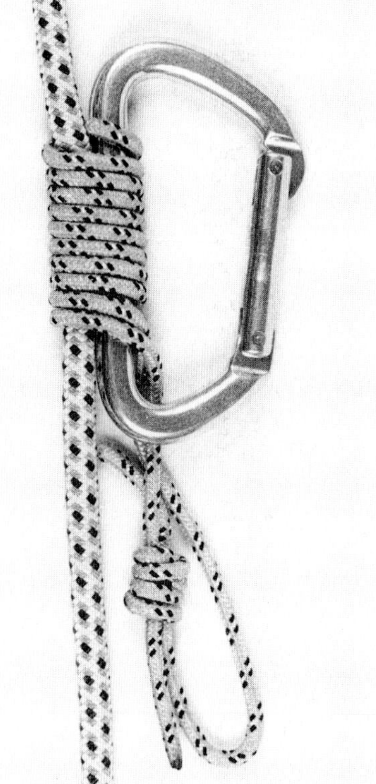

8.6

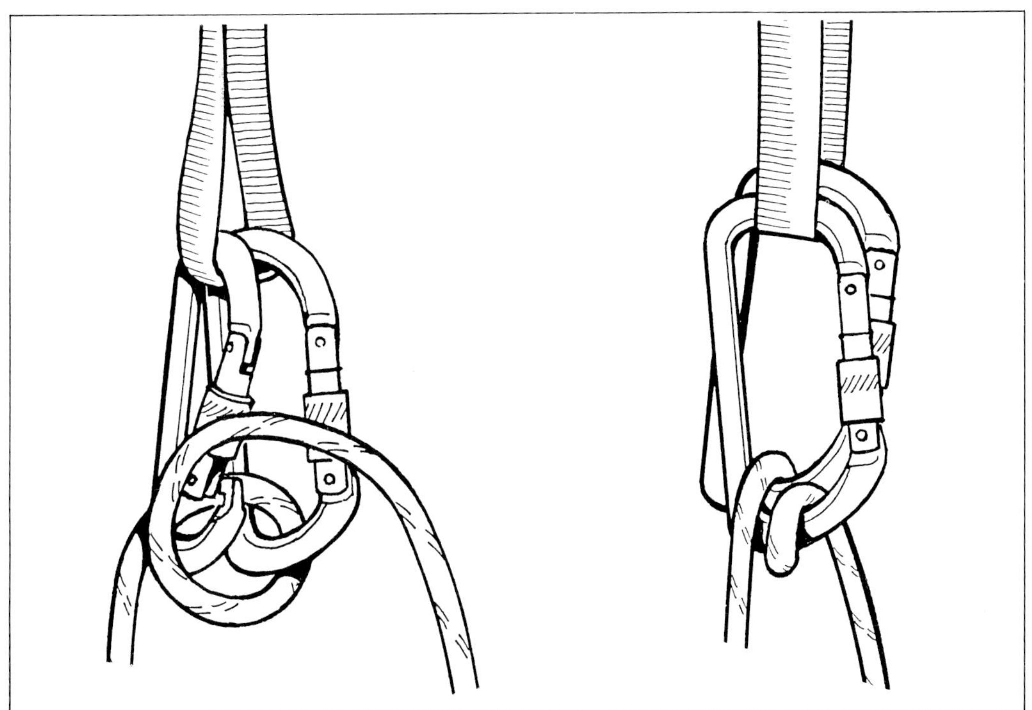

8.7

using two prusik loops, one to the harness and one to a foot, is simple and comfortable. A prusik loop is tied round the rope at about chest level and linked into the harness. If a harness is not worn, a sit sling must be improvised (see Chapter 9, page 141.) A second loop is tied to the rope below this and one or both feet put in it. The length of these loops can be altered by using slings, knotted if necessary, to obtain the best position. Stand up in the foot loop to unweight the upper loop and slide it up as far as it will go. Sit down on to this top loop to unweight the lower knot, move it up and repeat the process [*fig. 8.8*]. If the knots tighten up, they will have to be slackened off: this can often be done by putting the thumb against the loop of the knot and pushing it outwards. Because a prusik slides most easily on a taut rope, it may be necessary to hold the rope below the lower prusik to move it up. This becomes unnecessary once there is sufficient weight of rope hanging down below. Alternatively, the rope can be weighted by hanging a rucksack on the end or, if you are tied on to the end of the rope, weight the bight that forms as you prusik up the rope.

If the prusik to the harness is the higher of the two, when you stand up the seat prusik can be moved up at the same time; you can then sit in your harness and move up the lower one in comfort. The free rope below the prusiks can be trapped between the feet to provide tension while the lower prusik is being moved up. If the foot prusik is the higher of the two, more time must be spent hanging on your arms moving the harness prusik up.

There can be a problem when the rope runs hard against the rock as on the lip of an overhang. To move the knots up it is necessary to pull the rope clear of the rock with one hand or, better, to use the legs to push outwards. There may also be a tendency for the foot to slip out of its loop, especially when it is unweighted. This can be prevented by putting a lark's foot, an overhand slip knot, a clove hitch or extra turns round the foot. Some of these are painful when wearing rock boots.

The best safeguard when prusiking is a rope from above, but other back-ups are available. If using two ropes, you can prusik on one while protected, or even assisted, by the other. A slack sling can be clipped from the harness into the foot loop so that you are attached to both prusiks. As

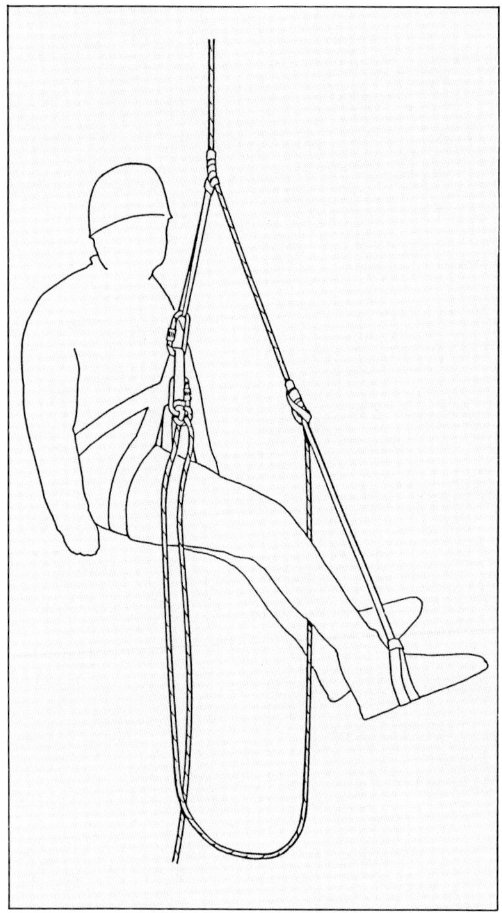

Fig 8.8 Ascending the rope using two prusik loops, in this case tape slings tied with a klemheist. The lower loop is fastened round the foot with a lark's foot to prevent it slipping off, and the rope is clove hitched into a locking karabiner on the harness as a safety precaution.

you ascend, a series of knots can be used to limit the length of a potential fall should a prusik fail. Figure-of-eight knots or clove hitches are tied in the slack rope and attached to the harness. Another knot is tied every 5m or so, attached to the harness and the first knot untied or the clove hitch adjusted. If prusiks do start to slide down the rope, there is a good chance that they will fail as a result of friction melting the loop.

As prusiking up a rope can be tiring, it is important to be efficient. Knots that are too tight and loops of the wrong length are two common reasons for problems, easily combated by having practised these techniques in a safe, controlled situation. As with any form of climbing, it should be the legs which do most of the work. If the rope is not hanging free, it is possible to brace one leg against the rock to help stability. When standing up in the foot loop, it is best if the upper knot is moved up at the same time: this reduces the time spent hanging on the arms. The optimum step up is with the knee bent at about right angles. Taking too-high steps results in leaning backwards and so more work for the arms. On a steep prusik there is a tendency to tip backwards, especially when wearing a rucksack. The foot loop, if long enough, can be put down through the harness to keep you closer in to the rope; a karabiner clipped into your harness and round the rope also helps maintain a more upright position. A chest harness, such as the Parisien Baudrier (see Chapter 9, page 141), clipped on to the rope is even better. An alternative is a sling attached to the hauling loop on the rucksack, taken over one shoulder and clipped on to the rope. This allows the rucksack to be used as a back rest. The rucksack can also be hung from the harness so that its weight does not tip you over backwards, or hung on the rope and pulled up afterwards.

If only one prusik is available, it is still possible to ascend the rope. The prusik is attached to the harness as before and the slack rope fastened round one foot by several turns or a clove hitch. Stand up in this and raise the prusik, sit back in the harness and re-tie the foot when in a higher position.

In an emergency any cord, such as nylon bootlaces, will serve as a prusik loop. A belay plate can also be used but it must be the lower of the two prusiks as it can only be moved up a slack rope. It may also have to be held to stop it sliding down when weighted, but this depends on the weight of rope below. Two karabiners can be used as an Alpine clutch. Again, they must be the lower point as they can only be moved up an untensioned rope. The karabiners are clipped through a number of strands of bootlace and then the clutch formed round them. This is a very comfortable and convenient method, but as the clutch runs only one way, it is awkward if you need to descend.

In an emergency anything will do as a prusik. Even a few karabiners, a wire nut and some imagination can be used to ascend a rope!

If no harness is worn, three prusik loops can be used, one for each foot and one under the arms and round the back. This is the traditional method, but it is neither very safe nor comfortable.

MECHANICAL ASCENDERS

Mechanical ascenders, also known simply as ascenders or as clamps, jammers, juggers or prusikers, besides their trade names, do the same job as prusik knots but in a more convenient way. They move freely up the rope but grip it when loaded. They seldom jam, can be removed and replaced very quickly and work on the normal range of rope diameters used in climbing. This form of ascending is often known as 'jumaring' after the Jumar clamp, the first popular ascender, which made its appearance in the 1950s and became a world favourite over the next two decades.

There are several kinds of ascender but all use the same principle, that of a cam which traps the rope against the main body of the device when loaded in the correct direction. There are two main types: those where the load is taken on the body of the ascender and a spring-loaded cam and those where the load is applied to a pivoting cam by a lever action [*fig. 8.9*]. The first type is the one most commonly used by climbers.

The spring-cam type of ascenders work by trapping the rope with the cam in a U-shaped channel. The face of the cam has a set of small, downward-pointing teeth or ridges which grip the sheath when initially loaded and this causes the cam to turn and compress the rope between the cam and the back of the channel. A safety catch prevents the rope from releasing accidentally and in some models acts as a handle to hold the cam open when you are attaching it to the rope. The body is usually formed from a bent aluminium alloy plate (though some are cast) and there are karabiner holes at the bottom and the top [*fig. 8.10*]. The cast types are fairly brittle and susceptible to damage by dropping or sudden loading and should be reinforced with nylon tape, taking in all the relevant parts of the frame. These tape loops are then used as the attachment point [*fig. 8.11*]. In a pair of clamps, one will be right- and one left-

Fig 8.9 A small selection of mechanical ascenders (from the top): a simple, lightweight ascender, a handled ascender, a Jumar and a lever cam ascender which has the advantage that it will work on a double rope.

handed. Some makes are colour coded but, when on the rope, the open side should face the user and away from the rock so that the cams and safety trigger are protected. Those which have a handle give better protection to the hands, especially where the rope runs against the rock. Some have no handle and use a karabiner through the attachment hole as the safety catch. This type is less convenient and can be dangerous in some situations if the clamp has to be removed from the rope and the user, but it is more useful as emergency or rescue equipment when its small size and weight is an advantage.

Many clamps are prone to slipping on icy or muddy ropes because the teeth clog up. If this happens, the teeth should be cleaned with a small, sharp implement or a stiff brush carried for the

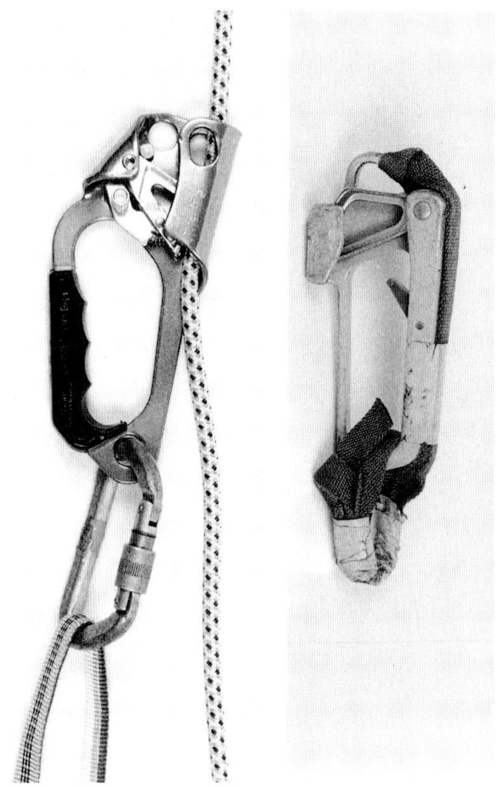

Fig 8.10 ABOVE LEFT: *A left-handed handled ascender of the spring-loaded cam type in place on a rope.*

Fig 8.11 ABOVE RIGHT: *A Jumar taped up for use in case of breakage of any part of the cast body. This is a right-handed ascender: the safety catch is the plastic lever under the toothed cam.*

purpose. (Lever cam ascenders, however, do not slip under these conditions as they have no teeth to clog up.) Unfortunately, because the teeth penetrate the rope's sheath, extensive use can damage the rope and tend to make the sheath creep over the core. There is also a danger of the sheath getting cut and sliding down the core with the clamp still attached, especially if the clamp is shock-loaded such as by a fall on to it. Most mechanical ascenders, though, do not work on double ropes while prusik knots will and most clamps cannot be released under load.

Using Ascenders

If a lot of jumaring is to be done, such as in big wall climbing, it is important to have your equipment correctly adjusted. Setting up is best done on a free-hanging rope and, if the angle to be ascended is not vertical then the system can be altered by adding or removing loops or karabiners. Various different systems are possible using two or three clamps attached to the feet, knees, waist or chest, but the majority are more applicable to long, free ascents most commonly found in caving. Anyone wishing to explore the intricacies of rope ascending is advised to turn to caving literature for this information.

The most efficient way to ascend a rope is to use the powerful leg muscles and direct this effort in a downwards direction. In other words, keep the body as near to the vertical as possible. The same stand-and-sit system of movement used with prusik loops can be used with one clamp to the harness and one to a foot. In this case the foot clamp can be put on the rope above the harness clamp; again, the upper sling can be taken through the harness. This method allows the harness clamp to be moved up at the same time as you stand up in the foot loop.

Another method uses two clamps, a pair of etrier or specially tied foot loops and some slings and locking karabiners. The clamps are attached to the rope, one about face and the other at chest level, and the etrier attached to them. When both feet are at the same level, one foot goes in the bottom rung of the etrier attached to the top clamp and the other foot in the middle rung of the lower etrier on the lower clamp. This means that the clamps are one rung length apart. The harness is attached to both clamps as a safeguard. Daisy chains or specially tied slings are used for this, the length between the top clamp and the harness being critical. The correct length is when the top foot and clamp are stepped up the optimum height: it should be possible to sit in the harness with minimal loss of height. The loop to the harness should then come tight at full arm's stretch. If the sling is too long, energy is wasted; if it is too short, too little height is gained with each step. To ascend, one clamp is pushed up at the same time as the appropriate foot is raised, and when the weight is transferred the other foot and clamp are raised. This system is really only suitable for rock which is vertical or less as the feet must be pushed against the rock for balance, but this quickly wears out the toes of your boots. However, by varying the length of the attachments to the clamps, it is possible to change from one system to the other as the angle of the rock changes. It is best if you are clipped into both clamps for safety and convenience.

It may be necessary to hold or weight the rope initially to slide up the lower clamp until there is enough tension in the rope to allow it to move up freely. Alternatively, the cam can be pushed down with the thumb so that the clamp lifts smoothly. When starting off on a long ascent, the first few moves will simply take the stretch out of the rope and getting going is often the hardest part as the rope bounces up and down. Stepping off a ledge to begin a jumar can result in a frightening drop as the rope elongates. This bouncing motion set up when ascending a rope can abrade it where it runs against any projections.

To stop the feet coming out of the étrier, a rubber band made from old tyre inner tube can be put round the ankle and used to hold the étrier in place. Thin, fingerless, leather gloves can save wear and tear on the hands. A chest harness can be clipped into the top clamp to help you maintain a more upright position, but this does tend to make things more cluttered. Again, extra security can be obtained by tying a knot in the rope below and clipping it into the harness at regular intervals.

It is also possible to descend using an ascender. The clamp must be unweighted before it will move, but in this case it must be raised slightly to disengage the teeth on the cam. The cam is then held open with the thumb while the clamp is moved down to the new position. The safety catch should not be released while doing this.

Because the clamp must be raised fractionally to be loosened, it is vital that it is never pushed hard up against an obstruction such as a knot, karabiner or another clamp. If it cannot be lifted, it cannot be removed from the rope or moved down.

9 Emergency Procedures

In climbing there is usually some element of risk: the bigger the climb, the greater that risk is likely to be. However, with foresight, planning and experience it can usually be kept at an acceptable level. Unfortunately, the unexpected can happen and you may then have to extricate yourself, your partner or someone else from a difficult situation. Most climbers will never have to deal with any sort of improvised rescue, but it is always better to be prepared than otherwise.

In climbing every situation is unique and every emergency different. For this reason it is better to be familiar with the various components which can be put together to solve a particular problem rather than learn set pieces. Know the building blocks of techniques, then construct the solution from these. If something goes wrong, you must work out exactly what the problem is, what will solve it and how this can be achieved. Sometimes this must be done under pressure of time and/or lack of equipment, and usually under the pressure of having to deal with the unfamiliar. The ability to think clearly, logically and imaginatively is the key to sorting out problems. Before each stage of your solution, run your eye along the rope, note all the attachments to it and ask yourself the question 'What will happen if ...?' before doing or undoing anything. Look at each link in the chain and, if its failure would be disastrous, back it up.

Nothing that is needed to effect some sort of self-rescue is particularly complex and the techniques often have other uses. No specialised equipment is necessary, although a small pulley can lessen the effort required. The pulley should be light, big enough to take the rope being used and capable of being put on that rope at any point.

The techniques covered here are broken down into improvisation, locking off, escaping from the system, lowering and hoisting. These can cover everything from making do when you forget your harness to having an unconscious partner hanging free on the end of the rope many pitches up a long route. Having the means and ability to belay, abseil and tie and use prusik knots is common to most of the techniques. If practising them, it is best to have a knife with you in case things do not work out as planned. Sometimes being able to cut a prusik, a sling or even a rope is the easiest, quickest and safest way out of difficulties. Any improvised rescue can present you with the unexpected and it is dealing with this that is the key to emergency procedures.

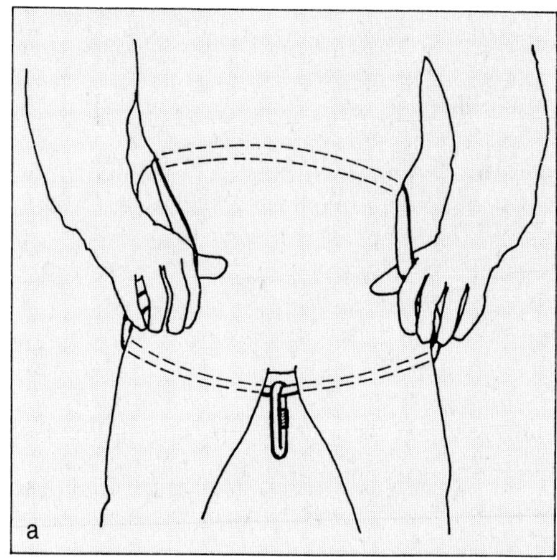

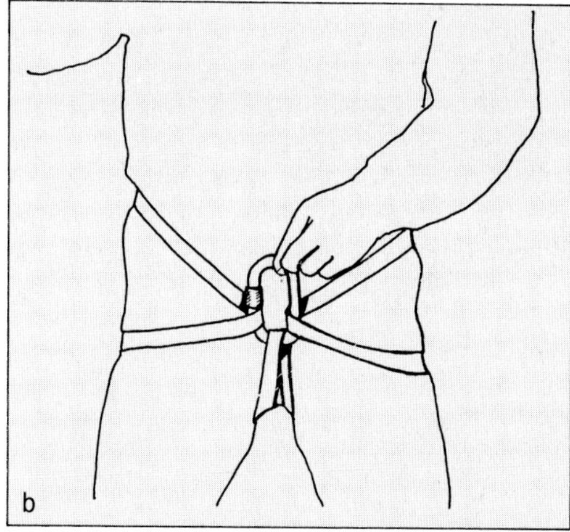

Fig 9.1 Making a sit sling from a double sling:
(a) Hold the sling on either side of the hips and let a third loop hang between the legs.
(b) Clip all three loops together with a locking karabiner or back-to-back karabiners.

IMPROVISED HARNESSES

Improvised harnesses can be made in a variety of ways but the simplest and most useful are made from slings.

Sit Sling

To make a sit sling or Dulfer seat, use a double sling. Hold the sling round your back with a loop to each side. Take another loop up between your legs and clip all three loops together at the front using a locking karabiner or back-to-back karabiners [*fig. 9.1*]. This can be clipped into the waist belt or rope for extra security. The knot or join in the tape is best put at the back of the waist where it is out of the way and less uncomfortable. If a double sling is not available, a short sling can be formed into a figure-of-eight shape and one leg put through each loop; it can then be attached to the waist.

Chest Sling

Also known as a Parisien Baudrier, a chest sling is made with a double sling. Put an arm through the sling, take it round your back and tie the two loops together with a sheet bend [*fig. 9.2*]. Ensure that this is tied correctly so that none of the strands of the knot can move to form a slip knot, which is dangerous. The loop left is used as an attachment point.

Full Harness

Full harness is a combination of the sit and chest slings. The rope is attached to the sit sling and the chest sling connected to the rope by a prusik loop which can be adjusted to give the best point of suspension. Alternatively, tie the chest sling with a longer sling and clip this into the sit sling. This loop is then tensioned up and tied in an overhand knot at the top and used as the suspension point. Various other methods are possible, depending on the gear available: the important points to look for are that there are no slip knots which can tighten up and the weight is mostly on the sit sling with the chest harness providing support. The standard double sling may be a little small for tying a sit sling or a chest harness on a large person or someone wearing a lot of clothes.

If only the rope is available, a sit sling and chest

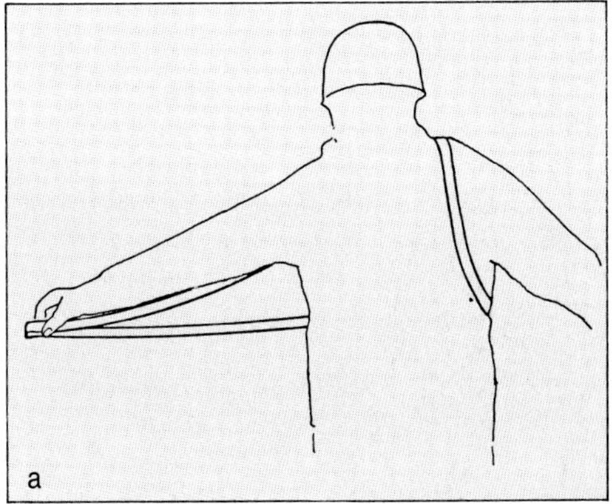

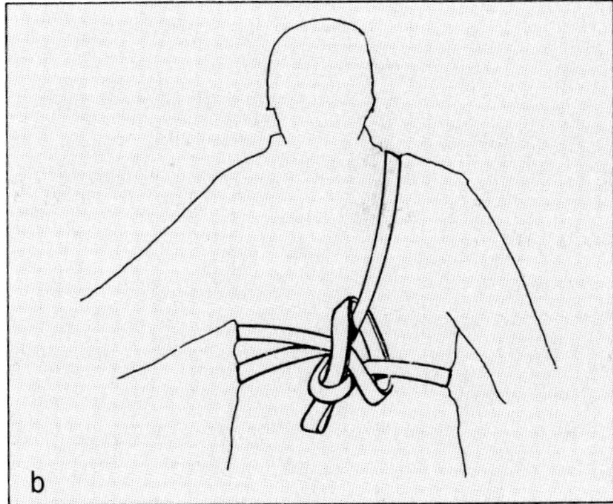

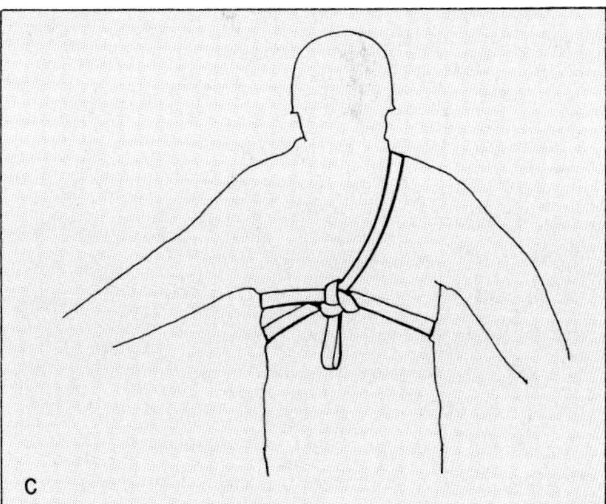

Fig 9.2 Tying a chest harness from a double sling:
(a) Put one arm through the sling and take it behind the back.
(b) Tie the two loops together using a sheet bend.
(c) Work the knot firm and ensure that no part of the harness can slide. The loop left can be used as the attachment point.

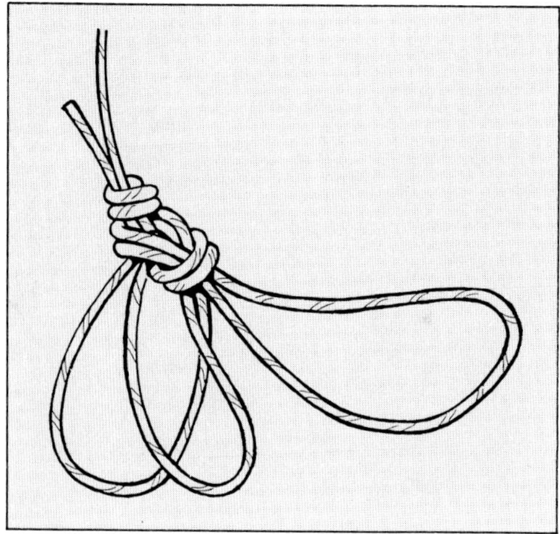

Fig 9.3 A triple bowline tied in the end of the rope.

harness can be made by cutting the required amount off the end of the rope. Alternatively, a triple bowline can be tied in the end of the rope. Form a bight from about 4m of rope, tie a bowline in this to give three loops of about equal length and finish the single end with a stopper knot [*fig. 9.3*]. Put this on with one loop round each thigh and the other round the waist or over the shoulder – the last method is the best as it puts the suspension point, the knot, above your centre of gravity. Like any improvised harness, this is not suitable for leading but will do for lowering or hoisting a climber [*fig. 9.4*].

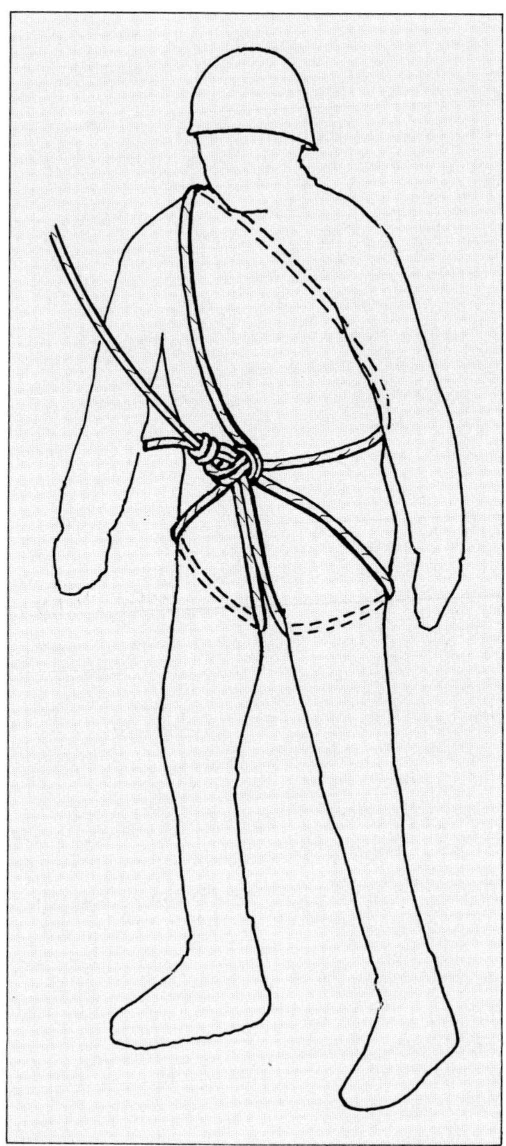

Fig 9.4 A triple bowline put on a climber with one loop round each thigh and the third loop round the shoulder.

HANGING FREE

If you fall off and end up hanging in space, the severity of the situation depends on the type of tie-on arrangement you are using. With a seat or body harness there is usually no real urgency; if you are on a waist belt, there is only limited time before you pass out and suffocate. In the latter instance the weight must be taken off the waist quickly and, if you cannot regain the rock or be lowered to safety, you have to do this yourself. The first and quickest thing to do is to turn upside-down so that your weight is taken on your hips which, although uncomfortable, is safer than hanging on your waist – provided, of course, that the belt is tight enough and you cannot slip out of it in this position.

There are several more satisfactory solutions to the problem. A double sling or a chain of shorter slings can be clipped on to the rope and stood in. The sling should be just shorter than the distance between the rope and the feet but it can be clipped into the belt, the knot loop, above the knot or attached to the rope with a lark's foot [*fig. 9.5*].

Alternatively, the double sling can be put on as a sit sling and attached to the rope. To do this,

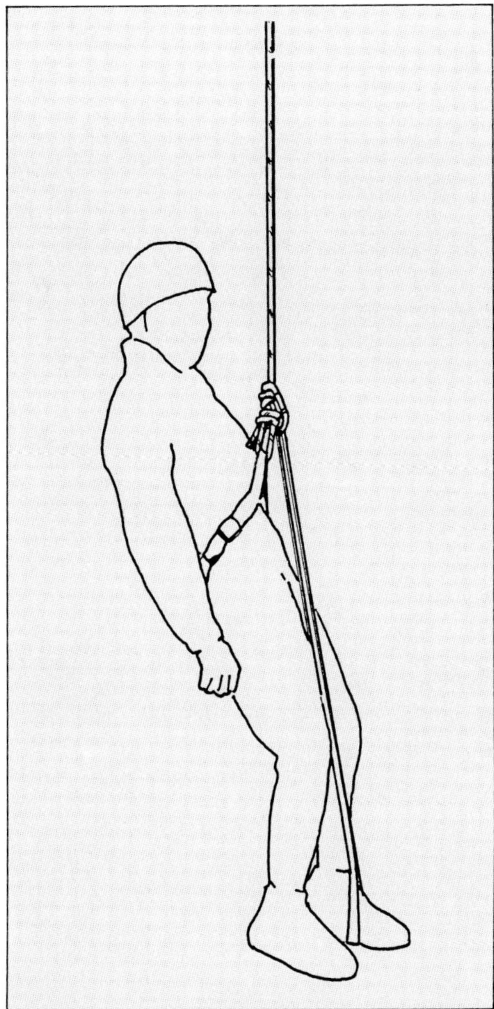

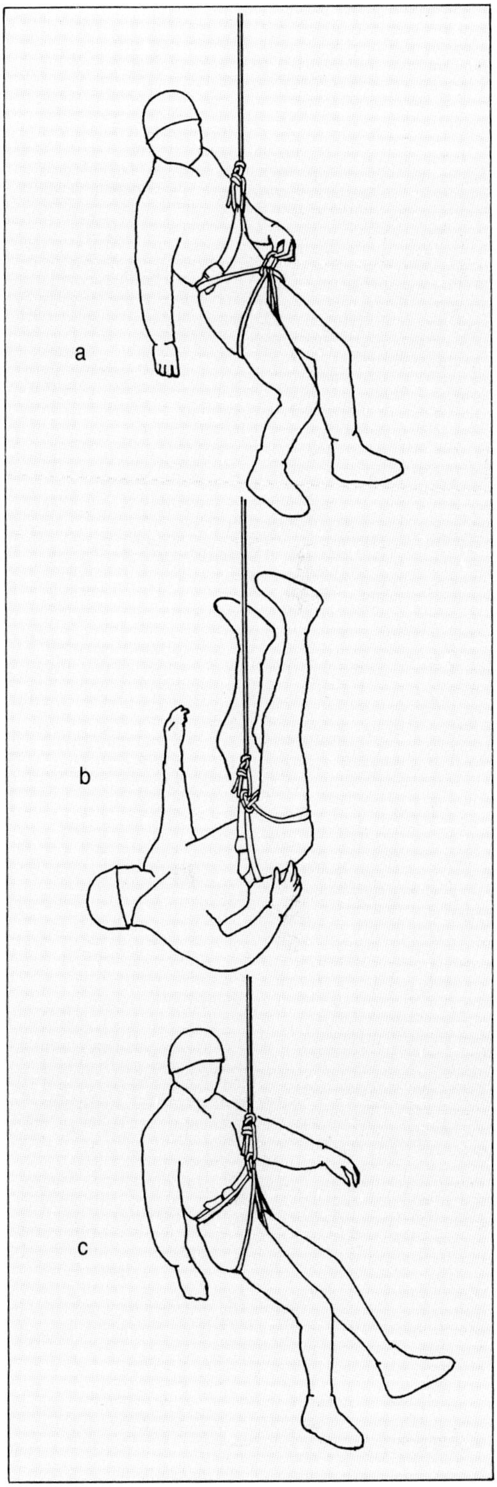

Fig 9.5 ABOVE: *If you are hanging free, the weight can be taken off the waist by standing in a sling, in this case clipped on to the rope above the knot.*

Fig 9.6 RIGHT: *Taking the weight off the waist in a free-hanging position:*
(a) Put on a sit sling.
(b) Turn upside-down and clip the karabiner into the knot loop.
(c) Turn the right way up again and your weight should then be on the sling rather than your waist.

turn upside-down and clip the karabiner into the knot loop or on to the rope above the knot. Turn back up the correct way and your weight will then be on the sit sling and you will be in a good position to start self-rescue [*fig. 9.6*]. If a prusik is

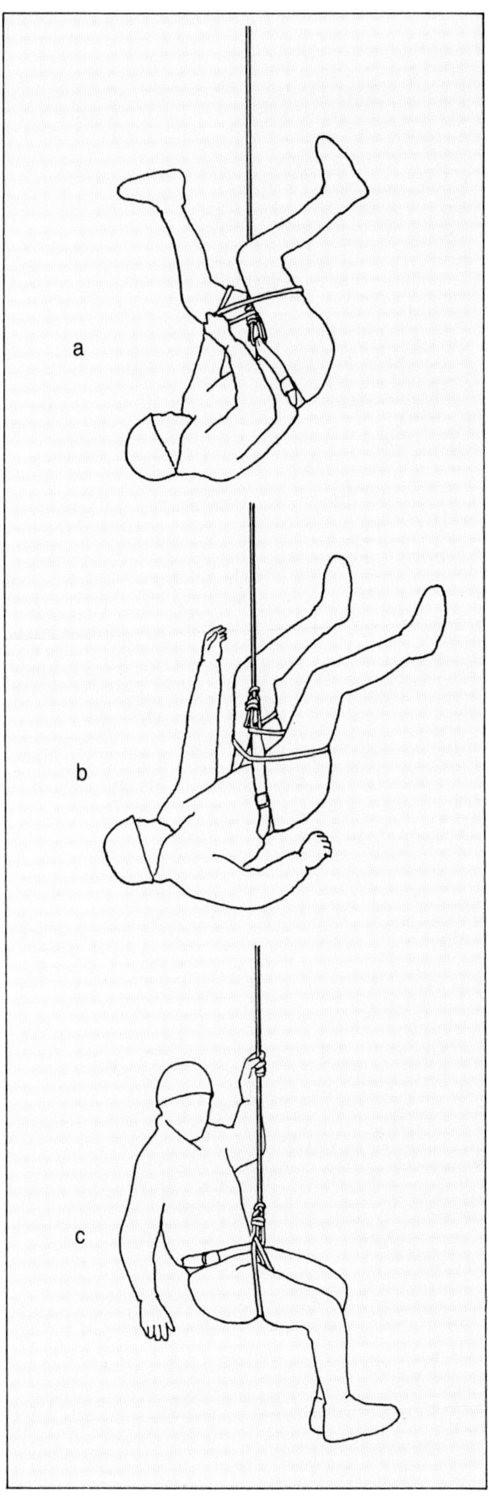

available, it can be put on the rope so that you can stand in it. The sit sling can then be clipped into that or another prusik loop and when the weight is off your waist you are in a position to start to ascend the rope.

If you have only a short sling, you have to use the baboon hang. Turn upside-down, put one leg on either side of the rope, put the sling over the legs and under the top of the thighs and then turn the right way up again. The rope will now run under the sling and up to the waist. This is very painful after only a short time [*fig. 9.7*].

LOCKING OFF

There are occasions during belaying, abseiling or lowering when it is necessary to lock off the rope while it is still under tension in order to free both hands. With any form of belay, lower or abseil this can be done by wrapping the rope three or four times round the thigh. The rope can also be stood on for extra security.

There are a variety of ways to lock off when using a belay plate, friction hitch or descender. These methods utilise a hitch which can be tied or untied while there is a load on the live rope. With a belay plate or descender, the dead rope is held in the braking position and a short bight of rope is pushed through the karabiner [*fig. 9.8a*]. A longer bight of rope is then taken from the other side of the karabiner and put through the short bight which traps it as the hand is taken off the rope [*fig. 9.8b*]. A further half-hitch is then tied round the karabiner for extra security [*fig. 9.8c*]. Ideally this hitch should be tied round the back bar of the locking karabiner, but if the gate is well

Fig 9.7 Using the baboon hang when hanging from the waist by a simple waist belt:
(a) Turn upside down, put one leg either side of the rope and put a short sling round both legs.
(b) Work the sling up round the thighs.
(c) Turn upright again and the rope will run under the short sling and up to the waist.

Fig 9.8 OPPOSITE PAGE: *Locking off a belay plate:*
(a) In the braking position a short bight of rope is pushed through the karabiner.
(b) A longer bight is taken through this and trapped by it.
(c) A half-hitch is tied next to it for extra security.

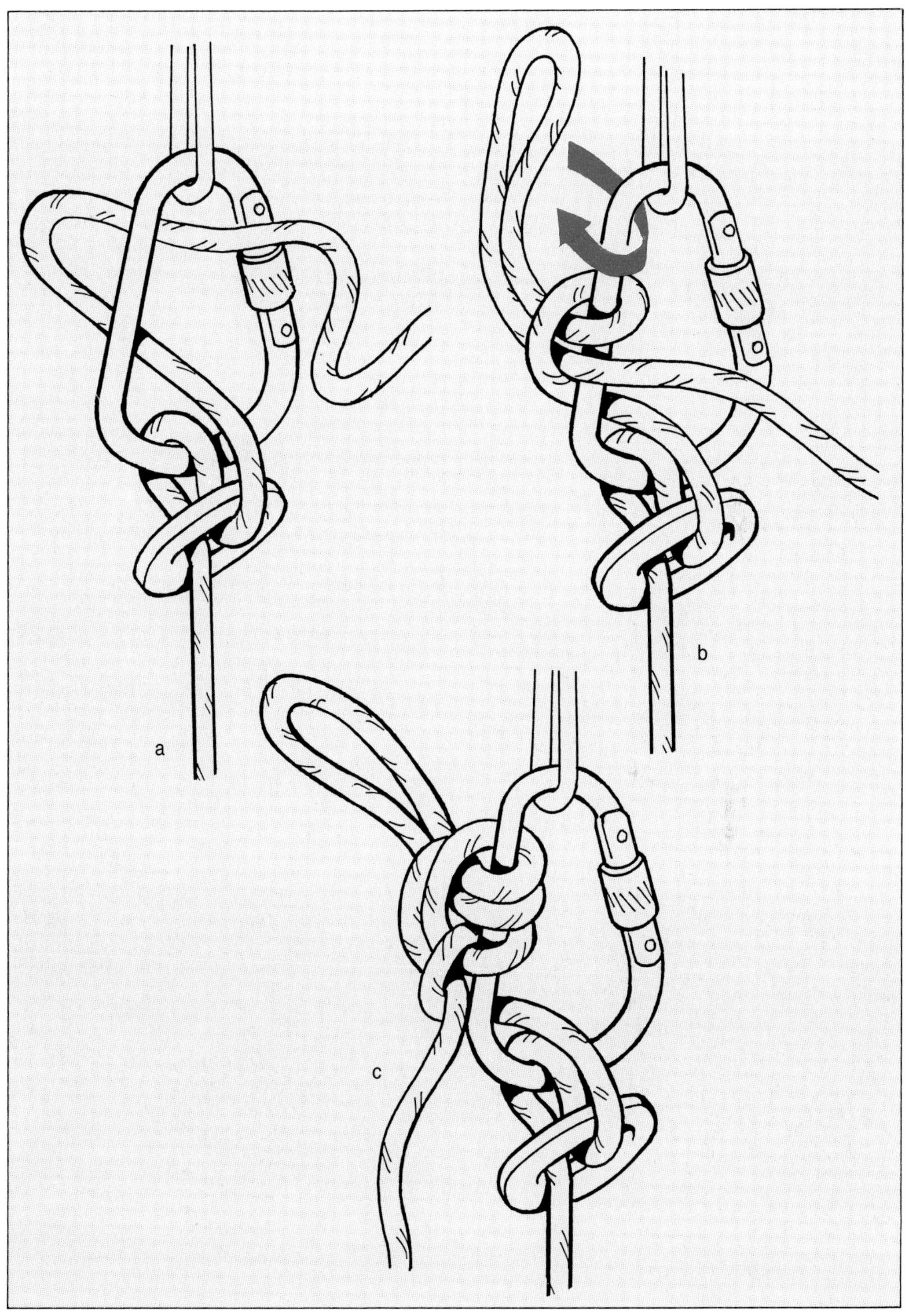
a
b
c

secured either side can be used. It is the way in which the rope is held that locks the device, rather than the strength of the knot. The advantage of this system is that it can be released under load. Untie the second hitch, then pull the free end of the long bight out. As this is pulled out behind the device, it is in the locked position, there is no jerk and the rope will not run accidentally.

When utilising the friction hitch, the same knot is used but it is tied round the load rope, again in the braking position [*fig. 9.9*].

With a belay plate an alternative is to tie an overhand slip knot in the dead rope and let this jam against the front of the plate. This is easy to do but can be difficult to release, especially if there are any twists in the bight that forms the knot. It can also give a jerk on the rope when released. To make a rope safe any large knot can be tied in the dead rope in front of the plate, but this can create problems if it is then loaded.

A figure-of-eight descender can be locked off by crossing the dead rope over between the load rope and the descender [*fig. 9.10*]. However, to do this means taking the dead rope into the running position, where slippage can occur. It may also require some strength to free it, which can cause a jerk on the rope. This cross-over still needs to be backed up as it can slip.

ESCAPING FROM THE SYSTEM

Escaping from the system involves untying yourself from the belay system and the rope while it is under tension. This may have to be done for a variety of reasons, such as having an injured climber hanging on the rope who cannot be lowered to safety and to whom you have to administer first aid or get assistance or organise his rescue. Escaping from the system depends on

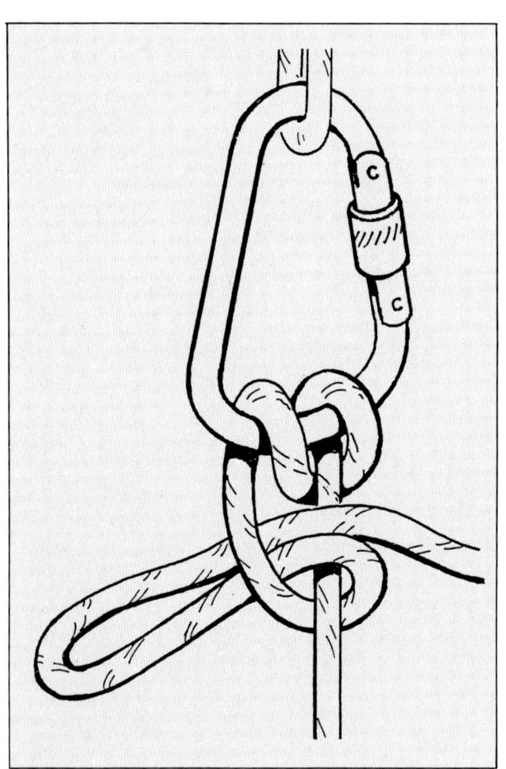

Fig 9.9 A locked-off friction hitch. A further half-hitch should be tied to ensure that it cannot accidentally come out.

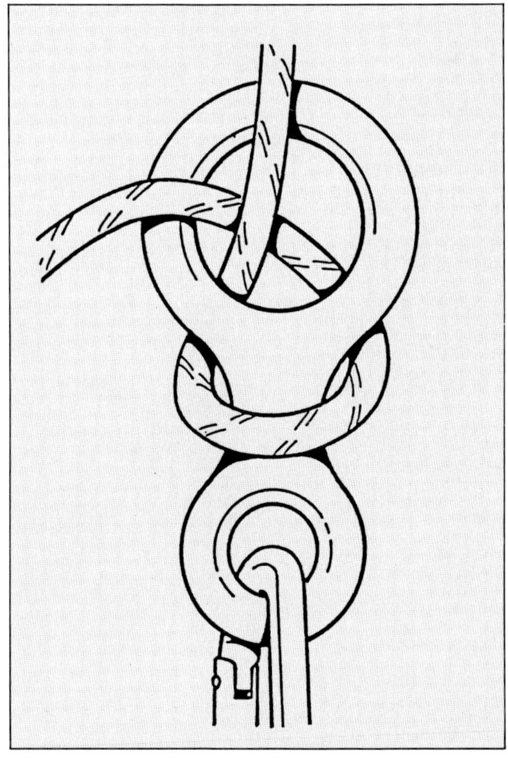

Fig 9.10 A figure-of-eight descender locked off by crossing the braking rope behind the load rope. This still requires further securing as it can slip.

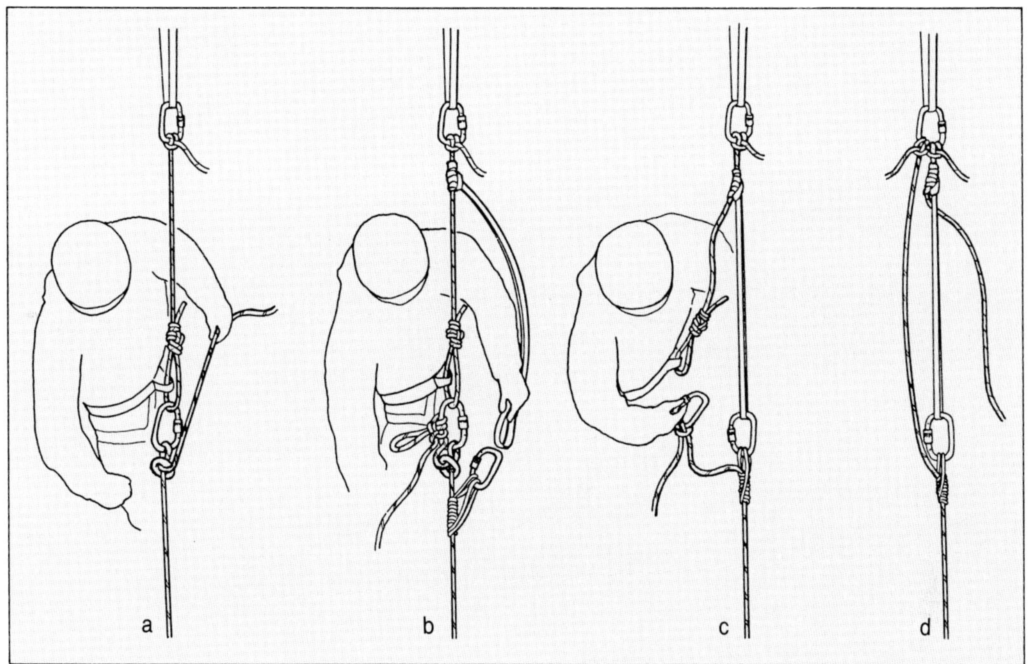

Fig 9.11 Escaping from the system where the belayer is attached to a single anchor with a clove hitch:
(a) The weight is held on the belay plate clipped into the knot loop.
(b) The belay plate is locked off and a French prusik attached to the load rope. As the belayer cannot reach the anchor, another prusik is attached to the rope to the anchor and the two clipped together.
(c) The French prusik is pushed down and the lock-off taken out so that the weight can be lowered on to the prusiks. The belay plate and karabiner can be taken off either before or after the rope is backed up to the anchor.
(d) The rope is clove hitched to the anchor as a back-up and the belayer can untie and escape from the system. To free the belayer's end of the rope, the French prusik can be pulled up the rope to put the load on to the rope back-up and so the end can be released.

the nature of the belay and other factors, but once the basic method is known other complications can be worked out.

The first step is to lock off the belay device to free both hands. Then attach a prusik, preferably a French prusik, to the loaded rope and clip the other end of it back into an anchor. If an anchor cannot be reached, put another prusik round the rope or ropes between yourself and the anchors and link the prusik on the loaded rope into this. Slide the prusik down the rope until it is tight, then release the lock-off and lower the victim until his weight comes on the prusik and so on the anchor. The belayer and the belay device are now by-passed by this prusik arrangement. Clip the main rope back into the anchor using a figure-of-eight, a clove hitch or a locked-off friction hitch as a back-up in case the prusik fails, then take the rope out of the belay device. You can now untie from the rope and so escape from the belay system [*fig. 9.11*].

Take care that the prusik on the load rope cannot foul anything such as an edge when the weight is lowered on to it. If you clipped the first prusik directly back into an anchor, part of the rope is now free for you to use for abseiling down to the victim or arranging a hoisting system. If you could not reach an anchor and used a second prusik, the weight has to be transferred back to the anchor by pushing or pulling the lower French prusik up the rope. With the load on the rope direct to the anchor, your part of the rope can be made available for other uses. In this situation a locked-off friction hitch is the best knot to use as a back-up because it can easily be released.

With some harnesses, when using a semi-direct belay, it is possible to escape from the system by locking off the belay device and then detaching yourself from the harness. The belay device must be attached to the knot loop if this is to be done.

Fig 9.12 The mariner knot tied in a long prusik loop which is attached to a loaded rope by a prusik knot. The mariner knot is formed by wrapping the loop three times round the karabiner and three times round itself and finished by tucking a bight between the strands.

LOWERING

The techniques of lowering are, in the main, the same as for belaying or abseiling. A body belay, descender, belay plate, friction hitch or karabiner brake can be used, but some methods tend to twist the rope, especially if one end is fixed and the twists cannot escape. The easiest way to lower is from a direct belay with the operator on a separate anchor point and holding the rope in a body belay. This provides a back-up and extra friction if required. The operator must always be in a position to brake or lock the device if necessary. This means that if using a belay plate or a descender the operator must be above the lowering point and if using a friction hitch he must be below it.

If a lower using two or more ropes has to be carried out, the knots joining them will have to by-pass the lowering system in a safe manner. The lower should be stopped about 10cm before the knot reaches the brake. The rope is then locked off in some simple way, such as by being held in a body belay, wrapped round the thigh and stood on. A prusik is put on the lowering rope below the brake and attached to an anchor. This is done using a mariner knot which can be released under load: it is tied with a sling or length of thinner rope which is wrapped three times round the karabiner then three or four times round itself, and finished with a bight tucked between the two strands [*fig. 9.12*]. The mariner is often tied with a long length of thin rope rather than a loop as this removes the chance of the knot joining the loop getting snagged up when you are lowering with it. The prusik is then pushed tight down the rope and a little more rope is let through so that the weight comes on to the prusik [*fig. 9.13a*]. The rope is then removed from the brake and replaced with the knot below it or, better, worked through the brake [*fig. 9.13b*]. The rope can be tied into an anchor as a back-up while this is being done. Then, with the rope held securely, the mariner knot is carefully undone and the friction it provides used to lower and transfer the weight back on to the rope so that the lower can continue.

A very good alternative to the mariner knot is a locked-off friction hitch which can be released under load. This can be tied in tape as well as rope slings. A French prusik, which can be worked up the rope, can also be used, but it must be far enough away from the brake to ensure that the load comes on the rope before the prusik reaches the joining knot.

HOISTING

Hoisting, a useful improvised rescue technique, is fundamental to crevasse rescue. Anyone venturing on to a glacier should be familiar with some of the systems described below, though they can be used for more mundane tasks such as getting a second over a crux or hauling a sack on a big wall.

In all these systems karabiners are used as pulleys and so frictional losses are high. One third of the effort can be lost with a rope taken round a karabiner through an angle of 180°. Using two karabiners reduces this loss a little, but a proper pulley is very worthwhile. Likewise, mechanical ascenders can be used in place of prusik knots. In any hoisting, especially on a cliff face, the lifters

Fig 9.13 ABOVE RIGHT: *Passing a knot in lowering a rope. In this case the knot used to join the ropes is a figure-of-eight which gives a flat knot which is less liable to snag.*
(a) The lower is stopped before the knot reaches the lowering device and the prusik attached by a mariner knot clipped into an anchor. The weight is then lowered on to the prusik.
(b) RIGHT: *The knot joining the ropes is then transferred to below the lowering device and the mariner knot used to lower the weight back on to the main rope.*

should be attached to separate anchors for their own safety. It is better if any pull is directed away from the cliff edge in case of failure which could cause an outward force or a stumble.

If a hoist is necessary, the simplest method is sheer muscle power, especially if there is enough assistance. It may help to put a prusik clipped back to an anchor on the rope. The prusik is pushed down as the rope is raised and can take the weight whenever required. If pulling on a rope, each person can be more effective if they use a prusik on the rope as a pulling point as long as the pull is directed along the line of the rope. With any hoisting there can be a great deal of rope abrasion, so any edges should be padded if possible.

Hoisting systems fall into two groups, assisted and unassisted, the former being the easier. In any hoist, however, the pulling effort required is reduced if the victim can walk his feet up the rock or ice; raising an unconscious person or someone hanging free is much harder work.

Assisted Hoist

The assisted hoist is simple and effective if the victim is not more than one-third of the rope's length below the rescuer. If using a belay plate, it is not even necessary to escape from the system to set this up. First the plate is locked off and a French prusik put on the load rope below the plate. This is clipped back into the belayer's harness or knot loop. Make sure that it is not long enough to go beyond arm's reach. Take a bight of spare rope, clip a locking karabiner to it and lower or throw this to the victim who clips it to the knot loop or other suitable point on his harness. Make sure that there are no twists in the ropes. The lock-off on the plate is then removed and the weight is taken by the French prusik. The victim pulls down on the middle rope, the only rope in the system that is moving towards him, while the rescuer pulls up on the third rope. The French prusik is held open by the plate as the first rope moves through it, but when a rest is needed the victim is lowered slightly and it will tighten and hold. Although not always necessary, this prusik acts as a back-up [*fig. 9.14*].

With belay methods such as the friction hitch or the body belay, the rope is locked off and a prusik used to hold the victim while the rope is arranged to run through a karabiner on the anchor or the belayer which will act as a pulley.

The main drawbacks to this method are getting the rope to the victim and communications. If both climbers are familiar with how the hoist works, these problems can be overcome fairly easily; but if they are not, the method can be difficult if the victim is out of earshot. Any runners have to be removed by the victim as he ascends.

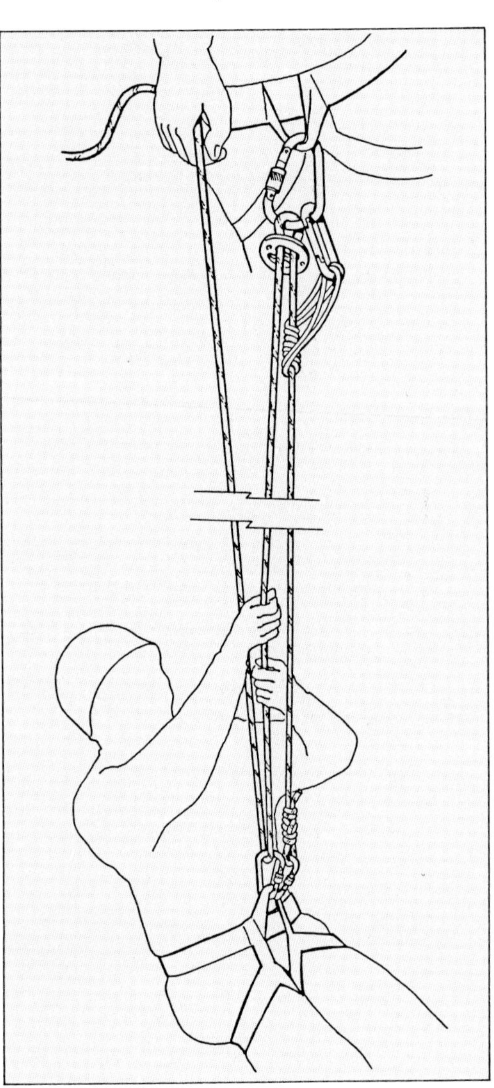

Fig 9.14 An assisted hoist, showing the arrangement at the belayer with the rope through the belay plate and the French prusik on the rope to the victim. The victim pulls down on the middle rope, the one which runs down to him, and the belayer pulls up on the third rope.

Stirrup Hoist

With a stirrup hoist the victim does most of the work and it can be used for half the length of a single and the full length of a double rope.

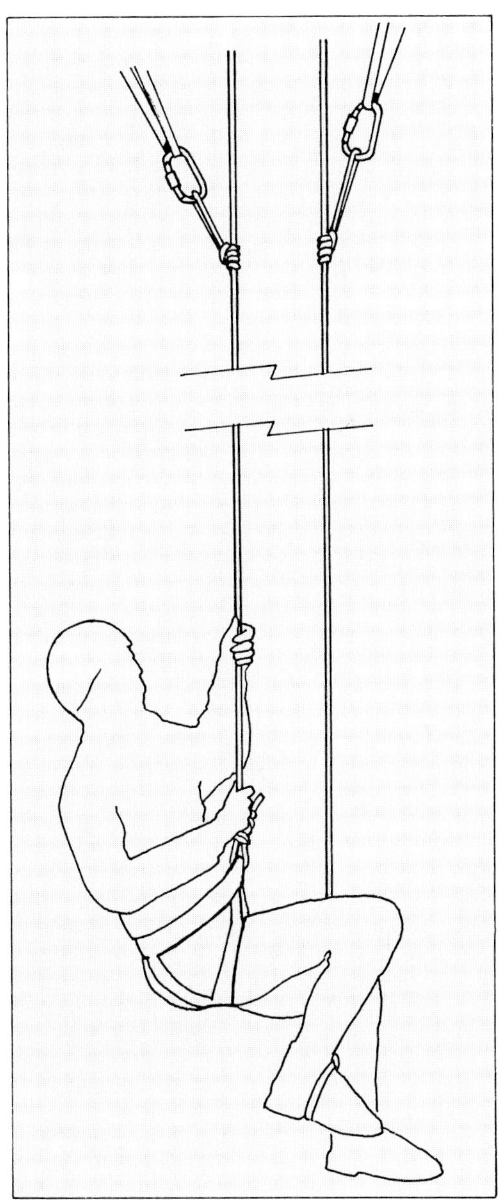

Fig 9.15 Stirrup hoist, showing one rope from the harness and the other to the foot. The foot loop is secured with a lark's foot and both ropes are attached by prusik loops to anchors. In reality both ropes would run close to each other to make stepping up easier.

Although several variations are possible, the simplest and most useful is where the victim is in a sit harness hanging on the rope. The free end of rope with a foot loop in it is lowered to the victim. Both ropes are secured through prusiks or clamps at the top. The victim stands up in the foot loop and the other rope is pulled up through the prusik until tight and the victim sits back on to this. The foot loop is then raised for the next step up and a repetition of the cycle [*fig. 9.15*]. The victim can run the foot loop through his harness or use a karabiner from the harness or a chest harness to keep closer to the rope and so make stepping up less strenuous.

The main advantage of the stirrup hoist is that it can be used when friction is such as to make hoisting impossible or the victim cannot (or has not the means to) prusik; also the rope does not cut into any edges as much as with other systems. Rope stretch, however, is always a problem with this method.

Unassisted Hoists

These require more effort from the rescuer and so strength plays an important part in their effectiveness. The actual method used will depend on a variety of factors such as the strength of the rescuer, the weight to be raised, the gear available and the location of the lifting site. A free hoist is easier to do if dealing with a dead weight, but if the victim can walk his feet up the rock its angle influences the effort required. Some of these hoists can also be used to haul sacks on big routes and in all cases the use of a pulley is recommended. With these hoists it is usually possible to exert a greater force by lifting upwards and using the legs rather than pulling down and using mainly body weight.

Yosemite Hoist

The Yosemite hoist is used primarily with lighter loads such as haul bags. The rope is taken through a karabiner or pulley above the operator and a prusik attached to the load rope and clipped into the anchor. A second prusik is put on the rope below the pulley and the load raised by pushing down on this while pulling up on the load rope. The load rope prusik is then slid down to hold while the foot prusik is moved up for the next step.

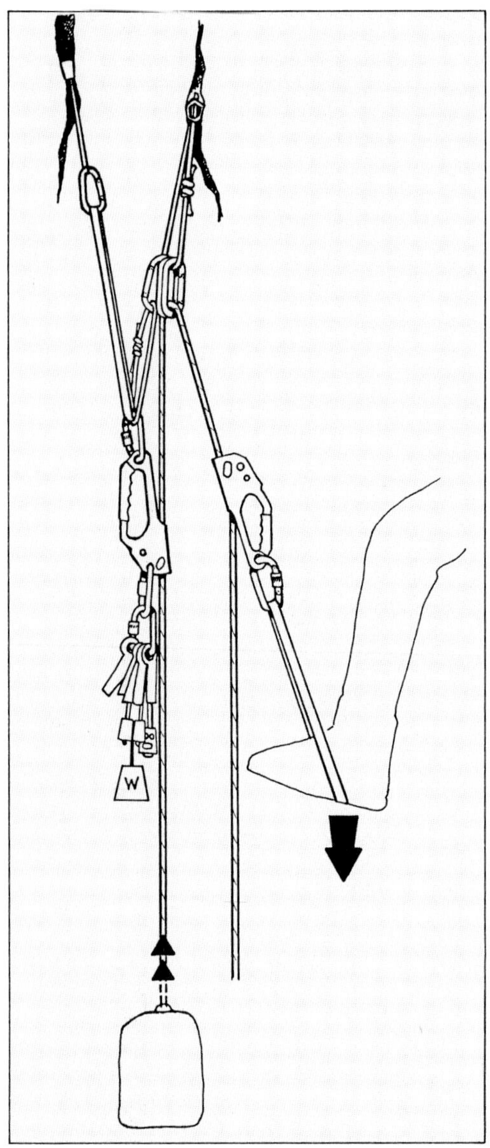

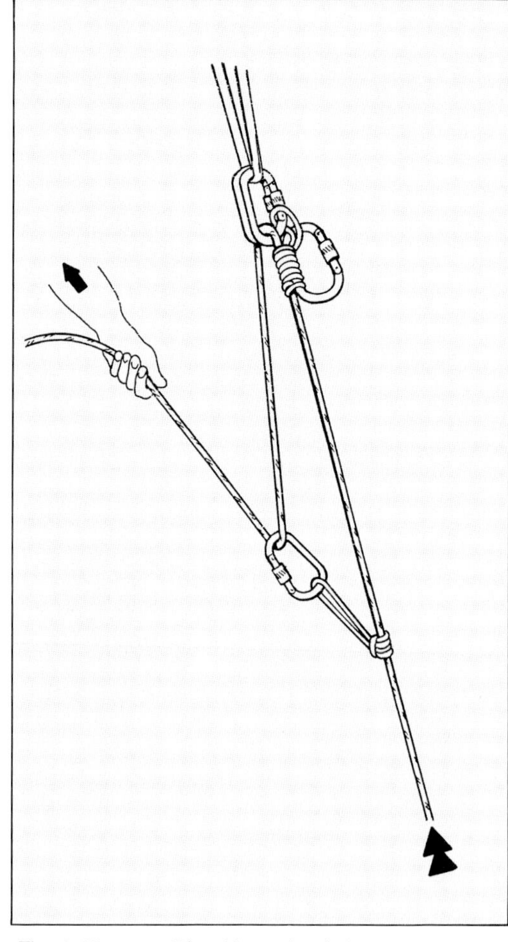

Fig 9.16 LEFT: *The Yosemite hoist set up using mechanical ascenders, with double karabiners as the top pulley. The more the force can be directed straight down, the more efficient this system is.*

Fig 9.17 ABOVE: *3:1 hoist with a Bachmann at the double karabiner pulley at the anchor and a simple prusik knot further down the rope.*

The faster and more usual type of Yosemite hoist uses mechanical ascenders: a weighted, inverted clamp is put on the load rope and the rope is pumped up through it using one or both legs on a clamp on the down rope [*fig. 9.16*]. Further advantage can be gained by using other pulleys and clamps.

Another version of this is to body haul. The inverted clamp is set up as normal, but this time the hauler attaches himself to the down clamp and to a separate anchor using a long sling or a few metres of rope. He then jumps or drops off the stance and uses his own weight to raise the load. When the load is held on the inverted clamp, he climbs back up and repeats the process.

Hip Hoist

The powerful hip hoist uses the strength of the legs. It works best on small ledges on steep walls. A high anchor point is arranged for a pulley system and the load rope put through this. The operator then attaches a prusik or an inverted

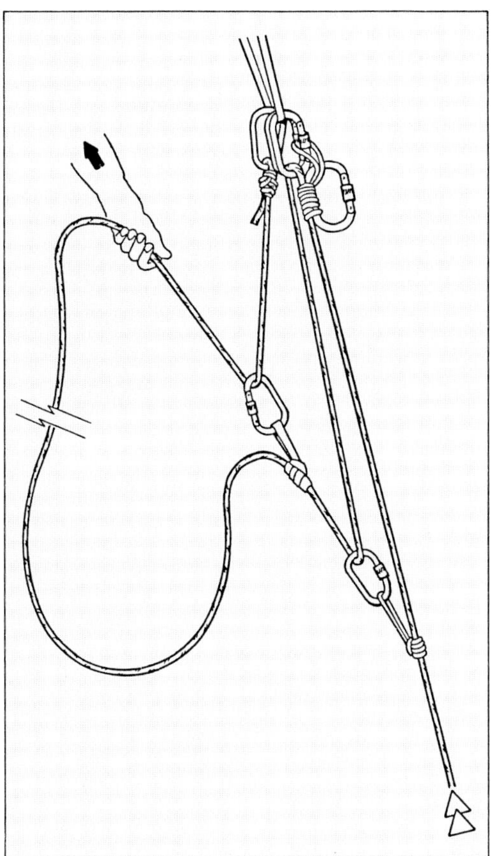

Fig 9.18 The 3:1 pulley converted by attaching another pulley to the original hauling rope, clipping the free rope end through this and into the anchor and pulling on this rope to give a 6:1 advantage but adding only one extra pulley to the system.

clamp to the front of his harness and puts this on the load rope. Lift is obtained by squatting down, sliding the clamp down the rope and then standing up, at the same time pulling down on the rope below the pulley. The rope through the top point must have some holding system on it to allow the pulling clamp or knot to be moved back down for the next lift. This can be a descender or a friction hitch, but both create work because the down rope has to be pulled through them. A French prusik can be placed below the pulley; however, as the gain on each pull is short, the loss through the knot stretching is significant. The best method is to use an Alpine clutch but as this works only one way you must be sure that no lowering will be needed. This hoist is most efficient if the hauler can stand with his heels on the very edge of the ledge with the top anchor well above so that all the effort is directed along the line of the rope and not at an angle to it.

Three-in-One Hoist

The three-in-one hoist is also known as the Z pulley system. It is usually necessary to escape from the system to set this up and it is from that point that its construction is taken. With the victim hanging on the rope which is attached to an anchor by a prusik loop and backed up by a knot in the main rope to the anchor [*fig. 9.11d*, page 147], two prusiks are put on the rope, one as near the victim as it can easily be placed and the other as close to the anchor as possible. The prusik used to escape from the system can usually double up as the lower prusik. The upper prusik must be a French prusik or a Bachmann and it is clipped into the anchor. With the back-up knot removed, the rope is taken through a karabiner at the anchor which now acts as the top pulley and then clipped into the lower prusik so that, by pulling up on this rope, a mechanical advantage of 3:1 is created. When everything is in place, the original prusik can be taken off if no longer used and, by pulling on the free rope, the victim is lifted. As the load rope moves up, the top prusik opens [*fig. 9.17*].

When the rope has been pulled as far as possible, the load is lowered on to the top prusik and then the lower one can be pushed down as far as it will go and another pull taken. When the load rope is being pulled, the top prusik opens automatically but grips when re-loaded. As there is some loss each time this happens, the top prusik should be as short as possible. If a Bachmann is used below the top pulley, ensure that the karabiner round which it is tied is larger than the pulley karabiner so it cannot be pulled through and inverted.

Variations can be constructed using the above method as a basis, but it is worth remembering that the increase in friction as extra karabiner pulleys are introduced can negate this advantage. A prusik and karabiner can be put on the pulling rope to act as another pulley. With the free end anchored and the rope taken through this karabiner, an advantage of 6:1 can be gained [*fig. 9.18*]. If a pulley is available, it is most effective if put on as close to the pull as possible.

Hanging Hoist

There are two occasions when a person hanging on a rope may need to have his attachment point to the rope changed: if he is unconscious and in a waist belt, and so needs to be placed in an improvised harness before he suffocates; and if he needs to be transferred to another rope for some reason – he might be an injured leader in a position where he cannot be lowered to safety and needs to be raised or lowered on another rope. In each case the casualty has to be raised to take his weight off the rope.

The rescuer first abseils down to just above the casualty and puts him in a sit sling and chest harness if required. A short prusik and karabiner are then put on the casualty's rope. A long sling from the casualty's sit sling is then taken through the karabiner on the prusik and the rescuer stands in the free end of this sling to raise the victim up so that the sit sling can be attached to that or another prusik on the main rope. This, however, is not easy to do, especially if the casualty is heavier than the rescuer. The same method is used to attach a chest harness to support the unconscious person fully.

If the victim is transferred to another rope, it is first tied on to him and he is raised in the same manner as before to take his weight off his rope which can then be untied from his harness.

An easier alternative is to cut the casualty's rope once he has been transferred to another rope or the rescuer. Ensure that the casualty is well secured before cutting the old rope and remember that tensioned ropes cut incredibly easily and it is possible to cut through more than you intend! If a casualty is transferred to the rescuer to descend with, it is important to have an abseil brake which provides enough friction for the weight of two people.

10 Pegs & Artificial Climbing

PEGS

Pegs, pins or pitons are basically metal spikes which are hammered into cracks in the rock and used for progress, protection or anchors. Their use in climbing has been a long and often controversial one which started at the beginning of the century. The first pegs, and those used up until the 1960s, were of soft steel. They were often poorly designed and manufactured and had comparatively low holding power. They worked by deforming to the internal shape of the crack into which they were driven and were more useful in softer rocks such as the limestone of the Eastern Alps where many hard and impressive routes were climbed using them for protection or direct aid. At the start of the 1960s pegs made of hard steel made their appearance. Developed for use on the granite walls of the Yosemite Valley in California, these pegs made of chrome molybdenum alloy were harder and stronger and could be driven into cracks which were too thin or poorly defined to take the soft European pegs. They were better designed, covered a wide range of sizes, lasted longer and rapidly replaced the older peg types. Using them, American climbers took artificial climbing to new degrees of difficulty and created some of the longest, hardest and most sustained aid routes in the world.

Where soft steel pegs often deformed so much that they could not be removed, 'chrome molly' pegs were usually recoverable and could be re-used many times. In Europe many aid pitches became pegged up, whereas in America pegs were usually taken out. This, however, had one major drawback: instead of the route being marked by a line of rusting metal, it showed as a series of scars caused by the repeated placing and removal of these pegs. The hard steel destroyed the rock and some popular aid cracks developed into a series of holes large enough to be used as holds for free climbing. This destruction of the rock took place everywhere but especially in popular aid-climbing areas, and with it came a growing awareness of the damage being done to

Fig 10.1 The repeated insertion and removal of pegs has severely damaged this rock, but at the same time it has opened up the cracks sufficiently to give free climbs.

the climbing environment in general. However, the expansion of nut protection and a rise in free-climbing standards occurred simultaneously, and these led to a general move away from the use of pegs and an adoption of a 'cleaner' code of ethics which placed greater store on leaving the rock in its natural, undamaged state [*fig. 10.1*].

In spite of this, pegs still have a place in certain aspects of climbing, in some areas at least. They are still used on many artificial or aid climbs which cannot yet be tackled by other methods and are still found on many free routes which cannot be adequately protected in a more natural manner: an occasional aid peg or artificial pitch can open up magnificent climbs which would not otherwise be possible. They are also used in situations when speed is important, such as in

Alpine climbing, in the Greater Ranges or when climbing in winter when the range of protection possibilities is diminished. Paradoxically, their use has also produced some superb free climbs by opening up thin cracks to create holds where previously none existed.

The majority of rock climbers today will never have to place a peg, though they may well use them for anchors and runners. Perhaps with time even these will disappear but, for the present, pegs look likely to stay around, in some places at least. The ethics regarding their use and acceptability seems to be about as complex and fragmented as any in climbing and relies heavily on historical precedent. If you feel the need to place a peg, find out local feelings on the matter first, but if a route has been lead without a peg it is unlikely to be generally acceptable; if contemplating placing a peg on a first ascent, ensure that it is absolutely essential. If a route has established pegs on it and they become unsafe, they should be replaced; if they are going to be there and used, they may as well be good. In the wider field of mountaineering the use of pegs is still generally acceptable; however, this too is changing to a cleaner ethic with greater respect for the rock.

Fig 10.2 A selection of pegs: angles, Leepers, Kingpins and knifeblades.

Peg Types

Pegs offer one main advantage over most nuts, for if well placed they can take a load in any direction. They can be divided into two main groups: flat, blade pegs and angles which have a V-shaped cross-section. These cover an overlapping range of sizes from hairline seams to wide cracks [*fig. 10.2*].

Blade Pegs

Blade pegs are of two types: the thinnest, knifeblades, which have the eye at one side of the blade, and the similar but thicker Bugaboos. Knifeblades and Bugaboos are also known as off-set pegs as the eye is located at one side. Thicker and generally narrower are Lost Arrows and Kingpins which have a centrally placed eye. These are described in terms of length and thickness, from short to long and from thick to thin. The thickness is measured next to the eye at the thickest part of the blade.

These pegs work by wedging in tight-fitting

cracks. In horizontal cracks both types are placed with the eye downwards; in vertical cracks offsets are placed eye-up so that when they are loaded the twisting action tends to pull them more securely into the crack rather than opening out the eye [*fig. 10.3*]. Knifeblades are primarily aid pegs and this should be borne in mind if using them as runners or as part of a belay system. With blade pegs a rule of thumb is that if they bend over 45° they can be expected to break.

Even smaller than the knifeblade is the rurp (Realised Ultimate Reality Piton), which is scarcely larger than a postage stamp. This is an aid-only peg and is used in incipient cracks where it can create its own hole in the rock. Rurps need to have a sling attached for use, in the bottom hole for vertical cracks [*fig. 10.4*] and in the central hole for horizontal ones. Those fitted with a swagged wire loop rather than tape are more robust and sometimes easier to place and remove.

Angle Pegs

Angles have a V-shaped cross-section and range in size from 12–50mm. The 20mm angle, because of its usefulness on granite, has come to be known as a standard angle, while those smaller than this are called baby angles. Above 50mm they are known as bongs and go up to 150mm. Large bongs are generally made of aluminium alloy which is lighter than chrome molybdenum and causes less rock damage. All these pegs work by a wedging and springing action and, when well placed, have great holding power. Similar to these are the Leepers which have a Z-shaped cross-section.

Angles and bongs are placed with the eye down in horizontal cracks and the eye across in vertical cracks [*fig. 10.5*]. Leepers go eye-down in horizontal placements and eye-up in vertical ones [*fig. 10.6*].

These pegs are susceptible to overdriving which can spread the sides too much and cause them to split along the back. They should not be placed so that they can bend backwards as this can break them. They must never be positioned with only two sides in contact with the rock as this is unsafe, yet they can still be difficult to remove.

These pegs cover a size of crack well able to take modern nuts and so are often redundant. They are also the ones which cause most rock damage, particularly when removed.

Fig 10.3 A knifeblade in a vertical crack with the eye uppermost so that any load will twist the blade more firmly into the crack.

Fig 10.4 A rurp in place in a hairline crack.

Peg Hammers

A peg hammer will normally only be carried when direct aid climbing on pegs is to be expected. On mixed Alpine and winter climbs an ice tool will fill this role. A hammer should be robust, fairly heavy, about 0.5kg in weight and be well-balanced and comfortable to use. The shaft can be of metal, wood, fibreglass or a composite construction, but should have a good grip and should dampen vibrations caused by the hammering. The striking surface should be a reasonable size and flat, and the other end can be either a long spike or a blunt pick. A spike is useful for cleaning out cracks, whereas a pick is good for delivering accurate blows to a small area – particularly handy when removing pegs from awkward placements.

A hammer should have some form of attachment, a cord or tape which is long enough to use at full arm's length. A holster is the most convenient way of carrying it.

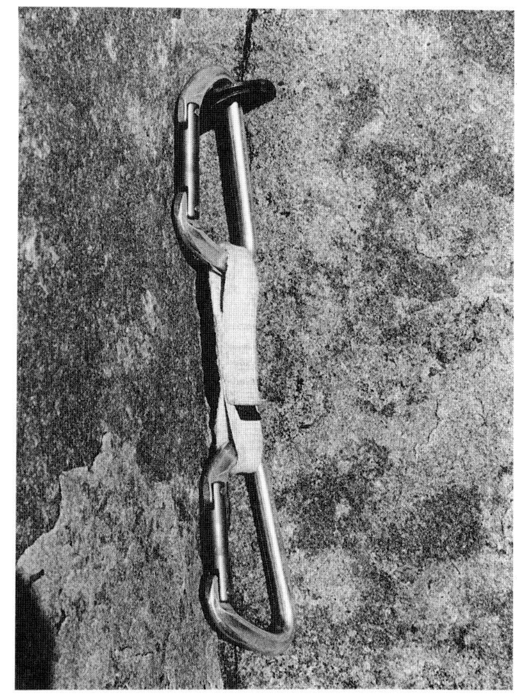

Fig 10.5 A well-placed angle in a corner crack with an extension and two karabiners attached and ready for use.

Peg Placement

The best place for a peg is in a solid, horizontal crack which takes the whole of it up to the eye and is angled down into the rock [*fig. 10.7*]. In the perfect spot the peg would be mechanically secure and could be placed by hand and one hammer blow. However, this is seldom the case and most placements are in vertical cracks where the peg must take a downwards and outwards force and resist a rotational shifting under load. The best pegs result from intelligent placing rather than cold-welding them into the rock, and horizontal placements are usually stronger than vertical ones.

First, find the best spot in the crack for a peg and select the peg that best fits it (rather than choosing a peg and trying to find a place for it). The best place is where the crack is locally wider and will grip the peg near the edges so that when loaded it wedges itself [*fig. 10.8*]. If there is a single high spot, this will act as a pivot point. The peg is then placed by hand: half to three-quarters of its length is pushed into the crack, depending on the peg's size and taper. It is then driven home with well-aimed blows to the flat surface at the head of the peg known as the anvil. It can be tested periodically by a light tap on the head along the line of the crack to see if it moves and, depending on the result of this test, hammered more. The hammer should bounce off the head of the peg when dropped on to it. A good peg will often look and sound right as it goes in and produce a rising, ringing note. A sudden change in note when the peg is hit but no longer goes in can

Fig 10.6 A Leeper with its distinctive Z-shaped cross-section in a vertical crack. The eye is up so that it will twist into the crack if loaded.

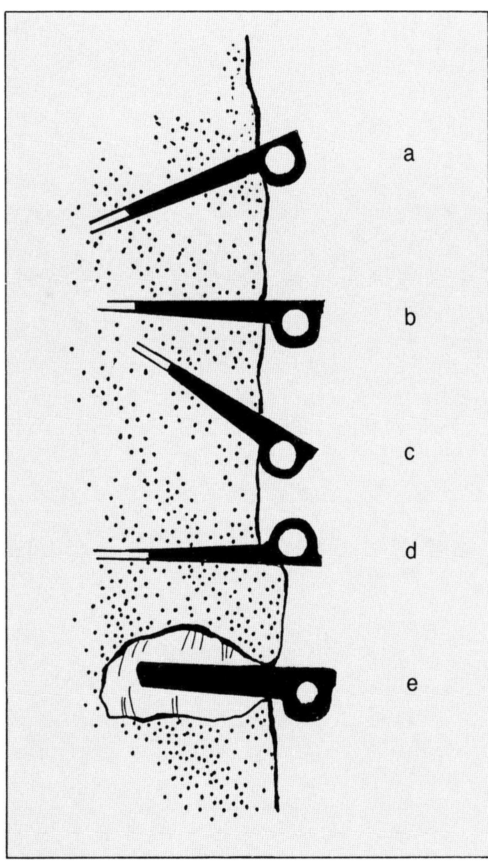

indicate that it has bottomed – that is, it has reached the back of a dead or rapidly narrowing crack and can go no further. In this case it should be removed and the next size up tried, or it can be tied off but should not be hammered further as this can loosen it. Although a rising note can indicate a good peg, it may not always: this sound can also be obtained from using an overlarge peg.

If pegs are to be used for aid only, they need only take a little more than body weight. For use as protection, however, they may be subjected to large forces. In this case it is better to err on the side of safety rather than the opposite, hammering

Fig 10.7 Peg placements in horizontal cracks:
(a) A perfect, mechanically sound peg placement.
(b) A very good, fully inserted peg.
(c) A much less secure peg which needs to be well driven in.
(d) An acceptable peg, although it would be better the right way up.
(e) A poor peg in a pocket.

Fig 10.8 BELOW: *Good and bad peg placements in a vertical crack:*
(a) A good placement where rotational movement is prevented.
(b) A poor placement at a constriction where any load would lever the peg out.
(c) A very poor placement where only a small part of the blade is in contact with the rock.

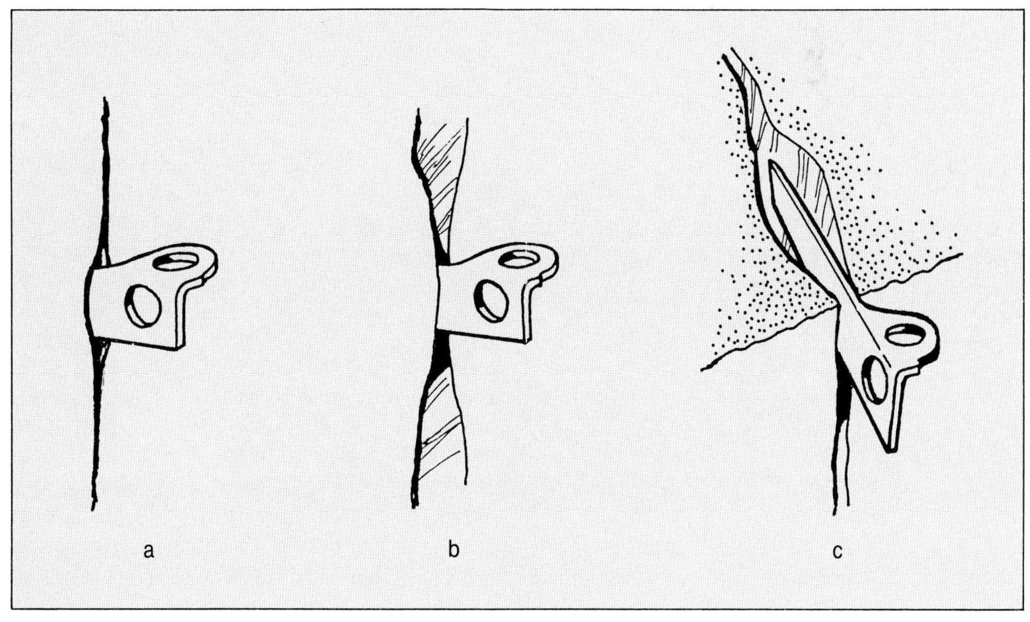

Fig 10.9 ABOVE: *A standard angle tied off with a clove hitch attached as close to the rock as possible.*

Fig 10.10 ABOVE RIGHT: *A knifeblade in a horizontal crack tied off with a lark's foot. A danger here is that, if loaded, the thin metal of the peg could cut the tape.*

Fig 10.11 BELOW: *A large angle tied off with a clove hitch; an extra karabiner is clipped through the eye to ensure that the tie-off cannot slip.*

the peg hard even though it may consequently be more difficult to remove. Overdriving, however, can lead to a loss in strength, particularly if the eye begins to deform.

Tying Off

Sometimes pegs will not go in up to the eye yet cannot be replaced by anything more suitable. If used with a karabiner through the eye, the peg may fail when loaded because of the increased leverage. These pegs should be tied off with a loop of rope or tape: tie-offs or hero loops are normally made from 10–15mm tape about 25cm long for aid climbing or up to 25mm wide for runners or belay anchors. These are best put on using a clove hitch with the cross-over part of the knot at the top as this will tighten up when loaded and stay in place. It should be put as close to the rock as possible and with very poor pegs it is best to use the thinnest tape to reduce the leverage [*fig. 10.9*]. A lark's foot can also be used or the loop wrapped round the peg for a complete turn [*fig. 10.10*]. The latter two ways are weaker but can be tied with one hand; unfortunately, if the peg pulls out it is liable to be lost whereas it may not be with a clove hitch. The peg can be linked into the tie-off using an extra loop or karabiner through the eye to prevent loss. Pegs such as large angles which have no defined head can have a karabiner clipped through the eye to prevent the tie-off from slipping off [*fig. 10.11*]. Bongs can be tied off using the lightening holes [*fig. 10.12*]. Pegs which slope steeply downwards when placed need not be tied off as little mechanical advantage is gained and the tie-off tends to slip down to the eye anyway.

One problem with tie-offs is that the loop can easily be cut on the narrow, sharp edges of the peg in a fall. If the peg is being used for protection, it may be better to use the thickest sling that will stay in place but does not put the load and hence the leverage too far out from the rock.

Fig 10.12 A bong tied off using the lightening holes.

Removing Pegs

You usually remove pegs by hammering them back and forth along the long axis of the crack where their tapered shape will assist them to work their way out. Hit the peg in one direction as far as it will go, then give it another couple of blows, but stop before any deformation occurs. Hammer it back the opposite way and continue to hit it. After this it can be driven back and forth more easily until it can be removed by hand. The spike on the hammer can be used as a lever at this point, but increases your chance of dropping the peg. Angles need not be hammered as far to each side as the narrow edges soon cut a groove which allows the peg to be removed. This cutting and grooving action by the edges occurs in even the hardest of rocks.

Some pegs are difficult to remove, especially if placed in awkward spots such as flared cracks or corners where it is not possible to hammer them effectively. If a peg will not come out relatively easily or seems likely to be damaged by removal, you should abandon it rather than destroy the rock or the peg itself. An old karabiner and sling clipped to the eye can prevent the peg being lost when it comes out, but always remove any good karabiners or tie-offs which will be damaged if hit by the hammer. If a chain of karabiners is attached to the hammer head and the peg, some stubborn pegs can be removed by swinging the hammer out and away from the rock to jerk the peg straight out. Pegs trapped behind expanding flakes or blocks may be taken out if you place a slightly larger peg near the reluctant one to expand the crack and so release it. This second peg should be large enough to remove fairly easily. Angles can sometimes be slackened off if you hit them across the line of the crack: the vibration and cutting action may be enough to break their grip. Large bongs may be taken out if you hammer them outwards from inside the crack.

Fixed Pegs

Fixed pegs are still a feature of many routes, both free and artificial. If a hammer is carried, they can be tested by a light tap with this along the line of the crack to see if they move and be replaced if necessary. Without a hammer, visual inspection and a limited amount of levering with what is available are all that is possible. Observe how much rusting has occurred and check the usual fracture spots such as at the neck and the eye where the metal is liable to have been more abused. Some *in situ* pegs are only there because they were poorly placed and so impossible to remove. This does not necessarily make them solid or secure.

Where cliffs are subject to freeze/thaw action as a result of water getting into the cracks, pegs can be loosened. This is particularly so in Alpine areas or where there is a definite winter season. Old tried-and-tested pegs can fail catastrophically because of this.

Where pegs are established and necessary protection on climbs, it would be preferable to have worthwhile pieces of gear rather than rusting relics of a past era. However, in many areas there is so far no agreed system as to who replaces these pegs and when.

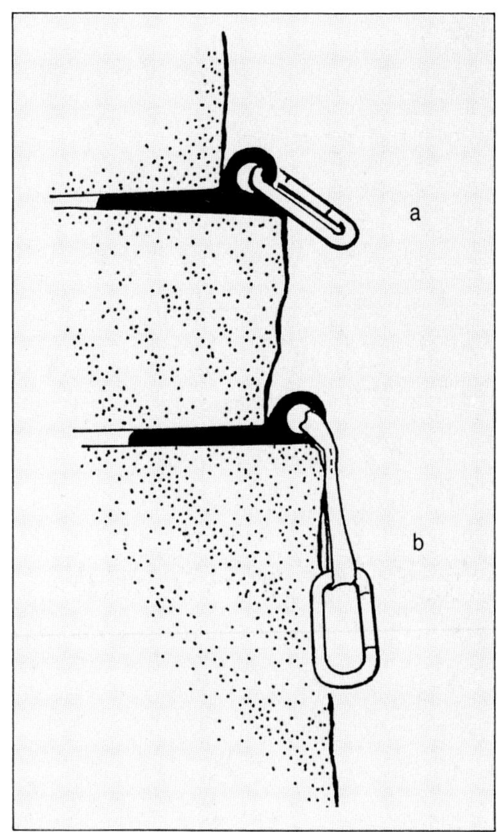

Fig 10.13 Placements in horizontal cracks at the back of ledges:
(a) A badly placed angle which would be levered out by the karabiner across the edge of the ledge.
(b) The better situation where the eye is threaded with a sling to reduce this levering action.

Further Considerations

Although there is an ideal way to place pegs, the configuration of the rock dictates just how each peg can be placed for maximum strength. Off-set pegs may not always go in eye-up – if the crack is in a corner, for example – and have to be inserted eye-down. If a peg has to be placed in a horizontal crack at the back of a ledge, it may not go in eye-down. It should be placed to get maximum blade in the rock, but it may be better to thread a sling through the eye if the karabiner could act as a lever over the edge of the ledge [*fig. 10.13*].

When using pegs on rocks such as limestone which have irregular and twisted cracks and holes, it may be better to use soft steel pegs which deform to the shape of the crack. These do less damage than hard steel pegs but can be difficult to remove.

Sometimes pegs have to be used behind sections of rock that are not totally secure. These expanding flakes are typical of granite and may be huge features. When a series of two or more pegs are placed in this type of crack, care must be taken to ensure that the second one does not wedge the flake outwards and cause the lower one to drop out. Use long-bladed pegs with little taper, place them in wider sections of the crack where natural wedging will occur and do not overdrive. It is as well to be clipped into the peg being placed in case the one in use is loosened by this. Nuts are better in these situations.

Stacking Pegs

On occasions when the correct size of peg is not available or the crack is not of a shape that any peg will fit, two or three may need to be used together to provide a placement. Basically the idea is to fill the hole in the rock with as much metal as possible. When using two pegs, you can drive them as a single one; when using three or more, you can place the last one between the others and use it to wedge them apart [*figs. 10.14, 10.15*]. Different sizes of angles and Leepers fit well together but it is possible to overdrive them and get one stuck inside another. When using stacked pegs, either clip into the eye closest to the rock or tie off the whole bundle [*fig. 10.16*]. A safety sling can be linked through all the eyes to save them if they pull out or on removal.

Imagination is the key to finding difficult placements; that and correct application of the principles of pressure and wedging and the

Fig 10.14 ABOVE: *Two stacked Kingpins tied off using a lark's foot.*

Fig 10.15 ABOVE RIGHT: *Two Kingpins and a blade stacked together. This stack is tied off with a turn of tape round the pegs to keep it as close to the rock as possible.*

Fig 10.16 BELOW: *An angle and a Leeper nested together to give a good placement. The karabiner is clipped through the eye of the angle which is nearer the rock to reduce leverage.*

reduction of leverage. Pegs and nuts can be used together – for example, a small nut can be held in place in a flared crack by driving a peg just below the nut itself and using the wire to keep the leverage at a minimum. In these days of sophisticated nuts, such techniques are usually called on only for thin cracks and shallow, flared sections where not even camming devices will work.

Carrying Pegs

Pegs are best carried on a rack in the opposite way to nuts: that is, on karabiners with their gates facing down and out so that you can take them off the karabiner using only one hand. Only two or three pegs should be carried on each karabiner otherwise it is awkward to remove them; off-sets are put on facing different ways – if they are not, they can nest inside each other and jam. Pegs are usually racked with the largest at the back and graded by size to the smallest at the front.

Care of Pegs

Pegs take a great deal of hammering and need to be checked regularly for fractures. These tend to form at points of weakness such as round the eye and the neck, and along the back bend in angles and bongs. Cracked pegs should be discarded before they break in use and further litter the rocks. Burrs and sharp edges should be filed off and the tips kept smooth and regular. This is to protect the hands as much as anything as the sharp, ragged edges often left by poorly aimed hammer blows can cut like razors.

OTHER EQUIPMENT

Skyhooks

Skyhooks are hard steel hooks which can be placed on tiny edges, crystals or in depressions, or even in drilled holes. They can be long or short and can have different types of points for use on different types of edges. Those which have a wide base are the most stable, but all must be used delicately as they are easily unseated. They stay in place better if they can be tied down to something such as a nut placed to take an upward pull.

Although primarily a tool of the artificial climber, the skyhook can be utilised to protect free climbs when nothing else is available and can be used to rest on or lower off climbs. If used for protection, it usually needs to be tied into place. If you are using double ropes, this can be done by using one rope to hold the skyhook down. A loop is tied in one rope far enough from the leader to leave him enough rope to reach easier ground or better protection. This loop is clipped into the skyhook and the second, by pulling down on this, holds the hook in place. The other, free rope is clipped into the hook and used as a runner in the normal way.

Copperheads

Copperheads are small pieces of a soft metal, such as copper, attached to a looped wire, which can be used as a nut or a hammered placement. It can be pounded into incipient cracks and grooves where the metal will deform and grip. Often the tip of a thin peg can be used to punch it in. Copperheads have the advantage over other malleable placements in that they can usually be removed. This can be done by linking a chain of karabiners to the wire loop and jerking them upwards and outwards.

Bolts

Bolts are sometimes used in aid climbing for progress or protection but, as in free climbing, the ethics regarding their use vary from area to area.

ARTIFICIAL CLIMBING

At some stage or other many climbers will resort to artificial aid. This can be either to make upwards progress or for resting on. Such aid can generally be anything apart from naturally occurring rock.

The usual point of aid used for resting is a runner, and you can either clip it into your harness or use it as a hand or foot hold. Alternatively, your weight can be supported by the second giving tension on the rope. If it is necessary to place an aid point for progress, remember that free climbing will be resumed above and if possible place the gear with this in mind. Although it can be awkward, try not to obscure holds, especially when climbing a crack.

No matter whether the aid section is only a pull on a nut, or a foot in a sling, or a long section of continuous artificial climbing, it is important to gain as much height as possible for the minimum expenditure of energy. Once you have decided that aid is necessary, full use should be made of it. As ever in climbing, try to make your legs do most of the work.

On long, hard free climbs, it may be convenient if the leader leaves a few slings which the second can use for aid on the more difficult sections, since he will often be carrying the heavier rucksack and speed may be more important than style.

If a longer section of aid climbing is expected (this will usually be mentioned in the guidebook), some extra gear will be required. This will depend on the difficulty and the length of the artificial sections but a basic gear list might include a set of étriers, a daisy chain, fifi hooks and a selection of extra karabiners, slings and technical aid-climbing gear such as pegs and nuts; ascenders may also be taken. The final selection, however, will depend on the grade of the climb to be attempted.

Gear

Before setting off on an aid pitch, it is essential to organise all the climbing gear carefully. Since so much gear may be required, a logical, systematic method of carrying it is vital. Much time and energy can be wasted as a result of poor organisation. The technical gear, nuts, pegs and karabiners, should be arranged on bandoliers which are more convenient when carrying large amounts of equipment, and it should be racked so that the gear most likely to be required is at the front and so most accessible. It should also be arranged so that it does not become tangled.

Etriers

Etriers are short ladders, nowadays usually of sewn nylon tape and generally with three rungs. Two etriers are normally used, but in some situations, such as on big roofs, three may be an advantage. They should have either a karabiner or fifi hook at the top. Fifi hooks are quicker and easier to use than karabiners but require more care. If a fifi hook is used, a thin length of cord should connect the etrier to the harness. This prevents the étrier from being lost should it be dropped, and allows for its speedier retrieval than when using karabiners. Experimenting will show the correct length for this cord but it is normally about as long as from the waist to the end of the fully extended arm and the cords to each étrier should be different colours to avoid the confusion which can result when switching them from side to side. A short loop of tape tied into the top of the étriers, which acts as a grab handle when stepping up, can be useful [*fig. 10.17*].

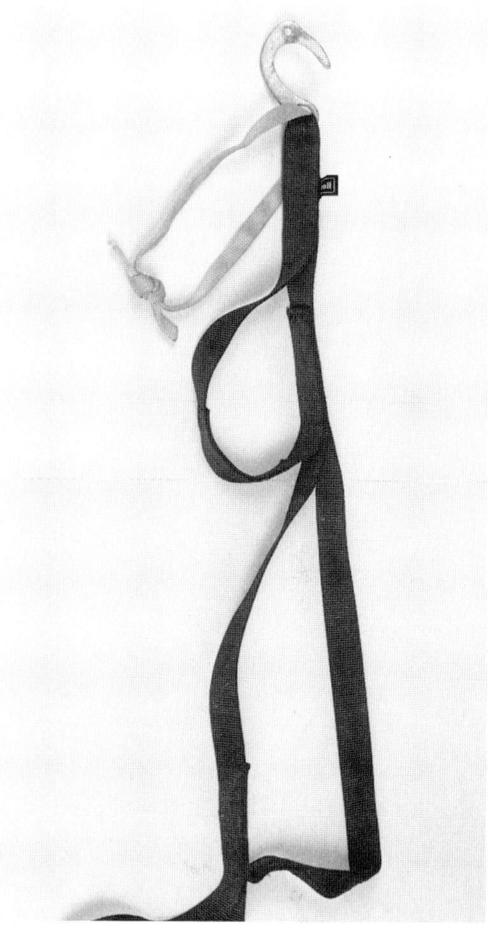

Fig 10.17 A sewn tape etrier with fifi hook attached and an extra tape loop tied through at the top.

It is often worthwhile attaching a daisy chain or cow's tail (a short tape sling used for resting) to the front of the harness. Daisy chains can be bought made up from sewn tape or are easily fashioned from 20mm tape knotted to form a sling and then tied with a series of thumb knots along its length. The finished sling should be about 70cm long and have a series of open loops some 15cm or less apart [*fig. 10.18*].

Climbing an Aid Pitch

There are several methods which can be used when aid climbing and the actual method usually depends on the angle of the rock, which can vary from a steep slab to a horizontal roof. Some of the techniques are very specialised; however, only a basic technique is described here, but it is one that can be modified to fit most situations. It can also be adapted by the individual to suit the gear being carried and the exact nature of the pitch.

Aid climbing can be strenuous and time-consuming, so being efficient is a priority and this begins with organisation and planning. If the aid points are far apart, greater height can be gained with each placement, but more energy is required to place gear high above your head and to stand high in the étrier. Sometimes the rock dictates where the aid must go; if there is a choice, you should try to find the distance which is most economical on time, energy and equipment. This will come with practice.

As the rope passes through so many karabiners on an aid pitch, great attention has also to be paid to avoiding rope drag by extending each point correctly. Friction through badly extended gear can soon slow down progress and squander energy. Sometimes on aid pitches it is even worthwhile descending to sort out gear which is causing rope drag. More often, however, it is necessary to descend to collect gear for re-use higher up.

Fig 10.18 LEFT: *A sewn and a tied daisy chain which could be used for artificial climbing.*

Fig 10.19 BELOW LEFT: *The etrier has been attached to the new aid point which has been tested and the end of the daisy chain clipped into it. The rope is then clipped into the point which is about to be left in preparation to moving up the etrier.*

Fig 10.20. BELOW: *The climber has moved up the etrier and re–attached the daisy chain close to his harness so that he can rest and reach the next aid point.*

PREVIOUS PAGE: *Yosemite's El Capitan; scene of some of the world's greatest big wall climbs. A climber can just be seen above the tower at the bottom of the photo.* (Adrian Liddell)

ABOVE LEFT: *A steep abseil.* (Martin Burrows-Smith)

LEFT: *On long aid climbs, extra gear may have to be taken. This can either be hauled or carried by the second, who is Jumaring up the climbing rope, and at the same time, taking out the gear.* (Martin Burrows-Smith)

ABOVE: *Crossing a gap by means of a Tyrolean Traverse. For protection a safety rope is being used to both sides. However, it can be dangerous to use a hand on the rope ahead of the karabiner, as it is easy for the fingers to become trapped.* (Stuart Wagstaff)

RIGHT: *When aid climbing, it is often an advantage to get into a resting position, in this case by sitting on one foot, whilst placing gear. Although this limits the reach in some situations, it does save strength. The rope has been arranged to run smoothly, in this situation by missing out gear.* (Allen Fyffe)

ABOVE LEFT: *If few runners can be placed on a pitch, it may be better to use both ropes as a single rope. Providing there is no rope drag, this gives increased safety in the event of a fall.* (Allen Fyffe)

BELOW LEFT: *On difficult mixed ground anything goes! Here the climber has one foot on ice and one foot on rock. The rucksack has been removed, both to make the climbing easier and to help keep a downward pull on the runner.* (Rab Anderson)

LEFT: *A classic winter chimney.* (Allen Fyffe)

RIGHT: *It is less strenuous to place protection before the start of the hard climbing. Here the climber has placed a runner and chopped down some of the over-hanging ice above before moving out on to the front of the bulge.* (Andy Cunningham Collection)

BELOW: *When seconding on steep ice, it is often possible to use the placements left by the leader. When this is not the case, the second can rely on less well-driven tools and so can conserve energy. As is common in winter a twin rope system has been used.* (Andy Cunningham)

ABOVE: *Drive-in ice screws are the quickest to place on steep ice. Here a natural ice foot hold is being used for a rest before completing the pitch.* (Allen Fyffe)

LEFT: *On steep, fluted water-ice, the tools must be placed carefully to avoid shattering the ice. With the knees slightly flexed, a good, comfortable position can be maintained.* (Andy Cunningham Collection)

RIGHT: *Often the most difficult section of an ice climb is the transition from steep, easier-angled ground. Here the climber is looking for some protection before surmounting the bulge that leads to the easy snow slopes above.* (Allen Fyffe)

ABOVE: *It is often possible to plot a route through a glacier from above. This is the upper plateau of the Freney Glacier, notoriously difficult and dangerous to cross.* (Alastair Cain)

RIGHT: *For climbing in extreme conditions, good gear and good organisation are essential. Although conditions are appalling, the climber is still able to use his belay plate properly.* (Iain Peter)

There are several ways of actually moving up using etrier but one system is as follows:

1 Place the aid point and clip a karabiner to it. Turn this karabiner so that the gate faces down and out for ease of use, and attach an étrier.

2 Transfer weight to the étrier and test the aid point. This can be done by easing your weight on to it or simply by standing up. At this stage watch the aid point for any signs of weakness or movement. If the point is sound, stand up in the étrier and give a small bounce to make sure that it is secure. If it fails, you will fall only as far as the last placement. If, however, the rope had been lifted up and clipped into this new placement, the fall would be further.

3 Clip in the daisy chain which is already attached to your harness: this acts as an extra point of security at this stage and later can be used for a hands-off rest. Clip in the rope to the aid point you are about to leave [*fig. 10.19*].

4 Climb up the étrier until the aid point is at waist level, re-clip the daisy chain as close to the waist as possible and rest. This means that the daisy chain is clipped into the point twice. Be careful not to exert too much outwards force on the aid point, especially if nuts are being used [*fig. 10.20*].

5 Reach up and place the next aid point, and continue as before.

Although this system seems complicated, it means that the length of fall and subsequent loading of the system are kept as low as possible, mainly from use of the daisy chain as a back-up. On very hard pitches two daisy chains may be used, and if this is done it is best for them to be of different colours.

This system becomes quite straightforward with practice and use. It can be simplified for easy aid climbing or for short sections of aid when slings can be employed instead of étriers. The étriers can be used on alternate points or they can both be clipped to the same point. In this case each foot has its own étrier, thus making moving up, resting and balance easier, particularly on rock which is less than vertical when a daisy chain may not be required. When standing in two étriers, balance can be maintained by crossing one leg behind the other; you can rest by sitting back on one foot tucked up behind you. If standing in two étriers and moving diagonally, always move the étrier at the side you are going to first. Whichever system and whatever gear are used, it is the legs which must do most of the work.

Aid Ethics

When aid climbing, try to observe the same ethic as in free climbing – that is, leave the rock as you found it. Obviously this is not always possible, especially if pegging is involved. However, bolting and chipping should not be necessary on a route which has previously been climbed without these. Always try to climb in a manner which fits in with the existing ethics and traditions of the area.

Seconding Aid Pitches

When following an aid pitch in conventional style, the second uses étriers. The basic method is first to unclip the rope from the aid point, attach the étrier and move up into a position where the aid point just left can be easily reached and removed. Move up the étrier and repeat the process. It is normally easiest to remove gear when it is at about shoulder height and this usually means staying in the lower rungs. Although it is best to stay standing or hanging in your harness to do this, the étrier can be sat in by slipping one leg through as far as the thigh. This is slower but can be useful for awkward placements.

If the climbing is very difficult or if food and equipment for several days are to be carried, it may be quicker and easier for the second not to climb the pitches but to follow by ascending the rope. If this is the case, the spare equipment, bivouac gear, food and water will be carried in a haul sack. While the second jumars, the leader hauls this up the pitch. Once again, this all evolves into a system which takes careful organisation and practice.

One such system could be:

1 A leads the pitch, belayed by B.

2 A arrives at the top of the pitch, sets up the anchors and gets ready to haul up the sack.

3 B releases the haul sack and A starts to haul it up.

4 B jumars up the rope, cleaning the pitch as he goes.

5 B arrives at the ledge and prepares to lead the next pitch or belay, as appropriate.

When following an aid pitch on ascenders, the second climbs the leader's rope. This can be a single or double rope: in the latter case the second jumars on one rope and is protected by the other. This can also make rope manoeuvres such as pendulums easier.

When ascending a lead rope, the aid point to which the rope is clipped must first be unclipped before the point can be removed. If the point is under tension, the top ascender must be removed from the rope and replaced above the karabiner. When the top clamp is re-weighted, the rope below it will be slack and the karabiner and the aid point can be removed. This is fairly easy if the rope is running in a fairly straight line, but if it is overhanging or diagonal this procedure is more difficult. As the top clamp is loaded, the lower one gets pulled upwards and can jam against the karabiner which can cause all sorts of problems. When moving on to the top clamp, the rope must be fed through the lower clamp at the same time to stop this from happening. This is not easy and practice is required: the more diagonal or overhanging the pitch, the more difficult the manoeuvre becomes. The lower clamp, however, can be replaced with a French prusik which can be moved down by hand when still loaded and so sometimes make the procedure easier. It is often better to second pitches of this nature in conventional style.

Organisation on Aid Climbs

On long routes speed and efficiency are essential. It is important that the climbers work together as a pair, thus avoiding confusion and consequent waste of time and energy. Many people on long climbs prefer to lead several pitches before swapping the lead. This allows more resting time and a smoother flow. When swapping the lead, it is important to organise the belays so as to make this as efficient and easy as possible.

On many long routes it is better to dispense with rucksacks and pack the gear into a single bag which can be hauled up by the leader, while the second carries a rucksack with the gear most likely to be required during the day. A haul sack must be very robust since it has to withstand a great deal of abrasion, especially when being pulled up walls which are less than vertical. Those made from tough plastic tarpaulin are suitably durable. All fragile items, such as water bottles, carried in the sack must be well padded if they are to survive the rigours of being hauled. To stop the knot on the haul rope becoming badly frayed by the rock, a plastic bottle with the bottom cut off can be slipped on to the rope before the knot is tied and moved down over it to protect it.

The Yosemite hoist, body hauling or the hip hoist are the usual sack-hauling systems. A back rope from the haul bag to the second is useful for freeing it when it gets jammed under roofs and in cracks and can also be used by the second as a back rope if required.

SECTION TWO

Snow, Ice & Winter Climbing

11 Equipment for Winter Climbing

This section of the book deals with the techniques of climbing on snow and ice. Although these are very varied and variable substances, the ways in which they can be dealt are basically the same whether at 8000m in the Himalayas, on an Alpine north face, on an American ice fall, or in a Scottish gully. There is a great difference between the black, glassy ice found on some Alpine faces, the brittle, vertical ice of frozen waterfalls and the white ice formed by repeated freeze/thaw action over a short period of time. Likewise, snow can vary from hard névé, which is easy to deal with, to seemingly bottomless powder or sun-rotted crust with every variation in between. Because of its variable and ever-changing nature, climbing on snow and ice can be complex and experience is a more important factor than when climbing on pure rock routes.

However, snow and ice climbs are only part of the picture here as winter routes are also considered, and these may mean not only climbing on snow and ice but also in spite of it. Many winter routes take lines on open faces where snow and ice are a hindrance rather than a help. Snow must be removed to reveal the rock underneath, yet this must still be climbed wearing crampons because of the thin slivers of ice that remain on it and verglass which may coat it. In some parts of the world such conditions are met only in winter, but they can regularly be found in Alpine areas, particularly after bad weather or at any time in the Greater Ranges.

The techniques of climbing on snow and ice are basic to high mountains or the winter season. They are not too difficult to learn in good conditions, but the sheer variety of conditions that a climber might encounter can cause problems. Which technique to use and when can be gauged only by experience, which, of course, usually takes time to acquire. In fact, it is technically easier to climb good ice than it is to climb rock of a similar grade. Rock requires a greater range of types of movement, whereas good ice may involve a repetition of the same manoeuvre for long distances. However, on ice the difference in the quality and frequency of protection can be large and conditions can vary dramatically over short distances and with the weather.

When climbing on snow and ice, rope management, belaying and protection techniques are the same as for rock climbing except that a further range of snow and ice protection is required. The main difference is in the time available. In winter daylight hours are limited, so there is usually pressure resulting from shortage of time; and spending too long on a route in cold conditions can also be physically unpleasant and eventually dangerous. Good, efficient rope work and belaying saves time and it is best that you rehearse these techniques thoroughly before setting out to climb in winter. Even when climbing on snow and ice in summer, as on an Alpine route, this time pressure still exists for the sun can make the climbing slower, less safe and less enjoyable as it affects the conditions, usually in a negative way.

Because conditions on snow and ice vary with the weather, it is seldom possible to do as much climbing of this type as on rock. There are no indoor ice walls to train on and few evening ice-practice crags; approaches to the climbs can be difficult, you can seldom boulder out the crux of an ice route or even fall off with impunity and bad weather can curtail all activity. Snow and ice climbing is rarely leisurely; usually it is physically demanding and often uncomfortable, but it can be intensely satisfying. Experience, cunning, inventiveness and a degree of boldness are needed to succeed on the harder of this type of climb, be it an Alpine face, a vertical ice fall or a rock climb with a thin veneer of white over it. The harder routes can demand not only the complete repertoire of snow and ice skills but also all the techniques of the rock climber as well.

When you take to the mountains in winter, it is necessary to add to the gear you already use for rock climbing. While the usual technical rock gear, nuts, Friends, ropes, slings and so on, is used in winter, extra specialist equipment must be acquired. It is also essential to uprate your clothing so that you are warm and reasonably comfortable when climbing in the often harsh, always cold winter mountains.

The lightweight boots used for walking to the crag in summer are not suitable for winter use. Their soles are too bendy, making walking and climbing on snow dangerous, and they do not take crampons. A suitable pair of winter boots has rigid soles for cramponing and step kicking but at the same time is comfortable enough to allow you to walk long distances [*fig. 11.1*]. Before buying, gauge the stiffness of the soles by trying to flex them either lengthways or across the width in your hands. Any flex at all indicates that the boots are not stiff enough. They must be high enough and stiff enough at the ankle to give support when front-pointing, yet they must not be restrictive when walking or using other crampon techniques. Good boots should also be light and warm. Unfortunately, the boot which fulfils all of these characteristics does not exist: instead, every pair is to some extent a compromise – good in some areas but weak in others. A good fit and the type of climbing to be undertaken will therefore usually be the deciding factors when making a purchase.

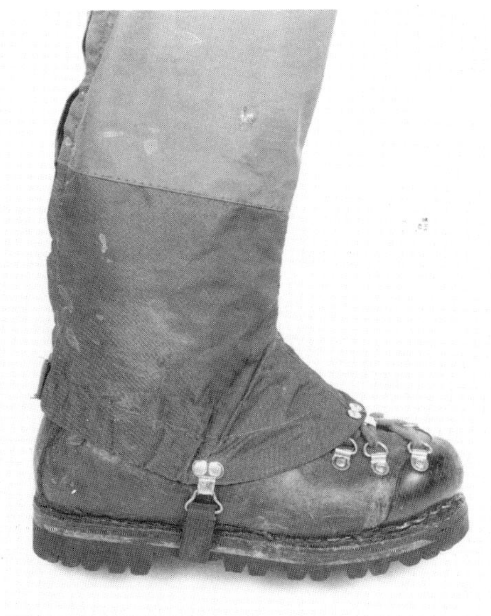

Fig 11.1 A good-quality leather boot. The toe has been reinforced with plastic for better resistance to wear.

There are two types of boot available: leather and plastic [*fig. 11.2*]. The traditional method of boot construction involves a layered mid-sole with leather upper and cleated rubber sole. Leather boots are good for ice and excellent for mixed and rock climbing. For many years they were the first and indeed the only choice; however, they have several significant drawbacks. Leather boots are not particularly waterproof and can even become waterlogged on multi-day routes. They require careful drying and regular waterproofing if they are to remain in good condition. They are often uncomfortable when new and require lengthy periods of breaking in. After a few months of wear, leather boots usually become extremely comfortable and, with occasional re-soling, may last many years. A single pair, as opposed to a double pair (that is an oversize outer boot used in conjunction with a warm, close-fitting, slipper-like inner boot) should be warm enough for routes that last one or at the most two days.

The alternative to leather is plastic. Plastic boots are both light and warm and are usually double boots. The outer, made of plastic, is rigid, durable and light but offers little in the way of insulation. The inner boot, of leather, man-made fabric or a combination of both, is padded to give a high degree of insulation. By varying the materials and type of the inner boot, it is possible to have a combination which is effective down to the lowest temperature extremes. Plastic boots are very rigid and light but are usually larger than the equivalent-sized leather boots and are thus more cumbersome to climb in, especially on mixed ground or on rock. They are waterproof, but this in itself can be a problem as condensation can build up inside the boot, causing wet and possibly cold feet. They have rubber soles similar to those of leather boots, but as the upper is not so hard-wearing it is rarely worthwhile having them re-soled. As plastic boots do not form to the shape of the feet in the same way as leather boots, the rocker (slight lengthways curve of the sole) which occurs naturally in leather boots over a period of time, must be built in to the plastic shell. This can make it difficult to obtain a good fit with some types of crampons.

When buying plastic boots, you should choose a pair that are comfortable immediately as they do not alter much in shape or fit with use. If, after a few days' wear, they prove to be uncomfortable, it is possible to have some outers (depending on the type of plastic) altered in a specialist ski shop.

Fig 11.2 Plastic double boots (left and centre) and leather single boot. The boot on the left is made from alveolite, which is very light but also very warm.

This is done by heating and stretching the offending area of shell; it is a fairly drastic solution to the problem of ill-fitting boots and is only to be considered after everything else has failed. The moulded construction method used in the manufacture of plastic boots allows a very pronounced welt to be added at both the toe and heel. This makes the fitting of clip-on crampons a simple and quick operation, more so than with leather boots whose welt tends to wear away quickly.

Plastic boots are cheaper, warmer and more comfortable than their equivalent in leather. However, at the higher standard of mixed climbing, leather boots may still be the first choice. Whichever boots are chosen, they should have good rubber soles with deep cleats for step kicking on hard snow. Both types of boots should be fastened by hooks or D-rings – usually a combination of both.

CLOTHING

While any combination of warm clothes can be effective, the use of a layered system of modern high-performance materials has a great many advantages and only one major drawback – cost!

A system of clothing which can be easily adjusted to suit different temperature extremes is best. This usually means a combination of shirts, sweaters and jackets which can be opened for ventilation or closed for warmth. For maximum insulation, a series of layers is best as the air trapped between the layers and in the clothes themselves is an excellent insulating medium.

For the first layer – that is, the layer next to the skin – most climbers choose some of the modern thermal underwear, which is not only warm and comfortable but also capable of wicking away moisture from the skin and so limiting cold, wet areas. On top of this can go a heavier shirt which, once again, is made of a non-absorbent material, either polypropylene or wool, and finally a sweater. As well as traditional wool sweaters, there is a huge variety of synthetic-fibre pullovers and jackets available, and those with zip-up fronts make ventilation easy. The pile fleece from which these are made has high insulation properties but is not very windproof. Wool and man-made fibres have their relative advantages and disadvantages but as long as the sweater is warm when damp, not too bulky and comfortable to wear, personal preference will be the deciding factor. The old adage that two thin sweaters are better than one thick one still holds true.

On the legs it is normal to wear long-john-type underwear with breeches or salopettes on top. These again are available in a great profusion of styles and materials, but any that are warm, comfortable and reasonably windproof will do. Those which are high enough to avoid cold spots in the lower back are especially good. Long trousers are more popular than knee-length breeches these days, but whether this is because of fashion or practicality is debatable. As in all aspects of clothing, personal preference in conjunction with price will influence the buyer's decision.

Good-quality stockings made from a mixture of wool and man-made fibres provide a sensible compromise between hard wear, comfort and warmth. These should be knee-length for maximum insulation, and a loop-stitched construction is best. Most climbers will wear one pair inside well-fitting boots: too many socks can result in tight boots which actually make the feet colder.

No matter which type of boot is worn, a gaiter of some description is required to keep the snow out of the top of the boots. These come in three basic forms: stop-tous, which are simply a cuff around the ankle; gaiters which cover the lacing of the boot and extend up the leg to just below the knee [*fig. 11.1*, page 171]; and overgaiters which cover the whole of the boot upper and sometimes the sole as well [*fig. 14.7*, page 209]. The type of gaiter used depends on the temperatures and conditions expected. In most situations a gaiter which reaches to just below the knee and covers the upper of the boot will suffice. This should have a zip closure which makes it easy to put on and take off and some form of strapping to hold it in place under the instep of the boot. It should fasten securely around the top. For more extreme conditions an overgaiter is best. This is warmer and more weather-resistant, the best models having a tight rubber seal which fits around the welt of the boot. The overgaiter is best used on snow and ice routes as it is easily damaged by mixed climbing or walking around on sharp rock. Overgaiters can be lined with fleece or similar material to provide extra insulation for the feet and lower legs. In exceptionally good conditions stop-tous will be all that is required. However, these do no more than prevent snow from getting in the top of the boots; they provide no insulation and do not protect the trousers from wear and tear.

Shell Clothing

The outer garments in the layer system are known as the shell. It can either have some insulating properties or, more commonly, be only a waterproof and windproof layer. For snow and ice climbing it is best to choose an uninsulated shell which is big enough to allow insulating layers to be worn below since an insulated jacket is usually too warm and impractical for normal use.

There are many good designs and materials available for shell garments, personal choice and price being the limiting factors. Modern materials, such as Goretex and Entrant, which are both waterproof and allow the body to 'breathe', make very efficient shell layers [*fig. 11.3*]. Shell gear made from proofed nylon is less expensive and just as waterproof but less comfortable to wear. For cold, dry conditions natural fibres, such as cotton ventile, are still among the best but least versatile alternatives.

A one-piece suit, with jacket and trousers combined, makes the ideal weatherproof outer shell. However, this is impractical for all but the most severe conditions as ventilation, changes of clothes and toilet visits are all very difficult. For these reasons a separate jacket and trousers are the better choice. No matter what material these are made from, there are several important design features you should look for. In the jacket a good hood is essential. This should be big enough to allow a crash helmet to be worn underneath it, and at the same time small enough to be manageable in windy conditions. A piece of wire to reinforce the rim of the hood can help here. When fastened, the jacket must be impermeable to spindrift and wind. This is normally achieved by having a full-length zip covered by a flap,

Fig 11.3 A well-equipped snow and ice climber. Rucksacks for use on snow and ice should be streamlined so as to avoid snagging, both when climbing and also when belaying.

which can be secured either by Velcro or by pop studs. Pop studs are better as Velcro can ice up and become useless in freezing conditions. When climbing, it is important to have good, secure cuff fastenings as well. These should be of a design which allows them to be tightened while you are wearing gloves, and the sleeves should be well cut so that they do not pull up when the hands are raised above the head. For convenience the jacket should have some pockets which can be used while you are wearing a harness: those at chest level allow easiest access.

Depending on weather conditions and the type of trousers worn, it may be necessary to wear some form of overtrousers. These can be either trousers finishing at the waist or the currently more popular salopettes, which are usually made from the same material as the shell jacket. Whichever type is chosen, they should have long enough leg zips to enable them to be put on or taken off when wearing boots and crampons. Those with reinforced patches will last longer but are heavier. Although salopettes are warmer, they can also be inconvenient as they will usually require the harness to be removed completely before they are fitted and make subsequent toilet stops more awkward. Make sure that trousers are not so baggy as to interfere with crampon technique.

There is a school of thought which suggests that, since overtrousers are often carried 'just in case', they provide an ideal opportunity for weight saving. Conversely, lighter, less windproof trousers can be worn, thus making the overtrousers an integral part of the clothing system, and as such they will be worn almost all the time.

As about one-third of the heat lost from a well-insulated body is from the head, a thin Balaclava is an invaluable aid to keeping warm. One that can be worn underneath the crash helmet is best and those of man-made fibre or silk are more comfortable than traditional woollen ones which can be itchy.

Gloves are perhaps, after boots, the most important part of the ice climber's specialist clothing. For straight ice climbing, shrunken woollen mitts are best. On first inspection these would appear to allow both wind and snow to pass through them. However, experience shows this not to be the case as the dense wool quickly traps a thin layer of snow on the outside which renders them both snowproof and windproof. The only disadvantage with this type of glove is that it is not waterproof and handling equipment can prove difficult because of the thickness of the wool used. For mixed climbing a thin pair of polypropylene finger gloves, together with a fibre-pile mitt with a waterproof covering, are best. For difficult mixed climbing the outer gloves can be removed, leaving the fingers still covered and protected. Before replacing the overmitts, as much snow as possible should be scraped off the inner gloves otherwise heat is lost from the hands in melting this snow. For this reason in all but the most extreme conditions many climbers choose to perform delicate operations with the bare hands, which are easily cleaned before returning to the warm, dry outer mitts. When climbing in dry conditions which are not extremely cold, ski-type leather gloves are very useful, though these have a very short life [*fig. 11.3*]. These are much favoured on hard routes because of the better grip they give on tools, and their extra sensitivity means that they need never be removed when handling other gear.

Since it could be extremely serious in many winter climbing situations to drop or lose a glove, a spare pair, or at least a single reversible mitt, should be carried. Gloves can be attached to the wrist by loops of cord, large safety pins or elastic which makes them much more difficult to lose. Whichever system is adopted, care must be exercised to avoid dropping a glove in case it is not attached and also to avoid the inevitable tangles.

Rucksack

You will also require a rucksack in which to carry your equipment. This sack will be bigger than that used for rock climbing: one of about 50 litres capacity should do for one-day routes. A rucksack which has no external pockets is best as it is less likely to catch or snag when you are climbing or to interfere with ropework [*fig. 11.3*]. A wide variety of styles and makes are available but one which is light when empty, simple and long-lasting, and has no external or rigid frame is best.

Harnesses

Although harnesses used for rock climbing can be pressed into service for snow and ice, it is best to have a totally adjustable system. A harness that allows extra clothes to be worn underneath without compromising its performance is ideal. This usually means a harness with adjustable waist and leg loops. The added buckles which are often a problem when rock climbing are well padded by the extra clothes worn in winter.

ICE AXES

An ice axe is the basic piece of equipment needed for moving on snow and ice. Inherently a simple tool, its uses are many and varied: it is used for balance and support, as a hold, as an implement for probing, clearing and digging, as a belay anchor and as an emergency brake.

Although the axe has changed over the years from the original long, crude Alpenstock to today's elegantly designed and engineered climbing tool, the parts of the axe have remained remarkably similar even if their precise role has altered. Because of increased specialisation in use the term ice axe now covers a wide range of forms, but a modern ice axe would still be recognisable to climbers from the last century, whereas more specialised ice climbing tools might not be.

The parts which make up the ice axe are the head, the shaft and the spike [*fig. 11.4*].

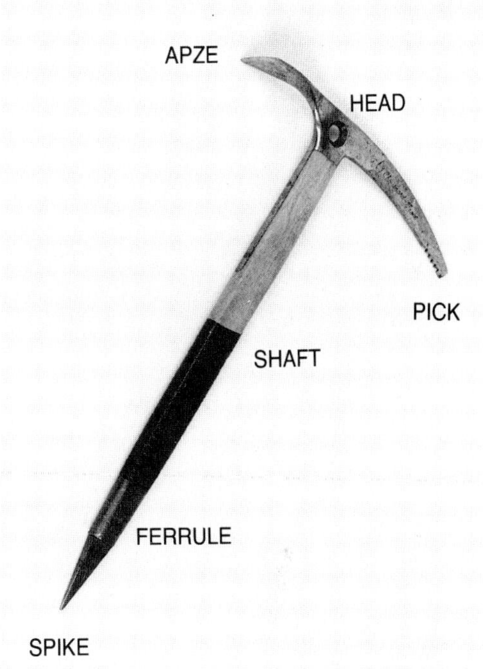

Fig 11.4 The parts of the ice axe. The shaft of this wooden axe has been taped up so as to give a better grip.

The Head

The head of an axe consists of a pick and an adze and is generally made of high-quality steel. The straight picks of the past, used for cutting, have given way to curved picks which are designed to hook in ice and stay there when pulled on. In general mountaineering axes the curve of the pick roughly coincides with the arc followed by the head of the axe as it is swung above the head. The bottom edge of the pick has a series of teeth which help it grip more effectively. These may be only at the front of the pick or may extend all the way back to the shaft, increasing in size as they do so; they give better holding power but are hard on hands and gloves. Although primarily a hooking implement, this design of pick can still be used for cutting.

The adze of the axe is mainly used for cutting and clearing. It may be flat or curved, straight-edged or scalloped, level or inclined. Generally a flat, straight-edged, uninclined adze is best for cutting.

The Shaft

The shaft of an axe is generally of a flattened oval cross-section to give a good, secure grip which does not pivot in the hand. It can be made of wood, wood laminates, metal, fibreglass or a combination of several materials. Wood, the traditional material, is the weakest but has good vibration-damping properties and 'feel' to it. Metal and fibreglass shafts are stronger but may be colder to hold, although many have a rubberised coating which improves insulation and grip. In general, with today's belaying techniques, the strength of the shaft is not as important as it once was: the 'feel' and balance of the axe are the main criteria influencing selection.

The length of axe chosen will depend on its main intended use rather than on any other factor. Generally, the bigger and higher the mountain it is to be used on, the longer the axe – up to about 80cm. For more technical climbing, a shorter axe – down to about 50cm – is easier to handle. A reasonable length for all-round use is about 60cm, although the actual balance of the axe cannot be ignored. Personal size and preference as much as logic will decide what length of axe will suit any individual, but for general use an axe whose spike almost touches the ground when held in a straight arm is a convenient length.

The Spike

The main function of the spike of an axe is to provide a sharp point so that the shaft can be driven into the snow. As long as it does this, its actual form matters little, although where the spike joins the shaft at the ferrule it should be smooth and tapered with no steps which could catch and impede its progress into the snow.

The Wrist Loop

Like the length of the axe itself, the length and type of wrist loop used depends on personal preference. Generally, however, the wrist loop is nearly as long as the axe. Its functions are to take some of the strain off the hand when you are using the axe for hooking in steep snow or ice; and to let you drop the axe when you need your hands for other jobs, such as placing protection or using rock holds (in these situations the axe simply hangs by the loop from the wrist). It is attached to the head of the axe either through the karabiner hole or by means of a hole specifically for it. It can be put on so that the pull on the pick is symmetrical and not twisting it out to one side, or tied so that it reduces leverage on the pick, whichever is felt to be the greater danger. The loop should be long enough to hold the axe near the bottom of the shaft so that its length can be used effectively. It can be held either over the back of the wrist or in the palm of the hand [*fig. 11.5*].

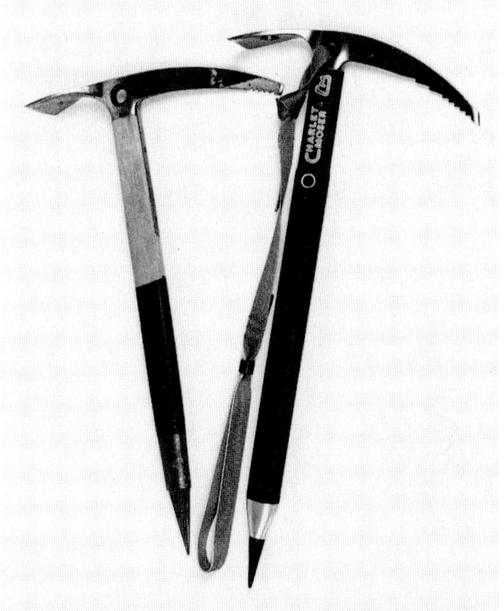

Fig 11.5 A metal- and a wooden-shafted axe. The wrist loop must be securely attached to the axe and may be adjustable, in this case by using the sliding ring.

Wrist loops may come with the axe, be produced commercially or be home-made. They should have a wide opening so that the hand can be inserted easily but have some form of slider which holds it tight against the wrist. A home-made loop can be produced from nylon tape and a short piece of hosepipe, tubing or tape.

It might seem that there is no reason not to use a wrist loop, and this is indeed the case in a climbing situation. However, in the broader mountaineering context the picture is not so clear-cut as the axe has a wide range of uses besides hooking. When used for security, the axe is held in the uphill hand, so must be changed over at each change of direction. The same applies when you are cutting steps, and in both cases the transferring of the wrist loop takes time and interrupts the flow of movement. Conversely, it does allow a better grip to be taken of the shaft and so relieve some of the strain of cutting, for example. In the event of a slip when the axe is used successfully for self-arrest, the loop is again no problem; but if control of the axe is lost, the falling climber is then attached to a sharp, pointed instrument which could cause injury. In some cases more serious damage has resulted from contact with the axe than from the fall. Letting the loop dangle free is not the answer as it can easily snag on crampons and trip you up, especially in windy conditions. If the loop is not on the wrist, it should be wound round the head and shaft and secured using the slider. An alternative is to have a wrist loop which is easily removed and attached only when you are about to start climbing.

Carrying the Axe

When the axe is not needed, it can be carried on the outside of the rucksack either in the loops provided or under the compression straps at the side. The spike, pick and adze should be well covered to prevent catching, cutting or tearing clothing, people or the interior of vehicles. In very crowded places such as cable cars, the axe is best carried in the pack or in one hand.

On terrain where the axe is occasionally required, it can be carried with the shaft parallel to the ground, spike forward and pick down to minimise the danger of impaling yourself if you slip. An alternative is to slide it down diagonally between the straps of the rucksack and the back. It can then be retrieved easily with one hand when needed but is not in the way. Remember to take it out before removing the rucksack or you run the risk of losing it.

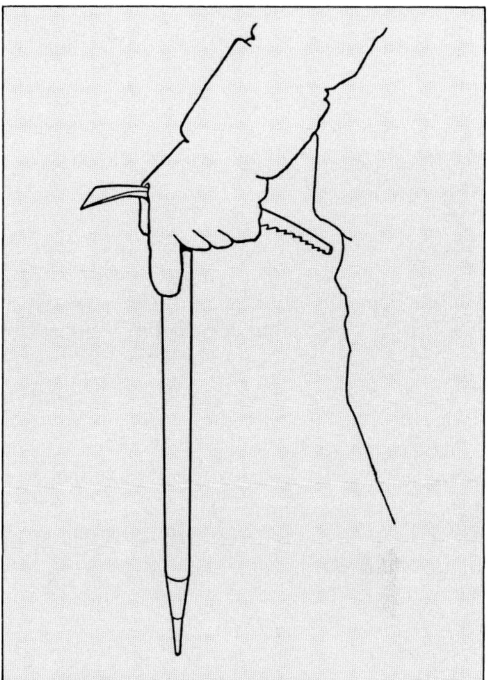

Fig 11.6 How to hold an ice axe.

When moving on snow slopes, hold the axe in the uphill hand where it can be driven into the snow for balance and support [*fig. 12.4*, page 180]. It is held with the adze facing forward, the pick back, the thumb under the adze and the index finger down the line of the shaft [*fig. 11.6*]. This is the basic grip used in self-arrest. It can be carried with the pick facing forwards but, although more comfortable and perhaps safer in a slip, it needs to be re-positioned to use for self-arrest. Many ice tools, particularly those with steep picks, are more comfortable if carried in this way.

12 Snow Techniques

Snow is one of nature's more variable materials: it can be as insubstantial as powder or nearly as hard as ice. There is a whole spectrum of snow types which grade from soft to hard, and as snow grades into ice, the way the climber deals with it changes. The technique used depends on slope angle, snow type, situation and the needs at the time. However, for the climber the factor that separates snow from ice is that in snow steps can be kicked, whereas on ice crampons are required. Although some step kicking is done while wearing crampons, it is necessary to be proficient at this without them. Time can be saved and progress speeded if a few steps can be kicked to negotiate a snow patch. It is not unknown for steps to be kicked by a climber wearing rock boots in otherwise summer conditions.

Soft snow generally presents few technical problems but much labour. Moving through soft snow, which can be waist- or even chest-deep, is simply hard work with few if any short-cuts. In any group it is the first person who does most of the work creating steps or even a trough through it. The lead should be rotated as often as necessary and energy saved by avoiding ploughing individual furrows. In the worst conditions crawling on all fours may be the fastest way to effect progress. Using ski sticks can make moving through deep snow easier: telescopic ski-mountaineering sticks are the most convenient as they can be made smaller and carried in the rucksack when you are actually climbing. In fact any mountain travel is made easier by using ski sticks as they take considerable strain off the joints and the spine, especially on downhill sections. They are particularly good as an aid to balance on slippery ground, in boulder fields, in windy conditions and when carrying a heavy rucksack.

If a lot of climbing in deep-snow conditions is contemplated, as in the Alps in winter, learning to ski and use ski-mountaineering equipment is the best solution for efficient travel. Snowshoes are an alternative but are slower and less effective on steep slopes.

However, for basic movement on snow an ice axe and a suitable pair of stiff boots are the main requirements to begin with. Once snow becomes harder or steeper, steps will have to be produced to allow safe progress and these can be made either by kicking or cutting.

KICKING STEPS

When kicking steps, the axe is held in the normal manner with the pick pointing backwards and the thumb under the adze. This way it can be used for both support and balance [*fig. 12.1*]. There are several ways to kick effective steps but in all of them the prime requirement is a positive step which is angled into the slope.

Direct Ascent

This type of ascent goes more or less straight up the fall line – that is, the shortest line up any particular part of the slope. Steps are kicked directly into the slope by swinging the boot an appropriate number of times to produce a secure step, usually deep enough to take half the foot and angled slightly down into the slope. On the hardest snow, however, a step a few centimetres deep may have to suffice. The main part of the technique is to conserve energy by using the weight and momentum of the swing to make the step. As the snow hardens, more effort is needed to produce a positive step; as the snow steepens, more vigorous kicking is required because it is more difficult to swing the foot as freely. In all cases, for security and efficiency, the body is held vertically and moving in a positive manner helps to produce better steps [*fig. 12.2*].

The axe is normally held in the stronger hand and driven vertically down into the snow for balance and security. It is moved only when the climber is standing securely in two steps. At steeper angles – about 45° – the axe is driven into the snow at a higher level. Both hands can be used for this. If it does not penetrate fully, the shaft can be held just above the snow to reduce leverage.

Fig 12.1 Using the axe for security and balance. It is carried in the usual manner with the thumb under the adze, the forefinger down the shaft and the remaining fingers under the pick.

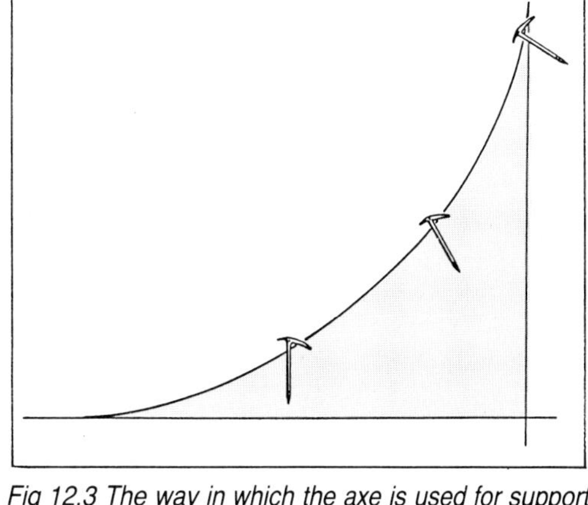

Fig 12.3 The way in which the axe is used for support on different snow slopes: this varies in angle from the vertical on easy slopes up to about 45° to the slope on vertical snow.

Fig 12.2 Kicking steps straight up a slope of hard snow where positively formed steps are required. The axe is held in the stronger hand and used for support while the step is being created.

On snow steeper than this the axe is driven in at a greater angle to give more support until, on vertical snow, it is pushed down and in at about 45° to the surface [*fig. 12.3*].

Climbing soft, deep snow, such as is often found below a cornice, is a matter of creating steps and distributing the weight as much as possible while pushing the axe and perhaps the arms into the snow. Alternatively, it may be a matter of digging and kicking a trough in the snow and wallowing up that. Steep, hard snow is treated like ice.

Diagonal Ascent

Diagonal ascent is the usual way of kicking steps up moderately angled slopes as it is the least tiring. The actual angle of ascent varies, although about 45° to the fall line is convenient for many open slopes. The steeper the slope becomes, the lower the angle of the diagonal. The steps themselves are created with the side of the boot and should be horizontal, angled slightly into the slope, nearly as long as the boot and as wide as is required for safety. The kicking action along the slope allows the cleats on the boot sole to act in a saw-like manner to form the step.

When ascending diagonally, you are in the more secure position of balance when the inner foot is ahead of, and above, the lower foot [*fig. 12.4*]. In the following step, with the outer foot above and ahead of the inner foot, your weight is concentrated on the inner or lower leg and so on only one step.

During diagonal ascent the axe is held in the uphill or inside hand and driven into the snow for balance and security. It is moved up into its new position when you are in the position of balance. Again, you should stand vertically to use these steps properly. When it is time to change direction, there are several options. In soft snow a step large enough to accommodate both feet can be kicked and the new line started from it. It may be possible to turn into direct ascent and, when in a secure position, swap the hand holding the axe

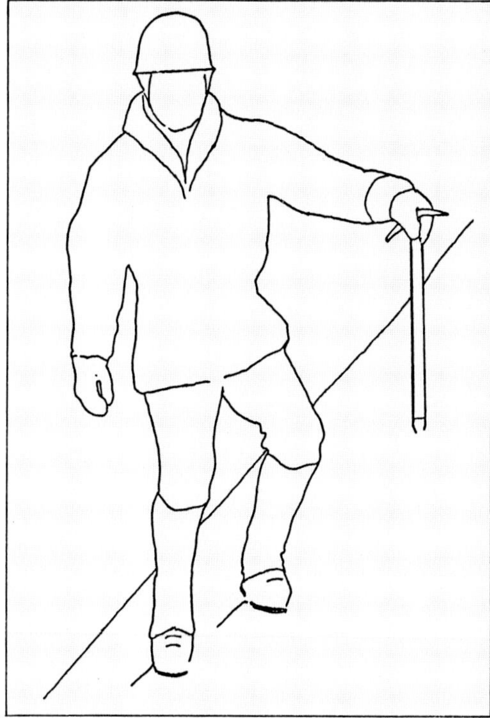

Fig 12.4 Standing in the position of balance in diagonal ascent with the feet on steps which are horizontal and angled into the slope and the axe held in the uphill hand.

and begin the next diagonal. On harder snow another way is to drive the axe into the slope, stand up and pivot on the upper foot while bringing the other foot up so it can kick the first step of the new line. The hands are swapped over on the axe so that, when you are facing uphill and pivoting, the axe is held in both hands. The last method is to adopt a position facing uphill with both hands holding the axe but with the feet splayed in opposite directions prior to starting the next line of ascent. The exact method used will depend on the angle of the slope and the hardness of the snow, but the aim is to make any change of direction smooth and controlled, rests being taken on the diagonal in the position of balance rather than on the turn.

Traversing

On easy angled or soft snow, steps can be kicked in the traverse when facing along the line of travel, but on steeper and harder snow it is best to face uphill and kick directly into the slope. The axe is placed in the snow at an appropriate level between waist and shoulder height and moved when you are secure. Each foot has to kick its own step, the feet being alternately together, then apart. It is usually best to avoid step-kicking traverses, diagonal ascent being easier [*fig. 12.5*].

Descending Steps

Creating steps in descent is a less natural way of creating steps. The type of steps used are plunge steps and are made with the heel of the boot. Stand upright facing down the slope and step forward and down, driving the heel into the snow with a positive, stiff-legged movement, almost a vertical drop on to the heel. The toes are kept in the air and care taken not to rock forward out of the step by dropping the front of the boot. Plunge steps must be done in a positive and confident way, even with a slight hop to direct more weight through the heel. If you are going straight down, the axe is held in the stronger hand ready to use for security should it be required, although the arms can be held out to the side for balance [*fig. 12.6*]. The axe can also be driven into the snow below and used for safety while you are moving into a position below it where it can be removed and replaced. This, however, makes the actual stepping action less positive and movement slower.

If the snow becomes too steep or hard to allow plunge steps, face into the slope and kick steps with the toes while using the axe for support. The distance between the steps when descending like this can be longer than on ascent.

CUTTING STEPS

Although cutting steps has now been superseded by the use of crampons, it is worth remembering that at one time this was an important technique. All the major Alpine north faces, almost all the big Scottish gullies and many of the world's major peaks and faces were scaled by climbers cutting steps with a single axe. Cutting steps encouraged a greater appreciation of the subtle variations within the snow and ice and forced climbers to be

Fig 12.5 Kicking steps in a traverse. The feet must next be brought together and then this position re-established. The axe is being used for security in the dagger position where it is held by the head and the pick driven into the slope.

Fig 12.6 Plunge steps used on the descent. The axe is held in the usual position.

imaginative in their use of the medium. To cut steps up a big Alpine ice route required a finely developed style which wasted no blows; Scottish gullies demanded a tenacity to hang on one-handed and cut steps up near-vertical ice in often awful conditions. All over the world step cutting ascents were made in times that are still impressive today. However, modern snow and ice techniques have taken much of the drudgery and pain out of snow fields and ice pitches and now permit them to be dealt with swiftly and often easily.

That is not to say, however, that step cutting is a thing of the past. Although it is now fashionable to say that steps need never be cut, this denies you a useful and versatile technique but one which does need to be practised to get the best out of it. Steps may still be required in several situations: crampons can break, be lost or forgotten; climbers can become tired, unsteady or injured. It may be quicker to cut a few dozen steps than to put crampons on and take them off soon afterwards, and in some places this may be so awkward or dangerous that it is safer to cut steps for a while. A patch of neve on a rock route can often be dealt with by a single axe and this can save the whole party carrying ice tools and crampons. On more tiring climbs steps are cut for stances and for resting. Learning how to cut a few common types of steps is a worthwhile investment.

When step cutting was the order of the day, the ice axe was made for this job with a basically flat adze and a straight, chisel-like pick. The adze was used primarily on snow and the pick on ice. Modern axes, with their curved or inclined and toothed picks, are designed to stick and hold and this makes them less suitable for cutting. However, much cutting can be done with the adze provided that it is sharp and used correctly, although steeply inclined adzes make poor cutting tools. In most cases, having a wrist loop taut to the wrist takes some of the arm strain out of cutting.

Step Patterns

The pattern of steps up a slope depends on the size and shape of the slope, its angle and the consistency of the snow or ice. Basically, however, if you imagine the line of tracks your feet would leave if you walked up the slope kicking steps, that is the pattern of steps you should cut. If hand holds are needed for balance or the slope is restricted in width, the steps will go straight up in an alternating 'left, right' fashion.

In the case of a less steep slope permitting a choice of line, the least tiring way to ascend is to zig-zag upwards. The actual angle of the diagonal line of steps to the fall line will depend on the slope, but the spacing and line taken follows that which a step-kicking climber would produce, between about 45° and 60°. On slopes of medium steepness a single line of steps will suffice; when the slope is steeper still, a double line may be required.

Types of Steps

If steps need to be cut, it would normally be on snow too hard to allow the kicking of adequate foot holds, or on slopes too steep to balance on comfortably. The actual type of steps cut depends on several considerations: the hardness of the snow or ice; the angle, size and shape of the slope; the use to which the steps will be put; and the competence of the party using them. There are, however, a few basic points which usually apply. Steps should be cut in a positive manner while the climber is standing securely in two steps; the pattern of steps should allow comfortable movement yet still be economical of effort; each step should form a positive hold angled into the slope; and the weight of the axe and the way in which it is used should do most of the work, not brute strength and ignorance. The best way to make any cutting efficient is always, after the first blow, to cut away from the initial hole so that snow can be broken out and the adze does not stick.

Fig 12.7 Cutting slash steps in diagonal ascent. Each step is as long as the boot, angled into the slope and at right angles to the fall line. The climber is in the out-of-balance position where the outer leg is ahead of the inner one.

Slash Steps

The quickest and most efficient type of step to cut in a diagonal zig-zag pattern is the slash step. This is cut while the climber is facing across the slope with the axe held in the uphill hand. The axe is swung in an arc so that the adze enters and leaves the snow as part of this swing. The weight of the axe does much of the cutting and the step produced should be as long as the boot, horizontal and sloping inwards to give a positive hold [*fig. 12.7*]. The pendulum action of the axe and the angle at which it cuts into the snow are critical. The angle is adjusted by changing the position of the hand on the shaft and by tilting the inside shoulder towards or away from the slope [*fig. 12.8*]. If the arm/axe length is too short, the adze will miss the slope; if too long, the adze will cut in at too steep an angle and stick. In good, hard névé a suitable step can be formed with only one swing, although two or three are more usually required. Reaching too far forward makes the step harder to cut as the adze will stick more and produce a step which slopes backwards. Too steep a line of steps is difficult to use, particularly when moving the outside foot.

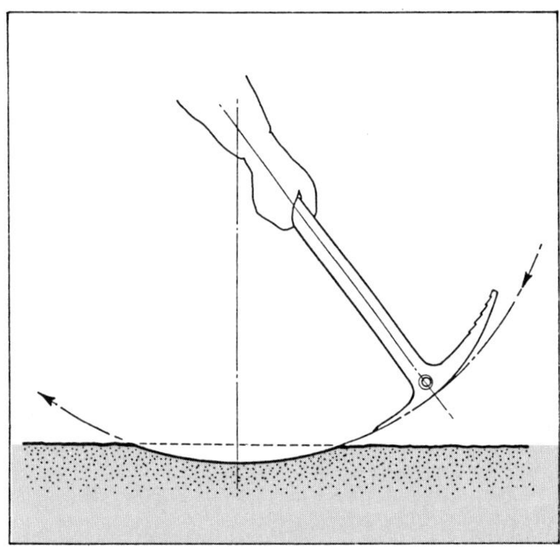

Fig 12.8 A side view of the pendulum action of the axe used to cut slash steps.

To change from one diagonal to the next there are several methods, some of which are elegant and efficient but require practice. The simplest method is to cut a large bucket step, stand in it with both feet and change the body position and cutting hand. The axe is planted firmly with either the shaft or the pick in the snow and used for security while you change direction.

While moving up from one step to the next, the axe can be driven into the slope to give security if required. As the slope steepens, it becomes more difficult to bring the inside foot through between the slope and the weighted leg. It is then better to cut two parallel lines of steps, one for each foot.

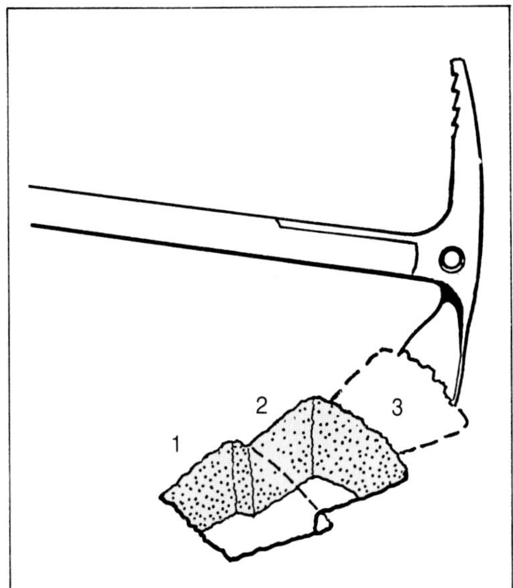

Fig 12.9 Cutting side steps. After the first blow, each subsequent blow cuts into an existing hole so that the step is cut from the heel to the toe.

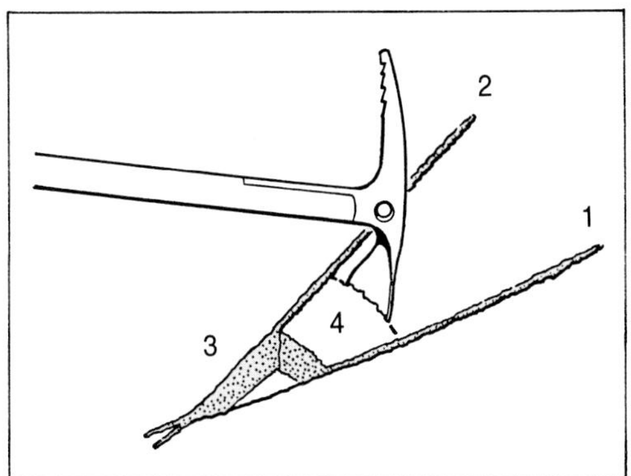

Fig 12.10 Cutting slab steps. The pick is used to make the two initial cuts and the adze then used to remove the snow between them.

Side Steps

In shape and pattern side steps are similar to slash steps but are cut with a series of vertical blows down into the slope. After the first cut, which produces a small hole, subsequent blows work from heel to toe or away from the body to produce a step which is horizontal and angled into the slope [*fig. 12.9*]. Side steps can be used on a traverse or a low-angled diagonal where slash steps could not be cut. They can also be cut in ice when the pick may be used. To prevent the pick sticking, a sharp upward lever at the end of the blow helps to break it free.

A variation on the side steps is the letterbox step which is cut in at right angles to the slope. The letterbox step is thus angled inwards and so is very secure. Like the side step, it can be cut with one or two hands and can be fashioned easily with the outside hand, allowing the inside hand to rest against the slope for balance. To change direction a large bucket step is used. Letterbox steps are fairly time-consuming to produce but are easy and safe to use.

Bucket Steps

Bucket steps can be of various sizes, depending on the use to which they are to be put. They slope inwards and are roughly semi-circular in section. They are cut with a simple downwards action of the axe, unless the larger versions are being made when a horizontal cut is angled into the slope then cuts are made downwards into the snow above this. The upper snow, being undercut, will break away more easily. The inside or outside hands or both can be used. These steps can generally be made more secure by an increase in size but their production owes more to strength than technique, although the principle of always cutting towards an existing hole applies here.

Bucket steps can either be small to take the front of the boot, medium-sized for both feet for resting or changing direction, or large for a stance. They can be cut in any pattern from horizontal through diagonal to straight up the slope.

Slab Steps

The slab step is an esoteric step used in slabby snow in the diagonal zig-zag pattern. In certain conditions this step can support your weight when steps kicked in the same snow will break up into slabby blocks, making uphill progress very tiring. First, two intersecting lines or slashes are cut in the snow with the pick of the axe to give a V-shape pointing towards you. The step is then chopped out with the adze, working from the heel to the toe [*fig. 12.10*].

Pigeonhole Steps

Pigeonhole steps are used in direct ascent or where it is steep and icy enough to require the hands for security or balance. As each step serves as both a hand and foot hold, it must be large enough to take the front half of the boot and have a pronounced lip to give a positive hand hold. Much of the shaping is done with the adze cutting down into the slope. After the initial hole in the ice is formed, further downward cutting will produce a good lip at the outer edge. Clear out any loose chips of ice to improve the grip before using.

The pattern is again the one that the feet would naturally make if going straight up the slope: that is, alternating left and right and a little more than hip width apart. Because cutting on ice is very tiring, as few steps as possible are formed, the distance between them being near your maximum step-up. Cut as many steps as possible before moving up and try to cut at least two ahead above shoulder height as they cannot be cut efficiently below this level. If the angle allows it, cut with both hands; if one hand is needed for support or balance, you are in for a long, hard bout of cutting.

Descending Steps

Steps can only be cut going downhill if the slope is not too steep. If good hand holds are needed for support, cramponing or abseiling is usually the quicker and safer alternative.

Slash steps are the best and most efficient type to use for descending; in fact they can be cut more effectively going down than up because of the better body position. Face across the slope and cut with the outer or downhill hand to form a step directly below the feet. The lower foot is then stepped down on to it, the upper foot brought down to occupy the step just vacated and the process begins again with cutting a step. Each step is cut from the position of balance and the inner hand can be used for balance and support if required [*fig. 12.11*]. An alternative is to cut a double line of steps with the line for the lower foot slightly ahead of the one used by the upper foot.

To descend diagonally, cut slash or side steps in the required pattern. Either step down one foot at a time, as when going straight down, or step the lower foot down and forward in the normal manner but bring the upper foot through between the slope and the weight-bearing leg which must bend to allow it to be placed on the next step. This action, however, rolls the weight-bearing foot outwards into a less secure position [*fig. 12.12*].

Fig 12.11 Cutting slash steps in direct descent. The climber is about to move the uphill foot down to the step just vacated when the lower foot was moved down, and once this is done the next step will be cut.

Fig 12.12 Cutting slash steps in a diagonal descent. The action of reaching forward tends to make the higher foot lift up off the step.

SELF-ARREST

In most aspects of climbing, prevention is better than cure, and this certainly applies to movement on snow and ice. Mastery of the techniques which will prevent a slip or a stumble is the first priority, but everyone should be able to save themselves should a trip turn into a slide. Anyone can trip up, and it is vital to regain control as soon as possible for the human body can quickly reach alarming speeds when sliding on snow slopes. The techniques for controlling such slides are known as self-belay and self-arrest. It is important that the skills described here are mastered in safe, controlled conditions before they can be relied upon in a real emergency.

The ideal place to practise is on a concave slope which has a safe run-out: that is, no protruding rocks or dangerous drops. This allows an out-of-control climber to slide to a safe and gradual stop, and also offers increased steepness and realism for use as your skills improve. A good run-out is vital, as you will find it difficult to relax and concentrate on the techniques if the consequences of failure are injury! Helmets should always be worn when practising any skills on steep snow slopes and it is also wise to ensure that little skin is left exposed to the abrasive qualities of rough, hard snow surfaces. When practising self-arrest, you should try to slide at a realistic speed, and in poor snow conditions a waterproof nylon jacket tucked into overtrousers helps make this possible [*fig. 12.15*, page 186].

Fig 12.13 Self-belay on hard snow where the axe must be grasped next to the surface of the snow to prevent it from being levered out. The feet are about to be kicked into the slope to help prevent a slide.

The Self-Belay

On a suitable slope the first skill to master is that of the self-belay, which is used to prevent a slip or fall from developing into a high-speed slide. The self-belay depends for success on speedy and positive execution. With the ice axe held in the correct position in the uphill hand, and the pick pointing backwards, the shaft is driven vertically into the slope should the climber stumble. It must be driven in as far as possible and the free hand grips the shaft at the surface of the snow to reduce leverage [*fig. 12.13*]. At the same time every effort should be made to kick the toes into the slope to gain some purchase. In soft snow conditions you will be able to drive the full length of the shaft into the slope, but when this is not possible your weight should be centred over the vertical axe. This reduces the leverage at the spike but still applies maximum force at the point where the shaft enters the snow, allowing some purchase to be obtained. These seemingly simple actions do take considerable practice and it will soon be discovered that if the axe is not driven in vertically, or the actions not performed at the split second when the slip occurs, they will not work.

On slopes of harder snow, or even ice, it is not usually possible to stop a slide by plunging the axe shaft into the slope. Instead the pick of the axe must be used. For this to be effective the pick must be stuck into the slope immediately – difficult to achieve when the axe is carried in the normal manner with the pick pointing backwards. To overcome the inevitable delay in changing your grip on the axe head so that the pick points forwards, it is best to plan ahead and change over before any problems arise. This has the disadvantage that the axe cannot be used for self-arrest, and so unless you are very confident that you can stop yourself with the pick alone the technique is best used only on easy-angled slopes.

It should be realised that a self-belay is only of any use when you have full confidence that, should it occur, the axe will hold your full weight while you replace your feet in the snow. If you are unsure of the security provided by the axe in a given situation, it is time to change the method of progress, perhaps to rope up and belay, fit crampons or cut steps. If you choose to continue, it should be with full awareness of the possible consequences of a fall which cannot be stopped by the self-belay. You must also realise that a failed self-belay can make subsequent self-arrest more difficult.

Self-Arrest or Ice-Axe Braking

If you fall on a snow slope and the attempt at a self-belay fails, some other method of stopping must be quickly adopted. The best method is to use the pick of the ice axe forced into the snow to bring you to a halt. This is known as self-arrest or ice-axe braking. The skills necessary to perform a successful self-arrest must be learned and practised before they become dependable. These techniques are practised on a similar concave slope to that used for the self-belay and the same clothes and equipment needed. Crampons should not be worn when practising as any mistake in the positioning of the feet can easily result in serious injury from them. Wrist loops should also be removed or, if this is not possible, they should be tied up out of the way. Since the slope used for practice should have a safe run-out, it is better to slide to a stop at the bottom if control is lost than to attempt to regain control of an axe whirling around at the end of the wrist loop, risking the possibility of impaling oneself at the same time.

To achieve a level of competence in ice-axe braking it is best to divide the technique up into progressive stages and to ensure that each stage is mastered before progressing to the next. It is also best to master each stage using alternate hands on the head of the axe.

There are many different methods of ice-axe braking, but the method described below is effective and can be adapted for any slide which occurs.

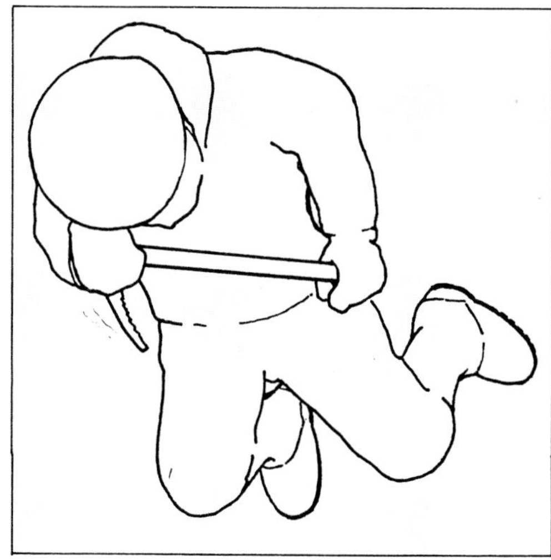

Fig 12.14 The basic ice-axe braking position as seen from underneath with most of the weight concentrated on the pick of the axe and the knees.

Fig 12.15 Dressed for practising ice-axe braking with full waterproofs and a helmet. The axe is held across the chest in the correct position and the climber is sliding on his back before rolling over into the basic braking position.

The Basic Braking Position

This method of ice-axe braking is based upon the usual way of holding the axe, whether in ascent or descent. With one hand on the head of the axe, the other hand grasps the end of the shaft and the ferrule. The spike is covered by this lower hand, both to protect your body and also to reduce the chance of the spike catching in the snow. If the spike is free, it can catch and the axe can be wrenched from your grasp.

The axe is held across the body with the adze under the right shoulder (assuming that the right hand is on the axe head), and the left hand and spike by the left side. This is the basic braking position which will always be used [*fig. 12.14*]. When you are lying on the slope, the pick is forced into the snow by pushing down with the right arm and shoulder and, if necessary, pulling upwards on the end of the shaft with the left hand. This allows the chest to be used as a pivot, providing more leverage on the pick. It is crucial that the adze of the axe is kept firmly pushed into the hollow just below the collar bone. If the axe is not under the shoulder, it becomes impossible to exert sufficient force on the pick. This can happen if you lift your head up away from the snow as this automatically lifts up your shoulder as well. In the correct braking position the brim of the helmet should be in contact with the slope. To maximise the pressure on the axe head, most of the weight is on the adze and your knees, with the stomach raised off the slope to help achieve this. The knees should be apart to give stability and the feet should be lifted up, well clear of the snow. If the feet are put down on to the snow while wearing crampons, they catch, causing you to somersault and lose control. Practise with the feet up as if you were wearing crampons; in a real fall you can use the feet to brake if necessary, but only when a conscious decision has been made to do so and when crampons are not being worn.

From a position lying face down on the snow, arch your back, withdraw the pick from the snow and begin to slide. The slide is easily arrested by gradually exerting pressure, through the shoulder, on to the axe head. If this pressure is applied too quickly, the axe tends to snatch at the snow and may either be torn from your grasp or pulled from its correct position under the shoulder. If the axe is displaced from its position under the shoulder, it is inefficient to attempt to pull the body back on top of the axe head unless you are fairly strong; instead, the back should be arched, the unweighted axe withdrawn from the snow, relocated under the shoulder and pressure reapplied. This is best practised as a series of start-stop slides.

If you master the technique described, you should be able to brake to a stop from a fall where you are face-down on the snow, sliding feet first.

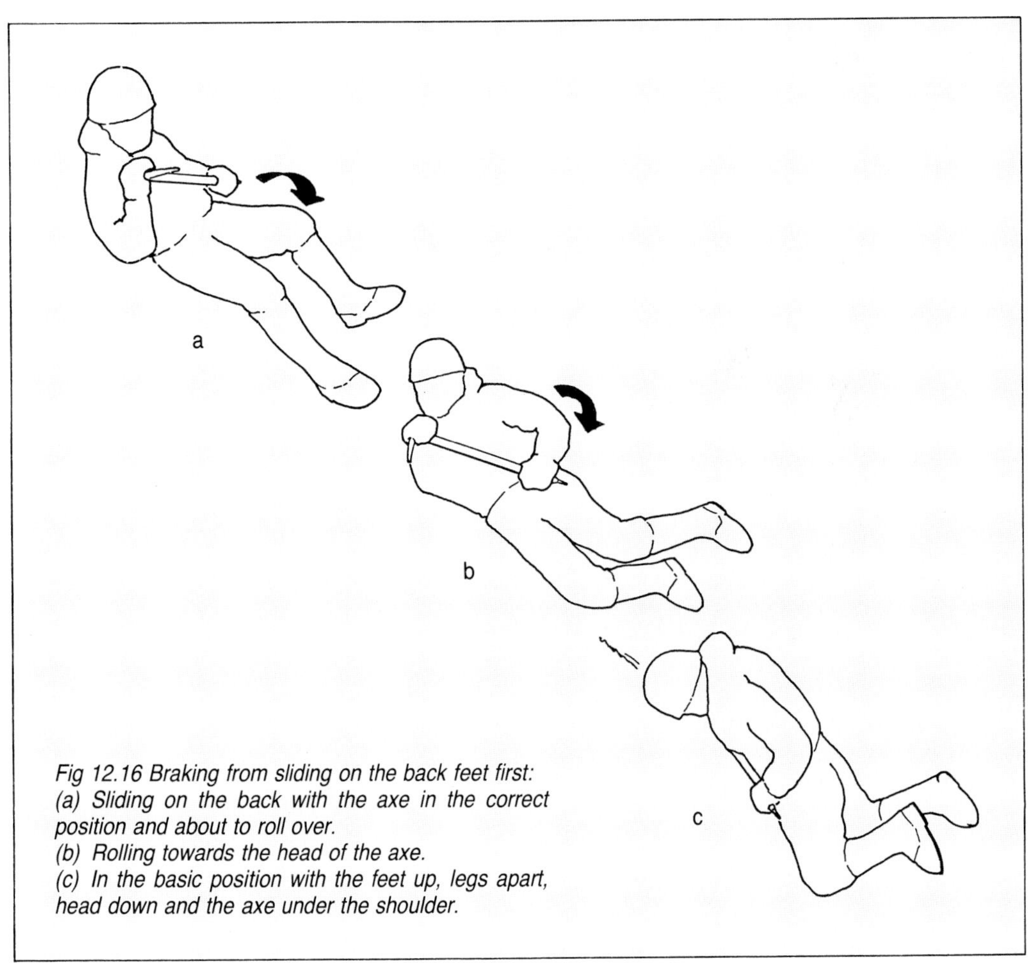

Fig 12.16 Braking from sliding on the back feet first:
(a) Sliding on the back with the axe in the correct position and about to roll over.
(b) Rolling towards the head of the axe.
(c) In the basic position with the feet up, legs apart, head down and the axe under the shoulder.

Sliding Feet First on the Back

If you should fall so that you are sliding feet first on your back, you must roll on to your front to get into the basic braking position. This is done by rolling towards the head of the axe – never towards the spike: it is too easy for the spike to catch in the snow and be wrenched from your grip. It is best to think of this manoeuvre in three stages:

You are sliding on your back, the axe against the chest with the feet held up, away from the snow [*figs. 12.15, 12.16a*].

You roll over, towards the head of the axe. The pick of the axe does not make contact with the snow at this stage, nor do the feet [*fig. 12.16b*].

Pressure is applied to the head of the axe by pushing the shoulder into the slope and exerting an upwards force on the end of the shaft [*fig. 12.16c*]. Ensure that the rest of the body is stable and under control. This pressure is increased until the slide is arrested. It is important that the roll is completed before the pick makes contact with the snow, otherwise it will be impossible to exert sufficient force on the axe head.

Sliding Head First, Face Down

For the series of manoeuvres involved in halting a head-first slide with the face down, a step should be cut at the starting point for the feet to hook into, so that the correct position can be attained in a static situation. The aim here is to use the pick as a pivot point for the body before braking as described above.

When you are lying face down and with your head pointing down the slope, hold the axe in the usual grip, but this time with one arm straight and out to the side. The pick should be level with the shoulder and as far out to the side as can be reached easily [*fig. 12.17a*]. If the arms are relaxed, causing the axe to be carried in front of the head, any bumps or undulations may cause the axe to smash into the face.

If the pick is planted out to the side the body will swing around [*fig. 12.17b*]. Do not leave the axe in too long since at high speeds it is possible for the body to swing through a greater angle than the desired 180°.

When you have spun around, withdraw the pick from the snow and, by arching the back, replace it under the shoulder [*fig. 12.17c*]. This allows braking to take place as before [*fig. 12.17d*]. Experience will quickly show how much force should be applied to the axe to gain the correct amount of turning momentum. In hard, icy conditions, a quick stab may be all that is required, whereas in softer snow the axe may have to be left in the snow for longer.

This sequence can be built up in practice from a static position (with your feet in a slot for security) to greater speeds as confidence is gained.

Sliding Head First on the Back

The important feature when stopping a head-first slide on the back is movement, as the ice axe initially provides only resistance to work against: it does not solve the problem on its own. You must not only turn over this time, but also pivot around.

The axe is held, with the head in the right hand and the left hand round the end of the shaft, level with the right hip and some way out to the side [*fig. 12.18a*]. When the axe is in the correct position, the right arm is straight.

Plant the axe in the snow and pull the upper body up on the shaft and towards the axe head, simultaneously throwing the legs out in the opposite direction – away from the axe head – and pivoting the body around the axe [*fig. 12.18b*]. It may be helpful to kick the legs out to the side and think about 'unwinding'. The axe should then be removed from the snow and braking completed in the usual way [*figs. 12.18c, 12.18d*].

To begin with a step – preferably a large bucket seat – can be cut in the slope and this is used to sit in while getting the feet pointing uphill. It is helpful to push the axe into the snow for support while doing this. Again, it is best to start from a static position.

The above is an outline of the basic skills required to stop when sliding in a controlled situation. You must practise with both hands until these skills have been perfected. It is also worth experimenting with tumbling and rolling falls. In an uncontrolled or tumbling fall this rolling must first be stopped. This is done by throwing the legs and arms wide apart, thus forming a star or spread-eagle shape [*fig. 12.19*]. This should stop you tumbling and cause you to slide, and from a sliding position the appropriate braking man-

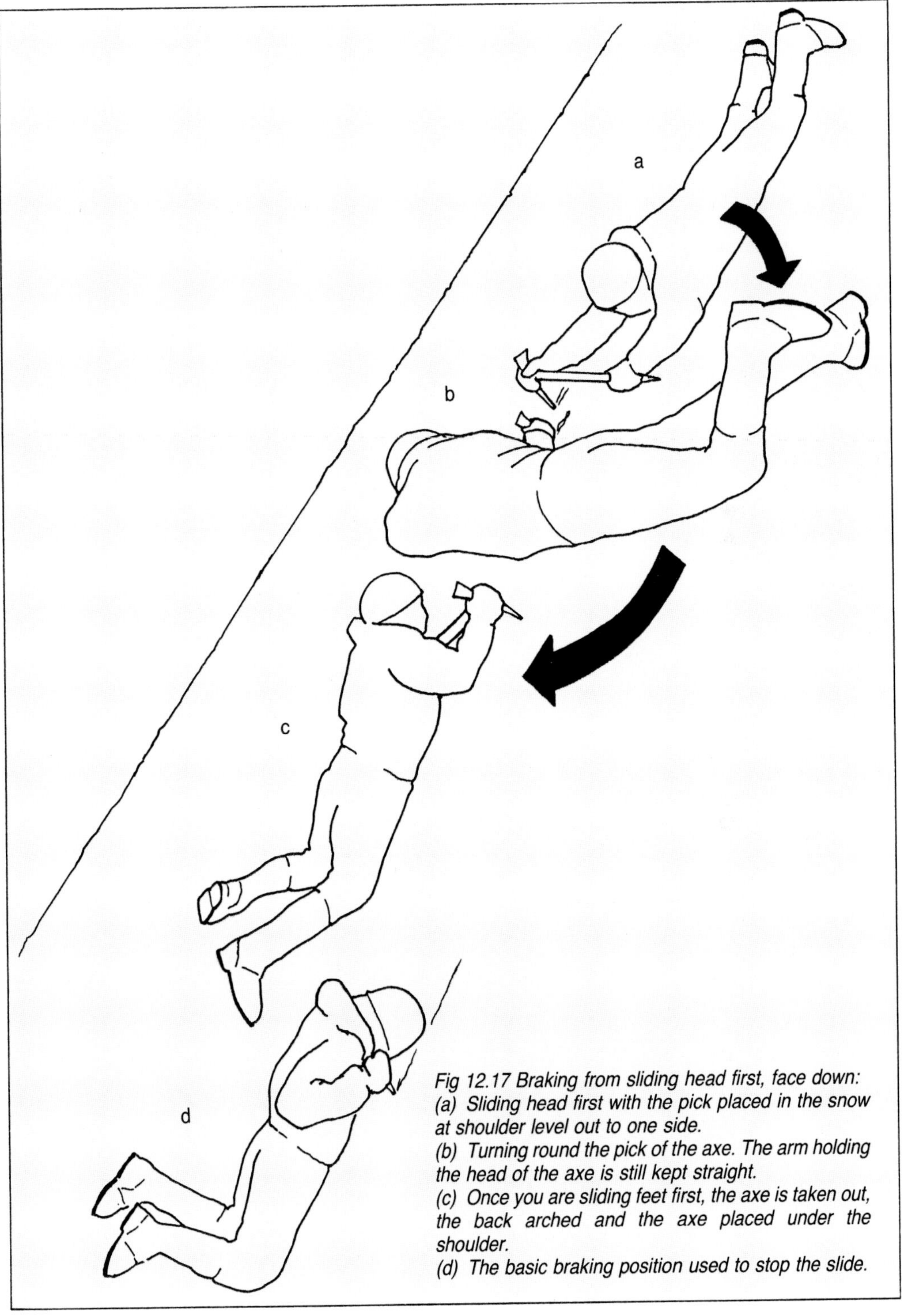

Fig 12.17 Braking from sliding head first, face down:
(a) Sliding head first with the pick placed in the snow at shoulder level out to one side.
(b) Turning round the pick of the axe. The arm holding the head of the axe is still kept straight.
(c) Once you are sliding feet first, the axe is taken out, the back arched and the axe placed under the shoulder.
(d) The basic braking position used to stop the slide.

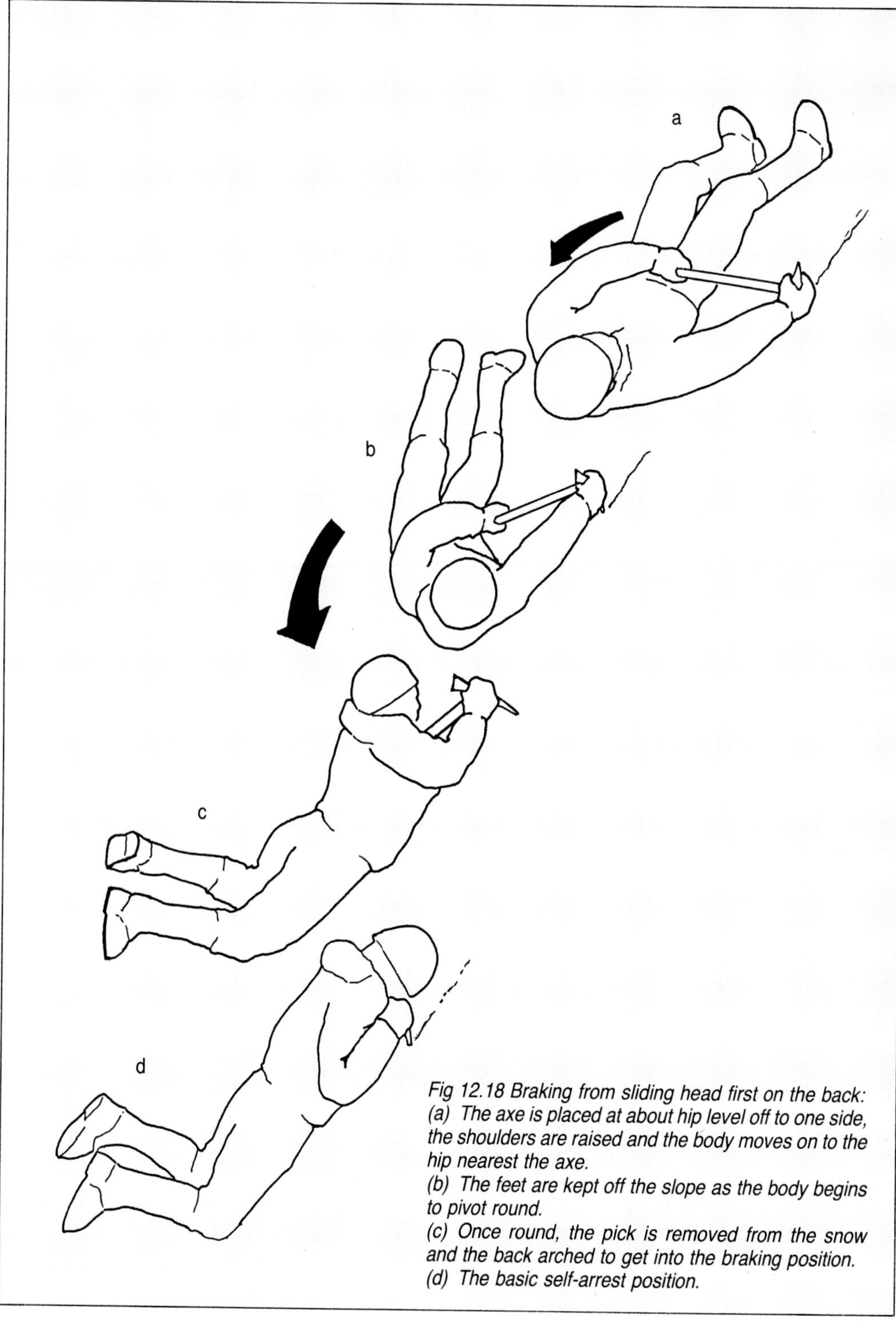

Fig 12.18 Braking from sliding head first on the back: (a) The axe is placed at about hip level off to one side, the shoulders are raised and the body moves on to the hip nearest the axe.
(b) The feet are kept off the slope as the body begins to pivot round.
(c) Once round, the pick is removed from the snow and the back arched to get into the braking position.
(d) The basic self-arrest position.

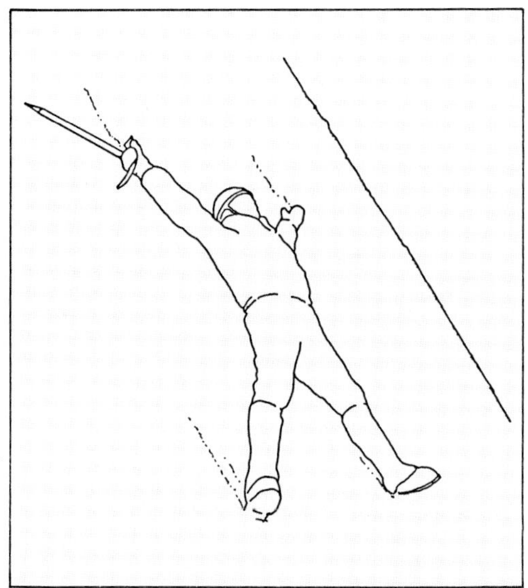

Fig 12.19 The spread-eagle position used to stop tumbling. It also has the advantage of putting the potentially lethal ice axe well away from the body until it can be used for braking safely.

oeuvres can be carried out. Great care should be taken with the axe when practising this.

Although it is best to practise all these 'exercises' at relatively high speeds, it must be appreciated that real self-arrest must take place as quickly as possible. In a real emergency there is no time for careful organisation and rearrangement: the braking must be an instinctive reaction. The further you slide, the more speed increases, making the fall much more difficult to stop. In all these examples, the importance of keeping the feet up has been stressed: this is for safety reasons in case you are wearing crampons when you fall. However, if the snow is very soft, it may be necessary to use the feet to increase the braking effect. When this is the case, the pick of the axe will rip through the snow and so the shaft may have to be used instead. Should this prove necessary, the hand at the end of the shaft should be moved up the shaft and the spike then forced into the snow.

It is vital that you are equally proficient with either hand, as the time taken to change hands may lead to so much speed being picked up that stopping is impossible. It is also worthwhile practising when kitted out with equipment you are likely to be wearing during a climb, such as a

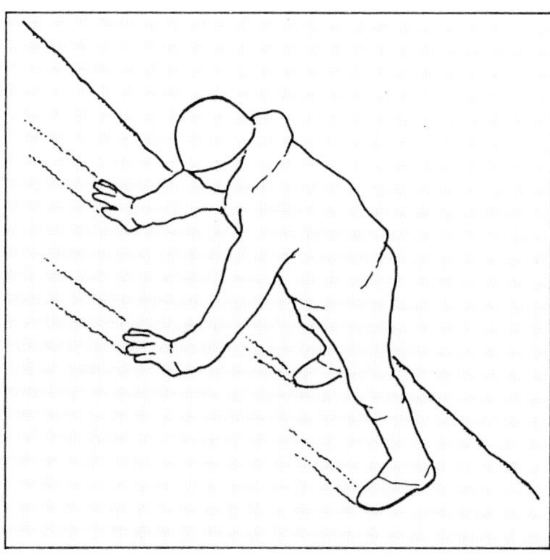

Fig 12.20 The position for braking with no axe where all the weight is concentrated on the toes of the boots.

rucksack and special clothing, so as to appreciate some of the factors which can affect a slide and how difficult it can be to stop.

If the ice axe is ever lost in a fall, you must make every effort to stop by using your arms, feet, hands and legs. If the snow is soft, this is quite easy, but in conditions of harder snow it can prove very difficult. One technique which is reasonably successful is to get into a face-down position on the slope and slide feet first. You then push out from the slope on your arms, and so form a wedge, sliding with most of your weight concentrated on your toes [*fig. 12.20*]. This will usually bring you to halt. It is a technique useful to skiers as well!

GLISSADING

Glissading can be a fast, efficient and exhilarating way to descend a snow slope, yet it can also be an invitation to disaster. What may begin as a glissade can end up as an uncontrolled slide or worse. Before starting, various precautions should be taken, the main one being that anyone who glissades must be competent at ice-axe braking. Glissade only where there is a safe run-out and the whole of the proposed descent can be seen, and ensure that there is no avalanche danger. Never wear crampons when glissading but do protect

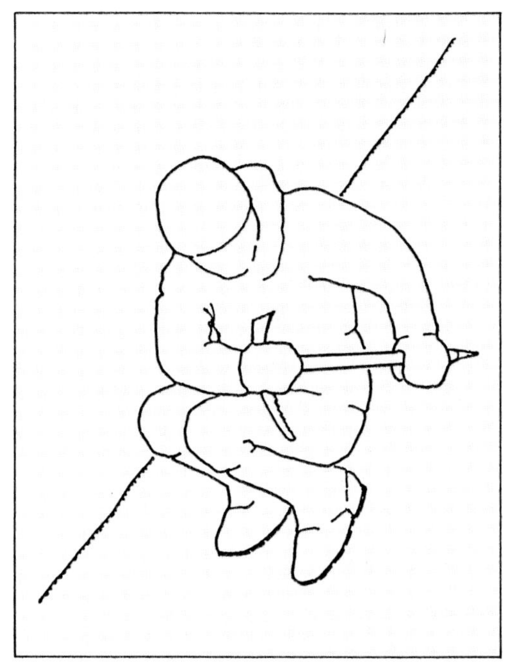

Fig 12.21 ABOVE LEFT: *The standing glissade position with the knees flexed and the arms held out from the sides for balance.*

Fig 12.22 ABOVE: *The crouching glissade where the weight is on the feet and the axe is used for control.*

Fig 12.23 BELOW LEFT: *The sitting glissade position with the axe shaft used as a means of control.*

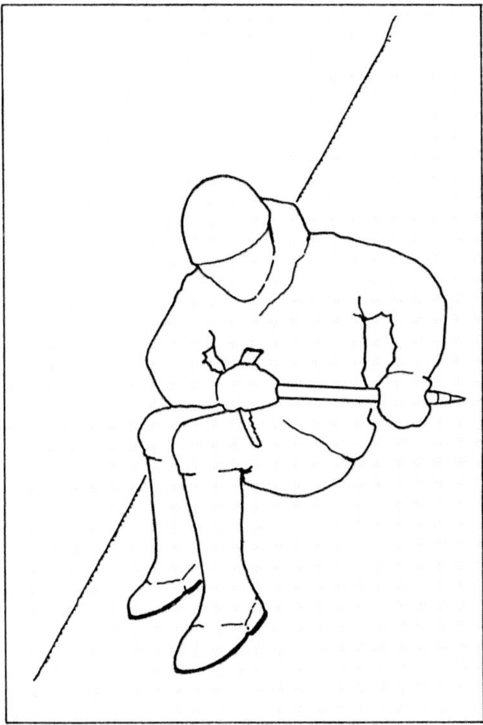

the hands with gloves and wear a helmet. Note that different clothes have different frictional properties, so some people may slide faster than others.

There are several methods of glissading but the one you choose will depend on your ability, the nature of the slope and the hardness of the snow. The best type of snow is firm enough to bear your weight yet soft on the top. These conditions are more often found later in the afternoon when the surface snow has been softened by the sun. However, patches of snow of different consistency can easily cause upsets and must be guarded against: glissading from a sunlit slope into the shadows can mean going from ideal snow to crusty ice in a few feet with predictable consequences.

There are three types of glissade, not including the involuntary one which is more properly referred to as a slip or a fall.

Standing Glissade

The standing glissade is the most comfortable, elegant and efficient method which permits the most effective steering and turning. It also gives the best views of the way ahead. It is, in essence, skiing without skis. Stand in a relaxed upright position with the knees and ankles bent forward and the feet about hip width apart. Hold the arms out from the sides to aid balance; the axe may be held in either hand, though the stronger one is more advisable. One foot can be slightly ahead of the other and your weight should be over the balls of the feet [*fig. 12.21*]. Leaning too far forward can cause your toes to catch; leaning too far back can make your feet shoot out from under you. Turns are effected by rotating the body in the desired direction and at the same time turning the feet so that the boots are on their uphill edges. As in skiing, an unweighting action assists the turn; bend the knees and ankles a little, then make an upwards motion to reduce the weight on the snow while turning. To slow down, put more weight on to the heels by rocking back slightly to dig them in. Alternatively, turn across the slope. To stop, turn the feet fully across the slope and use the uphill edges of the boots to create greater resistance. If the snow is slow or the angle too low, skating-type steps can be used to make progress.

At all times look out for changes in snow conditions which could cause problems and be ready to use the axe to stop.

Crouching Glissade

The crouching glissade is done in a low, crouched position with the axe held at one side of the body with one hand on its head and the other grasping the shaft above the ferrule. Squat down and slide on your feet and drag the spike in the snow for balance. To brake, put more weight on the shaft of the axe to push the spike into the snow. In general, this is fairly stable and slower than the standing glissade, but it does not readily allow turning and edging with the boots to control the speed [*fig. 12.22*].

Sitting Glissade

The sitting glissade is simply a matter of sitting on the snow and sliding down it. The axe is held at one side and the spike used as a brake as in the crouching glissade. Lying back and lifting the feet increases the speed; sitting up with knees bent and feet on the snow slows you down. Speed is controlled by increasing pressure on the spike of the axe and the heels. Turns are not possible, but it is the method which works best in soft and deep snow [*fig. 12.23*].

13 Snow Belays

Snow anchors come fairly low down the list of preferences for a secure belay, but on many occasions they may be all that is available. Snow can be unstable and made up of several differing layers, its consistency can vary from place to place and it can be difficult to assess the security of any anchor placed in it. An anchor in hard, consolidated snow may be as good as a rock anchor; in poor snow it may be useless. The actual type of anchor selected depends on the equipment carried and the nature of the snow itself. In general, the more consolidated the snow, the less the difference between the various snow anchors in terms of holding ability.

When placing any snow anchor, the more information you have about the snow cover, the better. If the locations of any hard or weak layers are known, it is possible to make a better decision as to what type of anchor to use and where to place it. This information is readily obtained by digging a snow pit as for the assessment of avalanche conditions. Even pushing the axe into the snow and noting the differing resistance of the layers can provide a great deal of useful information. (See Chapter 24, page 311.)

BELAYING ON SNOW

With any snow belay the actual stance taken is of greater importance than with rock anchors. It should enable the belayer to absorb some of the force with his body before the anchor is loaded. A low sitting stance is best as this is shaped so that the belayer is pulled down into it, rather than off it, in the event of a fall. The stance should be straight across the fall line and angled down into the slope; two appropriately sized and shaped footsteps are cut or kicked below it [*fig. 13.1*]. This can be extended further by cutting out a saddle-shaped stance behind which the belayer can brace [*fig. 13.2*]. If the slope is too steep to permit a good sitting stance to be taken, a bucket stance of the same general type should be cut for the belayer to stand in.

As snow belays are used when no better rock or ice protection is available, there is a good chance that a leader will not be protected by running belays and so could fall the full length of the rope. This puts a downward force on the belayer and, although this can be severe, it will often be more

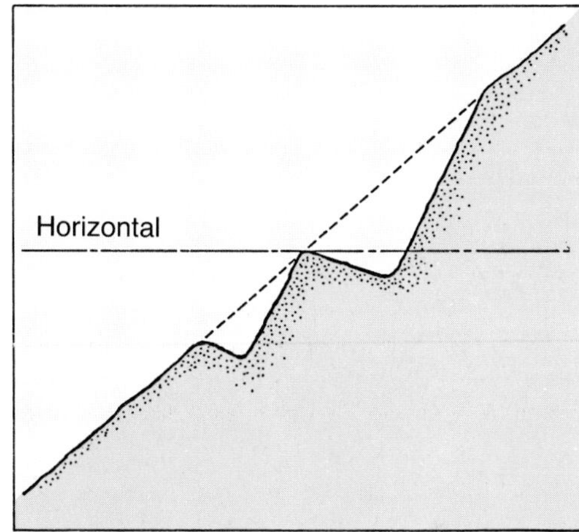

Fig 13.1 Cross-section of a stance in snow showing how it and the footsteps are angled into the slope.

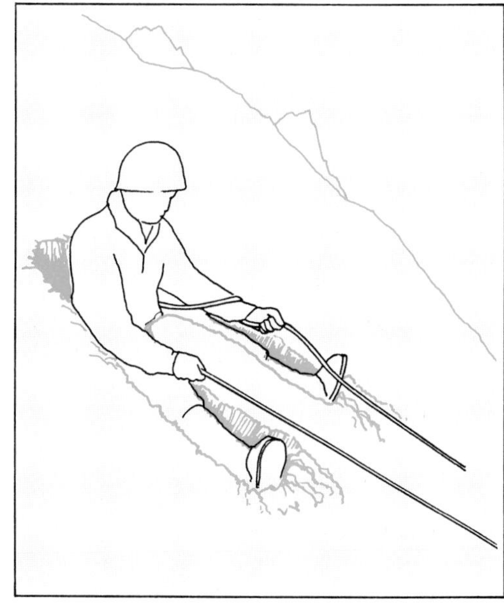

Fig 13.2 A body belay in a saddle-shaped stance.

of a slide than a free fall. When using a snow anchor, it is best to give a body belay in most situations. Besides being dynamic, the belay should also be indirect – that is, with the belayer's body placed between the force and the anchor so that it will take some of the force and act as a cushion for the snow anchor. The rope should go below the rucksack but above the ropes to the anchors to keep the point of pull as low as possible. If you are using a waist belt, giving a body belay is simple; but if you are wearing a harness, more care must be taken. The front point attachment can be converted to a rear attachment with a cow's tail or the live rope arranged to be at the same side of the body as the rope to the anchor. The live rope can also be taken through a karabiner clipped into the knot loop to re-direct it.

In a fall the dead hand is brought across the front of the body in a controlled manner to increase the friction and the braking. The speed at which this is done depends on the nature of the terrain, the speed of the fall and the amount of rope left to work with. If it is safe to let the leader slide, he can be stopped fairly slowly. If there is a chance that he may hit an obstruction or drop over on to steeper ground, he must be stopped more rapidly. The slower the braking, the less the load on the anchor. Do not try to grip the rope with the hands as this is ineffectual, particularly with icy or snow-covered ropes, and in some situations can be dangerous, but concentrate on bringing the dead hand across the front of the body. If a second slips, he should not be able to apply much more than body weight if the rope is managed properly. If a leader falls on to a running belay, the force of the fall will be upwards and the belayer's weight will act in a dynamic manner as he is lifted up. However, if the leader does get a good runner, it may be better to change it to a belay and take advantage of its increased security.

Another problem with belays on snow is the lack of opportunity to double up on anchors. On a rock belay, if an anchor is not good enough on its own, others can often be placed to give a sound attachment; on snow this is not generally possible. If an anchor is in poor unconsolidated snow, so are any others placed nearby. It is critical that snow anchors are loaded from the correct direction; usually this is straight down the fall line. This makes load sharing difficult to arrange unless the anchors are put directly one behind the other and a suitable distance apart.

Another difference between rock and snow anchors is the degree to which they can be checked. A rock anchor can be inspected visually and tested in other ways but a snow anchor, once placed, may be completely out of sight. It is also easier to build up experience of rock placements as they are used continually on rock climbs and tested more frequently by falls. Snow anchors may be placed regularly but hopefully fall tested very infrequently. Unless an anchor is loaded, you do not really know how strong it is and for this reason practice with snow anchors is invaluable. Select a safe slope such as would be used for ice-axe braking practice, place the various anchors and, by pulling on them, load them as much as possible. Try to find out how they fail and why, and build up experience of the anchors in a controlled situation before committing yourself to them.

When placing an anchor in snow, it is usual to try to disturb the snow which will be in front of it as little as possible. In some conditions, however, you can strengthen the anchor by compacting the snow by stamping it down before placing the anchor. This consolidation must be done over a fairly large area and works best in snow which is fairly damp and so will compact well. The anchor is then placed near the top of the compacted area.

It is also worth practising holding leader falls with a dynamic body belay to gauge the forces involved and the technique required to stop a fall in an appropriate way. It is easier to fall if the 'body' goes down the slope head first on its back. This way the slide is safer and faster and any strain is taken on the hips. Practise only in a safe place with a previously tested anchor.

Besides providing protection as a rock anchor would, some forms of snow belay can be used in a more temporary manner. That is, certain snow anchors can be arranged very quickly to provide protection when it is needed, to the extent of being placed when a fall seems imminent or has even occurred. These temporary anchors are of more use in a second fall, although they have been used to arrest leaders. However, to set them up in time does require fast reactions and a thorough understanding of the anchor's uses and limitations, and needs to have been practised in safe conditions on numerous occasions.

SNOW ANCHORS

Deadman

The deadman is a spade-shaped alloy plate, about 20×25cm, pointed at the bottom, reinforced at the top and with a wire about 2m long attached to its centre. It may also have lightening holes and angled wings to improve its stability. If correctly placed, it not only resists a force but also digs itself deeper into the snow and increases its holding power. Of all snow anchors it works in the widest range of snow conditions, although the harder the snow, the stronger it is [*fig. 13.3*].

The angle at which the deadman is placed is critical: it should be 40° to the snow surface. To find this angle, place the axe at 90° to the slope (use the plate's shape to achieve this if necessary), bisect this right angle and tilt the plate back another 5° [*figs. 13.4, 13.5*]. Push the plate into the snow and, using it as a guide, cut a slot at right angles to the fall line and at 40° to the slope. The depth of this slot depends on the hardness of the snow, but it should normally be at least 25cm; the softer the snow, the deeper the slot. This cutting is most easily and accurately done standing at the same level as the plate and looking across at it. In very unconsolidated snow it can be placed at the back of a horizontal step but still at 40° to the slope [*fig. 13.6*]. A vertical slot for the wire is cut straight down the fall line [*fig. 13.7*]. First mark out the slot, then cut from the bottom to the top so that the pick, adze or shaft does not continually stick in the snow. This slot is deepest at the plate and tapers up to the surface at its downhill end. It should be at least as long as the wire – about 2m – to ensure that the pull comes on to the plate at the correct angle. Use the pick or the shaft to

Fig 13.3 Two deadmen, showing the swaged wire, the reinforced top for hammering and the lightening holes. The deadman which has the wire wrapped round for carrying has wings to stabilise it.

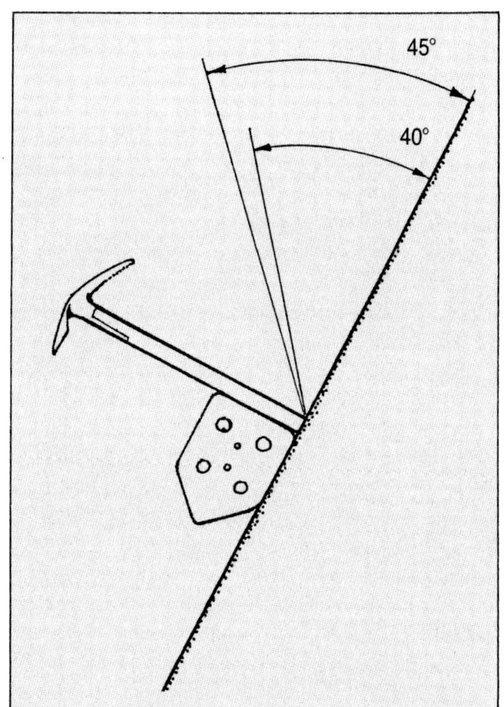

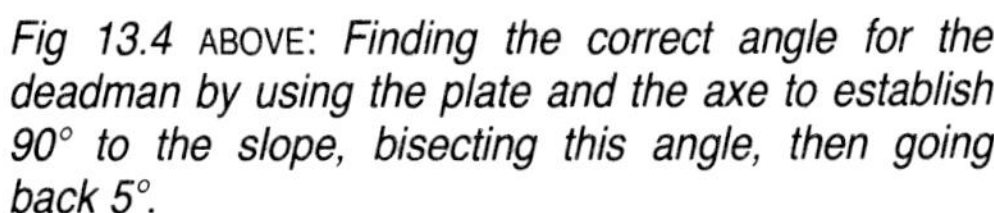

Fig 13.4 ABOVE: *Finding the correct angle for the deadman by using the plate and the axe to establish 90° to the slope, bisecting this angle, then going back 5°.*

Fig 13.5 BELOW: *Placing the deadman at 40° to the slope, using the axe at right angles to the slope as a guide.*

Fig 13.6 ABOVE RIGHT: *The deadman placed at the back of a horizontal step but still at 40° to the slope.*

Fig 13.7 BELOW RIGHT: *With the plate at the correct angle as a guide, the slot for the deadman has been cut at right angles to the fall line and the vertical slot for the wire is being excavated using the pick.*

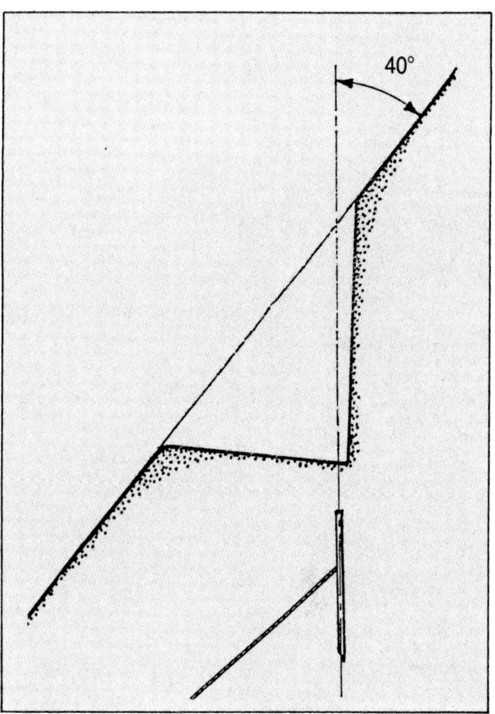

make this slot and try to disturb the snow in front of the plate as little as possible as it is this snow that provides some of the anchor's strength.

Once the slots are cut, put the deadman in the horizontal slot, hold it firmly against the front face and hammer it in until it is below the bottom of the slot. As it was flush against the face of the slot at 40° to the slope, it should maintain that critical angle as it is hammered into place. While you are hammering it in, keep the wire taut with one hand so that it goes down to the bottom of the vertical slot [*fig. 13.8*]. The internal angle between the wire and the plate should be 50°.

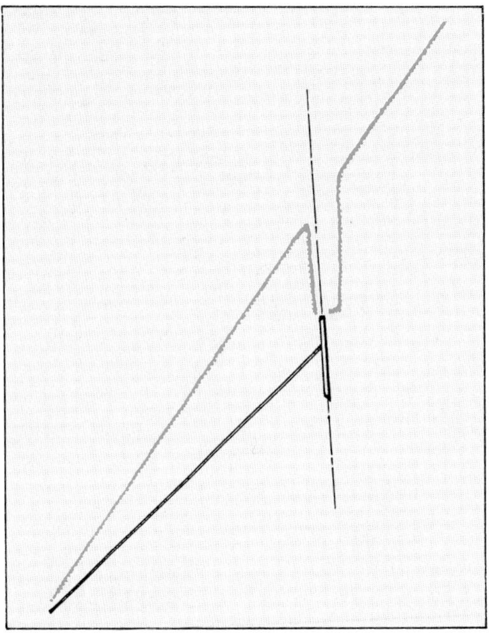

Fig 13.8 ABOVE: *A correctly placed deadman which has been put in down the front face of the angled slot.*

Fig 13.9 BELOW: *Faults in deadman placement:*
(a) At too shallow an angle the plate will cut down through the snow.
(b) At too steep an angle the plate can pull up and out.
(c) With a bend in the wire the plate can be forced upwards if the wire is loaded.

If the deadman is placed at too shallow an angle, the plate can cut down through the snow too easily and will eventually pull out where there is a weakness [*fig. 13.9a*]. This will be at the stance if not before. If it is too upright when loaded, it can pull up and out [*fig. 13.9b*]. A bend in the wire can also result in the plate being pulled up and out [*fig. 13.9c*].

As the deadman functions best in hard snow, it may be necessary to clear any layers of soft snow from the surface. If it is placed in soft snow lying on a hard or icy layer, the anchor could fail if loaded. When the plate pulls down and hits the hard layer, it will probably not penetrate but change angle and skid down above it.

When the deadman is in place, it should be bedded in firmly by using the axe as a lever through a karabiner on the bottom of the wire. The leader can then clip his rope into this karabiner and, protected from above, cut a stance at a suitable spot. As the angle of pull is critical, the stance must be low enough to ensure that this is down along the slope in a straight line between the plate and the belayer. The easier-angled the slope, the further the stance will be from the plate to ensure that the plate is above the level of the belayer [*fig. 13.10*].

To use a deadman belay on flat or nearly flat ground such as at the top of a climb, it is placed exactly as before, at 40° to the slope, and the

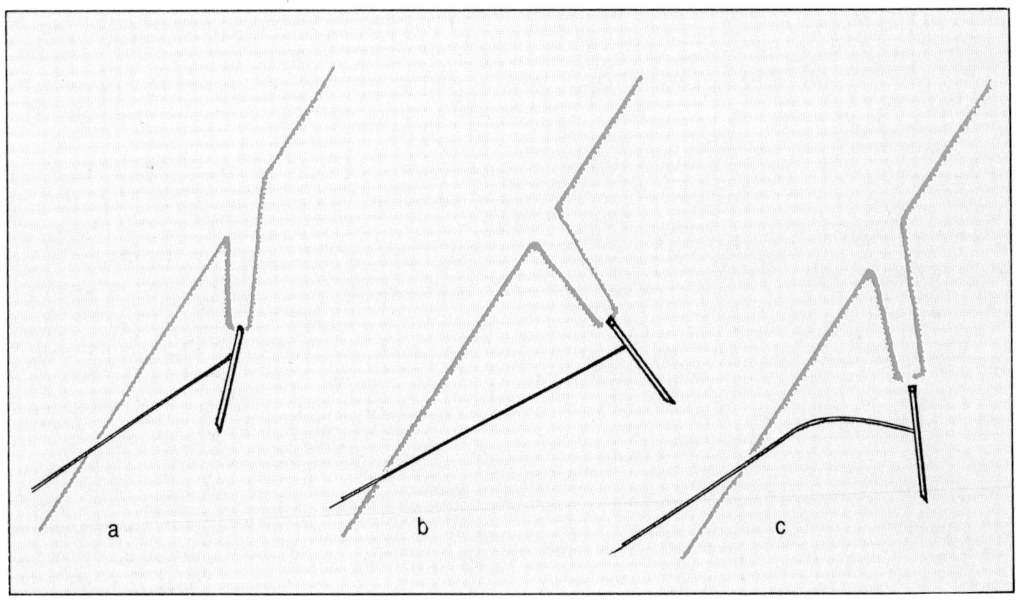

Fig 13.10 Using a deadman as the anchor. The belayer has a good saddle stance situated far enough below the plate to ensure that the pull is directed down along the surface of the snow and not outwards from it. An indirect body belay is being used and the dead rope is hanked round the axe so that it does not get snagged.

belay taken normally. Care must be taken to ensure that it is well back from any cornices [*fig. 13.11*].

The deadman is the only type of snow anchor routinely used for runners on snow and ice climbs. The deadboy is a smaller version of the deadman, but its use is limited.

Snow Stakes

Snow stakes or snow pickets are made of angled or T-shaped aluminium, pointed at one end and with a swaged wire loop or attachment hole at the top. They may also have lightening holes and can be from 0.5–1m long. You place a snow stake by hammering it into the slope as far as it will go with the inside angle facing downhill. The angle at which it is placed depends on the angle of the slope. On easier-angled slopes it is placed vertically or a few degrees back from the vertical. As the terrain steepens, the angle of placement becomes closer to 45° to the slope. In some snow conditions it can be put at the back of a horizontal step.

Snow stakes can be awkward to remove and may need to be cut out, so are often used when the anchor is to be left in place. They are more suited to poor snow and ice where a deadman would not work properly. Such conditions are often found on high mountains, particularly those in hot climates such as the Peruvian Andes.

Snow Bollard

A snow bollard is a simple and effective anchor, particularly useful in hard snow. A horseshoe-shaped slot is cut in the snow with the open legs facing downhill. The slot is normally cut with the adze and should be about 5–10cm wide and 10–20cm deep. It is deepest at the top, tapers up to the surface at the bottom of the legs and is slanted in cross-section to form a lip [*fig. 13.12*]. When cutting, work on the outside to avoid disturbing the snow which forms the bollard. Its size is determined by the hardness of the snow and is normally at least 1m in diameter in hard snow and up to 3m in diameter in soft snow. It should not be cut so that the legs join together to form a teardrop shape as this produces a weaker anchor isolated from the main snow slope.

Increasing the bollard's size can increase its strength but does not overcome its main weakness which is the rope cutting in. This can be reduced by padding the back and shoulders of the slot with anything that increases the effective diameter of the rope, such as spare gloves, hats, scarfs, overtrousers or other clothing, rucksacks or bivi bags. Axes and hammers can also be used, in which case they are pushed vertically into the snow at the shoulders, the widest points of the bollard, where the rope cuts in most [*fig. 13.13*].

When making a bollard, look very carefully for weak layers into which the rope could pull and so cut. It is best constructed to take advantage of the hardest snow and this is the main factor which

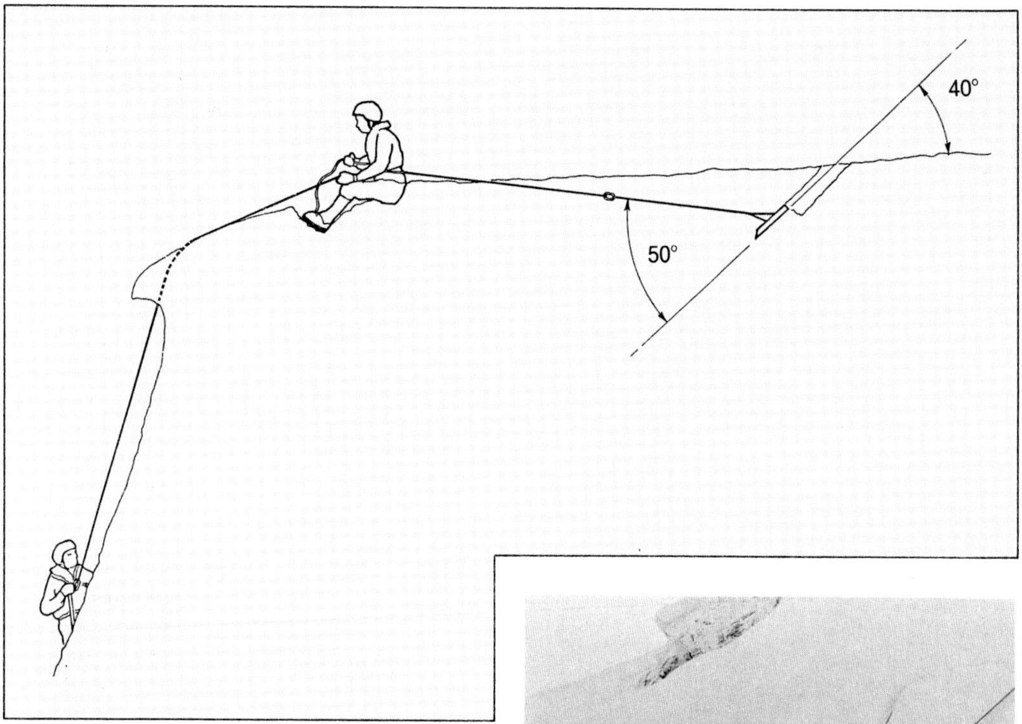

Fig 13.11 ABOVE: *Using a deadman on flat ground. The plate is still placed at 40° to the slope; the belayer has a good stance cut into the snow and is using a body belay.*

Fig 13.12 RIGHT: *Using a snow bollard as an anchor. The stance is situated far enough below the bollard to ensure that any pull is along the surface of the snow.*

Fig 13.13 BELOW RIGHT: *A snow bollard, showing the undercut back which keeps the rope in place and the axes placed at the shoulders to reinforce the bollard and prevent the rope from cutting in.*

decides the depth of the slot. Although it can use up a lot of rope, especially in soft snow, it requires no extra gear. A bollard in hard snow can be very strong and can be used as an abseil point without abandoning any gear. Even with a shallow snow cover it is often possible to construct a secure bollard where nothing else could be used.

Buried-Axe Anchor

To make a buried-axe anchor, first cut an adze-width slot at right angles to the fall line and a little longer than the length of the axe. This slot can be down into the slope at an angle of between the vertical to about 40° to the slope, but it must not slant outwards from the slope. It should be as deep as can be cut comfortably – about 0.5m in normal conditions – and dug to take advantage of any hard layers in the snow. Another slot at right angles to this and about one-third of its length in from one end is then cut down the fall line. This tapers from the depth of the horizontal slot at the top to the snow's surface about 2m lower down [*fig. 13.14*]. Try to disturb the snow below the horizontal slot as little as possible. The vertical slot is cut with either the pick or the shaft of the axe to keep it narrow, although the adze may be used in the initial part of the preparation.

A sling is then attached to the axe by means of a clove hitch put on with the diagonal strand of the knot at the back of the shaft so that if loaded it will tighten up. The sling is tied so that it is half-way along the axe in terms of surface area and pulls symmetrically on the axe. This attachment point is about two-thirds of the axe's length towards the head and is generally close to its point of balance. Securing the sling there distributes the load evenly along its length and decreases the chance of it pivoting and so coming out.

The axe is then placed, pick down, in the bottom of the slot with the sling in the vertical slot. The axe is pushed hard against the front wall of the slot for its full length to reduce twisting [*fig. 13.14.*]. The stance is arranged well below the axe and the belayer tied tight on to it.

Unlike the deadman, the axe does not cut down when loaded and relies on resistance to be effective. One problem is that the axe can pivot and pull out if not loaded correctly. Snow from above the slot can be packed down on the axe to help reduce the chance of this happening in some conditions. It is normal to use a sling on the axe, though it is possible to clove hitch the rope directly on to the axe shaft. This does not allow much range of movement when organising the stance, but in either case ensure that the stance and all other cutting has been done before burying the axe.

If another axe or ice hammer is available, it can be used to reinforce the buried axe by pushing it vertically into the snow immediately in front of the horizontal axe. This second axe is put through the sling at the top of the vertical slot [*fig. 13.15*]. An alternative that can be used to increase area and resistance when the snow is not deep enough

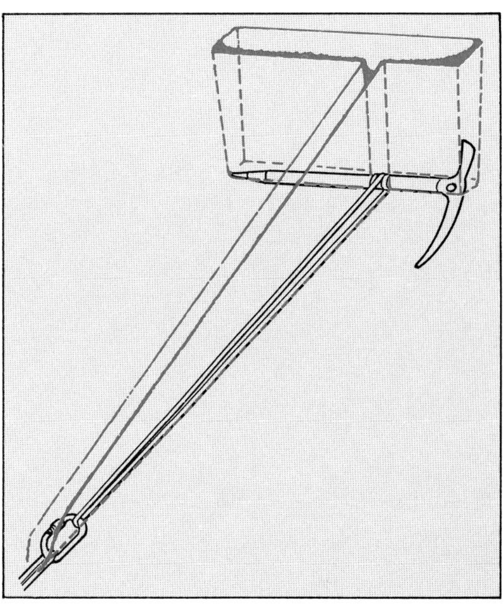

Fig 13.14 To make a buried-axe anchor, a specially shaped slot is cut. Then an ice axe is buried horizontally with a sling clove hitched round a point half-way along in terms of surface area.

to take a vertical axe is to use two tools horizontally. In this case the sling is clove hitched round both axes at their point of balance but with the axes facing in opposite directions.

T-Axe Anchor

The T-axe anchor is similar to the reinforced buried axe but the first axe is placed vertically, or a few degrees back from the vertical, behind the horizontal axe. A sling clove hitched to the head of the vertical axe is run over the horizontal axe and into a slot down the fall line. In this case the horizontal slot can be fairly shallow, only just deeper than the axe itself. The vertical slot is also shorter and less deep but must still be arranged so that the pull is along the surface of the slope [*fig. 13.16*].

The advantage of this anchor is that it is fast to construct as less cutting is required and it can take advantage of any hard layer of surface snow to provide resistance. Two long tools are not necessarily required as the horizontal axe can be replaced with anything suitable such as a peg hammer, ski sticks, tent poles or even a suitably shaped rock. The disadvantage is that more

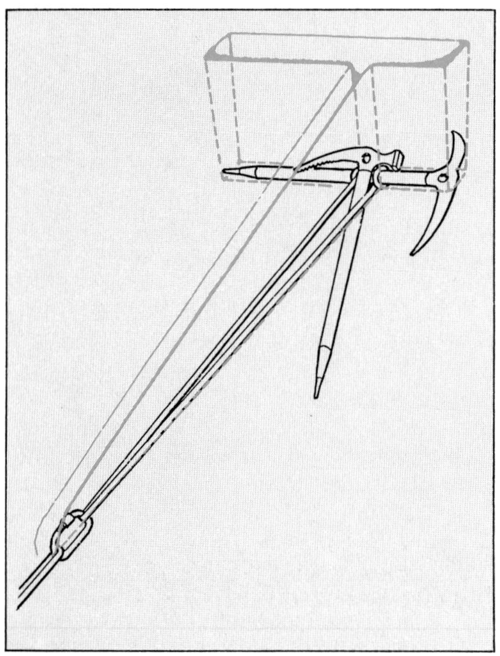

Fig 13.15 A reinforced horizontal axe: a hammer has been driven vertically through the sling in front of the horizontal axe.

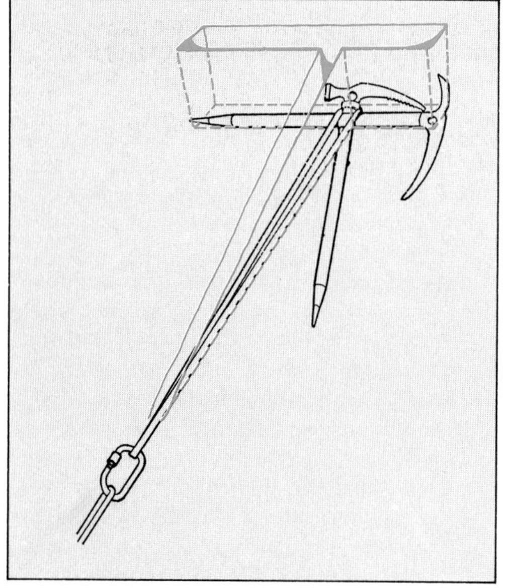

Fig 13.16 T-axe anchor in which the vertical hammer has a clove hitch round its head and is placed behind the horizontal axe. Normally the longer shaft is put in as the vertical placement.

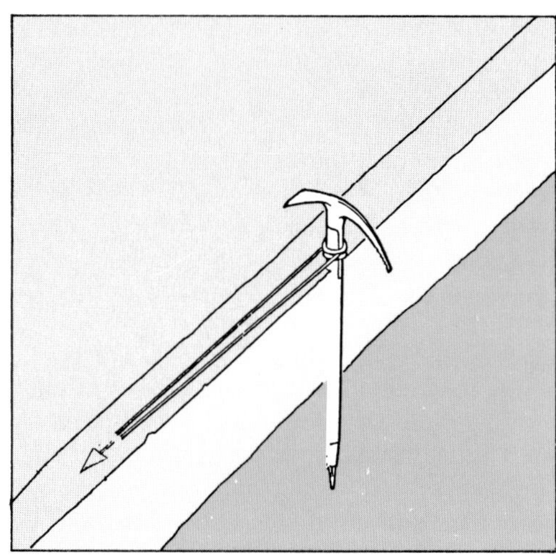

Fig 13.17 Vertical-axe anchor with a sling clove hitched on to the shaft at the surface of the snow.

experience is required in judging the snow conditions as this anchor can fail if not placed correctly or if the lower layers of the snow are much weaker than the surface.

Vertical-axe Anchor

The vertical-axe belay is the traditional unreliable type of snow anchor. The axe is placed in the snow vertically or at an angle of up to 20° back from the vertical with its head of the axe (and the wider cross-section) across the slope. A sling or the rope is attached to the shaft with a clove hitch which is put next to the snow surface [*fig. 13.17*]. Alternatively, a karabiner through the eye in the axe's head can be used. This type of anchor is prone to failure as a result of the leverage, lack of resistance and the tendency of the axe shaft, particularly if wooden, to break [*fig. 13.18*]. It can, however, give a more acceptable anchor in snow which is so hard that the axe has to be hammered in for its full length. This does the head of the axe little good and other forms of axe anchor are still better and stronger.

Foot Brake

The foot brake, often called the New Zealand foot brake, uses the axe for a temporary belay. It can be set up rapidly and, with practice, even be used by a party moving together.

To construct it, push the axe vertically into the snow as far as possible. Face across the slope and place your uphill foot directly against the axe so that it is braced by the foot. The axe head is pushed firmly downwards by the uphill hand. The live rope is then run across the top of the boot, round the back of the shaft and round the boot again. The rope is held in the downhill hand and pulled back against the ankle to create friction and a braking action [*fig. 13.19*]. When load is applied, the axe is pulled against the bracing foot which is firmly stamped into place. The uphill hand continues to exert downward pressure on to the head of the axe.

Fig 13.18 LEFT: *The not unusual consequences of using a wooden-shafted axe for a vertical-axe anchor.*

Fig 13.19 BELOW: *The New Zealand foot brake. The rope is run over the boot, behind the axe and round the ankle. Friction is increased by taking the rope uphill; the uphill hand maintains downwards pressure on the head of the axe.*

Fig 13.20 ABOVE: *The foot brake in hard snow where the shaft of the axe cannot be pushed in up to the head and must be braced behind the knee.*

Fig 13.21 LEFT: *The standing axe belay. The belayer is using a shoulder belay and, as the rope runs through a karabiner on the head of the axe, any force will be directed down through the belayer and on to the vertical axe beneath his feet.*

This form of belay is dynamic – the rope must be allowed to run and the braking done in a controlled manner. The degree of braking depends on the position of the rope at the ankle; moving the hand uphill increases friction. If the rope is held firmly, the initial jerk in a fall will probably cause the anchor to fail. In hard snow when the axe will not go in fully, it can be braced by the lower leg and the knee [*fig. 13.20*].

To use this while moving together (see Chapter 18, page 254) a loop of rope is carried so that it is in place round the top of the axe shaft and, if needed, the axe is thrust into the snow with the rope in place. It must be stressed that this form of belay is more suitable for a second fall and in any case requires fast reactions and much practice.

Standing-Axe Belay

The standing-axe belay, also known as a stomper belay, is a quickly arranged temporary belay which uses the axe pushed vertically into the snow. A karabiner, preferably a locking one, is clipped through the eye in the head of the axe and the live rope clipped through it. You then stand either directly on top of the axe with both feet, which can be awkward when wearing crampons, or brace one foot securely on the axe head and face downhill. A shoulder belay is given by taking the rope up and over one shoulder from behind with a twist round the dead arm [*fig. 13.21*]. Alternatively, the rope can be taken in through a belay plate or friction hitch attached to the waist belt or harness. If the rope is loaded, the force is directed down through the belayer's body on to the axe. This method of belaying is suitable only for fairly small forces such as second falls or when belaying on flat ground at the top of a climb or on a glacier, and should be practised before being used. It can also be employed on slopes if they are not too steep, in which case a horizontal step about 0.5m square is cut or stamped into the snow and the axe pushed in up to its head in the centre of this platform.

14 Crampons, Ice-Climbing Tools and Their Use

CRAMPONS

As early as 1574 reference was made to the use of crampons in the mountains. Initially used by hunters and shepherds in the European Alps, the early examples consisted of simple heel units, with spikes to penetrate the snow, which were strapped to the heels of the boots. Over the years these were developed, mainly in the Eastern Alps, until in 1910 crampons similar to those in use today were produced by Oscar Eckenstein. Although crampons were used in the Alps in the nineteenth century, it was not until the 1950s that they became popular in Britain and the USA, when improvements in reliability, strength and design led to their more widespread adoption. The more modern designs not only gave increased security on icy ground but also led, with improving technique, to big savings in time, an important consideration when snow and ice climbing.

Construction

The original hand-forged crampon has been almost totally replaced by the modern stamped or formed method of construction. Increased knowledge of the behaviour of materials used in making crampons, when subjected to low temperatures and constant flexing and bending, have led to the manufacturing methods used today, with the emphasis on strength, lightness and optimum performance [*fig. 14.1*]. In its original form the crampon was a metal frame with downward-pointing spikes which were strapped to the sole of the boot. Later two front points were added and, although they are based on this early design, today's crampons have continued to develop, using hi-tech plastics and metals and different

Fig 14.1 A hinged, twelve-point crampon correctly laid out for fitting. The buckles are always to the outside of the foot: this is the right crampon.

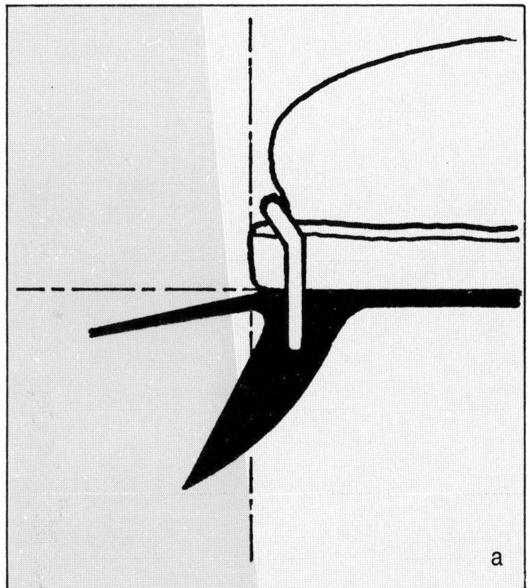

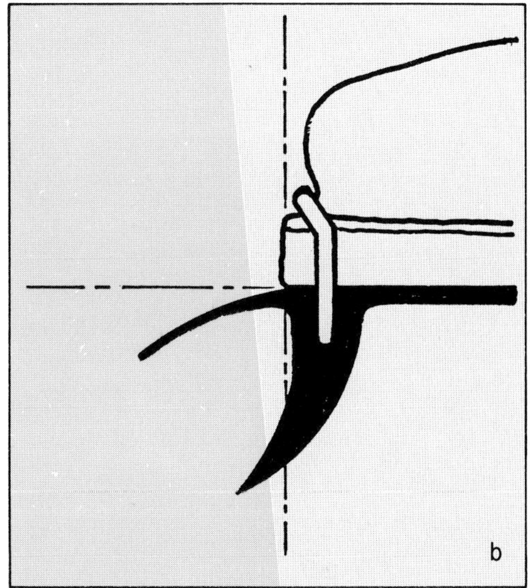

Fig 14.2 Inclined (a) and curved (b) front points of a crampon. Some people find the inclined points less secure and more difficult to place.

numbers and configurations of points.

All crampons, no matter what their type or age, strive to solve the same basic problems: they must be a good fit on the boot sole (adjustable to different sizes and styles of boot); and they must give the optimum performance for the conditions in which they will be used. Within these parameters there is a great deal of variety, choice and specialisation. Today there are two main types: general-purpose or all-round crampons (that is, those which are a compromise and so useful in all branches of snow and ice climbing); and technical ice-climbing crampons (those best suited to steep, hard ice).

The General-purpose Crampon

The general-purpose crampon has ten downward-facing and two forward-facing points and is hinged in the middle [*fig. 14.1*]. There are normally four points to the rear of the hinge and eight in front, so that the hinge sits under the instep of the boot. The hinge is a vital part of the general-purpose crampon as it helps to lessen the chance of crampon failure caused by the constant flexing which can occur when crampons are fitted to boots which do not have fully rigid or flat soles (the latter is a particular problem with the cheaper plastic boots).

The points on this type of crampon will be of average length (about 2cm) and the front points may be either inclined or curved [*fig. 14.2*] but will always be at right angles to the downward-facing points.

Technical Ice-climbing Crampons

The crampon which has evolved for technical ice climbing perhaps varies the most from the original concept. It is normally rigid, so giving a very stable platform under the boot, and has longer points than the general-purpose crampon. The front points are either inclined or curved but may be parallel to the downward-facing points [*fig. 14.3a*]. The type of front points used will depend a great deal on the preference of the individual climber. However, there are three main types: *Curved points*, designed to take into account the swinging action of the foot and so strike the ice at the correct angle for maximum penetration. They are often backed up by two other points, which give a 'lobster-claw' configuration [*fig. 14.3b*] and thus a more stable placement; *Inclined points*, normally at an angle of 45° to the horizontal and mechanically very secure when placed, though some people find them awkward to use [*fig. 14.3c*]. In very hard ice *Vertical points* penetrate more easily but are not so good in soft conditions when they provide less support and may even cut downwards.

Characteristics from all of these crampon types

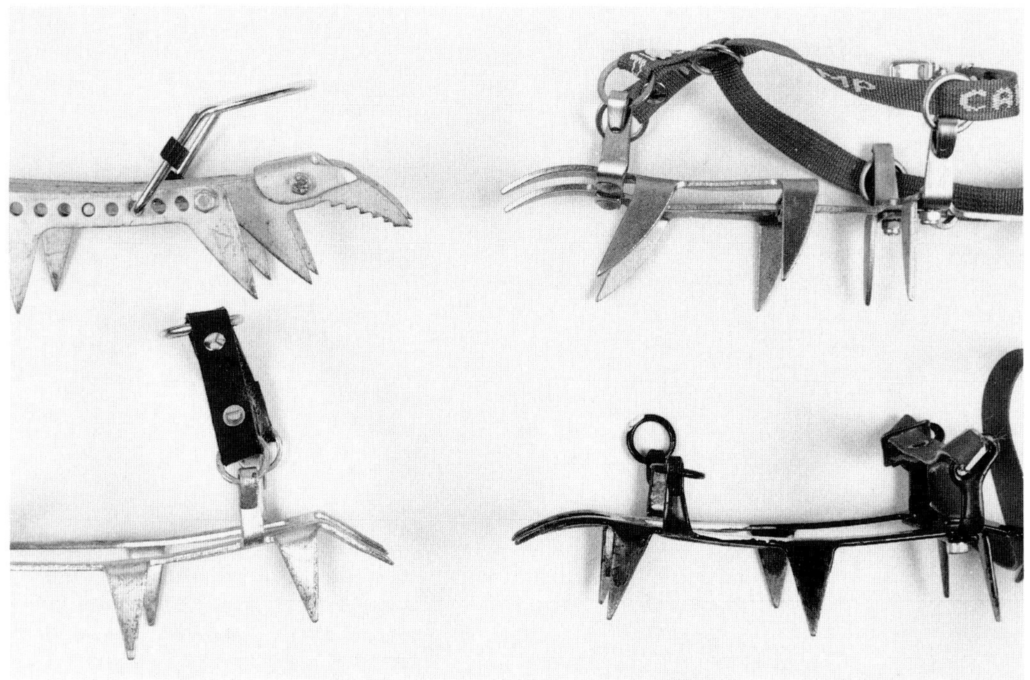

can be combined to produce a general-purpose crampon which would work well in most conditions [*fig. 14.3d*].

Crampons for Mixed Terrain

When climbing on difficult mixed ground, you need to be able to function on both rock and ice. The crampon you use must therefore fill two very different roles: not only must it be good on ice, but on rock too. Climbers on mixed terrain have thus adopted a crampon with shorter points which can be carefully adjusted so that they lie very close to the edge of the boot [*fig. 14.4*]. This cuts down on leverage when rock climbing and allows precise placement, but also permits the crampon's use on ice. Many climbers use an old, worn pair of general-purpose crampons for mixed climbing.

All of the above crampon point arrangements have their advantages and disadvantages, and as with other parts of your gear it is how well you know them and how well you use them that counts. Crampon design is constantly changing, and it is easy to imagine that the 'latest and greatest' will make all the difference. This is seldom the case: the crampons which you trust and with which you are familiar are almost always best, the only exception to this rule being in very specialised situations when the more extreme designs come into their own. Steep, brittle waterfall ice is such an example, when the single vertical point provides an alternative solution.

Fig 14.3 Four different styles of crampon:
(a) TOP LEFT: *The 'foot fang', a specialist, rigid ice-climbing crampon.*
(b) TOP RIGHT: *Lobster-claw points, which are very good on soft ice and snow.*
(c) BOTTOM LEFT: *Inclined points.*
(d) BOTTOM RIGHT: *General-purpose crampons with curved front points.*

Fit and Attachment

The type of crampon used depends on the sort of climbing being undertaken. In many cases a general-purpose crampon will meet most requirements and also be suitable for learning the different cramponing techniques.

For the best performance the crampon must fit the boot well. When it is correctly fitted, the boot can be lifted and the crampon will remain attached with the straps still undone [*fig. 14.5*].

The front points should protrude by about 2cm, although this varies with different designs [*fig. 14.6*]. After adjustment, ensure that all nuts and bolts are fully tightened; it may be wise to apply some Loctite adhesive since loosening of these bolts can be disastrous.

Attachment of crampons to the boots can be by traditional straps or clip-on bindings. Most general-purpose crampons are of the strap variety. Although these may be slower to fit to the boots, they offer unrivalled security and it is important that all crampon users have some experience of the strapping technique – if only so that an emergency repair can be made to the clip-on variety. French-style straps, with a ring at the toe of the boot, are also popular, but difficult to fit correctly. When fitted, the ring should apply tension over the front of the boot [*fig. 14.7*].

Clip-on crampons are available in a wide variety of attachment types [*fig. 14.8*]. These should be inspected carefully for their fit to the boot and their mechanical reliability. The manufacturer's instructions should be followed carefully when adjusting and fitting such crampons. Always remember that the binding materials themselves may stretch or the boot may compress, resulting in a less-than-perfect fit: a good fit at home may not necessarily be a good fit in the mountains and the necessary tools for adjustment should be carried on the first few excursions.

Crampons with clip-on bindings are particularly good when climbing in very cold conditions or

Fig 14.4 A well-fitting crampon used for mixed climbing. Notice the short, stubby points which cut down on leverage when using rock holds.

Fig 14.5 The crampon should be a snug fit on the boot.

Fig 14.6 Checking the length of the front points using a straight edge across the toes.

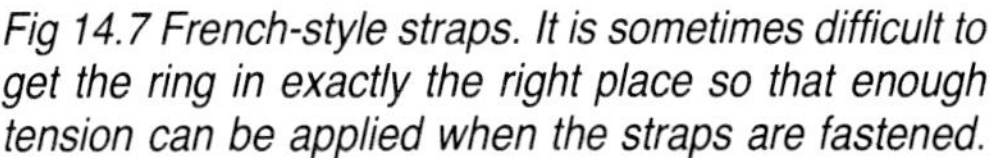

Fig 14.7 French-style straps. It is sometimes difficult to get the ring in exactly the right place so that enough tension can be applied when the straps are fastened.

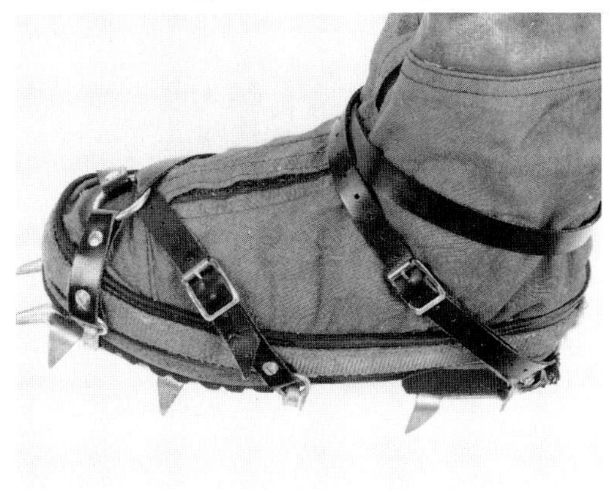

on mixed terrain when they may have to be fitted and removed regularly. They are quicker and easier to fit than strap-on types, and after a little practice it is possible to fit them without removing your gloves – a great advantage in sub-zero temperatures.

Unless a crampon is fully adjustable, the exact nature of the fit will depend on the shape, and to some extent the size of the boot. If the width at the front is fixed, for example, a narrow, pointed boot toe may protrude too much, making only part of the front points available. A square, flat toe, however, may result in overlong points. The boot and the crampon should be matched to give the best possible fit.

Attaching the Crampon to the Boot

When fitting the crampons, it is important that they are a light spring-fit. To fit them, first find a convenient rock or area of flat, hard snow which allows each one to be spread out and full body weight applied before you do up the bindings. If it is impossible to find such a site, the back of the rucksack or a deadman laid on the snow can be used. Trying to fit crampons while in a sitting position is slower and more awkward, and leads to less secure fastening as the crampons do not sit correctly on the soles of the boots.

Lay each crampon on the prepared site so that all of the rings, straps and buckles lie to the outside of the framework [*fig. 14.1,* page 206]. The buckles are always to the outside of the foot, where they cannot snag and catch. This makes the identification of the left and right crampons easy.

Fig 14.8 Clip-on crampons are quick to fit, and with practice they can be fitted even when wearing mitts.

Fig 14.9–14.11 Fastening strap-on crampons.

Make sure that the boot sole is free from snow (it may be necessary to tap the boot with the ice axe) before stepping into the crampon.

Fasten traditional straps by first passing the long, heel strap around the ankle of the boot and then securing it in the appropriate buckle [*fig. 14.9*]. Ensure that the strap lies neatly and is not twisted or pressing on the ankle above the cuff of the boot. The front of the crampon is now fastened as follows: pass the strap across and forward, then through the outside ring from the outside, and back towards the leg [*fig. 14.10*]. Neatly fold it over and pass it to the other front ring, again entering from the outside, but this time exiting to the front [*fig. 14.11*]. Once again, fold over neatly and bring back to the remaining buckle. Crampon straps should be pulled as tight as is comfortable. Be careful not to hinder the circulation to the toes (rarely a problem). When you have finished, about 4cm of strap should protrude.

With French-style straps the back strap is again fastened first, and this time the front strap is passed through the ring and then back to the securing buckle. It is important that when these straps are fitted to the crampons the ring sits in the correct place at the toe of the boot. It should be as shown in *fig. 14.7* page 209, otherwise the correct tension will never be achieved. The disadvantage of these straps is their lack of flexibility. If other boots are used, the straps have to be altered to fit, and even putting on a pair of gaiters can alter how well they fit the boot.

Fig 14.10

Fig 14.11

With clip-on crampons the toe is placed underneath the front retaining bail and the tensioning lever then applied to the rear welt. The exact method depends on the particular system used, but most are similar to those shown in *fig. 14.8*, page 210, and will include a retaining strap to hold the heel lever in place.

As boots have altered in material (from leather to plastic), so the ideal attachment method has also changed. Leather boots have a thin welt which is further eroded by use, and this makes it difficult to attach the toe bail of clip-on bindings. With the advent of the plastic boot with its more robust and prominent welt, clip-on bindings have become the norm. Plastic boots are also warmer than leather ones, rendering the addition of bulky gaiters unnecessary, and this in turn makes the more flexible and easily adjustable strap system redundant.

Crampon straps obviously play a very important role, even in clip-on bindings, and must be chosen and maintained meticulously. Nylon webbing straps are prone to slippage when used in spring-loaded buckles and should be avoided [*fig. 14.12*]. If it is necessary to use nylon straps, these should be fastened by means of two D-rings. These give a secure fastening but are prone to icing up and subsequent difficulty in removal. Neoprene rubber-coated nylon straps with pin-type buckles are the best form of straps as they are easy to use non-stretch and do not ice up [*fig. 14.11*]. All straps and attachment systems must be inspected regularly and any doubtful pieces should be replaced long before failure occurs.

Depending on the style of crampon and whether the boot has a narrow or wide heel, it may be necessary to fit retaining heel bars. If these are not supplied with the crampons, they can be easily improvised from stiff wire. They prevent the boot from sliding backwards, but need not be more than a loose fit on the rear heel welt [*fig. 14.13*]. Some crampons have a post here, making heel bars unnecessary. They are also unnecessary on clip-on crampons.

Maintenance of Crampons

It is important to keep an eye on the condition of crampons' straps and buckles. A sensible pre-

Fig 14.12 Some nylon straps slip in spring-loaded buckles. When buckles like this are used, only nylon straps with good surface texture should be chosen.

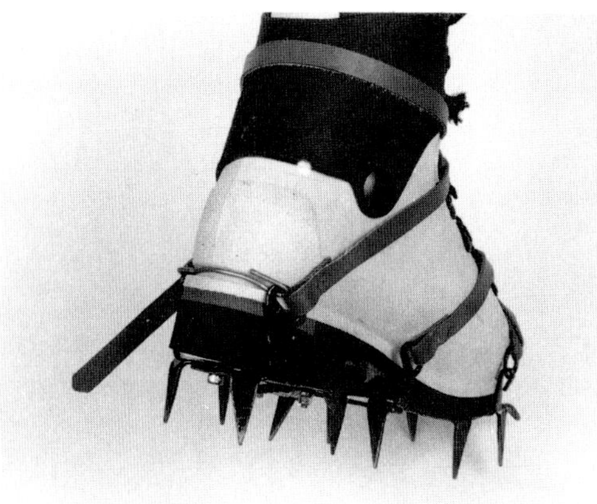

Fig 14.13 A crampon heel bar.

caution is to double-rivet all strapping as rivets can often fail. When the crampons become blunt, the front points should be sharpened in the same way as a chisel: that is, from the top downwards and in a forward direction so that the cutting edge is at the bottom. The downward-facing points should be sharpened along their edges and not their sides. Avoid sharpening to too keen a point as this is easily blunted, resulting in poor performance. It is best to sharpen fairly regularly and not allow the points to become too rounded, resulting in a lot more metal having to be removed to obtain sharp points. All sharpening is best done by hand as the heat produced by grinding tools can spoil the temper of the metal. Nuts and bolts should also be checked regularly as well as areas of possible metal fatigue. These include the base of the attachment posts, hinge areas and the side bars of rigid crampons. The cables and levers of the clip-on system should also be examined for signs of wear and tear or looseness.

Use of Crampons

In the early days of the crampon, different techniques evolved in different countries. The French developed a flat-footed technique (known as the French technique) in which all of the downward-facing points were used. The original French crampons had no front points, and the technique was most suitable for the softer ice and névé found in the Western Alps. The Germans and Austrians, on the other hand, favoured the use of the front points (called front-pointing). The discerning climber will use a hybrid of the two techniques, changing position and style as demanded by the terrain and the changing conditions of the snow or ice. In general, however, the French technique works best on easy-angled slopes (less than 45°) and front-pointing on steeper slopes or hard ice.

French Technique

As with all aspects of cramponing, French technique (or flat-footing) depends upon balance, confidence and commitment to the crampons. When mastered, it is a safe, quick and efficient method of travel over easy-angled snow and ice, and also a convenient way to rest on steeper slopes. To begin with, however, it can appear strenuous and awkward. The technique depends for its success on your trusting each foot placement, and this trust is best achieved by practice in a safe situation. Once you are proficient in it, you will find that French technique provides the basis of all cramponing on easy-angled terrain.

French technique is most easily learned on an easy-angled slope of hard névé. The slope need not be large but should present little in the way of danger should a stumble or trip take place. The basic technique on an easy-angled slope is different from normal walking in that the edges of the feet are not used; instead, the ankles are flexed and the feet kept flat [*fig. 14.14*]. However, because of the danger of the points snagging in the clothes, an open-stance gait, with the feet about hip width apart, should be adopted, and for

Fig 14.14 The French technique. As the angle of the slope increases, the toes must point more and more down the fall line if all of the downward-facing points are to remain in contact with the ice.

safety reasons all baggy trousers and gaiters should be well tucked in. Many crampon accidents which could easily be prevented are caused by spiking clothing and tripping up.

Concentrate on making sure that all of the downward-facing points are placed firmly in the slope. The pressure needed to make the points bite is less than imagined, body weight and the correct presentation of the points being enough for a secure placement. Excessive force is unnecessary and tiring, not only because of the effort involved, but also because the constant jarring on the legs causes fatigue in the calfs, knees and thighs. The ice axe is carried in the uphill hand and used only for balance (like a walking stick). In fact, trying to use the axe on easy terrain is more liable to cause a slip as it encourages poor body position through leaning forward. It is important to appreciate the holding power of the crampons and trust them, independent of the axe. When confident on an easy-angled slope – that is, you are capable of walking around without having to look at the crampons or at the terrain – progress to slightly steeper slopes.

In all stages of flat-footing avoid using the edges of the crampons. Flex the ankles and knees away from the slope in the traverse position and, as the slope steepens, point the toes farther and farther downhill. As the slope becomes steeper, the flat-foot technique becomes more awkward and more difficult, mainly because the ankle joint cannot flex particularly well inside stiff boots. To go uphill it is easier to proceed diagonally, with the feet pointing more up and down the slope rather than across it. This allows the knees as well as the ankles to flex and so maintain the all-important ten points of contact.

The ice axe is kept in the uphill hand and used like a walking stick as an aid to balance. On a diagonal ascent it is vital to resist the temptation to edge the crampons, as this can result in their breaking free and slipping. On 15–30° slopes progress is made with the feet pointing in the direction of travel. This is diagonally at around 35–45° to the horizontal, and in a two-step sequence.

With the axe planted, the downhill foot is brought in front of and then above the uphill foot and placed on the slope [*fig. 14.15.*]. This is the out-of-balance position, and so is less stable. It is important that the ice axe remains in the support position during this manoeuvre. Once the downhill foot has been positioned and the points firmly planted, the lower foot is brought up and placed in front [*fig. 14.16.*]. Body weight should

Fig 14.15, 14.16 When using the French technique, it is best to ascend slopes diagonally, using the axe for support in the uphill hand.

always be on top of the crampons and not leaning in towards the slope. Nervousness and lack of trust in the crampons can result in an unbalanced position and this in turn makes the crampons twist and sheer away from the slope. When in balance – that is, without the feet being crossed – you can reposition the ice axe and continue.

Each time the axe is repositioned, it should be far enough uphill and forward to allow you to regain a balanced position – that is, to take two steps – before having to move the axe. At all times on snow and ice look for flat spots or irregularities in the surface which can be used as natural steps to ease progress and provide resting spots.

The pattern of steps is similar to those used when ascending a similar slope without crampons, or zig-zagging. To change direction plant the ice axe firmly above and hold the head of the axe with both hands for balance. From the balanced position, take the uphill foot up and back to point in the new direction, and then place the downhill foot in the out-of-balance position at the same level as the other foot but pointing slightly uphill [*fig. 14.17.*]. As the body turns into the slope, the inside foot is moved to point in the new direction and slightly uphill. You are now facing in towards the slope and standing with feet splayed slightly outwards. Balance is regained by bringing the other foot into the new direction of travel. You are now in balance with the uphill foot advanced, facing in the new direction, and should be holding the ice axe in the uphill hand [*fig. 14.16*]. The changes in direction should be planned well ahead and, if possible, an easier-angled section chosen for the turn.

It is often easier to cut a quick step which allows both feet to be turned at the same time. Either way, practice is very important as many of the slips or falls which occur when cramponing do so at this stage.

As the slope grows even steeper, it becomes necessary to turn the toes more and more down the fall line. This places more strain on the ankles and thighs and is useful only in short stages [*fig. 14.18*]. Ensure that body weight is kept over the crampons and the axe used for support.

Using the axe like a walking stick may not give enough support on steeper slopes, so a different way of holding it must be adopted. Hold the axe across the body with the inside hand as close as possible to the ferrule while the outside hand is on the axe head. By distributing the weight so that 70 per cent is in the inside hand and 30 per cent in the outside hand, a balanced position can be achieved when the spike is driven into the slope. Though this is a somewhat 'old-fashioned' technique, it is useful on glaciers and as an exercise in cramponing.

Fig 14.17 Turning a corner when making a zig-zag ascent.

If even more support is necessary, the pick of the axe can be driven into the ice and the inside hand placed on the axe head, but this can overrotate the body resulting in the crampons losing their grip. Most of the body weight is still through the feet, the axe being used only for balance.

As you move around on snow and ice slopes of varying steepness, you will learn not only the skills of cramponing and movement on this terrain, but will also quickly become aware that the snow and ice is not a solid and uniform mass. Instead it exhibits a vast range of textures, hardnesses and consistencies which will help or hinder, and you must learn to differentiate between these and to choose the route accordingly.

Descending

When descending easy-angled snow, it is best to face directly down the fall line. The feet are kept flat so that all points grip the snow and are placed in a positive manner [*fig. 14.18*]. The ice axe can be used like a walking stick or held in the braking position, ready in case a slip occurs. As the slope steepens, the pick can be used for support. It is rare, however, that the pick will be used in this way when facing out since it is a strenuous and often precarious technique. If it is necessary to use the pick for support, it is best to face into the slope and descend by facing in and front-pointing [*fig. 14.19*].

Balling up

Although crampons are ideal for moving on snow and ice, there are some situations in which they can be a hindrance rather than a help. Wearing them while walking on rocky ground can be awkward, particularly in windy conditions when it is easy to turn an ankle or trip over the points. Being higher up can make balancing more difficult, and baggy trousers can easily be snagged, leading to a trip or stumble, especially when you are tired. The ability to cut steps, and so deal effectively with any snow patches, makes it more likely that you will take off your crampons when they are not required. This not only makes your movements safer and easier, but also extends the life of your crampons. The convenience of clip-on crampons is clearly an advantage in such a case.

Another situation in which crampons can be awkward, create extra work or be dangerous is when they ball up. In some snow conditions, particularly if the snow is wet, large balls of snow can stick to the crampons. The extra weight of these is tiring to lift and they prevent the crampon points from gripping properly. Rigid crampons tend to ball up more badly than those with hinges. The best way to deal with the problem is to knock the snow off regularly, either by using the shaft of the ice axe or by tapping the crampons against rocks. You can, unfortunately, knock lumps out of the shaft of your axe doing this, particularly if it is wooden, and it is another reason for taping up the shaft. The crampons can also be put in polythene bags or purpose-made covers, or their frames can be lagged with sticky tape to stop the snow from sticking to them, but this is not always a safe alternative. The framework of the crampon often provides valuable grip and if the snow is such that the points do not penetrate into a hard enough layer to grip, the smooth material round the crampon may give a treacherous slippery footing.

Fig 14.18 As the slope becomes steeper, the thighs take more and more strain, especially in descent.

Fig 14.19 Using the front-pointing technique to descend. A gear carrier is being used on the climbing belt as a holster.

ICE-CLIMBING TOOLS

Ice-climbing tools are specifically designed for use on steep ice, whereas an ice axe is multi-purpose. As well as a pick, an ice-climbing tool can have either an adze or a hammer head. The shaft and spike are much the same as on an ice axe but the shaft is usually metal or fibreglass rather than wood. Generally it is shorter, between 45 and 60cm being the most common length. This allows easier use in constricted situations such as gullies and chimneys.

The pick on an ice tool is the main reason for its existence. It should hook securely in ice, yet still be easy to remove. The pick can be inclined, have an extreme curve or be banana-shaped (that is, have a reverse curve) and, in the case of the inclined pick, can be solid or tubular [*fig. 14.20*]. Within the basic shapes minor variations exist but all have teeth on the lower edge: these vary in detail but generally increase in size from the tip to the shaft. Some picks have a few teeth on the top and others have a sharp upper edge to aid the removal from the ice. The thickness of the pick affects its performance; thinner picks shatter the ice less but pull through more easily in soft or marginal placements. Besides catering for different preferences, some picks work better than others in certain types of ice. For example, the inclined tubular pick is more effective in cold, brittle water ice where it does not shatter the ice as much as a solid pick. However, it can easily be damaged if it hits rock and this makes it unsuitable for mixed or thin ice routes where the curved or banana-shaped picks function best.

Hammer heads are used when placing rock or ice pegs and, as long as they are large enough for this, there are few differences between them worth consideration. Adzes, on the other hand, come in a variety of types as on an ice axe, but inclined adzes for hooking on snow or soft ice are handy in some situations. More inclined adzes are better to hook with, but are less suitable for cutting [*fig. 14.21*].

Wrist loops are essential on ice tools and most have specific attachment points in either the head or the shaft. These are situated so as to give the best pull on the pick. Some picks have a hole further out from the shaft for a wrist loop which can be used to reduce leverage when used on thin ice. When the hands are needed for other tasks, a loop attached to the head is best as the tool can be dropped and left to hang free from the wrist where it is out of the way. It is, however, less easy to retrieve from this position. A loop which goes through the shaft below the balance point is easy to grasp again as it hangs head down in the correct position for picking up, but the tool gets in the way more when you are using your hands. This loop may also catch when you are pushing the shaft into the snow. The former system is better on mixed routes, the latter on pure ice climbs. A head attachment can be altered by taping or tying the loop on to the shaft below the balance point if required [*fig. 14.22*].

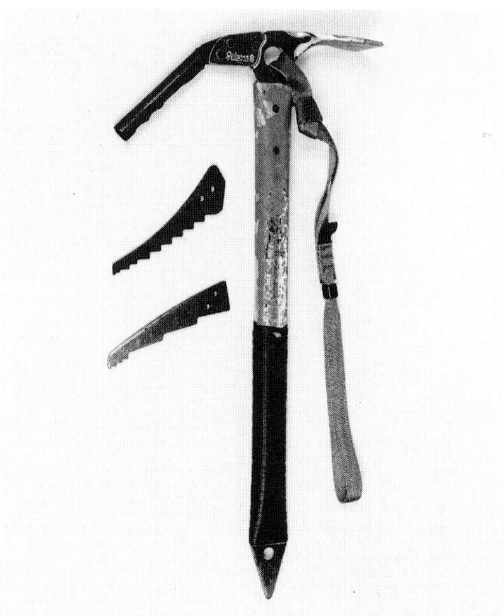

Fig 14.20 Three different interchangeable picks
FROM TOP TO BOTTOM:
(a) Tubular.
(b) Banana-shaped.
(c) Curved.

Other refinements include extra weights which can be added to the head of the tool to alter its weight and balance. Another feature is the modular head. This allows different picks, adzes and hammers to be fitted to suit different types of climbing; and the pick can also be renewed when bent, broken or worn down by use and sharpening [*fig. 14.20*].

Placing the Pick

Placing the pick of an ice axe or ice-climbing tool is not too difficult but some people do find it awkward to begin with. This is due to lack of accuracy rather than lack of strength and practice

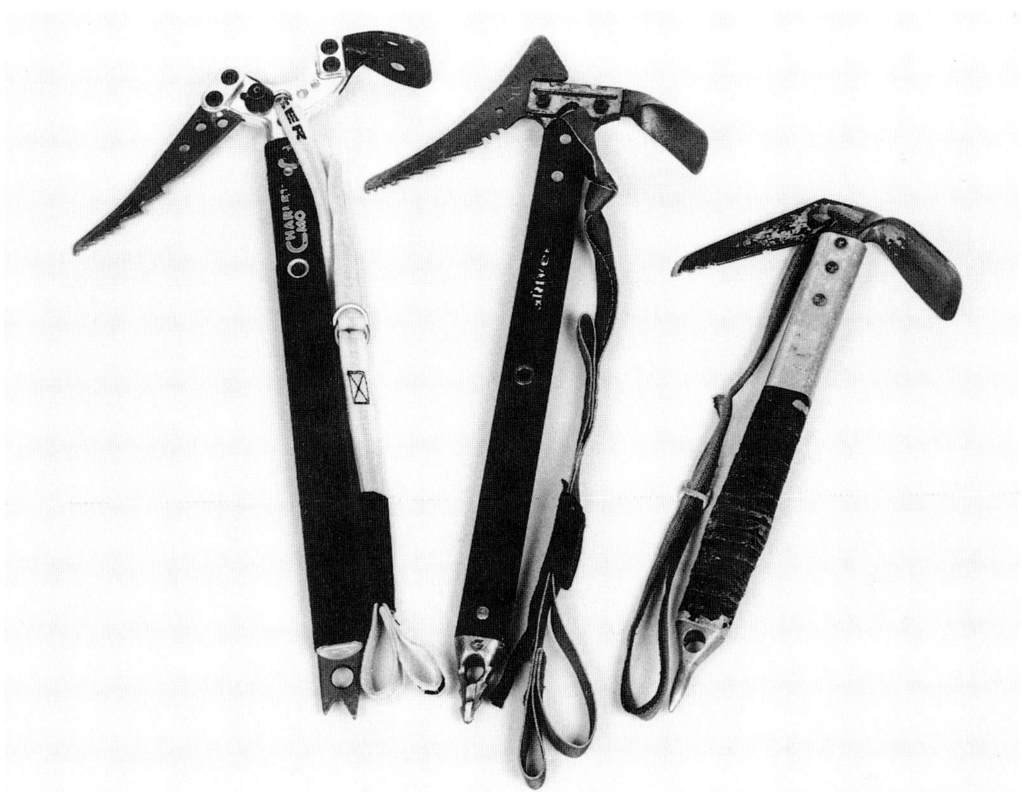

Fig 14.21 Axes are available not only with different picks but with different adzes as well.

soon improves their performance. There are difference in technique depending on the type of pick used, but in all cases the shaft should be held just above the ferrule to make best use of the leverage and momentum of the head to ease placement. The further up the shaft the tool is held, the less efficient the placement will be. Adjust the wrist loop so that it is the right length and aids holding the shaft at the correct place, and also helps to steady the tool during its swing.

In the case of a curved pick a smooth, rounded swing from the shoulder will place the tool efficiently with the weight of the head doing most of the work. Using the whole arm here means that the arc of the swing and the curve of the pick roughly coincide for an easy placement [*fig. 14.23*].

In the case of an inclined pick the action is more of a sharp, downward, chopping movement with the swinging action coming from the elbow. A full swing as used with a curved pick will result in the top edge of the tool hitting the ice and bouncing off. When using a banana-shaped pick, the action is very similar but more of a swing is possible. In both cases, however, a forward wrist action at the end of the main movement helps the pick to penetrate and also keeps the knuckle clear of the ice. Tools which have an extreme curve are also best placed in this manner.

Front-pointing

At the same time as the French technique was being perfected in the Western Alps, Austrian and German climbers were using the front-point method. Front-pointing is better suited than the French technique to hard, steep ice. It is a fairly natural style of climbing ice which, although easy to learn in a basic form, takes more practice to develop into a confident, economical technique [*fig. 14.24*].

Front-pointing on hard snow is basically a similar movement to kicking pigeonhole steps on soft snow, except that height is gained by kicking

Fig 14.22 ABOVE: *There are several different ways of attaching the wrist loop to the axe, all of which have their own advantages.*

Fig 14.23 LEFT: *When swinging a curved tool, a full, rounded swing should be used. Here the climber is standing in balance while the axe is replaced higher up.*

the front points into the slope and stepping up on the platform thus formed rather than by kicking a step with the toe. A deliberate tapping motion is all that is required to set the points. Too much force can cause the crampon to rebound as well as being very painful on the toes. When placed correctly, the two points behind the front points (the secondary points) also bite into the slope [*fig. 14.25*], helping to make the crampon more stable. Some crampons, especially those with 'lobster-claw' points, are specially designed for this purpose.

Good body and foot positions are the key to successful and economical front-pointing. The

Fig 14.24 Front-pointing on steep snow. A good belay site, well out of the way of any falling snow and ice, has been chosen.

feet must be kept horizontal [*fig. 14.26*] and the points inserted at the correct angle: that is, with the feet at right angles to the slope so that both front points bite equally. If the feet are splayed out, the points can glance off or only one point can grip. A slight flex at the knees helps balance and eases the strain on calf and thigh muscles [*fig. 14.27*]. For maximum stability the feet should be placed about hip width apart. It is the front points, together with the leg muscles, which provide almost all of the upward momentum when climbing on ice and they must be trusted if good crampon technique is to be achieved.

The technique for front-pointing on hard ice is very similar to that used on snow. However, on ice it is necessary to kick the points home more vigorously than on hard snow, though excessive force can set up vibrations in the ice which weaken the holding power of the points. Once the points have been placed, they should be moved as little as possible when stepping up since any movement tends to lever and twist them out of the ice, especially if it is thin [*fig. 14.28*].

Fig 14.25 When the climber is standing on front points, the secondary points bite into the ice and give a more stable platform.

On ice the secondary points of the crampons play an even more important role than on snow.

Fig 14.26 Good, horizontal foot placements are essential on steep ice.

Fig 14.27 A relaxed body shape is less strenuous when climbing and so conserves energy.

When correctly placed, they greatly increase the strength and stability of the crampon platform. Rigid-soled boots and well-fitting, sharp crampons are essential for this type of climbing. The angle of the feet is critical. If the heels are raised from the horizontal – a natural tendency when a climber is tired or in difficulty – the front points tend to 'pop' out of the ice or be levered out by the toe of the boot: not only is this very insecure, it is also very tiring. The same thing happens if the heels are dropped, but this is less likely to occur as the secondary points are in contact with the ice and so give some indication when the heels are too low. The feeling for the correct position of the feet comes with practice and experience.

It is often difficult if not dangerous, to experiment with technique on an actual climb, so bouldering on ice, just as on rock, is very valuable. If a good site is chosen, it is possible to practise cramponing skills and also to experiment on steeper and thinner ice in relative safety. Care must be taken when jumping off when wearing crampons as it is very easy to twist an ankle or worse. For this reason, and also because it is easier to climb up than down, many people top-rope when ice bouldering. When climbing in this manner, it is worthwhile experimenting without the ice tools for short sections as this is not only ideal training in crampon technique, but also good practice for mixed climbing and climbing on ice hand holds.

American Technique

The French technique and front-pointing can be combined to give the American technique [*fig. 14.29*]. This is a very economical way to crampon and is ideal for the ascent of long, uniform slopes and for resting on steeper terrain. While one foot front-points, the other uses the French technique. When moving diagonally, the lower foot, which is easier to flex, is flat-footed. This results in the feet being in a 'three o'clock' position. The flat foot is

Fig 14.28 On thin ice the points will tend to sheer out of the ice if they are moved at all. These crampons are a poor fit on the boot, the heels of both crampons being very slack.

the resting foot, and left and right can be alternated as such to give both legs some respite from the more strenuous front-pointing. American technique is also a very useful way to turn corners when using pure French technique in a zig-zag ascent.

Removing the Pick

To take the pick out, pull it up and down to loosen it and lift it out. Never waggle it from side to side as this can bend or break it. Stubborn placements may have to be loosened by sliding the hand up the shaft and banging the underside of the head with the hand. Try to take the pick out in the reverse of the line which it followed on its way into the ice. If the worst comes to the worst, you may have to cut it out using another tool. In all cases keep your face out of the way as tools which come out with unexpected ease can be painful if they strike you.

Fig 14.29 The American technique is very good for saving energy and resting alternate legs.

Modifications and Care

Axes and ice tools may have to be modified to suit individual tastes and requirements. Wrist loops may have to be added or changed; shafts which are slippery to hold – wood or fibreglass, for example – need to be adapted to give a better grip. Various tapes such as zinc oxide tape, some non-plastic insulating tapes or polyisobutylene (PIB) self–amalgamating electrical tape can be put on the shaft in overlapping spirals starting about half-way down and continuing to the ferrule. The overlaps, which face upwards, improve the grip but do not catch when the shaft is driven into the snow. An alternative, but one which is hard on hand wear, is a coating of non-slip varnish or varnish mixed with fine sand. Some shafts which have a smooth, rubberised coating may need to be roughened to improve the grip.

The teeth of a pick may also have to be altered. If too few or too small, they can be enlarged using a hacksaw or file rather than a power grinder which can overheat the metal and ruin the temper. Too large or prominent teeth, however, can make removal of the pick difficult and they may have to be filed down. Only experience of using the tool will tell you what, if anything, needs to be done. On some picks, especially thicker ones, it is worth sharpening the top edge to make removal easier.

The corners of the adze and the spike may be too sharp when new. Blunting the adze corners, but not the main edge, can reduce the chance of accidental cutting in some situations such as ice-axe braking. Too sharp a spike is dangerous if the tool comes out suddenly when pulled and then impales the user. The spike needs only to be reasonably sharp.

Cutting edges become blunt with use and should be sharpened regularly to obtain maximum performance. A pick should be sharpened to a chisel point by working equally at both sides to keep it symmetrical. Avoid making the taper too long and the point too narrow as this increases the chance of blunting or bending if you hit rock. The adze should also be sharpened to keep a good edge on it. Modular heads need the fixing arrangement checked and tightened regularly, especially the hammers which can loosen off with the shock of pounding pegs. All heads should be checked for cracks which are most likely to appear where there are weaknesses in the metal such as at holes in the pick and where they join the shaft.

Choosing the Correct Tool

The choice of what to use generally depends on the nature and difficulty of the climbs to be tackled. It is usually better to have a pair of matched tools rather than two of differing size, type and balance. Specialised ice tools give placements that feel more secure, especially on steep ice, but they are less convenient on moderately angled slopes. The more extreme pick and adze shapes often perform poorly when cutting, tending to stick at each blow. On the other hand, the 'classic' curved pick of an ice axe is placed with an easier, more natural swinging action on any angle of ice and fulfils several other functions better. Although difficult climbs are done with curved axes, the greater security of the steeper picks is generally preferred for the hardest routes. The axe's versatility, however, is preferable on traditional Alpine routes and on high mountains in general where there may be long stretches of moderately angled snow and ice. But the above are only general observations and personal preference is usually the deciding factor.

For most climbs on steep ice it is normal to carry an adze and a hammer but other combinations are possible. On all but the steepest ice these tools are used for support and balance, the legs and not the arms providing most of the upward momentum. They should be regarded as aids to balance, not as hand holds on which to pull. However, on sections of very steep ice it is necessary to pull on the tools in order to gain height, but even then good crampon work and thoughtful use of the feet can make this less strenuous. A pure ice climb with little or no snow work may be best tackled with two hammers so that ice pegs can be placed with either hand without swapping tools. On snowed-up rock routes where much clearing may be required, using two tools with adzes allows this to be done with either hand. In this case a hammer is carried for placing pegs and also as a spare in case another tool breaks.

Dagger Technique

This is a very quick way to climb, both upwards and downwards, on snow fields and easy-angled gullies. It allows one, or two, ice tools to be used in a fast, secure and economic manner. In the true dagger technique the hands are placed on the heads of the tools and the picks are then driven into the slope at waist height [*fig. 14.30*]. Progress is then made by 'rocking' the body weight from

Fig 14.30 Dagger technique.

tool to tool while keeping the arms straight. In this way your weight is used to push the tools into the slope, and most of the propulsion comes from the legs. Alternatively, the hands can be slid up the shafts of the tools until just below the head and the axe is then pushed into the snow like a dagger. This is slower and more strenuous to perform than true dagger technique, but can be useful. With either method, if only one tool is being used the other hand is placed on the slope for balance.

Using a Single Tool

When using a single ice axe to climb ice, place it as high as is comfortable and then, with one hand just above the ferrule, place the other hand on the axe head. Move up until the axe is at shoulder height and, with the feet securely placed and standing in balance, remove the axe and replace it higher up [*fig. 14.32*]. In this way the axe is used for support at the crucial time: that is, when you are moving. When removing the axe and replacing it higher up, balance and good crampon work are essential.

Sometimes more than one blow is needed to get a good placement and this is often the result of not hitting the ice squarely with the pick. If the first effort is not satisfactory, strike again at the same spot: after a few blows the pick should be secure. Although the tool is primarily an aid to balance it is also a 'portable belay' in case the feet slip. If the ice stars (that is, a series of cracks radiate out from the pick) and then dinner-plates (that is, a dish-shaped portion of ice detaches itself), this is cleared away and the pick replaced in the same spot as the ice underneath should be less brittle. Watch your own feet and the second when clearing these lumps of ice away.

One of the secrets of efficient ice climbing is driving a pick in the correct distance. Overdriving wastes time and energy and can even destroy the

Fig 14.31 ABOVE: *When pulling over a bulge on to easy ground, take care to keep the feet horizontal.*

placements. The pick should be secure but not stuck and it is experience that will help you to find this happy medium.

Using Two Tools

As the terrain grows steeper, it becomes more difficult to remove a single axe without losing balance, so an ice tool for each hand is required. When climbing like this, three points of contact, as in rock climbing, are maintained whenever possible. Although you have two good hand holds, the legs still do most of the work. It is very tiring to perform a series of pull-ups on axes with the feet hanging uselessly underneath. On steep ice the crampons are still placed horizontally or the front points will glance off or be levered out.

Fig 14.32 BELOW: *Good footwork and balance are important when using only one tool.*

Particular care must be taken at junctions between steep and easy ground because when pulling over on to easier-angled terrain the heels tend to lift, and a positive effort must be made to keep them down and so keep the points in the ice [*fig. 14.31*].

Moving from the vertical to the horizontal is one of the more difficult techniques on ice. Place the tools firmly on the easier-angled ice, but as you front-point up, change from a pull on the tools to a mantelshelf type of position. The points are worked up until it is possible to step flat-footed on to the easier-angled ice. If you start to lean forwards as you move up, the heels are lifted and so lever out the points.

When climbing with two tools, the best sequence of movements is to place both tools high and then to move up in a series of small steps. Big steps are strenuous and unbalanced. When the tools are at shoulder height, position the feet hip width apart for balance and at the same level. Remove one tool, and reach up and place it as high as is comfortable. Avoid overstretching as this is strenuous and can cause the heels to lift. Hold the higher tool securely, then remove the other and place that above. Now move the feet up in a series of small steps. Avoid large steps as these are more tiring and make you pull harder on the tools rather than use your feet. Take care not to place the tools too close together as any disturbance caused, especially when placing the second tool, may cause them both to fail. This is particularly important if the ice is brittle and prone to dinner-plating [*figs. 14.33, 14.34, 14.35*].

Vertical and Overhanging ice

On vertical ice the technique is altered slightly. The arms do more of the work and energy conservation becomes the key. The amount of vertical ice that can be ascended ultimately depends on the climber's arm strength. However, strong arms without good technique are no guarantee of success. When pulling on the tools, it is best to grip the shafts lightly, relying on the wrist loops rather than the strength of your grip for support [*fig. 14.36*]. There are a great many ways of attaching these loops, but so long as they pull along the shaft and allow the axe to be gripped just above the ferrule, any safe method will do.

When starting off on a long pitch, you must be sure that you have sufficient strength to climb it. It is difficult to climb down vertical ice – especially if this is necessary because of a lack of strength! Protection should be organised before setting off on the vertical section and any protection to be placed *en route* should be well planned in advance. Try to have the appropriate piece of gear readily available and if possible cut a step to stand on before attempting to place the gear.

On very steep ice place the tools as high as possible and a little further apart than normal. This helps avoid the danger of pieces of ice hitting the face and, should a tool pull out unexpectedly, it will be away from the head. Always go for good, secure placements. It is very tempting, but risky, to make do with a poor placement. Although marginal placements may have to be used when the ice is poor, this is a different state of affairs from a badly placed axe. Avoid overdriving the axes since their subsequent removal uses up a great deal of energy. The feet should be slightly further apart than on easier-angled ice since this helps to avoid 'barn-dooring' when removing one of the tools. The overall body shape should be that of an X [*fig. 14.35*]. Avoid moving up higher than shoulder height on the axes and rest with the arms straight and the weight on the skeleton [*fig. 14.36*] – if it is possible to rest on overhanging ice!

Traverses and Descents

Traversing on steep ice is precarious and strenuous. Place one axe at a 45° angle and lay away on it in the direction of the traverse [*fig. 14.37*]. The other axe is then placed vertically out to the side. Move underneath this axe and repeat the process [*fig. 14.38*]. The feet are moved either in small sideways steps or can be crossed over – a more difficult method [*fig. 14.39*]. It is sometimes easier, especially on very steep ice, to keep both the axes vertical and to settle for less sideways distance for each placement.

When down climbing on steep ice, try to hook the picks into the holes created on the way up; failing this, place a tool as low as possible, transfer the weight to this tool and place the other at the same height. The feet can now be moved down and the process repeated. It is extremely difficult

Figs 14.33–14.36 A sequence using two tools on steep ice. On steep ice as much weight as possible should be taken by the wrist loops rather than the climber's grip. In Fig 14.36 (bottom right) a climber is resting on steep ice with his arms straight and legs slightly flexed.

to place an ice tool below shoulder level as it is not possible to get an efficient swing with it. Down climbing is a very strenuous procedure, and if possible some overhead protection should be arranged. If this protection is good, lowering off or abseiling is the obvious choice. If the protection is not good, it is best to down climb carefully using the runner as a back-up .

Unlike in rock climbing, conditions constantly change on snow and ice routes, and while good ice can be climbed using the same movements repeatedly, many routes require an open mind

Fig 14.37 ABOVE: *Moving to the left on steep ice. The right tool is being used to lay away.*

Fig 14.38 ABOVE: *The left axe is placed vertically and the climber then moves underneath it.*

Fig 14.39 BELOW: *The feet can be either crossed over or moved sideways in small steps.*

and a wide variety of techniques for successful ascents. Few pitches can be overcome by the straightforward bash and pull of front-pointing. Instead, you must look to more subtle and economical ways of climbing, which not only save in energy but will also make the climb more interesting and enjoyable.

If is often possible to bridge out in chimneys and gullies, so relieving the strain on the arms. Natural rock and ice holds can also be used for rests, to place protection or ease the strain in aching calf muscles. Many natural features also provide ideal placements for hand tools. Spaces between flutings when waterfall climbing are a good example of these. When seconding a pitch, careful use of the holes left by the leader's placements can reduce the amount of energy expended by the second. On many occasions natural rock or even ice holds can be utilised, again saving in time and energy. In some situations the adze can be employed, especially in unconsolidated snow or ice. If the snow is soft, it may be necessary to drive the axe shaft into it at a suitable angle and then pull or push down on the head. This is especially useful in the soft snow found below or when surmounting a cornice.

Climbing good-quality ice is generally straightforward. Problems can occur, however, when moving on to poor ice or snow, as often happens at the top of steep ice pitches where the angle drops back and soft snow can accumulate. This is when a pick will not grip; instead, it simply pulls through. Sometimes the adze can be used to hook with, but more often the shafts will have to be utilised. They should be driven in as far as possible with the widest part of their cross-section across the slope. A few blows are usually

Fig 14.40 A steep ice pitch on Ben Nevis.

needed to get the shaft in far enough. Move your hands down to hold the shaft just above the snow surface to reduce leverage; then, with as much weight on your feet as possible, move up. Try to get as high as possible each time before replacing the tools.

As you become more proficient in climbing on snow and ice, you will soon realise that one of the most important aspects of this branch of climbing is mental control. Any single move on even the hardest ice route would be relatively straightforward at ground level. It is the ability to climb well under pressure, not simply gymnastic ability, which makes a good ice climber. You must strive to find the required calmness and composure, together with just enough boldness. It is very easy for the inexperienced to climb themselves into a situation from which retreat is all but impossible [*fig. 14.40*].

15 Ice Protection

Protection on ice can be better than that on snow but is unlikely to be as good as is found on rock. There are various types of protection that can be arranged on ice, both for belays and runners.

ICE PEGS

Ice pegs are usually made of aluminium alloy, stainless steel or titanium but, because of their size, the weight of the material from which they are manufactured is an important consideration. Tests have shown that ice pegs can take forces of 500–2000kg, depending on the type, the length (usually between 15–30cm), the angle of placement, the temperature and, of course, the quality of the ice. In the right conditions they give good, solid anchor points. Most ice pegs are circular in cross-section and their strength is related to their size. How well they resist an outwards pull is related to the size of any external threads. The best angle of placement for all ice pegs is at 100° to the slope – that is, 10° uphill from a right angle to the slope – and they should be placed with the eye facing downwards and flush with the ice. It is often necessary to clear away an area of surface ice to get the best placement [*fig. 15.1*].

Ice pegs can be divided into three main categories: drive-in/cut-out, drive-in/screw-out and screw-in/screw-out.

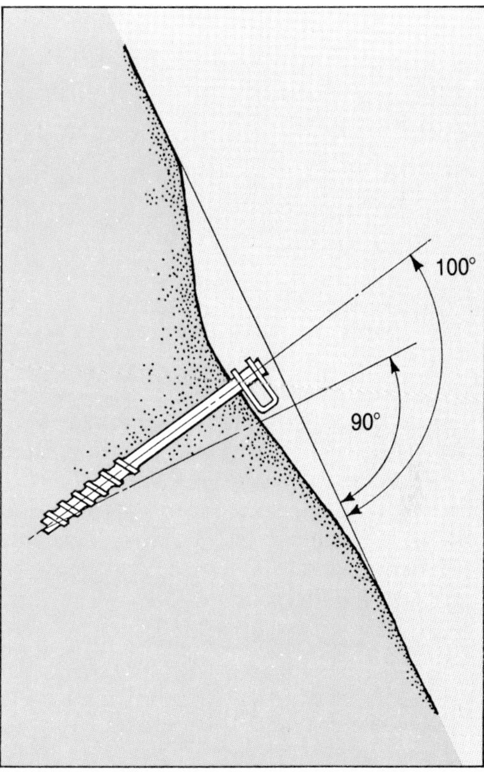

Fig 15.1 An ice peg correctly placed at 100° to the slope with the eye facing down and flush with the ice. An area round the head of the peg has been cleared of surface ice both for ease of placement and to enable more solid ice to be reached.

Drive-in/Cut-out

The drive-in/cut-out type of ice peg is outdated. It is tubular, half-round or has a very long blade and is simply hammered into the ice. To remove it you have to cut it out of the ice for virtually its full length. The time and effort required for this is one of the main reasons for its unpopularity unless it is to be left in place, when its low cost is in its favour. A more modern version is shaped like the head of an ice tool.

Drive-in/Screw-out

There are several types of ice peg in the drive-in/screw-out category. The most basic type is the solid, round peg with a thread cut into much of its length. It is hammered into the ice and removed by unscrewing. It does not hold particularly well as it has a small diameter and a fine thread.

A better type is the Warthog which has a spiral sequence of lumps or warts down its length [*fig. 15.2*]. It is placed by hammering into the ice at 10° up from a right angle to the slope. In brittle ice the hammer blows should be lighter than normal to reduce the chance of the ice cracking. As the peg is driven, it may rotate a little in a clockwise direction because of the spiral warts. To get the eye facing downwards it can be started off with the head slightly in the anti-clockwise direction to anticipate this rotation.

Fig 15.2 A small selection of Warthogs, showing differing degrees of spiral protrusion and types of eye.

Snargs are tubular drive-in/screw-out pegs. The surface of a Snarg has a fine thread and usually a slot to help in clearing ice from the interior of the tube. It is placed by hammering [*fig. 15.3*].

To remove these pegs use an axe or hammer to unscrew them in an anti-clockwise direction. With a good placement, however, a peg may be frozen in place and so much leverage can be put on it that it can be twisted and ruined. Hammering it further into the ice before unscrewing helps to break this grip. Another aid to easy removal is to chop away some of the ice round the peg to reduce the distance it must be unscrewed. The core of ice must be removed before re-use (see below).

Screw-in/Screw-out

There is a wide range in the screw-in/screw-out category of ice pegs, from simple thick wire corkscrews to sophisticated tubular screws which have the greatest holding power of any ice peg and are now the most popular type [*fig. 15.4*]. To place one, first chip a small hole in the ice using a pick. Put the peg in this and screw it into the ice: the initial hole helps the teeth at the end of the screw to bite. In many cases a little light tapping with the hammer may be required to get the screw started, even to the extent of hammering until the peg starts to turn under the blows. Once the teeth are biting, it is screwed as far as possible by hand until too stiff, then the axe or hammer is used as a lever to place it fully. The head should then lie flush with the ice and the eye point downhill [*fig. 15.1*, page 229; *fig. 15.12*, page 238].

Among pegs of this type, those with a wide diameter and thin walls are the easiest to place

Fig 15.3 A selection of drive-in/screw-out tubular ice pegs, or Snargs, which show a variety of eye types and different sizes and lengths of outer thread. The slot to aid clearing the ice core can also be seen.

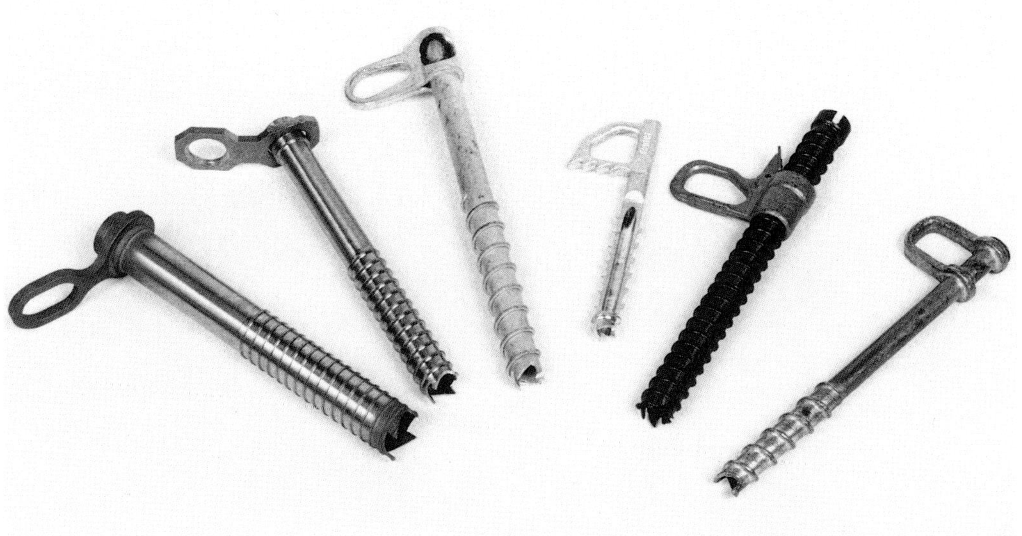

Fig 15.4 A selection of screw-in/screw-out ice pegs of the tubular type, showing a range of different sizes, diameters and numbers of teeth. An example of the ratchet type is also shown.

and the least likely to crack the ice, and work best in a wide range of conditions. They may have two, three or four cutting teeth; the more teeth, the easier they go into the ice. Large-diameter, thin-walled screws with good sharp teeth can often be screwed directly into the ice by hand. To ease placement a ratchet can be used: this can be adapted from machine tools, although some tubular screws are fitted with their own ratchet on the head, forming a fast but unfortunately expensive type of ice anchor.

To remove, unscrew the peg using an axe or hammer as a lever to begin with. Tubular screws need to be cleared of ice before they can be used again. As the tube is placed, it extrudes some ice, but a core of ice remains in the tube and this has to be removed before the peg can be replaced. Attempts to re-use a tubular peg in its 'blocked' condition will fail and may even damage it. The colder it is, the more difficult this ice is to remove. Warming the tube loosens the ice core: it can be warmed with body heat by carrying the peg inside clothing (unpleasant but effective) or by using a lighter (convenient but often impractical in windy conditions). The core should then be pushed out with a suitable tool such as another narrower peg, but this will only work if the ice is not still frozen in place. Another method is to blow into the tube and melt the sides of the core with warm breath. Tap the screw regularly to knock out the loose pieces of ice and work from both ends, taking care not to let the peg freeze to your lips in cold conditions. Many tubular screws have a slot in the end to aid removal of the ice core by means of a pick, and some may have a slight internal diameter taper, which also helps. Some are made semi-circular, apart from the cutting teeth, to get round the problem of blockage but these pegs are weaker. A coating of graphite in the tube can aid the removal of frozen ice. In warm conditions blocked pegs can be hung in the sun and left to thaw out.

Other Considerations

Placing pegs in good, thick ice normally presents few problems apart from hanging on while you do so. However, ice is not always so accommodating. In many cases the surface of the ice is less solid and has to be cut away so that the peg can be placed in the lower, more solid ice. The area of cleared ice should be large enough to allow easy access to the head of the peg both for insertion and extraction. In some situations, such as on easy-angled or rotten ice, the peg may be more secure if a horizontal step is cut and the peg placed vertically downwards at the back of this platform. When placing some types of peg, particularly those that are hammered into the ice, the ice may begin to crack, especially in cold conditions when it is more brittle. At first it will star – a series of cracks will radiate out from the point of entry of the peg – and then dinner-plate – a dish-shaped portion of ice will fall off. If the ice is thick enough, the peg should still be placed in the same spot since the lower ice is less liable to crack up in a similar way [*fig. 15.5*]. When clearing ice off, remember that the second and your own front points may be in the firing line below.

When placing pegs in thin ice, try to gauge where the greatest depth exists by the colour, the formations and the situation. The ice at the top of a step is often thicker than the steeper ice below it. If a peg goes in normally, then suddenly meets great resistance, stop screwing or hammering it. Depending on how far in it is and what the alternatives are, you can either try inserting it in another place or tie it off using a clove hitch. Although ice pegs are quite weak if tied off, it is often a case of something being better than nothing. If a peg is overdriven into the underlying rock, it can be made unusable. This is particularly true of tubular pegs, especially the screw-in ones. Once the cutting teeth are damaged or bent, it may not be possible to use the peg again until it has been repaired. This can be done by sharpening it with a file; Snargs can be re-sharpened with a round file or a cone grinder on a drill; tubular screws may have to be cut back at each tooth to form a new cutting edge, particularly if they have been bent.

If a peg suddenly begins to go in very easily during insertion, it probably means that the ice is hollow and backed by air or snow. The nature of the extruded core in tubular screws will often confirm your suspicions. Placements in this type of ice are generally poor and can fail at low loads.

Because the eye on an ice peg takes a severe pounding every time it is placed or removed, fractures can develop in this area, particularly since some types are welded on. If there is any chance that the eye is suspect, it is better if the peg is placed eye up and a sling doubled through it so that the load goes directly on to the main body of the peg.

Fig 15.5 Starring and dinner-plating round a Warthog. Once this surface layer has been cleared off, the peg will probably not break up the deeper ice.

On winter climbs of the more open, buttress type and in gullies in poor conditions, the ice may not be thick enough for even tied-off pegs. A reasonable alternative is to place an ice peg in frozen turf, vegetation or earth. Since this is often re-inforced ice, it can give a good anchor provided that the material in which it is fixed is large enough and well frozen in place. At least it will not star or dinner-plate. Warthogs are best for this; tubular pegs are not suitable as the cutting edge will be destroyed by hitting stones and gravel.

In conditions above freezing point there is always the danger of pegs melting out. Try to place them in the shade on sunny days or even cover the head with snow to slow down this loosening. It is liable to be more severe if the peg is weighted, when pressure melting also takes place. Longer and larger-diameter tubular screws perform better in these conditions.

Ice Bollards

Ice bollards provide excellent anchors in many types of ice but they are time-consuming to produce. The ice bollard is the same horseshoe shape as the snow bollard only smaller: 30–50cm across and 10–15cm deep with a pronounced lip behind which the rope or sling is seated [*fig. 15.6*].

To make an ice bollard, first mark its shape on the ice and cut round this, initially with the adze. Once you have produced a rough outline, the final shaping and forming of the lip is carried out with the pick. This is generally more easily done with a curved rather than an inclined pick, and in the case of some tools it may be better to do all the cutting with the adze. This stage of production requires a degree of care as it is easy to split or shatter the bollard if you are too enthusiastic; on the other hand, too much caution will mean that you will take too long. Often, scraping rather than cutting is more effective and will reduce your chance of breaking the bollard with a badly aimed blow.

Using natural features in the ice can reduce the amount of effort required. A bollard can be cut more easily at the top of an ice step than on a uniform slope. When using a bollard, it is essential that the pull is downwards as much as possible as it is stronger in this direction and there is less chance of the rope or sling sliding off. If a bollard is used as part of a belay, ensure that the rope between it and the belayer is tight at all times to keep it securely in place. If a bollard is used as a runner, put a long sling on it and perhaps weight it as well to decrease the chance of it lifting off.

Ice-Screw Thread

The ice-screw thread is a useful type of anchor, especially if not much gear is available. It is created by placing and removing a wide-diameter tubular screw twice so that the holes connect. The holes are made at about 45° to the face of the ice, usually in the horizontal plane, but they can be at other angles depending on what shape the ice is [*fig. 15.7a*]. A length of rope or tape is then threaded through the tunnel (a piece of wire with a hook on the end is invaluable for this) and tied to form a loop. This gives a multi-directional anchor, and the longer the screw, the bigger and stronger the thread can be made [*fig. 15.7b*].

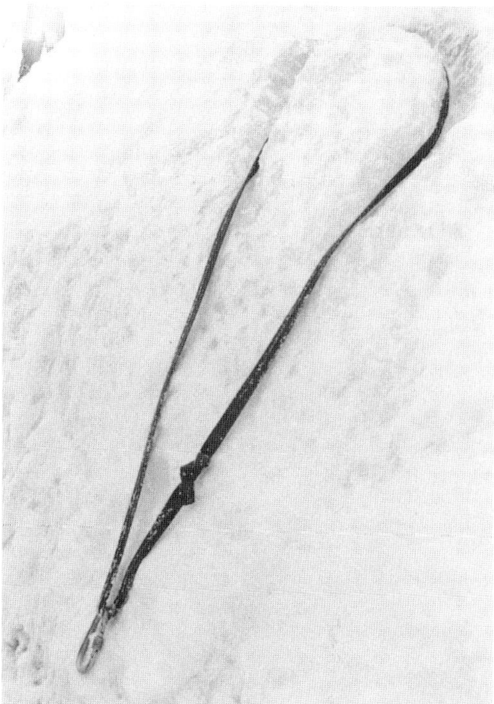

Fig 15.6 An ice bollard cut where the change in angle of the slope makes cutting easier. Using a double sling helps to keep the angle of pull downwards on the bollard and make it more secure.

Natural Ice Protection

Variations of the ice bollard can be made by using natural ice features. Ice bosses may form below icicles and icicles can grow to form thick ice pillars, both of which can be used by putting a sling around them. Several icicles can grow together to form a curtain of ice, and by cutting one or two holes through this a thread can be arranged. In such cases the strength of the runner may be marginal but perhaps better than nothing. With this kind of protection make sure that the pull comes downwards as these features are better able to take a pull from that direction. An outward pull can often shatter the ice.

Sometimes a gap may exist behind ice which is too thin to take ice pegs. You can utilise this gap by cutting a slot and putting into it anything which will jam, such as a deadman or a centrally tied-off ice peg. An open mind and an eye for possibilities are what counts in more marginal situations on ice.

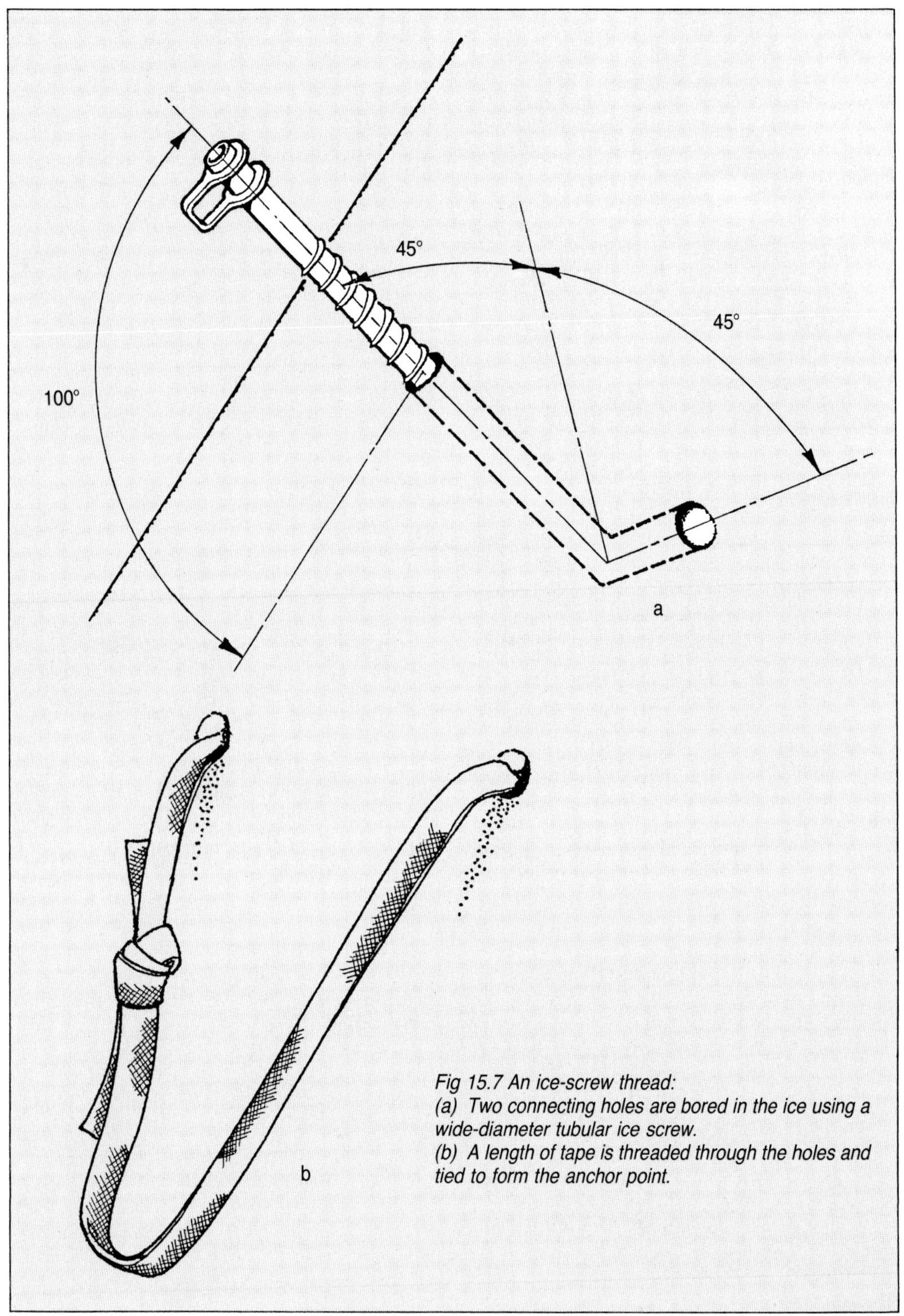

Fig 15.7 An ice-screw thread:
(a) Two connecting holes are bored in the ice using a wide-diameter tubular ice screw.
(b) A length of tape is threaded through the holes and tied to form the anchor point.

Placing Protection on Ice

Placing protection on ice is often more difficult than on rock. Although ice pegs are fairly simple to use, they do require the use of both hands. If the ice is thick enough, these pegs can go anywhere, so it is the position from which they are placed that becomes important. On ice part of the question of safety is whether to go on with few runners or use up strength placing more and so increase the chance of a fall that way. Ice climbing is about decision-making as much as any other aspect of the sport [*fig. 15.8*].

When climbing ice, the protection can be placed in the same way as on rock: where it is convenient and before the start of any steep sections. Looking ahead to plan where runners can be placed and where it is better to keep going is usually a good idea [*fig. 15.9*].

If the ice is not steep enough to require you to hold on with your hands, an ice peg can be placed while you are standing in balance on crampon points; or, more easily, from a previously cut step. Alternatively, a balanced position is attained using natural features which allows the hands to be freed [*fig. 15.10*]. One tool is driven securely into the ice at a convenient spot and the wrist left through the wrist loop. This frees the hand that

Fig 15.8 Climbing on ice can often be serious because of the lack of opportunities to rest and place protection, as on this steep but thin cascade of ice.

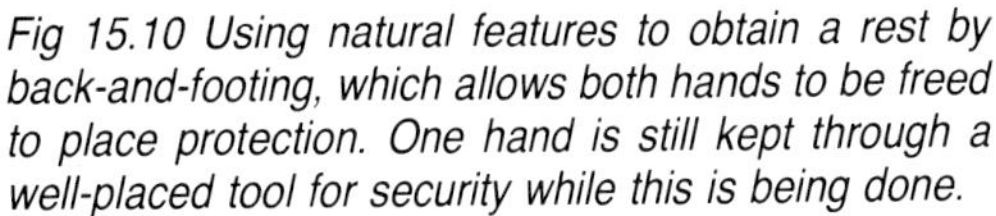

Fig 15.10 Using natural features to obtain a rest by back-and-footing, which allows both hands to be freed to place protection. One hand is still kept through a well-placed tool for security while this is being done.

Fig 15.11 Placing an ice screw. The climber is using the easing in the angle to rest his right leg by flat-footing. Security has been obtained by slipping the left arm through the wrist loop of a well-placed tool which also has a rope looped over the pick to act as a temporary runner. At this stage the hammer is also providing a safeguard but will soon have to be removed to act as a lever to screw the tube in fully.

has held the tool for working, yet still provides some security. The rope can be looped over the pick to act as a temporary runner. This works best with an inclined pick and can be used in any situation when protection is being placed. If a step is cut in the ice before the peg is placed, it provides an opportunity to rest the legs as well as making the placement easier.

On ice too steep to permit standing in balance without hands, natural resting positions such as easings in the angle or bridging positions should be sought out and used. Where no such opportunities exist, a tool must be used to hold you in a suitable position. One tool is placed as solidly as possible and the hand that has been holding it then slipped through the wrist loop as far as the elbow. By hanging from your crooked elbow, you free both hands to place the ice peg [*fig. 15.11*]. Clipping a sling between your harness and the placed ice tool gives you a safeguard while placing the peg in both these situations.

An alternative is to place one tool as fully as possible, perhaps using the other to hammer it in, and attach a sling or cow's tail from the axe to the harness. You can then sit in the harness with the weight off your arms and most of it off your legs and place the protection from this position. When clipping into the tools, do not use the wrist loop itself, because once it is under tension you cannot get your hand back into the loop again as it is pulled shut. A small, separate loop on the shaft or the spike can be used for this. Alternatively, some wrist loops have a separate attachment for the purpose.

Although this is a convenient way to place gear,

Fig 15.9 OPPOSITE PAGE: *Using ice protection. The leader has placed a runner before embarking on the steep ice where the opportunities to stop comfortably are limited. The second is anchored to the rock to one side, out of the way of any ice knocked down by the leader.*

it is considered by many to be a form of aid as the climber is not relying on his own skill and strength to climb the route. Different areas have their own code of ethics regarding this practice and they should be respected by anyone climbing there. In general, the bigger the route, the more this form of runner placing is likely to be acceptable. On an Alpine ice route a few rests on an axe are unlikely to make much difference to the final outcome; on a short ice fall resting and placing gear in this way can reduce a climb to an exercise in aid climbing on ice.

Fig 15.12 A well set-up ice belay with two fully placed ice screws and the ice tools tied in to provide extra security. The belayer is giving an indirect body belay to reduce the chance of shock-loading the anchors.

Ice Belays

When belaying on ice, the same principles apply as on rock. The anchor points must be secure, above waist level and linked in a safe, load-sharing manner.

When the leader reaches the top of the pitch where, it is to be hoped, there is the possibility of creating a stance, he first drives one tool securely into the ice and attaches himself to it. He then places the first anchor and clips into it. Then, protected from above, he can cut a suitable stance. On ice it is often better to cut a long, narrow stance as this requires less work and to stand on it in a heel-to-toe fashion facing sideways. He next places another anchor. This should be off to one side of the first and at a different level so as to decrease the chance of the ice cracking between the two points. If possible, the anchors should be in separate pieces of ice to spread the load. He then ties on in a load-sharing manner and belays as he would on a rock route. The anchors should be far enough above the stance to ensure that the angle formed between the two points and the belayer is as small as possible to avoid unnecessary strain. If the anchors are suspect, a more dynamic system, such as a body belay, should be adopted [*fig. 15.12*]. Extra security can be obtained by placing another anchor off to one side, the side from which the next pitch starts, and running the live rope through that. This can make the rope easier to handle and also means that the leader has protection immediately he starts the next pitch.

Ice tools can also be used as extra anchors. One or both tools can be hammered into the ice. Some picks even have a raised portion at the top of the head to make this easier to do. The tools can then be tied into using the hole in the head or the wrist loop if it is strong enough. Another method is to place both tools so that they cross in a shallow X. A sling is then put on to both shafts by tying a clove hitch round them at the point where they cross.

16 Climbing in Winter

When climbing in winter, the short days and the threat of bad weather makes fast, efficient climbing a priority. Even when the weather is good and time plentiful, a route can become unpleasant if too long is spent belaying on a constricted stance in freezing conditions while being bombarded by snow and ice from above. Winter is not the season for slow, inefficient rope work, belay organisation and anchor placement. The basic skills are best mastered on warm summer rock and should be well practised before this type of climbing is tackled.

A great deal of time can be saved, not only when climbing but also in other areas. This can start long before the foot of the route is reached with good organisation and preparation, beginning with the initial purchase of equipment. Ropes which do not absorb water are better for use on snow and ice as they do not get as wet and freeze as readily as untreated ropes and consequently are stronger, easier to handle, run better and so save time and energy. The choice of karabiners, too, can make a difference: lightweight ones which are smaller are less easy to handle when wearing mitts or gloves and their weight saving is of little significance when you are equipped for a winter route. Screw-gate karabiners can freeze up and be awkward to operate, and in some conditions back-to-back karabiners are a better alternative. The kind of harness or tie-on arrangement you need may well differ from the one used in summer, and unless the harness is fully adjustable it is unlikely to fit properly in both seasons because of differences in clothing. In fact, some of the reasons for wearing a harness on rock climbs, such as repeated falls, hanging in space or many abseils, may not be relevant on a winter climb – at least, not in the lower grades. When selecting a harness for winter use, different design features should be considered: is it convenient to put on when wearing boots and crampons?; could extra clothing be donned or removed with minimum inconvenience?; could holsters be fitted easily?; and is it easy to give an indirect belay while wearing it? On climbs where a lot of snow belays or marginal anchors are likely and so an indirect tie-on and body belay is preferred, a waist belt may be the best answer. However, when attempting more difficult climbs, the reasons for using a harness outweigh the inconvenience of doing so.

Gear should always be checked before you leave for a climb. Crampons and axes should be inspected for loose nuts, bolts and straps and sharpened if necessary. Spare gear should be packed in the bottom of the rucksack, where it is to be hoped that it will remain, while items which are likely to be used should be kept handy. Climbing equipment appropriate to the route to be attempted should be taken. Although protection may be poor on some winter climbs, it is often necessary to carry a fairly wide selection of gear to ensure that any suitable crack can be utilised. This varies with the climb and the conditions, but on a buttress route there is seldom the need for a large number of ice pegs: on an ice-fall a deadman may be unusable and rock anchors limited; where there is plenty of vegetation, drive-in/screw-out pegs are more versatile than tubes. Try to anticipate what may be needed, not only for your intended route but also for any other you may find yourself on as a result of changes in plan caused by conditions or by too many other climbers on the route you hoped to do.

The way in which gear is carried can also influence the speed of a climb. Bandoliers are the best system of gear racking in a leading-through climb when they can be swapped quickly at stances. To take twenty or more karabiners off a harness and re-rack them on another takes time, particularly in bad weather, and increases the chance of dropping and losing equipment. Gear is carried on the bandolier in the normal manner with the larger pieces at the back, grading round to the smaller pieces of protection at the front. Deadmen are notoriously difficult to carry and can be a hazard, especially in high winds. To carry them wrap the wire round the plate, push the swaged loop through a suitable hole and clip with a karabiner. They can then go at the back of the bandolier or be clipped to the bottom of a rucksack strap. An alternative is to carry deadmen in the top of the pack on the principle that if a snow belay is needed, there will be an opportunity to create a step and take the pack off to get at them.

Leave for the route in plenty of time, using a head torch if necessary, as it is better to have spare time at the end of the day than walk back in the dark when tired. Unless the cliff is well known to you, however, there is little point in arriving much before first light if locating the route is not simple. Gear up at a suitable spot early rather than later when it maybe more awkward to put on crampons, harness and helmet or an unnecessary stance has to be cut. It may well be worth having something to eat at this stage as once on the climb it will be less comfortable or convenient. One person, the leader of the first pitch, should rack up at this point, remembering, of course, to put on his rucksack before the bandolier and slings go over his shoulders. The second takes the rope and when the foot of the climb is reached he can uncoil it while the leader with the gear arranges the anchors. As few winter routes start from flat ground, an anchor and a belay at the bottom is usually needed. As the rope is uncoiled, it can be draped in hanks around an axe stuck in the snow to prevent one end sliding off down the slope. As soon as the anchor is found, it is worth clipping the rope through it to give some security while tying on. Because communications in winter are often difficult, establish a system of non-verbal communications at this point rather than have long delays on the climb. Four or five definite tugs on the rope for 'Climb when ready' is simple and effective.

Once you are on the route, you can save time at stances with a little forethought. Set up a spare attachment point for the second to clip into when he arrives at the stance so that he is safeguarded while the rope is arranged for the next pitch and the gear is sorted out. If one person is to lead the whole climb, having the stance and belay organised for this saves time but will still take longer than leading through. Another way to save minutes is for the leader to have the gear ready for the second to collect when he reaches the stance. Hanging it on an axe in the snow in a safe position or from an anchor point is convenient and relieves the leader's neck of the weight. When you are taking in the rope, save time and potential tangles by draping it in hanks round an axe, your leg or over the ropes to the anchors. This is particularly useful in windy weather.

Once the route is completed, it may be necessary to descend fairly quickly. Having already read and noted the descents in the guidebook and worked out the best way to navigate back to safety in the valley or hut is far easier and more pleasant than struggling with a map and compass by head torch in a blizzard. It is often in conditions like these that other decisions need making, such as whether to stay roped up or not, which descent to take and what gear, if any, to take off or put on.

Although ice-axe arrest can be used to stop a slip on snow, when actually on a climb it is less likely that this would be effective unless on a straightforward slope. In winter a fall rather than a slide can be more serious than a fall from a rock climb. One of the reasons for this is the difference in frequency and quality of the protection: longer falls are a real possibility. You are also likely to be wearing a rucksack, which increases the chance of a head-first fall as you will have a higher centre of gravity; and you will be carrying things such as axes and ice pegs which can cause stab wounds in a fall. Crampons can also cause a lot of damage: in even a short fall, if the points touch the snow, ice or rock, they can catch and result in ankle injuries. There seems little that you can do to prevent this, but try to keep your feet well away from the slope. Even when bouldering on ice, try to jump rather than fall off.

MIXED CLIMBING

Mixed climbing can mean several different things depending on the context in which it is used. In the Alps mixed routes are those which have both rock and ice pitches; in other places the term is used to describe climbs which have free and aid pitches. A mixed winter route is one which includes moves on snow, ice and rock; it is a combination of summer and snow and ice techniques used in a winter situation. This type of route often offers more technical climbing than pure ice routes and calls on the whole range of your climbing skills. To tackle it, the ability to rock climb while wearing crampons is fundamental and virtually every rock technique may have to be used. On this type of route ice and turf placements, rock hand and foot holds, axe hooking and torquing moves may need to be used. Decisions such as whether to clear the snow and ice off an area in the hope of finding protection and rock holds or to try to climb on poor placements and whether to use rock holds with your gloves on or off have to be taken regularly, making mixed routes a very satisfying type of climbing, for some at least. Experience and decision-making become more important on mixed routes and every situation is unique. Routes can vary considerably according to weather conditions as the snow and ice cover changes in thickness and hardness. A thick cover of hard snow may permit better placements but make protection more difficult to find; thin ice may offer hard climbing but reveal the usable rock features, and so on. The hardest mixed routes depend so much on conditions that they may not be climbable unless these are right.

Fig 16.1 Using a rock hold with one foot and ice with the other. When using crampons on rock, small holds can be stood on with the front points as long as they are fairly positive.

Rock Climbing in Crampons

Climbing rock while wearing crampons is very similar to climbing rock in very stiff footwear and using the toe of the boot [*fig. 16.1*]. Crampons whose first points are vertical rather than angled forward are the best for this type of climbing and the safest holds are positive edges. Small holds are stood on with the two forward-facing points, while larger ones can take the first two downward points as well. Although this can be disconcerting at first, good grip is obtained even on sloping holds because of the biting action of the points, all your weight being concentrated in a very small area. It is even possible in crampons to use small horizontal cracks which could not normally be utilised even when wearing rock boots as the front points can be slotted into the cracks. Climbing like this, however, is very tiring on the calf muscles, but having shorter points means less leverage and strain. Old crampons whose points are too short for ice climbing are often ideal for mixed routes. Likewise, articulated crampons are slightly better than rigid ones on this type of ground and leather boots give a better feel than plastic. Straps rather than clip-on bindings may also be preferable because of their greater security as this type of climbing can put a lot of twisting forces on the crampon.

Axe Hooking and Axe Torquing

Techniques more specific to mixed routes than any other are axe hooking and axe torquing. When hooking, the pick or the adze is placed on, or over, a suitable rock hold and this is used to pull up on. Banana-shaped picks and inclined adzes work best in such a case. The pull should be steady and straight down as, unless the hold is very incut, there is a chance of the pick pivoting off. In this situation the tool is being used as a large skyhook.

Axe torquing is using the tool in cracks. The best and simplest are the same as good nut placements where a part of the tool is slotted into a crack and pulled down to a constriction where it wedges firmly. The width of the crack determines which part of the tool is used: the pick, the adze, the hammer or the shaft. Where the pick joins the shaft can also be used as it is often wider or has fastening nuts and bolts which will jam in a

Fig 16.2 Mixed buttress climbing in winter using rock foot holds while climbing in crampons and torquing with the ice tools in the thin crack in the corner. Constant pressure must be kept on the tools to make sure that the picks are twisted firmly in place.

crack. More difficult torquing occurs when the crack is wider than the pick and narrower than the next-largest bit of the tool and does not constrict. Here the tool must be kept in place by twisting or torquing. In diagonal cracks this twisting happens naturally when the shaft is pulled down on. In vertical cracks it is more difficult as the head must be kept under constant pressure by twisting the shaft to one side to maintain a grip.

Torquing in wider cracks is done using the adze or hammer head when the part of the tool is turned and fitted into the crack, then twisted so that it grips. Flat adzes and rectangular hammer heads are the best shapes for torquing and the more steeply inclined picks and adzes are more difficult to get into cracks. In the case of a wider crack the whole tool can be fitted diagonally inside and twisted and pulled down on it so that the head and the spike grip. In horizontal cracks the pick, head or shaft can be used, depending on the size and depth of the crack. When using the head, the shaft is pulled down on to provide the necessary twist, but it is even possible to use this as an undercut by changing the pull to upwards when above the tool. Holding the shaft nearer the head reduces the leverage and strain in this sort of placement. Techniques such as hand traversing and laybacking are carried out using tools in the same way as on rock.

With these techniques all tools tend to have their good and bad points and their performance is related to the size and shape of the cracks on the climb. Personal preference is usually the main criterion for choice. All the techniques put immense strain on the tools, especially if the pick or adze is not fully in the crack. This is not generally the use intended for the product by the manufacturer, so equipment damage is to be expected if a large amount of mixed climbing is done [*fig. 16.2*].

Abseiling on Snow and Ice

Abseiling from snow or ice anchors is no different from abseiling on rock except that the ropes may be frozen or coated with snow and this can affect the performance of the friction device used. Some such devices clog up with ice, whereas others may give less control: only experience will reveal how any device will act with any particular rope. On any abseil, however, the descent should be smooth and controlled with as much weight as possible taken on the feet. On snow or ice there may be the opportunity of retrieving the abseil anchor once down. This can be useful when equipment is limited, but getting it right is obviously critical, so it is best to practise the procedure in controlled conditions before trying it for real.

Abseils from Ice

It is possible to abseil off an ice bollard and, by putting the rope round it, leave no gear behind as the rope should run freely on the ice. However, in certain conditions, pressure melting and re-freezing can result in the rope becoming stuck. Using a sling gets round this problem and can keep the pull on the bollard in a better direction – that is, downwards – as much as possible, especially at the start of the abseil. Ice-screw threads make good anchors as they require little gear and are multi-directional.

The third option is to use an ice screw which can be recovered once you are down. To do this, a tubular screw is inserted for part of its length at 100° or even slightly more to the slope and the abseil rope hung over the top of it. The tube is placed with the eye up and a piece of cord or tape attached to the eye and wound round the tube in the direction which will unscrew it when pulled. This cord is attached to the appropriate side of the abseil rope by a prusik loop, and when the rope and the prusik are pulled on retrieval, the cord unscrews the peg and it should drop out [*fig. 16.3*]. To ensure that it will unscrew, enough turns of cord must be wound round it, and in some conditions it may be necessary to insert the screw, remove it and then replace it to make sure that it is fairly free to turn.

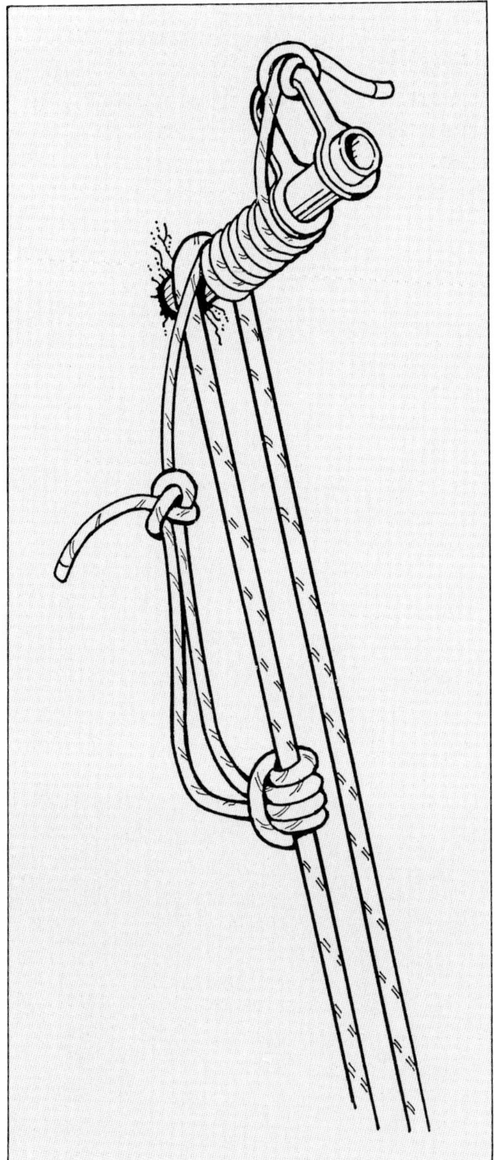

Fig 16.3 A retrievable ice screw. The rope to which the prusik is attached is the one which would be pulled to unscrew the tubular ice screw.

Abseils from Snow

When abseiling off snow, the obvious anchor to use is a snow bollard as no equipment need be left behind. If the snow is soft or badly layered, the rope may need to be padded to stop it cutting in too much. If this is carefully arranged, the gear used for padding can be attached to the rope so that it also pulls down. Making the slot round the bollard wider than usual renders this easier. Old bollards should be checked to ensure that they have not been too severely undercut by previous ropes pulling round them.

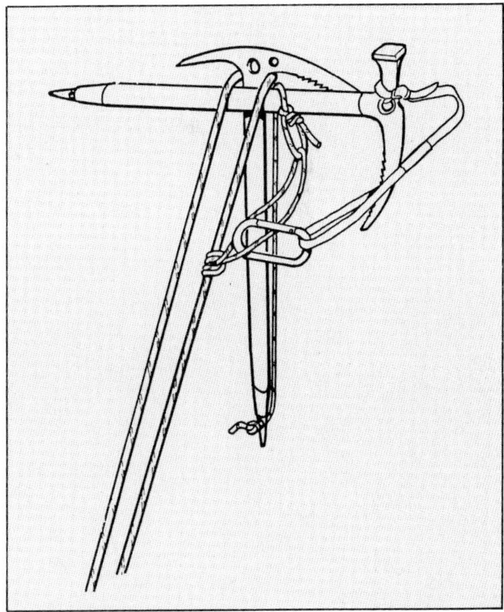

Fig 16.4 A retrievable ice axe. The rope to which the prusik is attached is the one which would be pulled to pull the vertical axe up and out.

It is also possible to abseil from an ice axe and retrieve it from below. A length of cord is attached to the spike either through a hole or by a clove hitch just below the ferrule. The axe is then placed vertically in the snow and another tool laid horizontally in front of it. The abseil rope is put round the back of the vertical axe, over the horizontal one and down the slope to be descended. The cord is taken up the vertical shaft, over the horizontal one and attached to the appropriate side of the abseil rope via a prusik knot. When the side of the rope with the prusik attached is pulled, the cord running over the horizontal shaft pulls the vertical axe up and out. The horizontal tool is loosely attached to the prusik so that it too is pulled down. If you are using a snow stake, the arrangement is exactly the same. In either case, stand well clear when recovering the tools for obvious reasons [*fig. 16.4*].

If the snow is such as to make this type of abseil anchor a necessity, take care that the ropes do not cut so far into the snow that they are difficult to retrieve. It may be necessary to cut away or compact the snow at any steeper sections such as cornices.

SECTION THREE

Alpine Climbing

17 The Alpine Experience

For many climbers Alpinism is the next obvious step after climbing on the lower crags and ice cliffs. While this may seem to be a relatively straightforward progression. Alpine climbing is inherently different from crag climbing. It demands a high level of mountain awareness (knowledge of weather, objective danger, navigation and the other mountain climbing skills needed for survival in potentially serious situations) by participants at all levels – from the glacier walkers to the climbers who ascend the *grandes courses*. It is perhaps this great diversity that makes Alpine climbing such a popular and challenging branch of climbing.

Alpine-style climbing covers everything from one-day routes to ascents on 8000m Himalayan peaks. It is a style of climbing which is as appropriate in New Zealand, Canada, South America and the Himalayas as it is in Europe. Alpine-style ascents are normally considered to be those which are done in a single push by climbers carrying all their own equipment. This may be an ascent of a snowy 3000m dome in the European Alps, a big face in South America or a multi-day push on a Himalayan giant.

It is often difficult to decide where crag climbing ends and Alpinism begins; and perhaps, at the end of the day, it is not necessary to make a distinction. Suffice to say that any route which involves an approach, an ascent and a subsequent descent, and which requires navigational, route finding and other mountaineering skills, will qualify as an Alpine route. It is not even necessary to specify a minimum length; instead, the overall character, the feeling of remoteness and situation of the route are more important in classifying it. One of the great features of this style of climbing is the feeling of commitment which is necessary for success at any level, whether it be a high-level glacier walk or a difficult and serious mixed climb. It is partly this commitment, when combined with the more unpredictable aspects of environment, such as weather and avalanche risk, which makes this such an exhilarating and challenging sport.

BIGGER MOUNTAINS

The all-important basic knowledge of mountains and how to move around in them is best acquired on low-level crags and hill-walking excursions. All the skills necessary for safe ascents of higher, longer routes can be learned while climbing at lower altitudes in summer and, even better, under winter conditions. Many of the smaller mountain ranges in the world, such as the Scottish Highlands, make ideal training grounds [*fig. 17.1*], providing as they do an excellent introduction to route finding, navigation, general climbing skills, snow and ice techniques and, perhaps most important, a development of the climber's awareness of risk and objective danger.

When you begin Alpine climbing, it is best to do so in a reasonably controlled manner which allows you to become acquainted both with the special problems of longer climbs and with those presented by the varied terrain. Many people at this stage may seek the services of a mountain guide, who will be invaluable not only in guiding the climber to the summit of his chosen peak but also in showing the approach required by this type of climbing. Failing this, it is best to make the transition slowly. Many of the lessons of Alpinism have to be learned by trial and experimentation, and obviously it is best to do this in as safe and controlled a situation as possible.

INTRODUCTIONS TO ALPINE CLIMBING

You may choose to start your introduction to Alpine climbing by progressing first of all to

Fig 17.1 OPPOSITE PAGE: *Typical mixed climbing terrain in the Scottish Highlands. Ground like this provides an excellent introduction to the mountaineering skills required for longer routes on higher mountains.*

longer and more serious ridge walks, often on mountains which are around 3000m high. This allows you to become accustomed to longer and more strenuous days, but still in a relatively safe environment with which you are familiar.

High-level Glacier Walking

For those whose aspirations lie more in mixed climbing and the ascent of snowy peaks, one of the best introductions is to link a few glaciers together [*fig. 17.2*] as a traverse and make a journey through a high mountain area. This quickly illustrates the problems of moving on glacial terrain and will provide opportunities to practise crevasse rescue and route finding in this often hostile environment. It also allows you to see at first hand how the mountains change, both with altitude and according to the time of day. Although glacier walking is often used as an introduction to the Alpine arena, the glaciers themselves should always be treated with respect [*fig. 17.3*] and you should always follow the basic rules of roping up where necessary and carrying sufficient gear to deal with any emergency. Many mountainous areas of the world have strings of convenient glaciers that can be linked together to form interesting traverses which, as well as providing useful information for future climbing trips, offer worthwhile excursions in themselves. The High Level Route from Chamonix to Zermatt and many of the treks in the Himalayas, Canada and New Zealand typify this type of Alpinism.

Fig 17.2 Glaciers can often provide entertaining routes through mountain areas. The climber is using a single axe, and the other hand is being used for balance on this 40° ice slope.

Alpine Mountaineering

Most Alpine areas of the world are covered by comprehensive guidebooks and maps and these can be studied to give an idea as to what is feasible for your party. In this type of climbing it is very important that all members of the rope are equally committed and equally skilled. Many Alpine trips have been ruined by partners who do not share the same ambitions or motivation and so the choice of a partner is of vital importance in any Alpine project.

It is best to climb at several grades below your normal standard when visiting an area for the first time as the routes may be graded and timed in a way with which you are not familiar. Short, established routes with well-marked approaches offer ideal opportunities for acclimatisation and familiarisation with the new area. As you become more familiar with an area and the style of climbing, as well as with your own limitations and aspirations, it will soon become obvious which routes are and which are not possible.

Acclimatisation

To begin with, many find it difficult to proceed with the care and caution which is an essential part of Alpinism. Easy ground and low technical difficulty often give rise to a false sense of safety, security and competence [*fig. 17.4*]. It takes some time for the body to become acclimatised to the reduced oxygen available at higher altitudes – above 2500m many people will initially feel quite breathless and tired. The body acclimatises best when not pushed too hard in the early days. This means that the first week should be spent getting used to this rarefied air, best done on easy routes of increasing altitude rather than on hard, technical problems. One of the most difficult aspects of

Fig 17.3 A complicated Antarctic glacier which is sourced from an ice cap.

Alpinism to come to terms with is that not all the routes can be climbed just when you like. Conditions and weather can often conspire to keep some routes out of condition for several seasons. This means that you must be both patient and flexible in your choice of routes. Try to avoid attempts on routes which are out of condition as failure is not just very frustrating but usually also leaves you in no fit state to take advantage of good conditions when they do arrive. In poor or unsettled weather short, one-day or even crag routes which do not involve a big expenditure of time, energy or commitment are best as they can be quickly abandoned should conditions on the higher peaks improve.

OBJECTIVE DANGER

One of the main differences between climbing at lower altitudes and in the high Alpine regions is objective danger. This is the term used to describe risks in the mountains which occur naturally and are often difficult to predict. Rock fall, avalanches, serac falls and lightning all come into this category. At first it seems that these are all 'acts of God', potential accidents which can happen to anybody at any time. However, careful observation soon shows that different places are more at risk at different times: for example, rock fall is normally worse in the afternoon sun when ice thaws and so releases debris which may in turn cause larger slides of rock and ice. The avalanche risk may also increase at clearly defined times of day, depending on slope aspect and weather conditions among other factors. Careful study of a mountain will show that stone-fall couloirs, areas of serac fall and so on are often best passed very early in the morning, or perhaps even at night when the temperature is lower and ice holds things together. It is for this reason that many north faces and mixed climbs are ascended entirely at night. It also explains why it is often necessary to start a sunny rock climb before dawn and so avoid the stone fall which can often threaten the approach to an Alpine climb.

Fig 17.4 A well-equipped party moving competently on a wet glacier. Although the terrain looks easy, there may be many crevasses under the snow surface.

Every climb, and indeed every glacier, will present its own special problems, but careful observation often reveals evidence of possible dangers. When any signs of rock or ice fall are observed, great care should be taken in the route planning, and if it proves necessary to cross the danger area, every effort should be made to move as quickly as possible. Objective dangers can never be rendered completely safe but they need not always be accepted as random, uncontrollable risks.

LIFE IN THE VALLEY

On any Alpine trip the actual time spent in the mountains will probably be only half of the time available. Alpine climbing is strenuous and time-consuming and the weather is often unreliable and unpredictable. These factors combine to make it essential that you live in as comfortable and relaxed an atmosphere as possible when in the valley. Since finance is often limited, many climbers choose to camp, but this can often cause problems in the more popular Alpine areas as overcrowding and pollution have made wild camping almost impossible to find and, indeed, organised camping sites can be crowded at peak times, especially in the popular centres. In most areas of the European Alps very good low-cost dormitory accommodation can be found. These dormitories offer an ideal base with cooking facilities, showers, and usually places to store equipment when away from base. It is important to eat well when in the valley, so that the body recovers after a climb and the 'batteries are charged' again for the next ascent.

It is very easy for inexperienced Alpinists who become impatient with bad weather to find themselves out of sequence with the weather patterns and consequently to achieve little actual climbing. Although often very difficult, the decision to be patient and not climb in mediocre weather must be made so as not to miss out on any of the good weather that does occur. In most circumstances it is best to wait out periods of bad weather and go back to the mountains only when the weather shows definite signs of improvement, rather than to rush off in bad weather and so get clothes and equipment wet, necessitating a delay when good weather finally arrives.

It is worthwhile progressing up through the grades so that fitness, acclimatisation and climb ing form are at their peak before you attempt longer and harder climbs. It is very tempting to try a difficult climb after several weeks of bad weather – often 'pretending' that the routes planned for that period have somehow been climbed! The correct choice of route, one which is actually feasible, is perhaps the greatest of all Alpine skills. It is all too easy to spend a season waiting for a 'plum' route to come into condition and in the interim to waste good conditions and time.

EQUIPMENT FOR ALPINISM

When making the transition from rock and ice climber to that of Alpinist, it would seem at first that much new and specialist equipment must be acquired. This is not the case: if you have chosen your rock and ice gear wisely, you will find that it will serve you well in all mountain arenas. There are, however, a few special considerations to be made when choosing equipment for Alpine climbing.

Because of the nature of the climbing, routes are frequently long, sometimes taking several days and often serious, so the gear must be very dependable while also being lightweight. This compromise between strength, reliability and weight is one which is difficult to achieve. Fortunately, modern materials have made the equipment lighter and stronger than previously – for example, twenty of today's lightweight karabiners weigh only ½kg as opposed to the 4½kg of the steel karabiners of twenty years ago. This use of modern alloys has also affected ice-axe and crampon design, both items now being lighter and more dependable, and although these do still break, the breakages are few and far between. It is important to recognise the advantages and disadvantages of lightweight gear, and, as equipment is replaced or renewed, careful choices must be made based on proven strength, weight and durability.

Perhaps the biggest single change to make in the gear taken on an Alpine route, as compared to a route on a smaller mountain, is in the relative amounts of technical and survival gear carried. It is common to rock climb in shorts and a T-shirt while carrying no spare clothes, whereas in many hill walking and mountaineering situations spare clothes, navigation gear, food, first aid and emergency bivouac equipment are carried. In Alpine climbing there is always an element of compromise: can a full rack of rock and ice gear be carried as well as a full complement of safety and survival gear? In many cases the answer will be no. The amount and type of gear carried will depend on the type of route, the difficulty of the climbing, the likely temperatures, the number of nights to be spent out and the overall situation.

It is helpful to look at some different types of Alpine climb and the different problems they pose. First, consider the ascent of a difficult route in the northern hemisphere. The route is predominantly a rock climb, but with a long glacier approach and a difficult and complicated glacier descent; it faces west; it is some 800m long and has some difficult rock climbing in its lower third. Since the climb is quite long, it is common to start the difficult rock in the afternoon sun after walking up from the valley that day. This means spending one night out on the face. The climbing on a TD+ route is reasonably difficult (pitches of V+ and V1) and most people will choose to wear rock boots, which means carrying mountain boots in the rucksack. (See Chapter 21, page 286, for information on route grades.) Bivouac gear and food, a good selection of rock climbing gear, equipment for the glacier and some basic navigation equipment for the descent are needed.

This quickly adds up to a large pile of equipment, so weight-saving decisions must be made. Would one axe between two be sufficient? Are sleeping bags necessary? How much of the climbing gear will be required? Could the climbing be done in mountaineering boots? The answers to these questions will vary, but the same questions are asked before every Alpine climb, be it in the European Alps, North or South America, or even at the start of an Alpine ascent in the Himalayas.

In comparison with this, when attempting a difficult ice face, you might elect, for safety reasons, to climb almost entirely at night and to hope to finish the climb in a single push. Obviously speed is a very important consideration in this case and the less gear carried, the faster you can move. The equipment carried for the glacier will double up and be used for climbing (this will mean using slings in place of prusik loops), and the amount of rock climbing gear taken will be much reduced – being replaced by some more ice screws. No bivouac gear will be carried and the route will be started from a hut if possible. This results in carrying less and consequently moving faster, but with a reduced safety margin should the route take longer than expected. It could also be argued that this approach is in fact safer, if everything goes according to plan, as you are less exposed to the vagaries of the weather and changing conditions, and hence at less risk.

With this in mind, the choice of gear becomes critical. Every mistake is not only a weight penalty, but also a time penalty!

Special Considerations

It makes a great deal of sense *always* to wear a helmet when climbing on an Alpine route. Not only are objective dangers, like falling rocks and ice, commonplace, but so too is that other – often more real – danger of being struck by rocks kicked off by other climbers. Wearing a helmet is not the great hardship it once was. Gone is the heavy, vision-restricting and uncomfortable headgear of yesteryear to be replaced by light carbon-fibre helmets which, while being much lighter, are also much stronger and more comfortable to wear.

There is now a bewildering variety of designs and types of boot, from fully stiffened plastic-shelled boots with overboots, to lightweight rock boots. The final choice will depend on the kind of climbing to be undertaken. Rock boots have only a limited use in Alpine climbing, mainly because they will almost always be used in conjunction with a stiff boot which has a cleated sole. They will not accept crampons and, with their smooth soles, are lethal on snow and ice. However, as standards continue to rise, these are becoming more and more a part of the Alpinist's rock climbing attire. A few, very specialist overboots are available which are extremely light in weight, consisting of a stiff sole attached to a pull-over gaiter which can be worn on top of rock boots. Their advantage is in their lightness (useful for when they are carried on climbs) but their disadvantage is that all the walking and climbing done in them is while wearing tight-fitting and often uncomfortable rock boots. They are most useful for short approaches to difficult climbs. Some people even wear rock boots as an inner to their plastic boots, in an effort to save weight but without compromising performance – if not comfort!

The type and amount of clothing worn on an Alpine route will depend very much on the altitude of the climb and its aspect. In Europe cold north faces contrast dramatically with their south-facing neighbours, often receiving only a few hours of sunshine in the early mornings or late afternoons. For this reason the Alpine rock climber, while on the sunnier south faces, will choose lightweight clothes which offer freedom of move-

Fig 17.5 Preparing for an Alpine bivouac. A head torch which can be attached to the helmet is an essential part of the Alpinist's gear.

ment together with a waterproof and windproof shell. On colder climbs fabrics and garments which allow the body to 'breathe' and are warm and light, even when wet, have vastly reduced the amount of extra clothing that need be carried.

Gloves and mitts are essential and warm, thin, lightweight thermal gloves are now standard equipment, usually worn inside a waterproof overmitt. Thick woollen mitts are excellent when on snow, ice or mixed routes.

The technical climbing gear is very similar to that used in other branches of climbing, the only major difference being the quantity (weight) of gear actually taken on the routes. Modern materials have helped lighten this load (titanium ice screws and even ice axes, and Kevlar slings, are only a few examples); however, the resultant weight saving is fairly small and is of little importance on most Alpine routes. A more important consideration should be in the type (style) and length of axes and hammers chosen. For most routes these will be longer than used for pure ice climbing: a length of 55–60cm will usually, depending on the size of the user, be ideal. The ice axe should be of a gently curved variety unless very steep ice is expected. On pure snow routes even longer axes may prove useful, but these are a disadvantage in situations requiring more technical climbing and on rock pitches. In most Alpine climbing two half-ropes are recommended because of their versatility, both in ascent and descent, and also the extra safety margin they offer. When the possibility of an abseil descent exists, it is worth carrying 10m or so of nylon tape which can be cut into lengths and used on abseil points as required. This saves the cannibalisation of the climbing rack.

Other Alpine Essentials

As well as the fairly standard gear requirements outlined above, you will also need to carry:

- A water bottle capable of holding about one litre. This should be strong and leakproof.
- Good-quality glacier glasses. These are essential and must give a high degree of protection against infra-red and ultra-violet light. They should have side shields to give complete protection. Those with glass lenses are best optically as they offer the best protection and suffer least from scratching; however, glass lenses break more easily than plastic ones.
- A head torch that is easily attached to the helmet and has a long-lasting battery, preferably one which can be operated easily while you are climbing and wearing gloves. A halogen bulb helps increase vision during night climbing [*fig. 17.5*].
- A small repair and first-aid kit on most routes. This should include some crampon spares (a long, thin strap with a quick-adjust buckle is useful here), a torch battery and spare bulb, a spare pair of light sunglasses (one pair between two climbers should suffice). A Swiss Army or similar knife can also be very useful.
- Bivouac equipment, if an overnight stop is envisaged on the climb.
- Maps, guides, compasses, altimeter and so on, as required.

18 Glacier Travel

It is important, before venturing onto a glacier, to have some understanding of what it is and how it behaves. A glacier is a mass of ice which, under the influence of gravity, flows outwards from the permanent snow field where it originates. Wherever there is permanent snow (over many years), there will be glaciers. The height at which this permanent snow occurs varies with latitude from almost 6000m in some areas of the Himalayas to sea level in the Polar regions. This accounts for the existence of glaciers at vastly different altitudes throughout the world. It is interesting to note that Ben Nevis, in the Scottish Highlands, where there is so much ice climbing, only just fails to reach the crucial altitude, around 1500m, at which permanent snow would be present at this latitude.

These permanent snow fields are dependent not only upon low temperatures for their existence but also upon a winter snow fall sufficiently large that the spring and summer thaws fail to remove it. Whenever there is an excess of snow left over from the previous year, a permanent snow field begins to grow. It will continue to increase in size until the weight of snow is such that the pressure it exerts turns the snow to ice which then moves downhill under the force of gravity, thus creating a glacier.

As the build-up of snow and ice increases, the pressure continues to rise and this pushes out the air trapped in the snow pack eventually to form hard, dense, airless ice deep in the glacier [*fig. 18.1*]. As this glacier continues to move downhill, it melts, mostly from the surface, a process known as ablation. The glacier continues to advance until its downhill end, or snout, reaches a position where, over the years, accumulation at the glacier source is balanced by this ablation process. This may be a long way below the snow line [*fig. 18.2*].

In most mountain situations the glacier flows in the bottom of a valley, usually as a long tongue of ice. Where the glacier exists in flat, snowy regions, it forms an ice sheet or ice cap [*fig. 17.3*, page 249]. As changes in climate occur, glaciers advance or recede. A particularly good example of this can be found on Mount Kenya where the glaciers have shrunk dramatically since they were first observed. The glacial recession we are experiencing at present has resulted in the level of the sea rising by some 8cm in the last one hundred years.

The ice which makes up the bulk of the glacier is neither a solid nor a liquid. Instead, the intense pressure turns it into a semi-malleable plastic material soft enough to flow at slow speeds. This does not apply to the crust of the glacier, which is under less pressure and so is hard and brittle [*fig. 18.1*].

Some of the faster glaciers, such as are found in Greenland, may move as much as 20m a day, but a figure of 1m or less is more representative of the speeds attained by most of the world's glaciers (the Mer de Glace, in the Mont Blanc range moves at around 25cm per day). On the 'surface' of these moving ice masses (which have been found in the Antarctic to be almost 3000m thick in places), is a crust which may be as much as 60m thick. This crust is brittle in comparison with the main glacier, and is carried along by the ice underneath. It is this crust which, when subjected to excess stress, cracks and fractures to give the features most important to the mountaineer: crevasses, bergschrunds, ice falls and seracs. These different features are caused by stresses and pressures working through the glacier, the different kinds of crevasses being named according to the direction of these stresses. Marginal crevasses [*fig. 18.3*] are the result of differential drag against the valley sides; transverse crevasses develop where the glacier flows over a convexity or steepening of its floor. When the steepening is very pronounced, ice falls and seracs are the result. These particular features are unstable and pose great objective danger to mountaineers [*fig. 18.4*]. They can also occur where the glacier flows

Fig 18.1 OPPOSITE PAGE: *A section through a glacier, showing its approximate composition. Only the upper part of the glacier will fracture and form crevasses. Below about 50m the pressure exerted by the weight of the ice is so great that the ice becomes malleable and so 'bends and flows' rather than fracturing.*

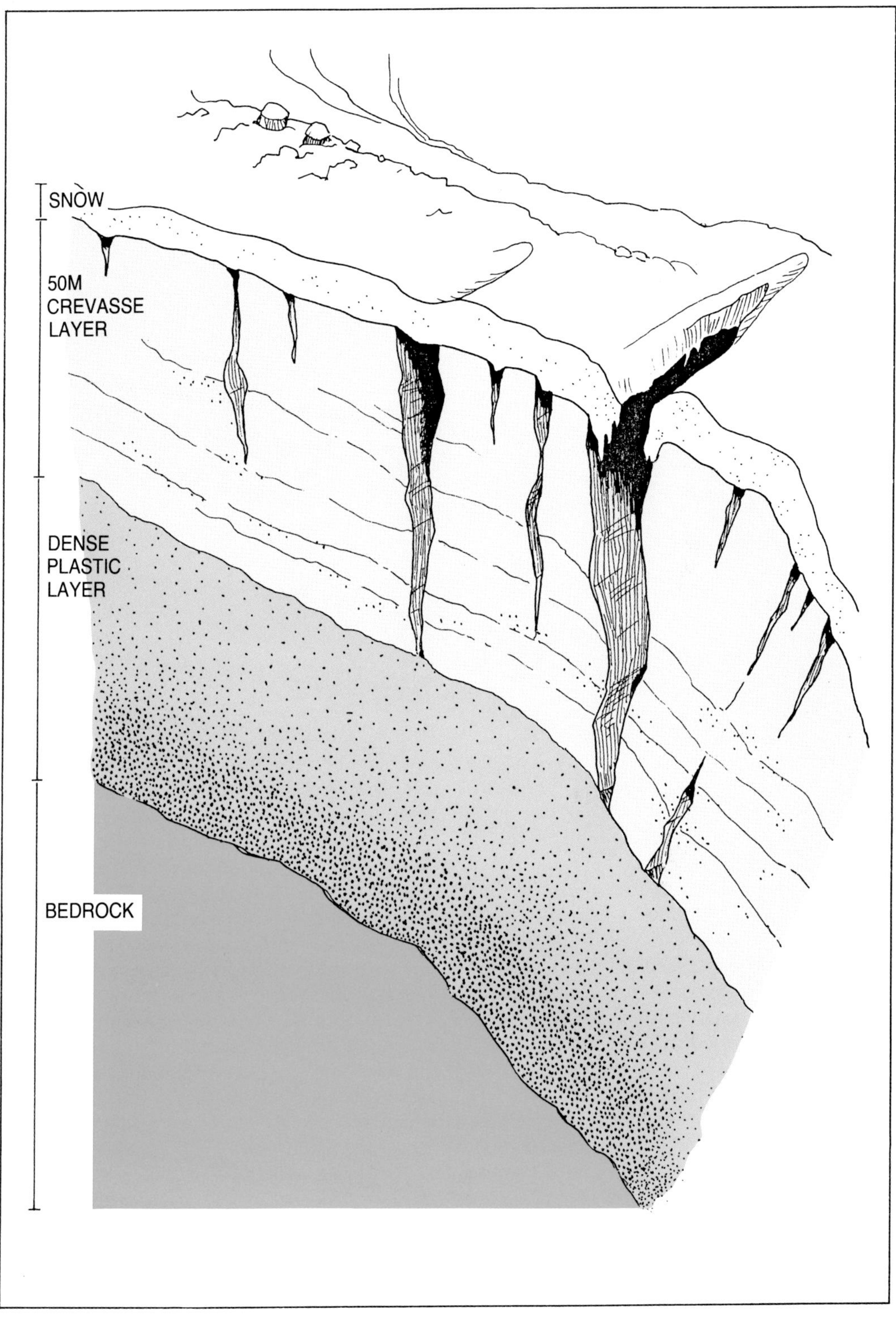
SNOW
50M
CREVASSE
LAYER
DENSE
PLASTIC
LAYER
BEDROCK

Fig 18.2 Approaching the snout of a dry glacier. Morainic material and open crevasses can be clearly seen.

over a cliff, resulting in a hanging glacier which will constantly shed large blocks of ice. The first crevasse on the glacier, which occurs at the point where the glacier tears itself away from its upper edge, is called a bergschrund. A bergschrund can pose a serious problem as it can be very difficult to cross. The bergschrund is the only crevasse which may reach through the glacier crust and into its core.

All crevasses are a by-product of the glacier's flow and as such they are not permanent features, some opening while others close. However, their overall position remains roughly constant and so areas of bad crevasses will remain so from year to year as the physical features which cause them are permanent.

As these huge ice masses move downhill, they grind and pluck at the ground over which they flow and become full of rocky material. The material embedded in the ice acts like an enormous file, shaping the terrain. In this way erosion removes huge amounts of material and is responsible for the shaping of many of our mountain areas [*figs. 18.2, 18.3*]. This crushed rock is called moraine. When it is deposited in ridges along the edge of the glacier it is lateral moraine; along the centre, usually where two glaciers meet, it is medial moraine; and at the snout of the glacier terminal moraine. It is this morainic material which gives the glaciers their characteristic surface flow-lines [*fig. 18.2*]. Moraines can often be used as crevasse-free passages in glacial areas, but sometimes are so loose as to be positively dangerous.

Occasionally outcrops of rock withstand the ravages of the glacier and protrude through the ice. These isolated islands of rock, surrounded by ice, can make useful landmarks but can also cause crevasses to occur, especially on their uphill sides. All in all, the glacier is a powerful, changing

Fig 18.3 The main mountain features:

1 Summit
2 Hanging glacier
3 Bergschrund
4 Permanent snow field
5 Snow line
6 Medial moraine
7 Lateral moraine
8 Glacier snout
9 Glacial stream
10 Couloir
11 Rognon
12 Crevasses
13 Glacial erratics
14 Pinnacle, aiguille or gendarme
15 Seracs
16 Col
17 Ridge or arete
18 Truncated spur

medium, which poses many problems, of which crevasses, seracs, avalanches, falling moraine material and the difficulties of navigation on an ever-changing but sometimes featureless surface are just some that the mountaineer has to face.

CHOICE OF ROUTE

With a basic knowledge of glaciers, the climber possesses a great deal of information to help him in the choice of route through glaciated regions. Often the guidebook for the area will give advice as to the best place to cross the glacier, usually supported by the use of relevant landmarks – for example, 'Keep to the left bank of the glacier until level with the Gross Rognon, head into the centre of the glacier and follow the medial moraine until the col can be gained.'

A map of the area will also contain much information. The places where the most serious crevasse problems exist often coincide with a steepening of the glacier (shown on a map by contour lines close together), or perhaps a bend in the glacier [*fig. 18.2*]. When approaching the snout of a glacier, take care not to be channelled off to the side by the marginal crevasses which always point in towards the centre of the glacier, increasing in width as they approach the valley sides [*fig. 18.3*]. The map does not show the exact location of individual crevasses but may give an accurate picture of their extent and approximate positions.

As well as the information available from written material, local knowledge should never be overlooked or underestimated. Local climbers and hut guardians will have crossed, and watched others cross, the glacier many times and their advice should be sought whenever possible. Care must be exercised when crossing snow bridges (tongues of snow stretching across crevasses) as they can collapse without warning. If in doubt, a temporary belay should be rigged.

It is important that a glacier approach is accomplished with the minimum of energy and time expenditure if the ensuing route is to be a success. This approach is often undertaken in the dark, so good preparation – perhaps even a reconnaissance the previous afternoon – is worthwhile. It is invariably safer to cross a glacier in the cold of the early morning, when surface drainage is at a minimum, with no melt water and the surface of the glacier frozen hard.

Even when the glacier is well known to the individual, it should still be treated with respect and caution and care must be taken with route-finding decisions.

MOVEMENT ON GLACIERS

Sometimes the surface of the glacier may be covered with snow. This covering is different from the main bulk of ice which makes up the glacier because it changes from season to season: in winter and spring it is more plentiful than in late summer and early autumn. When covered with snow in this way, the glacier is described as a wet glacier; when free from snow, as a dry glacier. The climber's approach to these different surfaces will vary a great deal.

Fig 18.4 Steep climbing in an unstable and unpredictable ice field. These can present very serious mountaineering obstacles.

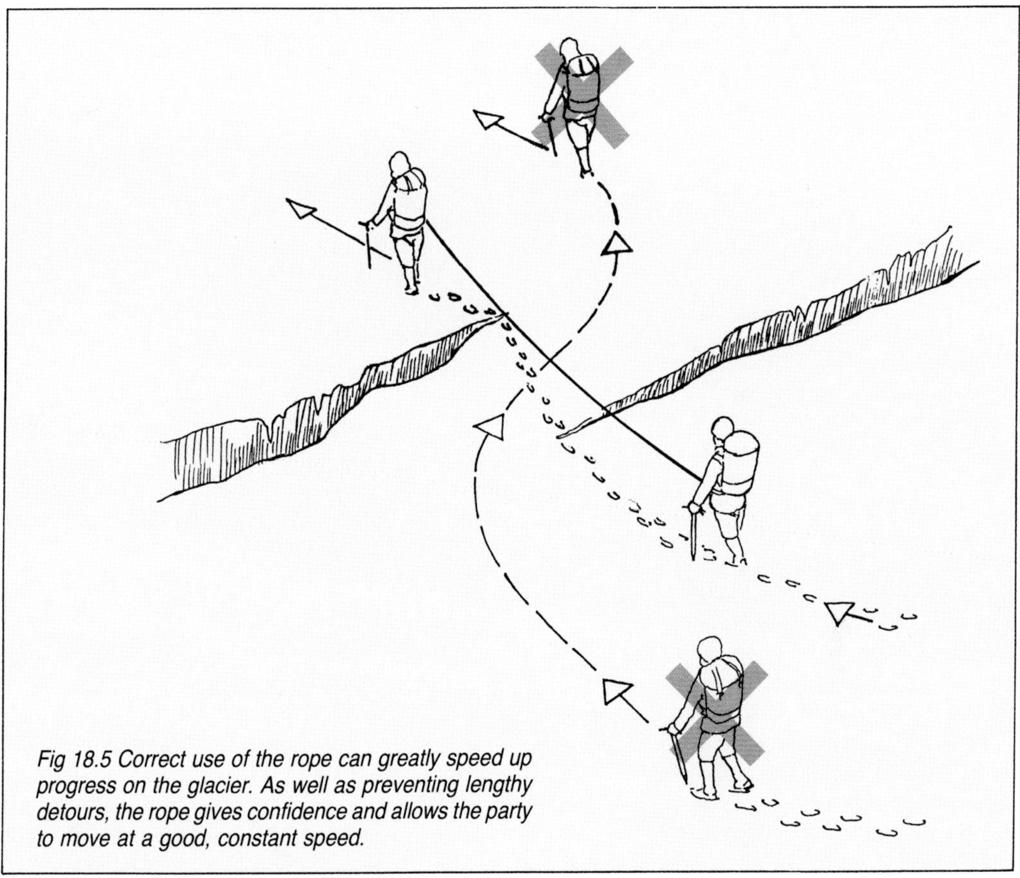

Fig 18.5 Correct use of the rope can greatly speed up progress on the glacier. As well as preventing lengthy detours, the rope gives confidence and allows the party to move at a good, constant speed.

Movement on Dry Glaciers

If the glacier is completely dry, any crevasses should be clearly visible and so easily avoidable [*fig. 18.2*]. Sometimes the glaciers may be so complicated that, although the crevasses are visible, it may still be very difficult to find a safe passage through them. Such cases should be treated in a similar fashion to a wet glacier. If all the crevasses are easily visible, and route-finding straightforward, it is not normally necessary to rope up. If there is any doubt, however the rope must be deployed.

Use of the Rope on Glacial Terrain

On all wet glaciers and some dry glaciers, the use of the rope is vital to safe and speedy progress. It is impossible to overstress that most accidents occurring on glaciers happen to people moving around unroped. Even the smallest of crevasses on a well-trodden path can open up below the feet of the unwary. As well as providing safety, the rope, when used correctly, will also speed up travel as less time will be wasted making needless detours and dangerous leaps over 'suspicious' patches of snow [*fig. 18.5*].

When moving roped-up on a glacier, the size of group should be given careful consideration. A group of three or more offers the greatest degree of safety [*fig. 17.4*, page 250]; groups of two have many weaknesses. However, two climbers roped together are much safer than if they were to move as individuals!

Rope Management for a Group of Three

In a group of three, the most experienced member of the party ties on to the front end of the rope. It is to be hoped that he will have the skills necessary to spot and avoid crevasses into which the unwary may fall. All other members then tie on to the rope as normal, depending on the type of harness being worn. The first and last man attach themselves to the beginning and end of the rope and, assuming 45m of rope are in use, the second man ties on 25m behind the first man. The rope is then shortened by taking coils around the shoulder until 15m of rope separates the climbers [*fig. 17.4*, page 250].

Shortening the Rope

To shorten the rope, take it from the tie-on point up over the right shoulder and under the left arm [*fig. 18.6*]. Using this first coil as a guide, wind as many coils as necessary around the body [*fig. 18.7*] until the desired amount of rope is left. (This will take some practice but a complete arm span is around 2m.) Then secure the coils by tying an overhand knot around them and the main rope [*figs. 18.8, 18.9*] and clip the loop back into the harness or knot loop with a locking karabiner [*fig. 18.10*]. The first and last men have no choice as to the direction in which they take coils, but the second man, and anyone else on the rope, take the coils in the direction of the leader. The distances between climbers will vary, depending upon the number in the party and the seriousness of the glacier. The more serious the glacier is, the more rope should separate the first two climbers. Obviously, as more people join the rope, the amount of rope available becomes less. However, the length of rope between the first two should never be less than 10m. The problems raised by the first man pulling the second into a crevasse are very grave indeed. Each member should have some coils around the shoulder as these fulfil a double function. In the first instance they act as an improvised chest harness [*fig. 18.11*] – if a full chest harness is worn, the manufacturer's instructions should be followed exactly – helping to keep the unfortunate climber in an upright position should he fall. Second, this extra rope makes his subsequent extraction from a crevasse a much quicker, smoother and easier operation.

Having attached themselves to the rope, the climbers attach a French prusik to the rope as follows: the leader and last man attach the prusik to the rope, so that it hangs within easy arm's reach; and the middle man attaches his prusik to the rope going to the leader [*fig. 17.4*, page 250]. This prusik also has duplicity of use – it can be a 'handle' on the rope should it be necessary for the belayer to hold someone falling into a crevasse. A sharp backwards pull on this handle is often enough to allow the leader to regain balance and so avoid a crevasse fall. The 'prefixed' prusik is also very useful as the first stage in prusiking out of the crevasse and as a quick attachment point for a belay, should this be necessary.

Fig 18.6–18.10 Shortening the rope.

This preparation should take place on 'dry land', not on the glacier itself. When moving on to the glacier, each member of the party should carry an ice axe and, if the glacier surface so dictates, crampons should be worn. At all times on the the glacier the rope *must* be kept taut between the climbers. All the systems of rescue and protection rely upon this for their execution and success.

Equipment for Glacier Travel

The amount of 'extra' equipment carried on a glacier excursion depends very much on the type of climb to be attempted. If it is a rock climb, some extra gear must be carried for the glacier

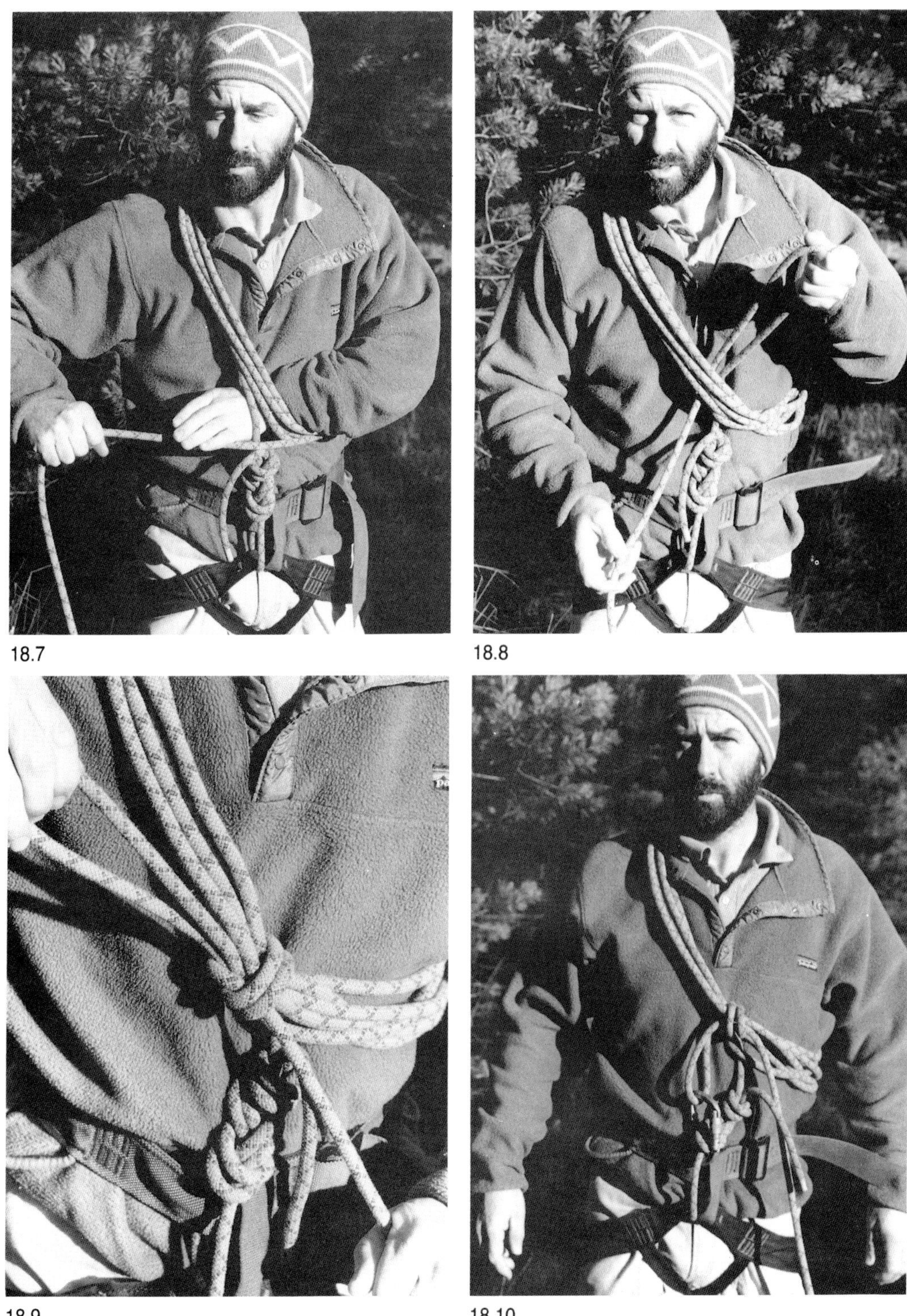

18.7

18.8

18.9

18.10

Fig 18.11 Chest coils not only shorten the rope, they also keep the climber upright in the event of a fall. The inset diagram shows how the rope cuts into the edge of the crevasse when loaded, sometimes to a considerable depth.

phase of the approach. The minimum requirement per person is: one double sling, one short sling, two prusiks – it is best to have one long (1m) and one short (50cm) prusik loop and these should be made up from 5 or 6mm cord and tied with a double fisherman's knot. Two locking karabiners and at least four karabiners completes the technical gear; however, enough equipment must be also be carried to allow a belay to be constructed. This is normally a snow belay, which will be fashioned with the ice axe, but it may be worth carrying a long ice screw as well.

There are many lightweight pulleys [*fig. 18.12*] and mechanical ascenders available which make crevasse rescue easier, but these are not strictly necessary – all of their functions are easily replaced by karabiners and prusik loops.

When moving on a glacier, attention should be paid to the clothes worn. Temperatures on the glacier can be uncomfortably high, especially in the late afternoon, and then there is a temptation to remove clothes. In the event of a fall into the depths of a crevasse very low temperatures are experienced, and the lightly clad can fall an easy victim to frostbite and hypothermia. Gloves

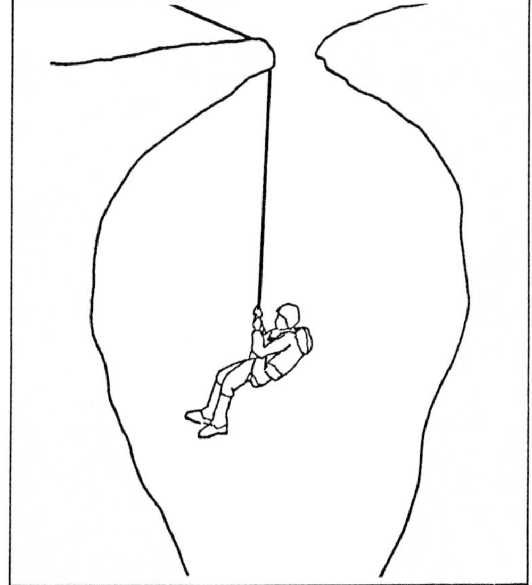

Fig 18.12 TOP: *Lightweight pulleys can greatly reduce the friction present in all hoisting systems.*

Fig 18.13 ABOVE: *In some crevasse falls the victim may be hanging free in space.*

should be worn on the glacier to protect the hands. Thin, lightweight, leather gloves are useful as they do not interfere with rope handling.

Arresting a Fall

If roped up as described, anyone falling into a crevasse should be safely held by their companions without excessive difficulty. For this to be accomplished easily, the person holding the fall must be alert and, above all else, there must be no slack rope in the system. This means that loose coils of rope (which are impossible to control) should *never* be carried in the hands while moving on a glacier.

Whenever someone falls into a crevasse, the rope will begin to cut into the snowlip at the edge of the crevasse [*fig. 18.11*]. This cutting effect of the rope is often enough to arrest the falling climber; however, as soon as the leader begins to fall, the rest of the group should move smartly backwards to make the connecting rope as tight as possible. If the leader actually falls into the crevasse (unlikely if the rope is tight and his companions alert), a braced sitting position with the heels well dug in is adopted as quickly as possible by the rest of the team. This low position is very stable and strong and should halt the leader's fall. It will be found that it is easier to hold the leader in ascent than in descent, but the above rules apply in both cases.

CREVASSE RESCUE

In many crevasse rescue situations, it is possible for the victim to climb out quickly unaided. This is more likely to happen if the team members on the surface were prepared, with ice axes in hand and wearing crampons. When anyone is attempting to climb from a crevasse, the rope should be kept tight by those on the surface moving backwards to take up any slack. In any rescue, the quickest and easiest solution will normally be best – do not start to rig a complicated hoisting system until it has been established that the victim cannot rescue himself.

If it proves impossible to climb out up the side of the crevasse, the next-easiest alternative is for the fallen climber to prusik up the rope. These techniques have already been covered, but there are a few complications which can occur on the glacier.

If you have fallen into a crevasse, you will be disorientated, panicked, perhaps hanging upside-down and possibly injured. The first priority is to get into an upright position and to establish your condition. You should then try to communicate your situation and intentions to those on the surface. If uninjured but hanging in space [*fig. 18.13*], it should be a relatively simple procedure to ascend the rope back to the surface in the

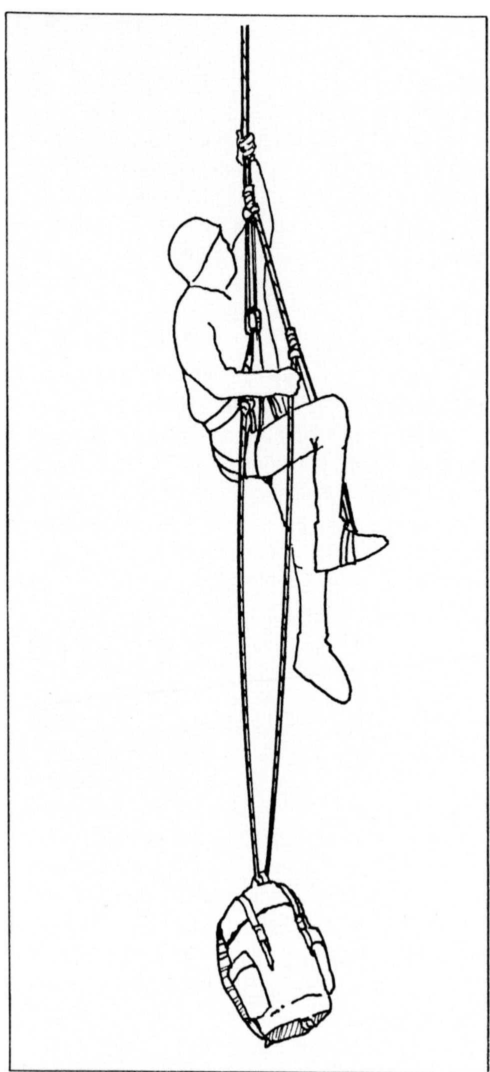

Fig 18.14 When a climber is prusiking out of a crevasse, the rucksack can be used to weight the rope. This makes it much easier to slide the prusik knots.

following manner. Push the short prusik already attached to the rope as far up as possible. This will later be used as the waist attachment [*fig. 18.14*]. Next attach the second (long) prusik, which will be used as a foot loop, to the rope below the short one. If necessary it can be lengthened by attaching other gear [*fig. 18.14*]. Place your foot in the foot loop and, with all your weight supported by the harness, slide the bottom prusik as far up the rope as possible, normally to just below the small prusik. By standing up in the foot loop, you take the weight off your harness. This allows you to clip the short, upper prusik into your harness and then slide it as far up the rope as possible. By weighting this prusik, you unweight the foot loop and it can be slid up the rope as before. These processes are repeated until the surface is reached.

It may sometimes be necessary to remove the rucksack, especially if it is heavy. In this case it should be attached to the bight of rope which forms between the harness and the lower prusik. This makes the effort involved in prusiking less since the rope will be held under tension allowing the loops to be moved more easily.

When the top of the crevasse is reached, it may be necessary to hack away the overhanging lip. This is sometimes possible from inside the crevasse but is normally easier from above. When the lip is being cut away from the surface, it is important that the prusiking climber be warned before great chunks of snow come crashing down. Those on the surface must be well anchored while moving around the edge of the crevasse, usually with enough slack to allow them this freedom.

Hoists

In some situations self-rescue by ascending the rope is not possible, perhaps because the fallen climber is injured or does not have the necessary skills or equipment needed to climb or prusik out. If so, those on the surface must organise a hoist to extricate their companion. It is here that the extra coils of rope carried around the shoulder are used.

Having arrested the fall, the second man on the rope maintains his position, holding the weight of the fallen climber. The back man (assuming there are three on the rope) eases the strain on the rope and checks that the second can support the load on his own. If so, the back man moves forward and prepares a sound anchor in front of the second; alternatively, the second can prepare this anchor by allowing the back man to take more of the fallen climber's weight [*fig 18.15*]. The prusik on the rope in front of the second is clipped to this anchor and those on the surface ease the load on to it. The second is then free to remove his shoulder coils and so escape from the system. The prusik should now be backed up by tying a suitable knot in the main rope and clipping this back to the anchor [*fig 18.16*].

Next decide exactly which sort of hoist is to be used – if the fallen climber can help at all, an assisted hoist is best. Failing this, a 3:1 hoist should be used. In both of these it is necessary to protect the edge of the crevasse from the further cutting effect of the rope by padding the edge with an ice axe, rucksack or similar item. In extreme cases the rope may have cut in so deeply that it is impossible to release it. In such a situation the spare rope between the second and back man can be used for the hoisting system, but the edge of the crevasse must be well padded before this rope is loaded. Pulling by those on the surface should always be away from the crevasse edge, so that a slip or failure in the system does not result in more people falling down the crevasse!

Very rarely the victim may be injured in the fall and require some first aid before being hoisted out. This usually means another team member abseiling into the crevasse. If this is necessary, the rescuer should try to prepare the lip of the crevasse on the way down so that he can prusik out easily himself. A back-up anchor should also be arranged.

A Rope of Two

The risks inherent in glacier travel are greatly increased for a rope of two. The ability of the members to hold each other in the event of a fall is much reduced. If either of the pair falls into a crevasse, it is much more difficult for the partner to arrest the fall; hence the possibility, especially in descent, of their both ending up in the crevasse is that much greater. To overcome this danger it is sensible to increase the climbers' separation on the rope, usually to not less than 15m. This allows

Fig 18.15 Preparing an anchor from which to hoist. Most of the fallen climber's weight is being held by the back man on the rope.

more braking time, and if braking is not successful, it allows more rope to run over the crevasse lip, increasing the cutting and braking effect this gives. Another useful technique is to tie figure-of-eight knots at 1m intervals in the main rope [*fig. 18.17*]. The knots catch in the groove cut in the lip of the crevasse as the rope pulls through it in the event of a fall. These figure-of-eight loops may then be used to climb out simply by clipping two slings alternately into them. This system is particularly effective if the climbers are of different size and braking power.

For a group of two to operate safely on glacial terrain it is essential that both are well practised in the techniques of crevasse rescue and prusiking. The same systems and rules apply as for ropes of three; however, the difficulties involved in hoisting in a 1:1 system should not be underestimated. For such an emergency it is useful for ropes of two to carry lightweight pulleys [*fig. 18.12*, page 263] which help to cut down the friction inherent in any hoisting system.

Fig 18.16 Never leave anyone suspended from a 5mm prusik: it should always be backed up – in this case by a figure-of-eight knot tied back to the anchor.

Avoiding Crevasses

Having plotted a safe route, and deployed the rope, there are a few more precautions you can take.

When on a glacier try to walk at right angles to the crevasses whenever possible [*fig. 18.18*]. This reduces the chances of the whole group standing on top of the same snow bridge and so risking disaster. Approaching at right angles also lessens the theoretical distance anyone should fall. In areas of bad crevassing it makes sense for the leader to probe the ground ahead in an attempt to establish the security of the snow and any snow bridges. This can be done by using the ice axe or, even better, a ski stick which has had the basket removed [*fig 18.19*]. Experience will soon show the types and thicknesses of snow bridge which will bear the weight of a person! If in any doubt as to the security of a bridge, a detour should be made to the end of the crevasse. When making this detour, keep back from the crevasse edges as the hole that is visible on the surface is no indication of the width of the crevasse underneath [*figs. 18.13* page 263; *18.20,*page 268].

If it is necessary to jump a crevasse, a tempor-

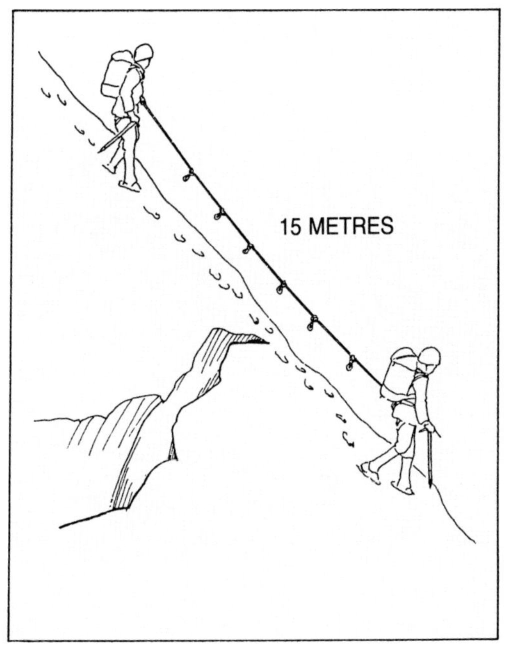

Fig 18.17 ABOVE: *Figure-of-eight knots tied in the rope greatly increase the braking effect caused by the rope cutting into the edge of a crevasse in the event of a fall. (18.11a)*

ary belay can be set up both before and after the jump. When jumping crevasses, it should be noted that the far edge of the crevasse may not be as solid as the edge from which the jump takes place. It is best to fall forwards on landing and to drive the ice-axe shaft into the snow, so that if the feet plunge into the crevasse, it may still be possible to scramble out on the far side. It will be easier for subsequent jumpers as they will jump on a tight rope towards the belay. In many cases a 'long step' is sufficient to bridge the gap. A party used to moving on glaciers will manage this without stopping or hesitation, each person adjusting his pace and organising the rope to allow the person ahead complete freedom of movement. Sudden tugs and tight ropes must be avoided in mid-jump!

At all times the leader must be watchful for slumps or hollows in the snow surface which can often indicate the existence of crevasses below. If it proves necessary to cross a suspect patch of snow, crawling on all fours or even with the

Fig 18.18 BELOW: *Crevasses should be approached at right angles whenever possible.*

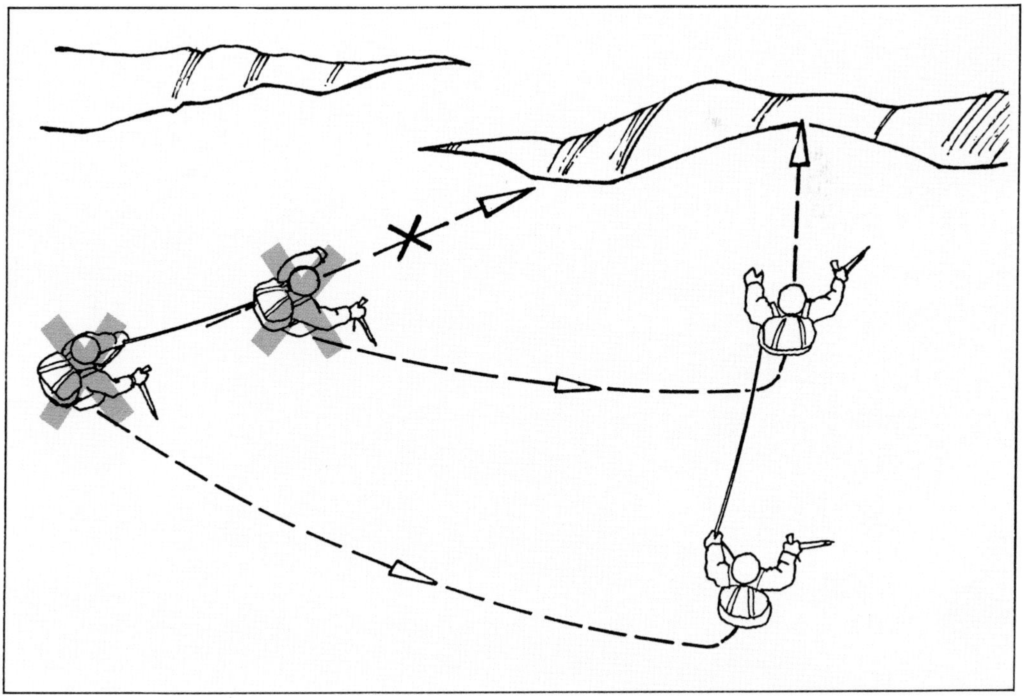

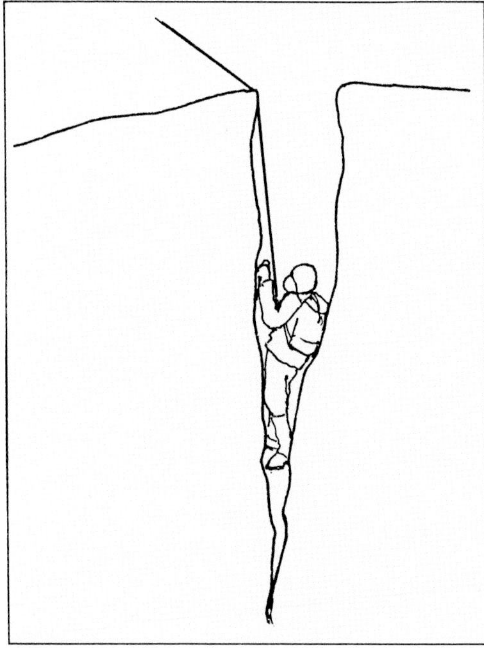

Fig 18.19 ABOVE: *Ski sticks make very effective crevasse probes when moving on complicated glaciers. On this Himalayan glacier four climbers are roped together for extra safety.*

Fig 18.20 LEFT: *Some crevasses narrow at the bottom and this can present extra difficulties in that the fallen climber can become tightly wedged.*

whole body flat out can be an effective way to distribute body weight more evenly.

Different-coloured patches of snow may also be a sign that crevasses are lurking underneath. Any abnormality in the glacier surface should be treated with caution.

MOVING TOGETHER

One of the most important skills in Alpine climbing is the ability to move quickly and safely over easy ground. What is regarded as easy ground will, of course, vary from person to person

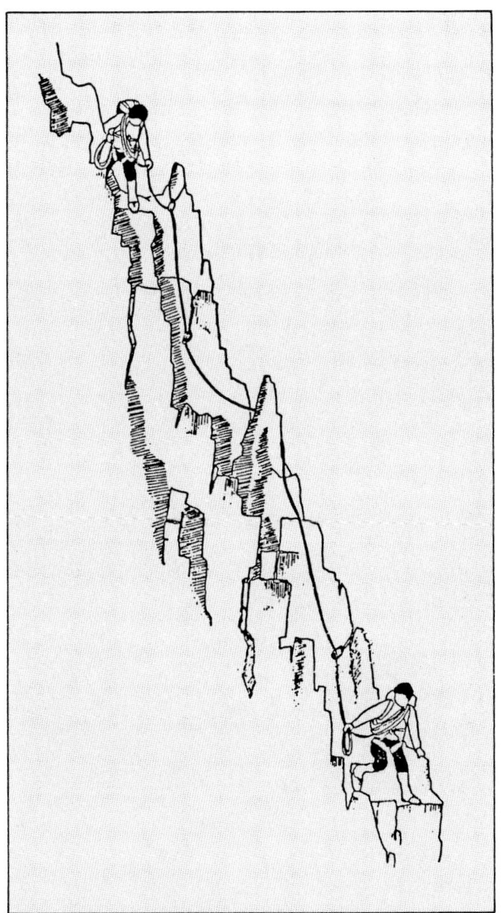

Fig 18.21 Intelligent use of the rope can allow two climbers to move together quickly and safely.

and from route to route, but will generally include snow slopes of up to 40° and grade I, II, and III rock (see Chapter 21, page 287, for information on grading). Very early in the career of every Alpinist it becomes obvious that normal pitching techniques are unsuitable and perhaps even dangerous on long routes which contain sections of easy ground. This may be because of the time required to organise belays and, of course, the time taken by individual climbers is twice that of climbers moving simultaneously. If the full rope length is strung out between climbers, there can also be an increased danger from falling rocks knocked off by the slack rope. On easier ground it is possible to move very quickly and this can make it difficult for the belayer to manage the rope quickly enough. This in turn makes the leader's life difficult as he must constantly fight and tug for slack rope.

On easy ground, several solutions are possible. You can continue to pitch the climb (common among inexperienced Alpinists), which is safe in terms of the risk of falling off but unsafe on grounds of speed and the time spent in dangerous areas. In most situations this is not satisfactory, unless one member of the party is less experienced than the others, or is sick or injured and therefore more likely to fall.

Another alternative is to remove the rope altogether and to solo. This is very quick, but also potentially dangerous. When soloing, you are at an increased risk from the simple things often ignored by roped teams such as the odd loose hold, collapsing snow steps, avalanches or slips and stumbles. Even the smallest of errors can have consequences out of all proportion to their original seriousness. Although often used by climbers on easy ground, and as a quick solution, soloing should be rejected by all but the most competent and experienced.

The best approach to climbing easy ground is to 'move together'. This describes the action of climbers who, when climbing at the same time, are roped together but make no use of conventional belaying techniques yet still use the rope to safeguard their progress [*fig. 18.21*]. This is not as contradictory as it at first seems! Most people's initial reaction to the prospect of being tied to someone else who is climbing, but effectively to be soloing, is one of abject horror. Visions of any mistake resulting in the whole rope plunging from the mountain immediately spring to mind – the infamous 'one off, all off' situation. However, this should not be the case: moving together can become a safe, secure and quick way of climbing.

A prime requirement for moving together is that the team should be of roughly equal ability and completely happy on the terrain on which they intend to use the technique. If this is not so, the best climber should go first on the uphill sections and last on the downhill sections – the same technique as used by mountain guides. This allows the most competent man the better opportunity to safeguard both himself and his companions. For best results the rope between climbers must be kept taut at all times – very difficult with a lot of rope in use, and so the rope must be shortened. This is best done in the same way as for crossing a glacier. Each climber takes some coils around their bodies, then, if it becomes necessary at a later stage to increase the amount of rope between them, it is possible from either end [*fig. 18.10*, page 261]. This is especially important on a ridge where short, difficult pitches requiring conventional belaying techniques may be encountered. It also means that the weight of the redundant rope is shared. Having shortened the rope, climbers should be 10–15m apart. The exact distance will be determined by the ground: the more difficult the rock the greater the separation. This distance should, however, never be more than 15m as any more rope is unmanageable when climbers are moving together.

Fig 18.22 The leader can often turn a runner into a direct belay by using a friction hitch. This can be a quick way to give the second extra security when the climbers are moving together.

The nature of the terrain dictates the exact

technique required. If it is very easy (perhaps a steep hillside with no difficult steps), belays are not taken. Instead, the rope is shortened until some 5m separate the climbers [*fig. 18.22*]. In the event of a stumble it should be possible for the lead man to hold the second, assuming that the rope has been kept tight. It would be more difficult, but still possible, for the second to hold a falling leader in this situation. This technique should be used only on the easiest of terrain where a fall is extremely unlikely [*fig. 18.23*].

On pitches of grade I, II or even III rock it is still possible to move together – but this time the technique used is more akin to a 'damage control exercise'. As the leader progresses, he can safeguard the party either by using running belays or by flicking the rope around any spikes or other natural belays encountered, so that there is always one anchor point between the two climbers. Obviously the leader could fall a fair distance in this situation but, it is to be hoped, not all the way! As usual, the frequency and quality of the runners will determine the size of any potential fall, but, by the nature of the technique, a sizeable fall could be possible [*fig. 18.21*].

It is normal for the leader to continue in this fashion until all of the runners are used up and subsequently collected by the second man. The roles are then reversed or the leader brings up the second, belaying him as normal, and collects the gear before setting off again. There is a danger that in the rush to move quickly the leader might allow a situation to develop where there are no runners on the rope. It is very important that the second man keeps the leader informed when he is removing the runners, especially the last one between them.

When moving together in this fashion it is vitally important that you fully appreciate the risks involved and climb accordingly. It can be beneficial for the leader and his second occasionally to take a few hand-held coils of rope as this allows for a little thinking time should a slightly tricky move be reached, and also in an emergency the extra time thus provided could allow the

Fig 18.23 On snow slopes rope up close together and use the ice axe for support and security.

repositioning of the body to make the holding of a fall easier. These coils must never be looked upon as a hand-held belay which can be deployed in a second – this is *never* possible. It is more likely that the slack rope will add to the distance of the fall. You must be sympathetic to each other's movements and avoid unnecessary and unbalancing tugs or jerks on the rope. It is crucial that the rope between you remains as tight as possible without inhibiting progress. This is the real skill of moving together: the ability to maintain a constant speed whether moving on flat ground or grade II rock. A real difficulty arises when opposite ends of the rope are engaged in different standards of climbing and yet only 10m apart. This may be the time for the second to gather a few hand-held coils as he approaches the leader or for the leader to pause for a moment and give the second a tight rope for the difficult section [*fig. 18.22*].

On snow slopes you should rope together so that you are only some 5 or 6m apart and each step upwards should be protected by using the axe as a self-belay [*fig. 18.23*]. The rope can be carried already around the head of the axe, so that, in the event of a fall or slide, it may be possible to belay the party by pushing the shaft into the snow while keeping your weight on the axe head [*fig. 18.24*]. It must be appreciated, however, that any fall in this situation could have disastrous consequences and, if there is any chance of one occurring, belays should be taken and the climb pitched as normal. It is often possible to climb at the edge of the snow field and so make use of rock belays as outlined above. Moving together on snow slopes is serious climbing and care should be taken when judging the snow conditions and the avalanche risk. The extra time and effort required to plunge the axe farther than normal into the slope can pay dividends should the leader slip as it is then more likely that the second could control and arrest the fall. However, if the snow is hard, pitching in the normal way may be faster.

You should be well practised in the skills of taking coils so that you may vary the techniques as appropriate to the terrain. Those who have difficulty or are not familiar with shortening the rope will find themselves occasionally moving together on inappropriate ground and so in a potentially dangerous situation. At all times climbers must be alert to the availability of runners such as rock spikes, natural threads and quickly placed nuts [*fig. 18.21*, page 269]. The effectiveness of your own bodies as belays should not be underestimated, especially on ridges, where having someone on either side of the ridge (or ready to assume that position!) may be the only protection available.

Fig 18.24 If the rope is kept around the axe shaft, an improvised belay can be organised very quickly, especially if the axe shaft is plunged into the snow with every step.

Only experience, practice and an understanding of both the grade and the type of ground to be encountered can enable a party to move together safely. It should be remembered that this system is designed for use on easy ground where a fall is not expected and the terrain offers enough belays to make protection a fairly simple and quick task. There is no point in moving together if it takes too long to find each anchor point, but at the same time it may occasionally be necessary for the party to move without intermediate anchor points for short distances. Although dangerous, this must be accepted as a risk and subsequent drawback to the technique.

The type and quality of the rock will play an important part in the safety of the technique. A crenellated granite ridge can provide a profusion of spikes, whereas water-worn limestone slabs may be lacking in natural anchors of any kind. Sometimes it is desirable to move together on ice fields, where the protection and security offered by the ice axe are not enough. In this case the leader places ice screws as runners between himself and the second. When they are used like this, there should be at least two screws between the climbers.

Above all, moving together requires a finely honed sense of judgement and a high level of mountain awareness. When these are present, it can be one of the most satisfying and quick methods of movement in the mountains.

19 Alpine Rock, Ice and Mixed Climbing

ALPINE ROCK

On most mountains a variety of skills and techniques are needed for a successful ascent. However, as you become more proficient and skilled, you may wish to specialise in one particular aspect of the sport. The Alpine rock climber has chosen to combine his Alpine and crag climbing skills and attempt longer and harder climbs. These may be pure rock like some of the north faces in the Italian Dolomites, or a climb similar to the Freney Pillar on Mont Blanc which has a complicated and dangerous approach and finishes almost on the summit of Europe's highest peak. These are extreme examples, both offering Alpine rock climbing at a high standard. There are countless Alpine rock climbs of all standards and lengths all over the world which, while being enjoyable in themselves, are also ideal training or introductory routes for big walls or mixed climbs.

There are many important differences between Alpine rock and crag climbing. In many cases these differences are obvious and usually are merely exaggerations of situations found on crag routes, such as exposure, loose rock, route-finding difficulties and perhaps aid moves. Consequently there are some worthwhile specialist techniques which help the climber to overcome these problems.

Situation and Quality of Rock

On a typical long rock climb, differences in rock quality will be encountered. It takes practice and skill both to recognise the areas of poor rock and perhaps avoid them, or, if necessary, to climb over them safely. Experience of the specific rock type is invaluable – colour of rock on limestone, for example, is a good indication of quality: yellow rock is usually loose and unstable, whereas grey is solid. Some rock types have horizontal bands of loose rock sandwiched between harder, more solid layers. These often show up from below as a series of ledges and overhangs.

As well as the danger of a fall from pulling off a hold, falling rock is also an important consideration. In areas of extremely unstable rock, the amount of rock fall can often be enormous – usually worse if you stray off the line of the route. It is possible to pull off blocks which can themselves start further rock falls. While this may not be a major consideration, and may present no immediate danger to the perpetrator, it could easily hit the rope, the second or other climbers below. When climbing, you have a responsibility to guard not only your own safety but that of other mountaineers too.

The problems of loose rock are generally less when on established routes – in many cases reduced to the odd loose hold; but if more than this, ample warning is usually given in the route description or guidebook. It is foolhardy to tackle long, loose sections without previous experience of this type of climbing. The feeling of exposure, seriousness and commitment of even easy climbing on a loose face, with few secure belays, should never be underrated. Although ascent may be straightforward, it may be difficult to retreat. It is worth bearing in mind that a hold which may support the rock gymnast may not support the same man carrying bivouac gear, ice axes and food for several days.

When on a long Alpine route, try to plan the belays carefully so that the second is protected by being below an overhang or bulge or, if this is not possible, at least positioned out of the direct line of stone fall. Never neglect the possibility that rocks may fall from high above, perhaps as a result of the natural action of frost and sun or, more likely, of other climbers. If a block is pulled off by accident, always yell a warning – not once but three or four times. On routes with loose rock great care of the ropes should be taken as they are easily cut by falling stones, perhaps without your being aware until it is too late. The ropes themselves also require careful management if they are to avoid knocking off loose rocks.

The exposure and situation can also be unnerving for the inexperienced. This can usually be cured by climbing medium-length routes which are within your capabilities before attempting longer, harder climbs. You may find routes on slabby rock less intimidating than steep limestone walls, but this will depend on your previous climbing experience. Exposure should not be a real problem if a sensible build-up has been made prior to the big climb.

If you are climbing as a rope of three on an Alpine route, it is often possible for two seconds to climb at the same time. If climbing on a single rope, tie a large figure-of-eight or Alpine butterfly knot, so that a loop using 3m of rope is formed some 2m from the end of the rope. One second ties on to the end of the rope as usual and the other clips into the loop. Provided that they both climb at the same speed, the leader can take in the rope as normal. If double ropes are used, the seconds tie on to the ends of the rope and the leader can belay them individually. This is better for the seconds but more difficult for the leader as his rope management is more awkward and his protection options are limited.

ALPINE ICE AND MIXED CLIMBING

The ascent of a long and difficult face is, for many people, the pinnacle of Alpine climbing. It is rare that such a face will be entirely rock; more likely it will be a combination of rock, snow and ice. When this is the case, it is usually referred to as 'mixed'. Mixed climbing offers many challenges to the mountaineer – it requires a high degree of competence in both rock and ice climbing as well as a deep understanding of the mountains and the risks involved.

In mixed climbing, more so than in any other branch of Alpine mountaineering, there is a degree of uncertainty with respect to the climbing conditions, the weather and, perhaps most importantly, the eventual outcome of the venture. This uncertainty can be the main attraction for many; for others it may serve only to turn the ascent into a lottery, seemingly a game of chance, where skill plays only a small part in ensuring success. As a successful mixed climber you must place yourself firmly in the first category: you should feel that every decision is important while at the same time constantly evaluating the risks, the conditions, the route finding and the climbing. If this has no appeal or offers no pleasure, perhaps mixed climbing is not for you. Many people find mixed climbing frightening; and for the skilled technical performer there is seldom a chance to climb at 'the limit', as the technical difficulties encountered in mixed climbing are rarely of the first order. Instead, the hard sections more often yield to cunning, determination and, above all, experience. It is as well, in the initial stages, to be open-minded about mixed climbing: after all it is not necessarily for everyone! If, however, you find it to your liking, it offers a vast amount of exciting, committing and truly satisfying mountaineering – more than enough to last several lifetimes.

Choice of a First Mixed Route

A mixed route of medium length, which can be comfortably climbed in a day and which presents no altitude problems, is an ideal introduction to harder mixed climbing. Longer routes at higher altitudes, no matter how straightforward, should wait until later when more experience and a higher standard of fitness and acclimatisation have been gained. On many mixed climbs speed is directly proportional to safety. Try to choose a route initially where conditions are stable and predictable and so will have less of an effect on the outcome. For the first route of the season, or in an unfamiliar region, choose a short glacier approach and preferably a route which can be seen from the valley. This makes it possible to establish the conditions of the glaciers and so help in the planning of further routes. If a long approach is chosen and conditions are more difficult than expected (perhaps because of deep snow), it is possible to arrive too late at the foot of the route. Prior inspection also allows you to plan your gear and approach to the route, and answers questions like: Is the rock free of snow? Are conditions good? Will a fast time be possible? Will a bivouac be necessary? All of these facts play an important part in the preparation for the route and also the style in which the route is eventually climbed.

When choosing a route, ensure that it is of equal appeal to all members of the party and pick a route suitable for the individual strengths of the climbers. Since speed is very important, it is obviously best to let the better rock climber lead on the rock sections and the ice climber on the ice. If you hope to go on and climb harder routes together, use these initial forays as an opportunity to get to know each other and to organise gear and equipment.

The climbing skills needed for mixed routes are no different from those used in rock and ice climbing at lower altitudes. The expertise lies in deciding when to use the various techniques. It may be better to use an aid point, which would enable a short, difficult section between two ice pitches to be climbed with crampons on, rather than to spend time removing and subsequently refitting the crampons. Perhaps an icy chimney or gully could be climbed by bridging on the rock to either side, thus making crampons unnecessary. Experience is the best guide in these situations, and each must be treated on its own merits. Parties climbing on mixed routes must be prepared to move together (see page 268) at every opportunity when it is safe to do so, since the time saved in this way can be considerable.

Hard Mixed Climbs and *Grandes Courses*

Above all else, climbers attempting a hard mixed route must have a high standard of climbing skill and fitness. It should be appreciated that no matter their condition, *grandes courses* are never easy. Although famous north walls, like that of the Eiger, are occasionally climbed in super-fast time and would seem to offer no excessive difficulties (in this case the hardest rock pitch is grade V), do not be fooled. A thin veneer of ice can make such pitches virtually impossible; conversely, a warm spring may also reduce the ice fields, leaving blank bands of slabs where 40° neve fields were expected.

Having established that you climb well enough to attempt such a route, it is advisable to do some homework and find out as much as possible about the chosen objective. Special note should be made of variations in the route, regions of safety or danger in different conditions and areas of the face which are particularly prone to stone fall or other objective dangers, and you should try to locate the best bivouac sites. It is also useful when viewing the route to try to spot landmarks and indicators of progress which will be encountered on the climb itself. It can be surprisingly easy to get lost on a large complicated face, especially if no attempt has been made to learn and understand the overall topography. Establish, if possible, exactly what constitutes good conditions for that route as this will affect the time taken. It can be beneficial to speak to someone who has done the climb that season, and any other information gleaned from knowledgeable climbers can be helpful. However, beware of the base-camp scaremongers. Such people abound in Alpine climbing and will always have a disturbing story or a few well-chosen negative words about conditions or difficulties, often simply to cover up their own inabilities and failures. Listen to everyone but treat the information carefully and, in the end, make your own judgements.

Try to find out about emergency descents and escape routes: there may even be an equipped abseil descent nearby. An ascent of the proposed mountain by an easy route beforehand is often time well spent, offering both acclimatisation and knowledge of the descent, which may have to be done when tired and perhaps in the dark.

Before setting out on the route, find out about local weather conditions and try, if possible, to see a weather map for the next few days. The forecast provided in Alpine areas can be unreliable and may err on the side of extreme caution. If possible, it is best to read the map for yourself and so construct your own forecast – at least you then know whom to blame for bad weather!

It is important to eat and rest well before the ascent. Mountaineering abounds with tales of late-night drinking sessions before big routes – these are seldom true. Lots of rest and good food, high in carbohydrates, are the best preparation.

On the Route

The approach to a long, difficult route should be treated with as much respect as the route itself. Time and energy wasted at this stage can have serious repercussions later. Leave for the route and the climbing at the correct time: if it is predominantly an ice route, this may mean starting at midnight; on the other hand, if the most dangerous section of the climb is a few hours from the base (perhaps an area particularly prone to rock fall), it may be best to start in the afternoon and bivouac in a safe place below the danger area. This allows the danger zone to be crossed at first light with an increased margin of safety. These are, of course, only examples and every situation must be judged on its merits.

When climbing on easy-angled ice and snow, try to move together whenever possible. When belays are taken, they must be good: it is foolhardy to belay on axe picks which, although speedy to place, offer little security. If you feel a belay is necessary, take the extra time required to construct a good one. If using belays on ice, place runners so as to reduce the load any potential fall will exert on the belay. It is often possible to climb at the edge of ice fields and so make good use of rock belays at the border.

On most mixed routes double ropes are best as these offer the greatest flexibility. Ropes of 8.5mm diameter are becoming increasingly popular because of their light weight. Ropes of 50 or even 55m may also be useful but at times the extra length can be more of a hindrance than a help. A double rope also allows for a quicker and safer descent should a retreat be necessary. Choose stances carefully: it is often quicker to split a difficult pitch than to wrestle with rope drag. When belaying, avoid stances exposed to stone fall, either natural or caused by the leader. Be especially careful of avalanche funnels, couloirs and stone chutes and try to plan the pitches so that as little time as possible is spent in these danger areas. Many teams find it best to lead several pitches at a time before swapping leads, thus allowing a longer rest and recuperation period for both leader and second.

It is beneficial to eat and drink throughout the climb – stick to a 'little and often' routine – and try to keep up fluid intake. In an active day at altitude the body needs 2–3l of liquid, and although it is seldom possible to have this quantity available, it gives an idea of the figure that should be aimed for.

The Descent

On reaching the summit, the climb is by no means over. An Alpine descent can be as difficult and as trying as the ascent. Make sure that the correct descent is taken (prior knowledge is useful), but do not hesitate to change any pre-made plans if conditions turn out to be different from those envisaged. The condition of the climbers and the proposed route must dictate the method of descent. Although it is slower to abseil, in poor conditions or when you are very tired it is often the only solution. In some situations it may be safer to bivouac and descend after a rest. However, a change in the weather at this stage could leave you in an even worse predicament. Above all, the concentration of the party must not be allowed to lapse – the true ascent of an Alpine climb is over only when the safety of the valley is reached.

20 Mountain Huts and Bivouacing

MOUNTAIN HUTS

Mountain huts and refuges have been around in the mountains from time immemorial. Wherever man has lived either among or close to mountains he has built temporary living accommodation. In days gone by this accommodation was used by shepherds tending their flocks (as was the case with many of the European Alpine huts), by travellers passing through the mountain regions who have required a place to stay the night and by hunters and trappers. Many of these huts are still in existence today and many more have been rebuilt, replaced and in some cases even relocated as the demand by mountaineers and other hill goers has replaced that of the original users.

Throughout the world these huts have their own traditions of use, and it is the duty of all mountaineers to find out about the customs and codes of practice prevalent in the area they hope to visit. In a great many cases the huts themselves have been in position, relatively unaltered, for many years, and it is only the careful and sympathetic use by both mountaineers and local people which allows this system to continue.

Most huts in use by mountaineers are situated in close proximity to the foot of the more popular routes and climbs, which makes them ideal bases and starting points. The huts will normally be placed at the tree line or on a safe rocky promontory above the glacier. It is often convenient to split the approach to the climb itself by stopping overnight at a suitable hut, since the approach to many climbs is often a lengthy affair. Using a hut allows time to rest, the drying of gear and boots, and also means that less equipment need be carried – that is, tents or bivouac gear. Huts will often contain route books which give advice on good local climbs and their recent condition.

Types of Mountain Hut

Mountain huts can be divided into two broad categories: those which have permanent or semi-permanent keepers or guardians and those which are unmanned throughout the year. It is the unguardianed variety which are most commonly used by mountaineers throughout the world and, because of their freedom of use, those at most risk from unsympathetic users. In many parts of the world these huts are used not only by mountaineers but also by fishermen, hunters and naturalists as well as members of the local population (farmers, shepherds, foresters and so on). These unguardianed huts (bothies, cabins, cabannes or shacks, depending on the area) are often owned by the local landowner and it is under his sufferance that they are available for use. For this reason every effort should be made to obey any special instructions posted in the hut, such as avalanche warnings (perhaps there may be blasting to release threatening avalanches deliberately), and to try at all times to behave in a courteous and low-key manner.

Hut Etiquette in Unguardianed Huts

There are a few basic rules for the use of these huts.

Open fires should never be built in the area surrounding a hut as these quickly lead to the destruction of local woodland and are a major fire risk. Fires, if necessary at all, should be restricted to proper fireplaces inside the hut and all wood collected for them should be done so in a careful and considerate manner.

It will be common to find other users in these huts and efforts should be made to ensure that all users feel welcome and comfortable – not overpowered by the larger group.

Since there is no guardian, there will be no one around to clear up any mess or garbage left behind. When you descend from the hut, all rubbish must be carried away and disposed of properly in the valley. If the hut is found to be damaged in any way (perhaps by weather or vandals), temporary repairs should be made and the damage reported as soon as possible to the relevant authority. In many cases there is no money to rebuild these huts which would be

ABOVE: *An ice axe or ski stick can often be used to probe dubious snow bridges or possible crevasses. The real danger here is not the obvious crevasse but the partially hidden one in front of the leader.* (Martin Doyle)

RIGHT: *When traversing a corniced ridge, care has to be taken to stay well clear of the edge. Here a low traverse below the possible break-off has been followed.* (Allen Fyffe)

ABOVE: *Ascending fixed ropes in the Himalayas. On a long route it may often be quicker for the second to Jumar.* (Allen Fyffe)

LEFT: *Alpine rock climbing can give climbing in superb situations but often at a moderate standard.* (Adrian Liddell Collection)

RIGHT: *On long Alpine rock climbs it is often more convenient to carry mountain boots in the rucksack and to climb in rock boots.* (Iain Peter Collection)

LEFT: *Sometimes it is not possible, or advisable, to remove crampons whilst rock climbing. Here a tricky rock slab is being negotiated at altitude.* (Allen Fyffe)

RIGHT: *A long traverse, necessary to avoid the extremely dangerous snow conditions on the ridge crest.* (Iain Peter Collection)

BELOW: *On mixed climbs, or in low temperatures mountain boots are worn, even for hard rock climbing.* (Iain Peter)

FAR LEFT: *Ski sticks can be very useful when carrying a heavy rucksack or load in deep snow. Rucksacks with compression straps make the carrying of cumbersome objects, like tent poles or skis, easier.* (Iain Peter)

LEFT: *An early start on a big Alpine North Wall.* (Chris Forrest Collection)

BELOW LEFT: *Alpine huts are usually situated close to main centres of climbing, in this case in the Bregaglia.* (George Reid)

RIGHT: *Camp sites on mountain faces are often precarious in the extreme!* (Allen Fyffe)

BELOW: *Powder avalanches, in this case started by a falling sérac, can reach 200mph and be devastating.* (Iain Peter)

OVERLEAF: *In South America, where snow is often subjected to intense sunlight during the day and freezing temperatures at night, large mushroom-type features and honeycomb snow can form. These are unpleasant to climb on and feel very insecure.* (Iain Peter)

allowed to fall into disrepair and eventually removed.

Many unguardianed huts have been bought by or are administered by local climbing clubs or other interested organisations. Huts in this category may well require prior booking, usually a simple process of contacting the club secretary who will make all necessary arrangements for access and so on. In these cases there will normally be a small charge for the use of the hut. In all cases local mountaineering clubs or trekking organisations will be able to give advice and details regarding the huts in their area.

Although some organisations may make a charge for the use of their hut, it may be unlocked and not subject to booking, as in New Zealand and parts of the European Alps. In this instance there will be a box in the hut or an address where money should be deposited or sent. Defaulting on payment will only result, in the long term, in the removal of this type of facility. Many huts have a telephone or radio for emergency use and may well contain a comprehensive first-aid kit. If the kit is used, efforts should be made to replace all items used.

Guardianed Huts

The best examples of guardianed huts are in the great network of refuges which cover the European Alps, although they do exist elsewhere in the world. In Europe these huts are owned mainly by the Swiss, Austrian, French or Italian Alpine Clubs and are often guardianed for as many as six months of the year (the spring ski touring season and the summer months). When the hut is unguardianed, in the autumn and winter, it is still available for use but provides a much lower standard of accommodation.

Guardianed huts should be thought of in much the same way as unguardianed huts: they are not hotels and the guardian is not a servant. His job is to make the visitors' stay as comfortable and easy as possible – a far from simple task when he may have 200 visitors and only 150 beds! The hut is his home and visitors should treat the refuge accordingly. The guardian's job is a difficult one, starting each day as it does as early as 2am and continuing until 10pm. The visitor must do everything possible to help the guardian. For this reason the refuge system has its own special code of conduct, which is often confusing for the first-time visitor.

Use of Guardianed Huts

The accommodation in guardianed huts is in the form of mixed dormitories where people will normally sleep in long bench-type bunks, usually in two tiers, with perhaps as many as twenty people in each tier. Blankets are supplied, making the carrying of sleeping bags unnecessary. In most huts a simple restaurant service is available, both for evening meals and for breakfast. In the normal way of things it is not necessary to book ahead for either a bed or meals. However, large groups (four or more) would be well advised to book in advance. This can be done either by telephoning direct to the hut or through the local Alpine Club office. The cooking facilities available vary according to the part of the world in which the hut is situated, and you should enquire about them beforehand if you are planning to visit an unknown region. In France and Italy, for example, a special room is set aside for cooking your own food. No stoves are supplied, so these and other cooking utensils must be transported from the valley. In Switzerland, on the other hand, the price of a night's accommodation includes the cost of your food being cooked by the guardian. This food should be simple and easily cooked; indeed, it is usual for visitors to prepare it before handing it over to the guardian for cooking.

In the European Alps, if you choose to bring your own food, you pay only for the night's accommodation. It is possible to have a reduction on this charge by joining a group which has reciprocal rights: for example, the British Mountaineering Council, the Alpine Club, the Austrian Alpine Club and so on.

The first duty on arrival at the refuge is to check in with the guardian. He likes to know as soon as possible how many people plan to stay that night (as opposed to making a day visit), and also their intended itinerary for the next day. This enables him to group people together in dormitories in such a way that there is minimal disturbance to others the following morning. In most cases the guardian will prefer bills to be settled at night as this means less hassle in the morning, allowing a quicker, smoother start to the day.

The guardian will also have a wealth of knowledge and advice on routes and passages in that locality.

It is a good idea to arrive at a refuge or hut in the early afternoon. This allows time to dry off socks, boots and clothes in the afternoon sun and, most importantly, it gives time to reconnoitre the way ahead. It is sensible practice to check out the proposed route in daylight rather than stumble around in the dark the following morning. Try to find some good markers, such as pointed rocks or other distinctive features, which will indicate the start of the path. If necessary, small cairns can be built, but these should always be knocked down the next day after they have fulfilled their purpose. It is often best to fit crampons outside the hut in the morning rather than walk for five minutes and then attempt to fit them in the dark, perhaps on uneven ground. It may also be useful to prepare the rope and other equipment necessary for the glacier the previous afternoon rather than struggle in the cold and darkness of the morning. Above all else, preparation is the key to success at this stage – pack rucksacks the night before, leaving out only essential items for that night and the following morning – for instance, head torches, glacier gear (if necessary) and warm clothes for wearing in the morning. If you are in doubt, consult the guardian as to starting times and any other information concerning the proposed route (the route book often provides this in unguardianed huts).

Fig 20.1 A bivouac on a North American big-wall climb. A long attachment, rather than the usual tight tie-in, gives both security and freedom of movement.

BIVOUACING

Bivouacing is the name given by mountaineers to a night spent out in the open, either before, on or after a climb. (In most bivouac situations only rudimentary camping gear will be available – not usually including a tent!) This may be a planned night out, as in the ascent of a long route, or an enforced stop, perhaps brought about by darkness, injury or other delay. Depending upon the skills you have at your disposal, bivouacing can be a comfortable, relaxed affair or a terrible, long, cold night spent perched on a tiny, exposed ledge [*fig. 20.1*]. Bivouacs can form the most memorable part of long climbs, offering a rare opportunity actually to speak to one's climbing companion! No one is a 'natural' bivouacer – those who appear to be especially good have usually put a great deal of thought into the subject or, more usually, had more practice.

When preparing for a climb, you must decide whether or not a bivouac is likely. This should be a realistic decision based upon previous experience, taking into account the time spent on previous routes, compared to guidebook time, and the conditions expected on the climb. (Guidebook times are the average times taken by competent climbers operating under good conditions.) Assimilate all available information at this stage, remembering that because a route takes a set number of hours in the guidebook you cannot always expect to climb it in that time. The time taken may vary greatly depending on conditions.

There are several possible options to consider

as regards bivouacing: a bivouac is not likely; the route might be achieved in a single day but any delay will result in a night spent out; a bivouac is unavoidable. It is best to evaluate these alternatives separately and change the equipment taken and the plans made accordingly. If it is decided that a climb, and subsequent descent, can be done in a single day, it is not necessary to take any extra bivouac gear. In fact, to ensure the completion of the route in the allotted time, as little extra as possible ought to be carried. On one-day routes, you should have a fair idea of the likely weather conditions and so the amount of spare clothing can also be rationalised. If cutting down on gear like this, however, whether for speed or simply for lighter sacks, you must be aware of the consequences of not keeping to time. A night out in the high mountains with insufficient equipment or clothing can vary from being a cold and miserable experience to one which is very dangerous. This is especially true if hard climbing has to be tackled after an exposed night out, often when you are in a tired and weakened state. Even on one-day routes some spare food should be carried, as the energy and comfort derived from it in the event of a bivouac is of considerable value.

When the possibility of a bivouac exists, you are faced with one of the more important decisions of Alpine mountaineering – to take bivouac gear or not? Obviously each situation, and team of climbers, will merit a different approach, but there are a few basic guidelines which can be followed. First, try to decide whether a bivouac is likely to occur on the ascent or descent. A bivouac on descent is often preferable, as there is not the same pressure on you throughout the night: you know that the climbing is finished and only downhill remains. If you bivouac near the top of the route, on the other hand, weather, stone fall, avalanche and further climbing can remain for you to worry about, making rest difficult. If you think you can reach the top of your route and begin the descent, you may elect to reduce your bivouac equipment and trust to ability and speed to see you through; an extra sweater and a stove might be all that is required.

The value of a stove in a bivouac situation should not be underestimated [*fig. 20.2*]. It

Fig 20.2 Efficient, economic stoves are invaluable on bivouacs. Here a tower stove is being used. The advantages of this are that it cannot topple over and is resistant to draughts.

provides thirst-quenching drinks from melting snow as well as morale- and energy-boosting hot drinks. Lightweight re-sealable gas stoves which burn mixes of propane and butane are best. One cylinder of gas will easily last two people a night, even if subjected to a lot of use, although its efficiency is reduced in low temperatures and at high altitudes. These drawbacks can be overcome by using more efficient fuel, like propane/butane mixtures, and a tower stove. It is best to concentrate on fluids when cooking and to take powdered fruit drinks (which can be drunk hot or cold) and warm beverages like soup, tea or hot chocolate. All food carried should be instantly edible, so as not to waste valuable fuel in cooking it. Ready-to-eat food can also be consumed throughout the day to keep up energy levels, and energy is saved as the only fuel that need be carried is for melting water.

When you decide that the bivouac is more likely to occur on the ascent, it is worthwhile increasing the amount of gear taken. Bivouac bags, made from material that 'breathes', are a valuable extra item. These are both windproof and waterproof and greatly increase comfort and warmth without an excessive weight penalty. Another valuable item is the closed-cell foam mat, which offers dramatic reductions in heat loss for only a small gain in weight. A small pad of this material carried in the rucksack at all times, both for the comfort it offers in the rucksack and for use in an emergency bivouac situation, is very worthwhile.

Since the bivouac is still only a probability, it is not worth the increase in weight that a sleeping bag would involve. The old adage, 'If bivouac gear is carried, it will be used', is very true in this situation. A reduction in the weight of bivouac gear carried will often result in an increase in speed and remove the necessity of a bivouac.

It is extremely difficult to do many long climbs without a bivouac. When you are getting ready for such a climb, the bivouac gear must be chosen carefully to give a balance between comfort and warmth, without at the same time being too heavy. All of the gear already mentioned – bivouac bags, stoves, food – needs to be taken and many climbers will choose to take a sleeping bag as well. The quality of this sleeping bag, and indeed that of any spare clothes carried, will depend upon the temperatures likely to be encountered. In the European Alps a lightweight down bag or, even better, a very light synthetic one is all that is required, whereas in Alaska or the Himalayas, a full-weight down bag is necessary.

Bivouacing Skills

When it becomes obvious that a bivouac is unavoidable, you should try to find as good a site as possible. This usually involves stopping climbing before absolutely necessary so that a site can be found and organised before darkness falls. The site should be as flat and comfortable as possible, preferably with enough space to lie down. Ideally the ledge should have good belay points close by and be protected from falling rocks, ice and other objective dangers [*fig. 17.5*, page 252]. The bivouac site which satisfies all of these criteria is seldom found, and you must decide how good a site you can expect to find – big ledges on granite walls are often very rare, just as a safe ledge with good belays is equally rare on some limestone walls. Having found a suitable site, spend some time making it as comfortable as possible: protruding pieces of rock and ice should be removed if possible and small retaining walls built to prevent you rolling around in the night [*fig. 20.2*]. In many parts of the world a lightweight snow shovel is an essential piece of bivouac equipment. Snow holes and shelters are often the best types of bivouac, especially on high mountains affected by strong winds.

You must be belayed at all times in a bivouac situation. There have been a depressing number of accidents caused by climbers falling from bivouac ledges, either through rolling off the ledge while asleep, or by falling off while moving around wearing unlaced boots or perhaps even no boots at all. All tasks involving extensive movement, such as calls of nature or collecting snow for cooking, are best done before settling down for the night. The best method of tying on is to rig up a multi-point belay which is reduced to a single attachment point and then clipping into this. In very difficult situations, such as very small or steeply inclined ledges, where you must continuously hold yourself in position, it is useful to attach a prusik from the harness to the main anchor rope. This is then used to make fine adjustments to your position, and in extreme cases you can take tension from the rope and so avoid the discomfort of constantly sliding off the ledge. This prusik is used only in addition to a normal belay and should never be trusted on its own. Always ensure that neither you nor your partner become detached from the system, an often difficult task amid the network of ropes which can develop on a bivouac ledge. The extra security and reassurance offered by a firm attachment is of great value when it comes to resting and sleeping.

All other items of equipment should be secured as well. The consequences of dropping a boot or crampon on a long route do not bear considering. To avoid this, fix a length of rope, secured at both ends, which allows many articles to be attached easily and also allows quick and easy rearrangement of gear the following morning [*fig. 20.3*]. It is a good idea to fix small loops to your gear so that it can easily be clipped in. Items which will be needed throughout the night, food, snow or water and cooking gear should be arranged so as to be within easy reach. A good deal of body heat is wasted by needlessly moving around while in the sleeping and bivi bags. If at all possible, it is best to sleep close together on bivouacs both to conserve heat and also to make sharing the cooking possible. Urine bottles, of about one-litre capacity, are very convenient and save moving around at night. When bivouacing in low temperatures, these should be emptied immediately after use.

If it is necessary to bivouac on separate ledges, the climber who has the site that is easiest to move around on, or perhaps with a water supply, should do the cooking. Make sure that everything needed for this is in the appropriate place. When settling down for the night, organise ropes and gear so that if it freezes you are not faced with 100m of knotted and frozen rope the next day. No matter how tired you may be, most jobs are easier at night than the following morning.

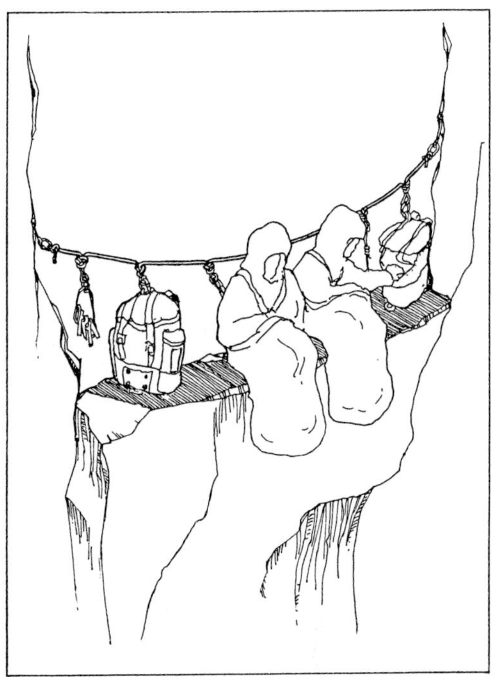

Fig 20.3 A system of loops, attached at both ends, makes the attachment of gear quick and easy.

When leaving the bivouac site, it may be necessary to take it in turns to get ready for the day ahead, particularly if the site is small and cramped. This avoids the possibility of becoming accidentally detached from the belay or inadvertently dropping or knocking things off the ledge. Everything possible should be done from the warm confines of the sleeping bag; only leave it when absolutely necessary.

Bivouacing proficiency comes only from thorough preparation, experience and organisation, allied closely to the careful choice of equipment and bivouac site.

SECTION FOUR

Appendices

21 Guides, Grades & Games

GUIDEBOOKS

Guidebooks are a normal part of most climbers' equipment, particularly when starting climbing or visiting an unfamiliar area. A good guidebook, properly used, can help you to get the most out of a day's climbing and cut down on time wasted finding a suitable route, climbing it and then descending. However, it is only an aid and the climber must still take responsibility for his own decisions and cultivate the skills necessary to reduce his reliance on the written words of others. Guidebooks are helpful but by no means essential and climbing without them can add an element of excitement and exploration that can be lacking on some of today's minutely detailed cliffs.

A guidebook will often contain, besides route descriptions, other useful and interesting information on access, approaches, descents and accommodation. A full explanation of the grading system used, rescue procedures and historical notes are usual too. Sometimes there will be sections on geology, glaciology, flora, fauna, conservation and perhaps notes on the prevailing ethics in the area covered. A well-written guide can make interesting and informative reading which can contribute much to the enjoyment of a climb. Some guidebooks are comprehensive and include every route in an area while others are selective and describe only some of the climbs, usually the better ones – in the writer's opinion at least. The latter usually cover a wider area, are intended for visiting climbers and tend to include less non-essential information, while the comprehensive guide is for regulars and may devote more space to ancillary information such as the history of climbing in that area.

Guidebooks vary in style according to their writer and what they are trying to achieve. This may be the description of as many routes as possible for the least amount of money, a work of some literary worth or something between the two. They can be amusing, prosaic, terse, elaborate, vague or precise, but most represent a large amount of work by their author. However, their main function is to allow you to find your chosen cliff or mountain, your route, the line of ascent and then the way down again. In general, the shorter the route described, the more precise the guide can be, even to the extent of specifying where vital holds are and how to use them. Other guides describing longer climbs may do little more than indicate a general line and single out a few important features. The longer the route, the more the climber must rely on his own resources and route-finding ability.

In general a route description for a multi-pitch climb will give you the route's name, length, perhaps some first-ascent details and then an introductory paragraph describing, if required, the approach, the general line and location and anything else of importance such as quality, objective dangers or protection. The start should be accurately described and related to easily located features. The usual format is to then describe the climb and this can be pitch by pitch or in more general terms.

Many guides cover a number of cliffs or mountains and have a general introduction to each section – often invaluable for setting out the main features of the face which are used for locating climbs. Many people who have difficulty with guidebooks do so because they have read only the description of the route they want and missed out this introductory material. To aid general route location, many guides have diagrams or photographs showing route lines which, when used in conjunction with the description, make finding and following the route easier.

As guidebook writers have different styles, you may have to try a few of the routes described before you become accustomed to the way the guide describes routes and rock features, particularly in terms of scale and distance. Different authors may pick on different features which they consider relevant. Slight differences in wording can mean large differences in route finding: for example, move, go, step, trend, traverse, work and veer all mean slightly different things and may be used to indicate different distances and directions in different guides.

Another way in which a route can be described is by topographical diagrams, (or 'topos'). These are most useful for climbs which follow fairly well-defined features or lines of fixed protection. They are a short, neat way of conveying information about a climb and, in this respect, are international. The symbols are fairly standard and easily understood and it is simpler to carry a sheet of paper rather than a whole guide, especially when climbing without a pack and wearing light clothing. Although they are not common, loose-leaf guides are excellent for only the appropriate page need be carried.

If a guide has to be taken on a route, carrying it in a pocket can be restrictive. An empty chalk bag is a good way of carrying a guidebook and is less liable to result in the loss of the book than the popular method of putting it down your shirt where it can be uncomfortable and drop out and be lost. Special guidebook covers which have a carrying loop are also handy.

GRADES

A grading system is intended to indicate the level of difficulty liable to be encountered on a route. Different systems have evolved in different countries, but for each the basic information to be conveyed is the level of technical difficulty. Although different systems are used in different areas, it is possible to translate one grade to another [*fig. 21.1*]. This is helped by the fact that most use a numerical system on the principle that it is more precise than words. However, even within an area in which a particular system is used there are liable to be local differences in the grades because of rock type, route length and historical development, which means that any comparison will be only approximate.

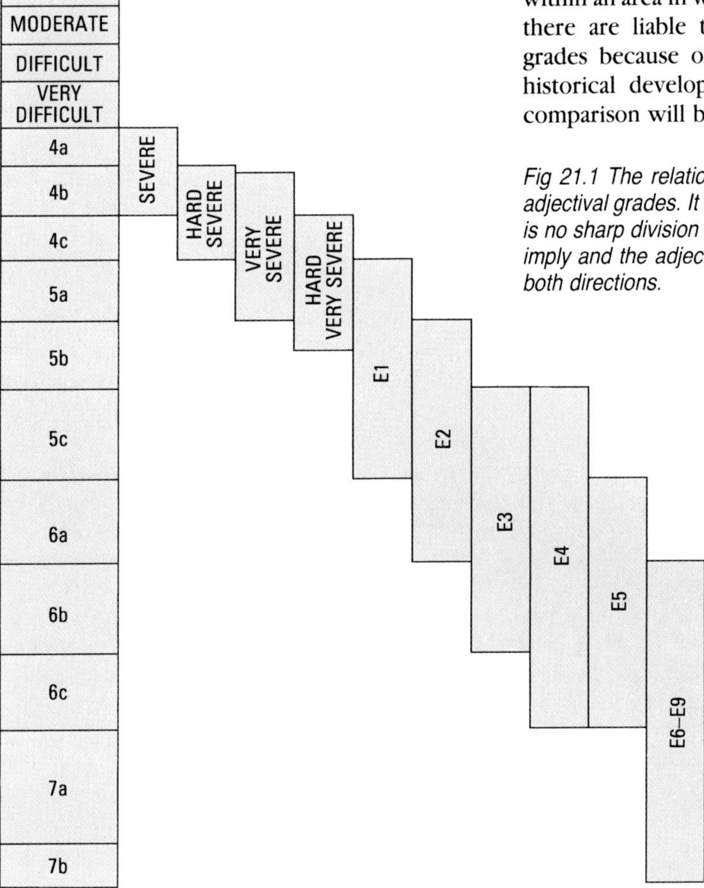

Fig 21.1 The relationship of the British technical and adjectival grades. It should be borne in mind that there is no sharp division between grades as this table may imply and the adjectival grades may extend further in both directions.

As grades are given for normal conditions, routes which are subject to the fewest outside influences are most likely to be graded accurately. Routes affected by changes in snow and ice conditions, weather, rock fall and variations to the line followed may give only a general indication of what an ascensionist can expect to encounter. Rock climbs can be graded with greater precision than Alpine routes.

When using grades, there are several factors to bear in mind. It is important to understand how any system works and this should be clearly explained in the guidebook. Grades indicate a band of difficulty and there will be a range within any grade. While the consensus of opinion will agree about the centre of the grade, either end of the range is often open to debate and a degree of subjectivity. When a route is first climbed, the first ascensionist grades it; this grade is then confirmed or modified by other ascents, but until sufficient repeats have been made the grade may not be certain. Grading may be done in a very individualistic way: some people grade hard, others easy, and a variety of factors can influence the first ascensionist's opinion. By the time most climbs reach a guidebook this uncertainty should have disappeared, but there is an element of doubt about the difficulty of obscure, unpopular, recent and rarely ascended climbs for some time. Even well-established routes can change their grade as holds fall off or appear, the rock becomes polished or vegetation disappears. Grades are only a guide to difficulty and not necessarily fixed and unchanging.

British Grades

The British grading system is, at first acquaintance, illogical and confusing, the result of the original grades being adapted to accommodate advances in standards and techniques. These original adjectival grades are Easy, Moderate, Difficult, Very Difficult, Severe, Very Severe, Hard Very Severe and Extremely Severe. Some of these may be further divided by the prefixes Mild or Hard. Although a climb graded Difficult is in fact now an easy route, in the early days of the system when climbers used nailed boots and hemp rope, this was the standard of the climb. The grade has remained the same but the level at which climbers now operate has risen.

At the other end of the scale the Extreme grade also fell foul of the rise in standards and by the 1970s had become almost meaningless as it encompassed a huge range of difficulty. To cure this, the Extreme range was split up into the E grades, from 1 to 5. This was left open-ended and now extends to E9.

While adjectival grades give an overall picture of how hard a climb is, the actual technical difficulty is shown by the numerical or technical grades. These derived initially from outcrops where top-roping was common and factors such as protection and rock quality were of little importance – only the difficulty of the moves counted. These were originally 1a, 1b, 1c, 2a, 2b, 2c, and so on up to 5c. This limit has now been extended to 8a but the lower grades below 4a are seldom, if ever, used. Technical grades are assigned to each pitch while the climb is given an adjectival grade. Used in combination, these give a better idea of the difficulties liable to be encountered when leading the route as there is a 'normal' technical grade for each adjectival one. For instance, a Very Severe usually has a numerical grade of 4c. A numerical grade lower than the norm may indicate a climb which is badly protected, on poor rock or is sustained; a higher-than-usual technical grade may indicate a more difficult but well-protected crux or a climb whose main difficulties are very near the ground [*fig. 21.1*].

Australian Grades

The Australian grading system is a logical one which goes from 1 up to 33 but is open-ended to allow further grades to be created as standards increase.

American Grades

Although more than one system has been used in North America, the most popular for pure rock climbs seems to be the Yosemite Decimal System. This initially consists of various classes in which hiking is class 1 and roped climbing is class 5. The difficulty of the rock climbing class was divided into ten sections from 5.0 to 5.9, but this has been extended to 5.14. Climbs of 5.10 and above are sub-divided into a, b, c, and d, but + and – may also be used. To give an overall grade for a climb,

BRITAIN	USA	AUSTRALIA	FRANCE	DDR	UIAA
	5.2		1	I	I
	5.3	11	2	II	II
	5.4	12	3	III	III
4a	5.5		4	IV	IV+
4b	5.6	13		V	V–
	5.7	14	5	VI	V
4c		15			V+
5a	5.8	16	5+	VIIa	VI–
		17		VIIb	
	5.9	18	6a		VI
5b	5.10a	19		VIIc	VI+
	5.10b		6a+		
		20		VIIIa	VII–
5c	5.10c		6b		
		21		VIIIb	VII
	5.10d		6b+		
	5.11a	22	6c	VIIIc	VII+
	5.11b	23	6c+	IXa	
6a	5.11c	24	7a	IXb	VIII–
	5.11d	25	7a+	IXc	VIII
	5.12a		7b		
6b	5.12b	26	7b+	Xa	VIII+
	5.12c		7c	Xb	IX–
	5.12d	27			
		28	7c+		IX
6c	5.13a	29	8a	Xc	IX+
	5.13b	30	8a+		X–
7a	5.13c	31	8b		X
	5.13d	32	8b+		
7b	5.14a	33	8c		X+

Fig 21.2 A comparative chart showing the main free-climbing grades. This can be only approximate as local variations and styles of climbing make direct comparison difficult and also fairly subjective.

as against the pitch grade described, the Roman numerals from I to VI are used. This takes into account the length, seriousness, average difficulty, exposure, rock quality and so on, with a I taking several hours while a VI is a long, serious undertaking which would normally last more than two days.

French Grades

French grades are similar to the British technical grades for climbs but in general the equivalent French grade is two higher than the British grade and starts at 4c. They are used primarily on pure rock routes rather than on Alpine climbs and, as many of these routes have fixed protection, this assessment of technical difficulty is the main requirement. Other relevant information is contained in the topo or route description.

German Grades

The German grading system uses Roman numerals from I to X. Above VII the sub-divisions a, b and c are used.

UIAA Grades

The Union Internationale des Associations d'Alpinisme (UIAA) grades were intended to be international but have not found widespread acceptance. They are mainly used in the Eastern Alps for mountain rock routes and for pitch gradings in the Western Alps (French grades are used for 'outcrops'). The UIAA system employs Roman numerals from I to X with + and – designations.

Alpine Grades

In the Western Alps routes are given an overall grade and rock pitches graded on the UIAA scale. The overall grades are F (*facile*, or easy), PD (*peu difficile*, or moderately difficult), AD (*assez difficile*, or fairly difficult), D (*difficile*, or difficult), TD (*très difficile*, or very difficult) and ED (*extrêmement difficile*, or extremely difficult). Above this is the grade ABO (*abominable*, which should be self-explanatory). Further refinement is with the use of 'superior' and 'inferior' or + and –. Artificial grades go from A1 to A5. These overall grades are used on Alpine routes of rock, snow and ice and mixed terrain and are often used for routes in the Greater Ranges. Sometimes the time for an ascent by a competent party in good conditions is also given as an indication of the scale of the undertaking.

For these routes the overall grade also considers factors such as the approach, the descent, the route's aspect, the ease of location, the nature of the stances, the quality of the rock and objective dangers, the exposure to weather and where the hardest climbing on the route lies. All these affect the seriousness of the route and may in fact be of greater significance than the actual technical difficulty. In the case of snow and ice routes the average angle of the climb may also be quoted as another indication of the climb's likely difficulty.

Snow and Ice Grades

Since the snow and ice conditions on winter routes can vary greatly, these climbs are harder to grade accurately. They may change in difficulty and seriousness almost day by day and this should always be borne in mind. The Scottish grading system seems to be the one most commonly used in ice climbing areas. This is a simple I to VI scale where grade I is a simple, straightforward snow slope and, at present, VI is an extremely serious and technically demanding climb. These grades were originally applied to the whole climb but are increasingly being used as pitch grades.

Artificial or Aid Grades

Aid pitches are indicated by the prefix A and range from 1 to 5. They are defined as follows:

A1 – good solid placements.

A2 – awkward-to-get but generally good placements.

A3 – poorer placements which could hold only a short fall.

A4 – placements which can take only body weight need to be used.

A5 – very serious with long sections of body weight placements.

Whereas A5 originally indicated a fall potential of 20m, advances in techniques and standards have raised this figure considerably. All the grades, in fact, can be translated into a potential fall distance run out above good gear. To give greater accuracy to the grades, + and – may also be added to the pitch grade and A0 may be used to indicate fixed gear. Aid pitches are more susceptible to grade changes as cracks are altered by repeated ascents and loose rock is removed.

Graded Lists

If all the climbs in a guidebook are listed in order of difficulty, an extremely accurate grading system is created. This, however, is not a feasible proposition because of the subjective nature of grading, no matter how many opinions are involved in the making of such a list. In spite of this, they can be helpful in establishing levels of difficulty, particularly when you are trying to increase your standard and work up through the grades, and they can always provide a focus for discussion and argument.

Fig 21.3 Soloing can be considered as the application of the ethics of bouldering to other climbing games.

CLIMBING GAMES AND ETHICS

Climbing is not a single sport but a collection of related activities. Just as running covers distances from 100m to the marathon and beyond, climbing encompasses a broad spectrum which ranges from boulders to the highest peaks in the world. There is a gradation in terms of scale, but for convenience climbing can be divided into a set of recognisable 'games'. An article on the subject, entitled 'Games Climbers Play', appeared in *Ascent* magazine in 1967. Written by the American climber Lito Tejada-Flores, this article defined seven climbing games and through these gave the clearest and most logical explanation that had, or indeed has, been written on this somewhat thorny subject.

Climbing is unusual in that it has no written rules, rather a set of ethics which exist as a set of negatives – things that you cannot do without incurring the displeasure of the climbing community. Ethics arose to maintain the challenge and feeling of achievement that climbing can give; they constitute a handicap system that maintains the degree of uncertainty as to the outcome of any attempted ascent. This handicap disallows certain types of equipment or procedures that would eliminate the uncertainty, which would permit an ascent based on other factors than the climber's skill and ability and this, to a degree, is related to the objective dangers that the ascent presents.

It can also be seen that the application of the 'rules' of a higher game to a lower one constitutes unethical behaviour. Pulling on protection on an Alpine route is acceptable in the interests of speed and safety, but doing the same on a free pitch is not. By applying the 'rules' of a lower game to a higher one, however, you can make a more stylish and therefore 'better' ascent. This has happened at the top of the spectrum as the expedition game is being squeezed by the super Alpine game. Even the most modern of the climbing games, competition climbing, can fit into the scale as an extension of the bouldering game since it is risk-free climbing in which the competitive element is overt and the reason for the game's existence.

This explanation is only a broad and general way of considering climbing ethics and is based on a traditional structure of the sport when routes were climbed from the bottom up. Styles of climbing also form a spectrum from, at one end, an on-sight, no-falls, no-rests ascent through all the various shades of meaning leading to a redpoint ascent. These mainly affect the crag and the continuous climbing games, especially where first ascents are concerned. How the route was put up becomes a matter of some importance when questions of abseil inspection, top-rope practice, pre-placed protection, resting on gear and even hold chipping are unanswered. These questions, though, are less important than what is said after the ascent. If everyone is aware of how any climb was (or indeed is) done, then they are in a position to make their own judgements concerning the difficulty and worth of the route. You can climb a route in any way you wish provided that you do not alter the rock. However, you should then be morally obliged to say exactly what you did. Misleading others either deliberately or by omission is simply another form of cheating. Pulling on a runner *in extremis* is understandable; forgetting about it afterwards is not. Satisfaction should come from completing a worthwhile route or climbing at your limit, not cheating at a higher standard.

Bouldering

Bouldering is the purest form of climbing in which almost all technical aids are banned and the climber and his ability are all that counts. Bouldering is solo climbing with its main emphasis on moves and sequences of moves, and it is in this game that the hardest technical moves are probably done. With the absence of objective danger and the risk of fatal falls nearly removed, the boulderer can devote all his energy and time to the actual climbing. Although the number of climbers who specialise in bouldering is fairly small. most play this game at some time or another for enjoyment, for training, to discover what they are physically capable of or simply for the social aspect. Despite the fact that bouldering is solo climbing, it is seldom a solitary activity and the competitive nature of many climbers can find an outlet here. For some, success in coping with the boulder problem is only part of the pleasure; competing with their peers is of equal importance.

Although bouldering is generally taken to heights where it safe, or at least non-lethal, to jump off, any unroped solo climbing is in effect bouldering. The 'rules' of bouldering, with its lack of material assistance, are applied to other more serious situations.

Good bouldering is, unfortunately, not found everywhere. The right mix of difficulty, variety and landings is a rare one and bouldering areas such as Fontainebleau near Paris have gained fame well out of proportion to their actual size. In many places the best bouldering is on short crags or the bottom of larger cliffs which often lend themselves to traverses. Even man-made structures such as quarries, buildings, bridges and walls can provide good entertainment and training.

When bouldering, it is still possible to hurt yourself, falling and jumping off being an integral part of the activity. It is easy to find yourself much higher up than you had anticipated. In these situations it is handy to have a companion who can 'spot' you when you jump (or fall) off – that is, someone to steady you or break your fall before you break a limb. It is best to jump off and try to aim for a suitable landing spot; having someone to steady you as you hit the ground can make landing safer. Also, having someone behind you when trying roof or layback problems can prevent you from landing on your head or back.

The Crag Climbing Game

The crag or outcrop climbing game is played on small cliffs where the length of the routes means that time is not a significant factor. Because of the limited size of the routes, the ethics are strict as to which type of protection and methods of climbing can be employed. In many places 'clean' protection, which does not damage the rock, is all that is allowed. This game is the one which is undergoing the greatest change at present as the search for new rock and greater technical difficulty has taken climbers into places where conventional protection is not adequate. Bolts have made their appearance and also changes in ways of tackling routes. The traditional bottom-to-top style of ascent, particularly on first ascents, is felt by some to be outdated. Into this scene has appeared French style (or redpointing) which is an attempt to rationalise the various alternative methods of doing routes. In a redpoint ascent any amount of 'cheating' may be indulged in if, in the end, the route is led in a single push and the runners are not weighted: there should be no falls, no lowers or rests on gear. Before this the route can be abseiled, top-roped, practised, yo-yoed or subjected to any other climbing method, but the

Fig 21.4 The crag climbing game, perhaps the most popular of the climbing games and the one which combines the hardest technical climbing with the problems of protection but generally threatens little in the way of objective dangers.

eventual ascent is open to no shades of meaning. This, however, requires regular and reliable protection, usually in the form of bolts; redpointing and bolts go together. At the time of writing this ethic is not accepted everywhere and tends to be restricted to only the hardest routes of a particular type. This is also related to the historical development of an area. What will happen remains to be seen, but crag climbing is being changed and may in the end split into two, each branch 'going its own way' and following its own codes of practice.

Continuous Climbing Game

Played on bigger cliffs than the crag game, the continuous climbing game imposes time pressure on the climber which is countered by a relaxation of the 'rules' which govern allowable protection techniques (notably pegs) and the acceptance of direct aid when necessary. Ascending the routes usually takes about a day. In climbing there is no strict delineation between the various games but a graduation from one to another, and climbs of this type are now tending to come into the realms and 'rules' of the crag climber.

Big-wall Climbing

Big-wall climbing is typified by multi-day ascents of technically demanding routes which usually involve free and aid climbing. On a big wall the full range of technical equipment is used. Not every pitch may be climbed by every climber, the second often using mechanical ascenders to cut down on effort. A variation on this is known as a capsule ascent, in which fixed ropes between suitable bivouac sites are used; this is more likely to be adopted in a hostile environment or at altitude.

Alpine Climbing

In Alpine climbing, objective danger as well as time pressure lead to a relaxation of what is considered acceptable practice. Because of the problems brought about by weather and climbing conditions, the line between free and aid becomes blurred as speed and hence safety become more important than style. This, however, is self-limiting as too much aid often cuts down on speed and makes success less likely. Alpine style is traditionally a two-man ascent in which all that is required is carried by the climbers.

Super Alpine Climbing

Super Alpine climbing involves the application of Alpine climbing to more serious and hostile mountains such as the Greater Ranges or the Alps in winter. The routes take longer, require a greater degree of commitment and are physically demanding. There are no constraints put on the climbers with respect to most techniques, except that the extensive use of fixed ropes as a continuous link with safety is not allowed. This is the most dangerous and committing of the climbing games.

The Expedition Game

The expedition game involves the conquest of mountains by almost any means. Big teams, large sums of money, fixed ropes and a pyramid system to put part of the team on top characterise this game. The mountains are deemed to have sufficient defences to require no handicapping of the climbers as the outcome will almost always remain in doubt. This is the dinosaur of the climbing games: big and old-fashioned, it has for years been rumoured to be dying out as the super Alpine game becomes the preferable way to climb even the highest and most difficult mountains. However, it is still around and probably will remain so while national interest and media coverage are required to sponsor expeditions.

The climbing games described above are the main traditional ones: most branches of climbing can fit in somewhere along the spectrum, their ethics being a response to the challenge, the pressure of time and objective dangers. The main types of snow and ice climbing, for example, can be fitted into the appropriate place in the scale by considering what is, or is not, acceptable in terms of equipment used either for progress or resting. The longer and more serious the route, the less restrictive ethics tend to be. As an example, Scottish winter climbing falls under the continuous climbing game: pegs are allowed for protection but aid climbing is considered to be unethical and the route should be completed in one day. Ice routes often change their character and difficulty in a short space of time and this makes any definition of what is acceptable rather more vague than on rock. Any alteration of the ice by the climber is also liable to be short-lived and unlikely to affect other climbers, whereas alterations to the rock are permanent.

22 Sea Cliff Climbing

Climbing on sea cliffs can give an extra dimension and present situations and problems not normally encountered on inland or mountain crags. An obvious difference is in the approach. Many sea cliffs have a descent down gullies or by abseil, and locating the descents from above can often be difficult. Ordinary maps may be of little assistance but good guidebook descriptions and detailed diagrams can help considerably. With an abseil approach, the route can have a sense of commitment not experienced on other climbs, especially if the abseil rope is retrieved once down and the only way out is up or by swimming. In many cases a separate abseil rope is advisable in case of unforeseen difficulties and to save wear and tear on the climbing rope as it is pulled over the edge of the cliff after each abseil. Even when you are below the cliff, it can be difficult to identify the routes as it may not be possible to get far enough away from the rock to recognise the features. Some cliffs have wave-cut platforms or beaches at their bottoms which may allow some moving above, though perhaps only at certain states of the tide, whereas others rise straight from the water. Before embarking on a route which is affected by the sea, tide tables should be consulted and enough time allowed to get both climbers up the first pitch. It is better to start as the tide is going out rather than coming in, particularly if the sea is at all rough. Tide tables can usually be purchased locally or found in local newspapers and it is worth knowing whether it is the time of a spring or neap tide when you are considering tidal access.

Some routes start after a sea level traverse and in such cases attention must be paid to the condition of the sea. Although every seventh wave may not be bigger, there is a pattern to waves which results in some being larger than average and it is these which can cause problems. It is worth studying the waves for some time before setting off on a traverse to ensure that there is no danger. Equipment should be carried so that, if you do fall into the sea, it can be abandoned quickly and not drag you down. Gear on a bandolier and the ropes in coils over the shoulder are better than a heavy harness and the rope tied on in some fashion. Falling in below many cliffs can be very serious because of undertows, currents and the danger of injury on the rocks. If in doubt, it may be best to turn back, wait for the tide to go out or rope up for the traverse.

When you are below the route, it may not be possible to uncoil the rope without its falling into the sea. If there is no suitable ledge for the rope, it can be hung in hanks across the belayer's leg or in a sling. Another method is to carry it uncoiled but fed into a rucksack, from where it can be taken straight into the belay device. Because of the noise of the sea communication can be difficult, so a system of non-verbal signals such as tugs on the rope should be agreed on before starting out.

Many sea cliffs are the nesting sites of birds, some of which are protected by law; any climbing restrictions noted in the guidebook or elsewhere should therefore be observed. Climbing over nesting or roosting birds is fairly unpleasant anyway and best avoided. Their nests can cover ledges and give dangerous footing, their droppings make holds less secure and the supposedly chalked-up hold may turn out, in fact, to be covered in guano. Smelling like rotten fish is one hazard of climbing where the birds are and some species can be disconcertingly aggressive.

Any *in situ* equipment found on sea cliffs may be in very poor condition because of the corrosive action of salt water and spray which is blown on to the rock. Some gear such as pegs can even be spotted at a distance by the line of rust stain which dribbles out from below them. All *in situ* gear should be treated with caution and it is not a good idea to rely too heavily on fixed protection unless its age and history are known. The heads of some pegs have been known to fall off at the first touch! Anything, unless made of stainless steel, is affected by this accelerated corrosion and should be treated with care.

Retreat can be difficult, especially if the route rises straight from the sea. Aiding to the top, moving on to an easier line or prusiking up an abseil rope are usually more attractive than

Fig 22.1 OPPOSITE PAGE: *Climbing on sea cliffs can present situations not encountered elsewhere and they often enjoy better weather than that experienced on inland and mountain cliffs.*

abseiling into the sea and swimming to safety.

Even at the finish of a route, the problems may not be over. The top portion of many sea cliffs can be of poor or vegetated rock which gives worrying climbing and belays may be a long way back from the edge. Stakes, found on some flat-topped cliffs, should be tied off with a clove hitch close to the ground to reduce leverage and the belay taken close to the edge. This improves communications, reduces the amount that the live rope cuts into the edge and decreases the risk of the rope knocking loose rocks on to the second. If the rope is not long enough to go to the anchor then back to the stance, it can be untied and attached directly to the anchor. The leader then ties back into the rope at an appropriate point using a figure-of-eight knot or a clove hitch into a locking karabiner. The clove hitch is better as it permits easier adjustment, especially when you are belaying close to the edge. There is, however, a great deal of stretch in a rope used this way, particularly a half-rope.

After you have climbed by the sea, all your metal equipment, such as karabiners, nuts, wires and camming devices, should be washed thoroughly in clean water to remove any trace of salt which will corrode them. A spray of a silicone lubricant will help to free any sticking parts, but wipe off the excess before further use as it makes the gear slippery to handle.

23 Navigation

For those who are content to climb near the road or civilisation and only in good weather, the ability to navigate is merely a convenience. However, those who use the mountains, and consequently encounter the risk of bad weather and poor visibility, should be able to use a map and compass. If attempting routes in the higher hills or in winter conditions, it is foolish to neglect your navigational skills. Besides equipping you with the means to move with confidence and speed in unknown terrain or bad weather, such skills can maximise your climbing time by permitting an efficient approach to the climbs and perhaps help avoid an unplanned bivouac on the return.

THE MAP

The ability to read a map – that is, to look at the map and relate what it shows to the actual terrain and vice versa – is fundamental to good navigation. Except in bad visibility, this may be the only skill required.

Conventional Signs

Maps use standard symbols, the conventional signs, to depict the features of the landscape. These are explained in the key (or legend), normally found at the side or foot of the map.

Scale

The scale of the map is the relationship of the distance on the map to the distance on the ground. This is generally given as a representative fraction such as 1:50,000. This means that 1 unit on the map represents 50,000 of the same units on the ground. For example, 1cm on the map is 50,000cm (or 500m) on the ground. The scale is one of the first things you look for when you pick up a new map as it influences how much detail the map shows and, to some extent, the area it covers. Maps of 1:50,000 are generally accurate enough for mountain navigation but those of 1:20,000 or 1:25,000, are probably better for more complex terrain.

Contours

For the interpretation of the terrain, the most important information given on the map is in the contours. A contour is a line which joins points of equal height above sea level. From their form the shape and angle of the ground can be interpreted. Contours are normally brown except when on glaciers when they are blue. The vertical distance between them is shown in the key, and the smaller this vertical interval, the greater detail the lines can represent. Every fifth (or index) contour is normally a darker shade. The actual height of the contours is given in certain places, so the height of any point on the map can be calculated. When you are looking at these figures on the map, the numbers should appear the right way up when you are 'facing uphill'. Where the ground is sufficiently steep there may not be enough room on the map to show all the contours so some are missed out; where it is steeper still, cliff symbols are used.

From the spacing of the contour lines the shape of the ground can be worked out. The further apart the contours are, the flatter the ground is. The closer they are, the steeper the terrain [*fig. 23.1*].

Spot Heights

Spot heights also indicate height above sea level and are usually found on definite features such as summits and cols.

Grid References

Some maps, such as those produced by the British Ordnance Survey, have a set of grid lines running

Fig 23.1 OPPOSITE PAGE: *Contours and shapes:*
(a) Uniform slope.
(b) Concave slope.
(c) Convex slope.

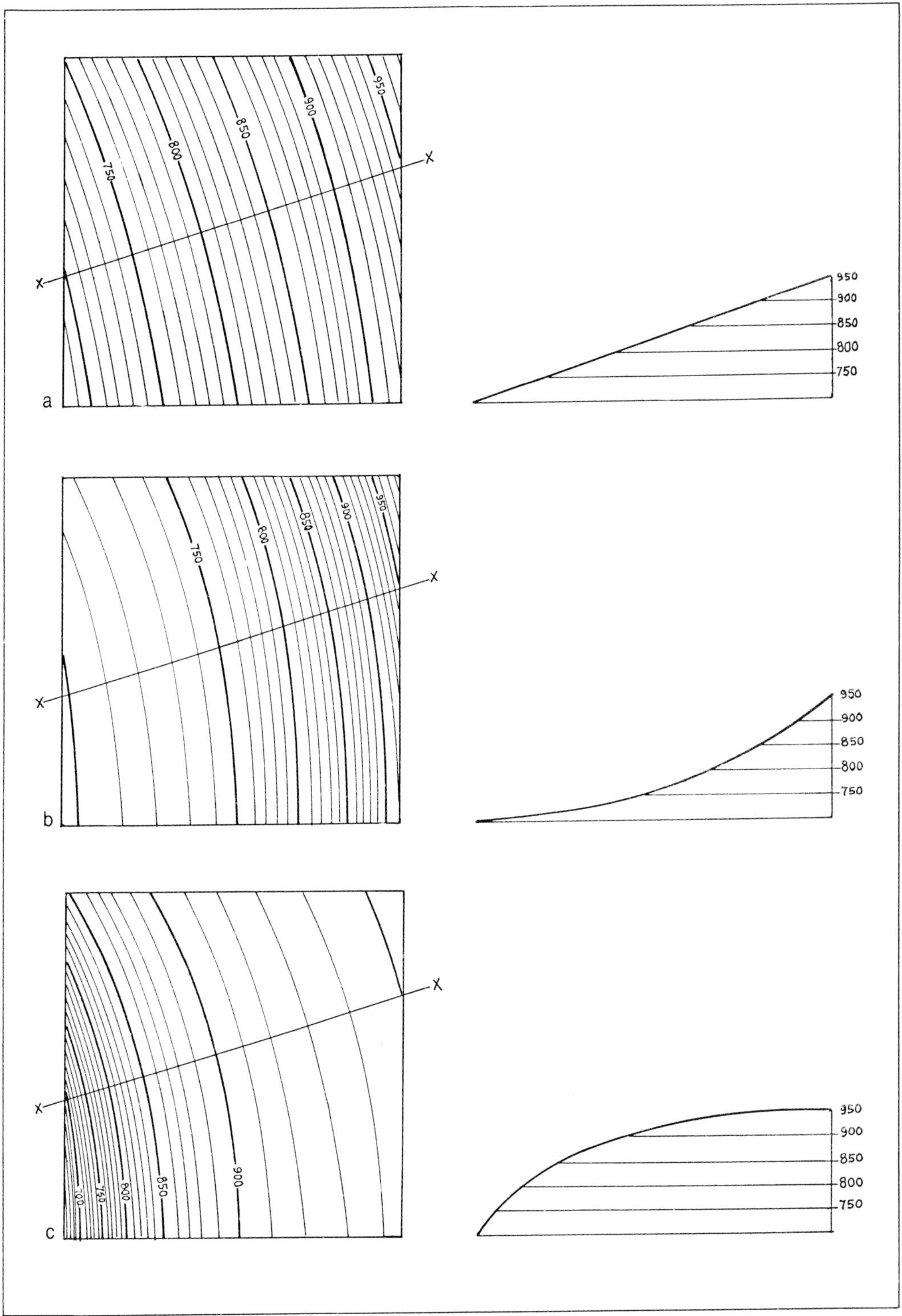

a
750
800
850
900
950
X
X
950
900
850
800
750
b
750
800
850
900
950
X
X
950
900
850
800
750
c
700
750
800
850
900
X
X
950
900
850
800
750

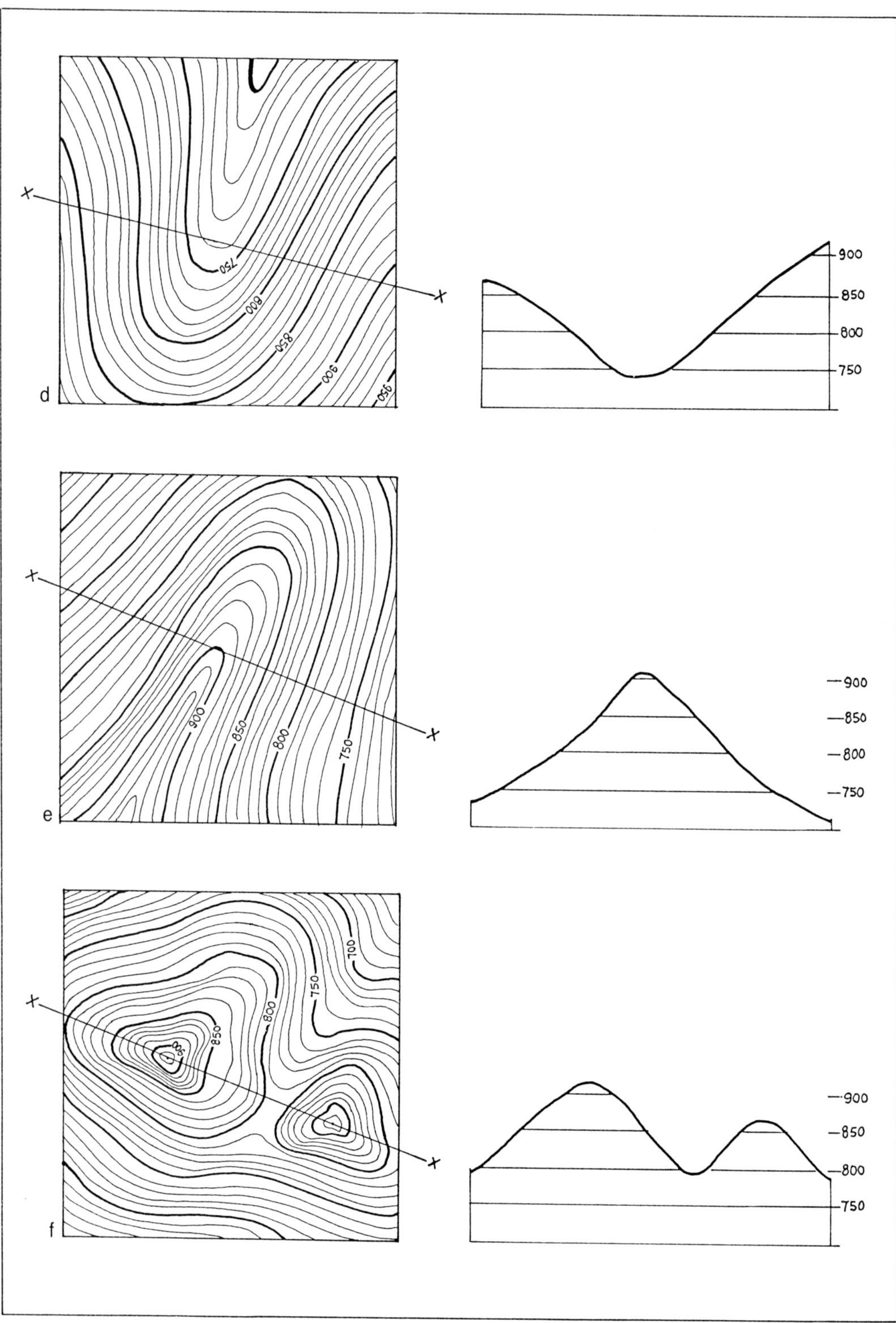

d
750
800
850
900
950
900
850
800
750
e
900
850
800
750
900
850
800
750
f
700
750
800
850
900
900
850
800
750

Fig 23.1 Contours and shapes, continued:
(d) Valley.
(e) Ridge or spur.
(f) Two tops separated by a col or a saddle.

north-south and east-west. These grid lines are numbered and divide the map into kilometre squares, each of which can be defined by these numbers. The four-figure grid reference of a square is the number of the north-south line which bounds the square on the west and the east-west line which bounds it on the south [*fig. 23.2*]. For greater accuracy the six-figure grid reference can be obtained by dividing the square into tenths numbered from 0 to 9 from the bottom left corner of the square [*fig. 23.3*].

The grid lines, particularly the north-south ones, are important when using a compass with the map and, if the map does not have them, they are well worth drawing on.

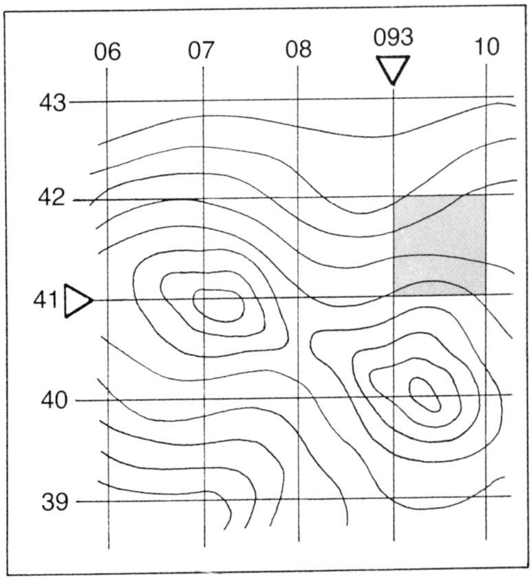

Fig 23.2 The four-figure grid reference for the indicated square is 09 41.

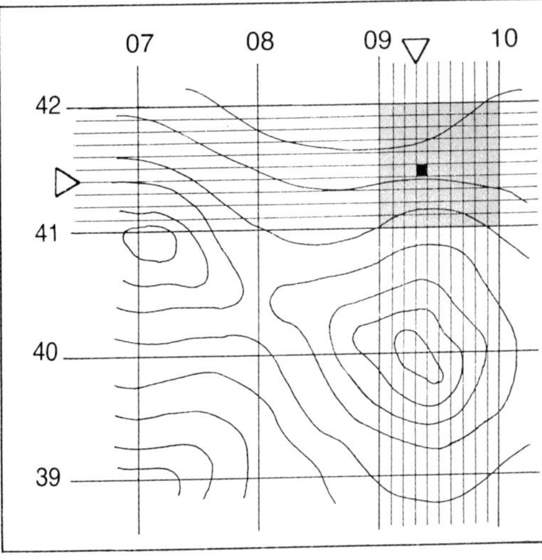

Fig 23.3 The six-figure grid reference for the indicated square is 093 414.

THE COMPASS

The most useful type of compass for mountain navigation is the Silva type which is light and simple to use. The main features are the transparent base plate, the magnetic needle and the compass housing, which is marked off in degrees round the rim and has an orienting arrow and parallel orienting lines on its base [*fig. 23.4*].

Before using the compass as a navigational aid, it is important to realise that there are actually three norths [*fig. 23.5*].

True North

True north is the direction from any point on the earth to the geographic north pole. This is of little importance in navigation and can be ignored.

Grid North

Grid north is the direction in which the grid lines on the map point.

Magnetic North

Magnetic north is the direction in which the magnetic needle of a compass points. This usually differs from the other norths and this difference (or magnetic variation, or declination) should be shown in the map's key. The magnetic north pole lies in the north of Canada and moves slightly from year to year. In Europe magnetic north lies west of grid north, while in the west of America it lies to the east. In parts of Britain, for example, the magnetic variation is 6° west, so any direction calculated from the map has to be corrected by the addition of this amount before it can be used on the compass. However, in other areas, such as Alaska, the variation may be as much as 30° east.

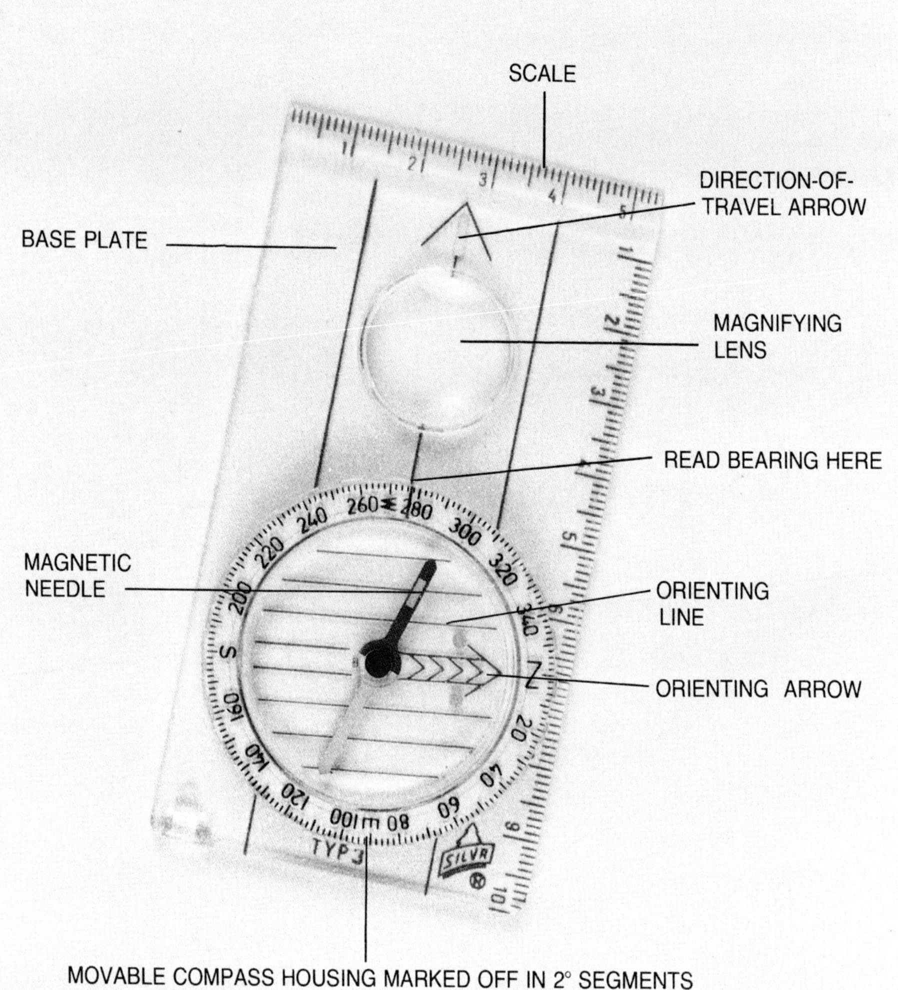

Fig 23.4 A Silva compass.

Setting the Map

Any map is more useful if it is set or orientated so that it lies the same way as the ground it represents. This can be done by eye: identify two points and turn the map so that the line that connects these points on the map corresponds to the line that connects these points on the ground. It can also be set using the compass, particularly if you are unfamiliar with the area or in poor visibility. Dial the magnetic variation on the compass housing and lay one edge of the base plate along one edge of the map or a north-south grid line. Hold the compass firmly on the map and turn the map and compass around until the magnetic needle lies within the orienting arrow and points to north. The map is now set.

Once the map is set, identifying features and relating the map to the ground is much easier. When using the map, ignore the 'right' and 'wrong' way up and get used always to setting your map as you travel [*fig. 23.6*].

The Compass and the Map

In bad weather or at night, when there are insufficient features visible by which to find your

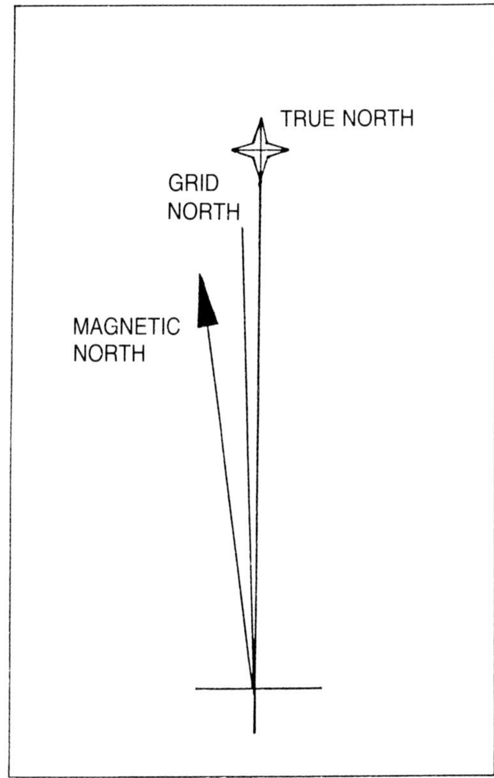

Fig 23.5 The three norths as they would appear in parts of Britain.

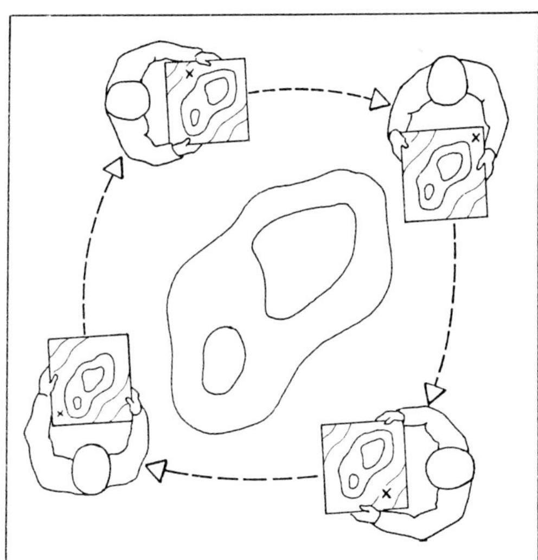

Fig 23.6 Walking with the map set. The map and the ground remain in the same orientation while the walker moves round the feature.

way, the compass and the map have to be used together. There are two main parts to this process.

Taking a Bearing

Taking a bearing is the first step in which the bearing or angle is measured from your location to your next destination. The north-south grid line is the base for this measurement – that is, 0° – and the compass is used as a protractor; the magnetic needle is of no significance.

Place one long edge, or line parallel to the edge, of the compass along the line joining your location, A, and your destination, B. The direction-of-travel arrow should point the way you want to go [*fig. 23.7*].

Hold the compass firmly on the map and turn the housing so that the orienting lines are parallel to the north-south grid lines and north on the housing points to north on the map. This is, by convention, at the top of the map [*fig. 23.8*].

Read off the bearing at the direction-of-travel arrow. Check by estimating the bearing by eye – for example, if the bearing is roughly north-east the bearing on the compass should therefore read about 45°. Doing this should ensure that a 180° error has not been made. This bearing is a grid bearing and must be corrected to allow for the magnetic variation to be usable. The variation is dialled on to the compass housing.

Following a Bearing

Once the correct magnetic bearing is shown on the housing, the compass can be used to indicate the direction of travel. As the compass needle is affected by ferrous material, it should be kept away from metal objects such as ice axes and cameras.

To follow a bearing, hold the compass firmly at about stomach level with the direction-of-travel arrow pointing straight ahead.

Turn round until the magnetic needle points to north on the housing and lies within the orienting arrow.

Sight along the direction-of-travel arrow to a marker directly in line. Walk to this and repeat with another marker directly ahead; continue in this fashion until your destination is reached [*fig. 23.9*].

Although not difficult, this does require some practice. The marker you sight on can be anything

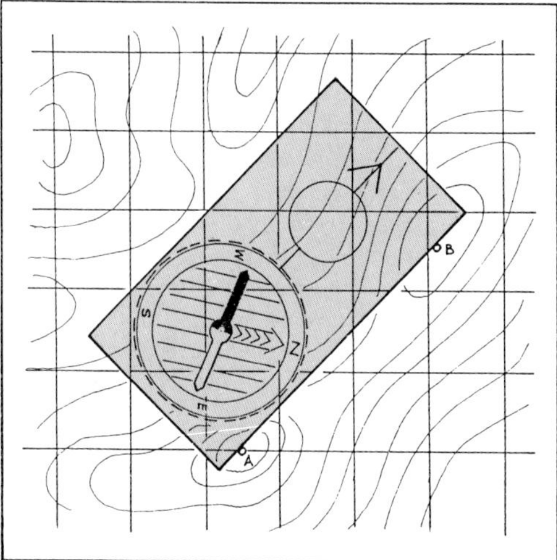

Fig 23.7 Lay the compass edge along your direction of travel.

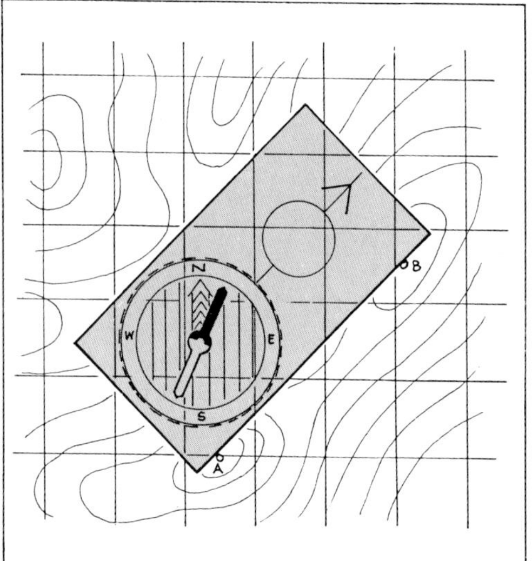

Fig 23.8 Turn the housing until north on the housing points to north on the map. Read off the grid bearing at the direction-of-travel arrow.

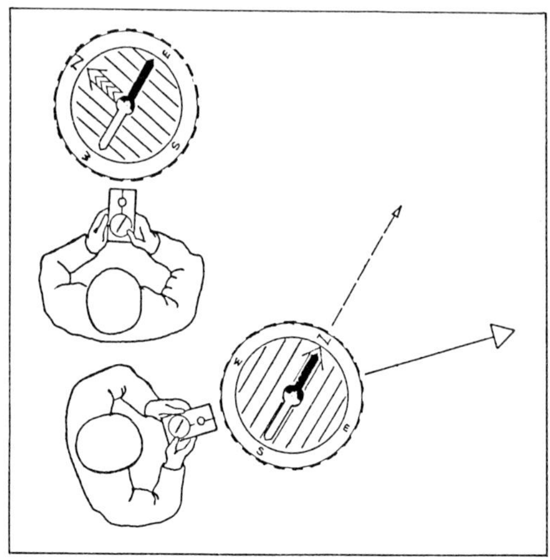

Fig 23.9 With the compass held firmly in front of you so that you are looking down on it, turn round until the magnetic needle lies within the orienting arrow. Sight along the direction-of-travel arrow to a suitable marker, then walk to it. Repeat the whole procedure until you reach your destination.

at all on the ground such as a rock, a boulder or a clump of vegetation. In winter, when fewer features are visible, the technique can be less easy to use, but old footprints, pieces of ice or snow or even changes in snow conditions can be used as markers. If visibility is zero, as in a white-out, one person can be sent ahead to the limit of visibility to act as a marker. This technique of leap-frogging unfortunately takes longer than the one outlined above and extra time may not be available. However, using a marker is the only way to ensure accurate navigation, as trying to walk straight while holding the magnetic needle at north is not possible for any distance. Even in very poor visibility there is usually some definition, even if only a few metres ahead. The longer any compass leg is, the greater the chance of error, so keep the legs as short as possible.

Some techniques which can be used to aid navigation are described below.

Attack Points

If going to a small feature such as a hut, go first to a larger feature nearby. This will be easier to locate and you can take a bearing to your destination from a known point on the larger feature. This keeps the important leg shorter and the large feature will be easier to return to if things do not work out on the final approach [*fig. 23.10*].

Aiming Off

If going to a point on a linear feature, such as a path or stream junction or a col on a ridge, take a bearing to one side of the feature. When it is reached, turn in the appropriate direction and

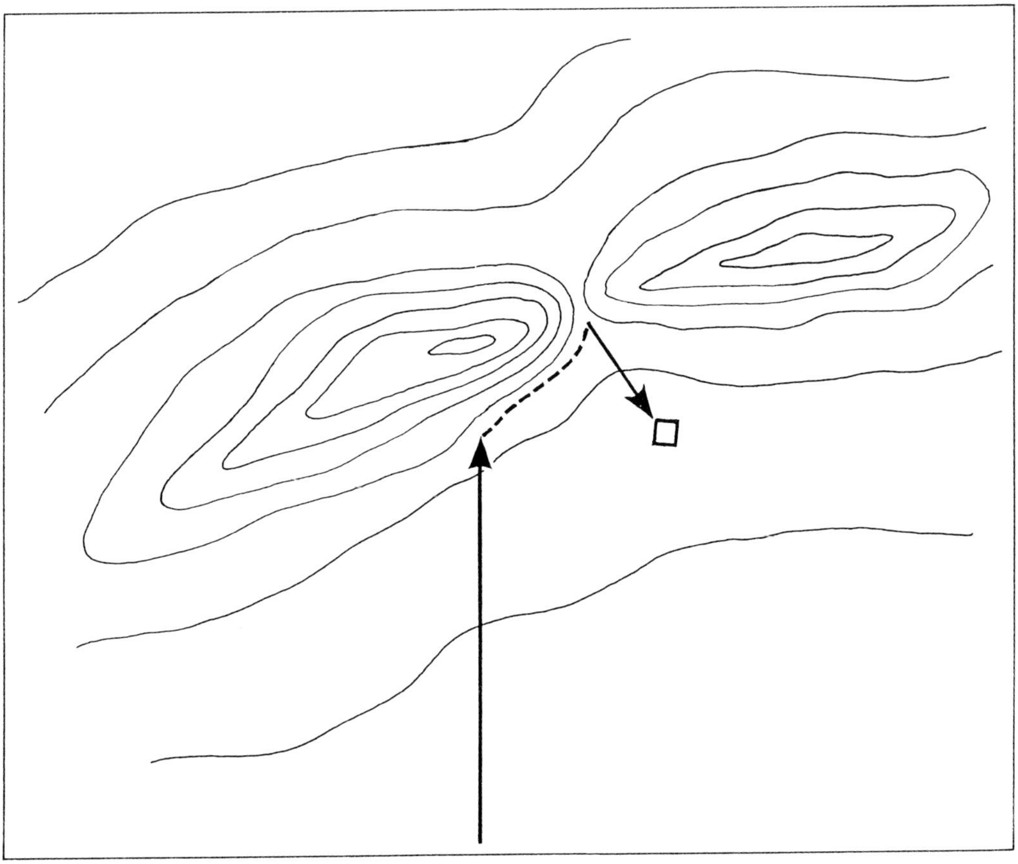

Fig 23.10 ABOVE: *Walk on a bearing to the obvious feature, the steep ground, and follow it to a definite point, the col, which is an attack point, and a much shorter and easier navigational leg then leads on to your destination.*

follow the linear feature to your destination. This requires less accurate navigation and avoids perhaps searching in the wrong direction if your destination is not hit exactly through following the direct bearing [*fig. 23.11*].

Boxing

If there is an obstacle in the way of a direct bearing – a crevasse, cliff edge or body of water, for example – it can be avoided by boxing. When the obstruction is neared, turn at 90° by aligning the compass needle to east or west, whichever is appropriate. Follow this for a set distance until the obstruction is cleared, then return to and follow the original bearing until on the far side of the

Fig 23.11 BELOW: *By navigating to one side of the objective, the stream junction, aiming off, you know that, when it is reached, turning downstream will lead to your objective.*

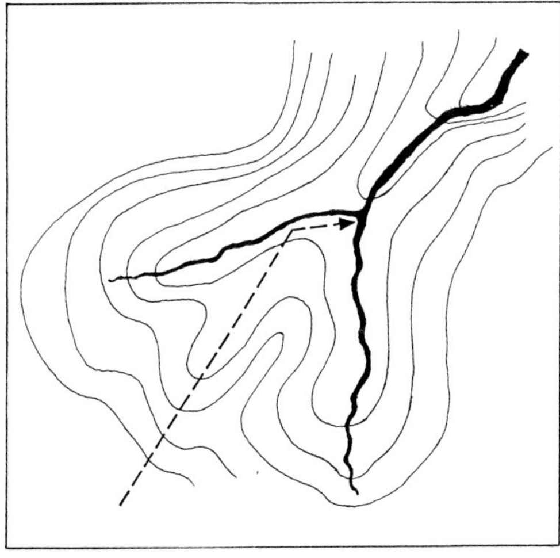

obstacle. Align the needle on either east or west (the opposite of the previous bearing) and walk on it for the same distance back to rejoin your original course. Using east or west to make the 90° turn avoids mistakes with calculations and keeps the main bearing on the housing [*fig. 23.12*].

Dog Leg

A dog leg is used to avoid danger or eliminate unnecessary ascent and descent. Choose a point on the map which takes you clear of the danger and go to this point. This will be a point which is marked on the map but does not exist on the ground: a boundary, number, letter or intersection of any two lines, for example. When this is reached, take a new bearing to your objective. If a physical feature exists which you can go to, this eliminates the need for a dog leg. The first point is simply something that you can take a bearing to and from. Keep the first leg as short as possible to reduce the chance of error [*fig. 23.13*].

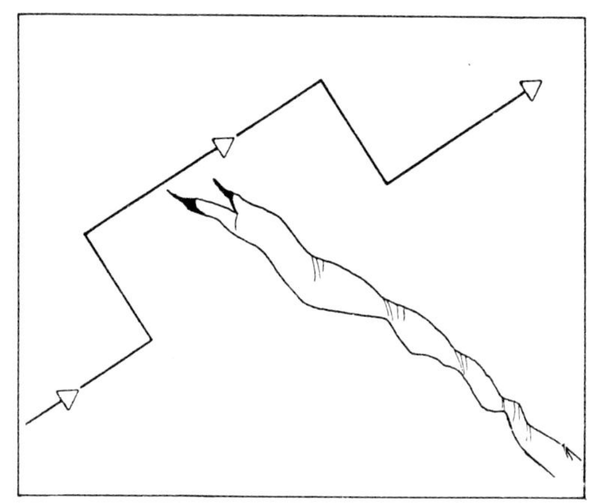

Fig 23.12 Boxing an obstacle, such as a large crevasse, by walking the same distance away from it and then back to it, allows the original bearing to be maintained.

Fig 23.13 BELOW: *Using a dog leg to avoid steep ground. The change of direction at X, the intersection of two grid lines in this instance, is marked on the map but is not an actual physical feature.*

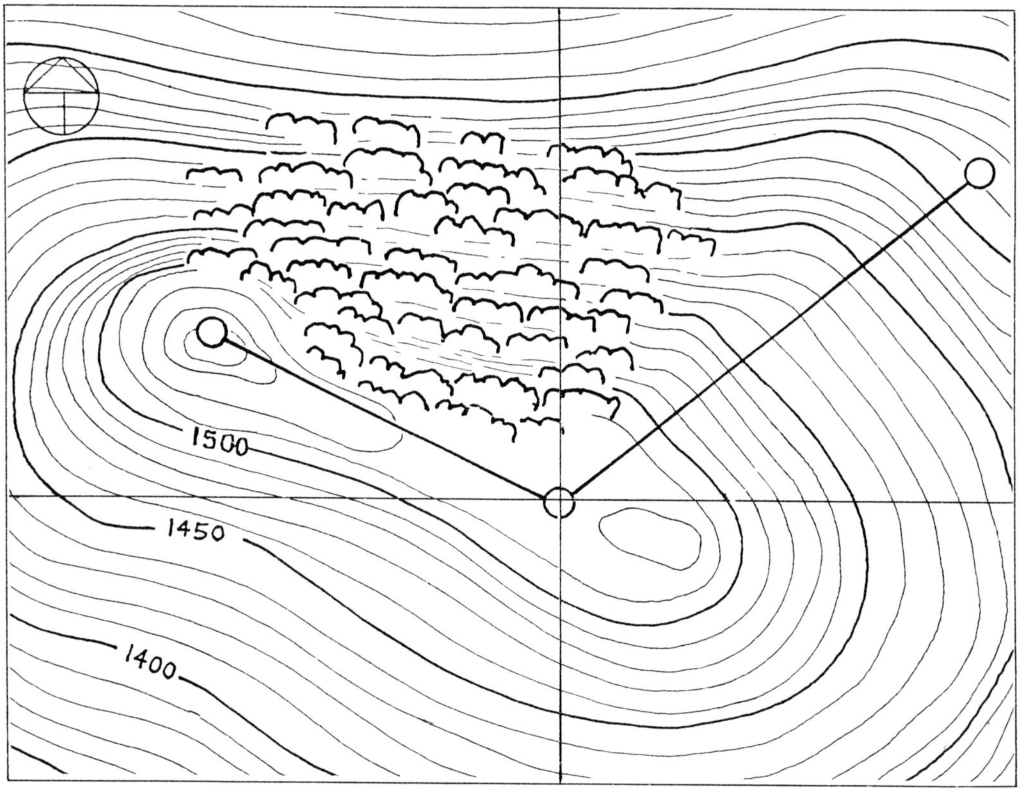

Slope Aspect

The aspect of a slope, or the direction in which it faces, can be a useful navigational aid, especially if you are unsure of your exact position. To establish the aspect, point the direction-of-travel arrow of your compass directly down or up the slope, turn the housing until north lies in the orienting arrow and convert this reading to a grid bearing for use on the map. Place the compass on the map and, keeping the orienting line parallel to the grid lines, move the compass in the region of your supposed position until the long edge crosses the contours at right angles. This should then indicate the slope you are on but not necessarily your height on it. This can be used to check your position at any time [*fig. 23.14*].

Checking

When travelling on a bearing, always compare the ground over which you are passing with the information the map provides. Changes in slope aspects and angles can give reassurance that you are going in the right direction and can alert you to any mistakes you may have made.

Identifying Features

Identifying a feature using a map and compass is the reverse of taking a bearing. Sight on the feature using the direction-of-travel arrow and turn the housing until the magnetic needle lies within the orienting arrow. Read off the magnetic bearing and adjust this to the grid bearing. Place one long edge of the compass on your position with the direction-of-travel arrow pointing away from your position and turn the whole compass until north points to the top of the map and the orienting and grid lines are parallel. The feature will lie along the edge or its continuation [*fig. 23.15*].

Checking Position

To check on your position using a known feature, take a bearing on it and convert this to grid for use on the map. This is known as a back bearing. Place

Fig 23.14 With the grid bearing on the compass, it is moved until the long edge crosses the contours at right angles. This is the line you must be on.

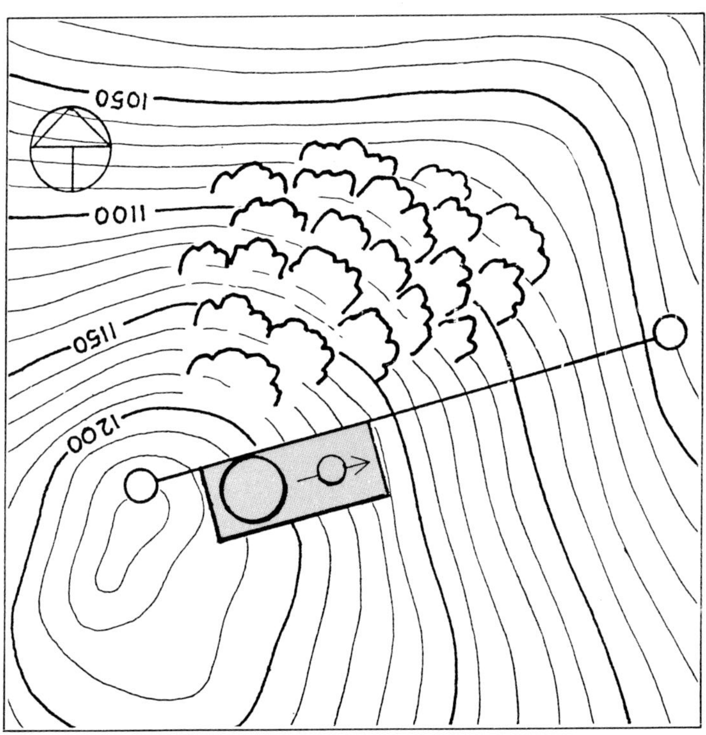

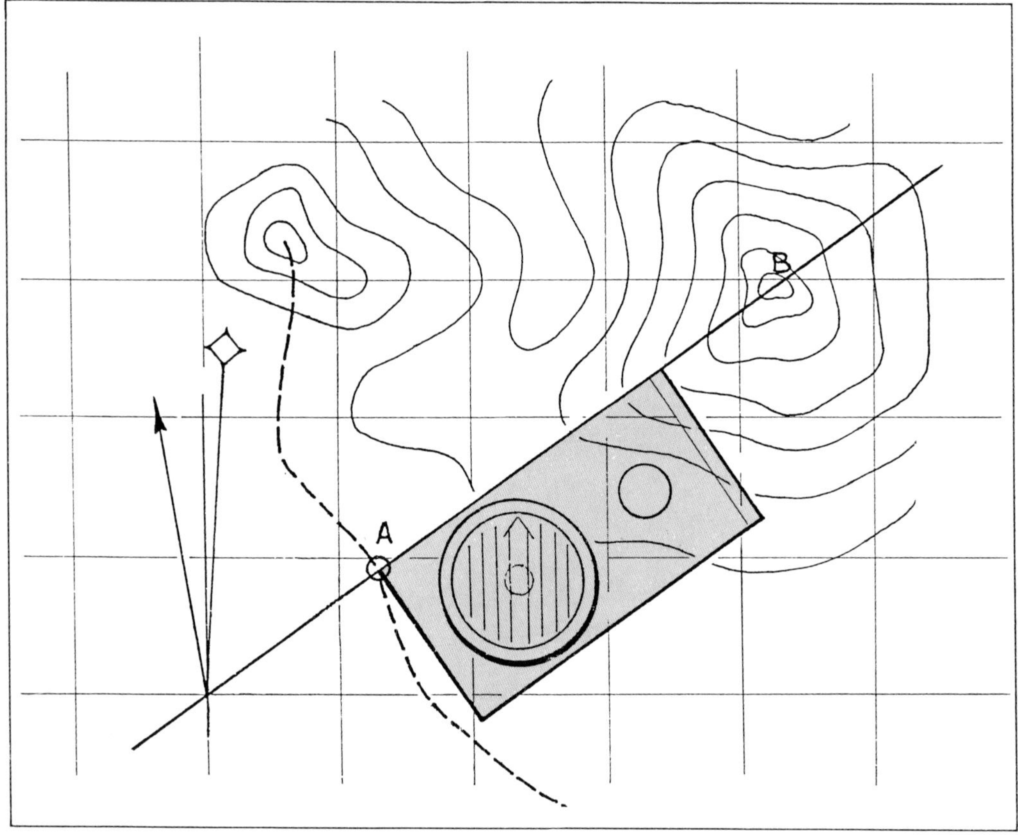

Fig 23.15 Find the grid bearing to B and place a corner of the compass on your location, A. Turn the compass until the orienting arrow points north and the orienting and grid lines are parallel. The feature then lies on the line or the continuation of it.

one corner of the compass base plate on the feature and turn it until the north points to the top of the map and the orienting and grid lines are parallel. Your position is then along this long edge or its continuation. If you are on a linear feature, this will give your position. The technique is similar to identifying a feature but different corners of the base plate are put on the known points.

If you are not on a long feature, you will have to take a second bearing on another known point: you will be at the intersection of the two lines. Repeating this with a third feature will place you in a triangle. This procedure, called taking a resection, is unlikely to be necessary if you can see well enough to identify two or three points. Using a bearing on to one feature, however, can be useful in sudden clearings in bad weather [*fig. 23.16*].

DISTANCE

The distance between any two points on the map can be measured and converted to suitable units using the scale. To estimate this distance on the ground, two methods can be used, both of which with practice can be accurate to within 10 per cent or better of the true figure. Estimation of distance is an important and sometimes essential tool in bad-weather navigation.

Pacing

To use pacing to estimate distance you must first establish how many double paces you take to cover 100m over various slopes and types of

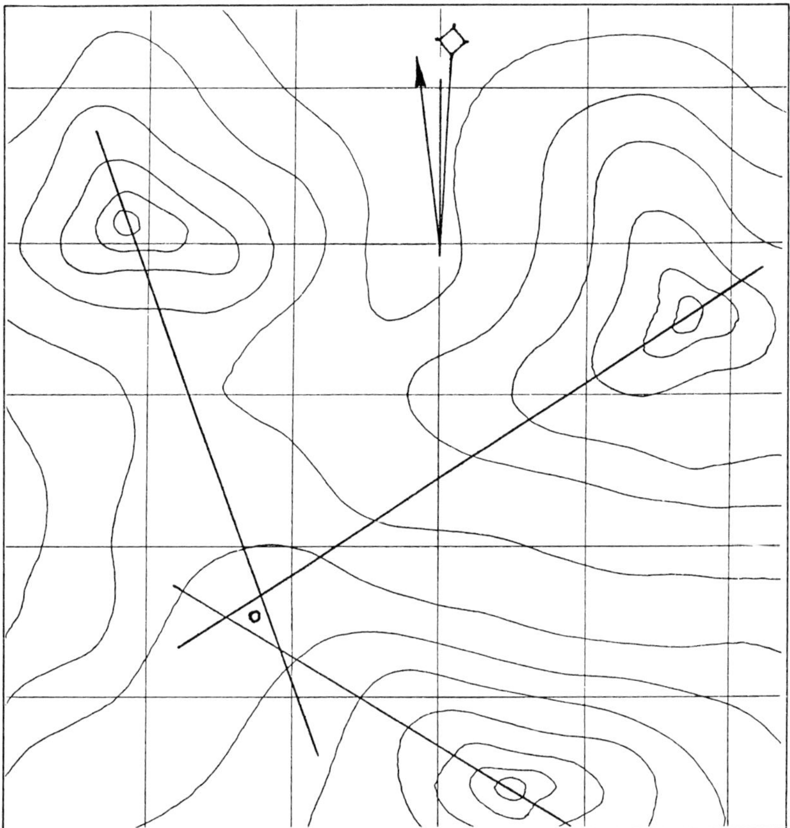

Fig 23.16 By taking back bearings on three identifiable features you can locate your position.

terrain. The average figure is sixty to seventy double paces on flat, easy ground but this can go up to one hundred on steep, difficult ground and will also increase when going downhill.

The number of paces taken for any distance depends very much on the individual but, once practised, this method can be very accurate. It is, however, best suited to fairly short distances and, rather than calculate the total number of paces needed, just tick off each 100m as they are covered.

Timing

It is useful when travelling longer distances to know in advance how long a journey will take. For this use Naismith's Rule which takes as its basis a walking speed of 3mph to which is added 30 minutes for every 1,000ft of ascent. In metric units this is 5kph and 30 minutes for every 300m of ascent, but it is more convenient to work things out in 100m units and 10m for ascent; in other words, work out the total time using 1.2 minutes per 100m distance and one minute per 10m of height gained. Going down is taken to be the same as walking on the flat but will be slightly less for long, easy-angled descents and more for long, steep descents.

This 'rule' is not fixed; it is a base from which to work and should be altered when appropriate. Variables such as fitness, the load carried, the weather, conditions underfoot, visibility and tiredness all affect the calculation, but with practice timing can be accurate and extremely useful.

THE ALTIMETER

Altimeters are barometers which are calibrated to indicate height instead of pressure. They are used to show height above sea level and are most useful when trying to fix a position on a long definite feature such as a ridge, glacier or climb, especially in poor visibility. In these situations, they can tell you how far you still have to ascend or descend to your objective, such as a summit. Although light and simple to use, they are unfortunately expensive. Those which are calibrated with a 10m interval are the best.

As an altimeter is affected by atmospheric pressure it will change not only when going up or down but also with the weather. For this reason it must be re-set at regular intervals, usually at a point of known height which can be established from the map. Unless this re-setting is done regularly, cumulative error can make the reading inaccurate and even misleading.

The altimeter's other use is in indicating changes in the weather, particularly after an overnight stop at a hut, camp or bivi. Check and note the reading when you stop for the night and before setting off look at the height indicated. If there is an apparent increase in height, there has been a drop in atmospheric pressure which may herald a deterioration in the weather. An apparent drop in height indicates a rise in pressure and a possible improvement in the weather.

24 Snow & Avalanche

The subject of snow and avalanche is a complex one, about which much has been written and theorised. An in-depth look at it is beyond the scope of this chapter; however, it is vital that all winter mountain users have a basic grasp of the systems and techniques which can be used to evaluate the safety of the snow-covered ground on which they will climb.

We tend to think of snow as a uniform mass, sometimes soft and powdery, and at other times hard and solid, but the structure of snow and the way it behaves on the mountain form a complicated science which the climber must try to understand. An understanding of where good conditions exist and what causes them can make climbing much easier, safer and more enjoyable. On many occasions 'local experts' can predict the conditions when outsiders cannot, and this is not through any exceptional local knowledge but from an understanding of the prevailing weather and that of the previous few days, and how these affect the snow cover.

SNOW FORMATION

Snowflakes are formed high in the atmosphere when super-cooled droplets of water come into contact with tiny dust particles. The moisture freezes around each dust particle nucleus and so a snowflake is formed. As this flake falls, it grows in size, either by further water vapour being deposited on the crystal (sublimation) or by a further water droplet freezing on to the existing crystal (riming). These crystals grow in countless different shapes and sizes but all have in common a basic hexagonal form.

Climbers are not so much interested in how snow forms as in how it behaves on reaching the earth, how it changes under the effects of wind and temperature, and what these different changes mean. Even the inexperienced snow and ice climber is soon aware that some snow is good and safe to climb on, whereas other areas of snow, perhaps only a few metres away, are soft, unpredictable and often downright dangerous. The processes which cause these transformations are explained later, but it is more important to understand the effect they can have on the snow pack, rather than how they actually occur.

From the time the snowflakes are formed in the atmosphere until they eventually revert back to water, they are constantly being changed or 'metamorphosed'. There are three basic processes which cause this change to come about: equitemperature metamorphism, temperature gradient metamorphism and melt-freeze metamorphism.

Equitemperature Metamorphism

Equitemperature metamorphism – or ET met. or destructive metamorphism – [*fig. 24.1*] is the process which causes snow crystals to be reduced from complicated branch crystals to those with a more rounded shape. This process works on all the crystals in snow packs which are at temperatures below 0°C. Crystals which form when there

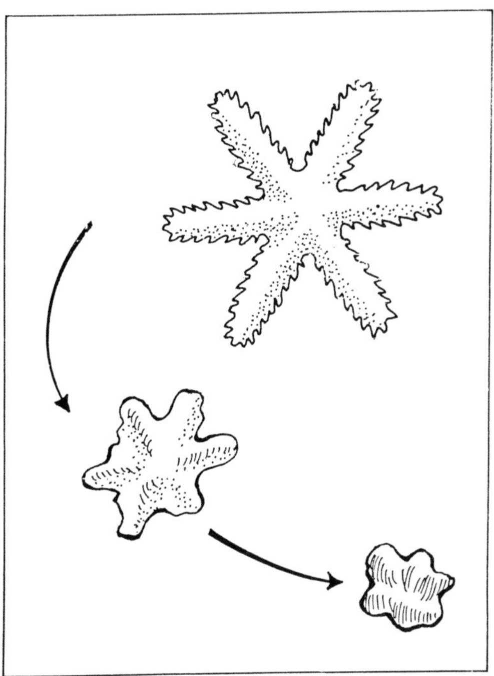

Fig 24.1 Equitemperature metamorphism.

is little or no wind are initially well linked together (by the interlocking of their crystal branches); however, as the ET process goes to work these interlinking branches are broken down, resulting in less cohesion between adjacent grains. This is why powder skiing is often better a short time after a snow fall rather than straight away. ET met. happens fastest at just below zero and stops altogether at −40°C. After some time bonds will once again become established between the crystals. It is from this that there arises the old adage, 'It is safe to climb twenty-four hours after a snow fall'.

Temperature Gradient Metamorphism

Temperature gradient metamorphism – or TG met., or constructive metamorphism – occurs when a temperature difference is maintained between the surface of the snow and the ground. The larger the gradient of this difference, the greater the TG met. effect. This means that a shallow snow pack lying on the ground, which is usually around 0°C, will have a high temperature gradient when there is a very low snow surface temperature. This allows water vapour to migrate through the snow pack, eventually resulting in the formation of large, unstable, cup-shaped crystals [*fig. 24.2*]. These may take as long as two weeks of sustained low temperatures to form and their formation is aided if air is free to circulate, perhaps because the snow is lying on grass.

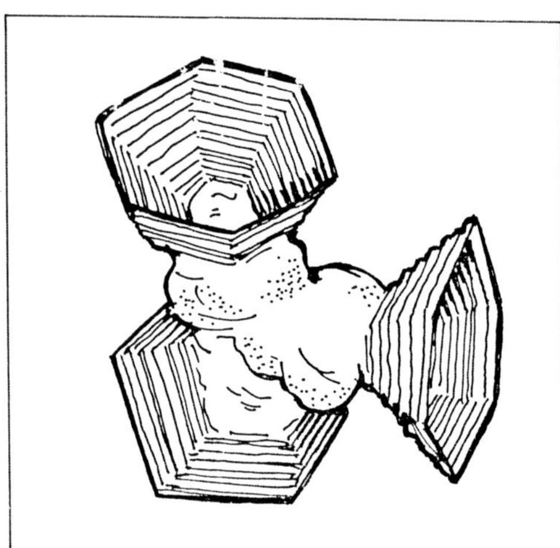

Fig 24.2 Cup crystals are formed as a result of temperature gradient metamorphism and give rise to a high avalanche risk. They may become buried under many layers of snow and so present a danger which is often hard to predict.

Melt-Freeze Metamorphism

Melt-freeze metamorphism – or MF met. – occurs when the snow pack or snow crystals are exposed to temperatures which alternate above and below zero. This results in the crystals' shrinking and being covered in a layer of water when above 0°C, and then subsequently re-freezing when the temperature drops below zero. An extremely stable snow pack quickly results.

Types of Snow

It is said that Eskimoes have over fifty words for snow. Fortunately, we need not go quite so far, but it is still worthwhile to be able to identify different snow types, and also be able to describe them accurately so that we can exchange notes about climbs and conditions.

Powder Snow

Loose, unconsolidated snow is called powder snow. It occurs when crystals fall in sub-zero temperatures and there is little wind. As already explained, these crystals are reasonably well bonded initially and so are fairly stable. However, after a short time the crystals are affected by ET met. and an unstable and avalanche-prone snow cover results. This unconsolidated powder is horrendous for climbing (or rather for wading) as it will not support the climber's weight and makes progress difficult, even on the flat. It is frequently encountered immediately after snow falls, at the foot of ice faces and at high altitude. Often the only means of progress is to 'swim' or crawl on the hands and knees. In extreme conditions it may even be necessary to remove the rucksack, place it in front and then mantelshelf on top – an extremely tiring and time-consuming procedure. Powder snow is also the name given by climbers to any snow which will not support their weight.

Wind Slab

Wind slab is formed by the effect of the wind on falling snow or by the accumulation of snow which has been eroded from existing banks and is subsequently re-deposited. As the wind blows the snow crystals, or picks them up from the ground, they are smashed up before being deposited on lee slopes or in wind scoops or hollows [*fig. 24.3*]. The speed of the wind determines whether the slab is hard or soft: the stronger the wind, the harder the slab. Wind slab makes up much of the snow occurring in the mountains since it is rare for snow not to be moved and deposited by the wind.

Firn Snow

Firn snow results from extensive ET met. It is old snow well bonded together and reasonably consolidated. If firn snow thaws or is exposed to direct sunlight, MF met. will produce neve.

Névé

Névé is the ideal climbing medium. It is hard enough to support the climber's weight but soft enough to allow easy penetration of crampon points. It is extremely stable and not prone to avalanche. Névé is usually formed by melt-freeze met.; it is made up of large crystals and has a high air content.

This is a simplified picture of the snow cover that is likely to be found on easier-angled ground, and relates more to large snow fields than to the more typical mountain terrain. Obviously gullies, couloirs, angle of slope and slope aspect will all affect the snow cover [*fig. 24.3b*]. When the processes of snow transformation have only just begun to act, or have acted only partially, it is common for a crust to be formed on the surface. If this crust is strong enough to support the clim-

Fig 24.3 Ground features and wind strength and direction can be used by the climber to predict where the less avalanche-prone areas will be. Ridges and buttresses often offer safe areas, while gullies and couloirs contain high build-ups of slab. Arrows represent wind direction, grey tints shows snow deposition.

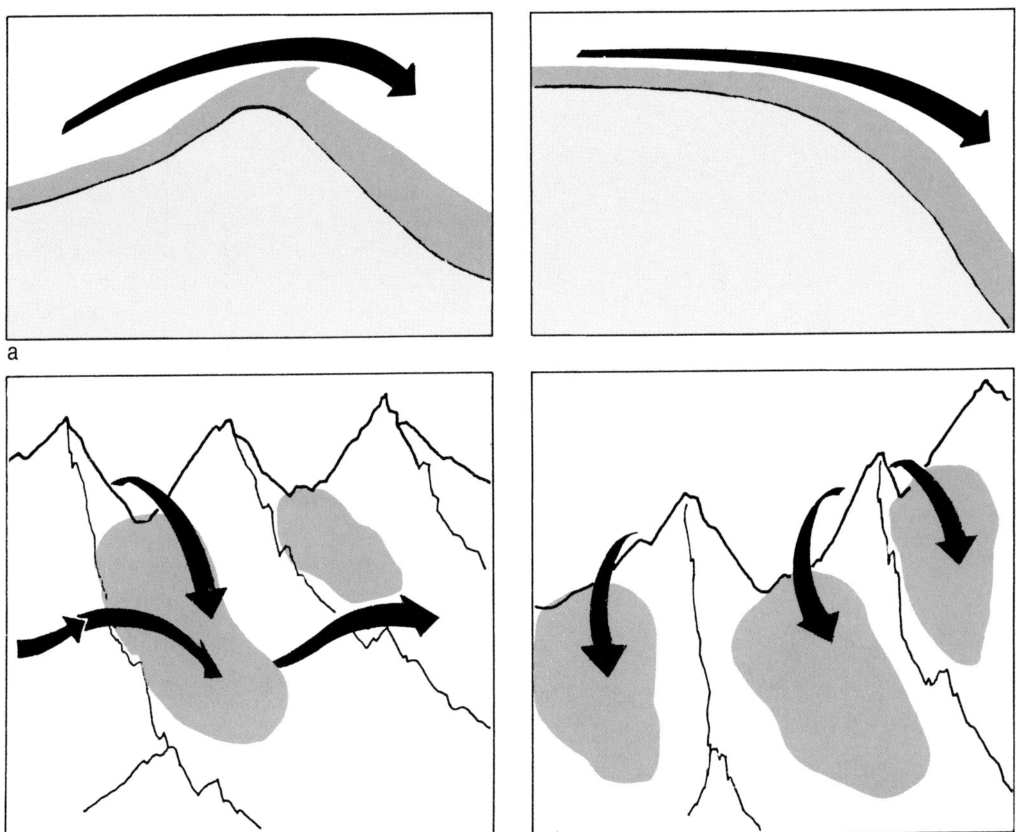

ber's weight, it causes no problems, but otherwise it can make for very tiring and strenuous trail breaking. This is known as breakable crust and it can be one of the most unpleasant snow conditions.

ICE FORMATION

Given time, all snow packs will eventually be transformed into ice. Ice can be formed either by further MF met. on neve, by the freeze-thaw action on melt water from the snow pack, by seepage from cracks or from rainfall. As with snow, ice varies in its 'climbability' and safety, and perhaps the best guide to the quality of the ice is its colour. Ice varies in hardness and texture depending on how it was formed and the temperature in which it exists.

White Ice

White ice results from the MF met. of neve and is perfect for climbing on. It has a high air content and so tends not to shatter or splinter. It is very stable but unfortunately rarely forms above 70°.

Blue Ice

Blue ice is very dense, has a watery hue and has little air trapped within. It is often formed by snow falling on wet rocks or natural seepage lines. The falling snow sticks to this moisture and freezes, often resulting in massive ice formations which are almost soft and plastic in texture. This is as a result of the high crystal, and therefore air, content in the make-up of the ice.

Water Ice

Water ice is formed directly from freezing water. It is clear in colour, has no air content and is usually very brittle. It is often seen in icicle or organ-pipe formations that can join up to give hollow structures which boom alarmingly when struck. In temperatures even several degrees below zero, there can often still be water flowing in and around the frozen features.

Black Ice

Black ice is formed when blue ice or water ice is exposed to extremely low temperatures and polishing by snow fall or avalanche. It is often encountered on steep north faces in winter and in the Himalayas. It is very difficult to climb on as it is extremely hard and dense and so resistant to ice-axe placements.

Sometimes snow and ice can be affected by sunlight, which can form a very thin crust on the surface. This crust can then promote a greenhouse-type effect, melting the snow pack underneath and causing the moisture to evaporate. The result is seemingly hard snow which turns out to be horrendously soft and deep. The South American Andes are notorious for this formation.

When rain comes into contact with sub-zero rock, verglas is formed. This is a very thin layer of ice which is extremely difficult to climb on. It is too thin for crampons or step-cutting, but at the same time effectively masks all of the rock's features and texture.

AVALANCHE ASSESSMENT AND EVALUATION

Avalanches can occur wherever snow lies. The snow cover (or snow pack) will support itself until the internal bonds and the bonds which hold it to the ground underneath become overstressed and break [*fig. 24.4*]. This results in parts of the pack becoming detached and sliding downhill under the force of gravity. This can occur under a variety of different circumstances.

When assessing the stability of the snow pack, the climber is primarily concerned with how well the snow is bonded together. Unfortunately, the snow is not a uniform mass but made up of layers deposited throughout the season. The climber must inspect these layers and the snow itself and so determine the stability of the snow pack [*fig. 24.4*].

Snow Profiles

One way to assess the different layers of snow is to dig a snow profile. This is a hole dug in the snow, preferably all the way down to the ground, which will give an indication of the different layers present in the snow pack [*fig. 24.5*]. When digging a snow profile, choose a safe site – that is,

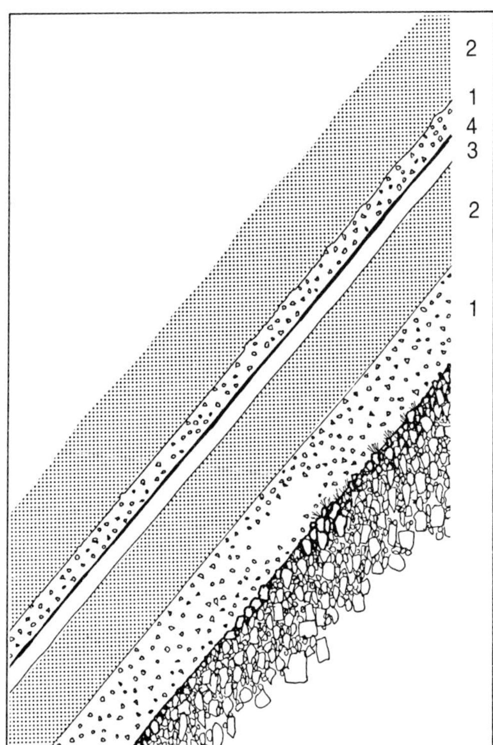

Fig 24.4 A section through the snow pack. This slope presents a high avalanche risk as there is a very soft layer (hardness 1) on top of a very hard layer (hardness 4).

one protected by rocks or in an area that is obviously not avalanche-prone. Try to select a site which is representative of the slope in question: that is, facing in the same direction (aspect) and at approximately the same altitude. The snow profile need not be too large and can be dug with a shovel or, more usually, with an ice axe. Although it is best to dig the pit down to ground level, this is not always practical or indeed necessary. Often, digging through the upper layers will expose a fairly consistent snow pack which will be stable and extend to ground level.

When the pit has been dug, prepare the back wall for examination by carefully smoothing it off so that the different layers and crystals are visible. First check for any visual differences in the layers. A high avalanche risk exists when there are large differences between adjacent layers in hardness, moisture content or crystal size. All of these eventually represent themselves as differences in strength. The first check to make is on the hardness of the adjacent layers.

Hardness Check

It is convenient to use a scale of identification of the snow layers which ranges from 1 (soft powder snow) through to 5 (hard neve). These hardnesses can be assessed by what can be pushed in to the appropriate layer: for instance, if a gloved fist can be inserted, the layer is likely to be very soft, perhaps of a hardness of 1; whereas if an ice-axe pick must be used, the layer will be of hardness 5. Where a difference of more than 3 between adjacent layers exists, the likelihood of an avalanche occurring is high. Where smaller differences exist, other factors must be taken into consideration before a final decision can be made.

Moisture Content

The moisture content of the snow pack must also be gauged as it too has an effect on the stability of the slope. When very wet, snow becomes dense and heavy and the lubricating effect of moisture can further increase its propensity to slide. Once again it is convenient to subdivide the moisture scale from 1 to 5. With a wetness of 1 the snow will be so dry that it is impossible to form a snowball; a wetness of 3 will allow a good snowball to form; and a wetness of 5 will result in wet gloves and large amounts of water being squeezed from the snow.

By the time tests have been conducted for snow hardness and wetness, any large irregularities in the grain size should also be evident. Look especially for large, round grains of graupel which are formed by rime ice sticking to falling snow crystals. These can provide an ideal sliding surface, acting in much the same way as ball-bearings do.

A final test can be done by cutting a shovel-sized wedge into the back wall of the profile [*fig. 24.5*]. This must be done carefully so that only the bonds at the sides of the wedge are destroyed and not those between the adjacent layers. If the shovel is then used to prise the wedge out, the amount of force required gives a further indication as to the strength of the bonds between the layers. This is a 'rule of thumb' test and only the experience gained from having performed the test many times before will allow you to form a realistic idea as to the snow's quality.

From the above it should be evident that a uniform or gradually changing snow pack is stable, whereas one which shows marked differences in hardness, texture, moisture content or grain size will have a tendency to be unstable.

Other Factors Affecting Avalanche Risk

The ground surface itself must also be taken into consideration, in much the same way as a snow layer, when assessing the risk of avalanche.

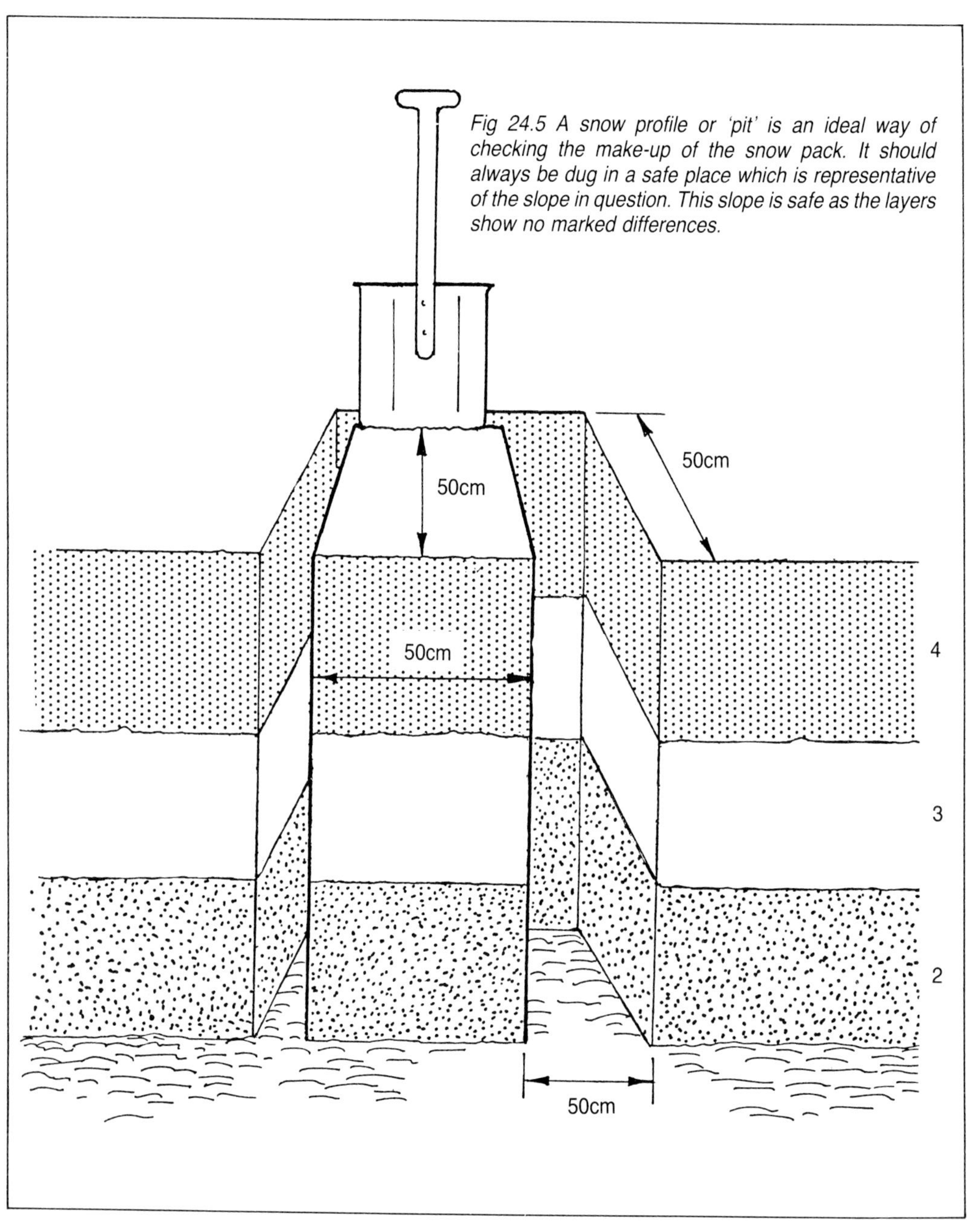

Fig 24.5 A snow profile or 'pit' is an ideal way of checking the make-up of the snow pack. It should always be dug in a safe place which is representative of the slope in question. This slope is safe as the layers show no marked differences.

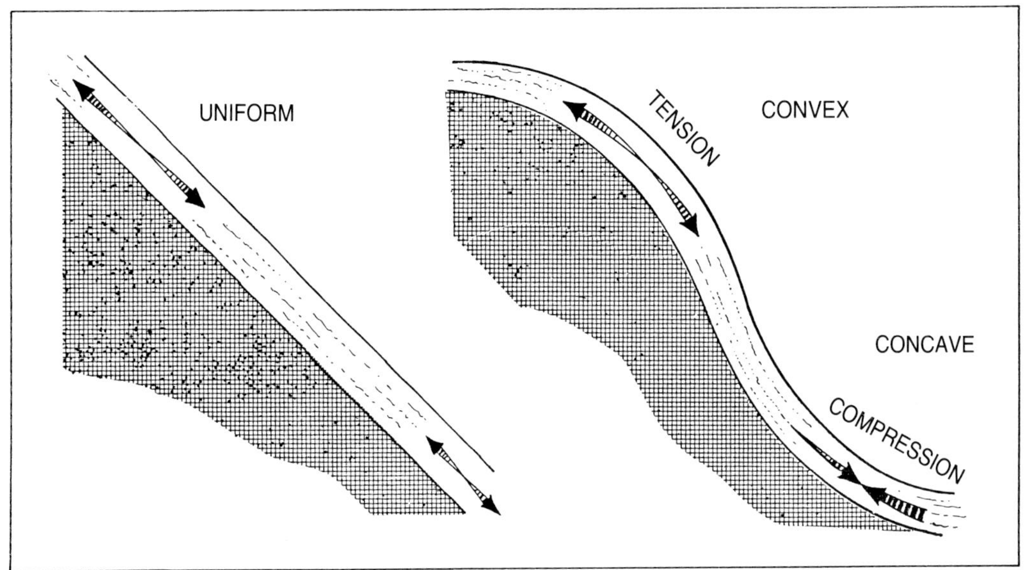

Fig 24.6 Different slope shapes affect the avalanche risk. Convex slopes place the snow pack under tension and so present the highest risk.

Smooth rock slabs and slopes of small scree pose a particular problem. They act in the same way as a very hard layer within the snow pack and are also prone to surface water run-off which can cause further weakening between the bonds joining the snow pack to the ground. Long grass gives a good sliding surface as the grass becomes flattened by the snow pack as it gradually slides downhill. This is further exacerbated by the grass shrinking as it decomposes. Layers of depth hoar or TG met. crystals may also occur at ground level and they are very unstable. Sometimes a weak layer can be formed where surface hoar (that is, the crystals formed when water condenses on the surface of the snow pack) are covered over by a fresh fall of snow.

The final factor which must be taken into consideration is the angle and the shape of the slope [*fig. 24.6*]. Convex slopes are much more prone to avalanche than concave slopes since a convexity sets up a tension within the snow pack, whereas concavity forms areas of compression. The slope angle itself is also very important, slopes between 20° and 50° being most prone to avalanche [*fig. 24.7*].

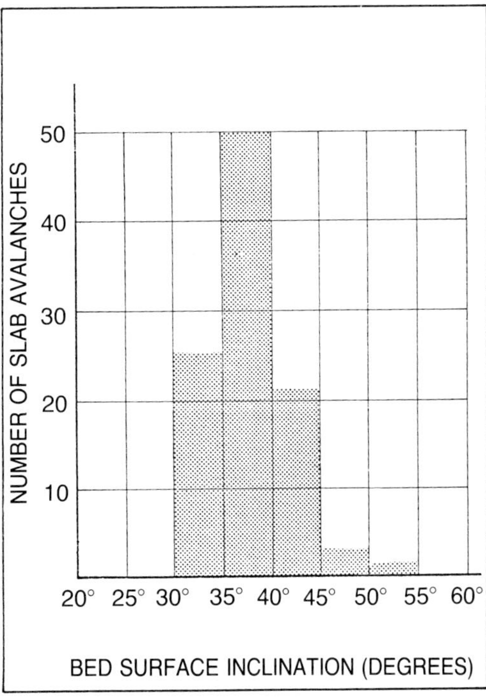

Fig 24.7 This graph shows the number of avalanches per slope angle. The easy-angled slopes (20–50°) commonly encountered at the foot of ice climbs are especially prone to slab avalanches.

Some Specific Avalanche Types

Wind Slab

There are several different types of avalanche but perhaps the most dangerous, and indeed the most common, is the wind-slab avalanche [*fig. 24.8*]. Wind slab is formed by the effect of wind on falling snow or on snow which is already lying on the ground (see page 313). It can be identified by its characteristic colour – it is 'chalky' in appearance and rather dull compared to other snow types. It has a very fine, smooth texture similar to cheese, and makes a very distinctive 'squeaky' noise when compressed. A good test for wind slab is to put an axe shaft into the snow pack and move it from side to side. Any 'squeaky' noises will indicate wind slab. Particular care should be exercised when identifying very hard slab as it can sometimes be easy to confuse this with neve.

When assessing the likelihood that a slab avalanche may or may not occur, the climber must consider the bonds which hold the slab in place. These consist of anchors at the boundary of the slab, bonds between the slab and the slope above, and bonds between the slab and the snow pack on which it lies. It is very difficult to assess the qualities of the first two, but the bond between the slab and the snow pack itself can be accurately determined by using the snow profile (page 314). The other major consideration is the angle of the slope. On slopes of less than 25° it is usually too shallow for the slab to slide and on slopes above 50° it is unusual for the snow to accumulate in sufficient quantities to cause a problem [*fig. 24.7*].

Fig 24.8 A typical slab avalanche. This slide is not full-depth – that is, the slab has slid on another layer of snow and not on the ground.

Powder-Snow Avalanches

When snow falls in windless or near-windless conditions, powder-snow avalanches may be expected. The risk will be dependent upon how much snow has fallen and over what time scale, but a fall of more than 3cm per hour, depositing in excess of 40cm of fresh snow, will represent a high risk. Powder avalanches will release when the sheer weight of the snow becomes more than the snow bonds within the snow pack can bear. Often this will release no more than a small slough of snow known as a spindrift avalanche, common when climbing in gullies or buttresses. This continuous release of small slides can sometimes be a good sign, indicating that there is no

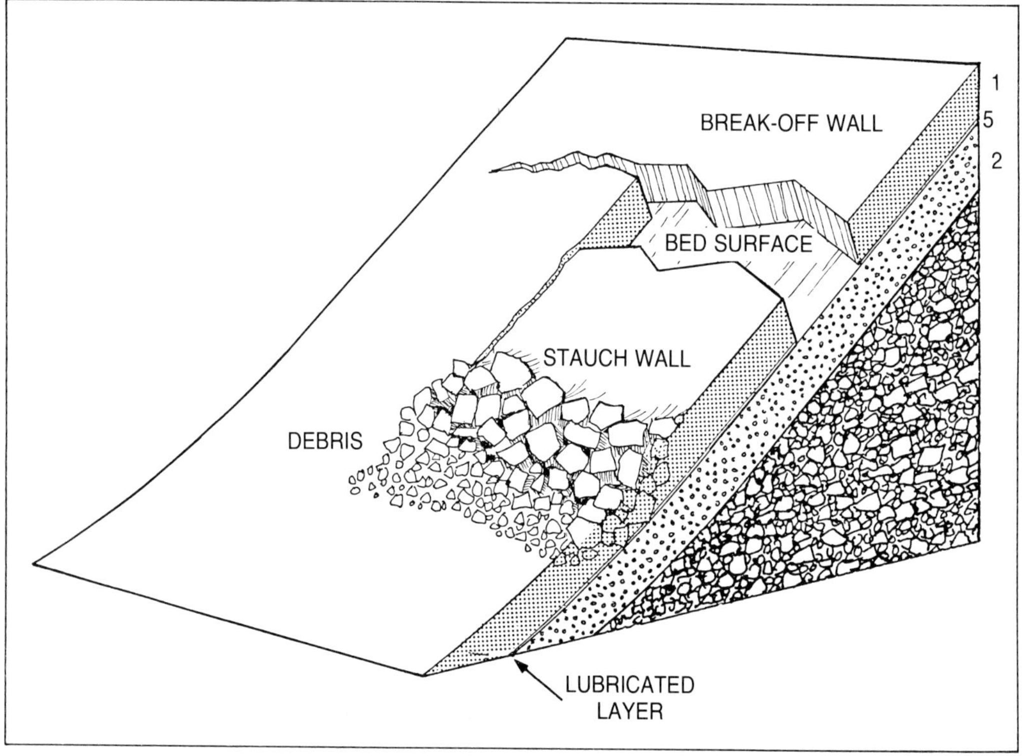

large accumulation of powder which later may release in a much more serious avalanche. Large powder avalanches can reach enormous speeds and push walls of air ahead of them which can be very destructive. Powder snow will become more stable when affected by the ET met. process or MF met. This is usually some twenty-four hours after it has fallen but will of course depend on the temperature: the colder the temperature, the longer it will take, and if it is below −10°C, these processes occur so slowly as to be almost non-existent.

Ice Avalanches

Ice avalanches usually occur either in warm weather when the ice thaws and suspended ice masses fall; or, in the case of seracs and ice falls, they can occur at any time [*fig. 18.3*, feature 15, page 257]. Seracs and ice falls are usually more stable when there are no rapid temperature changes, thus being more unstable in the first heat of the day and the first cold of the evening. However, the main cause of serac collapse is not temperature change but the irresistible force of gravity causing the glacier to move downhill. It is dangerous and sometimes even foolhardy to try to predict with any degree of certainty when or where a serac will fall. It is basically a matter of deciding how stable or unstable any of the towers or pinnacles of ice actually look.

Wet-Snow Avalanches

Wet-snow avalanches can occur at any time when the temperature is above zero. In such conditions it will be fairly obvious that the risk is present: there will be dripping water, sagging cornices and often snowballs will be seen rolling down from above. If these balls increase in size as they roll, the chances of a wet-snow slide are high. These avalanches are common not only in mild weather but also in areas exposed to strong sunlight, especially late in the afternoon.

Any rapid rise in temperature should be treated with suspicion as this will bring not only wet-snow slides but also a general increase in the avalanche risk.

CORNICES

Cornices are overhanging masses of snow which can form at any sharp change in angle but usually on the crest of ridges and plateaus. Formed by the wind, these petrified waves of snow overhang lee slopes and can be an obstacle and a danger to climbers. The wind, snow availability and the angle of the slope facing the wind are the main factors affecting their size and distribution. They form if the windward slope angle is between 42° below the horizontal and 18° above it, the optimum angle being 17° below [*fig. 24.9*].

Cornices can present problems when approached from any direction. From the windward side or going along their length, as on a ridge, the actual point where they join the ground is difficult to determine and they may be far more undercut than their appearance suggests. The break-off is often well back from the edge, not vertically above it. This means that a line well below the crest must be taken if at all possible. This can be difficult on a narrow ridge, so you should use rock anchors where you can when climbing roped; if you are moving together, each person should be prepared to jump down the slope opposite the cornice to counter-act the motion of the other should he fall through or the cornice collapse. If you are approaching or following a cornice in bad visibility, it is as well to be roped up.

Occasionally double cornices can be found on ridges, especially on higher mountains. In this case the cornices face opposite sides of the ridge and are due to changes in wind direction. Traversing them is like walking a tightrope.

When a cornice is approached from below, at least the problem is obvious. If it has to be climbed, this should normally be done at its smallest point which is usually at one side of a gully or where a buttress or ridge abuts the main line of the cornice. The second should belay to one side of the proposed attack point, preferably on rock, and if required a deadman runner placed before the final steepening. This keeps the belayer out of the line of fire of debris or even the cornice itself should it collapse. The actual method used to get over a cornice depends on its size and hardness, but with large cornices it is often worth traversing a long way to outflank them. If the cornice is composed of soft snow, a trench may be cut through it; if large, it may have to be tunnelled. Either way involves a lot of hard digging, usually with the adze, although using a bigger implement such as a snow shovel, a

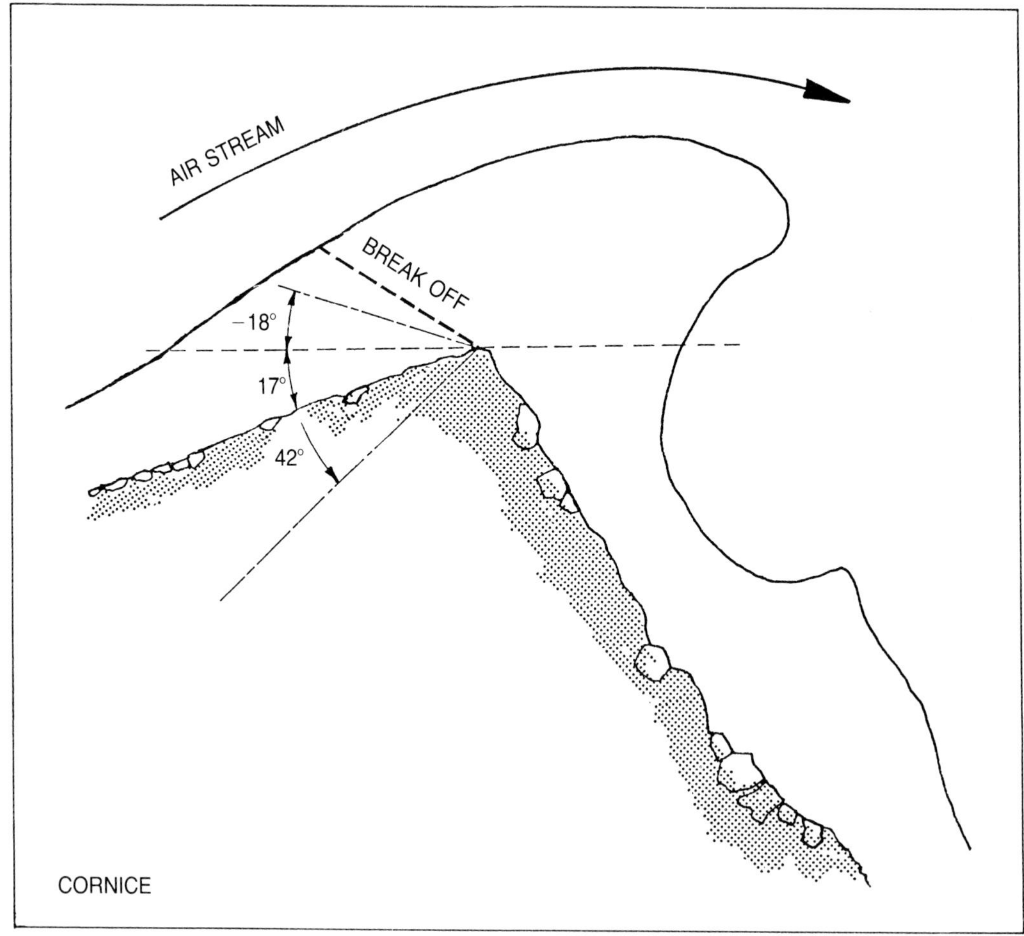

Fig 24.9 The make-up of a cornice.

deadman or even the hands can speed things up. Really large cornices may take hours of cold, laborious work to tunnel with the ever-present risk of weakening the cornice and causing it to collapse. Some cornices may be doubled or even trebled as they pile up on top of one another. It may be possible to surmount them individually, linking up the smallest points by moving along the slot that can form between them.

If the cornice is very hard, it may be possible to climb it with conventional front-pointing techniques, but kicking steps and using the axe shaft is the more usual way. Some cornices may require artificial techniques, with the shafts of axes pounded into the snow to act as aid points. This is a precarious and scary procedure as the snow in cornices often varies considerably in hardness over very short distances.

PRECAUTIONS FOR MOVEMENT ON AVALANCHE-PRONE TERRAIN

All climbers must make conscious decisions about the avalanche risk every time they venture on to snow or ice. While avalanche prediction is an imprecise science, if the basic tests and procedures outlined above are taken into account, the prediction of avalanches becomes more than a game of chance. Those people who are unlucky enough to be avalanched more often than is the norm should look carefully at their route planning and their knowledge of snow structure. Obviously the safest course of action is not to climb at all on snowy terrain and it is here that the crux of the matter lies. Somewhere between complete safety and danger lies an acceptable course and it is up to each person to decide where this course lies for them. Sometimes you may wish to climb when conditions are dangerous and unsuitable. At such times careful choice of a route can increase the level of safety and so permit climbing to take place [*fig. 24.10*]. After heavy snow falls, ridges and buttresses provide safer routes. However, it is not only the climb itself which must be considered but also the approach to and descent from the route and the possibility of avalanches which might affect it from above.

It may in some circumstances be necessary to cross a slope which has been judged dangerous. When this happens, it is best to cross one at a time so that only one person is exposed to danger at any time. The rope should be used to safeguard the person crossing and the slope either ascended or descended straight up and down. Sheltered positions, rock outcrops or any other ground features which offer cover and safety should be taken advantage of. If a slope has to be crossed, it should be traversed as high up as is feasible so that, if you are avalanched, there is less snow above to bury you. Convexities and steepenings in the slope should be avoided.

Fig 24.10 This section through a hillside shows how the terrain and wind affect the avalanche risk on a local level. Areas scoured by the wind are safer; areas of snow deposition more dangerous.

Survival if Caught

If you are avalanched, try to delay your departure from your position for as long as possible. The more snow that passes by you, the less there will subsequently be to bury you. In the case of a slab avalanche it is sometimes possible quickly to drive the tools in above the break-off wall and so maintain your position in this way. If this is not successful and you find yourself falling in the avalanche, you should try to manoeuvre yourself to the flow's edge. This can be done by rolling sideways. Since the head and shoulders are heavier than the legs, you will tend to roll in an arc and so reach the safety at the side. Alternatively, swimming motions are said to be successful in keeping you near the surface. In any event, try not to inhale snow into the lungs, and try to brake on the slope beneath. If none of this is successful, you should save your maximum energy for a last-gasp effort when you feel the avalanche start to slow down. Your life may depend on being able to fight to the surface at this time, again best done by means of swimming motions.

If you are buried, try to clear a breathing space

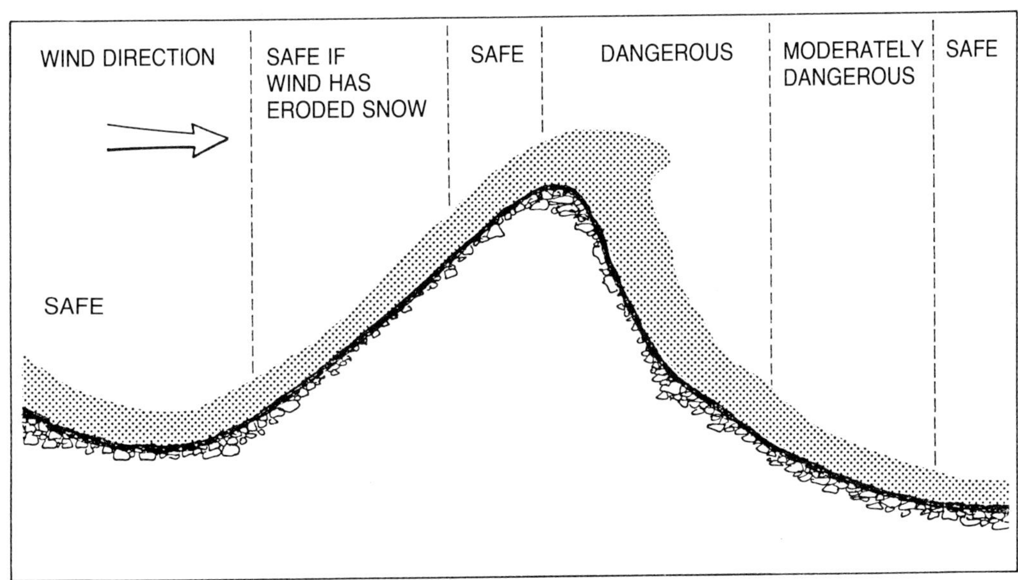

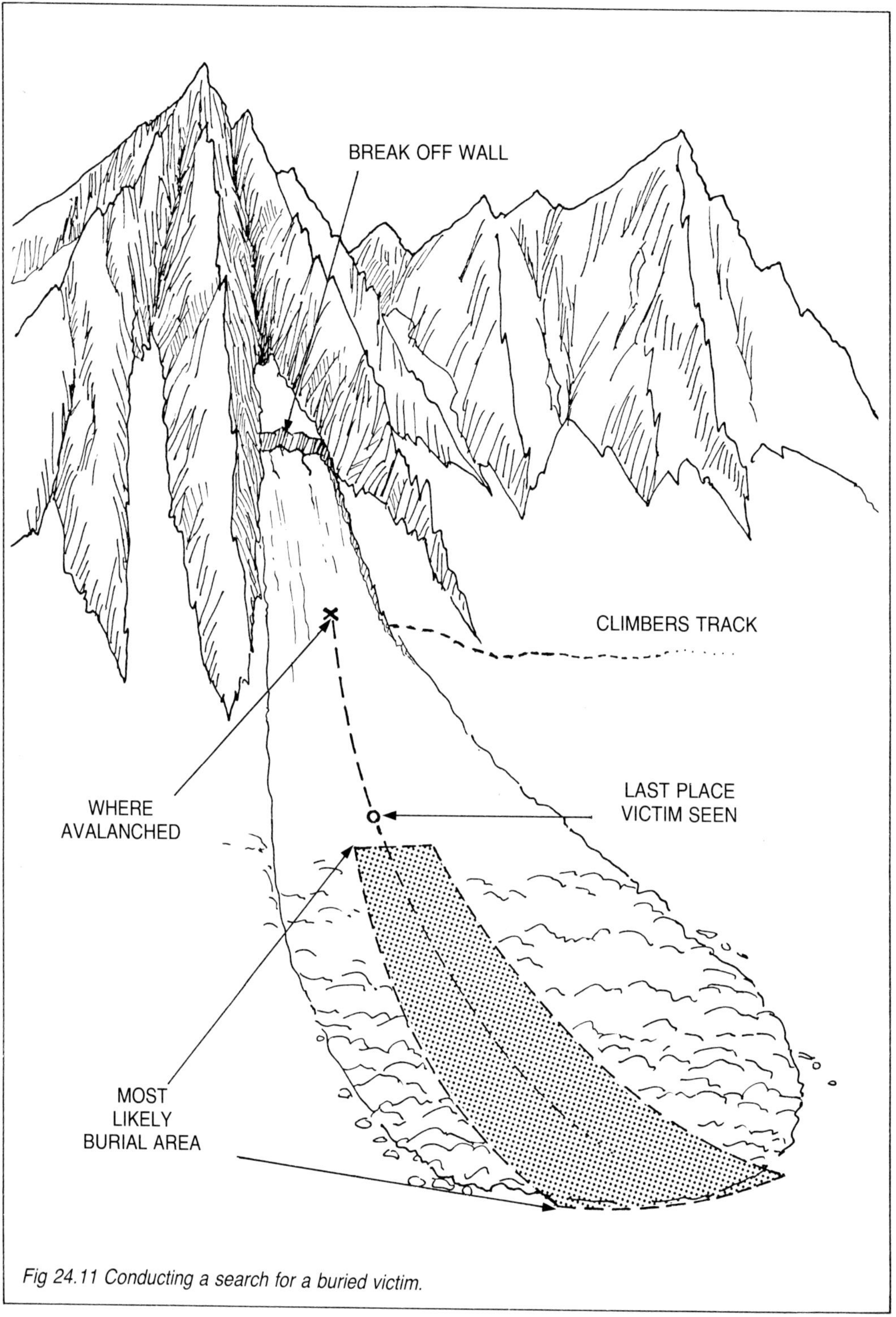

Fig 24.11 Conducting a search for a buried victim.

in front of the face: this is sometimes but not always possible just as the avalanche stops. If any part of you is above the surface, try to draw attention to yourself and free yourself from the snow. If you are completely buried, it is not usually possible to dig yourself out as even 20cm of snow can be enough to immobilise you. If this is the case, try not to panic but attempt to conserve the limited amount of oxygen available. Shouting is not only a waste of oxygen but also a waste of time as snow is such a good insulator that even people only a short distance away will not hear you.

Rescue

If you witness an avalanche accident in which someone is buried, mark the last place where they were seen and also the spot from which they were avalanched. The likely burial point will be below and on a line linking these two points. Conduct an immediate search for the buried person [*fig. 24.11*]. It is absolutely vital that this initial search is done as quickly and as thoroughly as possible. Unless help is very close by (no more than fifteen minutes away), no attempt should be made to seek outside help until the search has been carried out. Survival time decreases dramatically after one hour of burial [*fig. 24.12*].

The initial search is, in the first instance, a visual one: look for anything protruding from the snow – and also for clothing and rucksacks which have been ripped off by the avalanche and which may give some clue as to the burial spot. If this is not successful, the slope should be probed in a systematic manner with whatever is available – for example, ice axes, ski sticks and tent poles can all be used. The area of maximum debris accumulation is searched first and, if this is not successful, any places where a victim could be buried in the avalanche's path are also checked.

When the victim is located, the head and mouth should be cleared of snow immediately and any weight of snow constricting the chest removed. If the victim is not breathing, artificial resuscitation should be started immediately. Do not wait until the whole body has been exposed.

Fig 24.12 Survival time for an avalanche victim.

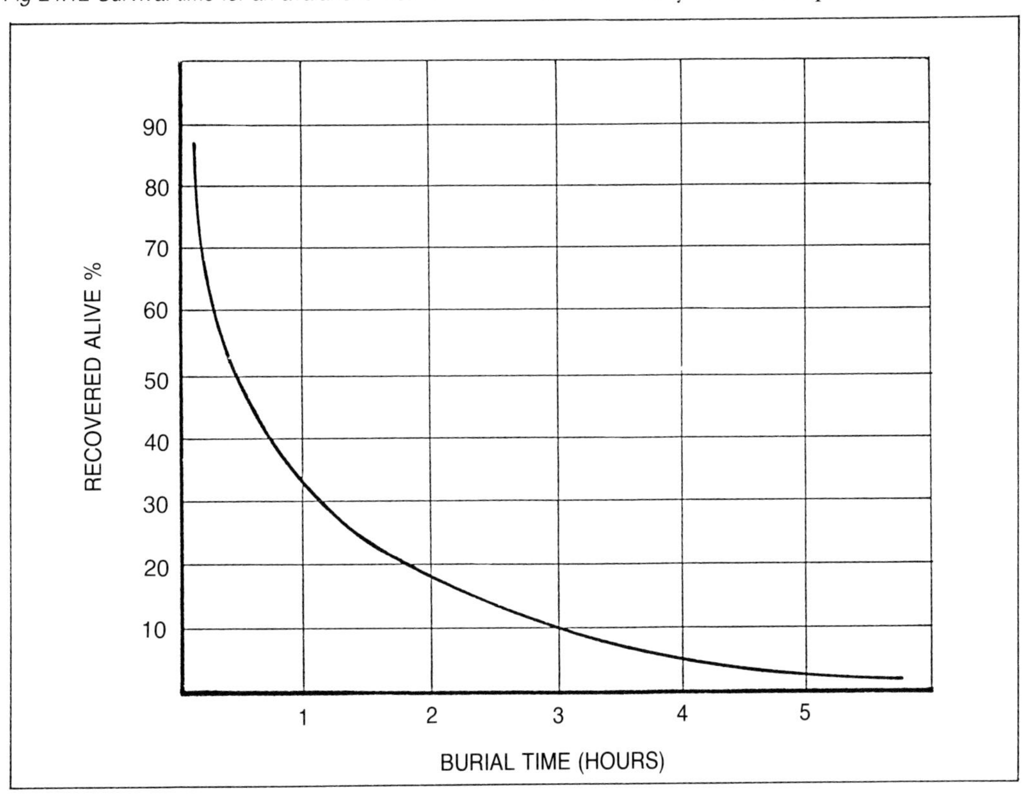

25 Snow Shelters

The use of snow as a building and shelter material has been known to man for centuries. The best examples of this use of snow are provided by the Eskimoes, whose igloos perhaps typify our idea of snow as a building medium. However, igloos require a great deal of time and energy to complete and in mountaineering are seldom the best form of shelter. In the mountains the quickest and most efficient shelter to construct will normally be the best.

It is important to make a clear distinction between the two main types of snow shelter: those that are planned (here called snow holes), for whose construction and subsequent habitation the correct equipment is carried, and those which are emergency bivouac shelters and require no special or extra tools for their construction.

The amount of energy required to fashion a snow shelter of either type should not be underestimated – two to three hours can easily be spent in hard digging (with the correct tools!) to complete a snow hole which will allow the night to be passed in only reasonable comfort. In an emergency this energy could well be put to better use.

The type of snow shelter chosen will depend on the number of nights to be spent in the hole, the number of people involved and the suitability of the site and the snow available. In very general terms the shelter should take advantage of the natural snow formations and ground features. There must be sufficient snow to allow the hole to be dug to the envisaged size and great care and judgement must be exercised as regards the condition of the site with respect to avalanche risk.

PRACTICALITIES

Tools

Having the correct tools for digging makes the task very much easier. If a full-sized hole is envisaged, at least one large and one small shovel are required. Both should be as light as possible, but also resilient enough to withstand the punishment of digging. It is useful if they are collapsible, which makes carrying them easier. Although some shovels are designed to be used on the ice-axe shaft, digging is much easier with a traditional T-shaped handle. As well as shovels, a snow saw is also very useful, especially when the snow is hard. A saw with a thin steel blade about 30cm long and with large offset teeth is best; it should also have a handle which is easy to hold in a gloved hand. For emergency bivouacs or snow shelters improvisation is the key; the ice axe, deadman and feet may often be the only digging tools available.

Choosing a Site

The first priority when choosing a site is that there should be enough snow for the proposed shelter. If in doubt, this can be tested by probing. However, experience will greatly assist in the location of likely sites: these will be in stream beds, underneath cornices, on the lee side of ridges or behind boulders.

Some sites may be prone to avalanche and great care must be exercised in their choice. If the shelter is to be used for several days, possible changes in weather and snow build-up must be taken into account. In strong winds many metres of wind slab can accumulate, increasing the avalanche risk, making burial and suffocation a real danger and making the subsequent relocation of the shelter impossible.

If possible, the shelter should be positioned at the top of a slope as digging and clearing of the debris is much easier when assisted by gravity. The snow under a cornice may prove to be softer, and easier to dig into, than that on the slope below. Steep slopes are easier to dig into than easy-angled slopes (that is, they require the expenditure of less energy for the same result) but may need more care when you are digging and moving around.

Digging the Shelter

It is easier to move snow around in blocks than as chips or powder and so it is best, if possible, to use the saw to cut a grid in the snow wall [*fig. 25.1*] and then to lever the blocks out using the shovel. If this is not possible, try to use the shovel in such a way that blocks can be hacked free and allowed to fall into space. Whenever you can, ensure that there is enough space to manoeuvre as digging in a cramped, confined area is inefficient and energy-consuming.

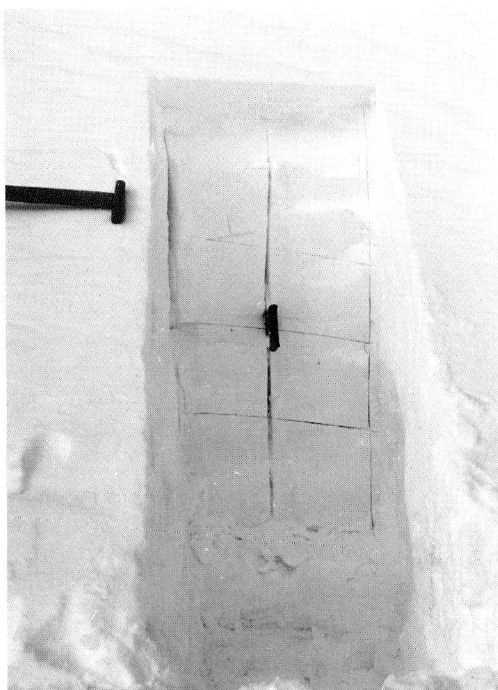

Fig 25.1 When cutting blocks, it is best to use the saw to form a grid as this greatly decreases the subsequent amount of work which must be done.

TYPES OF SNOW HOLE

Two-Door Hole

Digging a two-door hole is a very economical method of making a two- or three-person snow shelter. Choose a suitable and safe site, such as a steep bank of soft snow, and mark two doorways. These should be of shoulder width, high enough to allow unrestricted digging and 1.5m apart. Dig in a systematic and orderly fashion, both to reduce the energy expended and to make the removal of the debris much easier.

If the site allows the doorways to be positioned high on the slope, the removal of the excavated snow, under the influence of gravity, is easy; failing this, the excavated snow may have to be handled two or even three times.

The doorways should be dug parallel to each other until they are some 1m into the slope at the top [*fig. 25.2a*]. At this stage they may be joined together [*fig. 25.2b*] but avoid disturbing the

Fig 25.2a and b When digging a two-door hole (seen from the side and above), take care to leave a thick enough door pillar to support the roof. It should be at least 1m thick and 0.5m deep.

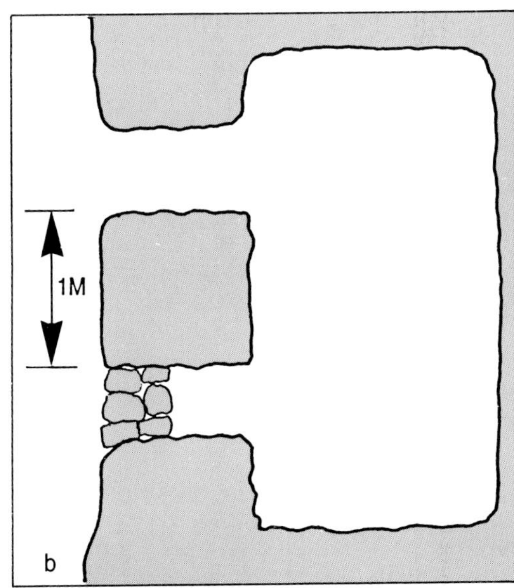

central pillar, from which the front wall of the hole derives its strength. When the doorways are linked forming a U-shaped tunnel, the hole can then be enlarged to the desired size. For three people this should be about 2m high and 3m square. For the most efficient use of this space, the floor/wall interface should be a smooth right angle and the roof/walls should be rounded off to a smooth finish [*fig. 25.3*], thus creating a half-sphere.

When the hole is nearing completion, the larger of the two doorways (or the least convenient for prolonged use) is blocked up with the remaining debris. This may have to be supplemented by blocks cut from outside or perhaps saved from the earlier digging [*fig. 25.4*].

Fig 25.3 The inside of a large, well-finished snow hole. This one could sleep seven or eight people!

Fig 25.4 When you are blocking up a doorway, use the snow bank to support the large blocks at the top of the door.

Snow Cave

The snow cave is similar to the two-door hole, but only one entrance is dug and the completed shelter is usually smaller in all dimensions, although it can be enlarged. The main disadvantage of this shelter is that only one person can dig at a time until the hole is well advanced. Not only is this slower but it also means that one person has no protection from the elements while the hole is being dug [*fig. 25.5*].

A good supply of air must be available inside the hole at all times. This can be difficult if drifting is taking place, as even large ventilation holes, including the main door, can quickly become snowed over. This drifting process can be insidious and difficult to spot. The lack of oxygen may not even be obvious until the stove or candle refuses to light, by which time the problem is acute. The best way to avoid this is by conscientious maintenance of an airway, which usually requires frequent bouts of digging, depending on the severity of the drifting.

In conditions when snow drifting in at the entrance is a possibility, the entrance should be extended by building a tunnel from snow blocks; this should be the same height as the door and about 1m long. This will stop the main hole from filling up with snow, and even if the tunnel becomes blocked the snow can be dug out and stowed inside the hole.

Holes which are dug in places frequented by others should be prominently marked so that they are easily seen and not fallen into. Not only does this preserve the hole but it also makes its subsequent re-location easier. If a number of holes are dug in the same site, the entrances should be linked together by a rope and the ends of the rope anchored inside each hole. If severe drifting is a problem, this makes it easier for people in adjoining holes to find each others' entrances, which are usually easier to clear from outside. Alternatively, tunnels can be dug in the

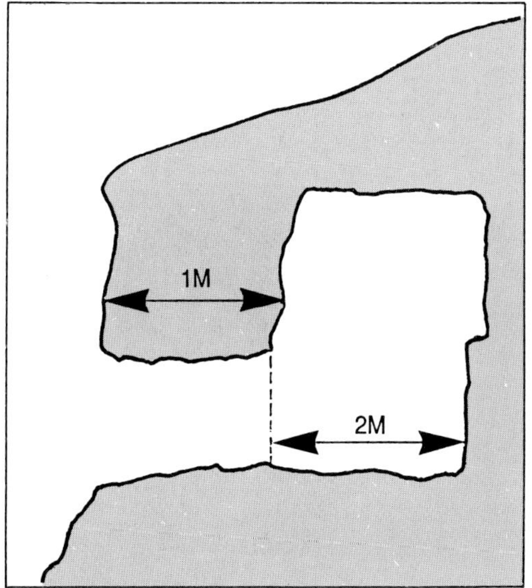

Fig 25.5 A section through a snow cave, seen from the side and above..

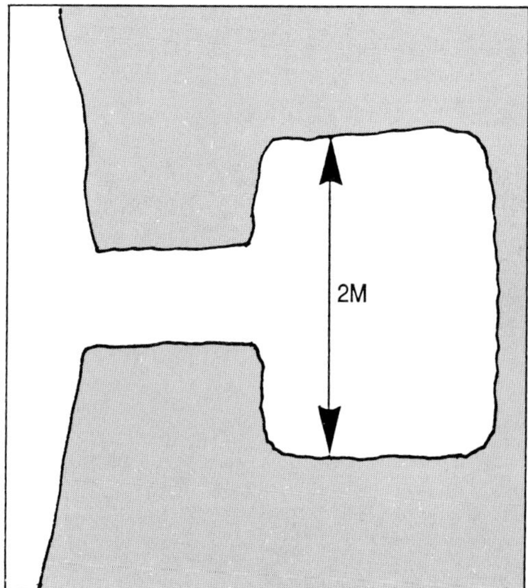

snow bank to link the holes together, but this is only feasible when the holes are close together.

Snow Mound

In cold, windless conditions when the only available snow is soft and powdery, the snow mound may be the only type of shelter possible. It relies upon the fact that disturbed powder snow undergoes a process of age hardening that makes the soft snow consolidate into a mass which can then be tunnelled into to form a shelter.

The powder snow is shovelled into a huge heap at least 3m in diameter and 2m high and left to consolidate for a minimum of two hours. Following this consolidation process, the centre of the mound is then excavated to provide a living space. The walls should always be left at least 50cm thick [*fig. 25.6*]. This shelter is useful only on flat ground with a thin covering of powder snow. It is more prone to temperature change and wind effects than other shelters.

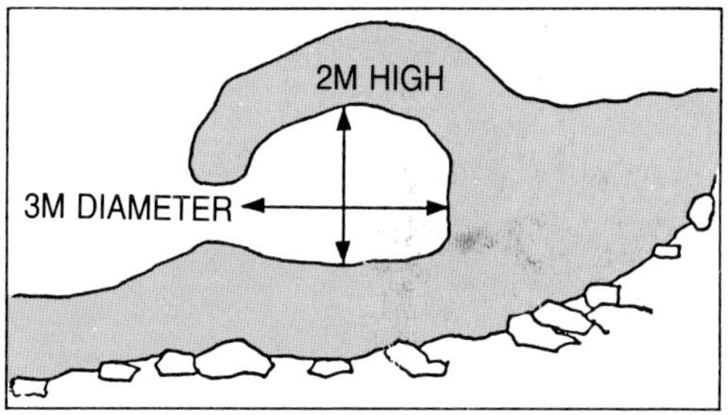

Fig 25.6 Soft snow mounds are good only in cold, windless conditions.

Igloo

In all but ideal conditions building an igloo is very time- and energy-consuming and requires a huge amount of good 'blocking snow'. This will normally be hard, wind-packed snow. Before starting construction, cut a large supply of blocks (this is a good test of the viability of the project as well as providing a ready supply of building materials). The blocks should be as large as possible and all approximately the same size. When sufficient blocks have been cut, mark out a circle of some 2.5m diameter on a suitable area of flat snow and, using it as a guide, make a circle of blocks laid end to end [*fig. 25.7*]. The joints between the blocks can be made a good fit by running the saw backwards and forwards along the joint between the blocks to remove the inside corners. When this initial ring is complete, cut it to form a tapering ramp as shown in the figure and add more blocks row by row until the characteristic igloo-shaped dome is formed.

Now cut an entrance hole at a convenient site. Remember that igloos are very susceptible to rises in temperature and wind strength.

Fig 25.7 Igloos are difficult and time-consuming to build. However, the building techniques employed are useful in other shelters.

In conditions which do not allow a full snow hole to be dug, it is often possible to dig in as far as possible and then to construct half an igloo on the outside [*fig. 25.8*].

EMERGENCY SNOW SHELTERS

By necessity emergency snow shelters need to be quickly and easily built – the exact type used depends on the circumstances, conditions and requirements pertaining at the time. It is best to allow the snow to dictate the final form and to take advantage of the easiest digging or blocking.

Bivi Hole

A bivi hole is most easily dug in a steep bank of soft snow. Tunnel inwards using the axe or another appropriate tool. Keep the tunnel small and circular, and of shoulder width if possible. When the tunnel is almost 1m long, cut a bench to sit on and a space for the head and shoulders. Once inside, away from the elements, the hole can be enlarged if needs be. This hole involves minimum snow movement and the quickest access to shelter from the wind [*fig. 25.9*]. When occupying a small hole like this, it is best to sit with the knees bent and the upper body hunched forwards. This keeps the area of body/snow contact to a minimum (only the seat touches the snow) and the rope or a foam mat can be sat on for insulation. You can block the doorway with your rucksack, or if it becomes too large you can use snow blocks to seal it [*fig. 25.10*].

Snow Grave

If it is necessary to build a shelter in a flat area, the snow grave is often the only possibility.

Mark a grid on the snow 2×0.75m [*fig. 25.11a*].

Fig 25.8 This shelter uses a shallow hole and an igloo combined.

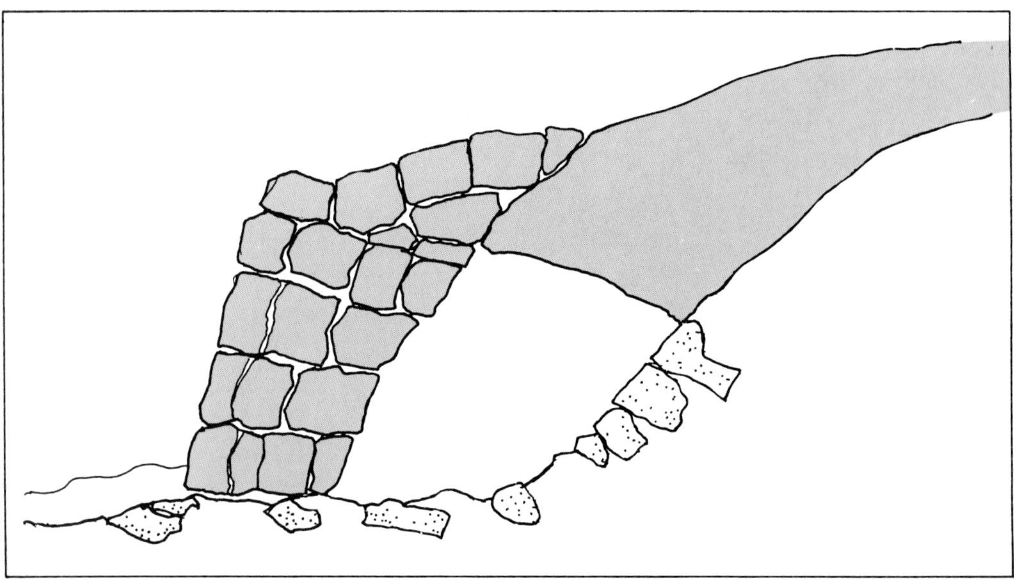

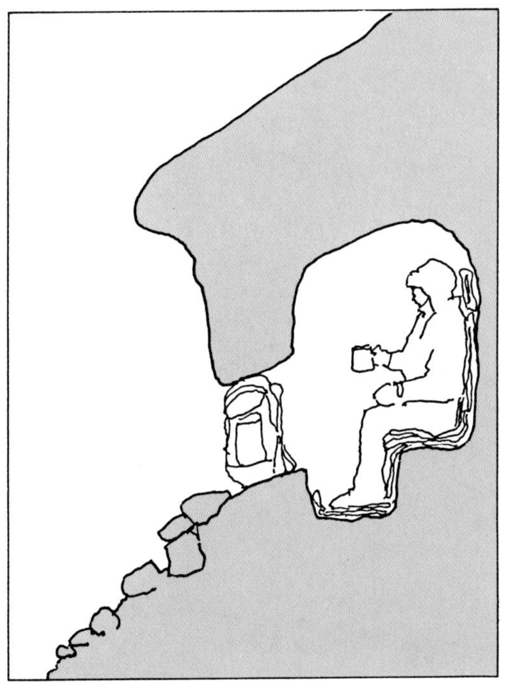

Fig 25.9 TOP AND ABOVE: *Digging a bivi hole involves minimum snow movement and is the quickest form of emergency shelter.*

Fig 25.10 ABOVE: *If the door to the emergency shelter becomes too large, blocks can be used to seal it up.*

Carefully cut out each block in the grid and store for later use. Then deepen the resulting hole and widen it to body size. If possible, leave a step to support the blocks [*fig. 25.11b*]. If this proves impossible (depending on snow type), it may be necessary to cut some larger blocks and to use these to roof the shelter. Position all the blocks over the trench apart from the last two: lay these alongside the head end. Enter the hole feet first and then slide the two remaining blocks over the open area above your head. It should be appreciated that this is a last-gasp shelter, as it is prone to being covered by drifting and involves the whole body being in contact with the snow. It does, however, provide some protection from the wind [*fig. 25.11c*]. As in any emergency shelter, try to have as little of the body in contact with the snow as possible. In a grave this means lying on your side with your knees drawn up.

ORGANISATION

The secret of any successful bivouac is the ability to improvise and the knowledge of how best to work with what is available. This comes only from practice and time spent in the construction of as many different types of shelter as possible. It is

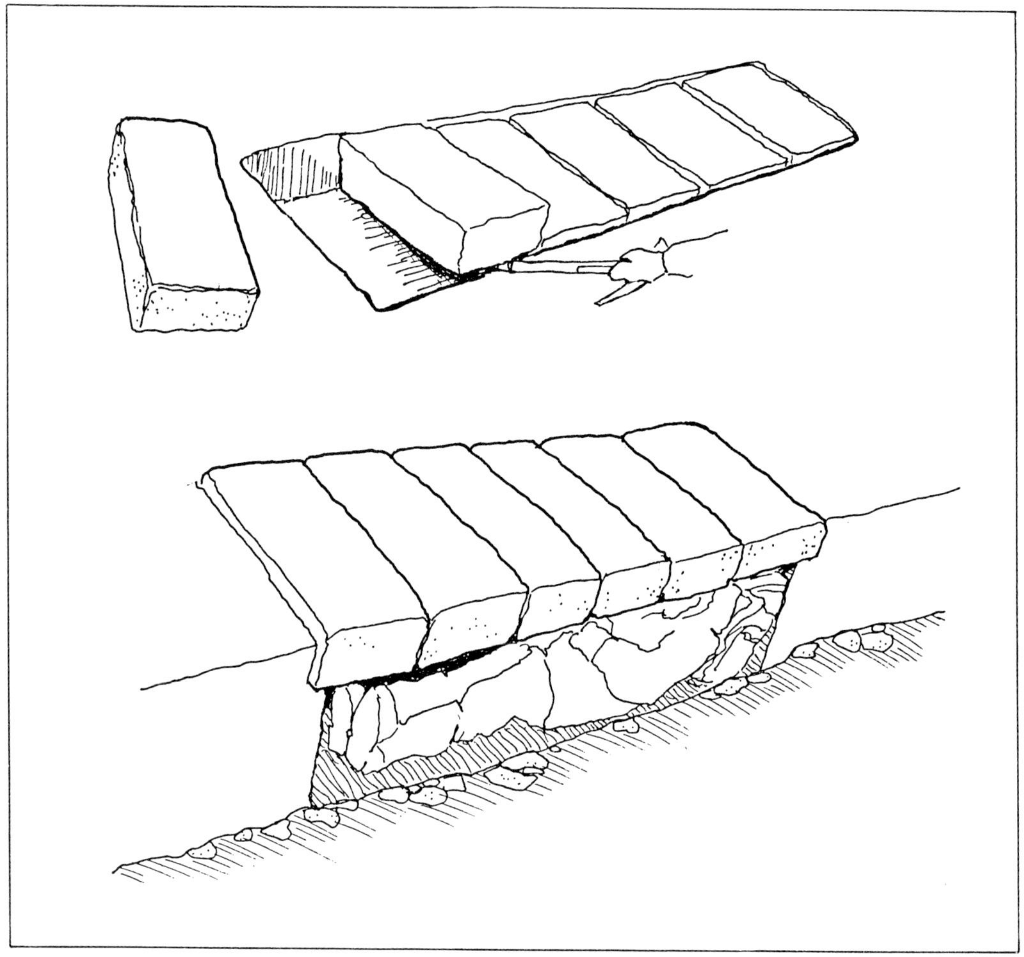

Fig 25.11 The snow grave. These are very prone to coverage by drifting but offer the only shelter on flat ground with a shallow build-up of snow.

also often possible to use a natural feature, such as a wind scoop or hollow, as the start of an emergency shelter. Make sure that all the possibilities have been explored before deciding on a site or type of shelter. Sometimes combinations of different types of construction are best. On a steep slope which has insufficient snow for a cave to be dug, you may be able to dig half a cave and then add half an igloo to complete the structure. On a gentle slope the downhill side of a snow grave can be built up to give a roomier shelter. Often the soft snow found under a cornice can be exploited – this can be good both for digging and block cutting. In glaciated areas good shelters can sometimes be found 'ready-made' inside crevasses and bergschrunds.

In some conditions it is not possible to cut large blocks and so supports for roofs and doors must be improvised. This can be done using ski sticks, ice axes or rucksack frames, depending upon what is available. If only small blocks can be cut, these can be used like house building bricks and built up in layers with snow stuffed in any cracks to act as cement.

Perhaps the most important and most neglected aspect of using a snow hole or shelter is the organisation of yourself and your equipment inside the shelter. In all cases the conservation of heat and energy are the prime requirements. Everything possible should be done from the confines of the sleeping bag: the less movement, the better. Ensure that the body is well insulated from the underlying snow by using close cell mats or air mattresses. This is especially important in emergency shelters, and a small piece of mat kept in the rucksack for just such a situation is invaluable. Alternatively the rope, climbing gear or the rucksack can be used as insulation between your body and the snow. Modern fabrics that can 'breathe', such as Goretex and Entrant, have made it possible to stay both warm and dry for long periods even in very cold and wet conditions and these should be used whenever possible. As well as being used for clothing, these materials are also made up into bags, which completely cover you, your gear and your sleeping bag. These are ideal for all bivouac situations.

When cooking in a snow shelter, make sure that a supply of snow for melting is readily available. Hack some blocks at the end of the digging phase rather than cut them from the inside of the cave and in the process cover the contents of the cave with ice chips. Prolonged boiling of fluids should be avoided as the steam created causes a glaze to form on the inside of the hole and this will subsequently cause dripping. If the hole is to be inhabited for several days, it may be necessary to scrape off this icy layer to allow the snow pack to absorb the moisture produced by the occupants.

A small brush is very useful for cleaning snow from the clothes and boots, so enabling them to be dried, packed away or used as a pillow. Shelves cut in the wall of the shelter make handy stores for gear, and candles placed on them cast a surprising amount of light as well as slightly raising the inside temperature.

It is vitally important to ensure that there is adequate ventilation in the shelter, especially at night and when cooking, as suffocation and carbon monoxide poisoning are real problems in conditions of severely drifting snow or at high altitude. Often the only sure way of maintaining this ventilation is by regular and thorough excavation of the entrance, perhaps as often as every hour if conditions so demand.

26 Training

by Ally Morgan

These days training for climbing is an accepted part of the sport and, to participate at the higher standards, a necessity. However, training at any level can result in improved performance and so enhance enjoyment and satisfaction. Improvement can show itself through a general increase in standard, an increase in climbing speed or the ability to make greater use of your time out climbing. The desire to train is born of an individual's personal perceptions of the sport, enthusiasm and motivation. It is only in recent years that climbers have sought out the kind of information on fitness and training that was regarded as the preserve of the athlete. Yet it is no easy matter to construct training programmes for the rock, ice or Alpine climber without first appraising the physical (and mental) demands that are placed on them. Upon analysis the specific requirements become clear but individual needs, personal strengths and weaknesses, availability of time and resources as well as lifestyle all have to be taken into account.

However, the fundamental principles of training theory are the same for everyone. These principles should be used to guide you towards the construction of your own training plan and allow you to research the various exercises and techniques from other literature. There is great scope for individualism and originality in training, which is in keeping with the sport itself.

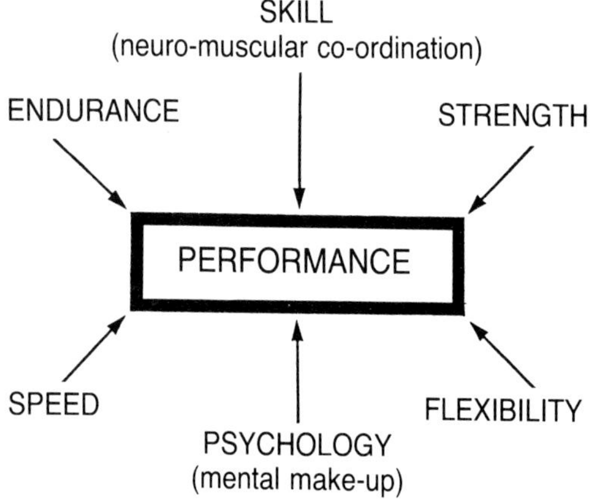

Fig 26.1 Aspects of training.

The model shown in *fig. 26.1* can apply to most sports and activities of a physical nature. If the profile of a climber is considered, it is seen that all the components shown in the figure require to be present, but being able to prioritise is the first step in devising an efficient and profitable training regime. It is appropriate to look at endurance, strength and flexibility in some detail, while also recognising the vital importance of technical ability and mental state in the improvement of performance.

ENDURANCE

Endurance is the body's ability to persist in physical activity and a measure of that quality is its resistance to fatigue and capacity to recover from such activity. The variable that is critical here is the intensity of exercise for it determines which physiological mechanisms are being challenged. These mechanisms operate at the heart/ lung complex and at the local muscular level with oxygenated blood being transported from one to the other via the vascular network. Hence, cardio-respiratory endurance is concerned with the efficiency of the heart and lungs, particularly the former, in delivering oxygen to the working muscles, while local muscular endurance is concerned with the function of muscle in the presence of this transported oxygen or, as also happens, in its absence.

Thus, energy for muscle action is derived from two sources. The aerobic system operates with vital oxygen, while the anaerobic system comes into play when no oxygen is available. The latter can occur either as a result of heart/lung inefficiency at high workloads or simply because even with a supply of oxygen around the muscle it is unable to utilise it. Muscles that are in a high state of tension due to excessive bulk or a very intensive workload can have their blood supply cut off. The penalty for invoking the anaerobic system is great because continuation of that level of hard work is short-lived (no longer than two minutes in a trained athlete) and unless there is a reduction in the intensity of output, the fatiguing by-product, lactic acid, accumulates in the muscle and eventually inhibits the quality of its function.

There is an obvious need, therefore, to ensure that your aerobic capacity is high so that you can perform efficiently and relatively tirelessly without having to step over the so-called anaerobic threshold and suffer the punishing consequences. Aerobic training can distance that threshold, but for anyone other than the occasional participant, training with an anaerobic emphasis is also vital if increased levels of performance are to be achieved.

Thus the following basic principles can be established:

- Develop and then maintain a high level of aerobic endurance. This is often referred to as general endurance and is regarded as the basis of all training.
- Training your muscles to function anaerobically, to resist fatigue and to recover faster is necessary if extreme use of the arms and legs is required. This component of fitness is known as strength endurance.

Aerobic Endurance

Improvements in aerobic capacity can be readily achieved by:

- Raising the pulse rate into a training zone which is 70-85 per cent of the maximum heart rate. This maximal figure is obtained by using the formula 220 minus one's age.
- Exercising at this level for a minimum of twenty minutes continuously and a sensible maximum of around forty minutes. Longer durations are possible with improved fitness, but it is questionable whether any increased benefit is obtained, particularly when it is balanced against the possibility of local injury.
- Training an optimal three times a week.

Running

Universally recognised exercise modes that challenge the body aerobically are running, cycling, swimming and circuit training (with or without weights). The all-over nature of these activities is particularly relevant to mountaineering. Running for aerobic development has one other important advantage. With increased availability of oxygen the main energy provision at lower levels of work is through the metabolism of fat, so enabling the body to retain limited stores of carbohydrate, the main fuel for more intensive, vigorous activity. For the rock climber a degree of weight control is the reward; for the mountaineer the body is better able to preserve the quantities of carbohydrate necessary to sustain long days in the hills. Anyone intending to implement a running programme should gradually increase the duration (distance) of their runs before improving their quality by attempting to reduce the time taken.

Variety in any training routine is desirable if optimal adaptations are to be made. Running on an interval basis from time to time, instead of continuously, has considerable merit. For example, intervals of five or ten minutes can be used with equal periods of active recovery in between. Such an approach, with shorter intervals and recovery periods, can also be adopted to challenge the anaerobic endurance capacity of the legs.

The same interval principle can be incorporated into a single run by varying the pace for specified amounts of time, or by allowing a change in terrain to dictate it. In this way the anaerobic threshold can be approached and crossed on occasions with these excursions challenging further the aerobic system and also, importantly, improving the efficiency of the recovery process from these more intensive bursts of activity. The relevance to climbing should not be missed here.

Greater variation can be introduced by devising a 'trim-trail' type of running circuit. Here, the run is interspersed with stations of exercises with or without specialist equipment. Body weight exercises such as pull-ups, press-ups, dips and sit-ups are ideal.

Circuit Training

Circuit training has stood the test of time as an effective training method, and if a circuit is constructed carefully, it can be yet another means of improving specific aerobic efficiency. Remember to apply the principles outlined previously:

- Work continuously from station to station for a

minimum period of twenty minutes, or alternatively as follows.

- Work on an interval basis with, say, five or ten minutes as the working time and a similar recovery period in between. Each period of activity could be equivalent to one complete circuit of the exercises.
- Use exercises that involve large muscle groups within whole body movements and try to avoid having similar exercises at adjacent stations.
- Aim to complete more circuits or parts of circuits in a set time before fixing the load and trying to beat target times.

Even more specific aerobic training can be devised by substituting real climbing moves on walls, boulders and outcrops for the exercises used in the 'trim-trail' or circuit approaches. There is much scope for originality here, and as long as the place of aerobic conditioning in your training programme is borne in mind and the appropriate principles applied, all work can be enjoyable as well as beneficial.

STRENGTH

Strength is probably the main quality that is seen to characterise the climber. The opportunity to climb longer or harder routes will be the reward for dedicated strength training, but it is worth remembering that a greater degree of conditioning in, say, the thighs, will also have the effect of reducing the amount of stress on the knees caused by years of walking, pounding and running downhill. Strength is indeed a fundamental component of the climber's make-up and a short investigation of this quality is necessary if we are to understand how to train for improvement.

Maximal strength is the maximum force that a muscle or group of muscles can produce against some form of resistance.

Explosive strength, sometimes known as power, is concerned with a high level of force being applied in a very short period of time, and the speed with which tension is developed in the muscle is critical in this type of situation. A dyno is a good example of the use of explosive strength.

Strength endurance, also referred to as local muscular endurance, is that component which bridges the gap between maximal strength and endurance by challenging the muscles to continue functioning without tiring. This quality is dependent on local mechanisms within the muscle that are concerned with the production of energy with and without oxygen. Training these energy pathways, most notably the anaerobic system, will without question improve your ability to 'stay on'. As mentioned, maximal strength levels are also significant in the ability of muscles to keep working when loaded, and so a development of this kind of strength is a prerequisite for gains in muscular endurance. Indeed, maximal strength is that basic element which influences not only strength endurance but also explosive strength.

Before discussing methods of strength training, it is worth considering the type of tension that is developed in a muscle when climbing and to use such specific information in constructing the strength programme. When a muscle shortens to overcome a resistance, as, for example, the biceps would if a pull-up were being done, the contraction is known as a concentric contraction. When the muscle lengthens to lower the body under control, the contraction is an eccentric one. Thus, strength training of an isotonic nature would be necessary to reflect this feature of movement in these two situations. When the muscle is static and possesses a degree of tension that is in balance with the resistance, an isometric contraction is said to be taking place. A climber in a locked-off position, or merely stationary, will be demonstrating isometric muscle action. It will be seen, therefore, that isometric work will be of value in supplementing the isotonic work in preparing for increased performance on rock or ice.

If muscles are subjected to systematic stressing under a training regime, the constituent fibres adapt by becoming more efficient, better organised and more responsive to impulses from the nervous system. Resistance training for strength is synonymous with weight training and that medium is the most important for climbers. Weight training is indicated for those wishing to develop the basic quality of maximal strength and they should use this as a foundation for strength endurance and explosive strength.

Specialist advice is recommended for those embarking on a weights programme since the 'point of entry' depends on the level of fitness and previous weight-training experience, and this has to be sensibly determined to eliminate the risk of injury.

Maximal Strength

The following schedules will prove useful, provided that the key principle of progressive overload is applied. A complete beginner should decide on the exercises to be performed and, using light weights, practise the correct techniques before starting a schedule. Such an introduction will also serve to tone up muscles and reduce the chances of muscle damage. For this reason and for simplicity, the use of machines as opposed to free weights is recommended here, but the latter approach lends itself more productively to the work of the experienced weight trainer.

All weight training systems are based on the use of a repetition maximum (RM). RM is the maximum load that a muscle or muscle group can lift in a given number of repetitions before failure. For example:

1 RM – maximum load that can be lifted once
10 RM – maximum load that can be lifted ten times

The De Lorme-Watkins method is suggested as a starting programme. Here, having selected the exercises which should be of a general and balanced nature, experiment to find the 10 RM for each.

Three sets of ten repetitions (10 RM load as basis)

Set 1 – ten reps. @ 50 per cent 10 RM
Set 2 – ten reps. @ 75 per cent 10 RM
Set 3 – ten reps. @ 100 per cent 10 RM

A recovery interval between sets of two to three minutes is taken. Initially failure will occur during set 3. It is the stimulus at this time that is mainly responsible for strength development. Progress to a new 10 RM is made when the original 10 RM load can be handled fifteen times during set 3.

After four weeks, progress from this method to a 'simple sets' system. Again use 10 RM as a basis but gradually reduce this to 8 RM over a number of weeks:

Three sets of ten (or eight) repetitions

Set 1 – ten (eight) reps. @ 100 per cent 10 RM (8 RM)
Set 2 – ten (eight) reps. @ 100 per cent 10 RM (8 RM)
Set 3 – ten (eight) reps. @ 100 per cent 10 RM (8 RM)

The same load is used on all sets with fatigue resulting in possible failure to complete the target of repetitions in sets 2 and 3. Progress is made by increasing the resistance appropriately when three sets of ten (or eight) repetitions can be achieved with correct technique.

For those who are more experienced the Berger method will prove more useful in effecting maximal strength gains. This operates on exactly the same principle as the 'simple sets' approach, except that a six-repetition maximum is used as the base.

The trend towards decreasing the number of repetitions and increasing the resistance can be continued with a method that would suit anyone who has been working with weights for a period of two years or more. The pyramid method of training uses 1 RM as a basis and involves the handling of much heavier weights right up to the lifting of maximum on occasions. It can be seen that from the establishment of the 1 RM to the times when a single repetition is attempted, great care, judgement and experience are necessary. It would be wise to seek expert help if you decide to develop the sophistication and effectiveness of your weight training in this way.

A typical schedule might be:

Four sets consisting of eight, six, four and two repetitions

Set 1 – eight reps. @ 50 per cent 1 RM
Set 2 – six reps. @ 65 per cent 1 RM
Set 3 – four reps. @ 80 per cent 1 RM
Set 4 – two (or one) reps. @ 90–100 per cent 1 RM

All pyramid systems are designed to produce a high level of fatigue culminating in maximum effort in the last sets. Progress is made by maintaining the pyramid structure and increasing in stages the weights lifted. The occasional re-test for 1 RM or maximal will provide considerable incentive and encouragement.

Advanced training routines worthy of investiga-

Fig 26.2 Climbing walls, if well designed and offering a suitable variety of climbing types and problems, can be one of the more enjoyable forms of training.

tion are: reverse pyramids, super-sets, pre-exhaustion sets and split routines.

For climbers, exercises such as pull-ups, sit-ups and dips should be included in weights sessions designed for maximal strength development by the use of weight discs attached to the body in a safe manner or, in the case of sit-ups, held on the chest. At this stage it is worth reminding enthusiasts that all work on the upper body and legs should be of a general and balanced nature with very little bias towards climbing specifically. This is because too much concentration on certain muscles early on in a training programme, and indeed at any time, can lead to chronic injury.

Strength Endurance

This ground work in the 'off season' can be followed by more specific strength endurance training which can be linked by first altering the emphasis with weights. Circuit training also plays a part here. Greater repetitions – up to twenty or thirty – with lower resistances become the order of the day until this form of increased duration of the work load can be applied to arm 'climbing' exercises such as pull-ups on a bar or ledge, rope climbs and traverses, rope-ladder climbs, wall climbs and traverses, bouldering and top-roping on outcrops.

Remember that at this time the aim is to overload more extensively the climbing muscles in the shoulders and arms in order to increase their ability to work aerobically and particularly anaerobically. The depletion of energy stores in the muscles, the production and tolerance of lactic acid during exercise and its clearance during recovery are characteristics of this phase of training. Such processes are conveyed by the feeling of being 'pumped', especially in the forearms, and by speedy recovery after shaking out.

The unfit climber, because of the very short time limit on pure anaerobic activity of this type, will get 'pumped' very quickly during a bout of climbing-type training that focuses on the fore-arms, upper arms and shoulders, while the trained performer will need to complete a far greater volume of work in order to achieve a similar effect. The technique of pre-exhausting muscles, using weights, before specific local work of this kind can cut corners in terms of effective use of available time for the well-conditioned climber.

It is vital to take into account the strength endurance properties of the muscles of the forearm when considering the principle of speci-ficity in climbing. Great strength in the shoulder and upper arm is of no use if the fingers are unable to maintain their grip on a hold. It is appropriate, then, that rock climbers subject themselves to 'fingery' work on ledges, edges, finger boards and climbing walls when training – but a loud word of warning here: such work should be built on a sound foundation of general strength condition-ing and its extreme specificity should never fool you into believing that this is the only form of effective training. The penalties for prolonged and continuous use of the fingers are conditions such as osteo-arthritis, which is a wearing-out of the joints' lubricating surfaces resulting from the protective synovial fluid being squeezed from between the articular surfaces of the bones of the fingers. The risk of this occurring can be reduced by warming up the finger joints before activity; avoiding prolonged static dead hangs using the fingertips; allowing the fingers to recover proper-ly between sets of 'fingery' work (give them at least ten to fifteen minutes) and between sessions on the gym or on the wall (they need two days in this instance); and trying, whenever possible, to wrap all the knuckles of all the fingers around the pull-up bar, ledge or hold.

Tendinitis, an inflammation of the membrane surrounding tendons, is another condition that can become chronic and, at worst, put climbers permanently out of action. Tendons allow limbs to operate at a distance from muscles and the small tendons that allow the muscles of the forearm to move the fingers are particularly susceptible to this kind of damage. These tendons

Fig 26.3 When high on a wall or a boulder problem, it is helpful to have someone to 'spot' you if you fall or jump off.

and the tendons running through the elbow and shoulder are subjected to great stress during training of the type described, and balancing the risk of injury to them against the motivation to perform better is a matter of common sense. As before, reduce the risk by warming up thorough-ly; make recovery periods between hard work-outs a matter of days; avoid extended exercise on the fingertips and recognise that too much muscle work of an eccentric nature, or lowering and down-climbing on just the arms when extremely fatigued, can stress the elbow and shoulder tendons, causing the condition or aggravating it if it already exists.

The isometric element in the strength endur-ance requirements of a climber can be acknow-ledged by holding positions – say, in pull-ups – for a length of time before continuing isotonically for a further period. To obtain full benefit from this kind of approach it is important that the arms are

Fig 26.4 Training can take place on a whole variety of structures and some, such as this bridge wall, offer excellent climbing and training, if of a limited type.

locked off in a number of different positions and not just in the most mechanically efficient one. One-arm lock-offs would be productive and even greater specificity would be achieved by them if the other hand busied itself by, for example, dipping into a real or imaginary chalk bag or placing and clipping a sling with a karabiner. However, training on climbing walls and bouldering in themselves offer adequate opportunities to develop isometric strength endurance.

Explosive Strength or Power

Explosive strength links maximal strength with speed and the degree of neuro-muscular co-ordination demanded implies further need for special training in this area. Speed in climbing was, and is, unnecessary for the majority of climbers. Controlled and deliberate movement on rock has traditionally been associated with good form, but explosive and dynamic moves are increasing in their application. Leg power is the key factor here as it is for the mountaineer preparing for driving body and rucksack uphill. In either situation power training will sharpen reactions and hone general motor control. As with strength endurance, it is best built on a platform of maximal strength training. The schedules described earlier would suffice, with particular attention being given to the concentric or shortening phase of each lift: it needs to be fast. The 'Power Clean' is an excellent all-round power exercise and certain forms of reactive jump training are beneficial to the knowledgeable, well-conditioned athlete who is seeking greater sophistication in training.

In concluding this section on strength it is worth reinforcing some of the significant principles:

- The optimal frequency of strength training sessions is three times a week. Muscles require at least two full days to recover from heavy work-outs.
- Exercise large muscle groups before the smaller ones during any one session.
- Overload muscles progressively. A system is required, therefore record your work.
- Do not overdo finger work.
- Maximal strength is the basis for strength endurance and explosive strength.
- Concentrate on general work before specific work.

FLEXIBILITY

Flexibility is a most neglected component of fitness and training, yet arguably it is the most important. A good range of movement in the hip and shoulder areas makes for more efficient use of the legs and arms when climbing. At the very least energy can be saved, and at the other end of the scale it can make the difference between success and failure. Flexibility and strength are closely linked elements. To train for strength without complementary joint stretching will lead to less suppleness, while to train for flexibility without strength training could result in weak, unstable joints.

This type of training tends to be unpopular with athletes of all sports because of the initial lack of obvious progress, the need for a high investment of time and the unexciting nature of the exercises. It is true that you would have to train every day for the best results, but many find that achieving the relaxed state necessary to bring about an increase in the range of movement in itself produces a degree of quietness and meditation that can be used positively and linked to mental training.

Stretching

Stretching can be defined as a process of lengthening muscles and tissue surrounding joints in order to prepare the body for the physical activity, as in a warm-up, or to help it recover from the muscular tensions that have developed during activity, as in a warm-down at the end of a training session or climb. In the latter situation it is important that all stretching is done gently and lightly, since tired muscles can more easily be damaged.

Flexibility Training

Flexibility training implies a much more structured approach that is designed to increase systematically the range of motion in a joint complex. To do this a committed attitude is vital, but the returns for a daily flexibility routine will be substantial. Those starting such a regime should seek out specialist advice; however, practice should adhere to the following principles.

A warm-up is essential to maximise the stretching effect and to prevent injury. Try to work up a slight sweat with some ten minutes of easy to moderate running or skipping before engaging in flexibility exercises.

There are many factors that limit the degree of movement in joints including age, sex, bony structure, type of joint and even clothing, but resistance to motion at the end of a particular range is mainly attributable to properties of the contractile element in a muscle and to the length of connective tissue that surrounds that muscle and, in fact, is a constituent part of it.

Any movement at a joint is brought about by a co-ordination of a muscle, or muscle group, that initiates the movement by contracting, and a reciprocal muscle, or group, on the opposite side of that joint that is allowed to stretch. This stretching of the co-called antagonist muscle, which is fundamental to the notion of flexibility, is controlled by two reflexes that originate from protective receptors in the muscle and its tendons. By inhibiting the myotatic reflex that brings about a reflex contraction of the antagonist when it is being stretched and by invoking the inverse myotatic reflex that causes a reflex relaxation in the same muscle, it is possible to maximise the amount of stretch in the contractile component of muscle.

Thus, stretch slowly to prevent a strong, opposing contraction of the very muscle(s) that you are hoping to stretch and hold each position for ten to thirty seconds or even one minute in order to ensure that the reflex that causes relaxation in a tense muscle is allowed to function. Greater effect can be obtained by consciously trying to relax, perhaps to the sound of soft, gentle music.

Research has shown that in order to bring about permanent changes in the lengths of connective tissue associated with muscle, the forces involved should be low and working temperature above normal. For best results, warm up, be gentle, increase the stretch slowly and prolong the stretch.

Perhaps one of the deterrents to sustained training is the mistaken association it has with pain. Stretching exercises should never be painful: this means that damage is being caused. Mild discomfort is one thing, but it is important never to persist with an exercise which causes pain, particularly if it is being felt at the extremities of the muscle in the tendons. Good technique is signalled by the feeling of stretch in the 'belly' of the muscle.

It is certain that fast, swinging, bouncing, circling methods of training are unproductive, as well as potentially unsafe, but such movements performed gently and slowly as part of a joint warm-up can serve to raise efficiently the working temperature of the joints. At this time a static approach is recommended where the 'end point' in any movement is gradually and progressively reached and held. This static method can be used in two ways, actively and passively, and it is important to employ both techniques for functional improvements.

Active Stretching

Active stretching involves the use of your own

muscles to move the limb into its most extreme position and to hold it there unsupported.

Passive Stretching

Passive stretching sees the joint moving through an even greater range because of the application of outside forces. In training this could involve the co-operation of a knowledgeable partner, while on the rock the bracing effect caused by, say, a wide bridge could stretch the joint slightly beyond its active range.

Therefore, there is a need to develop:

- Strength at the end of the range, especially isometric strength endurance, by exercising actively.
- A stretch capability that extends the active potential, by adopting passive techniques.

This is one way we can put into practice the 'hand-in-glove' principle related to strength and flexibility.

The passive work will result in an increase in the range of motion, while the active work will ensure that it can effectively be used without undue fatigue. Bias flexibility training in favour of passive exercises but neglect specific active movements at your cost. The passive stretch and active hold technique would seem to have much to commend it.

Climbers need to pay special attention to the shoulders and hips if they are to improve their technique. However, it would be wise to include a more general phase in each flexibility session in order to balance out specific development.

Remember:

- Commit yourself to flexibility training and persevere.
- Always warm up prior to stretching or flexibility training.
- Adopt a light stretching routine before and after any training session or climb.
- Develop flexibility by training for at least thirty minutes every day; however, three times a week will also produce results. Three sets of five to ten stretches on each exercise will suffice.
- Train in the morning rather than later in the day when muscular tensions develop.
- Be gentle: increase the stretch slowly; prolong the stretch; relax.
- Train actively and passively for best results.
- Avoid being a masochist – stretching should not be painful.
- Acknowledge the value of relaxation/meditation techniques, not only to improve the stretch but also as part of mental training.

This chapter has focused on three key components of fitness that apply to the climber: endurance, strength and flexibility. In the principles outlined there is a trend from the general to the specific. This and progressive loading have been highlighted and emphasised because the mistake that many climbers have made in the past is to train too specifically for too long and they have suffered the consequences. Be sensible about this. Results are achieved by a slow, systematic build-up over a period of months and years rather than by a furious burst lasting a few weeks.

TRAINING PROGRAMMES

It is usual to plan a training programme over a period or cycle of one year, but this is much easier to do when gearing the work to a fixed competitive season. A climber may be in action all year, yet this concept of periodisation should still apply, allowing for the absence of a 'season' as such. The yearly cycle is broken up into five phases (or meso-cycles) that reflect the gradual change of emphasis from general to specific.

Meso-Cycle 1 – General Phase

Six to eight weeks long

The base of aerobic endurance is laid at this time. Flexibility work is done regularly. Towards the end of the phase the emphasis changes slightly in favour of aerobic work on a local muscular level. Circuit training could be included.

Meso-Cycle 2 – Special Phase

Six to eight weeks long

The aerobic work has less emphasis, with strength training being the main constituent. A foundation

	OCT	NOV	DEC	JAN	FEB	MAR	APR	MAY	JUN	JUL	AUG	SEPT
ROCK CLIMBER	ACTIVE REST	GENERAL		SPECIAL	SPECIFIC			IN-SEASON				
MOUNTAINEER	GENERAL	SPECIAL	SPECIFIC (WINTER)	WINTER SEASON			SPECIAL	SPECIFIC (SUMMER)	SUMMER SEASON			ACTIVE REST

of maximal strength leads towards strength endurance and explosive strength development. Flexibility training continues on a regular basis.

Meso-Cycle 3 – (Sport) Specific Phase

Six to eight weeks long

Aerobic level is maintained. Strength endurance is emphasised with an increasing concentration on anaerobic work. Training becomes much more specific with gym, wall and bouldering assuming more importance. Flexibility training continues.

Meso-Cycle 4 – 'In Season' Phase

By the start of this phase the climber will be in a state of optimal readiness for the 'season'. The main emphasis should be on maintaining conditioning levels. This can be achieved by reducing the number of training sessions for endurance and strength to two or even one per week each, depending on the amount of climbing being done. Sustain the flexibility training as before.

Meso-Cycle 5 – Active Rest Phase

About four weeks long

The importance of this phase should not be underestimated. It is the time for a complete lay-off in order to allow the body to recover. Indulge in activities of a diverse and recreational nature – basically, enjoy an active holiday.

Two cyclical plans are shown above. One is for rock climbers and the other is for mountaineers who divide their time between rock climbing, summer mountaineering, Alpinism (possibly), winter rock, snow and ice climbing and winter mountaineering.

Remember that there should be a gradual change of emphasis from phase to phase and also within phases. This latter feature should be reflected in the micro-cycles that further divide each phase into weekly units.

An optimal frequency of training is three times per week for the components of endurance, strength and flexibility. An appreciation of how the body adapts to overload, by first recovering and then by having its performance temporarily enhanced through the process of super-compensation, will dictate the construction of the weekly micro-cycle.

Adequate recovery over a period of days is essential after intensive work-outs of strength training or extensive endurance sessions if they are not to be counter-productive. There is no evidence that sound flexibility work on a daily basis is harmful. It is probably best if flexibility training is done separately from other training – in the morning preferably; if not, it can be combined with a run or work-out, but you should avoid linking it with very hard sessions. Otherwise, flexibility training is preferable before the main session rather than after it, but remember the value of a light stretching routine as part of a warm-down.

Those with heavy training schedules should consider the use of split routines, whereby strength training can be done on consecutive days by splitting the work in such a way that different muscle groups are exercised. In this way local recovery can be made as training goes on.

Recovery requires an active approach rather than a passive one which might indicate 'rest'. Injuries apart, it is recognised that the recovery process after training is quicker if activity continues but at a much lower intensity. Thus, activity on the day after a very hard training session might be no more than a light jog and stretch.

By the same token, if maximum benefit is to be derived from such a hard session, the preceding day's activity should be appropriately lighter or have a different emphasis. It will be obvious that during the height of the climbing 'season' a hard work-out twenty-four hours or less before a day's climbing is likely to produce a disappointing time on the rock.

Having formulated your cyclical plan and then set about the construction of the weekly micro-cycles within each phase (meso-cycle), you are now ready to prepare each individual training session. The emphasis and level of intensity of each session will already have been determined, so now it is merely a matter of deciding content and order. Remember to include a thorough warm-up and acknowledge the value of a warm-down in promoting recovery.

Individual motivation and aspiration will decide the degree of training and commitment to it. There is obvious accuracy in the saying 'The best training for climbing is climbing', and for many this philosophy rests easily with them as they derive all the enjoyment they seek from their climbing activity. Others may prefer to express themselves differently by taking advantage of current theory and practice on training in the exploration of their own potential. Such dedicated enthusiasts should continue to appreciate the individual nature of fitness and fitness training – striving to devise programmes that are tailored to their needs and desires. They should avoid the tendency to become compulsive and neurotic about training and retain a common-sense attitude that allows for a flexible approach, particularly when injured or feeling below par.

The best results in training are based on a long-term structured commitment. Remember that gains are reversible if training ceases and that the longer the build-up, the slower the drop-off, if for one reason or another training has to stop.

DIET

No advice on training would be complete without reference to diet. Treat this aspect seriously, not only from a health point of view but also as an important contributor to improved performance. Much useful information on the subject is available in other books, so it will not be repeated here. Basically your aim should be to maintain a varied, balanced diet while recognising the advantages of carbohydrate and protein and the disadvantages of too much saturated fat.

27 Psychological Skills in Climbing
by Lew Hardy

Climbing is clearly a 'psychological' sport, and the purpose of this chapter is to introduce some of the psychological skills which can help you to improve your climbing while making it safer and more enjoyable. These are anxiety-control, self-confidence, attention-control and problem-solving skills. Just like physical skills they can all be learned and some people will learn them much more easily than others.

ANXIETY-CONTROL SKILLS

Every climber has experienced the negative effects of anxiety at some stage during climbing; and it is easy to think of examples of such negative effects, ranging from mild cases of 'sewing-machine leg' (a wobble produced by fatigue) to backing down from a route which is well within your capability. However, anxiety can also have several beneficial effects, provided that you can stay in control.

The symptoms of anxiety are usually considered to fall into two different categories – worry and physiological arousal. Essentially, worry involves thoughts or images about the consequences of failing or falling off, while physiological arousal is part of the body's natural defence mechanism – the famous 'fight or flight' response. Examples of physiological arousal include increased adrenalin, a dry mouth, sweaty hands and wanting to go to the lavatory. These symptoms are not necessarily bad: for example, increased adrenalin raises heart rate and therefore moves more oxygen to the musculature where it will be needed; increased sweat in the pores of the skin reduces the probability of it tearing; and going to the lavatory reduces the weight which you will have to carry. On the other hand, increased adrenalin also results in increased muscle tension – which is why climbers sometimes get 'gripped up' when they are anxious.

In an exactly similar way, worry can also play both a useful and a distracting role. For example, worry is a valuable source of motivation, not just to climb well but also, much more importantly, to concentrate and climb carefully. Lack of worry is probably one of the major reasons why so many accidents occur on relatively easy ground rather than on very difficult terrain. This is, of course, particularly noticeable in the Alps and other big mountain areas, where accidents frequently occur on descents. On the other hand unrestrained worry can be a source of immense distraction on a route, which at best results in hesitancy and a lack of commitment, and at worst leads to mistakes and serious accidents.

The key to all this is probably fairly obvious. If you are going to use anxiety to your benefit, or even just cope with it well enough to get up your route, you must be able to control both the worry and physiological components of it. There are many different relaxation strategies which can be learned to enable you to do this, but for our purposes they can be grouped into physical relaxation and mental relaxation strategies. Many top-class climbers acquire such control skills as a matter of course during their climbing. However, there is little doubt that many climbers of all grades would benefit from following a formal course in relaxation training.

At least two relaxation strategies immediately spring to mind as having a lot of potential for rock climbers. Progressive muscular relaxation (PMR) was originally devised as a technique to enable people to gain very precise control of each different muscle group in the body. It is therefore not just a relaxation technique. It can also have a direct effect upon performance by enabling you to 'smooth away' unwanted tension in a particular muscle group and thereby conserve energy.

Another technique which appears to have a great deal of potential for climbing is meditative relaxation. There are, of course, many different types of meditation, but they all work by slowing down the metabolism and occupying the mind with something simple and harmless to quieten and calm it. Meditative relaxation leads naturally into another technique called centring, which is extremely useful for regaining control of yourself when a situation is starting to slip away – for instance, when you start gibbering on the crux!

The following exercises may prove useful.

Exercise 1

1 Relax for a few minutes, focusing your attention on each exhalation of breath. Breathe easily and slowly, using your diaphragm. Notice how comfortable you feel with each breath out.

2 Next switch your attention to your body and slowly scan up it, starting at your feet and moving on to your calves, thighs, buttocks, back, stomach, neck, head and face, then back down to your shoulders, upper arms and finally your forearms and hands. As you scan your body, make a mental note of where it is tense. Do not try to change the tension; just be aware of it. Notice that, as you do this, your body relaxes itself!

3 After a few minutes, bring yourself back to the 'here and now' by taking five or six progressively deeper inhalations. After the sixth, stretch and get up.

Finally, if you do decide to learn some relaxation skills, try to choose a course or tape-recorded package taught by someone who knows what they are doing as good training programmes by necessity should contain a number of important safeguards.

SELF-CONFIDENCE

Perhaps the best inoculation against overanxiety is self-confidence. It will not necessarily help you to cope with anxiety once you are suffering from it, but it will reduce the probability of your becoming anxious in the first place. Although one person's self-confidence varies from situation to situation, it is relatively stable within each of those situations. For example, some people are very confident on well-protected overhangs but much less so on poorly protected slabs, while for others the situation may be reversed.

However, 'slab' people are likely always to lack self-confidence when faced with big butch overhangs, and their feelings about climbing slabs are unlikely to change this, no matter how difficult they are (within reason). Although this might seem fairly obvious, it does have one quite important implication. Mental skills, like physical skills, are specific to the context in which you train them. Another implication of the relatively enduring nature of self-confidence is that you cannot enhance it overnight. It takes quite a lot of hard work and planning to do so. Unfortunately,it does not seem to take quite so much hard work and planning to change it in the other direction!

The most powerful influence upon self-confidence is your previous experience. Consequently, a very good way to improve your confidence about a 'big' route is to plan out a programme of 'smaller' routes which are similar in style to it but which start off easy and gradually become more difficult as you go down the list. Since the weather is not a great respecter of plans, you should also include wet-weather alternatives in your programme, together with any physical and skill training which might be appropriate. Perhaps the most important thing about setting goals for yourself in this way is that you must perceive the goals to be realistic and worthwhile. Remember that routes which appear to be realistic when you are sitting at home reading the guidebook often do not appear quite the same when you are standing at the bottom of them!

Once you have got the basic idea of goal setting, you can use it in much more subtle ways to focus your attention upon specific aspects of your climbing technique, or your mental approach to a route. This requires you to be much more analytical about your strengths and weaknesses as a climber. However, the dividends of such an approach can be enormous, because what you are essentially doing is taking a negative statement about your present performance and transforming it into a positive statement which sets a goal for your future performance. For example, I am essentially a slow and cautious climber. When I am going well this is not usually a very big problem, but when I am climbing poorly I waste a great deal of energy literally just hanging about. Consequently, a very good goal for me to set when I am climbing poorly might be always to 'go for it' as soon as I have placed a runner.

Another good way to enhance your confidence about a specific route is to watch someone else do it first. Even better, if you get the chance watch several people. In the case of big mountain routes, it may be enough if you simply know other people who have done the route and can talk to them about it: the most important thing is that you are able to identify with them. Consequently, leading after a friend who is just a little bit better than you can often be quite a good strategy for enhancing your confidence about a 'new grade' but watching an exceptional performer leap up it three moves at a time will probably not be!

At a more general level, imagining yourself successfully climbing something can also be a very positive influence upon self-confidence. Some people find it very difficult to form images which are well-behaved. However, with practice anyone can learn to use imagery. It is just that some people need more practice than others. You can speed up the process by always relaxing for a few minutes before attempting to rehearse anything mentally. It will also help if you start by imaging only things with which you are very familiar. Remember: the more success you achieve, the more confident you will become about imaging and the easier imagery will become. Another thing which will help you to be more successful in using imagery is to obtain as much information as you can about routes in advance, so that you can make your images more detailed and vivid. Collecting such information is also very important in enabling you to plan alternatives into any programme of goals which you set yourself. If you do not do this and your partner does not want to do your first-choice route, all your mental rehearsal and preparation will be wasted.

Finally, always try to think positively about your climbing. Instead of saying you cannot do something, try to work out what you need in order to be able to do it; then work out a programme of goals that will enable you to achieve whatever it is you need.

ATTENTION CONTROL

When anyone becomes anxious, there is a tendency for them to attend only to those aspects of the environment which they consider to be important. Unfortunately, this apparently 'good' safety mechanism can have disastrous consequences in climbing. For example, beginners refuse to even look at their feet 'because it is their hands that hold them on'. Even worse, if beginners can be persuaded to stand out a bit and look at their feet, they will probably focus on the ground instead, 'because everybody knows that it is the ground which hurts you if you fall off'! Similarly, a leader who is badly 'gripped up' might typically search his field of vision as quickly as possible in a desperate attempt to find some 'straw' to clutch at – a hold, a runner placement, their second, anyone else on the crag. When you are really desperate, all sorts of things look as though they might help! Of course, a leader's problems are largely his own, and attending to distractions in this way simply clogs up the brain with useless information.

The net result of all this is that when you are anxious, your speed of perception is likely to be greatly increased, but you are also highly likely to make mistakes. These usually take the form of failing to see some holds while being totally preoccupied with others. Most climbers will be able to remember occasions when this has happened to them. What is required, then, is some means of ensuring that you focus your attention appropriately on those things which will help you – that is to say, some sort of concentration training.

One way to practise concentration is always to make a mental note of where all the holds are before you attempt to use any. You should try this from the ground when bouldering first, then from resting positions on routes. Try to relax for a few moments (for just one or two breaths) before looking for the holds: then, making a conscious decision not to try to work out how to solve the problem of your next move, focus your attention upon the rock and try to notice as many of its qualities as you can. Try not to think of it only as something that you climb on, but rather as a sculpture. When you see holds, observe their colour and shape as well as their size and usefulness. If your attention wanders to other things, quietly acknowledge the fact and then gently bring it back to the task in hand. Spend one or two minutes on the task before trying to work out how to do the next few moves.

Concentration is not about trying hard, it is about focusing all of your attention upon the things which are important. The sort of distractions that climbers have to overcome are, for example, worrying about a crux that they have not yet reached, or about how far above their last runner they are, or even thinking that they have not much further to go to the top of the pitch. The major difficulty in learning to concentrate is 'staying with the present'. This is not so much a case of continuing to focus upon the same thing as constantly switching your attention away from the previous thing as you make each new move. The following exercise will help you to gain this attentional flexibility.

Exercise 2

1 While you are bouldering, pause on a problem and relax for a few moments, then scan your body from your feet to your hands, exactly as you did in Part 2 of Exercise 1 (page 344). Again, make a mental note of where your body is relaxed, and where it is tense, as you scan it; but do not try to change it – just be aware of it.
2 Now focus your attention on the next section of the problem and link a sequence of moves together, keeping your attention focused on each move as you do it. Notice how good it feels! When you can do this bouldering, try it on easier routes.

PROBLEM SOLVING

One of the fundamental attractions of climbing is probably the satisfaction which can be derived from creatively solving problems while under pressure. It is a little like vertical chess but with big stakes! However, as explained in 'Anxiety-Control Skills' (page 343), large amounts of pressure are likely to bring with them worry and physiological arousal. Although high physiological arousal might be quite a good state in which to maximise physical effort, it is a very poor state in which to try to solve problems creatively. This situation is made still worse when the physiological arousal is accompanied by either high levels of worry or low levels of self-confidence – yet another good reason to adopt self-confidence and relaxation training in order to keep self-confidence high and worry and physiological arousal at manageable levels.

We should also train ourselves to solve problems creatively even though we are under pressure. The most obvious way to develop this ability is to practise problem-solving more often during bouldering sessions by constantly re-defining problems, so that you have to solve them rather than just repeat them. For example, see how many different ways you can overcome a problem using the same set of holds, or subtly change the holds allowed. (The latter version of creative bouldering is also quite good for developing concentration.) However, the exercise given below is probably an even more effective way of improving your vertical-chess-playing ability.

Exercise 3

1 Write down as many different ways of inducing psychological pressure in yourself as you can. These might include, for instance, physiological arousal (as after a run), fatigue (as at the end of a training session), time pressure (as when you have say, only one minute in which to complete a task), dual tasks (such as repeating the alphabet backwards) and so on.
2 Choose or define a fairly difficult problem on your climbing wall, or wherever you boulder, which is new to you.
3 Select one of the stressors which you wrote down in Part 1 (above) and try to solve your problem while under that pressure.
4 Choose another problem and try to solve that under a different stressor from the one you chose in Part 3. The more varied the nature of the problems you try to solve and the stressors you use to put yourself under pressure, the better will be the transfer of the skill you are learning to your 'real' climbing.
5 Notice that you can extend this exercise still further by having a friend try to distract you while you solve a new problem.

Mentally rehearsing a problem can also be an enormous help in problem solving since it not only helps you to warm up mentally for climbing but also lets you 'try things out' without falling off. However, just like problem solving, imagery ability is greatly impaired by high states of physiological arousal. Consequently, if you are going to use mental rehearsal to maximum effect when you are on difficult routes, you must first of all practise it on the wall and then on easier routes. A good way to start this process is to stand and mentally rehearse problems on the wall before you try to solve them. As you become better at this, you can practise traversing in to a problem and mentally rehearsing it from your position on the wall just as you reach the start of it. When you can do this, it is worth repeating the process with 'new' problems which you have not tried before. Finally, you can try mentally rehearsing problems when you are under pressure exactly as you did in the problem-solving exercise.

28 First Aid

All climbers should have an understanding of first aid, especially when climbing in remote and serious places where outside assistance is not readily available. You may need to help a member of your own or of another party who has been unfortunate enough to be injured. A practical knowledge of first aid in such a situation can literally mean the difference between life and death.

While it is beyond the scope of this book to provide comprehensive and detailed information, aspects of first aid which are particularly relevant to climbing and the mountains and which are not readily available in more routine first-aid manuals are included. Although a knowledge of first aid is vital, it is the ability correctly to assess the extent of an accident victim's injuries and to improvise with the materials available which are the keys to good mountain first aid.

FIRST-AID PRIORITIES

In any emergency the first aider's priority is to make sure that the casualty is breathing and can continue to do so. This is particularly important when dealing with unconscious casualties who can easily vomit and subsequently choke. If the casualty is not breathing, it may be because the airway – that is, the mouth, throat and the passageway to the lungs – is blocked. This should be checked and any obstructions – such as broken teeth, blood, vomit and the tongue – removed. Carefully mop up any debris in the airway with a stick around which a handkerchief or similar piece of cloth has been bound. When the airway is clear, start artificial resuscitation and continue until either the casualty breathes normally or is deemed to be dead.

If the casualty is unconscious but breathing, he should be quickly checked for other injuries, especially to the neck and spine, and, if none is found, placed on his front so that he is free to vomit without risk of compromising his airway. This is called the recovery (or coma) position [*fig. 28.1*]. Any casualty who has been unconscious or has vomited, or shows any signs of doing either of these should be placed in this position and his condition monitored at all times.

When it has been established that the casualty is breathing, he should be checked for serious bleeding. At this stage look only for life-threatening blood loss and ignore minor cuts and scratches. If the casualty is dressed for cold weather, check inside the clothing as large amounts of blood can often be concealed between the layers. Do not overestimate the seriousness of superficial head wounds, which can often bleed profusely but present no danger to life.

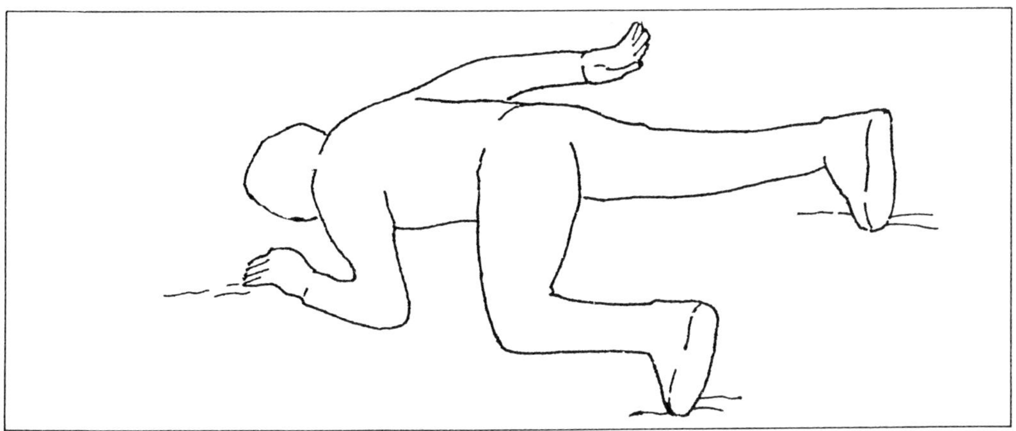

Fig 28.1 The recovery or coma position.

Severe bleeding is best stopped by direct pressure to the wound site. This is done by bandaging a pad, preferably a sterile wound dressing, tightly in place. If this first application of pressure is not enough to staunch the flow of blood, a second pad should be applied on top of the first and once again bandaged tightly. The pad should not be removed even when bleeding stops as this disrupts any natural clotting which has taken place. Elevation of the injury, assuming no bone fracture is present, also helps to control the bleeding. In some extremely serious cases it may be necessary to fix a restricting band or tourniquet above the wound site. Great care must be exercised, however, as restricting the blood supply for as short a time as twenty minutes can cause irreparable damage to the limb. A tourniquet should be considered only when the blood loss is such that life is threatened and it cannot be staunched by direct pressure. This is rare and is seen in the mountains only in injuries caused by rock or ice fall when limbs may be completely severed by falling debris.

When all bleeding has been staunched, the casualty should be examined for fractures or other injuries. This is best done from head to toe in a logical sequence so that no part of the body is overlooked. The conscious patient can help the first aider in identifying injuries, but serious injuries are not always painful or may be overshadowed by minor, less life-threatening injuries, and so the first aider must complete a check of the whole body. In the first-aid situation, and with the limited equipment available, it is seldom possible to treat fractures effectively in the field. The best the first aider can hope to do is to make the casualty as comfortable as possible and prevent any further damage or blood loss from occurring. Sometimes traction, gently but firmly applied, can do this and at the same time ease the pain. The offending limb can then be splinted – perhaps in the case of a broken leg to the other leg or to the ice axe or rucksack frame. Procedures and methods of treating fractures are well documented elsewhere.

Injuries to the head are unfortunately very common in climbing and all such injuries, apart from straightforward cuts, must be treated as serious. It is difficult to establish the severity of such an injury in the field and, since all severe head injuries require medical attention, help should be sought as a matter of urgency. The patient's condition should be monitored and any changes in pupil size, breathing rate or pulse rate noted and the medical authorities informed.

In most first-aid situations it is unwise to give food or drink. There are some exceptions – hypothermia and frostbite being two – but in most other cases this does nothing constructive and can in fact be dangerous. The casualty should be kept warm, reassured and readied for evacuation. Evacuation in the mountains is commonly done by helicopter, and if this is likely the site around the casualty should be cleared of loose material and prepared for a helicopter landing. Sometimes it may be impossible for an otherwise healthy casualty to walk, perhaps because of a broken ankle or knee injury, and in such cases it is often possible to transport him using a split rope carry or other improvised stretcher. The effort involved in any of these improvised carries should not be underestimated, and while they can avoid the need for costly and perhaps embarrassing rescue, they are suitable only for casualties with minor injuries and for situations which do not require lengthy evacuations.

HYPOTHERMIA

Hypothermia (or exposure) is the name given to the condition which results when the body core temperature drops below the normal 37°C. This happens when the body is cooled by the atmosphere and is unable to generate enough heat to maintain its normal temperature. As the temperature of the body core drops, so the body suffers a severe loss of function. A drop of 4°C results in disorientation; a drop of 7°C causes the casualty to lapse into a coma; and a drop of 10°C can be fatal. Heat is lost from the body not only at low temperatures; in windy conditions the 'wind chill' factor is usually more important than the real air temperature.

Climbers can avoid hypothermia principally by wearing the correct clothing for the conditions and by having a regular intake of high-energy foods. However, in some conditions, especially when it is cold, wet and windy, and the climbers are overextended physically, hypothermia can be a very real problem. If exhaustion, fatigue and low morale are added to the bad weather conditions, even experienced climbers can fall victim.

Recognising hypothermia in its early stages is not easy. In bad conditions people are often uncommunicative and everyone feels cold and weary, but abnormal behaviour of any kind, clumsiness (often an appearance of being drunk), sudden bursts of energy and disorientation should all be treated with suspicion. If the condition is not recognised early but allowed to progress until unconsciousness results, evacuation is a matter of extreme urgency, preferably under medical supervision, as death is usually not far away.

Since one of the first effects of hypothermia is to affect the decision making and rationale of the victim, it is very difficult, indeed usually impossible, for the victim to recognise the onset of the condition in himself. The only way hypothermia can be detected is for you and your partner to be aware of the possibility and to monitor each other's behaviour. This is not always easy in climbing as long periods are often spent apart, and so the 'buddy system' must be used whenever the opportunity occurs, usually at rest stops or belay stances. A quick test is to ask the possible victim to perform some simple arithmetic: counting from 100 downwards in sevens is an example, but this usually proves difficult enough at the best of times!

Exhaustion and hypothermia are very closely linked. As we become more and more tired, so we are no longer able to produce enough heat to keep our body at the required temperature. This exhaustion can result either from over-exertion or from an insufficient intake of high-energy foods; more usually, it is caused by a combination of both. The signs and symptoms of exhaustion and hypothermia are therefore often similar and are frequently found together. Anyone suffering from exhaustion in cold conditions should be treated as for hypothermia, and most hypothermia victims will be exhausted.

If hypothermia is suspected, it is vital that re-warming takes place immediately. This usually involves stopping and finding shelter, and any desperate urge to press on regardless must be overcome unless safety is very near. Hot drinks and food should be administered, and if this is done early enough it may be all that is required to increase the body core temperature of the victim. If not, more substantial shelter must be found, perhaps in a tent or snow hole, and the victim made as warm and comfortable as possible. Re-warm the casualty by placing him in a sleeping bag with a lightly dressed, healthy companion. A victim who has become unconscious will always required evacuation by stretcher, and even if he seems to recover after re-warming but before evacuation, he must still be moved by stretcher. After evacuation, re-warming should be carried out slowly and medical advice sought.

The best treatment for hypothermia is to avoid it altogether. Do so by using the correct equipment, eating sensibly and planning your routes conservatively. Mental state and fitness, as well as previous experience of bad weather, can all play an important part in the avoidance of hypothermia.

FROSTNIP AND FROSTBITE

When the body is exposed to sub-zero temperatures, especially in windy conditions, frostnip and frostbite can result.

Frostnip is the less serious of the two and, if spotted early, can be easily treated in the field without further damage. It is caused by the body protecting itself from the cold by sacrificing the extremities in favour of the core. This it does by shutting off the circulation to extremities, which then become cold and dead to the touch. Toes, fingers, ears, noses and cheeks are all common sites for frostnip. It makes the skin look white, numb and lacking in feeling, and a usual warning sign is when an area of the body can no longer be felt or is no longer uncomfortable due to cold – cold hands or fingers, say, which have not been re-warmed may no longer feel painful. On windy days frostnip is more likely to be suffered on the nose and cheeks.

Frostnip is treated by immediately re-warming the affected area, usually by direct application of body heat, either your own or (sometimes more easily) someone else's. The armpits, groin and mouth are the best sites for re-warming. If the sensation does not return within an hour, the condition should be treated as frostbite. Although it is often a real problem to stop and remove boots, cold toes which seem to improve unexpectedly (probably because they are frostnipped and so less painful than before) should never be overlooked. Rigorous self-discipline is essential if frostbite is to be avoided when climbing in low temperatures. Frostnip can be prevented by wearing good gloves, boots, clothes and, in extreme conditions, a neoprene face mask or scarf over the face.

Frostbite is the name given to the condition which occurs when frostnip is not treated quickly and effectively. With frostbite, however, the skin is not only numb and discoloured, but the cells within the tissue actually freeze. This makes frostbite a much more serious injury as it cannot be treated in the field, and if it is treated badly at base, tissue can be permanently lost.

There are two degrees of frostbite: superficial and deep. Both conditions look the same and are treated in the same way; it is only after some time that the difference can be appreciated. Superficial frostbite is when the nerves are damaged and the skin blisters but no tissue is lost, whereas deep frostbite is when gangrene occurs with subsequent loss of tissue. Frostbite occurs when the skin actually freezes, resulting in damage to the skin, the nerve supply to the skin and in extreme cases to deep tissue as well. It looks similar to frostnip but worse – the skin may be waxy or hard and frozen to the touch. There may also be blisters on the skin but these do not always appear immediately. Frostbite usually occurs only after prolonged exposure to the cold as on Himalayan expeditions or if part of the body is exposed to extremely low temperatures, perhaps as a result of a lost glove. Alternatively, prolonged exposure, perhaps as a result of wearing wet gloves or socks, at temperatures only a few degrees below zero can also result in frostbite. In all cases the quality of an individual's circulation will play a big part in determining his resistance to low temperatures and consequently to frostbite.

Frostbite is initially treated in the same way as frostnip, and if the affected areas respond to re-warming it is vital that they are not allowed to freeze again. This means that frostbitten feet are best left as such until base is reached as more damage can be caused to the feet if they are walked on after re-warming rather than while still frozen. If blisters occur, these should be covered with a sterile dressing and not burst. Re-warming should never be in front of direct heat, and if the tissue is actually frozen it should be re-warmed in hot water (at 40°C) but must not be allowed to become cold again. Medical attention, preferably by someone with experience of treating frostbite, should be sought immediately on return to civilisation.

Frostbite is best avoided by wearing the correct clothing and constant monitoring of the body extremities. Continual wiggling of the fingers and toes can keep the circulation active and so prevent cooling of the extremities. In all cases of frostbite, hypothermia should also be suspected. There is some evidence to suggest that small doses of aspirin, particularly if taken at altitude, can help prevent frostbite. It does this by 'thinning the blood' and so improving the ease with which it can circulate. Vaso-dilatory drugs have also been used to good effect. These work by increasing the circulation to the extremities and so are particularly useful for treating frostnip rather than as a frostbite preventative. Great care must be exercised in their use as any increase in the supply of blood to the extremities can result in excessive and dangerous cooling (hypothermia) of the body's core.

LIGHTNING STRIKE

Lightning is not a major hazard in the mountains, but can nevertheless be very serious. It is usually associated with cumulo-nimbus clouds and often occurs in afternoon storms in the Alps. An approaching lightning storm is normally a very impressive sight; as the storm moves towards you it is accompanied by the crash of thunder and the flash of lightning. The storm's distance from you can be worked out by measuring the time between the flash of the lightning and the peal of the thunder. When this time, in seconds, is multiplied by 3, it gives the distance of the storm in kilometres. As well as the visual and sonic warnings, metal objects may also hum and spark, the skin can tingle and your hair may literally stand on end.

A lightning strike is not always fatal, although a direct strike usually is. Most strikes hit the ground and people may then receive a secondary shock from the ground or rock through which it is earthing. This means that all easy paths for electricity such as chimneys, cracks and water courses should be avoided during an electrical storm. Rather than shelter under a roof, which may work like a sparking plug with you in the gap,

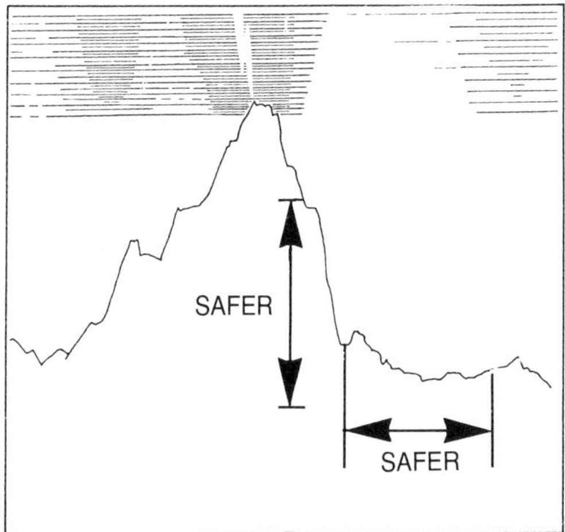

Fig 28.2 The frequency of lightning strikes on a typical mountain. The area below the summit has reduced danger as most strikes are drawn to the summit itself. The closer the lines are together, the greater the frequency of a strike.

or in a cave or under a boulder, it is safer to stay out in the open. Summits and pinnacles should also be avoided [*fig. 28.2*] as they are more prone to direct strikes. If at all possible, try to sit on something dry and have as few points of contact with the ground as possible. Avoid lying as any electricity, even small surface currents, will then pass through the body, usually with fatal results. A crouched, sitting position is best as any electricity passing through the body will then travel through non-vital regions. Wet ropes should be either discarded or at least piled up so that they do not work as lightning conductors. Take care when abseiling as many fatalities have occurred from non-fatal strikes stunning their victims who have then lost control of the abseil. If you do need to abseil during an electrical storm, use a safety rope or a back-up prusik.

If a companion is struck by lightning, begin artificial resuscitation and heart massage immediately. It is often possible to revive a seemingly dead victim if effective action is taken straight away. This initial first-aid treatment must be continued until the victim begins to breathe normally, or until all hope is exhausted. Victims may also suffer from flash burns and these should be covered with a dry, sterile dressing.

As with most problems encountered during climbing, prevention is much better than cure and a careful watch of weather conditions and forecasts can often, in conjunction with good planning, enable you to avoid lightning storms. This is especially true in Alpine regions where storms build up throughout the day, reaching a peak in the late afternoon.

HEAT EXHAUSTION AND DEHYDRATION

The body is affected not only by cold but by excessive heat as well. This can result in heat stroke and dehydration, both of which can be dangerous if left untreated. When suffering from heat exhaustion the casualty may well behave in a manner similar to someone experiencing hypothermia, but the skin is warm and dry to the touch and the victim often has a severe headache. Dehydration causes lethargy, muscle cramps and headaches; the urine is very dark brown in colour. All of these signs of dehydration can also indicate a failure to acclimatise well to altitude and in low temperatures can make the victim more prone to frostbite.

The treatment for heat exhaustion and dehydration is lots of fluid and, if possible, the body should be cooled. The fluids should be taken in small amounts regularly and no extra salt should be added, although mineral additives, like Isostar or Rehydrate, can be beneficial. Thirst is a poor indicator of fluid requirement, especially when climbing in a cold, dry atmosphere, and regular stops for fluid intake, even if this means lighting a stove, must be part of the daily climbing plan.

Heat exhaustion is best avoided by climbing in the cooler times of the day and adjusting the clothing for maximum ventilation. Protect the head against the sun – a white hat with a peak is an effective deterrent to sun-induced headaches. The back of the neck should also be covered.

SNOW BLINDNESS

Our eyes perceive only a small amount of the light radiated by the sun, and excessive exposure to the types of light outside our seeing range can be very harmful and painful to the eyes. Rays which have smaller wave lengths than the range we see (380–760nm) are known as ultra–violet and those which are greater than 760nm are called infra-red. It is the former which cause us most problems. At sea level most of this UV light is absorbed by the atmosphere and by water vapour and pollutants therein; but some does still reach the earth's surface. This does not normally present difficulties as our eyebrows and eyelashes shield the eyes from these harmful rays, which generally come from overhead. However, on snow-covered ground the surface of the snow reflects the UV into the eyes from below where there is no protection. This effect can be especially bad on cloudy days when the clouds themselves can also reflect the UV, causing it to become trapped between cloud and snow and thus greatly increasing its power. As the atmosphere is much purer and thinner at higher altitudes, there is less filtering of the UV rays and so very high levels can build up.

Over-exposure to UV light causes pain. Its effect is very similar to having sand in the eyes and it can even cause temporary blindness. It is best treated by resting the eyes in the dark, usually by covering with pads, and using antibiotic eye drops. Anaesthetic drops should not be used: although they provide pain relief, they also increase the time it takes for the eyes to heal. Although alarming for the sufferer, and potentially dangerous in some climbing situations, snow blindness is not serious and does not require medical attention.

Snow blindness can be avoided by conscientiously wearing good-quality sunglasses or goggles. Those which offer 100 per cent protection from harmful rays and have lenses which are dark enough to allow normal vision without your having to screw up your eyes are best. They should have side guards and be a close fit on the face so that light cannot enter from behind. Most good sunglasses and goggles bear labels showing the degree of protection offered; any which do not carry this information should be rejected.

There is no medical evidence to suggest that continuous exposure to sunlight can increase the eyes' tolerance to it; in fact, the opposite is true. People who do not wear eye protection are taking a risk with their eyesight. Should you lose, break or forget your glasses, effective temporary protection can be afforded by a piece of cardboard with two thin slits cut in it – one for each eye. Although obviously not ideal, this can prevent snow blindness in an emergency.

BLISTERS

Although not a serious problem, blisters can be very uncomfortable and spoil an otherwise pleasant day. It is best to prevent their occurring at all by applying a layer of sticky plaster or zinc oxide tape to the site of the rubbing. People who suffer from blisters invariably do so in the same places each time, and so these parts should always be protected before any walking is done. The sooner the offending site is treated, the less chance there is of the blister becoming a problem.

If the blister is allowed to develop beyond this stage, it is best treated by the application of a modern proprietary blister remedy. These products have an anti-septic, anti-friction jelly trapped between two layers of plastic and thus not only aid healing but also prevent further damage and make the blister comfortable enough for further walking to take place. If this is not available, the blister should be carefully burst with a sterile needle, dressed with a clean, dry dressing and covered in zinc oxide tape. If this adheres well, it is best left in place until base is reached. Sticking plaster which includes a gauze pad should not be used as the friction between the plaster, the gauze and the foot can exacerbate the problem.

Careful cutting of the toenails and ensuring that socks have no seams or holes can also help in the avoidance of blisters.

SUNBURN

Sunburn can be a particular problem for climbers on snow or at high altitude. Protection can be obtained by using a cream with a high protection factor – at least 8 for skin of average sensitivity and total block or factor 15 for more sensitive skin. The cream should be applied regularly to all exposed flesh, and special care should be taken to cover the inside of the nose and ears and the underside of the chin. Special creams and sticks are available for the nose and lips: these are usually total block and tend to need re-applying less often than ordinary creams. All sun-care products should be carried in a pocket where they are easily accessible and applied throughout the day. In cases of extreme sensitivity hats and scarves should be worn as protection against direct sunlight.

Glossary

Abseil The means by which a rope can be descended safely, the speed of descent being controlled by friction which can be produced by wrapping the rope round the body or by using an abseil device.
Abseil sling The sling used to anchor the abseil rope and facilitate rope retrieval once the abseil is completed.
ACU Active camming unit, a spring-loaded camming protection device.
Accessory cord Rope of between 4mm and 8mm in diameter which has a variety of uses, particularly for protection.
Acclimatisation The adaptation of the human body to the rarefied air and lack of oxygen found at high altitudes.
A cheval A way of climbing a narrow ridge or arête in which the climber sits astride the ridge and then shuffles along or up it.
Active rope The rope which runs between the moving climber and the person managing the rope. Also called the live rope.
Adze The wider, cutting edge on the head of an ice axe or ice tool.
Aid climbing Another term for artificial climbing.
Aid point A peg, sling, nut or bolt which is used for upwards progress or to rest on.
Aiming off A navigational technique used to make the location of points on a linear feature easier.
Alpenstock The forerunner of the ice axe, this was much longer, more cumbersome and originally used for glacier travel.
Alpine climbing Climbing which traditionally involves the problems of high mountains and glacier travel as well as the ascent of a peak.
Alpine clutch An alternative name for a karabiner clutch.
Alpine start The time at which many Alpine routes are started. An Alpine start can be any time from midnight onwards to avoid rock and ice fall which occurs later in the day when the sun melts the snow and ice. This also allows the snow to be climbed when it is in better condition after the freeze during the night.
Alpine style A style of climbing in which the route is ascended in one push by a party of climbers carrying everything they need. Each pitch is normally ascended only once and no fixed ropes are used. This style of climbing can be employed in the Greater Ranges as well as being usual in the Alpine areas of the world.
Alternate leads A climbing system in which two climbers on the rope take turn about at leading pitches. Also called leading through.
Altimeter An aneroid barometer, calibrated to read height rather than pressure, which can be used as a navigational aid or for weather forecasting.
Altitude sickness The result of ascent to high altitudes without proper acclimatisation. Can result in sickness, sore head, nausea and lassitude and can be severe and even fatal. Also known as acute mountain sickness (AMS).
American technique A cramponing technique in which one foot uses French technique while the other front-points.
Amphitheatre A very large recess in a cliff, often surrounded by steep rock above.
Anchor A point of attachment of a rope to a cliff. It can be a natural anchor such as a spike, chockstone or thread, or an artificial anchor such as a nut or a peg. To anchor is to attach yourself to such a point.
Angle peg A peg with a V-shaped cross-section.
Anorak Originally the Eskimo word for a windproof outer garment but now a general term for mountaineering jackets which are thigh-length, usually waterproof and have a hood.
Arête A narrow ridge of rock, ice or snow. The term can be applied to a smaller-scale cliff feature, in which case it is generally a steep and narrow rock ridge.
Arm bar A hold formed by bracing the arm across the inside of a wide crack.
Arm lock A hold in a wide crack formed by the arm which is fully bent at the elbow and locked in place by outwards pressure.
Artificial A term used to describe routes which can easily be abandoned once started on because of the proximity of less difficult climbs or easy horizontal features. The term can also refer to a climb which seeks out difficulty in spite of the proximity of easier climbing: that is, not a 'natural' line.
Artificial climbing Climbing which relies on the use of pegs, nuts and other equipment as the means of progress rather than as protection. Artificial climbing is generally confined to rock or ice which cannot be climbed by more natural means. Also known as aid climbing.
Ascender Mechanical device which is used for climbing a rope.
Aspect The direction in which a slope faces, useful in navigation and avalanche prediction.
Attack point An easily located feature which can be used as a point from which to navigate to a less easily located objective.
Avalanche The rapid downwards movement of a mass of snow and perhaps ice.

Avalanche debris The pile of material deposited when an avalanche comes to rest. This sometimes forms an avalanche cone.

Baboon hang A technique which prevents suffocation if hanging free suspended from the waist.
Back off Retreat from a climb because of weather, difficulty, prudence or cowardice.
Back-pack An American rucksack. To back-pack means to be self-sufficient when travelling in the mountains.
Back-rope A rope manoeuvre used by a second to protect him across a traverse. The rope is arranged so as to prevent a pendulum should he fall off.
Back-up A secondary connection which makes a system safe should something fail.
Backing up A method of climbing a chimney where the back is placed on one wall and the feet or knees are placed on the opposite one. The climber stays in place because of friction and opposed pressure and progress is made by pushing with the hands and the feet alternately.
Bail The toe attachment on clip-on crampons.
Balance Position of comfort where the climber's weight is taken on his feet and there is no strain on his arms.
Balance move A climbing move made without the security of a good hand hold in which the climber is relying mostly on his footwork.
Balling up The adherence of soft or wet snow to the soles of boots and crampons.
Bandolier Shoulder sling used to carry equipment.
Barn-door An uncontrollable outwards swing like a door opening – usually followed by falling off. Characteristic of difficult laybacks.
Base camp The lowest and usually the largest fixed camp on the ascent of a high mountain.
Bashies Soft aluminium blocks which can be hammered into incipient cracks and grooves for aid. Difficult to remove, they can be a form of visual pollution on the rocks.
Bearing The direction in which to walk to reach an objective. The grid bearing is determined by measuring the angle between location and destination on the map relative to grid north. The magnetic bearing is the angle shown on the compass that would be followed.
Belay The combination of a belayer, the belay method and the anchor to which he is attached. Together they permit a fall to be held by the rope. To belay means to manage the rope in a way that allows a fall to be stopped.
Belayer The person who manages the rope in such a way that he can arrest a fall should one occur.
Belay method The way in which a rope can be held or arranged which allows a fall to be stopped by converting some of the fall energy into friction.
Belay plate A metal plate or tube through which a bight of rope can be taken and then clipped into a karabiner. A fall is arrested by the friction of the rope and the plate as the rope is taken through a sharp S shape when braking occurs.
Belay seat Small nylon hammock which makes difficult or non-existent stances more comfortable. Now mostly replaced by comfortable harnesses.
Benighted To spend a night, or part of a night, on a route or mountain as the result of some miscalculation or mishap; an involuntary or forced bivouac.
Bergschrund The last big crevasse at the head of a glacier. It can often form a formidable barrier at the start of a route as the upper lip is often much higher than the lower one.
Big wall A climb, usually on rock, of such length and sustained difficulty that several days are required for its ascent. Artificial climbing is usual on big walls, as is the use of other specialised techniques such as sack hauling.
Bight A loop of rope which can be formed anywhere in the rope and can be of any size. The start of many knots.
'Biners An American abbreviation for karabiners.
Bivouac To bivouac (or bivi) is to spend the night in the open on a route or mountain. This can be in a suitable spot, at a bivi site or on a ledge, and with the requisite bivouac equipment, as is the case on climbs too long to complete in one day. *See also* Benighted.
Black ice Ice formed directly from freezing water. It is often mixed with gravel and polished by spindrift, so can be very hard and glassy.
Blind move A move which allows a hidden or unseen hold to be gained.
Boiler plates Overlapping and undercut rock slabs often found on granite.
Bold When used in climbing, this describes a route which has little protection and so requires a confident approach.
Bollard A rounded, upstanding piece of rock usually large enough to give a satisfactory anchor. A snow or ice bollard is similar in shape but cut out of a slope to provide an anchor.
Bolts Metal expansion bolts which are placed in pre-drilled holes in the rock for either protection or aid. As they can be placed almost anywhere, the climber rather than the rock determines their location. Controversial in some areas.
Bomb-bay A chimney which is wider at the bottom and narrow upwards. This downwards flare can be disconcerting to climb.
Bombproof Term used to describe anything particularly solid. Usually applied to anchors and running belays.
Bong A wide, V-shaped or large-angle peg.
Boot axe belay A way of creating an anchor and using the rope which gives a quick-to-arrange belay using a foot and an ice axe.

Boots Climbing footwear which ranges from heavy double plastic boots used for high-altitude climbing to very lightweight, tight-fitting, rock-climbing boots.
Boulder A very small cliff close to ground level on which a climber can attempt moves without the use of rope or other protection equipment. To boulder out a move is to make repeated attempts at it until the correct solution is reached.
Bouldering The practice of climbing on boulders or at the foot of higher cliffs. Generally, bouldering is taken to heights where it is safe to jump off and can be used both as training and as an activity in its own right.
Bowline A knot commonly used in climbing for forming a loop in the end of a rope.
Brake bar A metal bar designed to fit across a karabiner to provide friction when used as an abseil device.
Bridging A climbing technique in which the feet press outwards in opposite directions. This can be on either positive or friction holds. The arms can also be bridged, though primarily it uses the feet. It is commonest where there are two opposing walls, such as in grooves and chimneys, but can also be used in face climbing.
Bucket step A type of step cut in snow or ice which is generally quite large and half-round in shape.
Bulge An overhang, usually rounded in shape.
Buttress A defined rocky mass which stands proud of the main mountainside.

Cagoule Waterproof jacket worn in mountaineering.
Cam To jam in a crack by rotation and wedging against the sides.
Camming device An anchor consisting of a metal cam (or cams) which expands to fit any width of crack within its size range and can lodge in cracks which do not have any constrictions.
Ceiling A large, horizontal overhang. Also referred to as a roof.
Chalk Light magnesium carbonate, in powder or block form, which is rubbed on to the hands to improve their grip of the rock, particularly when they are hot and sweating. Carried in a chalk bag slung round the waist.
Cheating Using what are considered to be unacceptable means to succeed on a route and then hiding what methods were used by either lying or omission.
Cheating stick Length of wire or similar material used to clip out-of-reach aid or protection points.
Chickenhead Generally rounded, protruding lumps found on some igneous rocks such as granite which can be used for holds and sometimes protection.
Chimney A fissure into which most or all of the body can fit.
Chimneying The technique by which a chimney is climbed, usually by back and foot or back and knee.
Chock An alternative name for a nut.
Chockstone A rock wedged in a crack or chimney.
Chop Deliberately destroy the head of a bolt to make it unusable.
Chop route A route whose protection is so sparse that a fall from the climb would probably be fatal. Also used for a route with extreme objective dangers.
Classic abseil An abseil in which only the rope is used.
Classic route A climb that has an almost indefinable combination of line, history, situations and climbing which makes it outstanding. It can be of any standard.
Clean To remove all vegetation and loose rock from a route, usually prior to its first ascent. Also known as gardening. 'To clean a pitch' describes the action of the second who removes all protection or aid points placed by the leader.
Clean climbing Climbing using only equipment which does not damage or alter the rock in any way.
Cliffhanger Another term for a skyhook.
Climbing calls A set of standardised calls used between climbers.
Climbing wall Purpose-built training facility which is constructed to resemble a rock face. These are often built indoors to allow all-year-round training, although some are open-air structures.
Clove hitch A knot used in climbing, often to secure the rope to a karabiner.
Col A mountain pass or saddle.
Combined tactics Standing on your partner's back, shoulders or head to overcome a holdless section of rock.
Committing Used to describe a route or a move from which there is no easy retreat once it has been embarked on.
Compass An instrument which indicates the direction of magnetic north and is essential for mountain navigation.
Contour A line on a map which joins points of equal height above sea level.
Copperhead A type of nut with a malleable copper head which can be pounded into incipient cracks and corners and used for aid.
Corner A rock feature similar to the inside of an open book where the two walls meet to form an approximate right angle. Sometimes called an open book or an inside corner.
Cornice An overhanging mass of snow formed by the wind along the edge of a ridge or plateau.
Couloir A broad gully.
Cow's tail A short sling clipped from the harness to an aid point so that the climber's weight is taken on the harness. Alternatively, a short sling fixed to the back of a harness to allow the front tie-on to be converted to a rear attachment point.
Crack A fissure in the rock which can range in size from hairline to almost wide enough to admit a body.

Crack'n ups Anchor-shaped metal devices which can be used for aid in thin cracks, particularly old peg scars. They work by hooking and twisting.
Crag A fairly small cliff.
Crag fast Stuck on a cliff and unable to move up or down.
Crampon Metal framework with a set of downward-facing points and usually two forward-facing ones. A crampon is attached to the sole of each boot and used for climbing on snow and ice.
Cramponing Climbing techniques using crampons.
Crevasse A split or crack in the surface of a glacier. A rock crevasse is a similar vertical gap in the rock.
Crevasse rescue Method of extricating someone who has fallen into a crevasse.
Cruise A smooth, fluent ascent of a (usually hard) route.
Crux The most difficult section of a climb. The crux pitch is the most difficult pitch. The technical crux is the hardest move, but a psychological crux is the most worrying section to lead. These may or may not be the same place.
Cup crystals Large ice crystals, the result of TG met.

Dachstein Thick, pre-shrunk, woollen mitt used primarily when snow and ice climbing and in cold conditions.
Dagger technique Method of climbing snow or ice using crampons and one or two ice axes which are held by the head. A fast means of ascent but only if the slope is not too steep and the snow is of a suitable hardness.
Daisy chain A sling tied or sewn into numerous sections which allow it to be used as an adjustable sling.
Dead hand The hand that holds the dead rope. May also be called the braking or the control hand.
Dead hang Hanging by the fingers so that the whole body weight is taken on the arms. Used as a method of training, but bad for the joints.
Deadman A thin alloy plate with a wire cable attached to it which is used as an anchor in snow. A deadboy is a small deadman.
Dead rope The rope which has been round the belayer's body or through a belay device and which must be controlled to arrest a fall. Also known as the inactive rope.
Delicate Used to describe a move or climb which requires balance and poise rather than strength.
Depth hoar Fragile, hollow cup crystals which form in the snow pack as a result of a strong temperature gradient within the snow cover. Develops during long spells of cold weather making a weak layer in the snow pack and creating an avalanche risk.
Descender Mechanical friction device for use when abseiling. Also known by its French name, *descendeur*.
Desperate Used to describe an extremely difficult route or move.
Dièdre The French word for corner but used internationally.
Dihedral American term for a corner.
Dinner-plating The fracturing and falling-off of lumps of ice when hit with an ice tool or when protection is being placed on ice.
Direct aid Another term for artificial climbing.
Direct belay Belay method in which the force of a fall is taken directly by the anchors.
Double fisherman's Knot used for joining two rope ends.
Double rope System which uses two ropes, usually half-ropes, to provide security when climbing.
Drive-in Type of ice peg which can be hammered into the ice.
Duvet A down- or synthetic-material-filled jacket, very warm and often carried for use in a bivouac situation.
Dynamic belay Method of belaying where some rope is allowed to slip to reduce the impact forces generated by a falling climber.
Dyno A move in which the climber is using his legs to push dynamically upwards to reach a hold.

EBs Once the universal rock boots which took their name from Emil Bordenau.
Edging Technique of using small foot holds which are stood on with the edge of the sole. Edging boots are constructed so as to make standing on small edges easier and thus have a fairly stiff sole.
Eliminate A route fitted in between other climbs but which does not have a particularly independent line. To eliminate an aid point is to do the move without using it.
Escapable A climb which can fairly easily be abandoned for less difficult ground.
Etrier Short ladder, usually with three rungs and made of nylon tape, which is used to stand in during an artificial climb.
Exposure The term used to describe the amount of space below the climber, a combination of height above the ground and the steepness of the rock. Also another name for hypothermia.
Extension A short sling, usually of tape, used to lengthen a runner to prevent it from lifting out or to reduce rope drag.

Face Relatively unbroken or featureless expanse of rock.
Face climbing Techniques needed on faces, as opposed to crack climbs. Face climbing is often characterised by balance climbing.
Fall factor Indication of the severity of a fall obtained by dividing the length of the fall by the length of rope involved.
Fall line The steepest, shortest and fastest way down a slope. Usually applied only to snow slopes.

Ferrule Connection between the spike and the shaft of an ice axe.
Fifi hook An open metal hook, usually on the top of an étrier, to allow fast, convenient clipping into a karabiner. Also used as a quick means of resting if attached by a short sling to the harness.
Figure-of-eight The most useful knot in climbing which can be employed for a variety of purposes.
Figure-of-eight descender An abseil device consisting of two joined metal rings of different sizes.
Finger lock Hold in a crack obtained by twisting and wedging the fingers against the sides.
Firn *See* Névé.
Firnification Process by which snow is converted into glacier ice. Firn becomes ice when the air spaces between the grains are sealed off from each other.
Fixed protection Anchors which have been deliberately left in place for others to use. This can be in the form of pegs, bolts, nuts or threads.
Fixed rope Rope which is fixed in position once a pitch has been ascended to allow repeated ascents to be made easily or to act as a safe line of retreat to the foot of the climb.
Flake A thin slab of rock which is detached or partially detached from the main face. It can vary from a huge feature to a tiny hold. To flake out a rope is to uncoil it into a loose pile on the ground where it will run easily with no twists, knots or kinks in it.
Flared A term used to describe a crack or chimney which is wider on the outside and narrows inwards or upwards.
Flash To ascend on sight with no rests or falls but with the advantage of prior knowledge of the route. Usually used in reference to hard climbs.
Flat-foot technique The same method of cramponing as French technique.
Foot brake A belay ön snow set up using a vertical ice axe braced behind the uphill foot.
Fracture line The division between the sliding slab and the more stable snow above and at the sides of the avalanche.
Free abseil An abseil down overhanging terrain where contact with the rock or ice is lost.
Free climbing Climbing only using natural holds. Although the rope and other equipment can be used for protection, they are not used to make progress or for resting.
French straps Type of crampon straps which use a fixed ring at the front of the crampon. Also known as Scottish straps.
French style Style of climbing where any form of preparation and practice can be used as long as the route is finally led without weighting the runners. Also known as redpointing.
French technique Method of climbing snow and ice using only the downward-facing crampon points.
Friction climbing Ascent of rock which has few, if any, positive holds and relies a great deal on balance and foot work.
Friction hitch A hitch tied in a rope round a karabiner which provides friction and can be used to belay with or as a means of abseiling or lowering. Also called an Italian hitch, Italian friction hitch and a Munter hitch.
Friend Trade name for the original spring-loaded camming device.
Frigging Another name for cheating by pulling on runners.
Front-pointing A method of climbing snow and ice using the forward-facing points and perhaps the first two downward-facing points on crampons.
Frostbite Local tissue damage caused by temperature below freezing point.
Frostnip Mild version of frostbite characterised by white, doughy tissue.
Full-depth avalanche An avalanche in which the snow cover right down to ground level slides.
Full weight A term used to describe a rope which is strong enough for climbing with on its own. Usually used in connection with hawser laid ropes.

Gaiters Covering for the lower legs running from below the knee to beyond the ankle of the boot. Worn to prevent water, snow and stones getting into the boot. Some types cover the boot as well.
Gangway A ledge which slopes diagonally up across a face.
Gardening Cleaning loose rock and vegetation off a climb, usually prior to the first ascent.
Girdle traverse A route which crosses a cliff or face from one side to the other.
Gear General name for climbing equipment. Also applied specifically to protection.
Glacier A huge mass of ice usually confined to a valley and flowing downhill.
Glacier cream Cream worn as protection against ultra-violet radiation which is much stronger on glaciers than elsewhere because of the reflective nature of their surface.
Glacier snout The lower end of a glacier.
Glacier travel The techniques of safe travel on glaciers.
Glacis An easy-angled slab which can be walked up.
Glissade A controlled, sliding descent of a snow slope.
Goretex Trade name for a waterproof fabric that 'breathes'.
Grade The rating of difficulty given to a climb.
Graded list A list of all the climbs in an area arranged in order of difficulty.
Grande course A long, classic Alpine route.

Grapevine knot Another name for the double fisherman's knot.
Graupel Heavily rimed snow crystals like small hailstones. When present in the snow pack, they can form a weak, avalanche-prone layer.
Gripped Scared, particularly of falling off.
Groove An open feature similar in some respects to a corner but either at a more acute angle (a V groove) or a more obtuse angle (a shallow groove).
Guide Professional mountaineer who takes people up mountains or routes for a fee.
Guidebook A book containing descriptions of the climbs in an area.
Gully A large fault up a cliff.

Hail Frozen water droplets which have not come in contact with ice crystals.
Half-rope A rope of 9mm diameter or less which is intended to be used with another similar rope to provide a safe climbing system.
Hand jam The wedging of a hand in a crack to form a hold.
Hand traverse A traverse which has positive holds for the hands but not the feet.
Hang-dog Used to describe a climber who, after falling off a move, does not go down to the ground but rests on the runner, practises the move until successful and with this knowledge eventually leads the route.
Hanger The part of a bolt to which a karabiner can be clipped. Although it is usually fixed on the bolt, this is not always the case.
Hanging glacier A subsidiary glacier set at a higher level than the main glacier or valley. Hanging glaciers are often dangerous as they can have unstable ice cliffs at their lower end where they tumble into the main valley.
Hanging stance A belay location where there is no ledge to stand or sit on so that the belayer must hang from the anchors, supported by his harness or a belay seat.
Hardware Metal climbing equipment such as karabiners, nuts and pegs.
Harness Specialised item of climbing equipment made of wide nylon tape which is used to attach the rope to the climber and distribute the load in a fall. Sit or seat harnesses are fastened round the waist and thighs; full body harnesses go round the chest, waist and thighs and may be one-piece or consist of a sit harness and a chest harness linked together.
Haul sack Large, robust sack in which food, water and equipment can be packed and dragged up long rock climbs. An integral part of big-wall climbing.
Hawser laid A type of rope construction in which fibres are twisted into three strands which are then twisted into a rope. Now little used in climbing.
Heel hook A gymnastic move in which the heel is placed on a hold, often above head level, and used to take some of the weight off the arms, particularly when reaching for the next hand hold.
Heel-toe A foot jam across a crack using the heel and the toe of the boot.
Helmet Protective head gear worn by climbers as partial protection from falling rocks and ice and also in the case of head-first falls. Essential in some types of climbing.
Hero loop Alternative name for a tie-off.
Hexcentric Type of nut with an irregular hexagonal cross-section; it can work by wedging or by camming. Often just called a hex.
Hip belay Another name for a body belay.
Hip hoist A method of raising a load using the leg muscles.
Hoar frost Formed by ice crystals growing on exposed surfaces in moist, freezing conditions. It is easily removed and no real problem unless it obscures cracks in the rocks or becomes buried by subsequent snow falls.
Hypothermia The condition in which the body's vital core is cooled as a result of exposure to adverse conditions such as cold, wind, rain or snow. This can be a fatal condition and is often associated with exhaustion.

Ice axe The basic tool for climbing on snow and ice.
Ice-axe belay A belay set up using an ice axe as the anchor point.
Ice-axe braking The technique of using an ice axe to stop a slide down a snow slope.
Ice bollard A horseshoe-shaped trough cut in the ice to create a bollard-shaped feature which can be used as an anchor.
Ice fall A cataract of ice formed where a glacier flows over steep ground. It can also mean a frozen water fall or a steep ice pitch on a winter route.
Ice field A large area of relatively flat glacial terrain.
Ice hammer A tool similar to an ice axe which has a hammer head instead of an adze.
Ice peg A peg designed to be used in ice.
Ice screw An ice peg which can be screwed into and out of the ice.
Igloo Domed shelter made of snow blocks.
Impact force The maximum force inflicted on a rope when it holds a fall. Mainly determined by the fall factor and the weight of the falling climber.
Impact time The time during which the belay system is affected by the impact of holding a fall. Determined by the length of free fall: the longer the fall, the greater the impact time.
Inactive rope Another term for the dead rope.
Incuts Positive and inward-sloping holds.
In situ Used to describe equipment left in place.
Instep crampons Short crampons with four points which are worn under the instep of the boot for walking

on icy paths. No use for climbing.
Italian hitch Another name for the friction hitch.

Jam The wedging of hands, feet, arms, knees or legs in cracks to provide holds.
Jug A large positive hold – the term is derived from 'jug handle'. To jug is to use mechanical ascenders to climb up a fixed rope.
Jumar The original Swiss mechancal ascender which has given its name to the technique of ascending a fixed rope.

Karabiner Metal link with a spring-loaded gate in one side. It has numerous uses in climbing, the main one being as a connection between anchors and the rope.
Karabiner brake Friction-producing arrangement of karabiners used when abseiling.
Karabiner clutch A method of threading the rope through two karabiners which allows it to run in one direction but not in the other. Also called an Alpine clutch.
Karrimat Trade name for an insulated sleeping mat made of closed-cell foam.
Kernmantel Nylon rope of a core and sheath construction.
Kevlar A very strong type of static rope used as accessory cord.
Kingpin Trade name of a blade peg of medium thickness.
Klemheist A type of prusik knot.
Kletterschuhe Light climbing boots which generally have cleated and stiffened soles, little used nowadays.
Knifeblade Type of thin blade peg.
Knife edge A sharp-edged rock formation, often a ridge.
Krab Common abbreviation for karabiner.

Lassoo The technique in which a rope is thrown over a projection and then used for aid.
Layaway A layback done for only one move.
Layback Method of climbing a crack or an edge where the hands grip and pull in one direction while the feet press against the rock in the opposite, thus setting up opposing forces. The classic application is in a corner crack.
Leader The climber who ascends a pitch first.
Leading through Another term for doing alternate leads.
Leap frog Navigational technique used in bad visibility when one person walks ahead to the limit of visibility, is lined up on the correct bearing and is used as a marker.
Ledge A level, flat area on a cliff. It can be of any size.
Lee The side of an object which is sheltered from the wind.
Leeper Trade name for a peg which has a Z-shaped cross-section.
Leg loops That part of a sit harness which supports the thighs.
Lie back American term for layback.
Line The route up a cliff or mountain taken by a climb.
Live rope The rope between the belayer and the climber. Also called the active rope.
Lob off Term for falling off a climb.
Locking karabiner A karabiner which has some form of sleeve on the gate that prevents accidental opening.
Lock off To hold most of your weight on one bent arm while reaching up or placing protection; or to tie a loaded rope in such a way that both hands can be freed for other tasks but the knot can still be untied while there is weight on it.
Logan hook Type of skyhook which has a wide, stable base.
Lost arrow Type of blade peg similar to a Kingpin.
Lower off To use the rope and an anchor to be lowered to the ground or a stance.

Magnetic variation The difference between true or grid North and magnetic north expressed in degrees.
Manila rope The original type of natural-fibre climbing rope.
Mantelshelf A move used to gain a small ledge. It involves a pulling movement which is changed to a push when the ledge is at shoulder level. This is followed by getting one foot on to the ledge, then balancing up on to it. Also known simply as a mantel.
Marginal A runner of uncertain security which may fail if loaded; an aid point which will take body weight and no more, or a placement for an ice tool which could well pull out.
Melt-freeze metamorphism Melting and re-freezing process which affects snow.
Metamorphism The changes which occur within the snow pack.
Micro nut A very small wired nut for thin cracks.
Mixed route This can mean several different things but generally it is a route which involves different types of climbing. In the Alps a mixed route has rock and snow and ice pitches; elsewhere it can be a climb with both free and artificial pitches; and in winter climbing it is a route with rock climbing under snow and ice conditions.
Moraine Piles of debris carried down and deposited by a glacier. These ridges of stones, earth and rubble can be in three main forms: terminal moraine is found at the glacier snout, lateral moraine along the sides and medial moraine where two glaciers meet.
Mountain sickness Another term for altitude sickness.
Moving together The technique of using the rope to

safeguard two or more climbers who are moving at the same time. An important Alpine technique.

Nail To nail a crack is to use aid pegs to climb it.
Nails Nails designed for the sole of mountaineering boots, now totally replaced by moulded rubber soles, but the names, such as clinkers and tricouni, are still to be found.
Natural line An obvious feature or set of features which a climb follows.
Névé Permanent snow lying at the head of a glacier but more commonly used to mean snow/ice formed by repeated freeze/thaw action.
Niche A recess, generally quite small.
Nose A protruding mass of rock which can be anything from a few to a thousand metres in size.
Nut General name for wedge or hexagonal metal chockstone designed to lodge in cracks.
Nut key Stiff length of metal used to assist in removing nuts.
Nylon The man-made material from which climbing ropes and much software is made.

Objective danger Naturally occurring danger outside the climber's control and including things like stone fall, avalanches, crevasses, seracs and lightning.
Off hand A term used to describe a crack wider than finger width but too narrow to admit the whole hand.
Off width A term used to describe a crack wider than fist size but too narrow to admit the whole body. Generally a difficult and strenuous size to climb.
On sight A term used to describe a climb led without the advantage of prior knowledge. Usually used only in connection with hard climbs.
Open book Another term for a corner.
Opposition A technique in which one thing is arranged to pull or push against another to resist a downwards force. May be the body or climbing gear.
Outcrop A small cliff, less than a pitch in length and often much smaller than that.
Overboots Insulated covering for the foot and lower leg for use in very cold conditions.
Overgraded A climb which is generally felt to be easier than the grade given it in the guidebook.
Overhand A simple knot which can be used as a stopper knot. Tied in a bight of rope, it is the simplest way to form a closed loop.
Overhand slip A knot similar to an overhand but a bight of rope is included in the knot and when the appropriate end is pulled the knot comes out. Useful for locking off a belay plate.
Overhang Rock or ice beyond the vertical is said to overhang. An overhang is a sudden jutting-out of the rock.
Overlap An overhang which is not horizontal but generally very well defined and most common on granite slabs.

PAs The original specialised rock boots developed by the French climber Pierre Allain.
Palming Using the whole flat hand on a hold, usually on a rounded feature where friction is important.
Peak fee Money paid for permission to climb a Himalayan mountain.
Peel Yet another term meaning to fall off.
Peg Metal spike with an eye designed to be hammered into a crack in the rock as an anchor. Available in a variety of widths and types to cover a range of crack sizes. Also known as a pin or piton.
Peg hammer Tool used for placing, testing and removing pegs.
Peg scar Rock damage caused by the repeated insertion and removal of rock pegs.
Pendulum A swing on the rope. This can be intentional (as in the manoeuvre of the same name in which a climber hangs on the rope from an anchor above and swings back and forth to reach a new line of ascent) or accidental (as in a fall from a traverse). Also known as a pendule.
Picket A snow stake.
Pied d'éléphant A short sleeping bag which covers the body only up to the waist. Used in conjunction with a duvet jacket for bivouacs.
Pigeonhole step Type of step cut in ice of hard snow which can be used as a hand and a foot hold.
Pillar A tall, narrow column of rock jutting out from the mountain side and usually having its own summit.
Pin Another name for a peg.
Pinch A type of hold in which the thumb and fingers squeeze the sides of a feature. Also known as a pinch grip.
Pitch Section of a climb between consecutive stances.
Piton Another term for a peg.
Placement A spot in a crack where a nut can be placed. When an ice tool is driven into the ice, this too is referred to as a placement.
Plunge step Type of step created by the heel and used when descending snow without crampons.
Pocket Type of hold formed by a depression or opening in the rock. Can range in size from one finger to fairly large features. It is a characteristic of some limestone cliffs.
Porta-ledge A platform rather like a stretcher which can be hauled up a big wall as a stance and bivi ledge.
Positive If a hold is positive, it is good and sloping inwards; positive climbing means climbing on definite holds as against using friction or opposition techniques.
Powder snow Fresh, unconsolidated snow which generally has to be removed when climbing as it will not bear a climber's weight.
Pressure hold A hold which is used by pressing

downwards or sideways on it with either the hand or the foot.
Protection General term for the security provided by running belays.
Prow A rock feature shaped like a ship's bow.
Prusik The original sliding friction knot invented by the Austrian Dr Karl Prusik and now a general name for any such knot. To prusik is to ascend a rope using this knot.
Prusik loop A loop of rope or cord carried specifically to tie a prusik knot with.
Psyche out Be unable to do a move or a climb because of mental rather than physical shortcomings.
Psyche up To prepare mentally for a climb.
Psychological runner or belay A running belay or belay anchor which is so poor as to be of little real use in a fall but which may make the user feel slightly less unhappy about his lack of security.
Pumped A term used to describe the loss of strength and the feeling of pain associated with overworked muscles. Experienced when training and on strenuous climbs.

Quickdraw Originally a trade name for a type of short sling used as an extension but now often used to mean any such extension.

Rack The selection of climbing gear carried on a climb.
Rack up To organise the rack so that it is carried in a logical and accessible manner.
Ramp A diagonal slab running at an angle across a face.
Randkluft The large crevasse between the glacier and a containing rock wall.
Rappel The same as abseil. Often referred to as a rap or rapping.
Recess A small, shallow cave.
Redpointing Another name for French style.
Refuge A mountain hut.
Reverse To climb back down the section of climb just ascended.
Rib A slender ridge of rock.
Ridge The crest where two faces meet. It can be of rock, snow or ice and can be on a mountain or a much smaller feature.
Rime Soft ice deposited on the windward side of upstanding features by a moist wind. It generally has to be cleared off when climbing. It can also form on snowflakes, producing graupel.
Rock Trade name of a popular wedge-shaped nut which has curved faces.
Rock-over A very high step on to a foot hold which must then be stood up on. Usually there is little in the way of hand holds to help with this, so it is often a fairly dynamic movement.
Rognon A rock island surrounded by glacier.
Roof An overhang which juts out more or less horizontally.
Rope The actual rope used in climbing, or a party of climbers connected by a rope.
Rope down To abseil.
Rope drag Frictional resistance to the movement of the rope as it is pulled through karabiners and over the rock.
Rope length A climbing distance roughly the length of the rope.
Rope off To abseil off a climb.
Rope up The preparation required before starting on a climb or moving on a glacier.
Route An established climb.
Route finding Following a route from a description. Route-finding ability is the skill in finding the best way up a cliff or mountain when there is no description and the way is not obvious.
RP The original trapped wire construction brass-headed micro nut from Australia.
Runner Another name for a running belay.
Running belay Anchor placed on a climb and connected loosely or freely to the climbing rope by karabiner. Used to limit the length of a leader fall.
Run out The length of rope between the leader and the second. It can also be used to imply that a climb has little protection on it.
RURP The Realised Ultimate Reality Piton, the smallest peg, which is about the size of a postage stamp.

Sack haul A term used to describe the action of the leader on a difficult pitch who, when climbing with a rucksack, may elect to pull his sack up the pitch instead of climbing with it on. Alternatively, pulling up all the gear needed when on a big wall.
Safety rope A second rope used to protect an abseil or a prusik.
Salopettes Trousers or breeches which are chest rather than waist high.
Sandbag To cause a climber to start on a route on which he has difficulty by saying or implying that the climb is easier than it actually is.
Sastrugi Ridges of snow which face into the wind and are produced by wind erosion
Scoop A shallow, dish-shaped depression in a rock face.
Scrambling Simple climbing, usually at a standard below which graded climbing begins, which may or may not require the use of a rope.
Scree Loose rock debris covering the slope below a cliff.
Scree running Rapid descent of a scree slope by running and sliding through the stones. Only possible in scree made up of small stones.
Screw-gate Locking karabiner with a threaded sleeve

which can be done up to prevent the gate opening accidentally.
Second The climber who ascends a pitch after the leader.
Sentry box A narrow recess in a rock face.
Serac A pinnacle, block or tower of ice in an ice fall. Seracs are continually forming and falling and constitute a serious objective danger on some routes.
Serious Description of climbing or a route which is potentially dangerous because of objective danger, poor rock and anchors or lack of protection.
Shake out A position on a strenuous pitch where one hand at a time can be taken off the rock for a rest. To shake out is to flex and shake the hand to get fresh blood to the overworked muscles.
Shelf A small platform or ledge.
Shock tape Extensions with weak stitching designed to tear progressively and absorb energy in a fall.
Shoulder, giving a A method of combined tactics.
Shoulder belay An old-fashioned method of rope management in which the rope is taken diagonally up the back and over the shoulder.
Side pull Vertically aligned hand hold.
Siege To climb a route over a period of time, leaving the rope in place at the high point after each attempt. Now considered to be unethical in most situations but still a feature of expedition-style climbing.
Single rope A rope strong and safe enough to be used on its own to climb on; usually about 11mm in diameter, but may be as little as 9.8mm.
Sit harness Harness which goes round the waist and thighs. The climbing rope is attached to it and in a fall the force is taken on the back of the thighs, the part of the body best able to withstand it.
Sit sling Improvised harness made from a double sling.
Skyhook Metal hook which can be placed on small flakes and edges and used for aid. Occasionally used for protection or lowering off.
Slab An inclined sheet of rock generally lacking in large features but less than vertical.
Slab avalanche Snow avalanche which is released in sheet form from below a fracture line.
'Slack' The call used when more rope is required by the leader or the second.
Sling Loop of rope or tape which can be used in a variety of ways.
Smear Technique of friction climbing when as much as possible of the boot sole is placed over a sloping hold to give maximum adhesion. Smearing boots are very flexible rock boots particularly suitable for this.
Snap link Another name for a karabiner.
Snow blindness Temporary blindness caused by intense exposure to ultra-violet radiation reflected off the snow's surface.
Snow bridge A bridge of snow spanning a crevasse.
Snow field A large expanse of permanent snow.
Snow grave An emergency shelter dug in an easy-angled snow slope.
Snow hole A cave dug into a snow bank, used for accommodation instead of a tent.
Snow/ice Very hard, resilient snow formed by repeated freeze/thaw. The same as névé.
Snow line The altitude at which permanent snow begins to be found.
Snow pack The total covering of snow on the ground at any time. It consists of a number of snow layers.
Snow shelter An emergency shelter either constructed in a snow bank or built out of blocks of snow.
Snow stake A T-shaped or angled metal stake used as a snow anchor.
Soft slab Wind slab which loses its cohesion on release in an avalanche. It is laid down by light winds.
Solo To climb alone without the rope for protection. To rope solo is to climb alone while using the rope and protection as a safeguard.
Spectra Trade name for a very strong type of cord and tape used for slings and extensions.
Spike An upstanding finger of rock. Also the point on the bottom of an ice axe.
Spindrift Loose snow which is blowing about or falling down cliffs.
Split rope carry An improvised seat formed from a coiled climbing rope, used to share the weight of an injured climber between two people.
Spot To watch a boulderer with a view to breaking his fall or steadying him if he jumps or falls off.
Sprag A hold in a crack where the thumb pushes one way while the fingers pull the other way on an edge.
Stack To press or wedge two or more things together to form a wider and stronger fit in a crack. Fingers, hands, feet, pegs and nuts can all be stacked.
Stance A place on a climb where it is possible to sit or stand in reasonable comfort.
Standard Alternative name for the grade of a climb.
Standing axe belay Belay formed by the belayer standing on the head of the axe driven vertically into the snow.
Static rope Low-stretch rope which should not be used as a main climbing rope. Accessory cord used in short lengths, as on nuts, is often static.
Stauch wall The mound of snow pushed by the avalanche, which eventually becomes so great that it brings the avalanche to a halt.
Stemming Another term for bridging.
Step cutting Using the ice axe to create steps in snow and ice.
Sticht plate The original belay plate developed by Franz Sticht; now sometimes used as a generic term for all belay plates.
Sticky boots Rock boots soled with high-friction rubber.

Stirrup Alternative term for étrier.
Stomach traverse The traverse of a ledge on which it is not possible to stand upright. Progress is by lying on your front and wriggling – an ungainly and often precarious technique.
Stomper belay Another term for a standing axe belay.
Stone fall Stones and rock falling down a mountain or face which is caused by natural agencies such as the sun melting ice and freeze/thaw action. An objective danger on some routes, though much stone fall is caused by careless climbers.
Stopper Trade name for a wedge-shaped nut. Often used for a particularly good runner.
Stop-tous Very short gaiters which cover only the top of the boots.
Straddle A bridging manoeuvre.
Strenuous Used to describe climbing which is particularly tiring, especially on the arms.
Style The way in which a route is ascended, often in reference to the equipment used and the tactics employed.
Sublimation The ability of a substance to change from solid to vapour and back again without the liquid stage.
Super tape Name for a heavy, strong nylon tape. Originally a trade name but now a general term.
Sustained A climb or pitch is said to be sustained if difficulties are maintained at about the same level throughout.
Swami A waist belt of nylon tape wrapped round the waist and tied securely.
Swing leads Alternate leads.

'Taking in' Taking in the active rope. The call which is used to indicate that a leader is anchored and about to pull up the unused rope between himself and his belayer.
Talus Another term for scree.
Tape Nylon webbing which has many uses in climbing. Harnesses, slings and other items of software are made of tape.
Tape up To cover the hands/fingers with adhesive tape to prevent cuts and abrasions. Usually done to protect the hands when crack climbing. May also be done to alter the size or shape of the hands for specific climbs.
Technical When applied to climbing, this means that the moves are difficult to work out and execute.
Technical or three-cam unit (TCU)A range of different camming protection devices.
Technique The correct method to overcome any particular obstacle or climbing problem, usually in the best and most efficient manner.
Temperature gradient metamorphism (TG met.) The process which occurs when the snow pack is shallow and the surface temperature is very low. Causes depth hoar and cup crystals.
Tension traverse A traverse that uses support from the rope which is run through an anchor at a higher level than the climber. A tension move is one such move rather than a series of them.
Terrace A wide ledge on a face.
Thin A term used to describe difficult climbing on small holds.
Thread A natural anchor formed by a rock tunnel.
Through route A subterranean climbing route usually associated with chimneys and gullies.
Thuggish Used to describe brutal, strenuous climbing.
Tie-off A short sling, usually of tape, which is put round a partially inserted peg to reduce the leverage. To tie something off is to use a sling to reduce leverage in this way.
Tie on To attach the rope to the climber, his waist belt or his harness in a secure manner.
Toe jam Wedging and twisting the toes in a crack to create a hold.
Toe traverse A traverse which has small foot holds but no hand holds.
Topo Topographical diagram which shows the line of a route by a drawing rather than by words.
Top-rope To climb a route without leading it. The top of the climb is gained and a rope put down which then protects the climber from above. The term can also mean dropping a rope end to someone attempting to lead a route but who has got into difficulties.
Torque To twist part of the body or a piece of gear, such as an ice axe, in a crack so that it sticks.
Traverse To climb across rather than upwards.
Trigger The force which initially sets off an avalanche.
Triple bowline Bowline tied with a doubled end of rope so that three loops are formed.
T-stack Jam in a wide crack where the feet form a T shape.
Tunnel To dig a hole through a large cornice to get past it.
Twin rope Two ropes, each usually of less than 9mm diameter, which are used together as a single rope.
Tyrolean traverse Method of crossing a gap using a suspended rope.

Undercut An upside-down hold.
Undergraded Used to describe a route which is harder than the grade which it has been given, generally in a guidebook.
UIAGM Union Internationale des Associations des Guides de Montagne, the international association of qualified professional mountain guides.
UIAA Union Internationale des Associations d'Alpinisme, mountaineering's governing body.

Vegetation Any type of plant found on a climb.
Ventile A closely woven cotton fabric.
Verglas A thin tenacious film of ice on the rock which is caused by the freezing of water or water vapour when it comes into contact with a cold surface.
Via ferrata Spectacular paths in the Dolomites where ladders are used on the cliff sections.
Vibram Trade name for the first moulded rubber sole used on climbing boots.

Waist belay Alternative name for a body belay.
Waist belt Simple climbing belt, usually with a buckle closure, worn round the waist.
Waist line A tie-on method which uses a length of thin rope or cord wound a number of times round the waist to which the climbing rope is attached.
Wall A steep mountain face or a near-vertical portion of rock; a steep slab.
Water ice Hard and brittle ice formed by the freezing of running water, often blue in colour.
Wedge A wooden wedge used for protection or aid in a wide crack. Fortunately no longer necessary. Also a shortened version of wedge-shaped nut.
Well protected Used to describe a climb which has a large number of good running belays.
Wet snow Snow which is thawing.
White-out A condition of poor or zero visibility which occurs when falling, drifting or blown snow combined with a complete snow cover makes the ground and sky merge together.
Wind chill The effect of the wind removing heat from a body and making the temperature much lower than the actual air temperature.
Wind slab Snow which has been deposited by the wind and can form an avalanche danger. It can be soft or hard slab depending on the strength of the wind that has moved it, and it is most likely to be found on lee slopes.
Winter ascent An ascent of a route under winter conditions. This may be dependent on the prevailing conditions or be during a specific season. In the Alps the winter season is between 21 December and 21 March.
Wire Short name for a nut on wire. Alternatively it can mean to memorise the moves and holds on a hard climb so that it can be ascended with less difficulty.
Wrist loop A specifically tied or sewn sling used on an ice axe or tool which attaches the axe to the climber and makes hanging on the shaft easier.

Yosemite hoist A method of hauling used primarily with haul sacks on big walls and developed on the granite walls of the Yosemite Valley in California.
Yo-yo Repeated attempts at a route where the leader is lowered back to the ground or a resting place after each failure. An unethical war of attrition.

Zdarsky sack A bivouac sack named after Matthaus Zdarsky, an early ski teacher and equipment inventor.
Z hoist A type of improvised rescue; the same as the 3:1 hoist.

Index

Page numbers in *italic* refer to the illustrations